The Making of Markova

The Making of Markova

Diaghilev's Baby Ballerina to Groundbreaking Icon

TINA SUTTON

PEGASUS BOOKS
NEW YORK LONDON

THE MAKING OF MARKOVA

Pegasus Books LLC
80 Broad Street, 5th Floor
New York, NY 10004

First Pegasus Books cloth edition 2013

Interior design by Maria Fernandez

All photos are courtesy of the Dame Alicia Markova Collection at the Howard Gotlieb Archival Research Center at Boston University.

Letters written by Alicia Markova, Doris Barry, and Arnold Haskell are reprinted courtesy of Vivienne Haskell.

Anton Dolin's personal correspondences are reprinted courtesy of his nephew, Philip Kay.

Frederick Ashton's personal correspondences are printed courtesy of the Frederick Ashton Foundation, London.

Library of Congress Cataloging-in-Publication Data is available.

ISBN: 978-1-60598-456-8

10 9 8 7 6 5 4 3 2 1

Printed in the United States of America
Distributed by W. W. Norton & Company

To John

Contents

Preface

Book-Cadillac Hotel
Detroit, Michigan

Dec. 6th 1939

My Dearest One,

What a lovely surprise your cable was, as I had no idea you knew the date of my birthday, also many thanks for your sweet letter.

*Please don't be offended with me but the New York Season was so hectic & so much extra work that I was unable to see any of the people you told to look me up, but will try & see them when I return in the Spring. We are well on tour now & leave here for Cincinatti [*sic*] tomorrow. Shall be in Chicago for Xmas, Auditorium Theatre until Jan. 3rd, Seattle, Washington Music Hall Jan.18th, San Francisco Opera House Jan. 30th–Feb. 4th, Los Angeles Philharmonic Auditorium Feb. 9th–19th. Do let me hear from you & please send me a nice photograph to keep with me darling.*

*Life must be very depressing & trying at the moment, the papers here make things seem terrible & I try not to read them as it makes me so unhappy & homesick. Cheer up & keep faith as things must be alright [*sic*] in the end. We are doing wonderful business everywhere & I am enjoying great success. I know you will be pleased. Thinking*

of you my darling & only wish you were with me. My loving wishes for a happy Xmas & New Year.
With much love,
Alicia

P.S. When's your birthday dear?
Write c/o Hurok,
30 Rockefeller Plaza, N.Y.

In 1937, Alicia Markova fell in love with Stanley Burton, the recipient of that letter. The 26-year-old dancer was already the most celebrated British ballerina in the world. Her equally smitten beau was a charming 23-year-old businessman from a wealthy Leeds family known for arts philanthropy.

Then came the war. Though Markova wished to remain in London to be close to her family and loved ones, she was under contract to dance in America with the Ballet Russe de Monte Carlo. If she refused to honor that commitment, the company's manager Sol Hurok threatened a lawsuit that would have prevented her from performing anywhere in the world. Since Markova's widowed mother and three sisters counted on her income for support, she had little choice. She needed to earn a living.

So on September 29, 1939, Alicia Markova set sail from Southampton, England bound for New York on the S.S. *Washington*—one of the last American ships to make the crossing before the German bombings of London began. As soon as she was safely in her stateroom, the frightened ballerina wrote to Burton on shipboard stationery:

Dearest One,
Thanks so much for your letter & sweet telegrams.

God knows what the trip will be like. We had to stand for 4 hours in a line for passport examination before we arrived on here. Five people in the cabin! Well I must keep cheery.
My Love,
Alicia

Burton entered the British Royal Air Force (RAF), and the two wrote back and forth throughout the war.

Furnished Apartments All Service
Apartmentos Azteca
Hamburgo 29
Mexico City, Mexico

May 8, 1942

My Darling,

We arrived here yesterday after a very long & trying journey from N.Y. I felt fine yesterday but I woke up with an awful cold this morning. We begin rehearsals today & open our season here on Monday 11th. Do you realize dearest that apart from your cable I haven't heard from you since your last letter early in December? Do try & write to me more often as I still feel the same about you & get very sad & lonely when I don't hear.

When do you think we shall see each other again? I hope soon, although things seem so impossible. My contract with Ballet Theatre takes me until September 1943. If only this war would end I would fly back at once. You quite understand dear that the only reason I remain here is that I can earn more money over here to send back to the family than I could in England at the moment. I long to settle down & have a home again. This travelling & hotel rooms is beginning to drive me crazy. I am sorry my darling. I mustn't complain so much to you, when I think what you must have gone through it makes me feel quite ashamed. I will write again after we open. Until then.

All my Love
Alicia

P.S. I hope your family are all well.

Markova didn't return home again until 1948. By that time, Burton had met and married a woman named Audrey Solomon. Though the famous ballerina never publicly discussed or named anyone she was romantically involved with, she atypically reminisced about her lost love to a London newspaper reporter ten years later:

> "I'm rather lonely," she confessed in her Knightsbridge flat. "It is my sole regret—that I have never married.

"But I came so near to it. There was a man. . . ."

She paused and I waited while her memory slipped back two decades.

"He was very fond of me. I loved him too. It seemed certain that we would marry. Then the war came.

"I was in America. I did not return until the war was over."

She sighed. "People don't wait all their lives for you, do they? Perhaps, it was my destiny that I should not marry. I'm philosophical. Since that time, the demands of my career have always been great . . . so great."

—*Reynold's News*, London, 1958

Alicia Markova never did marry. Oh, there were men in her life, some famous enough to make for gossip-column fodder. She received several marriage proposals as well—at least two from multi-millionaires. But work always came first, making any committed relationship impossible.

When asked about the subject of marriage and children in a 1960 radio interview, Markova responded slowly: "I think in life, after all, we're not meant to have everything. When we realize perhaps we must sacrifice something, then I came to the conclusion that maybe this is the sacrifice I have to make . . . I feel one mustn't be greedy. I have many things to be thankful to God for."

Stanley and Audrey Burden had a long and happy marriage, with Markova remaining close to both of them throughout her life. Stanley saved all of Markova's love letters, and at some point after she returned home to England for good, he gave them all back—perhaps for posterity. They were found filed away with old newspaper clippings, buried in the roomy London flat Markova shared with her sister Doris. Now the letters are part of an astounding collection of material entrusted to Boston University's Howard Gotlieb Archival Research Center in Massachusetts.

Markova began sending her professional materials to the prestigious Gotlieb Center in 1995 when she was eighty-four years old, but the most personal items (including many revelatory letters) weren't made available until after her death in 2004. There would be 137 boxes in all—including journals, diaries, newspaper and magazine clippings, radio and television interviews, manuscripts, photographs, musical scores, costumes, keepsakes, and a lifetime of personal correspondence with some of the most famous ballet and arts luminaries of the 20th century.

The woman saved everything, from the mundane (a decades-old insurance bill for a fur coat) to the highly personal, including a poignant letter from Frederick Ashton despairing at the great success of lesser choreographers as he fought valiantly for recognition in "a cruel & frustrating war for me . . . I am getting on & have wasted 4 years of precious life & time."

I knew nothing about Alicia Markova before volunteering to help catalog her personal papers and belongings. As a longtime fashion/features/arts writer for *The Boston Globe* and numerous other publications, I became interested in Boston University's Gotlieb Center through its vivacious director, Vita Paladino.

Vita hired me to research and write introductory biographies of many famous collectees, from award-winning authors and war correspondents to celebrated film actresses and big band leaders. Many had overcome personal tragedies or societal prejudices to achieve their hard-won success, with each life story both unique and compelling.

While I worked on the project, Vita asked if I might also be interested in taking on the preliminary organizational archiving of a recent acquisition.

I would.

How about ballet dancer Dame Alicia Markova?

My first reaction was, isn't she Russian? Though my Odessa-born grandmother once tried to teach me the Cyrillic alphabet, I wouldn't be able to translate a word of the language. As it happened, I was confusing Markova with the Russian ballerina Natalia Makarova.

I soon learned that many people assumed Markova was Russian. Sergei Diaghilev had changed her name: "Who would pay to see Alicia Marks?" he had told her. The title "Dame" should have been an instant tip-off. Alicia Markova was British and the most famous ballerina of her generation.

I have loved ballet since childhood. Growing up in New York and later living in Boston, I had seen Baryshnikov as the Nutcracker, Fonteyn and Nureyev in *Romeo and Juliet*, and practically every illustrious company performing in those cities, from The Royal Ballet to the Bolshoi. Maya Plisetskaya's *Dying Swan* is still etched vividly in my memory.

Having a lifelong interest in modern art, I am also well versed in Diaghilev and Ballets Russes lore, especially the Russian impresario's genius in hiring the likes of Picasso, Matisse, Derain, and Miró (collaborating with Max Ernst, no less) as costume and set designers. Even Coco Chanel had worked with Diaghilev.

Markova, I soon learned, was Diaghilev's "baby ballerina"—the youngest dancer ever to be accepted into his Ballets Russes. She had just turned fourteen and was as timid as she was small. Many rare photographs and performance programs from those times are part of the dancer's archives. There were even rumors of an original Picasso drawing buried somewhere in the collection. (It was actually a Matisse.)

That all sounded exciting enough, but nothing prepared me for Alicia Markova's astonishing life story laid bare in her archives. Here was a woman far ahead of her times who overcame seemingly insurmountable odds with grace, determination, and an unflagging spirit of adventure. Markova's career is as improbable as it is remarkable.

In pre-World War I England, a frail, exotic looking Jewish girl—so shy she barely spoke a word until age six and so sickly she needed to be homeschooled—turned herself into a superstar and became the most famous ballerina in the world.

How famous? She guest-hosted Sid Caesar's *Your Show of Shows*, appeared on stage with Bob Hope and Buddy Holly and the Crickets, and had her own radio program. She was the subject of comic strips, crossword puzzles, and trading cards. Celebrated artists asked to paint her and *Vogue* made her a fashion icon. She was hired as an advertising spokesperson for everything from chocolates and potatoes (yes, potatoes) to shoes and cigarettes (though she didn't smoke). Her name alone could sell out a 30,000-seat auditorium—for ballet!

Markova appealed to both the opening-night glitterati and everyday people who had never seen ballet before her. There was even a racehorse named after her (the filly won a key race at 8 to 1 odds).

Markova was a workhorse herself, devoting every waking hour to perfecting her craft. She had a hardscrabble upbringing and a zealous drive to succeed.

In a radio tribute, good friend Laurence Olivier spoke of Markova's being "nicknamed affectionately 'The Dynamo,'—and understandably," he explained admiringly. "When you think she danced at least one act of a great classic ballet, and then a divertissement, *and* finale, every night of the week and twice on Saturdays—an unknown thing nowadays, and I'm sure would be considered impossible, because she didn't do it just for a short season, but for a number of years."

She not only pioneered British ballet—two of the three companies she helped launch are still in existence today—but she dared to go off on her own, becoming the first "free agent" ballerina, and the most widely traveled dancer of her era. She performed in parts of the world that had never seen ballet at all, let alone one of its greatest practitioners.

As the London *News Chronicle* reported in 1955:

> She is to the dance what Menuhin is to music, but unlike the violinist, she has no competitors in her field, for all the other leading ballerinas, from Fonteyn to Ulanova, work in the framework of established companies.
>
> Indeed, it seems as though Markova may be the last of her kind—the "rebel" dancer who is prepared to carry the full responsibility for her career on her own delicate shoulders.

Markova believed firmly in ballet for everyone, not just the elite. To that end, she not only performed in the world's grandest theaters with the most prestigious ballet companies, but also in more accessible popular venues, such as music halls, high school gymnasiums, and even a boxing ring. Though she flew *on* stage, she was down-to-earth once off, and it made her much loved by the public.

Several male impresarios, choreographers, and dance partners didn't share those sentiments. Markova's fierce independence and high artistic standards drove them crazy. Many needed her name to sell tickets, but bristled at giving her any personal control. Didn't she know ballerinas were supposed to be seen and not heard? Actually Markova was neither when it came to practicing, something she always did alone. She also never joined the company in daily classes, choosing instead to pay for private lessons. Markova wanted no distractions and this solitary endeavor gave rise to the myth that she rarely practiced at all, which was far from the truth.

Women in the dance world admired Markova's fortitude, among them Dame Margot Fonteyn, who said Markova "always remained my ideal and my idol."

Choreographers found her skills and determination a marvel. George Balanchine, Mikhail Fokine, Frederick Ashton, Léonide Massine, Jerome Robbins, Bronislava Nijinska, and Antony Tudor all created roles specifically for Markova. She was an invaluable muse to many.

Markova had to overcome poverty, sexism, anti-Semitism, and not being considered "pretty" enough to succeed. She was proud of her religion, which almost ended her career, and would become the world's first openly Jewish *prima ballerina assoluta*—the highest (and rarest) rank of a classical female dancer. And though often urged to have her prominent nose surgically "bobbed" to conform to conventional standards of beauty, Markova steadfastly refused. Compare that decision to one by Margot Fonteyn—who was both Catholic and very pretty. Upon being told by a famous choreographer that she was starting to look Jewish, the established ballerina immediately had her nose done over—an unfortunately botched surgery.

The Gotlieb Center archival materials offer many clues to what motivated Markova to always push on. Certainly her personal letters are a treasure trove, but so too are the countless scrapbooks of press clippings over the years. Markova was unusually open and candid with reporters.

Examined sequentially, the newspaper interviews demonstrate how the timid young dancer turned into a marketing genius, managing the media and her image with an uncanny flair. I've included many excerpts of news stories and performance reviews throughout the book. They illuminate not only much about the ballerina, but also the times in which she lived.

And then there is all that correspondence—boxes and boxes of it. While it was fun to read a charming note of thanks from Princess Diana or a Cecil Beaton luncheon invitation to dine with famed fashion designer Elsa Schiaparelli, it is the personal letters from the great dancers, choreographers, and impresarios in Markova's career that are the most revelatory. What a tale they tell of ego, flattery, hubris, and manipulation. The letters from Anton Dolin, Markova's most frequent dance partner and lifelong "friend," are positively Machiavellian.

Then there are the letters between Markova's sisters—Doris, who served as her personal manager and travel companion for many years, and Vivienne, who shared their London apartment. Doris's descriptions of horrendous stage conditions, unscrupulous managers, and Markova's increasing health problems are alternately disturbing and confounding. What drove the ballerina to keep up such a grueling, self-chosen life?

Markova clearly valued her friends, saving so many of their letters. She was obviously a good friend herself, judging from all the thank-you notes. She apparently never forgot birthdays or opening nights and made sure her gifts and flowers were delivered wherever her fellow artists were performing all over the world.

And she seemingly knew everyone. In addition to all the ballet luminaries of her time, Markova's address books are filled with a veritable Who's Who of the arts world, among them performers Charlie Chaplin, Laurence Olivier, and Gene Kelly, composer Igor Stravinsky, modern artist Marc Chagall, and pianists Arthur Rubinstein and Liberace—yes, Liberace!

Markova clearly valued letters from everyday fans—especially children and soldiers—all of which she saved and personally answered. A letter from a grateful solider during the war was in the same file as a jolly note from Noel Coward. People were people to Markova. She was enormously compassionate, always taking time to visit local ballet schools and fledgling companies to teach wherever she traveled, and devoting much time and money to numerous charities over the years.

But while Markova loved her public—she would spend hours signing autographs—she hated big parties, never getting over her shyness in a roomful of strangers. She could be great fun one moment, and severely depressed another, often retreating to her hotel room to read a book and listen to music alone. Markova herself was anything but an open book.

It is a very strange thing to read through all of someone's private papers, even if you have permission to do so. I had the pleasure of visiting Markova's sister Vivienne at her home in Bath, England. As lovely as she appeared in younger days, the sole surviving "Marks girl" is delighted to have her exceptional sister remembered anew.

While reviewing one of Markova's business files from the late 1950s, I came across an unsigned letter in her handwriting on Royal Opera House, Covent Garden, London stationery. Perhaps it was jotted down in her dressing room one evening, and then tucked inside her work papers. It is uncharacteristic and heartbreaking. Though she was a superstar to the world, Alicia Markova was only human.

March 24, 1958

Dear God,

I offer you my heartfelt thanks for giving me the power & strength to live and dance through the last two years. Since Rio, I have suffered such constant pain at times it has been almost unbearable. No one will ever know how much I have suffered mentally & physically. Only due to my faith in thee and the feeling that I must try & accomplish as much as possible to help people and make them happy (as time is limited for me) has kept me going.

Thank you dear God for helping me to live a good life and one that I could be proud of. I only regret that all the truth & knowledge I have acquired in my art & otherwise will be of little use as so few people seem to want it. . . . There is nothing here on earth to make me feel I want to stay so I am ready to leave at anytime.

Alicia Markova was forty-seven years old when she wrote that letter—still an in-demand performer and celebrity. She danced professionally for another four and a half years and lived to the age of ninety-four.

1

Another Pavlova

> Today Alicia Markova is not only the greatest English dancer, but one of the finest living exponents of the classic ballet. Giselle and Odette (The Swan Lake) are her most remarkable creations.
>
> Ever since childhood Markova has been compared with Pavlova; this is a great distinction, but also a heavy onus, and there are very few dancers, indeed, who would not crumble under it. Markova remains unimpaired and holds her own ground. This is a great achievement.
>
> —"America Meets a New Ballerina in Alicia Markova"
> *Dance News*, 1938, Anatole Chujoy

Few who saw Alicia Markova dance ever forgot the experience. Her technical bravura was astonishing. Her tiniest movement could break your heart. But it was her buoyancy—appearing to ever so slowly float through the air—that truly confounded and mesmerized audiences. And she did it all so effortlessly.

Sharing the stage with Markova, fellow dancers were stupefied. How was it possible that she never breathed heavily, perspired, or made a sound when she landed? Not even the softest thud. It was a point of pride with her.

At the Ballets Russes, Sergei Diaghilev insisted that the best ballerinas made as little noise as possible. More than anything, his youngest-ever prodigy wanted to please him, so Markova learned to dance silently.

"If Markova springs like a winged fairy, she comes to the ground just as lightly," wrote British dance critic Cyril Beaumont, "noiselessly in fact, always passing—ball, sole, heel—through the whole of the supporting foot. Of how many ballerine can that be said?"

Maybe she had some help from the size of her feet—only 4½ American (2½ British). They were so tiny that insurance companies refused to insure them. "The risk was too great," they said. Markova's foot anomaly also put them off. Her big toes were almost twice as long as the others. So when Markova danced *en pointe,* she supported her entire body on just one toe.

"Her weight had to be poised with absolute accuracy on the very center of the large toe," wrote a reporter closely observing the ballerina rehearse. "The slightest deviation could throw her off balance, cause wobbling and put strain on the muscles." But ask anyone who ever saw Markova dance. She *never* wobbled.

For choreographers, Markova was like a gift from the gods. She had a phenomenal memory not only for every step she ever danced, but for every balletic move she had ever *seen.* Moreover, she could do virtually anything that was asked of her. George Balanchine was in awe that at age thirteen, Markova could already execute supremely athletic step sequences formerly danced only by men.

But it was that ability to fly through the air that truly set her apart. Not soar—like Peter Pan or Rudolf Nureyev—just defy gravity for as long as she liked. "I saw her in *Les Sylphides* making her airborne entrance for the *pas de deux,*" wrote British dance critic Jane Simpson, "and it was quite clear, even to an already cynical spectator, that only her partner's restraining hands were stopping her from flying away."

It was otherworldly—an ethereal quality that made her the quintessential ghostly spirit of Giselle. Audience members would gasp, cry, and pinch one another. "Did we really just see that?" they'd whisper. And her fans came back again and again—even people who cared little for ballet—as if they were watching a magic show and trying to figure out the secrets of each trick.

"The more you see her the more you value her," wrote *New York Herald Tribune* dance critic Edwin Denby, someone who did care deeply about ballet. "[I]n every department of classic technique she is flawless. And she has all the peculiarities of physical structure that ballet enthusiasts gloat about—like the overlong arms, the lateral overmobility in the hip joint, the outward set of the arms, and of course the fabulously high arch—all of which add to the poignancy of the gesture because you seem to be seeing what is impossible to do. And she holds your eye on her. Not that she is sexy; she is very proper, but you watch her as intently as if you were perturbed."

Offstage Markova was just as intriguing—reserved, yet engaged; soft-spoken, but humorous and accessible; plain-featured, yet glamorous. What was going on behind those large dark eyes, one wondered? That air of mystery became one of her greatest assets on stage.

"Who Markova is, nobody knows," wrote Denby when reviewing her starring role in Antony Tudor's heartrending *Romeo & Juliet.* "What you see on the stage is the piece she performs, the character she acts. She shows you, as only the greatest actresses do, a completely fascinating impersonation, completely fascinating because you recognize a heroine of your imagination who finds out all about vanity and love and authority and death. You watch her discover them." Denby deemed Markova "one of the most poetic dancers of our times."

Those opinions were shared by many noteworthy critics, with laudatory reviews of Markova's performances awash in superlatives. She is "the perfect epitome of the classical ballerina," wrote the all-powerful dance critic of *The New York Times*, John Martin, and "probably the greatest ballet dancer who ever lived."

High praise indeed.

Another world-class ballerina, and Markova's closest lifelong friend, was the exquisite dancer Alexandra Danilova. Here was someone who really did know the offstage Markova as a living, breathing human being with a rollicking sense of humor and boatloads of insecurities. Markova was no supernatural creature of great mystery to Danilova. Nevertheless, she too only saw Markova's illusory qualities onstage.

I once asked the great Russian-American prima ballerina Alexandra Danilova what the difference would be between a

> very fine dancer—a soloist—and a real ballerina—it was to be a definition of the word "ballerina." She thought a moment, her eyes lit up and in her heavy accent she said, "Ah, Ballet is Giselle. Door of cottage open. Pretty young soloist come out. You happy and you say 'I hope she do well.' Another performance. Is also Giselle. Door open. Alicia Markova step out. She not danced yet. One step only, but you sigh and say, 'Ah! Ballerina!' You do not ask, you know. She is star. She shine."
>
> —Walter Terry, dance critic for
> *The New York Herald Tribune*

And she shined right from the start. In the 1930s, American choreographer/dancer Agnes de Mille and British prima ballerina Margot Fonteyn were ballet-school pupils in London. Along with the other students, they were completely riveted while watching Markova rehearse. Barely out of her teens, she was already the city's reigning star ballerina.

Markova was "both my inspiration and my despair," recalled Fonteyn, "because I could see equally clearly my vision of the ideal ballerina and the absolute impossibility that I myself could ever, ever resemble this tiny, ethereal being."

Agnes de Mille never lost her fascination with Markova, writing about her often:

> Always about her there was an aroma of sadness, a hint of death in the moment of consummated effort. This was her Jewish heritage, as it was Anna Pavlova's who made her world-wide reputation with a dance of death, the "Dying Swan." . . .
>
> Although English (born Lilian Alicia Marks), she was in face and body astonishingly like the Russian Pavlova—the same black-and-white beauty, the same serene brow, the dark, burning eye, the precise, patient mouth, the swanlike neck.

Ah yes, the inevitable comparison with Pavlova. It would happen again and again throughout Markova's career. Her likeness to the revered Russian dancer beckoned choreographers, beguiled the press, and gave continuity to the ballet world. When Pavlova died unexpectedly of pleurisy in 1931, hopeful eyes turned to the twenty-year-old Alicia Markova. It was both flattering and burdensome. Anna Pavlova was the most worshipped dancer of her time.

Agnes de Mille was a firsthand witness to Pavlova's enthralling stage presence and fame, recounting, ". . . her name was synonymous with the art—Pavlova, the Incomparable, was an internationally known slogan. She was as famous as Caruso and her position as unique. No one today approaches her power over the popular imagination. She half-hypnotized audiences, partaking almost of the nature of divinity."

But de Mille added, "I have seen two dancers as great or greater since." Alicia Markova was one of them. Anna Pavlova and her ghost would play an enormous role in the creation of her career, both literally and figuratively.

It was after seeing Pavlova dance and meeting one-on-one with the Russian star that nine-year-old Lilian Alicia Marks decided to dedicate her life to ballet. And when prejudice against Markova's Jewish faith and Semitic looks almost ended her career in England, it was her uncanny resemblance to Pavlova that inspired choreographer Frederick Ashton to hire her. Finally, for the London press, the constant comparison proved to the world that a British ballet dancer could be as talented as a Russian.

And there was so much the two ballerinas had in common, far more in fact than was commonly known. Both were Jewish—although Pavlova kept that a secret for fear it would end her career, whereas Markova wore her heritage proudly—with dark hair, very pale skin, and exotic, non-classical features.

Both were delicate and frail as opposed to the more robust muscular dancers of the time—such as celebrated prima ballerinas Matilda Kschessinska and Alexandra Danilova—with long torsos and arms, slender legs, and very thin ankles. This added to their vaporous stage presence, with a bird-like quality of seeming to hover mid-air without any noticeable exertion. And each was considered as fine an actress as a dancer, infusing classical roles with a stirringly emotive expressiveness.

Pavlova and Markova were also very small and sickly at birth—the former delivered two months premature, the latter at risk of dying along with her mother. They would both suffer through numerous childhood illnesses, some quite serious, such as scarlet fever and diphtheria. Once the leading cause of death in children, diphtheria was highly contagious, requiring immediate isolation. Having no siblings, Pavlova was nursed at home in the Russian countryside, her mother taking in laundry to support them. But ten-year-old Alicia Marks was quarantined in a special hospital ward where diphtheria patients often remained for several months. As her temperature soared, there were fears of heart damage or even permanent paralysis. Adding to the child's misery, the lengthy recuperation meant a lost opportunity to dance with the Ballets Russes.

Fortunately, both children completely healed in time, but their similar bone-thin physiques endured. The wispy delicacy of frame they had in common helped create a transcendental elusive quality on stage that always held audiences in thrall.

But of all the people who delighted in comparing the two dancers, no one was happier about their extraordinary likeness than Markova's mother, Eileen Marks—a ballet fan, who from the moment she discovered she was pregnant, wanted nothing more for her unborn child than she be another Pavlova.

In 1910, legendary ballerina Anna Pavlova made her first appearance on a London stage. Like Isadora Duncan, who caused a worldwide sensation when she introduced free-form modern dance to Europe in the early 1900s, the Russian iconoclast didn't fit the mold of a traditional classical dancer. Emphasizing expression in her movements over proper academic technique, Pavlova brought a natural spontaneity to what was then a rigidly controlled art form.

Not surprisingly, many of her peers disapproved. Audiences, however, felt differently. Just one year earlier, "La Pavlova" had drawn worshipful crowds in Paris while performing with Sergei Diaghilev's stellar Ballets Russes, earning press notices as sublime as her sometime partner, the incomparable Vaslav Nijinsky. At age twenty-nine, Anna Pavlova was one of the most celebrated dancers in the world, with legions of ardent fans. In her hometown of St. Petersburg, they proudly called themselves *Pavlovtzi*.

Needless to say, tickets for the star's London debut were in great demand, so 21-year-old Eileen Marks was very excited she would be attending. The pretty Irish-born newlywed had been to the Ballet of the Empire Theatre many times to see their classical Danish prima ballerina, the enchanting Adeline Genée. But this was Anna Pavlova!

The young Mrs. Marks was excited for other reasons as well. She was madly in love with her 21-year-old husband, Jewish mining engineer Arthur Marks. The former Eileen Mary Barry had even converted to Orthodox Judaism to be his wife—adding the Hebrew name of Ruth to her own—despite her strict Catholic convent upbringing and family disapproval on both sides. But that had all been smoothed over, with more good news to follow: the blissful bride had conceived on her honeymoon at the Metropole Hotel in Brighton. In December, she would give birth to the first of the couple's four daughters, Lilian Alicia. Seeing Anna Pavlova dance was just icing on the wedding cake.

Though one would have expected a dancer of Pavlova's renown to perform at the very grand Royal Opera House in Covent Garden, as Diaghilev's Ballets Russes would the following year, she was booked instead at a popular music hall, the Palace Theatre of Varieties. More shocking—especially to ballet patrons of today—the bill included Arley's Athletic Dogs and a film of former U.S. President Teddy Roosevelt at a British East Africa Big Game Shooting Expedition. Guns, somersaulting dogs, and toe shoes were a decidedly odd mix, but one that perfectly suited Pavlova's mission—later shared by Alicia Markova—to bring ballet to the masses.

Never mind the eclectic program. When Pavlova took to the stage to perform *The Dying Swan*—her signature role choreographed by Ballets Russes visionary Mikhail Fokine—the audience sat motionless and entranced, especially the starry-eyed Eileen Marks of Finsbury Park. She could recall every detail of Pavlova's performance even decades later.

"What was it about Pavlova that so captivated you?" a newspaper reporter asked Mrs. Marks for a feature story on her now-famous daughter. "The lithe, slim figure danced across the stage, the essence of beauty, of lightness, of grace," Eileen replied. "She seemed to defy the laws of gravity as she floated through the air."

One has to wonder if that reporter embellished Eileen's remarks just a little. He certainly continued the story with breathless prose:

> The mother-to-be sat in the auditorium. She was leaning forward. The classic grace of the figure on the stage had carried her right away. With bated breath, she watched every movement, her whole body thrilling to those lovely, easy-moving steps. And from her lips there came a whispered prayer—a prayer that her child should be a girl and should grow up to be a great dancer like Pavlova.

Though seemingly one of those too-good-to-be-true tales concocted by a public relations manager or the media, the story was in fact accurate. Eileen Marks *had* longed for a daughter as talented as Pavlova, and was quite vocal about it to family and friends. She had actually wanted to become a performer herself while growing up as one of seven sisters in County Cork, Ireland—but not as a dancer.

As Markova's younger sister Doris Barry revealed:

> Mother was quite a talented singer. She used to sing and act at parties occasionally, and once George Edwardes [a famous English theatrical manager/producer who occasionally worked with Pavlova] heard her and offered her an engagement. But her family frowned on the stage as a professional career and she had to refuse it.
>
> I suppose her talent did provide a hereditary influence in some way. But there was a more positive one in Alicia's case. For my mother always said, after she had to turn down that offer, that she would have a daughter who would dance like Pavlova.
>
> She used to go and watch Pavlova at every opportunity. Later, when we were children, she took us too. And Alicia fulfilled mother's dream. Two medical text-books have quoted her case as an example of prenatal influence.

And there was yet another prescient tale passed along to the Marks girls. When newly pregnant with Alicia, Eileen accompanied her husband to Cairo, Egypt, where he was working as a consulting engineer on the recently constructed Aswan Dam. As the story goes, the lovebirds were taking a romantic moonlight stroll in view of the Sphinx when Eileen suddenly patted her belly and whispered to her husband, "I often pray it will be a girl—and like Pavlova, even if she can dance only a quarter as well."

Talk about foreshadowing! Little Lily, as she was called early on, would acquire the nickname Sphinx in childhood for being mysteriously silent and remarkably composed. She was also strangely taken with Egypt at a young age, never tiring of playing Alexandre Luigini's *Ballet Egyptien* on the wind-up gramophone, even choreographing a dance to it complete with an elaborate Sphinx-illustrated program. But more importantly, Markova's future career would forever be inextricably linked to Anna Pavlova, whom she would so closely come to resemble.

⁂

It had been love at first sight when eight-year-old Anna Pavlova accompanied her mother to see Marius Petipa's sumptuous new production of *The Sleeping Beauty* in 1890 (later re-titled *The Sleeping Princess* by Diaghilev, and would have that name until 1944, when it was changed back to *Beauty*). Attending the matinee was a special treat for the pair, as the family could barely afford tickets. "You are going to enter fairyland," her mother told her, and she was right.

Boasting a glorious score by Russian composer Pyotr Tchaikovsky, the ballet was majestically staged and costumed at St. Petersburg's Maryinsky Theatre. The Imperial Ballet always put on a visually stunning spectacle. The company was famous for it.

Lead dancers in the production included the Italian star Enrico Cecchetti, creator of the internationally revered Cecchetti method of ballet training, still in use today. The Maestro, as he was later called, would personally teach it to both Pavlova and Markova in the coming years.

The Sleeping Princess was the longest of Tchaikovsky's ballets, with the original 1890 production lasting four full hours. For the intoxicated Anna, it wasn't long enough. When the curtain finally came down, she decided she had found her true calling. (Coincidentally, seeing Pavlova on stage would arouse the same ardor in Markova when she was the same age twenty-nine years later.)

Anna's mother was pleased that her daughter had been so taken with the performance, but was caught off guard by the child's incessant begging for dance lessons. Lyubov Fedorovna Pavlova let a few weeks pass, but Anna continued pleading. She longed to be a ballerina and dance on the Maryinsky stage. Eventually, her mother capitulated.

With great difficulty, Lyubov arranged for an interview at the Imperial Ballet School in Moscow; but when the eight-year-old was deemed too young and weak for their rigorous classes, Anna became despondent. She wouldn't even be allowed to audition until age ten.

That left plenty of time for a girl in a family of modest means to forget all about the ballet. Anna was an only child, described as obedient and docile. She loved her bucolic country home outside St. Petersburg and spent hours play-acting in the forest. She'll move on, thought her mother.

But Anna didn't move on and, upon turning ten, once again pleaded to be taken for an audition. Though her family could never have funded years of extensive dance training, the Imperial Ballet School was run by the state, so classes, room, and board were free to all students.

Despite fierce competition—seven or eight chosen out of a hundred-plus applicants—and concerns about Anna's slight, fragile physique, there was something so graceful and intriguing about this little girl's movements and her serious demeanor that she was accepted.

Some thirty-odd years later, Alicia Marks would give a similar impression in her audition before Sergei Diaghilev and his ballet master, Serge Grigoriev. "The child certainly danced well, but was extremely thin and under-developed physically; and though we both thought her promising, I could not imagine how we could possibly use her," Grigoriev later recalled. But Diaghilev had the final word. "We'll give her a chance to grow and study . . . then we'll see."

Despite her mother's prenatal dreams and predilections, Lilian Alicia Marks never uttered a word of enthusiasm for ballet as a little girl. In fact, she barely spoke at all.

"I was interested in most things around me. I just didn't speak much," Markova remembered. "I was very observant and listened a lot, but they were quite worried about me because I was so silent."

But Markova was also independent. She remembers herself as "silent, but not unsociable. . . . I used to visit our neighbors, wandering off by the time I was three and four to pay calls on them, and not necessarily to families with young children of my own age with whom I could play, but to grown-ups who welcomed me, and who would read stories to me."

When it came time for the six-year-old to enter school and she still wasn't talking, Lily's concerned parents took her to see a doctor. He assured them there was nothing really wrong, as their daughter was quite bright, well behaved and happy, but he recommended home-schooling until she became more vocal. Since Eileen had already hired full-time Irish governess Gladys Hogan (known to all as Guggy) to help with her growing family, that wasn't a problem.

The following year, a doctor would be called in again to examine Lily, this time for an ongoing physical ailment. It seemed the future ballet star had fallen arches. The recommended cure was to wear rigid, laced-up corrective shoes, which the fashion-conscious little girl detested. She was already sensitive about her "odd" looks, now only made worse by the unfeminine footwear.

"I didn't even look a typically English little girl of the period," Markova wrote in her personal memoirs, comparing herself to her three sisters. "I was not pretty. Doris was the beauty of the family, Vivienne was delicate, and Bunny as she grew older was also beautiful. I was the solemn-eyed, thin child who was dressed in sailor suits and with a hairstyle of great simplicity—longing inside for the frills and pretty clothes that my sisters wore."

Perhaps Eileen Marks thought a girly dress would only make Lily's sturdy corrective shoes look worse. As her eldest daughter was so quiet and well-behaved, she never complained. However, when Eileen asked what color she wanted for her first party dress, the five-year-old was quick to request black. After studying the most stylish women in the neighborhood, Lily had decided black was quite chic.

"Everyone laughed, but I wore a little black satin dress trimmed with white lace," Markova recalled proudly.

At age seven, Lily was anything but proud of her looks. She sported a severe "Buster Brown" (or Dutch Boy) haircut, cropped short with bangs, and was forced to wear unattractive, sturdy boots. What was worse, not only did the offending footwear fail to correct her fallen arches, but Lily's right knee also became problematic, often buckling under during playtime.

Markova remembered, "I also earned another nickname at this time, because of my legs. There was a racehorse called Tishy, whose legs seemed to move in improbable directions [and who apparently always came in dead last], and so of course in the family I became known as Tishy. And it is a name that stuck until I was grown up. Sometimes during the early days at Sadler's Wells [dance company] my sisters would call for me asking 'Where's Tishy?'"

Eileen and Arthur didn't realize the extent of their daughter's troublesome gait until one day while on summer vacation at the seaside.

"I was trotting along the beach when I was about maybe seven, and they noticed I was padding around like a duck," Markova told a radio interviewer years later. "I was taken to a specialist and he discovered I had flat feet, knock knees, and weak legs."

Forget just corrective shoes. Consulting physician Dr. Colman recommended rigid iron leg braces. Lily wasn't the only one upset at the news. Already concerned with her daughter's shyness, Eileen Marks was fearful the added stigma of appearing crippled would isolate Lily all the more. Mrs. Marks asked the doctor if there were any other possible corrective alternative.

"Thank God that man was interested in the ballet," Markova later remarked. "He asked my mother if she would be willing to experiment with him, and she said yes. He thought, having made inquiries about the exercises for classical ballet, that [these dancers] were turned out from the hips down, and he had in his mind maybe those exercises would strengthen me if I was sent for some lessons. And I was sent once a week on Saturday mornings. Otherwise, I probably would never have taken ballet at all."

Lily had actually wanted to become a physician—perhaps inspired by her many early trips to the doctor—with health and medicine a steady interest throughout her life. As a child, she was calm and helpful during illnesses and accidents, as when her quick actions once saved her sister Doris from losing a fingertip. Gushing blood didn't bother Lily a bit.

And with knee and foot problems, ballet would have seemed out of the question as a realistic pursuit. Markova often joked, "What would people say to a girl with throat trouble who announced her intention of becoming an operatic singer?" Even Eileen Marks had given up hopes of raising a baby Pavlova. Dance lessons were to be remedial, nothing more.

It was the well-regarded Thorne Academy in Muswell Hill that Lilian Alicia attended every Saturday. Run by two hard-working sisters, the school offered a variety of performance, exercise, and dance lessons for young girls. Four-year-old Doris, sent as company for Lily, took elocution classes with Madge Thorne, while Dorothy Thorne taught Lily what was then called "fancy dancing"—"Slide, push, hop. Slide, push, hop." Mrs. Marks never discussed her daughter's leg problems with either Thorne sister, not wishing her to be singled out for her infirmities.

Lily quite looked forward to her weekly classes. "I rather enjoyed it because I met other children and my younger sister came with me," Markova later recalled. "And we did all kinds of things, used Indian clubs and jumped around. It was fun!"

"Dancing lessons seemed to be the nicest kind of medicine," she later told her mother gratefully.

In addition to ballet *barre* and dance training, which did indeed strengthen her legs, Lily practiced skipping rope and swinging Indian clubs in time to music, a common form of exercise in Great Britain at that time. The latter built muscle control in her tiny wrists, so much so that as an adult she amazed many a choreographer with her ability to hold lifts. Léonide Massine took advantage of that strength, only to discover later that no other ballerina could duplicate the moves he created for Markova.

As Agnes de Mille wrote in her book *Portrait Gallery*, Markova looked "as fragile as Venetian glass. Her legs and ankles seemed so remarkably slender, her hands so tapering, one felt they would snap off with the first jar; actually, a tennis champion's wrist, or a surgeon's, was probably a weaker instrument. In those delicate bones she had the kick of a stallion."

Then, of course, there was her prodigious natural talent. Even with weak legs, baby Lily was known to dance on "tippy toe" around the nursery in carpet slippers that had strong leather soles and a stiff top. As an adult, Markova had vivid memories of being able to hold that "rise" for long periods of time, much to her sisters' amazement. It was Lily's favorite parlor trick.

You could have knocked Dorothy Thorne over with a feather when she first saw Lily perform. How could such a little thing master all those complicated dance steps with such apparent ease?

Some fifty years later, Miss Thorne spoke of those early impressions on the television show *This Is Your Life* honoring Markova: "She had a wonderful precision of movement that many mature dancers would envy. And she never seemed to get out of breath. And I realized even then, that even with so many talented dancers, a Markova only happens once in a lifetime."

Ironically, when Miss Thorne suggested private lessons for the gifted young Lily, Eileen Marks pooh-poohed the idea that a girl with weak legs and deformed feet could ever become a professional dancer. She had given up that dream long ago. Besides, Markova amusingly recalled, "My mother thought it was a dodge to get more fees out of her."

Perhaps music would be Lily's future, which was something Eileen could relate to a bit better. The child had a fine ear and enduring love of concerts, even as a toddler. When just two years old, she was completely taken with the sound of a brass band and Sousa marches, a favorite all her life. (Coincidentally, George Balanchine hummed marches for accompaniment when giving Markova private dance lessons at the Ballets Russes many years later, a warm reminder of home.)

Baby Lily had not just one, but two local parks with bandstand concerts to choose from. Her first choice was Clissold because she loved to feed the swans. (Yes, more foreshadowing.)

A family photograph from that time shows the smiling toddler in her white ruffled bonnet sitting in a park lawn chair while merrily conducting along with the concert band using a pencil as a "baton." Eileen hired a piano teacher shortly thereafter, and her eldest took lessons throughout childhood. Though she had to give them up when dance became an all-consuming pastime, that early training manifested itself throughout her career.

"When you watch Markova, the music seems to come *from* her—it's amazing, but somehow she is the music," a young dancer would comment on her idol almost fifty years later.

As a teenage dancer with the Ballets Russes, Markova spent her off hours attentively listening to the orchestra rehearse, scrutinizing the conductor's every movement. She could easily commit entire scores to memory and thought she might like to conduct herself one day. She could also remember the first time she heard any piece of music, always associating it with a time and place.

When appearing on the popular radio show *Desert Island Discs* in 2002, Markova's first record selection for her time as a "stranded castaway" was the *Merry Widow* overture: "This is the first tune I can remember," she reminisced. "My father used to hum it to me. He used to pick me up and sort of waltz me around and hum this tune. And somehow, I don't know, later in life it's been a very lucky tune for me."

Markova's first crack at show business was as the Marks family impresario when she was eight. With three younger sisters, she had a ready-and-willing "cast" for her original theatrical performances, including recitations, singing, and dance. Fortunately, she was now vocal enough, though still very soft-spoken, to put the other girls through their paces. Even infant Berenice, always called Bunny, was included—but more as a costumed prop—much to Eileen's dismay.

"Alicia would produce, design, choreograph, and teach the three of us all the numbers both dance, song, and comedy scenes, and also illustrate special programs which we would sell for the local hospital charity," remembered Doris, who was about to become a professional child actress and performer on the London stage herself.

In addition to the elaborately illustrated programs, the inspired impresario created exotic costumes to attract a neighborhood audience. Markova had already shown a real knack for clothing design, having access to luxurious fabrics and embellishments from her great-grandfather, who had his own colorful connection to the theater.

Abraham Marks was a supplier of decorative fabrics and ornamental trimmings to professional costumers and wigmakers—like Willy Clarkson, whose client list included the "divine" stage star Sarah Bernhardt. A widower, Abraham always enjoyed the company of his great-granddaughters, who were given free rein in his overflowing costume supply room at his home/workspace in Islington, North London. He held a special place in his heart for Lilian Alicia, whose middle name was selected in honor of his cherished now-deceased wife.

Lily became Great Grandpa's littlest apprentice, one with a surprising color sense and flair for the dramatic, turning remnants of brocades, velvets, and beaded silks into impressively regal outfits for her dolls. She was quite a talented sewer as well, later applying those skills to creating dresses and costumes for herself in her early days as a poorly paid dancer.

Arthur Marks was so delighted with his daughter's original plays that he constructed a concrete stage with lights and a canvas awning in their back yard, moving the gramophone out to the garden for performances. And he had more reasons to be proud. In addition to entertaining friends and family, Lily sold her painstakingly illustrated programs to raise money for the local hospital, an early indication of the importance she held for charity work, which would be a lifelong concern.

Arthur Marks was especially close to Lily, and she to him. He never forgot the painful decision he had been forced to make when Lily was born. During the problematic delivery, the doctor asked, "Which do you want me to save? Your wife or your child?" Markova's anguished father had chosen his beloved wife, as his own mother had died in his childbirth. That they both lived was a miracle Arthur never took for granted, and he would treat Lily as if she were the anointed firstborn son in a Jewish household.

"I was very attached to my father, perhaps because he hoped I would be a son," Markova explained many years later. "But when I arrived a girl, he said never mind and proceeded to groom me as head of the family—taking me with him to watch polo, football, and the races, and later teaching me to carve and choose wines."

And he used to read his favorite adventure books to her, especially the Western novels of Zane Grey. *Riders of the Purple Sage* was her favorite.

Lilian Alicia proved a boon companion at whatever activity Arthur Marks chose for the pair. Though notably quiet, she was always a very attentive listener (a trait that would endear her to numerous beaus throughout her life). And Arthur had a lot to pass on to his beloved daughter.

For a man in his twenties, the devoted husband and father was already well traveled. Before his prestigious engineering commission on the Aswan Dam in Egypt, Arthur had attended college in the United States where his mother had been born. He had also extensively toured South Africa and Kenya while mining gold there with his father.

Arthur would spend hours with Lily on his lap, showing her maps, photo albums, and souvenirs of all the places he'd lived, describing various locales in vivid detail. She was fascinated by his stories and had phenomenal recall decades later.

In 1949, for example, Markova made her first trip to Johannesburg, South Africa for a dance performance. Sent to interview her, a newspaper reporter couldn't believe the great ballerina had never been to the city before, as she already knew so much about the local customs, geography, and favorite food delicacies, which she gobbled up enthusiastically.

The Johannesburg *Sunday Times* reporter wrote, "Her manager, Alfred Katz, of New York, commented to me: 'She is strangely happy here.' He cannot say why, but he supposes it may have something to do with the ballerina's early associations, her father's snapshot album, and because her child imagination was stirred by the tales of early days on the brawling Rand [South African gold mines]."

Lily was always dreaming of exotic people and places, remembers her sister Doris, who later became her personal manager.

"One of our favorite games was traveling, using the lid of Mother's sewing machine and the upturned nursery table as our chariots, magic carpet, a ship, or even an aeroplane, and so we would pretend to visit foreign lands. Both Alicia and I were very interested in geography and I often think now, when we are in some far-off place, how our childhood dreams have become a reality."

Doris was four years younger than Lily, Vivienne seven, and Bunny eight. After giving birth to three successive daughters following Lily's troubled delivery, Eileen Marks became physically delicate and more a homebody than her husband. During that time, her eldest spent a great deal of time bonding with her father.

"Mother, to me, always seemed to be waiting for the next baby to arrive," Markova said years later. "When the First World War started [Alicia was four], Daddy got a car because he was doing war work, and whenever he went off he would pop me in the rear seat because I was very well-behaved. He took me to Arsenal matches when mother had to rest." Even when she was a toddler, Arthur encouraged Lily to shout "Buck up, The Reds!" while propped high on his shoulders at games.

Markova continued to actively root for Arsenal throughout her life, a fact her own fans found incongruous. "One doesn't expect Princess Aurora or the Sugar Plum Fairy to be interested in soccer," she joked. "I love it! What struck me at that first match? Oh, the marvelous movement of it all. And I had a great feeling of exhilaration. Those footballers were achieving something. I have delighted in achievement all my life."

Arthur Marks had achieved much by the time Lily was a little girl. He was perhaps proudest of formulating the product "Rubberine," a material so strong it was used during World War I to prevent tires on army vehicles from being punctured when fired upon. Arthur's many inventions and manufacturing ventures made him a very wealthy man.

As Markova recalled, "First my father had a Buick. Then when I was about seven, I was in a Rolls Royce." The fact that he would go bankrupt shortly thereafter was then unimaginable.

It was said that Markova inherited her love of music from her mother. But her photographic memory, analytical mind, and gift for arithmetic most certainly came from her father. As her sister's manager for many years, Doris was astounded.

"She was a wizard at mental arithmetic, which is most useful these days as she usually has the financial side of an offer or contract worked out much faster than I, who likes to do it on paper. This is an extremely practical side of her character that I am sure not many people know exists; no matter how busy she is with work and rehearsals, she always looks after her own personal accounts."

Indeed, Markova's storage files were filled with page upon page of her handwritten computations for costume, hotel, and traveling costs for herself and various dance companies she co-founded. Natural accounting skills would prove fortuitous, as keeping the books was a price she had to pay for professional independence. It was far more typical for *prima ballerina assolutas* to be loyal to one or two ballet companies throughout their entire careers—such as Margot Fonteyn's lifelong association with London's Royal Ballet—and, in turn, be nurtured and cosseted by management.

"How little the daily life of a ballet dancer in a large, permanent company has changed since Pavlova's youth," wrote Margot Fonteyn in the book *Pavlova: Portrait of a Dancer.*

> The dancers have no worries about the costumes or hairdressing, which are seen to by the wardrobe department and the hairdressers; shoes are given out by the shoe department and rehearsals are scheduled by ballet-masters to take place in the company studios, where pianists await with music ready . . . the dancer must dance and that is the single focus of energy every day.

And how much easier life would have been for Alicia Markova had she, too, taken that career path. With her quest for bringing classical ballet to audiences throughout the world, she was willing to relinquish that invaluable support and security system for freedom to travel.

Had he lived, Arthur Marks would have taken great pride in his daughter's self-reliance. When Lily was a small girl, he enjoyed talking about his own family's successes and resourcefulness. Arthur's great-uncle had chaired the committee that undertook construction of the iconic Tower Bridge.

As Markova remembered, "At week-ends my father—he was an engineer—took one of my sisters and me sightseeing in the City.

"That's how I first saw St. Paul's, Pudding-lane and the Monument. Daddy took us to Tower Bridge too. We thought of great-uncle as we looked at it and felt a proper family pride. I still do."

Arthur's father also had impressive credentials. He was involved with creating the first electrical lighting on theater marquees in London and New York. Little did he know that his granddaughter would one day see her own name up in lights.

Lilian Alicia Marks made her stage debut at an age when Anna Pavlova was still dreaming of ballet lessons. Upon the suggestion of Dorothy Thorne, Lily's governess entered the eight-year-old in a local weekly talent contest at the Athenaeum Cinema in Muswell Hill. It was held each Friday evening between movie showings.

Eileen and Arthur were a bit taken aback by the news, apprehensive that their daughter would freeze up on stage. After all, Lily was so quiet and shy around strangers and had already been pulled out of two different public schools. Her first year, severe whooping cough, scarlet fever, and German measles kept her home more than in class. Then when she returned the following fall, Lily had trouble with both her class work and fitting in.

Having been homeschooled until age six, she was way ahead of her peers in certain subjects, but behind in others. Spending so much time alone with her governess Guggy, Lily had also become accustomed to one-on-one teaching. At school, she always had her nose buried in a book, preferring reading to running around a playground. That hardly endeared her to fellow classmates. Markova later estimated that the sum total of her public school education was about two months.

"I envy people who have had serious education," she later confessed. "Mine was a combination of teaching myself or working with a governess, and then contact with the world of the Ballets Russes." But then again, Markova reconsidered, "there are not many girls who can claim Diaghilev, Stravinsky, and Matisse as their teachers."

It seems Markova always felt most comfortable on stage, much to her parents' relief and amazement. Not only was Lily a marvelous dancer—clearly extraordinary for her age—but she was also remarkably poised and self-confident in front of a large crowd.

"I often wondered what the Cinema audience must have thought when, probably expecting a broad comedian, a little slip of a child appeared in a white ballet dress and danced a rather sad dance with a rose to a Chopin waltz," Markova recalled. "As the dance went on, it got sadder and sadder and the pink rose I was holding fell to pieces, petal by petal, and the audience dissolved in tears. . . . It seems that even in those days I was to establish myself in a classic mood!"

The talent-contest winner was chosen based on audience applause, which was timed with a stopwatch. There was no question as to who won. The official prize was to be five guineas and a contract for a week's performance engagement at the Cinema. Due to her age, Lily had to turn the latter offer down, but she won far more that evening. Her parents realized Dorothy Thorne was right. Their daughter really was a gifted little dancer.

"I shall never forget the thrill I had when I literally 'stopped the show' and became beyond all doubt the winner," Markova proudly recalled. "I was so happy, not so much with the five guineas but with the appreciation and applause of my first public."

Moreover, performing seemed to bring the young Markova out of her shell. Now her parents would gladly pay for private lessons and see how she progressed.

That was music to Dorothy Thorne's ears. In the Academy's annual show that year, she chose Lily Marks for a starring role. Playing off the child's severe black hair and eyes—and dead-serious expression in one so young—Lily was cast as a cymbal dancer in *The Arabian Nights*. Her costume was almost comically elaborate, including a bejeweled breastplate and headdress worthy of a Wagnerian opera.

The overall effect on stage was compelling to say the least, and, combined with Lily's unique dancing abilities, the performance earned the moppet prodigy her first newspaper notices.

"Little Lily Marks made a great hit with an Eastern dance," wrote a critic from *The Sentinel* on February 21, 1919. One year later, the *Sentinel* writer was still impressed. "We always watch for Lily Marks, and this time, again, she did not disappoint us. There was something daintily suggestive in her Rose Poem dance to music by Chopin."

In April of the same year, Lily would wow an even bigger audience at a charity concert to benefit the Italian Red Cross at London's Strand Theatre. Here she shared the stage with many established celebrities, including comic actress Beatrice Lillie and British performer Jack Buchanan. Once again it was foreshadowing, as Markova would work closely with both stars in adulthood.

One would think Lily was getting all the attention at home, but the four girls were treated pretty much the same—which was fine with the budding dancer and a credit to her parents. Markova was extremely close with and devoted to her sisters throughout her life.

Besides, five-year-old Doris was already working on a career of her own. The Thorne Academy elocution lessons had paid off, and the young actress started appearing in several silent movies. A role in a film of Charles Dickens's *The Old Curiosity Shop* earned her the sobriquet "England's Baby Mary Pickford." Arthur Marks was enormously proud of both girls.

But for Eileen, there must have been a special bond when she tucked Lily into bed each night. Could she really have given birth to a baby

Pavlova? By the following summer, the little ballerina would share her mother's dream.

After spending the perilous years of World War I in America, followed by a lengthy tour of Mexico and South America, Anna Pavlova had returned to Europe at the end of 1919. Though she had been born in Russia, she now called London home.

There were several reasons. First, after being schooled and trained at the Imperial Russian Ballet (also known as the Maryinsky), Pavlova felt stifled by their restrictive policies. She chafed at being told what she could and couldn't dance. And how could she introduce the beauty of ballet to the world if her travel time outside of Russia was as severely limited as her repertoire?

While artistic independence was reason enough to leave the confines of the Maryinsky, it did not preclude Pavlova's living in her cherished homeland between engagements. Precipitating her permanent move to England was a man who would dedicate most of his life to her: Russian-born Victor Dandré.

It was an unlikely pairing. When they met, Dandré was thirty years old and a powerful member of the St. Petersburg municipal council, known as the *Duma*. As a government official, he also sat on the boards of many charities, often fund-raising through benefit performances at the Imperial Theatre. It was there that Dandré first took note of the Imperial Ballet's up-and-coming dancer, eighteen-year-old Anna Pavlova. He longed to know her better.

According to Pavlova biographer Oleg Kerensky, the teenaged Anna earned just £70 per year at the Maryinsky, not nearly enough to pay for a comfortable home and private dance lessons. But she soon found many "admirers" (as was then common practice for Russian ballerinas who often became mistresses to the rich and powerful) happy to subsidize her living expenses and provide her with elegant clothes and jewels.

Dandré would become her most generous admirer, and one who "presumably contributed towards the large flat in which Pavlova lived," writes Kerensky. Then, suddenly, it all went wrong:

> In 1911 Pavlova was summoned to an official enquiry into the accounts of the municipal duma and Dandré was arrested in connection with financial irregularities concerning funds set aside for the building of a bridge. It appears that Dandré had been appropriating public funds for his private purposes, including the support of Pavlova. But the exact facts will never be established as Dandré was released on bail and fled abroad before he could be brought to trial.

While they were not officially a "couple," Pavlova couldn't help but feel responsible for Dandré's exile. He was completely devoted to her and had embezzled government funds for her benefit. As payback, she took him on as her manager and partner, a move that surprised many. It was a job Dandré would hold and cherish for the rest of Pavlova's life. He was an able protector, traveling with her everywhere, save for her visits to Russia. There, he could never return.

But it was a fortuitous turn of events as it happened. Had Dandré remained a Duma official during the ensuing Russian Revolution, his fate would have undoubtedly been far worse than voluntary exile.

The pair chose London for their permanent residence, buying a home in the bucolic suburb of Golders Green near Hampstead Heath. In his touching biography of Pavlova, Dandré later explained how they came to live at the tranquilly situated Ivy House.

By 1912, Pavlova was earning an astounding £1200 per week for her seasonal four- to five-month bookings at the Palace Theatre in London. That made her a very wealthy woman, able to pick and choose among the most luxurious accommodations.

At first she settled in the elegant Hyde Park Hotel, chosen for its namesake garden-filled location. But there were always so many people about, making it impossible for Pavlova to take a leisurely stroll in the park without being mobbed for her autograph. She soon longed for her own private grounds where she could commune with nature in peace and enjoy quiet time between performances.

After a lengthy search, Dandré found the perfect spot. Only fifteen minutes from central London, Golders Green had country views and fresh air that reminded Pavlova of her childhood home in Russia. Ivy House in particular was a rather grand estate set high on a hill with open views for many miles. From the balcony, one could admire the isolated woodsy setting, multiple gardens, and large circular pond with bubbling fountains where the ballerina kept swans. She was frequently photographed with the graceful waterfowl, a not-so-subtle reminder of her signature ballet.

Dandré was informed that the famous British painter J. M. W. Turner had once lived at Ivy House, adding to the property's cachet. Known as "the painter of light," the 19th-century artist must have relished the floor-to-ceiling leaded-glass windows that made the sun dance throughout the expansive rooms all day long.

Then there was the dramatic, high-ceilinged grand hall—ideal for a ballet practice studio—and a large downstairs storage space, big enough to accommodate cumbersome scenery and costumes.

Pavlova was sold, and immediately arranged for her furniture to be shipped from St. Petersburg. There was need for quick action. To escape the current political turmoil in Europe, the Russian ballerina had booked a cross-country American tour for the 1913–14 season, perhaps followed by Australia. Knowing a welcoming retreat awaited her in England would be most reassuring.

But due to the outbreak of World War I in the summer of 1914, Pavlova would not return to London for another six years. (Markova would have a similar experience when forced to leave her homeland for America throughout World War II.) When Pavlova finally did come back to England in 1920, Ivy House would be her one permanent home and solace for the rest of her life. "I love London best of all," she told a British women's magazine in 1924, "and I look forward to coming back to my London home at the end of my tours."

In addition to herself and Dandré, Pavlova had quite a menagerie for company at Ivy House. She arranged for an aviary to be built inside the conservatory, filling it with a variety of exotic birds—and of course, there were all of the regal swans outside. Even though numerous pet dogs and cats were also allowed to roam freely about the grounds, the various species all seemed to get along. (Pavlova herself was allergic to cats—they gave her sneezing fits—but she enjoyed having them around nonetheless.) It was said every living creature at Ivy House had a name and Pavlova bid each one a personal good-bye whenever she left on tour.

Though they lived as "man and wife"—and Dandré was referred to as Pavlova's husband—no record of a wedding license has ever been found. The Russian impresario Sol Hurok, who proudly represented Pavlova on one of her American tours, claimed personal responsibility for having created the marriage myth.

"I myself married her off in the press," Hurok professed. "In 1925 the newspapers printed a story I gave them, announcing for the first time that she had been married to Victor Dandré—some of them called him her accompanist—seventeen years before." But he adds, "The truth is Pavlova was never married."

Many described the ballerina's relationship with Dandré as like father and daughter rather than lovers, but to the public it hardly mattered. If you wanted to get to Pavlova, you needed to go through Victor Dandré, and that's just who arranged a private audience for a very excited Lilian Alicia Marks, then nine years old.

In 1920, Eileen Marks was thrilled to learn that Anna Pavlova would once again be performing in London. It was the acclaimed dancer's first booking in the city since before the war, a seeming eternity in light of recent historic events. Pavlova was now thirty-nine years old, a world traveler, and still at the height of her fame.

In the past, Eileen had tried to make Lily aware of the Russian dancer's magic on stage and film, but with no lasting impression. Now that her daughter was a "dancer" herself, maybe the time was right. Arthur Marks offered to squire his daughter to the upcoming ballet divertissement so that Eileen could stay home with the other girls.

Pavlova was to appear at the majestic 2400-seat Queen's Hall, London's pre-eminent concert hall at that time. Still a tiny child at age nine, Lily had difficulty seeing over people's heads in large theaters, and Queen's Hall was constructed with perfect acoustics for concerts, not perfect sight lines. Eileen took that fact into consideration, securing seats in the upper circle with completely unobstructed views.

Though Lily had been taken to the theater many times, she was made aware that this particular performance would be something special. It was just as Pavlova's mother had told her as a child. "You are going to enter fairyland."

Waiting for the performance to begin, Lily carefully examined the deluxe printed program her father had purchased for her. The photos of Pavlova were intoxicating, even to a little girl.

As a woman who related to the camera as emotionally as she did an audience, the famous Russian ballerina was a photographer's dream. Pictures of Pavlova were always in great demand, whether she was posing alluringly in a magnificent, billowing tutu or modeling the latest fashion with one of her theatrically extravagant hats.

Lily couldn't get over the ornate costume details, lissome body positions, and chameleon-like expressions in all the photos. But she was especially taken with the photo of Pavlova nestled in the grass at Ivy House while lovingly cradling one of her swans. It was inconceivable that Lily herself would visit those picturesque grounds the very next day.

Live on stage, Pavlova had exactly the effect on Lily that she'd had on Eileen Marks and countless others. This wasn't ballet as the nine-year-old experienced in Miss Thorne's class. Pavlova was a revelation in her effortless grace, artistic movements, and passionate emotions, magically turning herself into a flower for her very first dance.

The solo had been added to Pavlova's repertoire when she toured the United States in 1915. While in San Francisco for a two-week booking, she had been captivated by the California poppies in full bloom everywhere she looked. The colorful flower closed its petals in the cool of each evening, opening once again in the morning to welcome back the sun. How marvelous, Pavlova had thought.

She was instantly inspired to create a new dance, choosing Tchaikovsky's moving "Melodie in E-flat" for accompaniment. Then Pavlova set about designing her costume, a poetic tour-de-force. Made of stiffened silk petals, each gossamer layer was scarlet red on the outside and a fiery yellow on the reverse, just like the poppy.

The material billowed about as Pavlova twirled joyously in the "sun," with a denouement that took the audience's breath away. The ballerina languidly drew each petal up and over her face until she was entirely encased in crimson. Then the stage would go dark.

California Poppy would be one of Pavlova's signature solos forever after. Lily Marks was beside herself. Since she was a baby, her two favorite things had been flowers and music. Now dance equaled their beauty. When asked what she would do when her performing days were over, Markova often replied, "As long as I have flowers and music, I'll be content." Pavlova voiced similar sentiments.

After seeing the Russian dancer bloom right before her eyes, Lily was convinced she had found a kindred spirit. She could picture herself walking in Clissold Park with the empathetic ballerina, pointing out her favorite flowerbeds and swans. She just had to meet Anna Pavlova in person and pleaded with her father to make it happen.

While most parents would pat their child's head and sweetly explain the impossibility of such a request, Arthur Marks was astonished by Lily's emotional entreaty. It was so completely out of character for his painfully shy daughter, who never spoke to strangers. He at least needed to make a good-faith effort on her behalf.

Of course, he really had no idea how to do that, but Arthur Marks was nothing if not resourceful. As befitted a proper businessman of the time, Arthur asked to leave his card at the stage door in hopes of taking Lily to Pavlova's dressing room after the performance. When told that unknown guests never gained such entrance—nor did famous ones—Arthur asked if there was anyone else he might speak with. "You might try Pavlova's manager, Victor Dandré."

Arthur did, but the answer was still a polite no.

The distraught father tried one more time, explaining that Lily was a talented ballet dancer herself, having already received good notices in London newspapers. Meeting Pavlova would mean the world to her.

It was exactly the right thing to say.

As Dandré later recorded: "When it was a case of parents wishing to choose the career of dancing for a child, Pavlova would refuse outright to give any advice, saying that she could only judge after the child had worked for two or three years under a teacher. Only then and according to the progress made, could one say anything definite regarding a child's aptitude and ability as a future dancer.

"If on the other hand, little girls having already had some tuition were brought to her, she generally agreed to see them, fixing some free hour for this."

It is likely Dandré thought Lily was a teenager, as he was told she'd already earned positive press reviews. That would make her eligible to be a potential *corps de ballet* candidate for Pavlova's company, always of interest to her. Thank goodness Dandré never asked Lily's age.

Would Arthur Marks be willing to bring his accomplished daughter to Ivy House the next morning to dance for Madame Pavlova at say, 11:30 A.M.? The dumbfounded father most certainly would.

Lily was over the moon at the news. She could barely contain herself while watching the second half of the Queen's Hall performance. As the curtain rose, she took a deep breath. There was her new idol dressed in a lavish 18th-century costume for a dance to another of Tchaikovsky's pieces, the "Belle of the Ball" Christmas waltz. With the knowledge that the two would meet the very next day, Lily found Pavlova even more electrifying. Arthur enjoyed watching his child's rapturous face even more than the onstage performance.

Before going home, Lily begged to join the large queue waiting for Pavlova to exit the theater. It was as carefully choreographed a performance as the one that had just ended on stage.

"The first sign of life would be that the chauffeur would light the interior of the car: this would produce a buzz of anticipation," revealed Margot Fonteyn's love letter of a book to the Russian icon, *Pavlova: Portrait of a Dancer.*

Next, the countless bouquets that admirers had sent to her dressing room would be ceremoniously trotted out one by one and carefully placed in the spacious limousine. Lily, of course, was in heaven watching the spectacle.

As each lavishly dressed person exited the stage door, the crowd would look up expectantly, than look down disappointed. Pavlova's well-to-do dinner companions always came out first. They too were carefully arranged in the car.

Finally, *La Pavlova* appeared, almost shockingly tiny offstage, but just as resplendent, most often covered in sumptuous furs.

> Nobody dreamed of daring to ask for her autograph, any more than they would ask royalty. She paused for a moment on the doorstep, then, amid a murmur of adoration, got into the car.
>
> Now the windows were lowered, and everyone had a final picture of the goddess, shining among flowers. She broke roses and carnations off her bouquet and threw them out to the

> happy crowd; and continued to do so as, very gently, almost imperceptibly, the perfumed and illuminated shrine moved away into the night.

As it was a warm summer's evening when Lily was in attendance, Pavlova relinquished her usual head-to-toe fur in favor of an absolutely enormous fringed picture hat—so dramatic that it drew audible gasps from the crowd. Markova would also become known for her face-framing hats and fashion sense, but as a proper Englishwoman, she favored a tasteful elegance over Pavlova's more startling, Slavic extravagance. And though Markova arguably became as celebrated a dancer, she maintained a far more modest life offstage, both in living quarters and theater exits.

"What ordinary ballet-goer had the chance of getting Pavlova's autograph after a performance, let alone of speaking to her!" wrote British ballet scribe D. P. Daniels. "Markova signs a pile of autograph books after each performance. . . . She makes very real concessions of time and energy to speak to people who want to see her for sincere reasons. . . . And by facing this 'light of common day' she loses no enchantment. Indeed, I think she gains a firmer place in the public's affection."

On the opposite end of the spectrum, Pavlova felt so strongly about maintaining an unknowable mysterious persona that, according to biographer Oleg Kerensky, "when efforts were being made to engage her to dance at a social function, she offered to reduce her fee from £500 to £300 if she would not be obliged to take dinner with the guests."

The multi-talented photographer/writer Cecil Beaton knew and revered Pavlova, later becoming close friends with Markova when he designed costumes for one of her performances. "I have a tremendous admiration for Markova," he would later recall. "At no time has she ever wasted her energies upon acting 'the star' offstage. First and last, she is a dancer, and, as an artist, a dancer exists only when she is dancing."

And dancing was exactly what nine-year-old Lily Marks would be doing for the great Anna Pavlova. To say that Eileen Marks was speechless at the news would be an understatement. The process of selecting a suitable outfit and packing all the necessary dancewear started late that night, only to be repeatedly checked and re-checked the following morning. Do you have your best tights? Where are your hair ribbons? It was hard to tell who was the most excited member in the household.

Once again, Arthur did the honors in escorting Lily to see Pavlova. They took the train from Finsbury Park, as it was faster and simpler than driving. Markova would relive that day for a BBC radio audience in 1975. Ivy House had recently been turned into a museum honoring Pavlova, and Markova was invited to visit and share her personal memories:

> It was a beautiful summer day with all the trees and the flowers and the birds singing. I remember arriving at the Golders Green station and walking up the hill with my father. And we arrived and it had two large gates, which opened. We came in and there was this beautiful foyer. And I remember looking in and seeing these huge baskets there, with the name Anna Pavlova on them. And I think they were all being prepared for her coming tour.
>
> [After Arthur Marks was given a stack of newspapers and escorted to another room, the luminous Pavlova took little Lily into her studio.]
>
> Well, naturally she gave me some advice about pointing my toes and breathing and technical things, but to me the things that really remained in my mind were two things one would never have expected.
>
> The first thing she said was that one must always take great care of one's health. And then she asked me to open my mouth. And like a little horse, I had to show my teeth. And she told me that the most important thing was to take good care of one's teeth. So for the rest of my life, I've always gone quite regularly to the dentist. That was one thing I have to thank her for.
>
> Then also, after I had danced, I naturally was perspiring and was warm. And she put her head around the door and asked me where my towel and cologne was for rubbing down. Of course I said I didn't know about anything like that. In a couple of minutes she was back with a large towel and a flask

> with a silver top—I've always remembered this—with A.P. on it. And with the cologne she started to rub me down so I wouldn't catch cold, and she told me this was very important: that if I were going to be a dancer the most important thing, never to catch cold.
>
> Now, there was one other little thing that I hate to say went through my mind. How will I ever make anybody understand that this really happened to me? I thought, could I steal the flask and take it home with me so that people will know I'm telling the truth. And then I suddenly thought, no—that would be terrible. I would be a thief!

One thing Lily did take from Ivy House that day was a lifelong love of the color mauve, as Pavlova wore a dress that color when warmly greeting her, putting the shy girl instantly at ease.

"Nothing else would suffice," Markova joked years later. When she bought her first bottle of rubdown cologne on the way home from the visit—a necessity, according to Pavlova—Lily selected one with a mauve ribbon. She planted mauve flowers in the family garden. Even as an adult, Markova's makeup case was custom-made of deep mauve leather, sumptuously lined in mauve silk moiré. Inside, the top of each brush, comb, and glass jar was inlaid with mauve enamel, including, of course, a mauve capped bottle of rubdown cologne.

Markova always remembered every single detail of her first meeting with Pavlova, even fifty-five years later in a radio interview at Ivy House. "You actually danced for her in her studio?" she was asked.

"Oh yes—a beautiful studio—not very large, quite high. It had a gallery that went all around it. I noticed first that there seemed to be a lot of very light ivory furniture. I was rather impressed with it because I myself have always liked very light things. I can't bear dark things around me."

Markova eventually owned much of that delicate ivory furniture, willed to her many years later by Pavlova's costume designer and close companion Manya Charchevnikova. (Manya planned to retire after Pavlova's untimely death, but after seeing how closely Markova resembled her former employer onstage, she volunteered to resume designing just for her.) Markova gladly loaned the ivory dressing table and other personal furnishings to the Pavlova museum (she also joined their board), but she kept two simple chairs for herself as a reminder of that auspicious first encounter with the Russian star. They remained in Markova's London flat until the day she died.

After discussing the furniture at Ivy House, Markova described the photographs around the room for the radio audience.

> . . . There's also a photograph of her in the garden with her cat, and another one with her swan. She loved animals, didn't she? She adored animals, and birds, and of course, nature really. With the swan—that was really amazing—because swans are really very vicious creatures. That proves what, shall we say, an enchantress she was to be able to hold that swan in her arms. . . .
>
> She had such a strong personality and she lived here very happily. Let's not say that her ghost is here. But I think by having this museum and the society, really it's for the younger dancer. I would like to see young dancers and young people and students come here because I think that's what would really make her very happy.

A visit to Ivy House had certainly made Lily Marks very happy. The great Pavlova had said she could be a really fine dancer if she applied herself. But the celebrated ballerina also added a warning: "Your life will be all work, and unless you're prepared to give up your pleasures, you should find something else to do."

Up until that point, dancing was just playtime for Lily. Classes were a very enjoyable form of exercise to strengthen her legs. She had astonishing natural gifts, so she didn't require countless, frustrating repetitions of steps to master them, nor did she feel competitive with the other students. And she surprisingly suffered no stage fright.

But watching Pavlova perform opened Lily's eyes to the true beauty of ballet. Little Anna had the same life-altering experience while watching the Imperial Ballet's sweeping stage production of *The Sleeping Princess*.

Lily Marks decided then and there that she would work tirelessly to become the best dancer possible. Like Pavlova, she would, and did, give up everything for ballet, just as her idol forewarned on that auspicious day. That both girls were so determined from such a young age and never wavered in their beliefs is truly remarkable.

Markova also shared Pavlova's mission to introduce and promote ballet throughout the world, each becoming the most widely traveled ballerina of her time. They visited secluded hinterlands and foreign countries that had never seen any ballet, let alone two of the art form's most illustrious talents; and no venue—including a skating rink and a football stadium—was beneath them.

"Pavlova was Miss Markova's ideal," her frequent dance partner Anton Dolin later told a reporter. "She was a great individualist, she says, and she went all over the world bringing her inimitable art to the people. Other ballerinas, such as Tamara Karsavina, were also great, but they identified themselves much more closely with the needs of the great ballet companies. Pavlova created her own magic . . . [both she and Markova] would much rather dance for an audience which knows little about ballet than for a so-called sophisticated crowd which thinks it knows everything about ballet."

Of course those constant travels came with significant sacrifice, as a *Yorkshire Evening Post* theater writer reported in 1950:

> I recalled Pavlova telling me, not many months before her untimely death, that one of the penalties of her kind of fame was to feel always a wanderer. She had made herself a beautiful home in London, but saw little of it.
>
> It is so with Markova. She has a small flat in New York and in the house of a sister in London a room is always kept for her, but she is rarely in either place for long.

Back at Ivy House at age sixty-five, Markova was asked what Pavlova did so differently from other dancers to achieve such fame.

"I could never compare. Because to begin with, I don't think dancers should be compared," she answered. "They should be individual. Naturally, we're all trained with the same technique, just as actors are all given the same words, but I suppose it's what one can do with those words or steps. And that was where Pavlova was unique."

Markova's often-repeated sentiments didn't stop people from drawing constant comparisons between herself and Pavlova. It was only natural, as the two shared the same oddly proportioned body type, facial features, and emotionally fragile stage presence. From childhood, both were considered so very "different."

From *Anna Pavlova: Her Life and Art* by Keith Money:

> As a student, Pavlova was talented and also different. . . . For such an apparently slight creature she had strong hips and thighs and a thorax that was not particularly waisted, so that the body, though immensely supple, flowed "all of a piece."
>
> . . . [It was] a body that fooled the Maryinsky selectors, and it went on fooling observers. Her muscles were steely; she was actually a racing machine, a hare. . . .
>
> Her natural talent, the curious poetry of her body, was so outstanding that nobody could ignore it, even though the idiosyncrasies were disquieting to some.

And so was her appearance. Both Pavlova and Markova shared jet-black hair and alabaster skin—a "black-and-white beauty," as Agnes de Mille generously called it—but neither dancer was considered classically beautiful, especially by "pretty" ballerina standards exemplified by Margot Fonteyn. In the case of Pavlova, her nose was too large for her face and she had wide gaps in her teeth. Markova also had a prominent nose—noticeably hooked in profile—and wide thin lips. (Those features gave her the look of "an etherealized Fanny Brice," commented a writer for *The New Yorker.*)

Markova's frequent dance partner Anton Dolin strongly advised that she get a "nose job," but the ballerina flatly refused. Choreographer Frederick Ashton and impresario Sol Hurok would make the same suggestion, also thinking it would be for Markova's benefit. To prevent further harangues, she asserted that altering her nose would change how she viewed the stage coming out of spins and jumps, and might put her off balance. Case closed.

Despite their less-than-perfect features, Pavlova and Markova were both extremely photogenic (and knew the ideal angles for posing) so their facial flaws weren't readily apparent to the public. Besides, they both had huge, seductive eyes, leading many reporters to wax a tad too poetic:

"When you talk to her you forget everything but her eyes," a London journalist wrote of Pavlova in 1924. "They are large . . . and mysterious. . . . They intrigue, they excite, they fascinate! You feel that they hide a wilderness of wonderful secrets. They are the eyes of a dreamer, a poet, an artiste."

Ten years later, another British journalist wrote the following about Markova: "I chatted with her for a short while in her dressing room and was captivated by the charm of her large dark eyes. Her hair is raven black—blacker than any I have seen—and she resembles the great Pavlova not only in her great love of dancing but also in appearance."

Those types of descriptions followed intimate, one-on-one interviews with the two ballerinas, with the added excitement of being up close and personal with the stage stars. From afar, dance critics could be more disparaging of the pair's looks, sometimes being downright cruel.

In the case of Pavlova, according to her biographer Keith Money, a Berlin dance critic in 1909 "made extraordinarily ungallant remarks about her personal appearance, writing that although her name was printed in fat letters on the program, she was thin as a skeleton, and her ugliness was off-putting."

Pavlova biographer Oleg Kerensky quotes another German reviewer covering the same performance: "Miss Anna Pavlova . . . showed as Giselle her strong mimic talent, her gracefulness and ease, and of course the whole bravura of her tip-toe coloratura. Unfortunately, she is neither beautiful nor specially well-built."

In Markova's case, comments on her not-so-perfect looks were used more as backhanded compliments, with critics lauding her talent as being so prodigious it could overcome her physical shortcomings. From Mel Heimer's "My New York" newspaper column in 1955:

> In a dreadful red wig and an absurd series of nightgownish costumes, Markova demonstrated once more the remarkable and seldom-seen talent of skill overcoming appearance. She is a plain woman, as Gertrude Lawrence was a plain woman—but Gertie had, and Markova has, the ability to make you forget their plainness once in full cry.

> The ballet, even in the big leagues as with the Ballet Theater, is the most tinselly of the arts. Its practitioners seem like small boys and girls wearing grown-ups' clothes and posturing like them. . . .
>
> However, Markova is—well, did you ever see Ted Williams swing a bat or Bill Terry play first base? The sports writers have a word for it. Ask the next one you meet.

New York Herald Tribune dance critic Walter Terry had this to say in a 1963 article titled "Ballet Stars Without the Body Beautiful":

> And what of another now-retired ballerina Dame Alicia Markova, who is classified as one of the great dancers of all time? The dancing Markova was terribly thin, her face was not pretty (by Hollywood standards) and there were other things that were wrong but she not only transcended the presumed flaws, she turned them into assets as her thinness became exquisite fragility, and her face, with its huge, luminous eyes, assumed a "mystique" that fascinated the world.

One thing all critics seemed to agree on: the combination of impassioned acting and exquisite dance technique is what sets the greatest prima ballerinas apart from the merely talented. It's what made performances by Pavlova and Markova so transformative and memorable, creating a lasting emotional bond between the dancer and her audience.

As British writer J. K. Prothero explained in his *Weekly Review* column in 1938:

> Mr. James Agate [noted American writer/critic] in a recent article suggested that it was part of a dramatic critic's function to estimate the acting of the artists in an opera as apart from their vocal capacity. In the same way it seems to me that as distinct from miming and the actual technique of ballet dancing it is of interest to analyse the dramatic talent of conspicuous performers.
>
> I was particularly struck the other night at Drury Lane by the acting in "Giselle," that charming traditional Victorian

> ballet. The part of the lovesick maiden who, learning that her lover was not a forester but a prince, commits suicide, was taken by Markova. There is something about this lovely and wistful artist reminiscent of Pavlova. One feels the same spiritual quality in certain moods—tender resignation, tragic acceptance with sudden piercing movements, and that fluttering up towards joy which animated Pavlova's greatest concepts. Markova plays the part as well as dances it and in this she stands above.

Markova wrote a belated response to that review in her autobiographical *Giselle and I*, making it clear that while flattered by the comparison, she could never be, nor sought to be, another Pavlova.

> I was stirred by this comparison, but I don't think I took it as a personal one. Neither have I done so since, though it has often been made through the years. I like to feel that perhaps it shows a similarity of aim. Pavlova gave her life to the ideal of bringing beauty and happiness to people through the dance, and I have tried to do this also, in my generation. No two artists or individuals are alike, but a shared ideal gives deep satisfaction.

But the comparisons were inevitable, especially from British dance critics in the 1930s, who for the first time were able to trumpet a homegrown ballet star. Alicia Markova proved that you didn't need to be Russian to become a world-class ballerina, and she changed the face of British ballet forever. Now London had its very own Pavlova:

> Markova to me grows more and more like Pavlova each time I see her, and if she continues in the way she is now going I see no valid reason why in the years to come she should not attain as great a position in the world of the dance as that occupied by the great ballerina whose death we all mourned nearly two years ago.
>
> —*Dancing Times*, 1932

> Fragile, quiet and utterly unaffected—such is Markova, prima ballerina of the Vic-Wells Ballet Company. . . . Markova's resemblance to Pavlova has been talked of before; but she is amazingly like her. That is why I asked for the picture, so that you could see for yourselves. Don't you agree?
>
> —*Yorkshire Evening Post*, 1935

> And of the many English dancers who have achieved fame, Alicia Markova (now appearing in the season of Russian ballet at Drury Lane) surely stands supreme. . . .
>
> She won the distinction of being the first English artiste to dance the leading role in a four-act ballet, when Tschaikovsky's [*sic*] Lac des Cygnes was revived for her. She was also the first English dancer to appear in Giselle, the "Hamlet" of the ballet.
>
> So uncanny is her resemblance to the late Anna Pavlova that she was offered a fabulous sum to go to Hollywood to star in a film based on Pavlova's life. . . . Markova felt it would be sacrilegious to attempt an impersonation of the greatest ballerina of all time.
>
> —*Theatre World*, August 1938

That last statement is another testament to Markova's ultimate respect for Pavlova's memory and strong desire never to impinge on her legacy in any way. Not only did she turn down the chance to play Pavlova on screen—which clearly would have been an enormous career boost to the young dancer—but she also refused to perform the Russian's signature role of *The Dying Swan* for over ten years, though repeatedly and relentlessly asked.

She finally gave in when pursued by none other than Mikhail Fokine, the visionary Ballets Russes choreographer who had originally created the role for Pavlova. Along with the American-based impresario Sol Hurok, Fokine begged Markova to take on the role "to keep the memory of Pavlova alive." She agreed on the condition that her performance clearly be designated a tribute to her idol and take place on January 23, 1942, the eleventh anniversary of Pavlova's death.

The first-ever audience for Markova's *The Dying Swan* was at the Boston Opera House. They were utterly transfixed, and from that day on, the role was as much associated with Markova as with her illustrious predecessor.

". . . [P]hysicians—or at least physicians who go to ballets—have commented with some astonishment on the way Markova's arms are attached to her shoulders," wrote Barbara Heggie in a 1944 profile of the dancer in *The New Yorker* magazine. "There is something avian about this, too. When she suddenly lifts her arms from her sides, it is as if she were unfolding wings. A critic once described her as 'a winged creature, inhabitant of the air.'"

"Markova's 'Swan' is a lovely, ethereal creature," wrote another dance critic upon seeing her first performance of Fokine's updated choreography. "Perhaps she has done her best to imitate Pavlova but she succeeds in being herself in this very beautiful interpretation which was staged last night as a tribute to the great Russian ballerina."

Markova had capitulated at just the right time. Seven months later, Mikhail Fokine would be dead.

Other famous choreographers were also drawn to Markova because of her eerie likeness to Pavlova. Frederick Ashton, for one, had his earliest successes in ballets he created for Markova. Ashton first saw her dance as a teenager with the Ballets Russes.

"During the Diaghilev season at the Princess Theatre I had sat in the gallery night after night watching her," he recounted in a later radio interview. "Apart from her work, her astonishing likeness to Pavlova fascinated me and I never dreamed that such a great artist would be interested in accepting an engagement from me."

For Léonide Massine, there was an added allure. The brilliant Russian dancer/choreographer had begun his career at the Ballets Russes, where he was well aware of Pavlova's negative feelings toward modern ballets.

As biographer Keith Money explained, Pavlova saw Diaghilev "as the arbiter of all that was destructively avant-garde," and though she respected his talents, "Pavlova had been personally offended by him."

> She could see that their current aims were divergent in many ways; she clung to the belief that the purest elements of the classical ballet vocabulary could, and should, survive, and that the old ballets from the Maryinsky era should be protected;

> Diaghilev, whatever his innermost beliefs, had built up the type of audience that looked continually for novelty, and here was precarious juggling of interests between the tenets of classicism and the aims of a theatrical adventurer.
>
> —*Anna Pavlova: Her Life and Art,* Keith Money

Unlike Pavlova, Alicia Markova was always game for anything new and exciting. How irresistible she must have been to Massine, able to provide an extraordinary technique on par with Pavlova's, but in someone all too happy to be the "vehicle" for bringing his latest innovative creations to life. And Massine didn't keep that sentiment to himself, as illustrated in the following scene recollected by noted Indian journalist and author Basanta Koomar Roy in the December 1943 issue of *Dance Magazine*:

> One evening when I was talking with Mr. Massine in his dressing room, on the art and philosophy of the Ballet, he suddenly walked out of the room, and in a minute returned with Alicia Markova. Without saying a word, he began to turn Markova around as a great dressmaker affectionately turns his favorite model in a fashion show. I was wondering within myself what it was all about. After a few moments I noticed that a certain angle of Miss Markova's profile resembled that of Anna Pavlova. Just then Mr. Massine broke his silence by saying:
>
> "Doesn't she look like . . . ?"
>
> "Like Pavlova, you mean," I said.
>
> "Yes."
>
> "Yes, a certain angle of her profile has indeed a touch of Pavlova; and the parting of her hair in the center accentuates that resemblance."
>
> "And she has a marvelous technique."

Imagine a choreographer dragging Rudolf Nureyev into his dressing room, spinning him around in front of an unknown writer—Massine didn't bother to introduce Markova—and comparing him to Vaslav Nijinsky in the third person. Alicia Markova was a huge star by 1943, yet she took the incident pleasantly in stride. (Roy later wrote a very complimentary profile on her.) She was used to it, as the comparisons only became more frequent after Pavlova's unexpected death in 1931.

In January of that year, the Russian prima ballerina caught pneumonia while stranded in the snow during a train derailment. She was on her way to perform in The Hague, Netherlands, and instead found herself seriously ill and bedridden in the city's luxurious Hotel des Indes. With the devoted Victor Dandré by her side, Anna Pavlova passed away, just hours after asking to hold her costume for *The Dying Swan* one more time. It was one week shy of her fiftieth birthday.

Dandré later presented Markova with several of Pavlova's ballet slippers and costume accessories as keepsakes. He was well aware of the pair's mutual admiration, though Pavlova thought Markova's brilliance was being wasted in the hands of avant-garde choreographers. She had told her so after attending a Ballets Russes performance in Paris.

"She was sitting in the box at the Sarah Bernhardt Theatre, I think it was," Markova later recalled. "And afterward she came backstage to pay her respects to the company. And of course, I was there. I was still the little one, the baby of the company. And she came over and said hello to me, but she was very disappointed."

It was not the tiny ballerina's dancing that dismayed Pavlova, but the non-classical role Diaghilev had selected for her. "I think I was in *Pas d'Acier* or something, one of the most modern works, and she said she was very sad to see me in a modern work."

That was yet another key difference between the two great ballerinas. As *The Telegraph* dance critic Ismene Brown wrote of the young Markova, "her undeveloped androgynous body and fearless male-type technique contrasted with the sophisticated femininity of Diaghilev's famed ballerinas, and was a valuable spark to the modern revolution. . . . Igor Stravinsky found her able to absorb new musical ideas readily, and—because of her emotional immaturity—the choreographer George Balanchine began to conceive a more abstract kind of female dancing, driven by music rather than drama."

But that "appetite for modernity," as one writer ascribed to Markova, never stopped Pavlova from admiring the little English girl's rise to fame. She even left Markova a fur coat in her will. It became one of her most prized possessions.

Another cherished memento was a floral crown Pavlova had worn in *Giselle.* Her former dresser and costumer Manya later presented it to Markova, and the dancer wore it for luck when first performing the role herself.

After Pavlova's death, watching Markova dance seemed to provide some comfort to Victor Dandré. In 1937, a British ballet critic reported, "Whenever Markova dances in London, M. Dandré, Pavlova's widowed husband, can always be seen in the stalls, acting as official 'fault-scout.' On the fall of the curtain he retires to the ballerina's dressing-room with notes of a few technical subtleties which might require attention—though they would be far too subtle to be noticed by the public!"

To Markova's credit, she always greeted Dandré and his "suggestions" warmly. She too enjoyed reminiscing about the great dancer who had shown her so much kindness.

"What can I recall of her gestures? They were not the important impression," Markova told a British reporter prior to a Pavlova tribute performance in 1956. "To a child in awe of the great lady she was so kind and simple. In minutes we seemed to have known each other always. . . ."

Pavlova herself once said to Markova, "If I had a daughter, she couldn't be more like me than you are."

Though that was true as far as the two dancers' appearance and performance styles were concerned, their temperaments were worlds apart. While Markova had great relationships with other talented female dancers—she remained best friends with Russian ballerina Alexandra Danilova for over seven decades—and often shared the stage with them, Pavlova wanted the spotlight to be hers alone.

According to Oleg Kerensky's biography, Pavlova left the Ballets Russes because fellow lead dancers Vaslav Nijinsky and the much-loved Tamara Karsavina received "too much publicity" in relation to herself. (Ironically, Karsavina's star rose for her portrayal of the title role in Fokine's *The Firebird,* a part Diaghilev first offered to Pavlova, and which she turned down because she thought Igor Stravinsky's music was "ugly nonsense." *The Firebird* would also be a great success for Markova.)

And when the beautiful Karsavina needed to take over the lead in *Giselle* due to Pavlova's early departure from the Ballets Russes, the latter refused to help her learn the part, though that was a customary practice in large companies. It was "a role which Pavlova jealously guarded for herself at the Maryinsky," Kerensky writes. "Pavlova was increasingly interested in ballet as a vehicle for a ballerina, herself."

Then there was Pavlova's notorious hot temper. She famously slapped several male dancers in front of audiences during performances, most memorably her legendary partner Mikhail Mordkin. The press ate it up. And it was said her jealousy was responsible for Mordkin's ballerina wife, Bronislava Pajitzkaya, being fired.

It would be a similar story with the Pavlova Company she founded and took all over the world. There was just one star—Anna Pavlova—with a talented male dancer to partner her, and a competent, though not stellar, *corps de ballet* of some thirty-odd dancers. As Kerensky writes, ". . . there would obviously have been no room in Pavlova's company for dancers with very big personalities and grand ideas of their own importance. English girls, being generally well-disciplined and modest, were ideal."

Markova was one of those "English girls" Pavlova approached to join her company. It was in 1929, right after Diaghilev died, and, with him, the Ballets Russes. Though Markova was frightened of her future prospects, she reluctantly turned the offer down. The eighteen-year-old was already a technically brilliant dancer with a burgeoning solo career, and knew she would never get a crack at lead roles while under contract to Pavlova, no matter how much she adored the star.

"It was funny," Markova recalled years later, "although she inspired me as perhaps no other dancer had, after four years strenuous work [with Diaghilev] I did not feel inclined to join her. I had worked from the bottom of the ladder and I determined to move on alone."

After Pavlova's death in 1931, Markova's likeness to her idol was seen as both good for ballet in general and useful to the promotion of fledgling British companies. It was shorthand for brilliant talent. As Anton Dolin told a British newspaper arts reporter the year the pair formed the Markova-Dolin Ballet Company in 1935:

> The spirit of Pavlova has entered Markova. She is the nearest approach to the divine Anna Pavlova that this or any other age will give us.

> Each time I see her dance, rehearse or dance with her, I am more and more conscious of this. The physical resemblance is extraordinary, at times almost frightening.

Agnes de Mille took this notion one step further in an essay on Markova she wrote for *The Atlantic Monthly* in 1953, later expanded in her 1990 book *Portrait Gallery*. De Mille mocked Markova for attempting to channel Pavlova when performing. "For quite a period, she even claimed the spirit of the Russian inhabited her body."

While Markova didn't mind the onstage comparisons, she emphatically denied any foolish transcendental connection, often refuting de Mille's contention in later interviews. The whole idea of Pavlova being her "spirit guide" was complete poppycock, as she told Maurice Leonard for his biography *Markova: The Legend*.

> People said all sorts of things because I resembled her and my mother told me that when she was carrying me she did think that it would be wonderful if I could dance just a little like Pavlova but, even knowing that, it didn't influence me. I had qualities she never had and her temperament was different, she couldn't have danced all those modern and humorous roles I did. A great lady and a superb dancer but we were different.

Truth be told, Markova was a better dancer technically, and Pavlova more emotionally thrilling. As Jennifer Homans writes in her history of ballet, *Apollo's Angels*, Pavlova's "dancing appeared spontaneous and elusive, as if painted from nature—like Impressionism applied to dance." That was why the romantic classics suited her so well.

The two dancers had opposite innate talents, needing to compensate for what didn't come naturally. Markova was a child prodigy when it came to learning difficult steps and technique, with an extra long big toe that aided her when performing *en pointe*. Being able to land and leap without the ball of her foot touching the floor added to the illusion that she was miraculously suspended in air. (Vaslav Nijinsky shared that skill due to his own remarkably strong toes.)

But Markova was considered a dancing machine in her early years, lacking an intuitive empathy on stage that took exhaustive Ballets Russes training to unearth.

In contrast, Pavlova's passionate nature seemed to ooze from her pores, even in her early student days. She had no trouble connecting quite viscerally with her audiences. But the fragile dancer's weak ankles, highly arched instep, and tiny toes proved a handicap in balancing and maintaining positions, something she worked very hard to correct.

To compensate for her problem feet, Pavlova unknowingly influenced the construction of ballet slippers for countless dancers who followed her. To relieve pressure *en pointe,* she was the first to curve and harden the toe area, while adding wood or stiffened leather for extra sole support. At the time, other dancers called this "cheating."

Ironically, Markova was one of the few ballerinas of her generation who did not dance on hardened shoes. As a New York reporter noted, "She wore only the soft slippers of the old Italian school which make the dancer depend entirely upon muscular strength for support," and when *en pointe,* muscular strength in just one toe. "Today, this successor to Pavlova has perfection of balance at all times and is the envy of other ballerinas who have three toes to stand on."

But as Jennifer Homans points out, Pavlova's "frailty turned out to be her greatest asset. Her dancing had a tremulous, fragile look—her arabesques and balances were, as Bronislava Nijinska [the ballet dancer, noted choreographer, and Nijinsky's sister] later recalled, 'insecure' and 'trembling . . . like an aroma, a breeze, a dream.'"

In her engaging memoir *Theatre Street,* Ballets Russes prima ballerina Tamara Karsavina wrote of her time at the Imperial Ballet School with the young Pavlova:

> Pavlova at that time hardly realized that in her lithe shape and in her technical limitations lay the greatest strength of her charming personality. Romanticism was not the fashion any more. The very figure of our dancers, as compared with the silhouette of those of half a century ago, clearly showed the reversion of taste from an idealized vision towards the attractions of more material charm. . . . Pavlova was destined

> to bring back to our stage the forgotten charm of the Romantic ballet of the days of Taglioni.

Unlike Pavlova, Markova's strong technique made her as suited to modern ballets as she was to the classics.

There was also the personality difference between the impassioned Russian and genteel English woman. "Every country, of course, has its admirable born dancers," Pavlova once said. "Some of the best performers of my company are English. But it is only in Russia, owing to the spirit and the customs of the people, that the atmosphere exists in which dancing flourishes best of all."

And Markova? Bronislava Nijinska paid her the ultimate compliment years before the two became great friends. It was at the Ballets Russes where Nijinska was a successful choreographer and Markova the youngest dancer. After watching the teenager blossom under Diaghilev's tutelage, she told her, "You have a Russian soul!"

Diaghilev had spotted it first.

2

Diaghilev's Prodigy

Her ballet technique was so astonishing at an age when most little girls are just learning to tramp through the minuet, that the impresario who paid her first salary billed her "The Child Pavlova" all over his theatre . . .

It nearly ruined her life. At least, that's how it seemed at the time.

—"Alicia Markova: A Life on Points"
by Kay Webb, *The Leader,* London

British pantomime is to England what *The Nutcracker* is to the United States—a much-loved annual Christmastime spectacle. But despite the name, English pantomimes are anything but silent and have nothing whatsoever to do with mimes.

The lively musical extravaganzas originated in Victorian times as a hodgepodge of comedic opera, vaudeville slapstick, and fairytales. Loosely based on a classic children's story (*Cinderella, Little Red Riding Hood,* or *Aladdin,* for example), each "panto," as the productions are frequently called, boasts classic heroes and villains, costumed animals, raucous comedy, singing, dancing, celebrity guests, and audience participation. Children are encouraged to shout warnings to characters in peril—"Look out, there's someone behind you!"—and parents are kept amused by pop culture references and adult humor assumed to go over the heads of the little ones.

Another panto signature is casting cross-dressing actors, such as a woman in the role of the male juvenile lead and a middle-aged man playing the obligatory elderly "Dame" character. Joining them on stage are numerous child performers, again much like *The Nutcracker*, and it was in one of those key roles that Alicia Markova made her professional stage debut. She was barely ten years old.

In the 1920s, producer George Shurley was in charge of one of England's foremost holiday season pantomime shows staged annually at the Kennington Theatre in South London. Though the performance schedule was limited to the winter months of December through February, Shurley worked on the enormous undertaking all year round, much like America's Macy's Thanksgiving Day parade.

One of his tasks was to find and book talented children for each panto, and to that end Shurley often attended public recitals at the top local dance schools. (His appearance always caused quite a stir.) And that's how the producer found himself in the Thorne School audience when little Lily Marks performed her *Arabian Nights* solo.

Shurley kept an all-important journal of potential future candidates for his productions, and there was no doubt Lily made the cut. It was hard to forget such a tiny girl whirling and prancing about in harem pants and operatic breastplate. So when it was decided that *Dick Whittington* would be the subject of the next Christmas pantomime, the producer sought out the parents of the bejeweled baby ballerina.

Unknown to most Americans, *Dick Whittington* is a bizarre folk tale loosely based on a real person—one Richard Whittington—a 14th-century London mayor famous for building the city's first public bathroom. (Shakespearean it's not.) Several centuries later, a back-story was invented involving a penniless young Dick coming to London with a cat as his best friend, a handy contrivance as the arch-villain was King Rat. A side trip to rid Morocco of their rat problem for the Sultan was later added (that's where Lily's oriental dance would come in) leading to wealth, love, happiness, and Dick's being named Lord Mayor of London. The End.

When contacted about a formal tryout for the show, Arthur and Eileen thought it would be a grand adventure for their talented daughter. Without telling her what was in the offing, Arthur took Lily to audition for George Shurley and his staff. As always, she performed impeccably. But the best part, as far as she was concerned, was being treated to tea and dessert cakes afterward, indulging what would become a lifelong passion for sweets.

Soon after, Shurley made an offer to hire Lily as the lead child performer in the 1920/21 production of *Dick Whittington*. She would dance three numbers per show, two shows daily, six days a week, from December 27th through February 12th, with a very generous weekly salary of £10.

Interestingly, Arthur and Eileen Marks accepted the engagement without ever discussing it with their daughter. It was not as if they needed the money at that time, and it meant a great deal of pressure on the ten-year-old, her love of dancing notwithstanding. As her sister Doris would comment many years later, "I think, perhaps, she missed a lot of the fun of girlhood: the other three of us must have had it for her."

Though Mr. and Mrs. Marks surely assumed Lily would be thrilled with the opportunity, the child's early entrance into show business was clearly the parents' desire, not the young girl's. More unsettling, Eileen allowed her daughter to perform with a mild case of chicken pox, though she kept Doris far away from her lest she too catch the disease.

Come opening night, Lily had no visible rash, but she did retain a light-sensitivity problem connected with the illness. The glare of the theater spotlights didn't help. Fortunately, at the beginning of the long Salome solo, a veil covered her face, which the ten-year-old chose to leave on throughout the number until her eyes improved several weeks later.

To Eileen's credit, however, she never became a pushy stage mother, nor did she spoil or pamper Lily. Quite the opposite in fact: she kept home life exactly as it had always been, with no favoritism among the girls.

When finally told of the momentous *Dick Whittington* booking, Lily reacted as she did to most everything. She cheerfully—and quietly—did what she was told. The physical and mental demands of such a rigorous performance schedule were clearly beyond the naïve child's comprehension, but government regulations were in place to watch out for her. Before Mr. and Mrs. Marks could sign the contract, there were many procedural hoops to jump through.

First and foremost, a special work license was required from the London County Council in Westminster because Lily was so young. The winter engagement wouldn't have been possible at all had she not turned ten on December 1st. (And had it been one year later, Lily would have been immediately disqualified, as the minimum age was raised to twelve.)

In addition to checking her health, the officials needed a guarantee that the child's education wouldn't suffer due to rigorous rehearsal and performance schedules. Underage actors were only permitted to miss school if they received at least twenty hours of weekly private tutoring. That was not a problem for Lily, as her governess was already homeschooling her many more hours than required.

As with any government bureaucracy, the licensing process proved lengthy, so by the time it was approved, Lily was one of the last cast members to be officially hired for the show. That was unfortunate for her, as it meant shuffling roles amongst the other children performers to accommodate the new "star." Jealousy would make for a less-than-welcoming start to her professional career.

Making matters worse was Lily's over-protective caretaker Guggy, who was a dispiriting, controversial presence throughout Markova's childhood, especially damaging at the Ballets Russes.

Guggy's real name was Gladys Hogan. Though she was Irish, like her longtime employer Eileen Marks, the similarities ended there. Where Eileen was winning and warm, Guggy was humorless and cold. Coming from a military family, the governess was raised to be organized, hardworking, and dutiful above all else. Never married, she seemed incapable of displaying affection, though she protected Alicia like a mama bear with her cub.

It's hard to understand why Eileen and Arthur gave Hogan such unfettered supervision of little Lily. No question Guggy was an enormous help to Eileen when the young mother had four small daughters and a large household to run. The governess was nothing if not efficient. But it couldn't have escaped either parent how domineering and controlling she was. For a child as painfully shy as Lily,

Guggy's defensiveness around strangers of any age only exacerbated the problem.

But who else would be put in charge of chaperoning Lily to, from, and at the theater as required by law—helping her dress, tutoring her between performances, and serving as all-around "protector"? Eileen Marks still had three young daughters aged six and under at home. Of course the child's longtime governess would get the job. Guggy may have had her personality defects, but in the eyes of Lily's parents, she was always dependable and trustworthy.

For her part, Guggy disapproved of the whole pantomime experience, thinking it beneath the well-to-do Marks family. To express her feelings of superiority, Hogan dressed Lily in a black velvet coat with an ermine collar for her first day of rehearsal. The two couldn't have made a worse entrance—the over-dressed little girl and her stern-faced governess—walking into the large practice room, above a pub in Soho, of all places.

Markova said she always remembered the smell—not beer as one might suppose, but a sickeningly sweet citrus aroma—as she and Guggy walked in. The other children were on break and were busily peeling and gorging themselves on oranges.

They all looked up with daggers in their eyes at the tiny interloper, having just been told she was to replace the thirteen-year-old Jessie Matthews in the lead juvenile role. Matthews, who would become a popular British musical/film actress in the 1930s, was a very pretty teenager and already a favorite among the other girls.

"I think the ermine caused these orange-sucking youngsters to hate the sight of me," Markova later joked. But it wasn't funny at the time.

Jessie Matthews remembered Markova as "the very shy little girl with big sad eyes. . . . I felt sorry for her because she had a very restrictive governess Guggy who whisked her on and off the stage and never let her talk to anyone. During the entire run, I never heard her talk at all.

"I met her parents, who were very sweet, kind people, and I don't think they had any idea all she did was work and study with no pleasure time."

Unlike the other children, Matthews was completely won over by little Lily the very first time she appeared on stage.

> [Markova] did this little dance and I stood watching her. And my sister was very angry and pulled me away and tried to stop me watching this little girl dance. And I said but I want to watch her. She's so sweet. She's so lovely.
>
> And she said she has no right to be dancing a solo in this pantomime. You are the prima ballerina! And apparently it appears, that Markova herself wanted to talk to me, and every time she came down early to talk to me, . . . [Guggy] pulled her away because she wasn't allowed to speak to me.
>
> And it wasn't until—oh years later—that we met in New York during the war at a party, and she recognized me, and she yelled out Jessie! And I said Alicia! And we ran across this room full of celebrities in New York and embraced. She said I've been longing to meet you for years, and I said I've been longing to meet you for years. . . . And then we sort of laughed and cried together. It was quite absurd.

Lily wanted nothing more than to laugh and play with the other girls at the rehearsal, but her "watchdog" was having none of that. As soon as the ten-year-old had finished her numbers, Guggy scooped her up and spirited her away to her dressing room for a nap or tutoring. Worse still, Lily's being the youngest performer in the production necessitated a private room for changing costumes and daily lessons—the London County Council insisted—making it all too easy for Guggy to keep her charge a virtual prisoner. Of course, the private room led to further jealousies among the children.

Little did they know that the solitary confinement was more like a punishment for the lonely young girl. It broke Lily's heart that they thought her snooty when she wasn't; and Guggy prevented her from convincing them otherwise.

George Shurley, however, was perfectly happy for his little star to have preferential treatment. He had known right away that Lily Marks was special. The combination of her tiny size and adult stage demeanor would be a guaranteed crowd pleaser, and he invented ways to emphasize both those traits.

Lily made three appearances in the panto, the first, ironically enough, as a poppy, the role Pavlova had danced that so won the girl's heart at Queen's Hall. But where Pavlova was the epitome of ethereal grace, Lily's entrance was played for laughs. The scene was a cornfield at harvest time and after a big theatrical number, the stage was suddenly deserted, save for a single small sheaf of corn. Suddenly—out pops this tiny girl. No one could believe that any living person could have been completely hidden behind this insignificant corn sheaf.

As this was Lily's first-ever professional appearance, it was the ideal entrance, because the audience applauded before she even began to perform. In her personal memoirs, Markova later explained the pressures she was under at that time, something she wasn't able to share with anyone else:

> My secret fear all through the rehearsals for Dick Whittington was that having always danced to a piano when I had appeared before on stage, I might not recognize my music when I heard it played by the Orchestra. I would lie awake at nights worrying myself to death about this, and not having the courage to confide in anyone.
>
> When at last the morning for the Orchestral Call, I was absolutely sick with fright as I waited shaking behind the cornsheaf from which I made my entrance. The music started and out I jumped, and was amazed to hear what then sounded to me the loveliest music I had ever heard, and I was aware that I could just go on dancing and dancing, the music was my inspiration.
>
> I had been fond of music since as a baby I had played the family gramophone at every available opportunity, but until that morning, I had not realized how much music really meant to me as a dancer. As soon as I could, I learned to memorize a score by ear, which is quite a hard thing to do, and also all the different instruments, and I have found it invaluable in my career.

With the audience already on her side, Lily made the most of her poppy pizzicato, delighting them all the more. They were equally charmed by her second appearance as a costumed butterfly. But neither of those roles prepared anyone for Lily's *denouement*—the harem dance at the Sultan's palace.

"It was my very big number which used to stop the show," Markova amusingly reminisced years later. "It was a dance not *en pointes*, [but] unusually in bare feet, and it was kind of a Salome dance—very dramatic. And I think I must have been very funny when I did that—this very serious child with two green stones on my fingers—you know which I used like snakes. There were all kinds of exotic movements."

Markova described the finale in her personal journals:

> I can remember that at the end I finished with about 32 bars of very fast pirouettes and then let out a piercing scream as I fell flat on my back. The audience gasped for a moment thinking I had hurt myself, but when they realized it was part of the dance, the applause would break out with a deafening roar.
>
> Frankly, I enjoyed lying there listening to it whilst I waited for a six foot tall "Slave" to come and carry me off. When I think of this scene, it was most effective and one most commented on. No one since has ever thought of letting me use my voice to such good advantage on the stage!

Falling backward at each performance had a more lasting effect as well. "You remember how in Giselle at the end of the Mad Scene, I lift my arm as if to tell Albrecht something, then fall suddenly backwards and crumple up?" Markova told a reporter years later. "It always took the audience by surprise. Well, I learned that fall in panto in Kennington."

And though few *prima ballerina assolutas* begin their careers in commercial theater, Markova thought it most instructive. "I loved it because I learned then about all the flying and the trap doors and quick changes and—how should I say—maybe I learned to be a professional when I was ten."

Another talent she picked up at Kennington was mastering the art of sleeping on cue, as Guggy insisted she take naps between performances. The adult Markova found that enormously helpful during exhaustive cross-country train trips traversing the United States in the 1930s and '40s.

Also of future value was Markova's new stage moniker. "Lily" was forever dropped in favor of her middle name, which was the same as her great-grandmother's. Alicia Marks sounded much more professional.

Though much of the promotional material for *Dick Whittington* had already been printed by the time Alicia's contract was finalized, George Shurley created a special add-on billing advertisement:

"LITTLE ALICIA—THE CHILD PAVLOVA—AS PREMIÈRE DANSEUSE."

It was a lot to live up to, but the press ate it up:

"Little Alicia, described as 'The Child Pavlova,' more than justifies the title."—*Sunday Times*

" . . . a wonderful youngster, aptly named 'The Child Pavlova,' who gives a solo exhibition of remarkable grace and beauty for one so young."—*News of the World*

"Little Alicia, 'The Child Pavlova,' is a very accomplished ballerina in miniature, and even in the trying dance of Salome suggested much of its grim power."—*Daily Telegraph*

Someone else who admired Alicia's *Dick Whittington* performance was dancer Anton Dolin, then going by his birth name of Patrick Healey-Kay (actually, Francis Patrick Chippendall Healey-Kay). Patte, as he was always called, later selected Anton for his first name after Chekov, with two successive stage last names: Patrikayev, suggested by Sergei Diaghilev, and eventually Dolin, which stuck.

At age sixteen, Patte was actively auditioning for professional dancing roles. The same year Lily was in *Dick Whittington,* he had tried out for a J. B. Mulholland-produced pantomime at the King's Theatre in Hammersmith. Though the teenager didn't get the part, Mulholland suggested he go see "Little Alicia" in Kennington, whom he called a "wonder child." The producer thought the two youngsters might dance together for him some day. He even arranged for two free tickets for a performance to which Patrick took his mother.

Dolin rather dramatically described his reaction to seeing Alicia on stage for the first time:

> There, in a circle of flame, dressed in an exotic Eastern costume, bejeweled, and with a veil over her head, was a tiny figure. . . . Slowly the veil was lifted, and the most serious face came into view. No make-up could ever have enhanced the oriental contour of her features. They were Sphinx-like. . . .
>
> Though she looked such a child, her dancing was sensational in its ease, attack, and precision.

Dolin kept poking his mother throughout Alicia's act. He was astonished. "I was extremely impressed with this little girl. I asked my mother for a bob [shilling] so I could buy her some flowers and I left them for her at the stage door."

They were delivered to the ten-year-old *danseuse* anonymously. Dolin would later fess up to being Alicia's secret admirer—pleasing her no end—when the two met later that year at the dance studio of Princess Seraphine Astafieva. It was the premier dancing academy in London, with an illustrious teacher right out of Hollywood central casting.

Born in 1876 to Prince Alexander Astafiev of St. Petersburg, Princess Seraphine Astafieva was a member of the Russian aristocracy. Equally noteworthy, she was a grandniece of the celebrated author Count Leo Tolstoy. And there was one more exalted connection: the Princess's sister-in-law was Mathilde Kschessinska, the beautiful *prima ballerina assoluta* of Russia's Imperial Ballet.

It seems Kschessinska was as captivating offstage as on, managing to become the mistress of Tsar Nicholas II and two succeeding Romanov Grand Dukes. (Facilitating behind-the-curtain rendezvous at the Maryinsky Theatre, "a secret passage led from the Grand Duke's box directly to the stage," according to dance writer Judith Mackrell.) Kschessinska claimed not to know which nobleman had fathered her son, but her future wealth was assured nonetheless. With that substantial inheritance, the retired ballerina settled in Nice on the French Riviera following the Russian Revolution. *War and Peace* indeed.

Princess Astafieva spent every winter holiday on the Cote d'Azur with her accommodating sister-in-law, a heavenly escape from the climate-challenged London. Though at opposite ends of the economic spectrum, the two had the world of ballet in common.

Like Kschessinska, the Princess had also studied at the Imperial Ballet School in St. Petersburg, where she became a member of the prestigious Maryinsky company. Tall, slim, and with beautiful long legs, Astafieva was known for an emotionally expressive, rather than classically romantic, balletic style.

Diaghilev thought her well suited to his experimental new dance company, inviting her to join the Ballets Russes around 1909. There she met Bronislava Nijinska, who later wrote in her memoir: "Sima [Astafieva], a dancer from the Imperial Theatre, was a charming, witty, cheerful person, and she and I became good friends."

That description would have been inconceivable to visitors at Astafieva's London studio in the late 1920s, where the aging Princess resembled nothing so much as a mercurial, and often frightening, Miss Havisham.

What would still ring true, however, was the Princess's lifelong love of an eccentrically dramatic wardrobe. While Nijinska often found the elaborate Ballets Russes costumes difficult to perform in—as did many of the other company dancers—Astafieva enjoyed the theatricality of it all.

In a Paris production of *Bayadère Enivrée*, Nijinska remembered her friend "carrying a peacock on her shoulder"—she never says if it was dead or alive—and "the vividly colored feathers of the bird's tail brushed the floor as she performed her oriental dance."

The Princess was equally at home in the jewel-studded, gold brocade costume she wore in the Paris premiere of Mikhail Fokine's *Cleopatra*, in which she gave one of her most famous interpretive performances.

By 1916, Astafieva had moved permanently to London where she became the first distinguished Russian ballerina to open a dance school in the city. She quickly gained an excellent reputation for being the best ballet teacher England had to offer.

Not surprisingly, the prideful aristocrat selected a historically important London building for her Russian Dance Academy and living quarters. "The Pheasantry" (named for the birds that had been bred there in the mid-1800s) was a landmark 19th-century building on King's Road in Chelsea. The ornate entrance was marked by an imposing wrought-iron gate, watched over by two formidable stone eagles. (Markova used to call them "vultures waiting for the tired and weary bodies to emerge from class.") Above the gate was an archway grandly depicting a chariot drawn by four horses.

By the early 20th century, the entrance to the school was as shabby chic as its proprietress. The initial impression was rather gloomy, as one had to pass through a maze of dark stone hallways before reaching the studios. Like Alice in Wonderland, one would disappear down the rabbit hole of passageways until reaching an uninviting door up several steps.

It was marked by a plate: "Russian Dance Academy." More than one student never made it that far.

For the brave souls who persevered, few ever forgot their first meeting with Astafieva, as Chilean dancer Doreen Young recalled:

> Fearfully, I rang the bell.
>
> The door was opened by a strange apparition in weird drapery and with straggly wisps of hair. I timidly asked for Madame Astafieva and the phantom answered, "Yes, I am" with a strong Russian accent. I managed to say I wanted to study with her. All she said was: "You come tomorrow at half-past ten." I was perplexed to find the great and glamorous teacher looking like a witch.
>
> Next morning I joined the school where I spent some of the happiest years of my life. . . . Madame was transfigured from the strange vision of the previous day into a beautiful woman with a commanding presence.

Once inside, the practice rooms were far less foreboding. The studio took up the entire first floor of the building, with light streaming through the large windows at each end and a grand open stone fireplace in the middle. Next to it was the bench where friends and hovering mothers of the pupils could sit and *quietly* watch their charges during class. But even spectators needed a strong stomach, as Princess Astafieva was a stern taskmaster, known to yell, shriek, and reprimand new pupils. That would inevitably lead to a flood of tears, but the Princess always softened to talent, and was a wonderful instructor.

Doreen Young eventually became quite close with her teacher:

> Occasionally, Astafieva took me with her on a shopping expedition, when she thought she needed some new item for her wardrobe. She never gave a thought to prudence, and would happily strip off her upper garments in full view of the other customers and of passers-by. I would jump about attempting to cover her, but usually only managed to get in the way. But somehow she always commanded respect, despite her eccentricities.
>
> She had the most beautiful legs, and never wore [anything] other than white silk stockings, but they were always wrinkled and covered with variegated darns, done by her well-meaning pupils. Somehow, she remained impressive even when dressed in odd frayed shoes, long white stockings, black bloomers, a black silk skirt shortened around the hips with string, a pyjama jacket, an oddment of wool around her shoulders, and a very odd piece of Shetland scarf swathed round her head in the shape of a turban. And, of course, the carrot-coloured wig which presumably she thought preferable to her own hair.

The Princess's face makeup matched her stockings—dead white, looking all the more startling with her heavily charcoaled eyes. As to her teaching demeanor, Astafieva's controlled grace and delicious phrasing was at complete odds to her Miss Havisham-like appearance—often wrapped in tattered chiffon while clutching a gold-handled teaching stick, cigarette holder, or both. She made a point of saying her skirt was "not really dirty, just near-white."

Even when quite frail and close to retirement (she would die of cancer in 1934), the Princess retained her extraordinary sense of style. In 1933, she accepted one of her last pupils, Dame Margot Fonteyn, then known by her birth name of Peggy Hookham. Astafieva made a quite indelible impression on Fonteyn when they first met:

> Tallish, aged about 60, worldly and elegant with slender legs and an indefinable mixture of the stylish with the slightly grubby that only such an aristocratic personality from Czarist Russia could hope to carry off successfully. . . .
>
> We [Peggy and her notoriously ambitious stage mother] arrived, apparently, on a day when she was sitting in the dark, inner room in a Russian gloom, both physical and moral. She did not want to accept any more pupils.

The main reason Peggy and her mother were so set on employing the retiring dance instructor is that they both were in awe of London's star ballerina, Alicia Markova. She was Peggy's idol and everything she wished to be as a dancer. Everyone knew Astafieva had been responsible for the young Markova's training.

Fonteyn might have felt better about her inhospitable introduction to the mercurial Russian had she known about Markova's own calamitous reception.

It would be a story repeated and retold throughout her life. There wasn't a reporter, interviewer, ballet critic, or fellow dancer who didn't find the tale entertaining and worthy of embellishment. It became like the children's game of "telephone," where a story is whispered from one youngster to another, each remembering different details—changing some and exaggerating others—until the last listener tells his or her version aloud and everyone laughs at the comedic distortions.

That the anecdote involved the world-famous Anna Pavlova made it even more irresistible, regardless of language or country.

The background story was straightforward. After Alicia finished her successful booking in *Dick Whittington,* Eileen Marks was considering the next step in her daughter's training. For the time being, the ten-year-old was back in Miss Thorne's class, soon performing in a charity matinee at London's Shaftesbury Theatre alongside pupils from the Dance Academy of Princess Seraphine Astafieva. Mrs. Marks watched from the wings as the Russian dance teacher encouraged and supervised each of her charges and, after making inquiries, decided this was the person who could best prepare her daughter for a serious career in the ballet.

First, here is the story in Markova's own words, followed by a selection from the countless retellings that appeared in print throughout the years. The tale becomes more and more amusing in its dramatic reinventions.

From Markova's personal journals:

> I can remember clearly the morning we set off to call on Madame Astafieva. My mother decided that for this auspicious occasion, she should accompany Gladys [Guggy] and myself and I was very happy that she was with us. We arrived as class was finishing and Madame came over to us; but when she saw my card introducing "Little Alicia—The Child Pavlova," she was furious and tore the card up and threw it in Mother's face saying: "You silly woman. Why do you waste my time with such nonsense? Child Pavlova!! It is outrageous," and she slammed the door on us.
>
> I was mortified but not so my mother. She was an extraordinarily sweet woman, famous for her great charm, but she was also Irish and for anyone to behave like that to her and her daughter was too much. She rang again and when Madame came to open the door she told her what she thought of her and also that she was making a big mistake by not at least seeing her daughter dance. Whether it was Mother's indignation or my tears of genuine disappointment that changed Madame's mind, we shall never know, but she condescended to let me dance for her.
>
> This made me happy as I felt sure that once she saw what I could do she would feel differently towards me. The number I danced was *Valse Caprice* which was one of my favorite pieces of music at that time. [It had been a favorite of Pavlova's as well.] At the end, Madame came over and threw her arms round me and kissing me on both cheeks said, "I shall be happy to teach you to dance, little one, but there are certain things that you will have to realize . . . you must work hard, terribly hard, and as you are so frail, you must be wrapped in cotton-wool and treated like a racehorse."
>
> These conditions didn't frighten me. All that mattered was that she had accepted me as a pupil and I knew in my mind

> and with all my heart I would do my very best to justify her hopes of me. So began a new life.

Compare that to this excerpt from the magazine article, "Alicia Markova," by Basanta Koomar Roy, *Dance Magazine*, 1943:

> "No-no-no! No-no-no! I won't teach the child that disgraces the great name of our Pavlova. There is only one Pavlova in the world, and she is our Russian Anna Pavlova. I won't teach this little thing. No-no-no! No-no-no!" cried the outraged ballerina.
>
> The mother was broken-hearted. Alicia was sad, and a little frightened by the explosive temper of the teacher. Slowly tears began to gather in the beautiful and tender eyes of the child. With her eyes glistening Alicia looked up into the eyes of the Princess. Tears in such precious eyes at once melted the heart of the Russian Princess. The tempest of her temper quickly subsided. She gently asked the child to dance for her.
>
> Alicia, nervous to the extreme, wiped her tears away; but she smiled sweetly and danced Rubenstein's [*sic*] Valse Caprice for Princess Astafieva. She danced it with such innate refinement, exquisite charm and technical precision that the Princess at once accepted her as a pupil. As a jeweler knows jewels, so Ballerina Astafieva automatically envisaged a great future for this child as a dancer.

From *Balletomania Then and Now* by Arnold Haskell. (Following a description of Eileen and Alicia Marks arriving at the Dancing Academy):

> "I am Astafieva. What you want, dahlink?"
>
> Everyone was always "darling" to her, including the coal-man one morning, to his great amazement and mine. There was a muttered explanation, a silence to gather up strength, and then the explosion.
>
> "You mothers are all alike. You are a *doura*, yes, a *doura*, in English eediot. You think because little girl can stand on toe

and wobble she just like Pavlova—yes? You don't know how long it take to make Pavlova, what work, what tears, what art. You don't know what it mean. Good-bye."

From the commemorative article "Classes with Astafieva," by ballerina Doreen Young, 1964:

> Much has been written about Alicia's entry into Astafieva's school; I happened to witness the entire episode.
>
> A card was passed in to Madame introducing "Little Alicia, the Child Pavlova." Madame was furious—but consented to receive Mrs. Marks and her daughter. They walked into the studio in very elegant clothes, Alicia crowned by a hat with enormous feathers. Madame said she would see the child dance, and we all hovered in the studio full of curiosity, instead of vanishing downstairs to dress.
>
> That delicate-looking little girl with her long, thin legs and short hair astonished us all. Here was something quite out of the ordinary. Madame, completely delirious with excitement, embraced her and profoundly understood the wording of Alicia's card: Pavlova herself had given permission for the use of her name, after seeing the child and guessing her destiny. [That of course wasn't true.]
>
> From that moment, Alicia became a pupil of the school and was greatly loved by us all. She always came accompanied by her governess "Guggie" as she was called, and had a very sweet and easy way with her fellow students.

The story just kept on going, well into the 1970s. Astafieva was in "a towering rage" and gave Mrs. Marks "the tongue-lashing of her life." There was plenty of "foot stomping." Alicia let out a "shrill wail and stood crying in utter despair." And so on.

Whatever the true specifics of that first meeting, Alicia Marks spent the next four years taking classes with Madame Seraphine Astafieva, who did indeed think the young girl a prodigy and came to quite adore her. Markova, in turn, became a most conscientious student, as she recorded in her personal journals:

> Known to her pupils in the classroom as Madame, she [Astafieva] was an awe-inspiring figure with an impressive personality. She wore pearl earrings and long strings of pearls knotted at the throat, her handsome head tied up in a turban to keep it warm (the turban being a very old Shetland shawl), white silk stockings, woolen knee-caps which seemed to accentuate her small, neat well-shaped feet, and her dress caught up in a sort of bouffant crinoline.
>
> And her stick!!! Always she had that thin long black stick with the gold handle, which would find its way round the ankles, knees, and elbows; even across the shoulders of some unfortunate pupil who was not getting the right angle or position. Sometimes it would be no more than a reminder or a caress, but at others it would sting hard as it emphasized a fault Madame was trying to correct. I was one of the lucky ones; with me the stick was used mostly as a hurdle for jumping over and an excellent one it made.

"[H]er classes were a revelation," wrote British dance critic Arnold Haskell about Astafieva. "By her link with the great tradition, her knowledge, enthusiasm, and vivid personality, she was beginning to do things with English dancers, and to break down the legend that they were only fit for the corps de ballet."

Not only did Astafieva provide Alicia with the best Russian ballet training available in England, but she also introduced her to the man who would forever change her life—the Princess's former employer and friend, Sergei Diaghilev.

The Ballets Russes impresario had great trust in his one-time soloist, often taking Astafieva's advice on which of her promising pupils he should hire for his illustrious dance company, including Patte Kay, the future Anton Dolin.

Unlike poor Alicia's initial encounter with Astafieva, Patte made an entirely different first impression on the Princess, according to his 1960 autobiography. In 1917, the thirteen-year-old arrived at the school dressed in "a pair of brown velvet knickers, a Little Lord Fauntleroy coat to match, thick woolen socks and black shoes."

It was August.

Only someone as eccentric as Astafieva could have appreciated such bizarre attire.

The two became very close, with Dolin riveted by all his teacher's colorful stories of her homeland and Ballets Russes days. Patte soon moved into one of the shared rooms at the Academy set aside for resident students, though the teenager often slept curled up on the sofa in Astafieva's bedroom, according to classmate Doreen Young.

"Madame adored him as a son," remembered Young. "Patte kept us vastly amused, always playing jokes and at one time was much addicted to throwing jugs of cold water over me."

Patte also loved playing jokes on tiny Alicia, "always the first to arrive and the last to leave," he would say.

"Her technique was really quite extraordinary," Dolin vividly recalled. "She used to really annoy all of us pupils in the class with the idiotic facility and ease with which she could execute all the steps. Frankly, it was quite annoying to see what was really quite a fantastic machine dancing without any emotion. Why she should have any emotion I don't know."

So, for fun, Dolin would take advantage of the unquestioningly obedient child. "After class I would rehearse with Alicia. I wasn't really strong in those days and Alicia was thin, light and pliable. And frankly, I used to boss her around. And she would do anything I told her to do.

"I put her on an arabesque and I'd just leave her there, go over and perhaps talk to Mrs. Haskell who used to come and watch the classes so often, eat a couple of chocolates that Mrs. Haskell had bought me—a box of chocolates—and I'd go back and there was Alicia still standing there on that damned arabesque. Didn't move."

Another remembrance of Dolin's was Alicia's "extraordinary fondness of cats." It seems the feeling was mutual. "Cats used to follow her around," said Dolin, "and Astafieva liked cats."

Alicia bonding with felines would be a recurring theme throughout her childhood, as Guggy desperately tried to prevent her charge from mixing with more suitable playmates—other children. The governess never let Alicia out of her sight, an emotionally crippling experience for the pre-teen who grew more and more unsure how to act with her peers. Dolin used to pinch her from behind or pull her hair while she was dancing in class just to get a rise out of her, but Alicia would continue to perform perfectly, as if nothing had happened.

"At that time, he treated me like a very small sister, teasing me and finding everything I did a great joke," Markova remembered. "Although I was rather upset about this, I looked up to him as a big brother—one that I never had."

Alicia's technique was so remarkable—able to turn thirty times on one *pointe*—that Astafieva used her as a teaching model; but unlike with her *Dick Whittington* peers, the other students weren't jealous in any mean-spirited way. They actually felt sorry for Alicia—always under Guggy's glare from the studio guest bench—and everyone could see that Alicia desperately wanted to be friends. It wasn't like the little girl was humorless, either. She was a very sweet child.

In her personal journals Markova reminisced:

> The early years of training I had at Astafieva's were invaluable to me; she was a hard task master, or should I say mistress—but she knew exactly what she wanted out of a pupil and did not stop till she had the required result. I would have danced until I dropped down dead if she asked me to do so. We all felt the same, such was the affection and admiration this incredible woman inspired in those with whom she came into contact. . . .
>
> Although Madame taught Classical Ballet, her ideas were for that time very modern. She would take one step and build the whole lesson round it. We would do it backwards, forwards and sideways without moving from the spot, or moving in all angles. With pirouettes too, she would call for one to one side, say the right, than two on the left, four right, two and a half left—which meant you finished with your back towards her, but all these commands were fired at you like firecrackers and to do them on the spot, as she asked, took very quick thinking and brain and muscle control.
>
> This was Madame's whole idea to develop precision and co-ordination of mind and body. Another thing she insisted on was that every step be done both ways, to the right and to the left. This is rarely taught, but I feel sure it is something which

> has helped me enormously as it has given me great balance control which is developed equally on both sides.

Each day, Alicia—with Guggy glued to her side—would take the long Underground ride from her home in Finsbury Park to the Pheasantry. She took classes for two hours every morning and then practiced in the studio all afternoon, often receiving private lessons from an instructor, or from her frequent training partner Anton Dolin. She also enjoyed watching and studying other dancers in rehearsal, finding it an invaluable learning tool.

It was while quietly observing her fellow classmates audition for Sergei Diaghilev that Alicia first met the great man. She had only been taking lessons with Astafieva for a few months when the world-famous impresario paid the school a visit in the late fall of 1921. The Ballets Russes was staging a spectacular full-length version of *The Sleeping Princess* in London and, as was typical of touring companies, needed to hire local dancers to fill out the *corps de ballet* and minor roles for the enormous production.

Astafieva had prepared her most promising students, including Patte Kay, and they performed one at a time for the imposing Diaghilev. Off in the corner leaning against the *barre* was tiny Alicia.

At ten years old, she was still a little slip of a thing, sporting a boyish "Buster Brown" hairstyle instead of the classic ballerina sleek bun. And while other dancers pirouetted in tights, Alicia still wore white cotton socks, only accentuating her young age and wafer-thin legs.

In her journals, Markova described the momentous event:

> One morning there was great excitement. Word went round that the famous Serge Diaghileff was coming to watch class to choose some dancers for his new production of Sleeping Beauty. We all felt sure that the star pupil Patrick would be chosen and we were very proud and happy when he was.
>
> Imagine my shock and bewilderment though, when as we finished class and were getting ready to leave, Madame suddenly came over and asked me to dance my Valse Caprice for Diaghileff. . . .
>
> I remember thinking that morning, this is the most important moment of my life and yet I do not feel nervous, only so

happy to have the great honor and opportunity to dance for a genius. How pleased too, I felt, that I was wearing my favorite practice dress.

When I finished my series of fouettes which were at the end of the dance and curtsied low, Diaghileff applauded and seemed much amused. "Would you like to join my Company?" he asked with a smile. I was speechless, utterly speechless. This was the most wonderful thing that could ever happen to me. Eventually I recovered my equilibrium sufficiently to reply, "Yes please, thank you very much. I would love to."

He kissed me and said "Goodbye, Douchka." I had no idea what this meant and had to get Madame to translate it for me when he had left.

"Douchka means little darling, and coming from the Maestro himself, this is a great thing," she told me. I treasured that word; it was all Diaghileff ever called me when he spoke to me personally, never Alicia, always Douchka. Even now whenever I hear it, it is like a dart going into my heart and I think of him, whom I loved so reverently. That day, I went home on air, certainly not on the Underground, in fact, I think I floated home on wings of elated thoughts.

This seventh heaven did not last long. My three younger sisters developed diphtheria one after the other and my poor Mother and Father were frantic with worry. I tried to console them, meanwhile gargling and doing everything the doctors instructed, but to no avail. Within a week, I had succumbed and was also in the fever hospital. Although I did not have the dreaded disease as seriously as my sisters, I was forbidden to dance for six months after I left hospital. This to me seemed the end of my career and I wept bitterly in my hard hospital bed. The doctors could not discover why my temperature continued to be so high. Little did they guess my hopes were shattered knowing I was lying there and I would not be able to dance in the "Sleeping Princess" at the Alhambra Theatre.

The Ballet was produced whilst I was still in hospital, so I missed being "Little Red Riding Hood" and more important still "Fairy Dew Drop the Smallest Fairy in the World," which was the part Diaghileff was having specially interpolated for me.

While Markova wrote those words as an adult, her disappointment is still palpable. She never seemed to get over the pain of her emotional roller-coaster childhood—absolute euphoria one moment, then dashed hopes or isolation the next. That scenario would be reenacted many times in her early life, especially when Guggy literally locked her away at the Ballets Russes.

Irene Webb was a matron at the convalescence hospital where Alicia was quarantined with diphtheria. The sad little girl stood out in her memory as a "bizarre, very quiet, very reserved" child, who wept with a despondency that far outweighed the seriousness of her illness. "Then I heard she was learning to be a dancer," Webb recalled, "and she had a great opportunity, which she had missed because of this illness—which was very sad for her. I told her she would have other opportunities, as we all do."

But Markova didn't feel that way. She decided her life was over. For any other child, that would seem to be a complete over-reaction. But Alicia's entire life was now wrapped up in dance. It was her way of getting adult approval. She feared emotional abandonment if she proved a disappointment. Everyone had been so excited that Diaghilev had "chosen" her. Now they would all feel she had failed.

Then something rather amazing happened. Sergei Diaghilev did not forget his little Douchka after she became too ill to take part in *The Sleeping Princess.* Once Alicia was out of quarantine, the Ballets Russes impresario arranged that two tickets be made available for her whenever she felt up to attending performances at the Alhambra Theatre. If Guggy could not take her, Diaghilev would escort her himself.

It was completely out of character for him to do such a thing. Diaghilev was known to dislike children and had only seen Alicia that one time at Astafieva's studio. Why would he care about a sickly ten-year-old?

But from the very start, there was a strange bond between the impresario and the fragile little girl, and it would last until his death. No one quite understood the mutual affection, but it was very real and undeniable. Neither was remotely demonstrative. They just seemed to connect on some strange spiritual level.

One thing was for sure: both the adult and child thought ballet was as necessary as breathing and couldn't imagine life without it. Alicia wasn't a mere spectator at *The Sleeping Princess*. She understood that Diaghilev was giving her an opportunity to learn, and she devoured the experience.

The Sleeping Princess was Diaghilev's pride and joy. It was his return to grand Russian classicism after the avant-garde, and he had borrowed heavily to pay for the lavish costumes and sets. (The sum was an astronomical £10,000, or roughly $330,000 in today's money.) He lost it all.

For Alicia, each performance was like a class. She carefully studied how the various prima ballerinas interpreted their roles, especially Vera Trefilova, and the magnificent Olga Spessivtseva—Diaghilev's acknowledged favorite. "Olga Spessivtseva and Anna Pavlova are like two halves of an apple," he once said, "but the Spessivtseva half has been in the sun."

As remarkable as Alicia's intensive study of the dancers was Diaghilev's instinctively realizing that she would do just that. When sitting next to her in the theater, he would point to various movements and sequences the ten-year-old should note. Did he already know of her phenomenal memory? She was a mere child but never forgot a step.

"That was where I think I started to acquire all the knowledge," Markova told an audience of Royal Ballet students many years later. "I saw all the great ballerinas, all the great artists. With the performances they alternated—so many artists. And I think at ten years of age, that set my very high standards."

As for Diaghilev, "From that moment on, I don't know, he became like a father, a second father to me."

And unfortunately, Markova would soon be in *need* of a second father.

It's not clear exactly when Arthur Marks lost his considerable wealth, but it seems to have happened when Alicia was about twelve. Her father invested the family fortune in what was purported to be a state-of-the-art cork invention, but his business partner proved unscrupulous. Arthur lost everything, and though his dishonest partner wound up in prison, the Marks family savings were wiped out.

There are various explanations of what occurred next. Doris later painted a picture of a less-than-disheartened father who had plans to go back into the gold-mining business with family members in South Africa. (Doris was only eight years old at the time.) As Doris and Alicia told biographer Maurice Leonard, "Arthur was without work again but was not too concerned as the family had plans to move to South Africa. In the end, they never did. Had they done so, the course of British ballet history would have been quite different. Arthur contracted pneumonia and died on 14 September 1924, Eileen's birthday. Alicia was thirteen."

Anton Dolin offered a different interpretation: Arthur "suddenly found himself penniless. The shock proved too much for him. His health collapsed, and he died with tragic suddenness, leaving a widow and four daughters to face the world with no visible means of support."

But there is one more explanation given by a one-time Ballets Russes dancer and lifelong friend of Markova, Alexandra Danilova. The story involves George Balanchine, with whom Danilova was romantically involved. She remembers the two of them being quite excited when Balanchine was hired by Diaghilev—the steppingstone that would result in his becoming one of the most celebrated choreographers of the 20th century.

When Balanchine joined the company in Monte Carlo, his first assignment was to create new choreography for "The Nightingale" with the teenaged London student Alicia Marks as his potential star in the title role. From Danilova's autobiography:

> While we were still in London [performing], Balanchine was summoned by Diaghilev to go with him and Boris Kochno [Ballets Russes artistic director] to see a young dancer. It seemed that Astafieva, a former member of the Maryinsky now living in London, had telephoned Diaghilev and told him about a little girl who had suffered a great tragedy: her father had lost all his money in America and committed suicide, leaving his widow and four daughters. One of them, Astafieva

> explained, was a very talented dancer. So Diaghilev, Boris, and George went to see this girl, who was named Alice Marks, and they liked her very much.

It is not implausible that the Marks family would wish to bury the fact of Arthur Mark's suicide in later years, or that Eileen never told her young daughters the actual circumstances of his death. And Danilova—who adored Markova—would never have invented that detail on her own. She clearly heard it from Diaghilev and Balanchine, who may have been privy to the true nature of Arthur's death through Astafieva. (Eileen needed to confide in the princess, whom she counted on to find Alicia paid work to help support the family.)

Adding to the mystery is a loving letter Arthur wrote to Alicia the day before he died. She was staying in Brighton with the Crewley family, who were lifelong friends of the Markses, while Eileen, Guggy, and the three younger girls were on holiday seaside. This strange arrangement of a split-up family vacation was a common occurrence for the Marks family, with Alicia often "farmed out" to various friends while all her sisters went off with Eileen. Once again, it illustrates Alicia's extremely odd upbringing.

Arthur was in London, presumably working, and wrote to Alicia on business letterhead stationery from *S.J. Feldblum, Limited, Government Contractors, London.*

> *S.J. Feldblum, Limited*
> *2, Pounds Buildings,*
> *75, Leadenhall Street,*
> *London, 13/9—1924*
>
> *My own beloved Lily,*
>
> *Thank you sweetheart for your nice loving letter sent to Auntie Alice's, which Uncle Max gave me this morning in the City—as I am not staying with them—so if you are writing dear, send your letters to 89 Queens* [the family home address in Finsbury Park].
>
> *I am so glad you are having a nice time & that the weather is fine—& I am sure you will always be happy at Auntie Sophie's—give her my love—*

Mummy dear, & Guggie & the children left yesterday for Folkstone & I had a few lines from Mummy to say she is enjoying it better than B'mouth. You are a good girl to write Mummy—God bless you & with my ever fondest love & kisses—

Yoursever loving Daddy.

Kiss here Daddy

One has to ask, is it likely that Arthur would be at work in his office if he were deathly ill with pneumonia? And if instead he were writing on business stationery from his sickbed, would his loving family leave him alone in the city and go off on a carefree seaside vacation?

But it would be equally strange for a man contemplating suicide to instruct his daughter to send all future letters to their home address instead of relatives where he had been staying. If Arthur did not kill himself, it seems more likely that he died suddenly of a heart attack following his disastrous business misfortunes than succumbing overnight to pneumonia. And if that was the case, why later say he died of pneumonia?

Whatever the case, the letter shows a man expressing his great love for his daughter, whether meant as a final farewell or not; and his death certainly left the family in dire financial straits. Alicia would now have to earn a living as a dancer.

The young ballerina's last paid engagement had been one year earlier, when she was twelve. She had been hired to perform at the London Palladium with the Russian Art Dancers organized by Nikolai Legat—the former dancer and respected ballet master from the Maryinsky Theatre in St. Petersburg. Legat's lovely ballerina wife, Nadine Nicholaeva-Legat, was the company's principal dancer and would be partnered with Anton Dolin in London.

An interview with a local newspaper just prior to the engagement illustrates just how unworldly the twelve-year-old Alicia was at the time:

> Although Alicia, who is just thirteen [she was actually twelve, but for legal reasons the press was told she was thirteen] has appeared many times on the stage, she is a delightfully natural child off it . . . a shy little girl with an elfin face and large dark eyes in a very short coat and poke-bonnet, hugging an enormous doll.

> "Yes," she said shyly in answer to a question, "I am most excited about appearing with real Russian dancers in a London theatre. I hope people will like me.
>
> "It is very hard work dancing," she continued. "I practice steps and positions five hours steadily every day.
>
> "Then I have also my lessons to learn with my governess besides. I like them too; but I would rather play with my dolls than do arithmetic or history," she added.
>
> "I want to be a great dancer when I grow up, like Mme. Pavlova. Before Madame left for America I went to tea with her. She was most sweet to me, and wanted to take me with her."
>
> —*Pall Mall Gazette*, 10/6/23

Known to drop by Astafieva's dance studio in search of potential corps members for her company, Anna Pavlova kept tabs on the tiny dancer who had so impressed her at Ivy House in 1920. As Markova never lied as a child, it is quite probable the Russian star did ask if she'd like to go with her on tour—but she may have meant when Alicia was a bit older. (Pavlova would formally invite Markova to join her company several years later.)

Markova studied with Nikolai Legat for many years, always citing his training as invaluable to perfecting her technique. In turn, both Legats found Alicia quite remarkable, even as a twelve-year-old. Years later, Nadine Nicholaeva-Legat told a funny story about the child's experience with the Russian Art Dancers.

> When she was a little girl studying at our ballet studio in 1923, my husband and I thought that Alicia was a very promising pupil, and that it would be of interest to the public to see her dancing as a child prodigy. At that time we had our own little company and we gave performances in several West End theatres.
>
> As she was under twelve years of age, we had to get a special license for her appearance. We received this permission, but with the proviso that she should, on no account, dance after nine o'clock. We arranged that her dance should come on a little before nine, as one of the first numbers of the Divertissement.
>
> One night there was extra applause for the preceding ballet, and this delayed the start of the Divertissement. There was

> a danger of Alicia not being able to appear that night at all, because her performance would take place after nine o'clock, which was against regulations.
>
> The little Alicia had foreseen all this, and was determined at all costs to appear. Knowing that there were only a few minutes before 9 P.M., and that these precious minutes would be taken up by the preceding dancer, she waited for the opening bars of music—which were not for her dance at all—then rushed on to the stage and began her solo, much to the annoyance of the girl who should have been dancing.
>
> She, thinking that Alicia had made a genuine mistake, also began her solo whispering tragically to Alicia that it was not her dance and that she must get off the stage. But Alicia, having great courage and determination, energetically continued and ignored the other dancer altogether.
>
> So there were on the stage at the same moment two dancers, one a child and the other an adult, performing quite different solos to the same music. Standing in the wings, I was greatly amused at this incident, feeling in my heart great admiration and approval for the child's spirit, courage, and self-confidence. Whilst everybody was prepared to scold poor Alicia, I said to my husband, "I like this; to me it is a proof that she will reach the goal of a great ballerina!" And I was right.

The dance Alicia was so eager to perform was a *Dragonfly* solo, originally made famous by Pavlova. While Markova had none of the emotional complexity of her idol at that time, her lovely rendition nonetheless earned her some very positive press reviews. That led to several offers for other professional bookings; but, on the advice of Astafieva, her parents had thought she should concentrate instead on lessons to perfect her technique. They could hardly argue with a woman who was offering her services for free, as Astafieva was already aware of the Marks's financial difficulties. Now that the family patriarch was gone, the situation had become even more desperate.

Markova was asked to speak about what happened next many, many times throughout her life. Here she tells the life-changing story to a group of eager dance students at London's Royal Ballet:

> He [Diaghilev] said he would come back and see me when I was in my late teens, which as we all know, is about the time you go into the corps. Well, he came back earlier as my father had just died.
>
> And I was just thirteen, and Fokine was to stage the dancers at the Drury Lane Theatre for "A Midsummer Night's Dream." They were putting a big production on there. So naturally, he heard from Astafieva about me.
>
> I auditioned, and it was set that I was to go into that, which of course was marvelous, because at that time, I thought if I had missed out on Diaghilev, Fokine was the next best thing. [Fokine had left the Ballets Russes in 1914.] And to be able to work with a great choreographer like that, and still have my classes, and also to earn a little money, which was important!
>
> Then Diaghilev heard that and he said, no, he would audition me again. I had to audition for him in Astafieva's studio. He brought [his choreographer] Madame Nijinska along and Boris Kochno, and Serge Gregoriev [*sic*]. And I hate to tell you. My audition went on for three hours!
>
> I think I was upside down, back to front, everything I ever knew I had to try out.
>
> So, that was that. I went home, and naturally, I continued working.

Alicia could hardly sleep anticipating the outcome. Then word finally came. Diaghilev was going to bring her into the Ballets Russes. As Madame Nijinska had a young daughter, Alicia and her governess would live with them. (Due to Alicia's age, Diaghilev insisted on a governess.) Eileen and Astafieva were thrilled—not to mention Alicia's euphoria.

Then suddenly, everything was up in the air once more, as Markova explained:

> . . . About two weeks later, the phone rang. Mr. Diaghilev came back and said I needed to audition again. So I thought, oh dear, another three hours!

So this time he said he was bringing Mr. Balanchine who had just joined the company. So apparently—I didn't know at that time—but in the past two weeks, Madame Nijinska and Diaghilev had had an argument, and she had decided she was leaving, and so Balanchine had just joined the company.

So then I think I had four hours of auditioning for him!

The phone call for Alicia to return *immediately* to the studio for an important audition came while she was devouring a hearty after-school meal with plenty of her favorite dessert cream cakes—a special treat at the home of Emmy Haskell. Mrs. Haskell was a wealthy patroness of the ballet who had met and become fond of Alicia at Astafieva's studio. Her largess would make the next stage of Markova's career possible.

Also at the lunch was Mrs. Haskell's son Arnold. Markova wrote in her journal:

> Mrs. Emmy Haskell, who was a great friend of Madame's and came almost every morning to see us work, she took an interest in me, became my dear friend and adviser, and when she took me to her lovely home in Queens Gate, I met her son Arnold and I found in him someone with whom I could feel completely natural, who understood me and also had a love of the dance which to me was a bond at once. I suffered from a natural shyness or rather reserve, especially with boys, but I never had this feeling with Arnold but could talk and confide in him as I did with my sisters. I knew he did not think me foolish for the ideas I had or for the ambitions I nursed in my mind.

Haskell, who was 6½ years older than Markova, was amazed one so young had so much passion for ballet. "I met Alicia at a Christmas party," he recalled. "As usual, I gravitated toward the first person who was willing to discuss dancing, and the first person was this child [she was just eleven], who was very shy, did not quite fit in, and was just as eager to talk dancing as I was. Immediately her whole outlook, her very great earnestness and her ambition, charmed me."

And this was before Haskell ever saw Alicia dance. As an only child, Arnold immediately befriended all of the Marks girls. "I saw a great deal of Alicia and her three mischievous sisters," he would write, "mischievous doubtless by contrast, for the only naughty thing she [Alicia] ever seems to have done was to wipe the floor with a facecloth, and she shuddered as it was told."

It's what everyone would say. Alicia was almost too good to be true. No child, they thought, could always be *that* well-behaved.

As Haskell later recalled in an interview with British dance authority Clement Crisp:

> I met her and her three sisters and she was always the very modest and rather retiring one. The youngest sister was quite theatrical even at the age of three. Alicia was the retiring one. Then I went to see her at class and to see her dance, and I really was so enthralled. Everything I said about child prodigies I took back, she really was quite remarkable.

Arnold often accompanied his mother to Astafieva's studio, and, as was true with everyone else who saw Alicia dance, he was mesmerized. "Her legs were like arrows, she danced as if she meant it, and there was nothing of conventional prettiness in the small child. She was then the complete ballerina in miniature," he wrote. It was significant that Alicia was not cute like her sisters. Even at age eleven, she looked and danced like an adult.

Between Alicia's obsession with ballet and her God-given talents, it is no wonder Arnold bonded with the young child. He saw in her the same thing his mother did—a future star.

Arnold often compared his relationship with the four Marks sisters and their penniless widowed mother as right out of *Little Women*, with Alicia in the Jo role, and he as the lonely and wealthy only-child neighbor, Laurie. The analogy was to prove even more prophetic when Haskell married Alicia's younger sister Vivienne many years later, just as Jo's sister Amy had married Laurie in the Louisa May Alcott novel.

But when they were all just children, it was the eldest, Alicia, who spent her after-dance class hours at the well-to-do Haskell home, being entertained by Arnold. As Markova noted in her journal:

> I spent the afternoon as I always did on my frequent visits to these very close friends, playing with a wonderful model farm

> that Arnold had. Farm is hardly the right word. It was really a village. We would have such fun together, especially when he had a fire and I was the Fire brigade and came rushing to the scene with a super engine with Arnold pretending to be the bell, making a frightful din! Sometimes we felt in a more serious mood and would sit and listen to Arnold's excellent collection of records, mostly ballet music.

The two became even closer after Arthur Marks died. "They were a very devoted family, but it was very difficult," Haskell revealed. "She [Alicia] in a way became an adult before her time."

Alicia certainly ate like one, forcing her to attend the most important audition of her life while over-stuffed with dessert pastries she had gorged on at the Haskell home. And the audition for Diaghilev and Balanchine involved far more than pirouetting flawlessly in her favorite *Valse Caprice*.

Balanchine was planning to revive Igor Stravinsky's *Le Rossignol* (The Nightingale) for the coming Ballets Russes season in Paris, and the idea of a tiny, whirling dervish of a dancer appealed to him for the title role. After Alicia had performed everything in her repertoire, including several *pas de deux* with Anton Dolin, Balanchine pushed the teenager even further. A firsthand account, again from Markova's personal journals:

> Balanchine started to ask me to do all kinds of things, including a lot of acrobatic steps. These I did rather to his surprise, mine too I might add. Finally he said, "Now please do for me two pirouettes in the air, like the men do." This seemed to me a little extraordinary, as I had never even tried to do one. Anyway, I attempted it and went round perfectly. He was delighted and said, "Yes, you will do." Do for what? I had no idea.
>
> The days went by and still we heard of no decision. Then I heard from Drury Lane that I had been chosen for "Midsummer Night's Dream." Madame [Astafieva] said that I must refuse to do it and I was a little puzzled as to why I should refuse when I had not heard from Diaghileff. She evidently had though, for when she told him that Fokine wanted me,

and unless he gave a decision right away he would lose me, he told her his decision to take me into the Company.

It was not until New Year's Eve that I knew. Madame gave a Russian party for Diaghileff and the rest of the Company and I was invited to bring the New Year in and dance for them. This I did: my Valse Caprice, and then a pas de deux with Pat [Dolin]. At the end, Diaghileff came over and, putting his arm around my shoulders, announced to all the Company that I would be joining them as the new member. There was silence. They all looked at me most suspiciously and thought that Diaghileff must be mad. It was unheard of that a child of fourteen should join the famous Russian Ballet, a very small and immature child at that.

The day of "baby ballerinas" had not yet dawned and Diaghileff had the whole world to draw from. But Diaghileff was quite sane and very serious and later discussed with my Mother the terms of my training:

No one ever had a contract with Diaghileff. [Actually, many did.] He did not believe in them, saying if an Artist could not trust him, then he was not interested in them for the Company. His way of using Artists in the Company was always what he thought the best for the Artist, so if they did not agree or did not like it, they just left.

My Mother was only too happy for me that I had been so honored by Diaghileff that I think she would have let me go for nothing, but he told her I would receive some money as a member of the Corps de Ballet, 800 francs (50 shillings) a month. He would also pay for Gladys [Guggy] to travel with me. Nothing was mentioned about my name, which fact filled me with curiosity.

I did so want a Russian name.

Markova fancied Olga. "I had visions of being Olga Tredova, or something marvelously Russian—you see." Diaghilev had something else in mind.

3

The Ballets Russes

> The rest of the company, to whom Diaghileff's loathing of children was well known, were baffled when he began calling Alicia "little daughter," took her to art galleries and concerts, and once allowed her to scold him when he kept her waiting a half hour in a hotel lobby.
>
> —Barbara Heggie, *The New Yorker*, 1944

The worst event of Alicia's young life—her father's death—would lead to arguably the best: becoming the protégé of the Russian-born ballet impresario Sergei Diaghilev. The sheltered and shy fourteen-year-old would now see the world through one of its acknowledged artistic geniuses.

With the formation of the Ballets Russes, Diaghilev reinvented (or rescued, as some would say) outmoded classical dance productions, creating in their place a vibrant, avant-garde forum for innovative choreography, revolutionary design, and transformative music. That the celebrated impresario chose to personally share this wondrous, self-created universe with a timid little *English* girl—with no sexual component, nor monetary or social benefit—is truly remarkable. He had never shown any interest in children before—or after—her.

There was no question Alicia Marks was different from other children. Like Diaghilev, she was deadly serious about ballet, loved everything about the theater, and shared his devotion to music and the visual arts. She had an amazing work ethic for one so young, diligently practicing and far exceeding the talents of any others in her age group.

She was also a sponge with a razor-sharp memory, not just for her own music and choreography, but for everyone else's as well. And she loved to learn. Even at ten, she listened wide-eyed and intently to everything Diaghilev told her and, though quiet, was uncommonly observant and intelligent.

Despite the language barrier, she seemed to understand everything quite clearly. The two never had trouble communicating, and though Diaghilev hated speaking English, he would do so with little Alicia when necessary.

The young girl had another endearing quality: she was *always* well behaved, described by her family as embodying an almost unnatural goodness—no childlike squirming, outbursts, or impatience. (And no pushy stage mother to annoy or interrupt. Her governess Guggy may have been a stern protector, but she was stoic and silent in public.) Though Alicia often received praise for her dancing, she did not feel special. She was never spoiled at home, and always felt unattractive compared to her three sisters.

"People said I appeared 'foreign,'" Markova wrote in her memoir notes, "certainly my thinness and my solemn dark eyes were far from conventional canons of prettiness of the children in the immediately post Edwardian era."

Diaghilev was also unhappy with his looks, particularly his oversized head. He was always fastidious about the proper haircut to mask the size as much as possible.

"No one ever knew what Diaghilev looked like. He never posed for photographs," said Markova.

Alicia's insecurities kept her modest and pliant, but also fiercely determined to succeed and very comfortable in the company of adults. In short, Markova was the perfect reflection of Diaghilev's ethos, and he would never find another person willing to obey him so unquestioningly and gratefully. Diaghilev's word was law. When crossed, he could be ruthless.

"He was a monster in a way," said Ballets Russes dancer Tamara Gevergeva (George Balanchine's first wife). "He was vengeful, he was selfish, he pursued his goal and nothing would stand in his way. If anybody turned against him or did anything he did not like, that was death.

"Yet, after a while, he would forget; he did the most awful things to people; then, when he needed them, he would charm them like a snake-charmer, and get them right back."

Like Markova, Diaghilev's early life had been far from secure. Perhaps he saw a bit of himself in his young dance prodigy, whose wealthy family lost everything, including their patriarch. The industrious showman had also been raised in a well-to-do household—his grandfather's twenty-room home and imposing country estate—only to have his parents squander their fortunes and force the family into bankruptcy, as Diaghilev biographer Sjeng Scheijen recently discovered. Like Alicia, Diaghilev would make the unpleasant journey from pampered child to family meal ticket.

Looking back on those times, Markova recalled sadly, "I had learned very early on that money was important, and that I must work to make it not for myself, but for my mother and sisters initially. It brought me face to face with certain harsh realties that children should not have to know about, and it taught me that I was sustained, and I dare admit, driven by the knowledge of obligation to other people."

By generously accepting into his world-famous company a mere novice—just turned fourteen when sixteen or seventeen was then the minimum age—the 52-year-old Diaghilev safeguarded Alicia from the necessity of taking on commercial engagements to earn money, with their requisite eight performances per week. Both he and Astafieva felt that such a demanding schedule would damage Alicia's still-growing body, and leave no time for proper balletic training to further strengthen her muscles and technique.

Ironically, she would work seven days a week for Diaghilev—as did all the members of his company—but her time was spent not in run-of-the-mill entertainment, but rather learning from the greatest arts talents of the time: ballet classes with Maestro Cecchetti, music tutelage from Igor Stravinsky, choreography lessons from George Balanchine, and personal costuming by none other than Henri Matisse.

"There were no unions then and we worked every day in the week, including Sunday, only different by not having class or rehearsal in the morning, and joy of joys, one could stay in bed until noon," Markova remembered. But even full workdays were a pleasure for the immensely appreciative novice, who later said she equated meeting Diaghilev to being granted an audience with King George V.

Art in all its spiritual forms was the major preoccupation of Diaghilev's life, and for whatever reason, he unselfishly bestowed his vast knowledge, access to master teachers, and star-making power onto this impressionable young girl.

Diaghilev actually considered adopting Alicia at one point—going so far as to broach the topic with Eileen Marks—but ultimately decided his precarious finances made that unwise for all concerned. (The impresario's answer to debt was typically to spend even more.) The idea that he would take such a major legal step is not as far-fetched as it sounds. Everyone in the company was aware of the pair's odd mutual admiration and emotional attachment to one another—and no one understood it.

For Alicia, who had been completely shattered by her father's sudden death, her relationship with Diaghilev seemed perfectly natural. Here was a man who delighted not only in her dancing, but also in the dancer herself. He was an instant father figure who actually enjoyed her company, just as her own father had; and he made those feelings quite public, calling her his "new daughter" or Douchka (little darling) in front of everyone.

She in turn endearingly called him "Sergypop," a fatherly term contrived from the impresario's first and middle names—Sergei Pavlovitch. (after his own father Pavel). Diaghilev thought it delightful.

"I knew he was the greatest man in ballet, but I was never afraid of him," Markova reminisced years later. "He gave me a feeling of security. He was very gentle and spoke quietly, hardly moving his mouth. He used to put his hand over mine when he talked."

Alicia's own undemonstrative public demeanor also appealed to the remote Diaghilev. She understood her place as a member of the Ballets Russes, never running up to the impresario for hugs or reassurance. He was the well-respected Director, and if he chose to compliment her or kiss her lovingly on the forehead, as he often did, she took it as a particular sign of doing well that day. If he did not, she never thought it a slight. Though he could instill fear in other members of the company, Diaghilev was always gentle with Alicia, and their mutual affection was something they both could embrace silently. Alicia never spoke to him unless spoken to first.

"He was my artistic father," she said proudly. "To have been discovered and developed by such a man was probably the greatest thing that ever happened to me."

Sergei Pavlovitch Diaghilev was born on March 19, 1872 into a family that was both prosperous—thanks to inherited vodka distilleries—and cultured. Though his mother died when he was an infant, it was not in childbirth due to his abnormally large head, as is often claimed, but rather from blood poisoning three months later. Fortunately for Sergei, when his father remarried, his stepmother couldn't have loved the boy more if he had been her own flesh and blood. Both parents stressed the importance of literature and dramatic theater, but were most passionate about music. They made sure their eldest son, as well as his two stepbrothers, acquired an early appreciation of noteworthy composers through study and attending recitals, concerts, and the opera.

Diaghilev also greatly enjoyed his singing and piano lessons and, like Lily Marks, gave poetry readings and musical performances for the family. In later years, he would surprise Ballets Russes members with his proficient piano playing at parties, often using it as a way to avoid conversation.

According to Sjeng Scheijen, Diaghilev's time as a law student at the university in St. Petersburg coincided with his family's spiraling money problems due to overspending combined with estate mismanagement and neglect. The eighteen-year-old was forced to subsist on a modest inheritance from his mother, setting some of that money aside for his family's care. He also supported his devoted former nanny, whom he'd invited to move in with him when his father could no longer pay her wages. (Sergei's deep attachment to this warm-hearted woman, who raised him after his mother died, may have been the reason he believed Alicia's governess Guggy would tenderly watch over her, not realizing the Irish spinster was anything but affectionate.)

While Markova's singular talent as a dancer was apparent from a very early age, Diaghilev came to his true calling after realizing that he was not especially gifted in any of the arts he so admired. He could play the piano well, but was no prodigy. He attempted singing, and was quite serious about composing, but without success. (When asked to review his compositions, Russian master of orchestration Nikolai Rimsky-Korsakov outraged the young Diaghilev by suggesting that his future lay *elsewhere*. Diaghilev never could take criticism well.)

And though Sergei admired and befriended painters Léon Bakst and Alexandre Benois in St. Petersburg (both of whom would be instrumental in Ballets Russes design), he was still merely a connoisseur of modern art, not a practitioner or an involved participant. "The dream and purpose of my life are to work creatively in the realm of the arts," a 21-year-old Sergei wrote to his idol Count Leo Tolstoy. But how to channel that enthusiasm?

Upon graduation in 1895, the 23-year-old finally settled on his career path, elucidated in a letter to his doting stepmother—the woman who had presciently taught him "never to utter the words 'I can't'":

> I am first a great charlatan, though with dash; second, a great charmer; third, cheeky; fourth, a person with a lot of logic and few principles; and fifth, someone afflicted, it seems, with complete absence of talent. I think I've found my true vocation: to be a patron of the arts. For that I have everything I need, except the money.

New York Times dance critic John Martin agreed with that personal assessment, writing of Diaghilev in his *World Book of Modern Ballet* (1952):

> The secret of his accomplishment lay in an erratic combination of perspicacity, taste, organizational genius, daring

> methods of exploitation (which, stripped of their elegance, would have won the admiration of P. T. Barnum), a disarming Slavic charm; an insatiable snobbery (in a man less cultivated and less well born it would have been accounted vulgar), which goaded him to know all the "best" people, artistically, socially, financially, and to beat them at their own game, as it were.

Making early use of those traits, Diaghilev managed to get funding from both the Russian government and wealthy sponsors, with the goal of promoting the country's culture—art exhibits, concerts, theater, and dance—throughout Europe. Though impressively executed and often quite successful, those productions were not without scandal and objections to Diaghilev's singular vision, particularly from the Maryinsky Imperial Theatre where he staged ballet. Yes, Sergei was charismatic and talented, but he was equally stubborn and cocksure of his abilities.

"Only a fighter and an absolute autocrat could have succeeded," wrote Arnold Haskell, who knew the impresario personally. "Diaghilev was a born dictator, but that rare thing, the dictator of discrimination and intelligence."

His unwillingness to compromise in any way eventually resulted in Diaghilev being fired from the Imperial Theatre and forced to leave Russia in search of employment elsewhere. He landed quite happily in France.

With home bases in Paris, and eventually Monte Carlo on the French Riviera, Diaghilev made excellent use of his vast experience in the fields of music, dance, and design (he had co-founded the influential Russian *World of Art* journal and exhibition society with Benois and Bakst). By forming the Ballets Russes, Diaghilev would create the first star-filled internationally touring ballet company not based in Russia. Even more importantly, it would be a catalyst for the reinvention of countless art forms for decades to come, while also inspiring everyday fashion and home decorating trends around the globe. (Future style doyenne Diana Vreeland, born in Paris in 1903, "maintained that Diaghilev's Ballets Russes was the only real avant-garde she had ever known.")

When the budding impresario had enumerated his qualifications for such an endeavor in the letter to his stepmother years earlier, he left out one crucial element. The man recognized talent when he saw it, with a vision of how best to exploit it.

After gathering the most highly acclaimed dancers, choreographers, composers, and artists of his day, the Russian became a magic-making puppet master, pulling everyone's strings with unyielding control. He knew when to tighten and when to loosen those strings, casually—and often callously—brushing aside close associates if they were no longer needed.

In a period of twenty years, Diaghilev oversaw the creation of eighty-five new ballets that forever changed the formerly staid worlds of dance, music, and design. Though underappreciated in his homeland, the impresario would finally soar in France, a high-profile vindication that brought him tremendous personal satisfaction.

"The theory of art for art's sake never enjoyed a clear victory in Russia," Diaghilev wrote in the first issue of *World of Art* magazine in 1898. Paris was the place to be for an arts revolution, and Diaghilev took full advantage. And one more slap in the face to his stuffy homeland: he *stole* their best dancers.

In the widely acclaimed 1909 premiere season of the Ballets Russes, the Paris stage was shared by Anna Pavlova, Vaslav Nijinsky, and Tamara Karsavina, all dancing to choreography by the brilliant Mikhail Fokine and to music by Nikolai Tcherepnin. The enchanting sets and costumes were by Diaghilev's longtime friends Léon Bakst and Alexandre Benois.

To that heady mix was added the sensuous—and scandalous—Ukrainian dancer Ida Rubinstein, a statuesque beauty from a wealthy Jewish family. Her performance of an erotic striptease in Oscar Wilde's *Salomé* would be banned in Russia for its brief nudity. Fokine had created that shocking "Dance of the Seven Veils" choreography specifically for Rubinstein, and the pair would once again cause a sensation with their first collaboration for the Ballets Russes in Paris: *Cléopâtre*.

Fokine first choreographed a Cleopatra-themed ballet (named *Egyptian Nights*) for the Maryinsky Theatre the previous year. But France was not Russia. In the Parisians, the choreographer had a far more sophisticated audience where sex and sensuality in art were concerned.

With magnificent Oriental sets and costumes by Bakst, the lavish ballet debuted at the Théâtre du Châtelet on June 2, 1909. Starring Rubinstein as Cleopatra, Pavlova as Ta-Hor, and Karsavina and Nijinsky as slaves, the one-act ballet was a showstopper. Along with similarly exotic productions, such as the Far Eastern-themed *Shéhérazade* the following year (also starring Rubinstein and Nijinsky), Diaghilev's Ballets Russes became more than just a successful dance company: it was a global trendsetter for the arts.

According to Charles Spencer, curator of the 1994 museum exhibit "Designers and Dancers of the Ballets Russes," Diaghilev's company "had the most tremendous influence not only on fashion and interior decoration, but on popular entertainment. It influenced novel writing on Oriental themes. It influenced the silent cinema, all those vamps and Rudolf Valentino. . . . But it also influenced theater in the wider sense."

At the same time he was promoting Orientalism, Diaghilev had the good box-office sense not to neglect romanticism. By pairing beautifully staged classics with more daring fare, the company could attract wider audiences. And to keep those seats filled, the arts visionary instinctively knew when exoticism had run its course. The follow-up needed to be even more trailblazing.

In the midst of World War I and its aftermath, a groundbreaking modernism—as exemplified by Pablo Picasso, Henri Matisse, Joan Miró, and Giorgio de Chirico, among others—was shattering all preconceived notions of realism and linear perspective in art. It was boldly geometric, unnaturally colorful, and pictorially challenging. Diaghilev had found his new direction.

Along with Georges Braque, André Derain, Maurice Utrillo, Max Ernst, and many others, the above-mentioned artists would be called upon to design sets and costumes for a new mode of contemporary choreography at the Ballets Russes. From Picasso's cubist treatment of Jean Cocteau's *Parade* (1917) to Giorgio de Chirico's surrealist graphics for *Le Bal* (1929), the Diaghilev company once again both captured and influenced the zeitgeist of the times.

"The era 1909–1929 was the Diaghilev era, because he crystallized what was going on, and not because he actually created it," wrote Arnold Haskell. "This does not detract from him; it puts his genius on another plane, and at the same time allows full credit to his collaborators."

It was at this creative juncture that Alicia Marks joined the Ballets Russes in 1923, and her timing couldn't have been more fortuitous. While exotic Orientalism had sold tickets in the early 1900s—as the littlest *Salomé* dancer knew well—the practitioners of cutting-edge modernism would dominate their fields for many, many decades to come. The friendships and working relationships Markova developed with composer Igor Stravinsky; dancers Anton Dolin, Ninette de Valois, and Alexandra Danilova; artists Henri Matisse and Pablo Picasso; and most importantly, choreographers George Balanchine, Léonide Massine, and Mikhail Fokine would remain a vital part of her life and future career long after the Ballets Russes came to its unexpected end. It also cemented her willingness to embrace new ideas. And she had a single Pygmalion to thank for it.

Markova's transformation under Diaghilev's tutelage began when she was just ten years old and accompanied the great man to performances of *The Sleeping Princess*. Now that she had been officially accepted into his company, those one-on-one lessons would start anew. The impresario and fourteen-year-old made a striking pair.

There was no missing Sergei Diaghilev in any room he entered. Vaslav Nijinsky's sister, the dancer/choreographer Bronislava Nijinska, got her first glimpse of the impresario at a ballet rehearsal with Mikhail Fokine when she was just eighteen years old:

> All eyes were on Diaghilev. He was an imposing figure: tall, rather heavy, impeccably dressed, carrying a walking cane and holding his hat in his left hand. . . .
>
> He was broad-chested and had a big, almost square head, slightly flabby cheeks, and a full lower lip. In his big black eyes there was always a look of sadness, even when he smiled. The expression on his face was at once menacing and attractive—like a bulldog's, initially discouraging all friendly overtures.

> Looking at him, I felt that it would not be easy to become friends with Sergei Pavlovitch.

The opposite would be true for Alicia Marks.

> "I was a very shy, timid person when I was young," she remembered. "Strangely enough, the one person who I suppose I should have been nervous with, Diaghilev, I never was. To me, he really was like a father. . . . [H]e perhaps sort of replaced my father dying, taking over shall we say, my artistic guidance and having me trained by the greatest ballet masters in the world . . . I mean sending me to museums, and to see dancers, and all the great artists I should."

It was such an odd sight—the two of them sitting together at performances. The large, imposing Diaghilev in his signature black suit and white dress shirt—matched by the shocking white forelock in his ebony hair—top hat and cane by his side as he intermittently toyed with a handkerchief always hidden inside his sleeve just under the frayed cuffs; and the pint-size dancer, dwarfed by the huge man, looking equally dramatic with her own severely cut jet-black bob, saucer-size sad dark eyes, and alabaster skin—almost disturbingly still and poised for a child. She would always remember him smelling deliciously of Guerlain's exotic *Mitsouko* fragrance.

They did indeed appear to be father and daughter, and their bond only got stronger during the London Ballets Russes season prior to Alicia's joining the company in France. As she wrote of those times in her diary:

> I did not dance with the Company that season in London, but Diag: [*sic*] asked Gladys [Guggy] to bring me down to the Theatre each performance and he would take me in front with him.
>
> I shall never forget how Diag: would take me with him through the pass-door of the Coliseum and to the settee at the side of the stalls and there we would sit and he would explain in the little English that he knew, that there were all different

styles of Ballets. Difference in characterisation, difference in scenic design, difference in music.

Having been brought up in the strictly classical tradition and been over-awed by Sleeping Princess, I was so excited and thrilled at the thought of seeing once more my beloved Ballet. But the first program I saw was Three-Cornered Hat, with décor and costumes by Picasso and music by de Falla. This ballet was completely lost on a child of my age, and when Diag: asked me how I enjoyed it, the answer was "I am afraid I didn't. I want to see the Company do a classical ballet on their points in lovely floating ballet dresses." Maybe the world will be surprised that I answered the great Diag: in this manner, but it wasn't impertinence. I always speak the truth. "Ah, Douchka, you must wait," he replied. And so my artistic education began. . . .

Each day I saw a different ballet, Blue Train, The Faithful Shepherdess, Cimarosiana, Prince Igor, and eventually Aurora's Wedding. . . . He wanted me to know and appreciate all of them, the details and elements, the artistic aspects of all they portrayed, whether I liked them personally did not count but I had to learn that there were different schools of Art, the classic, the Modern, and he wanted me to be attuned to both. "You have to learn about them," he said, "as they will be as important to you as your daily lesson in perfecting your technique. . . . I can only thank God he gave me all the attention."

What made this relationship all the more strange was Diaghilev's complete lack of friendship with other members of his company, save his lovers. Though the dancers "admired him; it almost amounted to worship;" wrote Arnold Haskell, "at the same time they were thoroughly scared."

"'Frightening' is a word used over and over," to describe Diaghilev, wrote dance critic and editor Robert Gottlieb, "—yet kind, even paternal, to the fourteen-year-old Alicia Markova."

No one could understand it.

Ballets Russes dancer Ninette de Valois (born Edris Stannus in Ireland) was asked by the impresario to take Alicia under her wing. (In the 1930s, de Valois would work closely with Markova in the founding of London's Royal Ballet.) Though known as self-assured and formidable herself, the 26-year-old dancer was completely intimidated by her demanding boss, making her all the more perplexed at the special relationship he had with this mere child.

"He was crazy about her," de Valois recalled, still in disbelief more than five decades later. "[Alicia] brought out a gentle side to Diaghilev that he showed to no one else." De Valois elaborated in an interview for a BBC television documentary on Markova:

> I think of course her history as an English dancer is absolutely unique. Here she was this great ballerina and Diaghilev really adopted her. He saw this child in London and was so interested in her, he just took her into the Company. She was much too young to appear with us then . . . not in any of the ballets at the beginning, she was too small—a very little thing even for fourteen. . . .
>
> He saw all these great qualities in her were going to come out with a little careful tuition and everything. But she's always had a wonderful mind applying herself to anything. I don't know anyone who's quite so reliant on herself.

That self-reliance would emerge after Guggy's departure from Alicia's life in the not too distant future, but for now it was the departure from home that was her singular preoccupation. Preparation in the Marks household was being handled with all the fuss and intrigue of Marie Antoinette's Austrian "hand-off" to France, albeit on a vastly more modest scale.

First was the issue of money. Though Markova later said her mother would have let her join the Ballets Russes for next to no wages just for the experience, that was not actually the case. She needed to earn a salary.

Then there was the additional cost of a governess. Diaghilev had insisted that Alicia have a chaperone, perhaps her mother, as he could not be a full-time babysitter for the immature teenager. Since Eileen Marks still had three young daughters at home, she decided to send Guggy instead, though her inability to speak French or Russian would be a considerable drawback.

While Diaghilev offered to subsidize the governess's salary, that small amount would hardly cover lodging and food for the pair once on tour. And it wasn't as if the Marks family could survive without Alicia's contributing something to the family coffers.

Fortunately, Emmy Haskell looked upon Alicia as the daughter she never had, generously providing an additional monthly stipend for her and Guggy. Equally magnanimous was the wealthy couple Valia and Nathan Golodetz. Valia had taken dance classes with Alicia at Astafieva's studio, growing quite fond of the little girl, whom she was convinced would become a ballet star one day. To make sure that happened, Valia and her husband offered to help support Eileen and the girls so that Alicia could concentrate on training with the Ballets Russes.

Next was the issue of clothes. Clearly not yet a fashion plate, Alicia Marks would now be living in soigné Monte Carlo and was in need of an updated wardrobe. Once again, the kindly Mrs. Haskell stepped in, having some of her own smart dresses cut down to fit the child, as well as remaking one of her fur coats. The devoted patron anticipated a need Markova would come to know well—how to stay warm on long unheated train rides from one performance venue to another throughout the frigid winter months. (Catching pneumonia on one such trip would lead to the sudden death of Pavlova years later.)

To Alicia, however, the most meaningful present was a joint gift from Emmy Haskell and her 21-year-old son Arnold, who had always looked upon the eldest Marks daughter as the little sister he never had. As a going-away present, the Haskells had a compartmentalized dressing case custom-made in mauve, Alicia's favorite color since her fateful first meeting with Pavlova. Markova treasured it and kept it her entire life.

Arnold Haskell enjoyed telling an amusing story about lunching with Alicia just prior to her joining the Ballets Russes. During the meal, the guileless teenager suddenly looked up from her plate and asked, "Who is this man Basket they are always talking about?" Haskell was puzzled for a moment, until he realized she meant Léon Bakst, the already quite famous Russian set and costume designer for the company. Oh, Alicia had so much to learn, Arnold thought to himself.

But first she needed to get to Monte Carlo, and the biggest hurdle was no longer money. The minimum age for a British resident to work abroad was sixteen, and Alicia had just celebrated her fourteenth birthday on December 1. Worse still, she looked even younger than that. What to do?

Diaghilev was nothing if not a rule-breaker, so he decided to just roll the dice—perfectly appropriate for the owner of a company that performed inside the most glamorous casino in Europe. Alicia would never be granted legal permission for a work permit, so why not just "sneak" her out of the country?

Poor Alicia. As if it weren't unnerving enough that she was leaving her family, joining the most famous ballet company on earth, and moving to a country where she didn't speak the language, the timid child also had to contend with the fear of being "handcuffed" at the border—she, who *never* broke the rules.

But Diaghilev had wisely chosen Ninette de Valois as travel chaperone for the little girl and her governess. There were other British female members of the company he could have called upon, such as Lydia Sokolova (born Hilda Tansley Munnings in Essex, England) or dancer/choreographer Léonide Massine's first wife Vera Savina (born Vera Clarke), but neither had the haute manner, imperial elegance, and French surname of de Valois to intimidate border patrol officials. Who would question the imposing beauty about her quiet companion when they crossed over into France?

The day Alicia was to set off on the grandest of all adventures, London was enveloped in one of its renowned blinding fogs. It was a real "pea-souper," as the Brits call it, and the type of weather that would eventually become associated with the ballerina. Maybe, Alicia thought optimistically, the thick haze would keep British officials from noticing the underage expatriate fleeing the country at Victoria Station.

But Diaghilev had another ace in the hole. Alicia would receive a foreign-sounding name. She had long fantasized about a new one: "I would spend hours thinking up all sort of weird and exotic names and would wait to ask Arnold and his mother at our next lunch their opinions," she recorded in her journal notes. "They knew I had set my heart on Olga, I suppose from my idol of the Sleeping Princess days, Olga Spessivtseva, but I certainly did not like Olga Marks—but Olga what?"

She found out at Victoria Station.

> I was saying Good-bye to my dear Mother and sisters and feeling a little sad at having to leave them behind, when the Regisseur, Serge Grigorieff began to call out the roll-call to make sure all the large Company were there. He came to Alicia Markova and no reply, again he called it—no reply. "You, little one," he said "You, Alicishka."
>
> Oh dear, I thought, not Olga, the same name with only one letter changed, and that is how Alicia Markova was born.

Also born at the train station was a lifelong friendship with Ninette de Valois. At their first meeting, Alicia was in awe of the cosmopolitan dancer. She was so polished, pretty, and impossibly chic. And she did indeed whisk Alicia and Guggy through French customs without incident.

De Valois was also pleasantly surprised, having expected to be saddled with a whiny brat. As she told Clement Crisp in an interview for a documentary on Markova many years later:

> I was one of these sorts of adopted aunts. I had to do everything, because of course the governess couldn't speak a word of French and disapproved of any country but England, so it wasn't easy. So I had to do a lot of work for her at that time, but she was a charming child. Almost too good. She was so obedient and so obliging to everybody. Very intelligent in a little quiet way and Diaghilev of course really was extraordinary. He saw she had French lessons, used to take her out to galleries and things.

And in perhaps his strangest role, Diaghilev became Alicia's personal morality cop. Saintliness was hardly the calling card of the Ballets Russes, nor of Monte Carlo for that matter.

In the 1920s, the Monaco principality was home to the only legal gambling casino in France, thus becoming the go-to good-time playground for the rich, royal, famous, and infamous. There was so much to do, or not to do, in the divinely decadent resort—from sunning, tennis, and swimming, to dining, drinking, and roulette. And of course there was the Ballets Russes for entertainment.

The company moved their base of operation to Monte Carlo in 1923 when the deeply in-debt Diaghilev received an offer he couldn't refuse.

In exchange for performing annually during the busy winter months, the Ballets Russes would gain a permanent home at the Casino's appropriately named Grand Théâtre. As Sjeng Scheijen explains, in one fell swoop "the deal would give Monaco the world's most prestigious dance company and end the company's money woes for good."

One of the Ballets Russes's most popular productions was a musical pantomime parodying Monte Carlo's well-heeled vacationers. With a libretto by Jean Cocteau, contemporary choreography by Bronislava Nijinska, and modern costumes by Gabrielle "Coco" Chanel, the satiric ballet was called *Le Train Bleu*. It was named after the luxury night-express train that chauffeured wealthy patrons to the gaming hotspot beginning in 1922. And it wasn't just the French who booked passage.

Looking to flee bone-chilling winters, pleasure-seeking Londoners—including the Prince of Wales, Somerset Maugham, and even Winston Churchill—would ferry across the English Channel to Calais, France, where the train trip commenced at 1:00 P.M. The French glitterati boarded in Paris or one of the other stops along the way, before arriving in the warm embrace of the Côte d'Azur the following morning.

As towns flew by, so did time, as one could dance (yes, dance), drink, and dine (five-course dinners lasted hours) in the wood-paneled cars with etched Lalique glass window screens. When just too exhausted to party on, passengers would retire to one of the deluxe, gilt-edged sleeping compartments painted the royal blue color that gave the train its nickname.

It was over-the-top opulence and rich excess all the way, a perfect prelude to that lovely capital of indulgence, Monte Carlo: home to too much sunning, too much gambling, and too much nightlife. That of course led to too much sex, often with whoever was currently available.

Like many artistic companies whose members spent most of their waking hours working and socializing together, the Ballets Russes was a hotbed of revolving romantic liaisons: heterosexual, homosexual, and bisexual. After his famous love affair with Vaslav Nijinsky ended disastrously, Diaghilev alternately became involved with Ballets Russes members Anton Dolin, Serge Lifar, Léonide Massine, and Boris Kochno—some more willingly than others. While sleeping with the boss was decidedly advantageous to one's career, ending the affair often meant lost creative opportunities.

Diaghilev was sexist to the extent that he would seek to dismiss female dancers who consorted with men "he found common or unsuitable for the Russian Ballet," wrote Haskell. "He was no hypocrite, he did not preach a morality foreign to himself, but the whole tone of these servants of art must be maintained. Nothing could be allowed to interfere with the quality of their work." It was far better that they should stick to their own kind, or else their paramours should at least be rich.

Alicia Marks was another case entirely. She was *completely* innocent—known as the "baby ballerina" of the company—and her "artistic father" would make sure she stayed that way. In this, he couldn't have had a stauncher ally than Guggy. Between the two of them, no alcohol or smitten beau would come near her lips; chocolate Ovaltine was considered a nightcap; and makeup was only for the stage, and even there, not too much.

Markova would later become known for her flawless stage makeup, passing along what she learned from her Ballets Russes days to numerous young dancers over the years. "He advised me," she would tell them, "'Child, the persons in the first few rows will see your makeup; therefore you must not use too much. As for the rest, they can't see your face anyway, and it is your body that must tell the story.'"

And that face and body better not be tan, Diaghilev added. It was his belief that ballerinas should look as white as possible to enhance the purity and delicacy of their movements. So the only interaction Alicia had with Monte Carlo's famous beaches was the view from her little balcony, where she longed to join the other teenagers joyfully basking in the sun.

Markova's good friend, actress Florence Desmond (whom the dancer met on the set of *Dick Whittington* when she was only ten), had a villa in the South of France where Markova often vacationed as an adult. Desmond laughingly recalled the following story during a radio interview:

> I don't suppose many people think of a ballerina being fun, but we get on and laugh all the time. The thing that did surprise me, I don't know why one thinks of a ballerina's being an all-round athlete, she cannot swim *one* stroke. She used to hang on to the ladder of my boat and just kick. . . . And she said, you see, when I worked with Diaghilev, we were never allowed to take any exercise except ballet, not even walking. So swimming was absolutely out.
>
> And always, she sat in the shade. She said, you see, I've never taken sun in my life, because again, Diaghilev insisted on us looking ethereal and looking very pale.

In later years, Markova would be grateful. Everyone remarked on her translucent, unlined skin well into her eighties.

Guggy took her guardianship of Alicia to alarming extremes. It was bad enough that the girl was allowed no simple pleasures, but when not dancing or watching rehearsals, she was made a virtual prisoner in their tiny apartment. Located in the affordable town of Beausoleil overlooking Monaco, the one-room bedsit had a kitchenette where they ate every meal together.

The same was true on the road. The two shared a single hotel room where Guggy prepared all their carefully rationed meals in a "hatbox stove" made popular during the war. It had a cooking ring and tiny saucepan inside, in which the governess boiled eggs. But rather than make the experience fun, as in a camping trip, "with Guggy it was a grim ritual without a scrap of pleasure," according to Anton Dolin. "There was a constant tension in that dreary top room."

When not in dance class or rehearsing, Alicia was expected to return to the studio apartment to study from her school textbooks. On all but performance nights, she was to be in bed by 6:30—Guggy sleeping on the bed beside her—and was never allowed to join the evening social gatherings with the rest of the company.

When dancer Alexandra Danilova stopped by the Beausoleil flat one afternoon to invite Alicia to tea, the teenager was unable to open the door because Guggy had locked her in for "safekeeping" while out running errands. Danilova was horrified. What if there was a fire?

Guggy's exacting discipline knew no bounds. She criticized Alicia's performances, punished her for getting marks on her ballet shoes (having been told that that meant she was landing incorrectly), and chided her for her "silly" musings in letters home to her mother and sisters, thus refusing to mail them.

Guggy herself would report on their daily life to family and friends. Knowing Alicia loved chocolates—coincidentally somewhat of an obsession with Diaghilev as well—the governess took control of the sweets given to her by other dancers, holding them back for any perceived dancing mistakes, treating her charge like a trained seal.

"Everything had to be done her way," Markova told a newspaper reporter many years later, describing the whole experience as a bit Dickensian. "She wanted to dominate. She had marvelous qualities, she would have died for one, but I would prefer somebody with a little warmth. She wouldn't let me do anything for myself, ever. I'm afraid I was very young in years and very naïve; I was wearing socks still. When I look back, I think, my God, it was frightening."

But it's not as if Alicia didn't realize the situation was abnormal at the time. What choice did she have? She spent every waking hour with the woman who, though almost cruelly strict and demanding, was also her full-time caretaker. "I was bathed, dressed, changed, as if I were a doll," she wrote in her memoirs. "In the theatre she supervised my every movement, dressing my hair, making me up, fitting and fixing my costumes, preparing my shoes; outside the theatre, when I was not in rehearsal or spending long hours watching rehearsals, Guggy became a kind of bodyguard." It was far more demoralizing than helpful.

There was no one even close to Alicia's age in the company, adding to her loneliness, and Guggy's implacable manner kept friendly overtures from Danilova and de Valois at bay. "She sat and watched everything and I wasn't allowed to talk to the other dancers in the breaks," Markova recalled sadly. "The only time I spoke to children my own age was when I went home for two weeks in the summer and saw my sisters."

No wonder Markova was often seen carrying on animated, if a tad one-sided, conversations with Pierre, the theater stray cat.

Guggy was also the cause of a minor kerfuffle between Alicia and Diaghilev, of which the whole company would learn. In order to educate the "little one" in all the arts, the impresario often arranged to take her to local shows and performances he thought she should see—a rarefied honor indeed. One day, he told the fourteen-year-old to meet him in his hotel lobby at four o'clock. Alicia begged Guggy to take her there at three, for fear of being late. And there they sat—four, five, six o'clock—still no Diaghilev. Markova would have sat there all night, but Guggy insisted that they leave, as Alicia's bedtime was 6:30. The governess literally dragged her overwrought little charge back home.

The next morning at rehearsal, Diaghilev asked Alicia in front of the entire company where she had been. In her always quiet, polite, and clipped manner, Alicia answered, "You said 4:00 and I waited until 6:30, and when you didn't come, I left." The company couldn't believe what they were hearing. First—why Diaghilev would make an appointment with this mere child was beyond them; and on top of that, she had had the effrontery to stand him up! One waited all night for the great Diaghilev if necessary.

But rather than explode, the impresario replied calmly, "What a pity," as he had planned to take Alicia to tea and outside the city to watch an exciting Spanish dance troupe. Though the conversation passed without incident, the story became Ballets Russes legend. No one other than a male lover had this type of relationship with Diaghilev, especially not a sexless, immature English girl.

Fortunately for Alicia, not even Guggy could prevent her from soaking in the warmth and unparalleled beauty of the Côte d'Azur. Their lodgings may have been third-class, but the views from the hillside town of Beausoleil were breathtaking and the local shop owners welcoming.

Alicia started every morning dining on tea and croissants on her sunny little balcony—the Mediterranean and splendors of Monaco at her feet. As she raced down the hill, she could see the famous clock over the entrance of the casino, keeping careful watch that she arrived on time for the ballet lessons she so loved.

Her days were quite full, beginning with morning class at 9:00 A.M. sharp, followed by watching or participating in rehearsals all afternoon, and more rehearsals or performances in the evening.

Little Alicia never forgot how lucky she was for the great opportunity given her by Diaghilev, and was determined to make the most of it. Her greatest terror was disappointing him. Diaghilev had *chosen* her. She must succeed at all costs to prove that his faith in her was justified.

If Guggy was the price she had to pay for joining the Ballets Russes, so be it. Markova chose to focus on the positive, as she recorded in her personal journal:

> That first year at Monte Carlo was an exciting one, full of discoveries and surprises. It was like being suddenly transported to Fairyland and instead of dreaming and imagining myself dancing as various characters, here I was actually doing it; the Ballets for me held the magic of the unknown and I loved every minute of my work.
>
> My first role of course was Little Red Riding Hood in Aurora's Wedding. I would enjoy acting this role. I understood it, the little girl going through the forest and meeting the terrifying Wolf, the byplay of trying to divert his attention and finally the fear as he carried me off—presumably to be eaten. These expressions came naturally to me, as I was R.R.H. as soon as I had my dress and cloak on. I was not a mature or sophisticated child, though I was fourteen, and Diag: did not wish that I should become aware of life and its complications too soon.
>
> I can realize now how he took care that I was unspoiled and sheltered from the intrigues that abounded in the Company. Therefore I found it much harder to portray other grown-up roles, as invariably I did not even understand the emotions that I was supposed to be expressing. I was acclaimed always for my dancing and infallible technique, but it took time for the acting element to develop in my work. How could a child dance Swanlake? This was an interesting experiment of Diag:s.

Alicia's innocence amongst wolves delighted Diaghilev. His life was filled with troubled love affairs, the histrionics of his artists, and unrelenting money problems. "Every penny went into his dreams. He handled millions, and died poor," wrote Haskell. Then there was this little angelic cherub in their midst. He relished showing her off, like fine china you only take out to impress important guests. And his first opportunity to do that presented itself shortly after Markova joined the company.

The Prince and Princess of Monaco were giving a very grand reception at their glittering palace in February, with Diaghilev asked to provide the entertainment. Only a few dancers were chosen, including Vera Nemtchinova, Alice Nikitina, and Anton Dolin. There would be one more, as Markova recalled well.

> I was so delighted when I heard Diag: had included my Valse Caprice, one of his favourite numbers, in the Programme. I felt very grown up to be going to the Palace and so late too, as a rule I was not allowed to go to any function at night that was not a performance at the Theatre. I can remember clearly after the rehearsal in the afternoon, we were all coming down from the Palace, along the winding road that always reminds me of a stage set or a scene that you see in exclusive toy shops where they exhibit moving toys going round and round on a turntable.
>
> We were all seated in the Hotel de Paris. As usual I was sitting very quietly, being seen and not heard as was my way, when Diag: turned round and said, "And how does the little one like her first visit to the Palace?" "It's lovely," I sighed, and thereupon, they all roared with laughter. I could not understand why, and felt hurt, but Diag: explained to me, here I was a little girl going to the Palace of the Prince of Monaco with all the great Stars of the Ballet, and when I was asked my reaction to this great event instead of uttering superlatives, I had simply said, "It's lovely" just as if I had been sucking a lollipop and he had asked how I was enjoying it.
>
> I found this explanation rather beyond me, but now I know what he meant. I can now understand how Diag: tried to

> keep me as simple and naïve as he could, whilst my serenity and self-possession attracted him, he admired my simplicity of thought even though I had heavy responsibilities on my shoulders. I was never precocious, and it was these qualities he saw in my dancing and wanted to keep.

Though the Monaco ball was attended by a Who's Who of European high society—including the Duke of Connaught and Lady Sackville-West—upper-crust British newspaper *The Sketch* began its colorful party review with the youngest person present:

> It is a long time since we applauded an infant prodigy. I suppose the description applies to the charming little Alicia Markowa [*sic*], who danced so divinely at the great reception given by T.S.H. the Hereditary Princess and Prince Pierre of Monaco at the great salon of the Palace on Saturday. The very skimmed top of the creamiest cream of Riviera society had been invited. . . .
>
> Mmes. Nemtchinovina and Tchernicheva were dazzling in some of the most effective pieces of the repertoire. But the clou [highlight of the show], I think, was the child Markowa. She and Anton Dolin were both congratulated warmly by the Duke of Connaught after their performance. I hope it won't interfere with their career if I say (I flatter myself, what!) that Markowa and Dolin are not those artists' real names. (You probably knew that before!) They are no more Russian than I am a Dutchman! But there you are, prejudice dies hard.
>
> —*The Sketch*, 2/18/25

Sadly, Alicia's beloved grandfather Abraham Marks never forgave her taking the stage moniker "Markova," calling it "an unpardonable affront to the family name." After she joined the Ballets Russes, he cut off all communication with her, unmoved that Alicia, a name she kept, was chosen in honor of his now-deceased wife.

It seems an unreasonable decision coming from a man who was once so close to his granddaughter. Though they were a very religious orthodox Jewish family—Abraham's wife Alicia was a contributing writer to the London *Jewish Chronicle*—Markova wasn't renouncing her religion, just her name—and dropping only one letter at that. In fact, "Markova" roughly translates as "the daughter of Marks." But Abraham felt any change was an insult, and sadly drifted out of Markova's life.

Life as a new "Russian" presented many other problems for the English dancer. The daily schedule for every member in the company was posted on a large callboard written in the native language of the Ballets Russes. Markova, Alicia soon learned, appeared as "MAP-KOBA," but deciphering the various ballet titles and their appointed rehearsal times proved far more difficult. Her wonderful ear for music carried over to a gift for languages; but that was because she could easily master sounds, not a strange alphabet.

After misreading the board one day, Alicia missed a key practice session, which always came with the penalty of a fine she could ill afford. When assistant director Serge Grigoriev discovered she wasn't playing hooky, but rather mistakenly resting in her room, he forgave the mix-up.

One might wonder why Markova didn't just ask one of the British ballerinas to help her with the language, but the teenager was too in awe of them, looking upon her fellow performers as revered "stars" rather than peers. She even kept a scrapbook of all the dancers, cutting out their photos and name captions from Ballets Russes programs and carefully pasting them in her keepsake album. It was just like any schoolgirl might do, but Markova was a *member* of the ensemble, not a stage-struck fan.

Also unheard of, Alicia shyly, and with a deferential bow, presented her favorite ballerinas with little bouquets at rehearsals whenever she could persuade Guggy to spare some change at the flower market. Though many in the Corps were understandably jealous of Diaghilev's young prodigy, the principal dancers quickly warmed to this practically mute, talented little girl who clearly worshipped them.

And how could they resist a co-worker who actually asked for their autographs? It was just too sweet for words when Markova opened her baby blue leather album, pen in hand, and asked politely for them to sign. The autographs were often as charming as the bashful girl who asked for them:

Lydia Sokolova, Paris June 1926
For beauty I am not a star,
There are others lovelier far.
But my face I don't mind
Because I'm behind
It's you folk in front get this jar!
Do you mind?

A mon petite amie.
Alicia Meilleurs soulaitations [*sic*]
Alexandra Danilova, London 1926

Alice á Alice un bon souvenir
Alice Nikitina
London, 15 Juillet 1926

Yours Sincerely
Vera Nemtchinova
My love to little Alicia

There was another constant reminder of Markova's age. She was so tiny that costuming her for the stage was a habitual problem, starting from the ground up. Before joining the Ballets Russes, Alicia had always performed in little socks and toe shoes. The sight of her beanpole legs supporting astounding leaps and turns only added to the audience's amazement.

Now her pale pink anklets, which she wore at all rehearsals, made her look even younger than she actually was in comparison to the other dancers. Everyone else wore the same uniform: a white shirt and black tights or knee breeches for men, and a plain black tunic or dress with black tights for women. (Female dancers were allowed to wear one bright color of their choice in a hair ribbon.)

Markova would gladly have worn black tights herself, but she was so small, none could be found to fit her. Interestingly, Diaghilev told her he hated black leggings, as they made it difficult to see if a dancer was moving the right muscles. Besides, he added, those dark tights were just a holdover from the "pretentious" Russian Imperial Ballet.

The impresario tried to institute a change to "flesh colored" tights, at one point, but the company rebelled. The dancers were required to pay for and maintain all legwear themselves, and complained the nude hose got dirty too fast.

For rehearsals, durable cotton or wool tights were the norm, with expensive silk reserved for performances. It was the only breathable material that clung to a dancer's legs without wrinkling, and it had such an elegant sheen.

All silk tights were ordered from Paris at great cost, then carefully washed and mended after each wearing. "Ballerinas were more sorely tempted from the paths of virtue by offers of silk tights than diamond bracelets," Markova joked years later.

Markova had exactly one pair of silk tights—a pale pink—that had been specially made for her performances as Little Red Riding Hood. But pink wouldn't do for her next scheduled appearance.

The "little one" had been such a success at the Monaco Royal Palace that Diaghilev decided to feature her once again at another high society party, this time in *The Salle de Musique* at the Monte Carlo Casino. A *pas de deux* from *Swan Lake* was selected, along with the shortest male member of the company, Nicholas Efimov, to partner her.

Classical white ballet tights were a necessity for any self-respecting swan, so a pair was expressly ordered from Paris. An even bigger thrill for Alicia was her costume. One of Vera Trefilova's old tutus was being cut down to fit her. What an honor!

The week before the performance, various parcels arrived from the costumiers—but no tights for Alicia. Not to worry; another shipment was due the following week. Come performance day, the final delivery arrived—but still no tights. Now the little swan was in trouble.

An attempt was made to bleach Alicia's pink Red Riding Hood tights, but the color wouldn't come out. So in a panic, a search party was sent off to locate small-sized white silk stockings that might be stitched to a waistband. (Diaghilev was quite the perfectionist. If he ever saw anything wrong—an errant safety pin, too much makeup, a misplaced dance step—he would have Grigoriev assess a fine.)

All too close to curtain time, Guggy came through, finding a pair of white stockings in an out-of-the-way shop in Beausoleil. As Markova's feet were so tiny, the stockings needed to be hiked up, stitched to a makeshift belt, and somehow affixed to her waist. She remembered an old pantomime costume trick of sewing pennies inside a waistband, as the weight in a tightly tied sash kept the legs from bagging. Guggy finished stitching her in just before she took to the stage.

"It seemed a very precarious business to me," Markova laughingly recalled. "I went on far more nervous of whether the pennies would drop out, than whether I should remember the difficult routine I had to dance. Sure enough, on the first lift in the *pas de deux* there was a dreadful clang, and I trembled not daring to look down. Imagine my relief when I saw that it was my partner Efimov's belt. I really should not have been so relieved as he used this to keep up *his* tights and the catastrophe was much worse!"

But that wasn't the end of their costume problems, as Alicia was about to experience her own wardrobe malfunction. It would not be the pennies.

When Markova first joined the company, Diaghilev asked that she grow her hair long so she could wear it parted in the middle and sleeked back like the other ballerinas. "The thing that Diaghilev adored was that the head be unadorned," Markova remembered. "But I had this little bob. What were they going to do with me? So they found me a black band with little diamonds [rhinestones]—very simple."

While Efimov was in the wings having his belt tended to, Alicia performed rapid triple pirouettes, one after another. As her head whipped around, so did the headband, eventually spinning around her neck like a hula hoop. It could have been worse: the headpiece could have flown across the stage or, worse still, hit Efimov when he came back on.

"Thank God I danced impeccably," Markova recalled. Diaghilev accepted her profuse apologies and was impressed that she had continued to dance flawlessly despite the distraction. But he warned her, "Everything must be stuck on with glue. Everything—there must be no excuses, you must stick it hard."

Markova asked the other ballerinas for advice, but would soon discover "Seccotine," a type of glue from England that remained flexible after drying. She would never be without it.

"From that day on, I never moved without adhesive. I still have that band to this day. And if I look inside it, my hair and skin is on the tape. I never danced again without everything firmly attached."

That often meant gluing jewelry and costumes to body parts. Markova even glued her foot into her toe shoes, something she demonstrated on American television some thirty years later.

And Alicia wasn't alone in her onstage wardrobe mishaps at the Ballets Russes. With Diaghilev frequently hiring famous artists and fashion designers as costumiers, outfits tended to be created for their visual impact, not ease of movement.

Côte d'Azur couturier Coco Chanel was both a personal friend of Diaghilev's and a successful businesswoman who invested money in his company. She was often consulted about the "look" of new ballets, as was Pablo Picasso (then married to former Ballets Russes dancer Olga Kokhlova). Dress rehearsal "fashion parades" were arranged by the impresario to solicit their opinions and suggestions.

When Chanel tried her own hand at costuming for the contemporary scenes of the satirical *Le Train Bleu*, she simply translated her signature *de la mode* styles for the stage. While audiences loved it, the performers were less enthused.

Consider poor Lydia Sokolova. Chanel presented her with a two-piece wool jersey bathing costume complete with rubber slippers that stuck to the stage. What could be worse? The ballerina also had to wear a tight bathing cap and oversized faux pearl earrings much like the costume jewels favored by Chanel's affluent clientele—the very ones who would be in the audience on opening night. The ear bobs were so large and cumbersome, Sokolova couldn't hear her orchestra cues.

Leon Woizikowski fared no better. He had to master grand leaps while wearing spiffy oxford shoes with his Chanel-designed golf knickers, shirt, tie, and striped long-sleeve sweater; and Nijinska's tennis dress came complete with a visor and full-size racket. Alicia's tights problem paled in comparison.

Markova was well aware of Chanel's status as the epitome of modern chic on the Riviera. Diaghilev had told her to study not only how "Coco" dressed, but also how she walked and sat. The teenager couldn't have found a more stylish role model, and the adult Markova would share her fashion idol's preference for understated elegance, black and white, and a few pieces of dramatic costume jewelry.

Since Alicia didn't have a growth spurt until age sixteen (one of the reasons it was the minimum age for dancers to join any *corps de ballet*), she was given fanciful character solos designed to highlight her marvelous technique, while masking the vast height discrepancy between her and all the other dancers.

"I was thought particularly suitable for roles which called for a fairytale illusion," she explained. And her choreographer for these parts would be Diaghilev's new hire, the untested George Balanchine.

Markova and Balanchine were much alike in their quiet demeanor, love of music, and fascination with the methods of Italian dance master Enrico Cecchetti, whose moves were considered small, precise, and graceful in relation to the grander, more elongated Russian style. They also shared a willingness to try anything new, especially step sequences never previously attempted in ballet.

And they both adored the effervescent Alexandra Danilova—so kind and sisterly to Markova, and Balanchine's longtime lover. While Danilova spoke some English, Balanchine did not, and he and Markova learned to communicate through mime.

The first major work assigned to Markova and Balanchine would be *Chant du Rossignol* (The Song of the Nightingale) in the spring of 1925. Both would succeed brilliantly, but they would get to know each other on an earlier collaboration of an opera ballet.

As Markova humorously recounted to a radio audience years later: "In the first scene I had to emerge from the fireplace as 'smoke,' wreathing and floating out on stage. In the second scene, I was a squirrel; and to this day, whenever I see one in the park, I instinctively compare the lightning movements of its front paws and its busy air of intense inquisitive excitement with the impression I had to give in *L'Enfant et les Sortilèges*!"

Markova's clipped pronunciation of the word "skwer-el" was as amusing as the story.

For Balanchine, little Alicia was like the Swiss Army knife of ballet. She had so many unexpected useful tools, able to pirouette and spin like a top without ever getting out of breath. And she could do acrobatic moves, like double turns in the air, normally only performed by men. She hadn't known she could do them until Balanchine asked her to try when auditioning her for the Ballets Russes at Astafieva's London studio. Diaghilev already had in mind a restaging of *Chant de Rossignol*, and wanted to know if

Balanchine thought Alicia capable of the role. She most certainly was, he quickly concluded.

The one-act ballet was based on a Hans Christian Andersen fairytale of a Chinese emperor who prefers the false notes of a mechanical bird to a real nightingale's melodious song. When the emperor is near death, the live bird sings him back to life after the clockwork one breaks down. It was a visually enticing allegory for the stage, first choreographed for the Ballets Russes by Léonide Massine in 1920, with Tamara Karsavina in the lead role.

But despite a score from Igor Stravinsky's opera *Le Rossignol*, and an innovative costume/set design by Henri Matisse, the production received a dispiritingly lukewarm reception. Diaghilev thought Balanchine might do better, and why waste the dramatic Matisse sets and costumes in storage?

The 21-year-old Balanchine desperately wished to prove himself to Diaghilev, and he couldn't have had a better partner in this goal. As the diminutive nightingale, Markova did indeed fly.

With conflicting class and practice schedules, Balanchine and Markova found that the best times to rehearse without interruption were later in the evenings or on Sundays. During their intense collaboration, Markova blossomed, as she explained to John Drummond in his interview anthology *Speaking of Diaghilev*:

> In the morning I would have my classes with Cecchetti and he would be instilling me to turn out, and then I would have to come in the evenings with Balanchine, and all these wonderful modern things he was giving me, all turned in. I found that rather confusing. In which direction do I go? And I think that was the first time it was explained to me that this is the difference between being a dancer and when you start being an artist. To dance you just turn out, but to be an artist, you have got to go in any direction.

Markova had supposed the role of the Nightingale would be similar to the classical Blue Bird in *Sleeping Beauty*, but Balanchine was nothing if not completely original. She later recorded her memories of the role in her journal:

> There were several acrobatic steps and dangerous looking ones that I did with Death [danced by Lydia Sokolova]. Poor Gladys [Guggy] would sit and watch in terror as I endeavored to do whatever Balanchine asked of me. I am sure she thought he would injure me for life with some of the things we tried.
>
> I must confess, I enjoyed the experiment and the results were well worth it. In fact, the pas de deux with death was acclaimed as one of the most exciting that had been seen to date. The climax where I was strangled by Death was most dramatic. I shall never forget how wonderful Sokolova was during those rehearsals. It was a great honor for me to be dancing with her but she never once made me feel this.

Lydia Sokolova later gave her side of that tale:

> I told her how lucky we both are to be alive because the urge I had to strangle her at every performance of Le Chant du Rossignol brought us remarkably near to "Murder in the Ballet." She was so tiny, all white, light as thistledown, gentle in movement, more like a sparrow than a girl.
>
> My role of Red Death required fierce, but restrained force. At the end of our dance together, I took off a long row of small skulls from my neck, put them over her head and twisted them as though to kill. [In the heat of the moment] I was sorely tempted to give an extra twist. Poor Alicia, if she had but known!
>
> —*Dance and Dancers* magazine, January 1955

Balanchine always wanted "more, more, more!" explained Peter Martins, the choreographer's later disciple and successor at the New York City Ballet. "That means more speed, more height, and more athleticism."

And that was true from the first. Alicia spent countless hours mastering Balanchine's inventive dance steps, jumps, and soundless landings that would soon make him the preeminent contemporary ballet choreographer in the world. In *The Song of the Nightingale,* he introduced stylistic movements never seen before, such as chain turns with alternating open and closed arms, which the young Markova compared to swim strokes. Balanchine was creating a new modern dance vocabulary that would forever change ballet, and his little nightingale was determined to fulfill his dreams.

London's newspaper *The Independent* would later comment, "Alicia's incredible virtuosity thrilled Balanchine. He included double *tours en l'air,* a turning jump from the male lexicon, and devised a diagonal of *fouettés* that gave the impression of a little bird hopping."

Richard Buckle elaborates in his biography of Balanchine: "He planned that she [Markova] should make her entrance as the Nightingale [in a cage] with two men holding her aloft by one leg. She then had to dive and be caught by two other men very close to the floor. [They once dropped her and knocked her unconscious.] Alicia thought working with Balanchine was like a lesson in arithmetic. 'Give me this leg, give me this hand'—and then suddenly the whole sum would come out right."

Another valuable lesson came courtesy of composer Igor Stravinsky, who, like Diaghilev, was often considered intimidating and brusque. But also like the impresario, Stravinsky couldn't have been more patient and gentle with the young Markova, as she reminisced years later:

> I remember the very first rehearsal with Balanchine. I started to cry, and they said what's the matter? I said I'm never going to be able to learn this. You know, this isn't music to me. What am I to do? And Stravinsky was so wonderful, I'll always remember, he just took me by the hand. He was very quiet. . . . And he spoke very little English, but somehow he found a few words for me.
>
> He said, "There's no worry. I'll be there for all the rehearsals, and I will conduct, and as long as I'm here, you mustn't worry, but there's one thing you have to promise me. . . . You've got to learn the scores by ear. You must learn instrumentation, orchestration and everything by ear," he said, "and then you'll never have any worries for the rest of your life." And he was so right.

Stravinsky's unique musical phrasing—as avant-garde as the abstract art of his times—baffled many over the years. That was certainly the case in 1942 when the composer again collaborated with

George Balanchine, this time on an unconventional commission for the Ringling Bros. and Barnum & Bailey Circus. The dancers? Pachyderms.

"'The Ballet of the Elephants' production was an attempt by John Ringling North to bring high culture into the circus and featured fifty elephants in pink tutus accompanied by female dancers," explained Matthew Wittman, author of *Circus and the City: New York, 1793–2010*. "The rhythm changes in Stravinsky's Circus Polka proved difficult for the elephants to grasp, and it was only performed intermittently." In contrast, once Markova mastered Stravinsky's distinctive cadences, she never forgot.

Theirs was another relationship that confounded company members. If Diaghilev was a father figure, then Stravinsky was like an Uncle, always calling Alicia "Petichka," which means little bird, like the nightingale. He supervised all her music education.

"He was very kind," Markova recalled. "He took me over to the piano, picked out certain notes and suggested that I should learn the instrumental sounds and not be afraid. 'Listen to the music and don't count,' he said."

And Stravinsky personally conducted the orchestra for Markova's rehearsals, a very uncommon occurrence. They would be friends for life, and work together again in the United States two decades later.

Alicia's innocence and naiveté endeared her to all the famous painters and composers (including Sergei Prokofiev and Joseph-Maurice Ravel) who drifted in and out of the Ballets Russes circle.

Dancer/consultant Marie Rambert, who would become instrumental in pioneering British ballet with Markova in the 1930s, worked for the Ballets Russes for many years. She remembered sitting between Pablo Picasso and Diaghilev watching Markova rehearse, each man remarking how utterly charming yet lightning fast she was. Her quick mastery of complicated moves was dazzling.

Diaghilev had explained to Alicia the significance of the creative geniuses in her midst, urging her to pay close attention to what everyone was doing around her. But while she was endlessly fascinated, as when watching Picasso sketch, she was oddly unintimidated, perhaps because all the older visiting "gentlemen" seemed to have a soft spot for the "baby ballerina."

"Stravinsky is my music teacher and Matisse teaches me art appreciation," she would tell her mother, like it was the most normal thing in the world. Perhaps those immensely talented artists appreciated a young mind eager to absorb everything they had to say after years of pushing against the establishment to validate what they were creating. Henri Matisse in particular was going through a brief critical slump in the mid-1920s, considered by some to be almost bourgeois when compared with the avant-garde Dada and Surrealist artists.

Markova's first official meeting with the fauvist master concerned his costume design for her starring role in *The Nightingale.* While the petite dancer was picturing a birdlike, brown-feathered tutu, she couldn't have been more wrong, as recorded in her personal journal notes years later:

> Just after we arrived in Paris, I had to go to the Apt. of Mme. Soudeikina, the well known costumier, for a consultation about my costume for Nightingale. I could hear several voices in deep discussion as Gladys and I mounted the dark stairway, and I wondered whether it was the designing of my dress that was the cause.
>
> When we entered the room I was rather taken aback to see Diag:, Boris Kochno [the artistic director], Igor Stravinsky and of course Henri Matisse all surrounding Mme. Soudeikina [who would later become Stravinsky's second wife]. Matisse had already decided I should wear white—"This fragile personality should always be dressed in white," he told Diag:, "white with diamonds—always, always—she is like a little Princess and so we must see she looks like one."
>
> Diag: seconded his emphatic statement full-heartedly and I inwardly grew a few inches taller and my small chest puffed out as far as it could with a mixture of pleasure and pride. I was not an attractive child by the usual standards and though used to compliments on my dancing I was a little starved for any about myself and suffered acutely from an inferiority complex about my looks. Matisse did not know how much he did to help me that day. With those words, I realized one could look distinctive without being pretty.

> I could see no design for the costume and I have since learnt that Matisse does not like doing one if he can help it, but prefers to work direct with the artist he is designing for there with him and the costumier on the spot. [In the future he would draw a costume directly on Markova's body.] I was more surprised still when Mme. S [Soudeikina] started to measure my feet, legs, neck—all this for a tu-tu?
>
> "Listen little one," Matisse was saying, "white silk tights all over, then white satin ballet shoes, large diamond bracelets around both ankles, the wrist of one arm, and the other just here above the elbow, a little white bonnet like a baby's and no hair to show. Please dear remember, no hair." I came out of my reverie of seeing my lovely ballet dress dissolving into the air to hear a heated argument in progress about the bonnet.
>
> "White georgette, studded with diamonds, trimmed with petite white ospreys," Matisse was instructing Mme. S.
>
> "Ospreys!" gasped Diag: "Mme. S, how much for these ospreys?" Mme. Thought a minute doing calculations in her mind and told him.
>
> "No ospreys," said Diag:
>
> "But please Sergevitch," pleaded Matisse, "the little one needs them round her face to soften the hard line of the bonnet and make her a little bird."
>
> "No ospreys," repeated Diag:
>
> Then Stravinsky entered the argument. He too thought they were necessary, but Diag: was adamant and still refused, and unexpectedly Stravinsky turned to Matisse and said, "Henri, we buy the ospreys between us, 50-50, yes?"
>
> "Yes!" echoed Matisse, and so I had my ospreys, and how I guarded them, as if they were gold, indeed to me they were more precious than gold, what greater gesture could I have from two such recognized artists?

Though the osprey feathers were heatedly debated, no one seemed to think twice about the fourteen-year-old appearing on stage in second-skin white silk tights with no covering. For all intents and purposes, she would look nude. And while performing publicly in leotards is *de rigueur* for ballerinas in modern times, the 1925 Paris production of *Le Chant du Rossignol* marked the first time any dancer had appeared so attired when Markova took to the stage. There had been brief nudity in ballet before, as in Ida Rubinstein's infamous "Dance of the Seven Veils," but not an entire ballet performed so exposed.

As Alicia's body was so tiny and underdeveloped, Matisse's costume didn't appear vulgar or salacious, and she most certainly looked like a little bird capable of flight. The virginal white color helped—a seemingly odd choice coming from one of the greatest colorists of all times. But Matisse saw only purity and innocence in the young Markova.

The Parisians were entranced, and both Balanchine's ballet and Stravinsky's "Petichka" received wonderful reviews.

"I'm very amused," Markova told a radio audience many years later, "because today, after all that, it's really the dancer's uniform and to think I was the very first dancer to ever appear in all-over tights."

The only existing photo of Markova in her Nightingale costume looks quite different from the one just described, and we can thank Great Britain's Lord Chamberlain for that. Less open-minded than the Parisians, the British authorities banned London-born Alicia Marks from appearing "practically nude!" at the Princess Theatre. (Admittedly, her body had begun to develop, becoming more "feminine," as Markova delicately explained in later years.) Matisse was hurriedly called in to modify his "indecent" design.

His solution was to create a transparent white tunic and narrow pant made from featherweight silk chiffon that fluttered as the nightingale danced. Both pieces were studded and cuffed in rhinestones, with the pant affixed to her legs by diamond bands around the upper thighs and below the knees. Markova thought it the height of fashion and the performance went on as scheduled, once again to great acclaim.

"Honors go to the 'baby' of the ballet, Alice Markova, who is only sixteen and dances wonderfully as the true Nightingale of Andersen's story," wrote one London paper. But another would prove prophetic:

> **Hope for an English Ballet**
>
> A feature of the Russian Ballet's production of Stravinsky's Chinese Ballet was the appearance of the youthful dancer, Mlle. Alicia Markova, as the "Nightingale." There was about

her a grace, an almost classic elegance, which was infinitely charming, and suggested future possibilities of great brilliance. She has something of that delicate fantasy in her appearance which is an essential attribute of a dancer of the first rank.

I learnt too, which interested me, that Mlle. Markova is English by birth—a consoling fact in these days of continental weeping and wailing over the dearth of native artists—and that she was schooled in the rudiments of her difficult art by Princess Astafieva.

—London *Graphic*, 6/8/27

Clearly the change of costume didn't affect the dancer's aerial birdlike impression on the audience. But several stage mishaps in other ballets did prove problematic, as when Markova found herself floating the wrong way mid-air in a production of *Faust*:

Again, my size seemed to fit me for the role of an angel. So, dressed in a golden wig and long white gown, I and a sister angel led Marguerite up to heaven, flying on wires which were intended to raise us slowly and gracefully until we vanished from view. But alas for the poor Director—nothing would stop the wires from twisting slowly round in the wrong direction, and we three with them, turning gracefully right away from the audience!

On another occasion Alicia was a last-minute replacement for a Ballets Russes dancer who became ill. It was for the opera ballet *Samson and Delilah*, a production in which Markova was forbidden to perform because of the orgy scene, which Diaghilev considered inappropriate for his innocent ward. But this was an emergency, so the ballet's choreographer, George Balanchine, quickly taught Alicia the role at the dress rehearsal.

No one mentioned, however, that during the actual production the set Temple thunderously collapses around Samson, and the *corps de ballet* all needed to quickly move toward the front stage floodlights and fall flat.

"I didn't know that," Markova later reminisced, laughing. "As the Temple collapsed—bricks, wooden planks, and everything in the building went flying—and it came down on top of me!" It would not be the last time Markova was knocked out by scenery. She also almost choked to death once when dancing *Giselle* in London.

> I was pirouetting quite alone across the stage when I felt something trail lightly over my face and neck, and then as I continued turning, I suddenly felt my throat gripped and my head jerked back. There was absolutely no one near me, and for a moment I was too frightened to do anything. Then, since it was the only way in which I could move, I began to turn back the way I had come. As I did that I saw what had gripped me. A long black cord, invisible in the dim light of the stage, had been left hanging from above, and, as I had turned, had caught against me and wound itself around my neck.

Learning what could—and often would—go wrong was a valuable lesson for Markova to understand early in her career. She also took advantage of every opportunity to study the ins and outs of ballet theater production.

When not taking classes or rehearsing, Alicia asked the company ballet master Serge Grigoriev for special permission to sit in the theater and watch Diaghilev supervise how the scenery was to be designed, built, and properly lit. "I found it totally absorbing and deeply exciting," Markova remembered.

She spent countless hours listening to the orchestra rehearse, observing the conductor's moves and melodic instrument changes—then memorizing the finished scores. She was so small and quiet that few people even knew she was there.

Markova also studied and saved every printed program, learning the importance of art and design in ballet. These were not the throw-away playbills of today, but rather sumptuously produced oversized booklets filled with original color illustrations of the costumes and sets by almost every modern artist of the day, most often Diaghilev's close friend Picasso. Dramatic photographs of the principal dancers in costume were also included.

In one picture, Markova looks the modern sophisticate in a fitted cap with a two-foot-high feather on top. (Clearly, a great deal of adhesive was needed to keep *that* headpiece in place.)

Diaghilev expanded Markova's art education by giving her a list of galleries and museums to visit in each new city where they performed. The two would later meet to discuss what she had seen and learned. Like few teenaged schoolgirls of her times, Alicia would come to understand cubism, fauvism, surrealism, and every other avant-garde movement in relation to classical art history.

Diaghilev also explained to her the mutual respect one should have "artist to artist," whether watching and learning from other dance companies, or respecting fellow performers at the Ballets Russes. Many years later, Markova passed on the impresario's guiding principles in a talk about the great man:

> He believed in, and encouraged, criticism, artist to artist. He spent his life striving for perfection in the world of art and would tell them that even the greatest artists experience doubts and fears, and need above all the encouragement of their fellow-performers.
>
> He taught the Company to strive against petty-mindedness and jealousies—to create a masterpiece among themselves as a whole, and to be generous and broad-minded in all other forms of art.

Unfortunately, that generosity to fellow dancers would be a principle lost on many of the ballet stars Markova would work with later in her career.

While Diaghilev offered the most comprehensive art education any student could hope for, it was Maestro Enrico Cecchetti who helped Markova perfect the dance technique that would make her famous. Once again, her timing was fortuitous. She was one of the last Ballets Russes dancers to benefit from the incomparable personal training with the famed Italian ballet teacher who had taught Anna Pavlova, Vaslav Nijinsky, and Léonide Massine. Cecchetti would soon leave the company to teach at La Scala in Milan, where he died three years later at the age of seventy-eight.

Markova almost missed the opportunity altogether, as she was assigned classes with Madame Cecchetti, the Maestro's ballet instructress wife. Madame was responsible for teaching all the members in the *corps de ballet*, with her esteemed husband's classes reserved exclusively for company principals and top soloists.

It was after finishing early one day that the Maestro first took notice of Alicia when he came to meet his wife and watched the end of her practice session. That afternoon, Grigoriev found Markova in her usual darkened theater haunt, watching the orchestra rehearse.

"Alichka, you are to go to the Maestro himself tomorrow morning," he told her, "and you take advanced class under his personal supervision." It was both a great honor and stroke of good fortune, though her lessons would now be far more physically and mentally demanding. Markova remembered well her first impressions of the barely five-foot-tall Cecchetti:

> Spotlessly clean and tidy, with a cherubic face and bald head with a sweet little fringe of white hair round the edge, he resembled strongly the Chief Angel on an American Christmas card. This resemblance was grossly deceptive as he was anything but angelic!
>
> Punctuality was a religion with him and even though you were on time for a lesson, according to him you were always late. He had a trick, or rather a habit of advancing his clock that stood on the piano ten minutes, and the consequent tardiness gave him an excuse to scream and whistle, especially whistle, all through the lesson.
>
> . . . Another idiosyncrasy he delighted in was to give nicknames to his pupils. A tall slim blonde he called "Asparagus," another short heavy girl he called "Korova" (which means cow in Russian). I was more fortunate in being christened "Petita," a mixture of French and Italian for "little one."
>
> The language problem was a sore one for me as besides having to learn the Cecchetti method, I also had to learn the Cecchetti tongue; his directions and instructions were always given in Italian with broken French and broken Russian interpolated. He did not and would not try to speak English.

> . . . Whilst looking the picture of kindness, the Maestro was a tyrant and possessed a very quick temper. When aroused, he would whisk out his cane and snap it over some poor unfortunate dancer's legs, or even send it hurtling across the room, and then the disgraced pupil who was the cause of this tempest had to go and retrieve it and very bravely take it back to the maestro and with a deep curtsey, or bow if a boy, return it with a sincere "Thank-you."

Markova would joke about this later when explaining her early education to young dance students:

> Now I don't think we're allowed to use canes today! We're not allowed to come anywhere near you. But believe me, in my time, oh, the people that would leave class in tears. . . . I think we can achieve a lot without being beaten by a cane. I think we can achieve with kindness.
>
> But my time? We'd have to do our grand jetés and the cane would be held up and you'd have to go over that cane. To get us to move and cover space—suddenly you'd find the cane put in, and it was like a hurdle you had to go up over it. But believe me, it didn't hurt one, because I survived.
>
> But I still believe we can achieve without that.

Cecchetti's harsh techniques and eccentricities aside, he prepared a ballet dancer like no other. There were so many invaluable lessons he taught the young Markova that would result in her future legendary stage presence. As she recorded in her personal notes decades later:

> My Russian training with Astafieva had been free and spacious, sometimes even wild; arms abandoned gesticulating like a windmill, whereas with Cecchetti you learned to dance by the compass, as he called it. . . . In other words, he "tidied me up" and more important still, taught me the meaning of *ballon*, the lightness for which I am renowned and which is always associated with my dancing.

> Another thing I have to thank the Maestro for teaching me is the art of making one's work look effortless . . . the theory of Diaghileff and Cecchetti being that everything danced on the stage had to give the impression of being easy and simple, and steps that drew attention by looking difficult were not allowed to be done.
>
> Diaghileff would say, "Ha, you think you're in the Circus, no? In the ballet all is pure and simple and beautiful to dance, if it is hard for you, go back to the classroom and practice some more until it is easy to do." . . .
>
> I think herein lies the secret of my technique. As young as I was, I absorbed both schools of training, the Russian and the Italian, welded the two together and discarded what for me was superficial, leaving a pure dance technique that I have practiced all through my career and which I still adhere to.

And Cecchetti helped Markova achieve the silent stage landings Diaghilev so prized:

> With Cecchetti we had to wear practically soft toe shoes, almost no blocks at all. His contention was that if the balance was placed properly and evenly distributed in the body with the weight taken in the correct muscles, there was no need for heavily blocked shoes. I found this true and always like to feel the stage through mine. It sometimes takes hours softening them down until I can feel comfortable enough to go on and dance a performance in them.

Markova never worked as hard in her life as she did for Cecchetti. Joining her in those rarified classes were two Ballets Russes members who would play key roles in the ballerina's future career. One was the Italian soloist Vincenzo Celli, who later became her most valuable private dance tutor in America; the other was the imperious Russian star Serge Lifar, whom she would do battle with in *Giselle* sixteen years later. Too bad Lifar seemingly forgot how fond he had been of Markova at the Ballets Russes. Known to be rather lazy, he relished the tiny Alicia as a partner since she was so effortless to lift.

Markova, however, was anything but lazy, recalling some particularly grueling lessons with Cecchetti:

> Sometimes they would go on for four hours or even longer if the Maestro felt like it. He would continue as long as he wanted to and even though one was dropping from fatigue, one dared not show it but had to give the impression that one was highly honored to be given so much of his time. . . .
>
> I feel that the secret of Cecchetti's method was to give perfect control, which enables the dancer to have complete freedom of movement.

Markova's steely self-reliance would be the next major lesson learned, although Cecchetti would not be the one to teach it. The process would be both emotionally debilitating and professionally humiliating.

As a fifteen-year-old, Alicia had performed in the most cosmopolitan of European cities, from Monte Carlo, Paris, and London to Milan, Vienna, and Berlin. She had met and befriended the greatest artists of her day and performed before royalty. But the teenager was still unsophisticated in so many ways, as Guggy did everything but dance for her.

That all came to a crashing end one evening in Monte Carlo when the governess found she suddenly could not get out of bed. Alicia called the doctor, who informed her Guggy was extremely ill with a high fever—it turned out to be advanced kidney disease—and could not be moved. For the very first time, Markova would have to go the theater alone.

She was to perform in *Le Carnaval,* with décor and costumes by Léon Bakst and choreography by Mikhail Fokine. Feeling utterly terrified, and dutifully worried about Guggy's health, the teenager sheepishly knocked on the door of Lydia Sokolova's dressing room, makeup case in hand. When Markova explained that her governess was sick and she needed some help, her British compatriot welcomed her in. But when Sokolova discovered that Alicia didn't know the first thing about stage makeup, she justifiably exploded, as Markova wrote in her personal memoirs:

> How old was I? How long had I been with the company? Here was I a member of the greatest ballet company in the world entrusted by Mr. Diaghilev with a second soloist role in one of the company's most important ballets, and I couldn't put my own makeup on. I should be thoroughly ashamed of myself.
>
> Sokolova was fiercely angry—but she was so for a purpose. The tears streamed down my face. I don't think I had ever cried so much before or so bitterly, for I thought that here was someone rescuing me from a disaster, and the disaster was getting worse. I wept on and on. I tried to explain that my governess would not allow me to do anything for myself. Through sobs, I gulped out my story for about ten minutes.
>
> Then Sokolova smiled. "Well, come along, ducky. Enough of this. Dry your eyes. You've learned a lesson you have to learn. You must be self-reliant. If you have any dreams of being an artist in the theatre you have to rely only on yourself. Will you promise me to remember that?" . . .
>
> Promise I did, and always after that—throughout the next 37 years of my performing career—I obeyed Sokolova.

As with everything in her young life, Markova took her new tasks very seriously and was a quick study. In a 1955 *Dance and Dancers* magazine dedicated to Markova, Sokolova reminisced:

> She used to sit beside me and watch how I made up for various ballets. In my dressing room she learned how to do her own. Few people in ballet today make up better than Alicia and I am glad that I possibly had something to do with that. . . .
>
> I like to remember that, other than her dancing, I admire her for her tremendous courage. She has the English determination to overcome difficulties she is sometimes confronted with—and always does. She carries on alone, flying all over the world giving infinite pleasure to a vast number of people. There is no other dancer but Alicia who does that.

Thanks to Sokolova, in later years countless newspaper and magazine articles would detail Markova's superb makeup skills and tips for the average woman. It was often emphasized how a "plain" woman could make herself so alluring.

Within days of Guggy taking to her bed in Monte Carlo, the teenage Markova would begin a lifetime of carrying on alone. It was one thing to run down the hill from Beausoleil to the theater by herself, but now it was time for the company to travel to Paris, and Alicia had never gone anywhere in her life unsupervised by her governess.

The doctor made it clear that Guggy could not be moved. Equally alarming for Alicia, her governess had begun to hallucinate. The Marks family would soon find out that in addition to succumbing to kidney and heart disease, their daughter's caretaker had been mentally imbalanced for many years, which had only exacerbated her controlling nature and obsessive domination of Alicia. Very soon, Guggy would die insane.

At the time, all Alicia knew was that the governess who devoted her life to taking care of her was now in need of care herself. Diaghilev had already gone ahead to Paris, so Markova informed Grigoriev that she would have to remain behind to tend to Guggy. The company left without her.

Within a few days a telegram arrived to the effect, as Markova remembered: "Report for rehearsal in Paris on such and such a date, or consider yourself no longer a member of the Ballets Russes." It was signed Sergei Diaghilev.

Markova couldn't believe her second father, whom she so fondly called Sergypop, would threaten legal action in such a time of crisis, but the impresario knew better. While it was he who had insisted Alicia be chaperoned, he hadn't foreseen how universally disliked Guggy would become by everyone in the troupe, clearly doing Alicia more harm than good. The fifteen-year-old would now need to break away from her suffocating governess.

And that's just what she did. Markova approached a pleasant Englishwoman whom she had befriended in their Beausoleil boarding house. With her help, care for Guggy was arranged and, with borrowed train fare and pocket money, Markova went to the station for her overnight trip to Paris. Having never traveled anywhere by herself before, she fought to stay awake the entire trip for fear of what might happen to her or her luggage.

Upon arriving at *Gare du Nord* the next morning, the exhausted and unwashed teenager remembered the name of the hotel her great friend Emmy Haskell stayed in during the Paris ballet season. With the little money she had left, Markova took a cab there, praying that Mrs. Haskell was already a registered guest. She was, and upon greeting her relieved charge, remarked on the poor, bedraggled girl looking exactly like a baby bird that had fallen out of its nest.

As she had done so many times before, Markova's fairy godmother came to her rescue, locating where the company was staying, seeing that she arrived there safely, and giving her enough money to live on.

And again Ninette de Valois was called upon to watch over Diaghilev's "little one," who didn't even know to bring her passport on the trip. As de Valois recalled many years later:

> She had no one. So of course she had to come into my hotel and I had to look after her
>
> In those days it was very worrying, such a young girl knocking about Paris, and there's a funny story attached to it.
>
> I did want one night to go out and dine with a friend of mine who was in the British Council there. And I said to him, "Look, you'll have to be very quick tonight. I can't stay very long because I've got this little girl on my hands I can leave at the hotel I think for a couple of hours, but I must get back."
>
> He said, "Don't tell me any more. If you do, Mr. Diaghilev will be in prison." It was utterly illegal to have an English child in any sort of company there without a passport.

During a hundredth-birthday radio tribute to de Valois seven decades later, Markova publicly thanked her savior once more for her kindness:

> I was put in your care and I thanked God every night because it wasn't so much the dance part, but how you taught me what I should eat, what would be good for me, what would give me strength. Not only that, but how to go shopping and how to buy everything, because at that time, we all had very, very low salaries. And so really, in a few words, you tried to teach me how to deal with life.

De Valois also taught Alicia how to stand up for herself, finding her blinding obedience disconcerting, as illustrated by the following story:

> From the very beginning, she [Markova] showed a remarkable personality and her self-discipline was extraordinary. In connection with this a small incident is very revealing. It was when her governess was ill and I had sole charge of Alicia during one of our Paris seasons. I had received an important telephone call and had to go out for a couple of hours. Before I went out I went up to Alicia's room at our hotel and found her sitting on her bed mending her tights. She was very meticulous about such things—always mending and washing. I told her that I had to go out and added, "don't move until I come back."
>
> When I returned two hours later, there she was in just the same place on the bed still mending her tights. Although I naturally meant that she should move about the hotel but not to go outside, it never occurred to her to do anything other than what she had been told.

Alicia was very lucky to have de Valois to teach her basic life lessons, while instilling her with some much-needed confidence. "For the first time, someone treated me as an equal," Markova said gratefully. The much older men at the company—Diaghilev, Stravinsky, Matisse—were kindness itself to Alicia, but she was just a sweet child to them. As she grew into a young woman, it would be de Valois and Danilova who taught her self-reliance.

The days of Guggy doing everything were permanently over. The deathly ill governess was institutionalized for her remaining days. In short order, Markova would officially become an adult. The process was not always a happy one.

With Guggy gone, Eileen Marks decided it was now time that she personally accompany her still-underage daughter on tour. Through the continued generosity of close friends, Alicia's three sisters were placed in excellent schools, with homes of various friends to stay in on breaks and vacations.

But while Guggy had governed Alicia's every movement, Eileen was the complete opposite. It was now sixteen-year-old Alicia who was in charge. It was she who spoke fluent French, knew how to make travel arrangements, shop, cook, and budget their money.

In Monte Carlo, Eileen would be sunning herself on the beach while Alicia took ballet classes, rehearsed, and took care of business. It was wonderful for the teenager to have a warm, loving presence in her life again, but her work schedule only became more demanding.

Then came the biggest blow. Alicia Markova had been a soloist with the Ballets Russes for two years, getting loads of attention and wonderful critical reviews for roles. She was the subject of feature stories in newspapers and magazines throughout Europe, and admirers sent bouquets of magnificent flowers to her dressing room. She had even received a marriage proposal from a young musician who had become infatuated with the shy dancer, often squiring her on dinner dates—supervised by her mother, of course. Markova had modestly declined.

And Markova knew the ropes. She had learned how to function on the road, sleep sitting up in the crowded second-class train compartments, and be the official luggage guard when other company members went in search of cheap lodgings. She worked hard, never complained, and was now well liked. The very high standards of Diaghilev and all connected with the Ballets Russes were now hers as well.

But at sixteen, Alicia had also grown a bit taller (she was still under five feet), and was now at the age when most young dancers join the *corps de ballet* to learn their craft. She had never done so.

One afternoon, Diaghilev pulled her aside to deliver some unwelcome news, as Markova recalled many years later:

> Diaghileff said to me, "You own the talents, but you have to start from the beginning, your place is in the last row in the corps and it depends on yourself whether you can grow into a solo dancer." I felt myself standing against the wall and was very afraid, but he said, "Once, there will come a day that you will thank me." He was right.

Though it was heartbreaking to hear, Markova accepted Diaghilev's decision gracefully. No other dancer had ever started as a soloist in a company half as grand as the Ballets Russes. It was an honor that one earned through disciplined training and proving oneself by slowly acquiring larger and larger roles. She knew Diaghilev had made a very special exception for her, and now she trusted in his judgment again.

"One can truly say that he was a genius," she told an audience of American college students in a speech following her retirement. "I think his real gift was having the ability to discover artists, inspire them, and develop them so they could express themselves. There is so much talent around, but talent can't always bloom alone."

By requiring Markova to virtually start over, Diaghilev taught her the discipline required of a corps member, resulting in a newfound emotional and physical maturity. She became a better dancer for it. When later interviewed about her time with the impresario, Markova revealed:

> He used to have a trick of occasionally not letting his star dancers dance the particular parts they most wanted to dance, and he would never let anyone feel that he or she was "indispensable" to him; and so he kept us all on the tips of our toes, in a sense of expectancy, but without "security"—and so probably getting the best out of all of us.
>
> But he must have been just and reasonable on the whole, or he would never have kept the whole huge company—and painters and designers and musicians as well—together for as long as he did.

Markova dutifully worked her way back up. She learned what it meant to be in perfect step with the corps and continued daily lessons with acclaimed Russian teachers Lubov Egorova and Nikolai Legat. They had both trained at the Imperial Theatre School in St. Petersburg—Egorova under Fokine—so Markova got the best of both worlds: Cecchetti's innovative Italian methods and the classically disciplined Russian mode.

Egorova was Serge Grigoriev's wife. On the publication in England of the former Ballets Russes director's book, *The Diaghilev Ballet, 1909–1929*, a London reviewer commented, "Grigoriev takes pride in recording that his wife, as ballet-mistress, so greatly improved Markova's elevation that in Diaghilev's words, 'she made her take wings and fly.'"

Markova's closer interaction with the company and girls her own age also taught her how to infuse her roles with more emotion.

"I was so shy and wooden in my dancing that the company nicknamed me 'Sphinx,'" Markova said in a newspaper interview years later. "But I soon noticed that the Russians in that company never hid *their* feelings, either on or offstage.

"Even the men, if they were unhappy in their work, burst into a flood of tears. I never went quite that far, but following their example and learning to express myself more freely was of enormous value to me as a dancer."

Yet despite her move to the corps, Markova grew ever closer to the delightful Alexandra Danilova, who would remain her best friend for life. On Alicia's birthday in 1927, Danilova and Balanchine bought their favorite little English girl her first bottle of perfume, *L'Aimant* by Coty. "[A]t that time it had just come out and was the new modern one for young people," Markova remembered fondly.

The gift was especially appreciated as the company was on tour in Budapest at the time, staying in a bedbug-infested hotel (often the norm). Everyone was miserable and covered in red marks, and the lovely-smelling cologne cheered Markova immeasurably. She was seventeen, and no one had ever thought to buy her perfume before.

For Diaghilev's part, he treated his "Douchka" the same as he always had—remaining both loving and protective—while continuing to shelter her from parties and wild nightlife.

The rest of the company was impressed that the former soloist took the demotion so well, and in time, featured roles were hers again. Glowing critical reviews followed.

But even as a more mature soloist, Markova was seen as an innocent in Diaghilev's eyes. While attending a dress rehearsal of the *Blue Bird* in Manchester, England, the impresario was upset to see Alicia dance the title role wearing a headdress of ostrich feathers and pearls, which he thought much too "vulgar" for her.

Diaghilev now took on the Matisse role from *The Nightingale* battle for expensive osprey feathers, insisting that Markova wear only real blue bird-of-paradise feathers and costume diamonds in her crown. Unfortunately, such precious plumes were hard to come by.

And just as Guggy had been called upon to locate hard-to-find white stockings in Beausoleil for *Swan Lake*, now it was Eileen's turn to work a miracle. According to Markova, the impresario reached into his pocket and pulled out two £5 notes which he handed to Eileen while speaking two English words everyone understood: "Go shop!" Eileen did, and her daughter was a true blue bird.

In *Cimarosiana* (1927), Markova danced exquisitely in a classical *pas de deux* with Serge Lifar—who would later be her bête-noir in *Giselle*—and in *La Chatte* (1929), she was delectably feline in the title role.

While Markova would originate many roles in modern ballets throughout her career, she was fortunate that *La Chatte* was not one of them. As she told John Drummond in *Speaking of Diaghilev*:

> Spessivtseva created it and had an accident, and then Nikitina took over and she hurt her foot, and then I went in. I was the third Cat. I was only sixteen at the time, but I was very observant. I had noticed that they complained so much about the floor because it was black, American cloth, terribly slippery in certain areas. And other areas, because of the very modern design, were like cotton, two surfaces, and I figured out that was causing the accidents.

Making matters worse—or better, depending how you look at it—*La Chatte* choreographer George Balanchine decided to take advantage of Alicia's special talents and add more complicated and difficult moves.

> I thought, I don't want to hurt my foot, I don't want to be put out, because it was a wonderful ballet, marvelous role. I had to solve this problem somehow, and this slippery floor, because otherwise I wasn't going to be able to do all these double turns in the air that Balanchine had given me and all these pirouettes on pointe which he had added, so I suddenly remembered when I danced on a ballroom floor, I used to have rubbers [sole grips] put on my ballet shoes.

So without telling anyone, Markova did just that. Unlike her predecessors, she never faltered. "The Cat of Alicia Markova was flawless," wrote a German critic. "She is an accomplished ballerina . . . one of the greatest dance talents of present times."

From London's *New English Weekly*: "Her [Markova's] success in this role played wonders in her artistic development and this rather shy English child acquired a personality of her own, literally overnight."

And from Paris: "Mlle. Markova has shown herself to be full of charm and talent, especially in 'The Cat,' where she revealed all the cruel seduction of the cat and the tender coquetry of the woman in love."

Alicia Marks had acquired a Russian soul.

At the end of the ballet season in 1929, Diaghilev once again requested a private meeting with his Douchka. This time the news was exhilarating, as Markova happily recalled years later.

"Sergypop explained to me I had been apprenticing all this time and working for him with no contract. And he told me the following year I would have a contract like everybody else and be working for myself and I would be paid more money. He discussed roles he had in mind for me, *Le Biches, Romeo & Juliet, The Firebird.*"

He also offered her the role of a lifetime—the lead in *Giselle*—which she would alternate performing with the great Olga Spessivtseva.

"To be a dancer wasn't enough for Diaghilev. He also wanted you to be a great artist," Markova often said. He now felt she was one, and in just a few months' time she would become a prima ballerina in the greatest ballet company then in existence.

Appropriately, the meeting took place where the relationship had all begun, in London while the company was performing at Covent Garden. Diaghilev remarked to several newspaper reporters throughout the run, "Watch the dancing of my little English girl, Alicia Markova. Her promise is remarkable."

Arnold Haskell, who had made frequent trips to Monte Carlo and Paris to see Markova's progress with the Ballets Russes, remembers Diaghilev confiding in him about little Alicia: "He genuinely loved 'his English girl,' and often told me, 'I will do big things for her when she wakes up.'" Now she had woken up.

To initiate his now not-so-little-one into adulthood, Diaghilev at long last allowed her to accept invitations to formerly forbidden parties and receptions, where the eighteen-year-old sipped her first glass of champagne. For the occasion, Emmy Haskell bought Markova her first designer evening dress—a sophisticated Lanvin gown in midnight blue that she kept until her dying day—worn with statuesque silver kidskin high heels.

The 1928/29 Ballets Russes season came to an end with Alicia Markova walking on air. When the company dispersed for their summer vacations, the former baby ballerina went to visit friends in the restful seaside resort town of Littlehampton, England, already looking forward to the coming fall.

On August 19, 1929, the carefree teenager picked up the evening newspaper after a relaxing day at the beach—shaded under an umbrella, of course.

The headline read: DIAGHILEV DEAD.

4

Starting Over

I became ill, verging upon a nervous breakdown, haunted by my own absence of future and also by my awareness of the total absence of any security for myself, my mother or my three sisters. At no time in my life thus far had I been called upon to make any more decisions than the fundamental one in my character of being ready to work hard and be obedient, and use what gifts God had been pleased to give me to the best of my ability.

I was, artistically, without any anchor; emotionally and physically I was a young woman possessed of a talent of the most special kind, one which could only be used in the rarefied and glorious world of the Ballets Russes. Now that world had gone, irrevocably.

—From Alicia Markova's personal journals

The timing of Diaghilev's death only added to the pain. Just two weeks earlier, the company had all been together in Vichy, France, south of Paris, for the final Ballets Russes engagement of the 1929 season. No one could have imagined that the August 4 performance would be the troupe's last.

After the seasonal celebratory farewell party, each member went on holiday to rest up for what promised to be another eventful year. Few knew that the impresario's physical and mental health had been in decline for many months. As Sjeng Scheijen reveals, the 57-year-old diabetic was suffering from painful boils, and was further distressed by his half-brother Valentin's imprisonment in a Russian concentration camp (where he would be executed soon after Diaghilev's death). As was typical of the showman, he tried to keep both facts hidden, but close friends couldn't help but notice his wan, sometimes frightening appearance.

Ignoring doctor's orders, Diaghilev continued to play the *bon vivant,* maintaining his manic work schedule and ceaseless social whirl. Everyone naturally assumed he would make a full recovery on summer break. Venice, his favorite of all cities, would surely be the tonic for whatever ailed him. But when he met up with Serge Lifar at the Grand Hotel des Bains de Mer—the very one where Stravinsky had astonished them all with his seminal score for *The Rite of Spring*—Diaghilev's health began deteriorating rapidly.

The unattended boils led to abscesses and blood poisoning accompanied by a dangerously high fever. Upon notification, the ever-loyal Boris Kochno—Sergei's great confidant, secretary, creative collaborator, and former lover—rushed to his side, soon followed by close friends Coco Chanel and socialite/arts patron Misia Sert. The wealthy women would volunteer to pay for Diaghilev's funeral, as few knew he was heavily mortgaged and basically penniless.

The ballet ringmaster died at dawn on August 19, early enough to make the late afternoon papers. The next day, Sergei Diaghilev's death would be the leading headline around the world.

Naturally, no one took the news harder than members of the Ballets Russes company. They had all just seen him. Future plans had been set. It seemed utterly inconceivable that he was gone. Worse still, they had all dispersed for vacation. Many, like Markova, were left to absorb the shock without the consolation of the group that knew him best.

Ballets Russes manager Serge Grigoriev was back in Monte Carlo when he received a telegram imparting the terrible news. A similar telegram awaited Igor Stravinsky upon his return home from visiting fellow composer and Paris neighbor Sergei Prokofiev. Stravinsky and Diaghilev had had a falling-out earlier in the year, a common occurrence between the impresario and his various artists; but after running into one another in London in July, the pair seemed destined toward a *rapprochement* that was never to be. Stravinsky was shattered, thereafter making annual pilgrimages to place flowers on Diaghilev's grave at the San Michele cemetery in Venice.

Alexandra Danilova never forgot the very moment she heard the news. She was summering in Nice at the Hotel Negresco, with her lover George Balanchine off working in England. While waiting for an appointment at her hairdresser's one afternoon, Danilova was offered the day's newspaper. Staring her in the face was the headline DIAGHILEV DEAD. From her memoirs:

> I remembered the last time I saw him, on the stage at the end of our season in Vichy. He made a brief speech about how well the season had gone. Then he said, "I can't kiss everyone, but you, Choura, I will kiss." And he came to me and kissed me twice—good-bye.

Balanchine, who was discovered, nurtured, and catapulted to fame by Diaghilev, was at least among fellow dancers when the front-page news reached him on location in a London film studio. He was choreographing a ballet sequence for the movie *Dark Red Roses* (1930) with Anton Dolin and former Ballets Russes performer Lydia Lopokova (then married to the British economist and Bloomsbury group member John Maynard Keynes. The couple would soon play a key role in the birth of British ballet). Dolin, who had skipped the last Vichy performance for the movie commitment, saw the headline in the evening paper. Diaghilev was his former lover, teacher, and star-maker.

Lopokova, who had always affectionately called Diaghilev *Big Serge*, wrote a moving obituary published in *The Nation*: "He leaves a big empty space which is impossible to fill. For he was a Life Force: something extraordinary which made the world more vital and moving than it can be when he is gone."

Though it would be natural for Diaghilev's closest associates to overstate his impact on the arts, he truly was one of a kind. For the past twenty years, Paris had been the Mecca for avant-garde artists of every field and from countries all over Europe. But it was Diaghilev who brought them together to work as a group, overcoming language and societal barriers to create something brazenly modern in ballet, even when it was inspired by the past. He had always asked one thing of each artist: "Astonish me." And they did.

John Martin, esteemed dance critic for *The New York Times*, expressed the impact of the impresario's death:

> When Serge Diaghileff died in 1929, the realization flashed like a bolt of unexpected lightning across the consciousness of the ballet world—a small and special world it was then—that not only a man but an art had died. He who had never choreographed, composed, designed, or danced in a ballet had been, nevertheless, the moving power behind the revivification of the art after its slumber of two generations, and over a period of twenty years had made himself its sole master, as both catalyst and manipulator.

But after the initial shock wore off, an artistic malaise set in. It wasn't just the end of the Ballets Russes, but the end of an era. As Martin continued:

> Now, to all intents and purposes, he had taken his work with him into the grave as if he were too jealous of it to leave it behind. . . . He had deliberately avoided establishing a routine of procedure: his artistic method was one of brilliant and dogged opportunism. . . . What remained was, ironically, only a heightened set of artistic standards which now would be all the more difficult to satisfy.

For Alicia Markova, Diaghilev's death seemed so personally cruel, she didn't think she could go on. He was her employer, champion, and adoptive father who, like Arthur Marks, had died unexpectedly, leaving her emotionally adrift and in dire financial straits. But this time it seemed worse, as Markova wrote in her personal journal:

> For the second time in my 18 years I had lost a father. The first time, when my real father had died, the emotional suffering was intense, but I had found a means of sustaining myself: subconsciously I had managed to compensate for this [loss] in work. Dancing had been a way of using and exorcising some of my grief then, and because our minds always seek a way to heal themselves, my brand new relationship with Diaghilev had almost immediately been that of a daughter to a new father (was it completely accidental that I had first of all mispronounced patronymic—Sergey Pavlovich—as Sergey Pop?)
>
> But now this new bereavement had come. And I was older and more able to understand the full depths of deprivation. I felt as much as when my own father had died. And there was no escape from it that I could see. At a particularly vital stage in my development, both as a dancer and as a young woman, I was alone. Artistically and emotionally I felt myself abandoned. It was not simply selfish grief: I understood enough of my feelings to grieve for Diaghilev himself and for my "family" of the Ballet Russe, but I also felt that I was completely lost. Where only hours before, the road had seemed clear before me, I could now see no way at all.

For the past four and a half years, the Ballets Russes company had been Markova's entire life. "My home and my roots were in the physical structure of the company itself, not in any town or house," she would write. "The gypsy life of the ballet made me a perpetual wanderer, and at this time I didn't realize how odd this was."

The only constant was Markova's bond with the company members themselves, with whom she spent her formative years. As she recalled years later in an interview:

> I was surrounded with people so much older than myself. To think that when I entered the company at fourteen, the people around me were Stravinsky, Matisse, Picasso, Prokofiev. They were these charming gentlemen to me, walking in and out of class every day, and I looked on them as my friends. . . .

> When I was young, I was very shy. To walk into a room with people just terrified me. At one time, I used to stutter and I think that was why for a little while, I didn't speak very much because I thought if I opened my mouth it won't go right.
>
> So I thought I'll just keep quiet. And perhaps, maybe that's why with the dancing, it was a wonderful form of expression for me because I didn't have to use my voice. I was able to express everything through the body.

Now she had neither her artistic friends nor the vehicle for expressing herself. And from an employment standpoint, the eighteen-year-old was in a far more precarious position than her Ballets Russes peers.

Alexandra Danilova, Lydia Sokolova, and Olga Spessivtseva were all experienced prima ballerinas and soloists, with established followings and name recognition. While Markova had received excellent reviews and critical praise during her tenure with the company, she had only just completed her apprenticeship in the *corps*, with the upcoming 1929/30 season to be her formal entrance into the higher ranks.

Years later she recalled her last conversation with Diaghilev: "The following season, as he put it, I'd be working for myself. I had served my apprenticeship very well and so the coming season for me would have really been wonderful. The new ballet that Lifar was going to do, new music had been commissioned, and many more roles. And above all, he was going to give me a very nice salary, because up until that time, as he'd said, I'd been working for him."

Even more thrilling for the young ballerina was the promise of alternating the lead in *Giselle* with the great Spessivtseva, who would personally coach her for the role. To dance this romantic classic was a dream come true.

Arnold Haskell had watched Markova mature from her earliest performances in Monte Carlo, as he later explained:

> The first time one noticed her was in Little Red Riding Hood where she was really quite charming and really gave the impression of fear from the wolf, and then she was marvelous as the Blue bird—not only light, but mischievous.

> Then Balanchine recreated the Nightingale for her. She was lovely in that. Then when one began to see her as an adult was in *La Chatte*. Nikitina sprained her ankle and Alicia stepped in. It was then that Diaghilev told my mother, the little English girl is waking up and there will be a big career for her.

But not in England, and not without Diaghilev and the structure of the Ballets Russes. When Markova received the devastating news of his death, she was visiting with family friends, the Crewleys, in beachside Littlehampton near Brighton. Until that moment, it had been like every other summer of the past five years, which Markova recalled in her journal notes:

> The "real" end of the season each year for the Diaghilev Ballet always came in London, where we played during July. Thereafter there might be a couple of weeks, unimportant we always felt, in Vichy or Le Touquet, although they helped keep the company in work.
>
> But for me the arrival in London meant that the end of the dancing year was in sight and that my mother and I would be reunited with my sisters. Doris was still living with a former secretary of my father's and attending a day school; Vivienne and Bunny were boarders at the Masonic school; their holidays and mine coincided, and for two months the ballet was left behind.
>
> I became once again the eldest of four, who—for some inexplicable reason—spent much of the year away from home. With the family gathered together again, all the mysterious excitement and the hard work of my "other" life as a dancer was forgotten: I was once again Alicia Marks.
>
> To reunite us properly, my mother always took furnished rooms in London as a base—all that we could afford, and I was able to go away to visit friends at the seaside in Bogner or Littlehampton or Brighton—and be by myself, without fuss. I didn't realize the basic split in my life, the crucial split that existed between Alicia Markova of the Ballet Russe and Alicia

> Marks who was in some way going to have to be responsible for a family and three sisters. My days were spent happily with the family, resting, reading, perhaps going out with a few friends. Markova was someone else. . . .
>
> I did not worry about the future, because I knew that Diaghilev was there and my trust and belief in him were absolute. He had replaced my father in my conscious and subconscious understanding of the world. . . .
>
> Asked if I had any close family, I might have said that the company was "closer" to me than my sisters, but these ideas never entered my head. What mattered, what I had to strive to reach, were the ambitions that Diaghilev had for me: in him I had a kind of super-father who could be absolutely leant on for the future. I need have no will, no dreams: Diaghilev willed and dreamed for me.

Utterly bereft at the news of his passing, Markova moved back to London to be with her mother and three sisters in their crowded two-room apartment. Adding to her discomfort, it was an especially hot and humid summer.

While tight quarters were nothing new for the world traveler, life in London most certainly was. After an almost five-year absence, Markova had no social circle to call upon. And with her unorthodox childhood as a performer, there were no old school chums to look up or favorite haunts to revisit.

She was an odd duck—one who had the most cosmopolitan views of theatre, art, and dance; had performed before kings and queens; and was a seasoned traveler—but at the same time, she was still awkward and inexperienced socially, all thanks to Diaghilev. Now that she was ready to come out of her shell, she was leaving a progressive, inclusive environment for a more closed and complacent one. Unlike France, England of 1929 had a clearly delineated class society, with strict rules of propriety and etiquette.

Those vast differences had manifested themselves when she was just fourteen and performing in *The Song of the Nightingale*. She could merrily pirouette in second-skin leotards in Paris, but was forced to cover up in her more puritanical hometown.

And things hadn't changed much in the past five years. Just a few months prior to Diaghilev's death, a London art gallery caused quite a scandal by displaying paintings of nudes done by famous writer/artist D. H. Lawrence. Many of those artworks were later seized by Scotland Yard on the grounds of indecency—but only after twelve thousand viewers had been through the exhibit to register their personal distaste for the "obscene" subject matter.

The city certainly had its share of modernists, but not nearly in the numbers, or with the public acceptance, found in Paris and Monte Carlo. There in France, for the price of a cup of coffee, one could sit for hours at a sidewalk café debating—and loudly arguing—about the future of art, culture, and politics. Or, in Markova's case, just listening to the lively conversations among Ballets Russes artists and their worldly friends made outdoor dining an invaluable educational forum.

Even on the hottest summer's day, the British wouldn't think of dining *al fresco*, let alone accepting passersby in their personal conversations. Markova felt stifled, figuratively and literally. She was used to starting her day on a breezy Beausoleil balcony overlooking Monte Carlo and the sunlit Mediterranean, devouring still-warm croissants from a basket delivered to her door. Then it was a quick run down the hill to the Casino rehearsal studio—the very one made famous in the beloved ballet film *The Red Shoes* (1948).

Now she spent her mornings eating traditional English cold toast in a hot, cramped kitchen. Worse still, she had nowhere to go. There were no ballet companies in England at the time, and few prospects for work. And as her family had so little money, she couldn't afford leisure-time entertainments to cheer her up.

Her depression only deepened when the following letter arrived from Monte Carlo mid-September:

Sept. 14, 1929

Dear Alicia,

I must inform you that I have received a letter from the judicial administrator of Serge de Diaghilev's successors, in which he declares that Serge de Diaghilev's enterprise has come to an end and begs me to inform all the "artistes" of the company about it.

This decision is taken by him with the consent of the successors of Serge de Diaghilev.

Yours Sincerely,
Serge Grigorieff

The former Ballets Russes manager took the time to handwrite what must have been dozens of those letters, perhaps as a small way of expressing his personal sadness at having to share the unwelcome news. Several months later Grigoriev attempted to revive a semblance of the company by contracting a season of ballet performances with the Monte Carlo Opera.

Markova was one of the dancers asked to participate, and jumped at the opportunity; but the season was short and lackluster without Diaghilev's energy and artistic input. Her one consolation was being able to spend time with close friend Alexandra Danilova again.

Markova had received just one other offer of employment. Soon after learning of Diaghilev's death, Anna Pavlova sent word inviting her to join her own traveling troupe. Pavlova had always favored proper English girls in her *corps*, as she felt they were brought up to be well behaved and malleable. Like them, Markova would have been relegated to a permanent supporting role, with absolutely no opportunity for advancement to solos or leads. Anna Pavlova was the only star in her eponymous company.

Additionally, Markova's first-class training would essentially stop. At the Ballets Russes, she not only took daily lessons with Enrico Cecchetti and Nicolas Legat, but also performed with them on stage. As the "toy shopkeeper" in *La Boutique Fantasque*, Cecchetti had quite enjoyed publicly using his ever-present cane on "spoiled American child" Markova. "He was an old devil," she would later tell an audience of young dancers. "He used to come round and he'd give me what for and nobody could stop him!

"Then again, in *Le Carnaval*, when I was doing Butterfly, Legat was Pantalon. I'd be taking my class in the morning under a very strict teacher. And in the evening, he was my partner on stage."

And Olga Spessivtseva was to personally teach Markova the role of *Giselle* in the upcoming Ballet Russes season, had Diaghilev lived.

It was the Russian tradition of experienced prima ballerinas training the next generation, but one that Pavlova summarily rejected. Though Markova idolized the incomparable Russian dancer, she just couldn't accept those terms if she had any hopes of becoming a prima ballerina herself one day. As time passed without any offers of work, Markova would mentally revisit that decision.

Back home in London after the Monte Carlo engagement, the nineteen-year-old thought she'd go mad. "I lived in a waking nightmare, devoid of hope or energy," she wrote in her journal. "My mother was wonderful in caring for me, and trying to sustain us."

The family had so much invested in Markova's career, which now seemed at an end to Alicia. But Eileen didn't give up hope, and found ways to keep her bereaved daughter busy until future employment opportunities came her way.

Encouraged by her mother, Markova took up baking and sewing to pass the time. Her newly mastered tailoring skills—a combination of *Vogue* patterns and her own innate sense of style—would actually be quite useful in the near future. When money for ballet costumes was tight, Markova would now be able to make or alter her own.

She also took up knitting, another fortuitous hobby, as Markova made an interesting discovery. While working on a bed jacket planned as a Christmas gift for an elderly friend, she decided to use extra thick wooden needles to create an airy, lacelike stitch. That way the wrap would be warm, but comfortably lightweight. The ballerina was so happy with the result that she decided to make practice tights using the same open-weave stitch—in her favorite color, mauve, of course.

That was a far more momentous occasion than one might suppose. Up until that time, dancers wore heavy leg warmers over knit tights at practice sessions during the winter months, and despite the cold, the wool made them sweat profusely. In Markova's case, perspiring heavily led to weight loss she could ill afford. But the new lacy tights were far more breathable, and also less restrictive, making it easier to perform complicated leg movements.

Later, when Markova was once again employed, other dancers asked if she might be willing to knit them a similar pair. She was happy to oblige, and soon the trend caught on. The ballet world has Alicia Markova to thank for the standard practice tights of today.

Sadly, Markova's original knit pair didn't get much of a workout in those bleak early days without Diaghilev. She occasionally attended a dance class at Astafieva's studio, but there was no money for daily lessons. And while the Princess surely would have taught her for free, Alicia wasn't a child anymore and no longer felt comfortable taking charity.

Markova was also embarrassed by her situation, not wanting anyone to know how destitute she really was. Astafieva had believed in her as a future star of the ballet, and now the promising young dancer couldn't even get a job. So Markova decided to practice at home instead, using the bathroom towel rack as a *barre*.

Though she couldn't help but feel sorry for herself, Markova realized there were far bigger problems going on in the world than the loss of a ballet company. The 1929 U.S. stock market crash was reverberating in economies around the globe and England was mired in high unemployment and related political unrest. Since the end of World War I, the country had begun the slow, painful process of modernizing energy and transport industries, as well as infrastructure. And the devastation and losses from that horrific war were still firmly etched in people's minds and daily life.

Slowly however, the Brits experienced some optimism in the early 1930s, especially in the middle classes. British social historian Juliet Gardiner referred to the period as one of both "high minded planning for a better world" and the less selfless desire for "an easier life for all." The middle class became a modern-day Oliver Twist—politely, but firmly, asking for "more."

More things—clothes, cars, modern appliances—and more free time to play: sports, vacations, reasonably priced entertainment. "The 'dream palaces'—the massive fantastical cinemas that proliferated and the audiences that filled them nightly—are eloquent witness to the desire for escapism, for a world of the imagination," explained Gardiner.

The zeitgeist of those times would play a key role in the next phase of Markova's career, as she sought to build ballet audiences among the new culture-seeking British public. The dancer would support her family not by performing in Opera Houses and grand theaters throughout Europe, but rather on the stage of popular movie palaces, providing live entertainment between film showings.

And as her star rose—eventually becoming England's first ever *prima ballerina assoluta*—the "exotic" Markova also became an endless source of fascination to all those women wanting "more." Stories about the ballerina's daily life, diet, fashion, and makeup tips would fill newspapers and magazines throughout Great Britain. She was a poor British girl who had made good, and millions of everyday women wanted to share a piece of her success, even if that meant just buying the same lipstick.

Markova would also do something no other ballet dancer had done before her, appearing on the intriguing new medium of television. The myriad publicity made Alicia Markova a household name.

But all that attention was still a few years off. First, British ballet would need to step forward and create public interest in classical dance. There had been a desire for a homegrown company for quite some time. It had just seemed a daunting proposition with Russians so dominating the world of ballet.

"At that time, I hate to say, it was thought that English people couldn't achieve very much in the arts as singers or dancers," Markova would later lament. "England was wonderful—they always welcomed great artists from overseas and companies and guests—but somehow they never considered anybody of their own could achieve the same pinnacle. So, the only thing left for one if you were a dancer, you had a Russian name, because the idea was the Russians were the greatest dancers in the world at that time, and if you were a singer in opera, you took an Italian name."

But the death of Diaghilev seemed a catalyst for change, giving "English Ballet an odd sense of release and the sudden loss of a hopeless feeling of inferiority," as dancer/choreographer Ninette de Valois later explained in her memoir. She and former Ballets Russes dancer/teacher Marie Rambert had each opened a ballet school in London in the 1920s with hopes of one day forming a homegrown company. De Valois teamed up with the eccentric theatrical manager/producer Lilian Baylis to achieve her goal. And in light of the socio-economic changes in 1930s England—as well as Markova's exceptional talents—their dreams would soon become a reality.

While Sergei Diaghilev had reinvented modern and classical ballet in France, the future of British ballet would be primarily in the hands of the three formidable women just mentioned: Ninette de Valois, Lilian Baylis, and Marie Rambert. Like many male impresarios, they were all enterprising, passionate, and single-minded, but also domineering, temperamental, and sometimes thoughtlessly cruel. Stories of Rambert and Baylis as stingy and tactless were legendary.

Of the three, de Valois was the only one with a trifecta of skills—artistic talent, business acumen, and farsighted vision—making her the biggest asset to British ballet in the long run. Another of de Valois's invaluable gifts was understanding how best to use the other two women to her advantage.

From Rambert, de Valois would poach underpaid talent; from Baylis, funding and a theater. None of the three thought ballet would be a moneymaking proposition. They worked hard for their art, not profit. And each was completely devoted to the promotion of ballet in England.

De Valois realized her calling while a soloist with the Ballets Russes. She longed to be Diaghilev, not Danilova, preferring to create her own works and company to dancing for someone else. Still in her prime, the 28-year-old chose to leave the illustrious Russian troupe with hopes of becoming a successful choreographer, teacher, and producer in England, a country sorely lacking a national ballet of its own.

De Valois was used to reinventing herself. The former Edris Stannus was born in Ireland with a name clearly unsuited to any marquee. "My mother gave me the name Ninette for the theatre when I was too young to say much about it, but I had a lot of French blood in me," she wrote in her autobiography. "I don't know anyone any more who calls me Edris. It's rather a serious little name, I suppose. You outlive it, rather, a name like that."

But the crisp-sounding Edris did indeed suit the high-minded, determined figure who, having been raised in an aristocratic military family, understood the necessity of a long-range plan of attack to meet her goals.

The first step was opening a private London ballet school for discovering and molding local talent. De Valois had mastered the Cecchetti method while studying with its creator for four years and felt she could ably teach it to others. A suitable location was found in Roland Gardens on Gloucester Road, and the determined Irish woman began taking students in 1926. To underscore the seriousness of her new venture, de Valois called her school "The Academy of Choreographic Art." The regimented, plum-colored uniforms were as officious as the name.

De Valois's next step was to find a repertory theater willing to take on a fledgling dance company. She smartly believed that alternating ballet performances with plays and opera would be a fiscally viable way to slowly build an audience. To that end, the statuesque de Valois marched across Waterloo Bridge in a hard-to-miss large floppy hat for an appointment with Lilian Baylis, a former music teacher who operated the Old Vic Theatre in London's West End.

Baylis was well known for presenting quality productions of Shakespeare and opera, but on shoestring budgets, allowing her to keep ticket prices affordable to all. While it was an admirable enterprise, some people attributed ulterior motives to her largess.

Baylis was "a woman of high religious fervour as well as entrepreneurial zeal, who saw theatre for the masses mainly as a means of clearing the drunkards off the streets," wrote Fonteyn biographer Meredith Daneman.

And though Baylis seemed concerned with the limited means of her audience, she had no such concerns for her performers' empty wallets.

As Baylis biographer Elizabeth Schafer explained:

> Staff asking for a pay rise were told that Baylis would have to ask God, and God's response was always the same: "Sorry, dear, God says No." And amongst underpaid Vic-Wells staff, Baylis's favourite prayer was reputed to be "Dear God, send me good actors but send them cheap." These anecdotes attest to undoubted truths about Baylis's management: last-minute, panic-stricken, under-rehearsed substitutions were common at the theatres; she did not flatter her performers; she underpaid actors of the caliber of Edith Evans and John Gielgud; and she was confrontationally public about her religious commitment.

Then there were all the careless insults to performers that popped out of her mouth uncensored. Some were mean and deflating, others oddly amusing. Baylis once informed an actress that her wig was so unsightly that it needed to be returned immediately to Berts, the wigmaker. When told it was the actress's own hair, Baylis replied, "I don't care. It will have to go back to Berts."

Though Baylis was decidedly unorthodox in her behavior, her success was undeniable. In addition to the Old Vic, she would later refurbish London's Sadler's Wells Theatre, where Markova performed her first *Giselle.* Actors such as John Gielgud, Ralph Richardson, Michael Redgrave, Alec Guinness, and Laurence Olivier also got their starts under her management.

In terms of a legacy, Baylis launched companies that would evolve into today's English National Opera, British National Theatre, and Royal Ballet. Not too shabby for a poorly dressed, gauche, and idiosyncratic religious zealot.

Hardly the epitome of tact herself, de Valois always defended Baylis: "I have no wish to join the ranks of those who succeed only in stressing her as a quaint character. In my opinion, this is to underestimate her wholly. Above all, she was a very real person, and it was from this quality that she derived the strength of purpose. Mentally, she was not unlike a sincere, shrewd, devout peasant."

And as de Valois further points out, Baylis "inspired affection and loyalty from those who worked with her"—the newly minted dance school teacher among them.

Floppy hat aside, Baylis hired de Valois to teach drama students how to move more gracefully, as well as choreograph various productions of Shakespeare and opera ballets for the Old Vic. As Schafer elaborates:

> Where de Valois and Baylis connected was in their total, almost ferocious dedication to the job in hand, their willingness to attempt what others assured them was impossible, and their pragmatic, strategic thinking. Both women were also capable of volcanic rage, particularly when faced with what they felt was laziness or sloppiness.

In that last regard, Lilian Baylis certainly made de Valois's job harder. Always looking for cheap labor, Baylis asked for volunteers among her office staff to perform as background dancers in various operas. Of course, it was left to de Valois to train them. According to Schafer, one of the volunteers had a "wooden hand"—hardly ideal for any dancer—whereupon Baylis promised to reserve "an excellent kid glove" for her exclusive use. Problem solved.

In the opinion of de Valois, the general standard of many charges put in her care was absolutely "terrible."

No wonder de Valois soon went in search of genuine talent for her work-in-progress ballet company. Everyone acknowledged that Marie Rambert had the gift of spotting and nurturing future stars; and amazingly, she was even more outlandish than Baylis.

Few teachers engendered the love-hate relationship among her students as did ballet teacher and school master Marie "Mim" Rambert (the former Myriam Ramberg). The American dancer/choreographer Agnes de Mille was one of Rambert's most devoted pupils. In her biography of de Mille, Carol Easton perfectly captured the Jekyll and Hyde personality of the mercurial Mim:

> The Polish-born Marie Rambert operated her Ballet Rambert, then called Ballet or "B" Club, on a shoestring in Notting Hill Gate. "Mim" had a tiny body that contained a large, contradictory personality. She was capable of great warmth, wisdom, and tenderness, but her miserliness and insults, hysterical outbursts and off-the-cuff organizational style drove people mad. She was an intense, opinionated martinet, who could on occasion be outrageous—turning cartwheels in Piccadilly Circus, for example, when well past fifty. She had high standards, ambition far beyond her resources, and an unerring eye for new talent.

Ultimately, Agnes de Mille, like two other soon-to-be-famous Rambert pupils—Frederick Ashton and Antony Tudor—found that their teacher's pros far outweighed her cons. In her own book *Dance to the Piper,* de Mille fondly remembers the "warmhearted," "motherly" side of Mim, who always took the time for tender "woman-to-woman" chats, an opinion shared by Markova. De Mille also finds humor in Rambert's thoughtless behavior:

> Sometimes, Mim merited a scolding. She behaved on occasion outrageously. She has been known to walk down the theater

> aisle and say to paid customers, "I would like to sit next to Lady Oxford, do you mind moving to the back row?" And she moved them to their astonishment although they had held their tickets for weeks.

While de Mille doesn't shy away from relating anecdotes of Rambert's chair-throwing furies and belittling vitriol, she attributes them to her teacher's perfectionism and frustration at her own lack of success as a dancer, making them forgivable offenses. There was certainly great praise, encouragement, and valuable personal training along with the outbursts—sometimes equally annoying—as Rambert could corner pupils for hours on end with her "helpful" advice. Many evenings post-performance, Markova and Ashton would sneak out of their dressing-room window onto the street to avoid Mim's all-night chats.

Born in Warsaw, Poland in 1888, Marie Rambert had worked with the best of the best after first falling under the spell of dance while watching Isadora Duncan perform in 1905. Soon a master of "eurhythmics"—the art of interpreting musical compositions through harmonious bodily movements—the 24-year-old was hired by Diaghilev to help Vaslav Nijinsky and Igor Stravinsky create the infamous primitive choreography for *The Rite of Spring*. Some say she was their referee, as the ballet's premiere resulted in a much-publicized riot.

Rambert briefly stayed on as a member of the *corps de ballet*, where she studied under Enrico Cecchetti. She would train with the Maestro again in London in 1918, but this time to learn his teaching methods, as the tiny, plump dancer with short legs and un-arched feet sadly realized that a career as a performer was just not in the cards for her. Rambert later claimed it was Cecchetti's strict, dictatorial classroom style that inspired her own, and, from Markova's personal experience, throwing canes and engendering tears were indeed par for the course. But from all accounts, Rambert was far more unpredictable than the Italian and a veritable emotional volcano.

In 1917, Mim met and married English playwright, critic, and theater manager Ashley Dukes, then a soldier, thus becoming a British citizen. With his support, Rambert founded her own London ballet school in 1920, soon discovering that she had an undeniable eye for talent and how to develop it. In the 1930s, Dukes would open the minuscule Mercury Theatre in which he presented new dramas by stellar writers including T. S. Eliot, W. H. Auden, and Christopher Isherwood, alternating those productions with his wife's Ballet Rambert.

Markova and other dancers often spoke of the Lilliputian-sized shared theater accommodations that had everyone falling all over each other. "The actors made great friends with our dancers, in spite of little quarrels over rehearsal rooms," Rambert wrote in her memoirs.

In 1926, Rambert gave Frederick Ashton his first choreographic commission and continued nurturing his fledgling career for the next five years. "Never accept the first solution," she taught him.

It wasn't until 1931 that Alicia Markova became Ashton's muse, and it was their collaborations that made Rambert's Ballet Club a quite "fashionable" success, as Arnold Haskell described it. Haskell was one of the original directors of the Ballet Club along with Ashley Dukes, who—it should be pointed out—loved his wife, not ballet. It was Haskell who first recommended that Frederick Ashton contact Markova—good advice for all concerned. Prior to the pair's triumph on the tiny Mercury stage, Haskell admitted that on many nights he was fully one-tenth of the ballet theater's audience.

The year 1930 was an *"annus mirabilis"* for British ballet, asserts dance writer Mary Clarke in her book on the history of the Sadler's Wells Ballet, as Ninette de Valois's company came to be called. That year "saw announcements of the establishment of a permanent ballet at Sadler's Wells and the formation of the Ballet Club [Rambert's company], and it witnessed the first performance staged by the Camargo Society, which was to be of infinite value and importance in publicizing and encouraging these twin nurseries of English ballet."

So why was it an *"annus horribilis"* for Alicia Markova? Until the end of 1930, none of those organizations contacted her with employment opportunities, despite the fact that she was one of the most technically proficient out-of-work ballet dancers in London. In the case of de Valois and Rambert, there was a desire to develop and groom pupils from the ranks of their own schools first, and it wouldn't be until 1931 that their companies would be ready for a dancer of Markova's caliber.

De Valois did make a concerted effort to keep in touch socially with Markova. Learning that her former Ballets Russes charge was both broke and depressed, de Valois insisted on treating her to dinner and a movie once a week. It meant the world to Markova.

The Camargo Society, however, was a completely different matter. The idea for some sort of organization that would promote modern British ballet was the brainchild of *Dancing Times* editor Philip Richardson. For help, he called on his friend Arnold Haskell.

"With Diaghileff alive, such competition as we might offer would have been comical," wrote Haskell in his 1934 book *Balletomania*. "Indeed, the fact that there ever could be such a thing as English Ballet had never occurred to me, not through any snobbery, but because I was well satisfied with things as they were."

But with Diaghilev gone, things were now different. Over a long lunch in October 1929—fittingly held at the Chez Taglioni restaurant, named for the celebrated 19th-century ballerina Marie Taglioni—the pair formalized a plan of action.

"Both Richardson and Haskell believed that there was sufficient talent available in England to produce not a substitute for the Diaghileff Ballet but something interesting and important in its own right," wrote Mary Clarke.

The many prominent and influential participants in that newly formed group, including almost every former Ballets Russes dancer then living in England, had lofty goals perfectly suited to Markova's talents. She was quite demoralized that over a year would go by before anyone thought to call her.

"It is significant that when the Camargo Society was formed in October 1930 [it was actually 1929] to try to keep ballet alive by a series of Sunday performances, Alicia was the only British dancer of any standing not asked to take part at the opening performance," admonished Anton Dolin. "That hurt her at the time when she felt that she might, with her international experience, be of service to British ballet."

Markova's disappointment would have turned to anger had she known the reasons she was overlooked. Jealousy of her flawless technique and an undercurrent of anti-Semitism both played roles in the openly Jewish dancer being left out of the "club." High-ranking

Camargo committee members—former Ballets Russes dancer Lydia Lopokova and her husband, and group treasurer, the celebrated economist John Maynard Keynes—were behind the painful snub, though few others realized what was happening at the time. Named for the celebrated 18th-century ballerina Marie Camargo, the Society intended to be anything but exclusionary.

As British dance historian Kathrine Sorley Walker explains:

> The aim of the society was production. A program of "original and classic ballets" was to be given four times a year at a West End theatre, on Sunday evenings and Monday afternoons when no commercial shows were staged. "Eminent composers, painters and choreographers" would be invited to collaborate, and "the best dancing talent in London or from abroad" would be enlisted. It was an ambitious scheme.

A gala inaugural dinner was planned to enlist supporters and subscribers and was attended by close to 160 of London's literary, arts, and social luminaries, including writer H. G. Wells, socialite/author Margot Asquith, and Bloomsbury veterans Lytton Strachey and Virginia Woolf. But the most publicized patron was one who chose not to attend. In declining, writer George Bernard Shaw sent his explanation in a postcard:

> These people are idiots in business. My joining the Society will—my own subscription apart—make not one farthing difference on their takings. Tell them to kick out all their Press agents and publicity experts, amateur or professional, and stick to their job, as Diaghilev did. He succeeded in delivering the goods, not by celebrity hunting and postprandial speeches.
>
> I can do nothing for them, as I neither dance nor compose nor plan ballets; and I have enough sense to keep out of the way under such circumstances. The notion that a dinner can act as a send-off to a ballet season—unless they can make the Lord Mayor drunk enough to dance a hornpipe on the table

among the walnut-shells—is beyond my patience. Intimate the same as violently as you can.

"This was read out and got us a lot of publicity as you can imagine," Arnold Haskell recalled in a televised interview years later. "That is how the Camargo really got going."

Though everyone thought Shaw's note quite amusing—and it found its way into print in several newspapers—the society's founders might have taken the content a bit more seriously.

"The Camargo Society was my first experience of a long life of committee work," Haskell recalled, more than a little exasperated. "I attended over a hundred meetings, two or three of which may have been of importance. I remember that a whole series was devoted to plumbing and lavatory fixtures and I asked myself whether I had become a balletomane for that. It is a truism that a work of art cannot be created by a committee."

In fact there were dozens of committees, each with a different fiefdom, including art direction, music, and décor. The task force for dance was of an especially high caliber—including Ninette de Valois, famous Russian prima ballerina Tamara Karsavina (then living in London), Anton Dolin, Marie Rambert, and Princess Seraphine Astafieva. Heading up that group and named "Choreographic Director" was the former Ballets Russes star Lydia Lopokova. Her husband John Maynard Keynes was put in charge of the Camargo finances. (Though Keynes was already a respected economist, it wasn't until 1936 that he became a political force in England with the publication of his seminal book *The General Theory of Employment, Interest, and Money.*) From the start, Mr. and Mrs. Keynes were quite the high-society couple, but their union was surprising to say the least.

The pair had met while Lopokova was performing in London with the Ballets Russes in 1918, when the Russian dancer quickly became a press darling and toast of the town.

"Lydia Lopokova was full of surprises," remembered fellow Ballets Russes dancer Lydia Sokolova. "She had not the appearance or physique of a classical dancer but to everyone's astonishment whatever she attempted came off. Few dancers have performed with such assurance or flown through the air as she did."

And Lopokova loved to shock, both with her scattershot appearance and her onstage antics. Sokolova thought both part and parcel of her friend's carefree personality, as in the following anecdote:

> She [Lopokova] was so gay and feckless, never taking any trouble about herself and always coming to bits on the stage. One evening when she was dancing the Mazurka in *Les Sylphides*, she arrived at the part where she had to perform a *relevés in arabesque* several times over. Her raised leg fell lower and lower; then to everyone's surprise, she stopped, tucked her hand under her costume and stepped out of a pair of tarlatan drawers. She threw them into the wings, picked up her music where she left off and carried on as if nothing had happened.

While Sokolova found such "accidents" entertaining, many of Lydia's fellow principal dancers did not. That type of thing happened too often not to be purposeful, they thought, and Lopokova was always quite masterful at upstaging her costars.

She was known to tie her ballet shoes loosely so they would become undone on stage, causing her to trip. Then she'd gracefully fasten them once again with a wink to the crowd. Audiences—and Diaghilev—adored her.

"Lydia had a remarkable sense of sincerity," claimed Sokolova, but she conceded, "always with a suspicion of naughtiness."

Lopokova's experience working for Diaghilev was the exact opposite of Markova's. Where the teenage Alicia Marks had placed herself totally in the hands of the controlling impresario, the Maryinsky-trained Lopokova had loyalties to no one, frequently dropping in and out of dance companies and people's lives as it suited her. The spontaneity of her career decisions matched the impish style of her dance—one that perfectly suited the modern choreography of Mikhail Fokine and Léonide Massine.

But no sooner had Diaghilev made her a star than the teenaged Lopokova deserted him—simultaneously breaking a long-term contract with the Imperial Russian Ballet—without thought to the serious consequences of both actions. "She should have been content with this, but success always seemed to bore her," wrote Arnold Haskell, "and she went off to seek the customary fortune in America."

After five years of often less-than-glamorous working conditions in the States, Lopokova rejoined the Ballets Russes where she once again became an international celebrity. She would walk out on Diaghilev without notice twice more, and it's a testament to her irresistible charm—and undeniable gifts as an audience-pleaser—that the impresario kept taking her back. Along the way, she broke many hearts—cowardly ending an engagement to American sportswriter Heyward Broun by mail—and entered into a bigamous first marriage in her twenties.

So it's not surprising that when Lopokova was performing in London in 1918, the "shameless flirt" hooked up with the unconventional, self-absorbed Bloomsbury Group—a name applied to them by others, not themselves. The legendary circle of cultural elitists became both famous and influential in early 20th-century England.

Members of the "unofficial" but like-minded group included writers Virginia Woolf and Lytton Strachey, painter Duncan Grant, author/poet Vita Sackville-West, husband and wife artist Vanessa Bell and writer Clive Bell, and economist John Maynard Keynes. The very definition of Bohemian, they all felt "above" the strict moral codes of the Victorian era, favoring instead open marriages and relationships: hetero-, bi-, and homosexual. Everyone seemed to be involved with everyone else at one time or another.

Fans of the avant-garde in all arts, the Bloomsbury set was quite taken with the audacious ballet star Lydia Lopokova, as well as her dance partner, the brilliantly innovative choreographer Léonide Massine. Clive Bell published essays on the pair.

Despite Keynes's homosexuality, "Lydia and Maynard" became a couple, though he continued same-sex affairs throughout their courtship. (One-time lovers Lytton Strachey and Duncan Grant each alternately had intimate relationships with Maynard, as he was always called.) Keynes found Lopokova's uncensored ramblings refreshing, and her silliness a welcome change from his deadly serious political and economic duties.

In turn, the flighty Lydia was "drawn to the promise of security and power" that Keynes could offer, according to Lopokova biographer Judith Mackrell.

The couple took up residence in Keynes's Gordon Square townhouse, living close to, and spending much time with, their Bloomsbury cohorts.

When working with Keynes on Camargo Society business, Arnold Haskell found Maynard and the Bloomsbury group to be insufferable snobs:

> I am no judge of his [Keynes's] quality as an economist but I felt at times that I had rarely met anyone more smug or arrogant. He was a fine writer and an enlightened collector of books and paintings but anything that his clique did not recognize as art could not be art. The whole thing was a game whose rules he made up as it progressed. I was immediately sensible of his knowledge and his cleverness but I felt that there was something incomplete and immature. . . . Keynes constantly ignored his fellow committee members.

Haskell also thought the self-professed bohemian lifestyle of the group tedious in the extreme: "Bloomsbury made much of personal relationships but never seemed to escape the squabbles associated with adolescent 'crushes.'"

And as modernists, they couldn't hold a candle to the Ballets Russes artists, leading many to scoff at the temerity of Duncan Grant and Vanessa Bell thinking their set and costume designs could pick up where Picasso, Matisse, and de Chirico left off.

Lopokova, on the other hand, was roundly adored by the Camargo Society powers-that-be. Though not beautiful, she was devilishly attractive, seductive, and amusing. With a delightfully quirky blend of Russian and English, her lively chatter was filled with laugh-inducing malaprops—she once told Anton Dolin he danced like a "cantaloupe," meaning antelope—and her ebullience in storytelling made her mean-spirited barbs somehow less hurtful.

Lopokova's great gift was her vivacious personality—one that carried over to the stage. Combined with Keynes's fund-raising skills for Camargo, they were a formidable pair.

The couple married in 1925, and though originally drawn to Lopokova's *joie-de-vivre,* the Bloomsbury group felt quite differently once the ditzy ballerina had officially "landed" Keynes. To almost everyone, the couple seemed a classic example of opposites attracting.

In commenting on the 1990 book *Lydia and Maynard: The Letters of Lydia Lopokova and John Maynard Keynes*, British journalist and writer David Pryce-Jones asserts that "almost the only attitude the two held in common was anti-Semitism, and both go out of their way to indulge in it."

The Bloomsbury group shared those sentiments, despite Virginia Woolf's husband being Jewish. As is often the case with public figures known to have made anti-Semitic remarks, those statements in no way preclude their having close working and personal relationships with Jews. But those sentiments certainly influence their behavior in social and business situations. As the de facto leader of the Camargo Society, Lopokova was easily able to exclude whom she wished merely by not inviting them into her circle.

"On all occasions, Lydia Keynes (still Lopokova to us all) was our most outspoken member," wrote Ninette de Valois in her memoirs. "She did not like committees; but having found herself a member of one, she did not suffer from any inertia or inhibition."

Judith Mackrell agrees: "Lydia rapidly found herself positioned as the Society's principal advocate, and during the following months, as Camargo geared up for its autumn season, it was she who also emerged as its main broker of power."

One way to insure her Queen Bee status was to hold committee meetings at the spectacular Keynes Bloomsbury home in Gordon Square. First, that allowed Lopokova to control the guest list, and second, she was able to impress one and all with her grand supper parties. As Mackrell points out, "lubricated by Maynard's claret," the group was far more inclined to follow the hosts' wishes.

The "in" crowd included Lopokova's friend from the Ballets Russes days Ninette de Valois, whom Lydia oddly called "Ninnie"; the talented British music conductor Constant Lambert; and the up-and-coming 25-year-old choreographer Frederick Ashton. (Though Lopokova met Ashton through Marie Rambert, Mim—who was Jewish—was decidedly not invited into Lopokova's inner circle.)

Lopokova and Frederick Ashton would become thick as thieves. They went everywhere together—Lydia, of course, footing the bill.

That relationship would later prove quite problematic for the Jewish Markova. From *Bloomsbury Ballerina*:

> Lydia had never liked the younger ballerina [Markova]. Whilst others might marvel at the rarefied beauty of her technique, Lydia simply thought her cold and, back in the Ballets Russes days, sniggered enjoyably over the gossip that Diaghilev was trying to find her a lover 'to warm' her up. [The opposite was clearly true.]

In 1930, Lydia Lopokova was thirty-eight years old and on the downside of a long career. Unlike Markova, who performed into her fifties, the impetuous Russian ballerina hadn't the patience or will to diligently practice every day. As she had never been a dancer of classic grace, Lopokova depended on her vivacity and athleticism in modern ballets to win over an audience. Now she was far less able to perform in that capacity, and she knew it.

Taking the young, talented Ashton under her wing—he was immensely flattered by the interest paid him by Massine's very own muse—she planned a comeback in contemporary ballets by the budding choreographer. Alicia Markova didn't fit into those plans, and neither did Marie Rambert, Ashton's teacher and mentor.

While Rambert was an obvious force in British ballet, and had been invited by Haskell to join the Camargo Society, Lopokova kept her at bay by closing ranks with Mim's competitor, Ninette de Valois.

"Lydia may initially have been fond of Marie, or 'Mim' Rambert, admiring her energy . . . but she now saw her and her studio as a potential rival to the Camargo Society," writes Mackrell.

In 1931, Lopokova felt Ashton wasn't spending enough time on the few yearly Camargo productions, focusing his energies instead on commissions for Rambert's Ballet Club, where her "rival" Markova was now performing. Lydia fired off the following letter to Maynard: "A Bombshell. Fred under influence of Mim is behaving disgracefully . . . I am disgusted yet I know he is a nice boy & it is a matter of influence, the Jewess dominates him at present."

Along with Markova, Rambert was seemingly unaware of Lopokova's anti-Semitic feelings toward her. Mim was nothing but warm and full of praise for Lydia in person, press interviews, and later, in her memoirs, where she called Lopokova "a delicious little person of irresistible charm."

Further fomenting Lopokova's rage against both women was the Ballet Club's production of the humorous *Façade* with Markova in the starring role dancing the "Tango" in 1931. Frederick Ashton had originally choreographed the part for Lopokova to perform in a Camargo premiere. How dare Mim give her role to Markova! Never mind that the choice was actually Ashton's. To Lydia, it was a Jewish conspiracy.

Lopokova's jealousy and shared anti-Semitism with Keynes had effectively kept Markova—soon to be the world's first openly Jewish *prima ballerina assoluta*—from being invited into the year-long planning process and grand premiere performance of the Camargo Society. But the younger dancer's immense and undeniable talents made it impossible to keep her out in the long run.

Lopokova aside, one might wonder why Arnold Haskell, Markova's childhood friend and avid follower of her career, hadn't invited her input early on. He was one of the founders of the Camargo Society, after all. But Haskell still regarded the nineteen-year-old as immature and inexperienced in many ways. When he visited the Marks household as a friend of the family throughout 1930, Markova's still underdeveloped body and frail appearance must have made her seem even younger than she was. To Haskell, Alicia was like a shy, sweet little sister.

As he reminisced in his 1951 memoir *In His True Centre*, "I can see her (Alicia) at the children's parties I gave for the four sisters, always choosing the least conspicuous part in any game or charade. No one could have been less of a theatre child." Haskell goes on to talk about taking Alicia to the zoo and the cinema when she was young, and what a "stranded, truly pathetic figure" she became when he visited her at the Ballets Russes after Guggy became ill.

"When Diaghileff died Alicia began a new and very difficult career," Haskell continued. "Ballet was by no means popular and there was no place awaiting her." Certainly not at the Camargo Society. Haskell could easily justify not having included the young dancer in any of his planning committees. She hadn't lived in England for the past five years, so had no knowledge of potential patrons, possible venues, or local arts professionals to contact. It is also probable that he assumed the choreographic committee would eventually contact her for performances, not knowing Lopokova's true feelings.

But there was more to it than just that, as Haskell wrote in a lengthy article on Markova for *Dancing Times* magazine in June 1931, a full twenty months *after* the Camargo Society was formed:

> One of the literary weeklies has called Alicia Markova "the white hope of English dancing." She has earned all the compliments that can be paid her, but this particular compliment will not bear analysis. English dancing is not in a bad way, on the contrary it has never been in a stronger position, and Alicia Markova does not shine as a solitary hope, but as an exceptionally fine performer among fine performers.
>
> . . . I find that Markova has gained enormously since the end of the Diaghileff ballet. She has spent the time profitably in discovering herself, largely thanks to the Camargo Society and The Ballet Club and the terms "colourless" and "lacking in personality" that were applied with some justice two years ago are ridiculous to-day. Personality she has in abundance, but there is still a certain restraint that must be broken down, before she can reveal herself more fully.

After Markova became an acclaimed star in England, Haskell didn't agree with his fellow critics' high praise. "Naturally, I was pleased at this success, pleased yet puzzled," he wrote. "This was not the Markova that Diaghileff had expected. She was light, and to the great public lightness is everything. She was precise, but she was totally lacking in the ability to portray the emotions and also in the really grand manner. To me she was lost somewhere between the artless child and the consciously artistic woman. They acclaimed her as a great ballerina. I could not agree, nor could I conceal my feelings from someone so close to me."

To the credit of both, Haskell's opinions never marred his close friendship with Markova, who accepted the criticism gracefully. Unfortunately, the result of those feelings back in 1930 was that Markova had to listen to her friend natter on about Camargo's goings-on when he visited, completely in the dark as to why she wasn't included, and too self-conscious to inquire.

It wasn't until January 1931 that she was asked to participate in any Camargo production, and that call came from Ninette de Valois who thought Markova perfect for a new ballet she was choreographing.

"*Cephalus and Procris* [1931] was Alicia Markova's first connection with the Camargo Society," writes British dance historian Kathrine Sorley Walker. "She was going through a very bleak time with few opportunities to dance and was disappointed that she was not included in the opening Camargo program—nor had she been asked to take any part in the setting up of the Society. Although she had been a Diaghilev dancer, she was of course, still very young, having celebrated only her twentieth birthday in December 1930. De Valois, however, who had known her and her ability from the time she joined Diaghilev, had complete faith in her potential, and chose her to create the role of Procris."

Haskell ended his *Dancing Times* profile on Markova with an odd confession that may explain some of his opinions and actions:

> I can say that I have known Alicia long before she was Markova. I have known her since her first exercise at the bar. She has steered a careful course through the dangers of being presented as a "miniature Pavlova," and today she is an artist of great achievement and still greater promise. The fact that I know her and her work so well has made me extremely critical. Personal association with an artiste invariably reduces the glamour and mystery, and sharpens one's critical faculties. There is the fear that one's swan will be a goose after all. Alicia at the age of eight was my first big hope, and I was terrified of disappointment. Up till last year I had doubts on many points. Today I can join the public wholeheartedly in my enthusiastic applause of Alicia Markova.

And there is an additional factor that played into Haskell's prejudice. In the *Dancing Times* piece, Haskell compares his childhood friend unfavorably to Pearl Argyle, another British ballerina then performing in Rambert's Ballet Club. Though Argyle's technique didn't approach Markova's, she was a lovely dancer and a great beauty. As Ninette de Valois said about Argyle, "Imagine what it must be like to wake up every morning and see that face in the mirror." In his feature article on Markova, Haskell compared the two dancers:

> . . . in the pas de deux from Les Sylphides Pearl Argyle has to perfection that dream atmosphere that Markova seems to lack. Here are ballets where facial expressions as quite apart from mime proper counts for a great deal and that is, perhaps, the cause for the failure, which may quite well be a failure of observation on my part.

Could it be that Haskell realizes that he prefers Argyle simply because she is so beautiful? It's hard to believe that Markova, who would be considered the greatest romantic classical ballerina of her time, lacked any "dream atmosphere" when dancing *Les Sylphides* in 1931. Just six months prior to Haskell's article, a New York writer said of her in a newspaper profile:

> I do not know whether it is the combined effect of the centrally-parted raven hair, the oval face, the lovely brown expressive eyes, the general air of fragility, and the atmosphere of dreamy serenity that surround her, but Alicia reminds me ever so much of Pavlova, whom it has been my happiness to meet on several occasions. She has Pavlova's grace, too, allied to the technique of Karsavina, with an indescribable something added that is essentially her own.
>
> To watch her dancing is fascinating in the extreme. She lives her roles, brings them a rhythm, an understanding interpretation, an intensity that one has hitherto associated only with the continental dancer.

That article appeared in *The American Hebrew*. Clearly, Markova's looks were to taste. She more closely resembled her Jewish father than her bonny Irish mother like her sisters did. Perhaps if Arnold Haskell had seen Pavlova dance when she was eighteen, he would have found faults with her as well. It would take time for both dancers to grow into their distinctive looks.

Markova was well aware of the fact that she was not considered conventionally pretty, as her sisters were, and it made her all the more insecure. It also cost her several potential job opportunities as she languished in 1930, as related by Anton Dolin:

> At that time her beauty had not bloomed to its present fullness. . . . On several occasions I wanted to have Alicia as my partner when I was engaged by Sir Oswald Stoll at the London Coliseum or in the revues in which I appeared . . . I was always given the same answer, "She is not pretty enough." Today they would think differently.
>
> Alicia had some bitter and discouraging years before she saw her name in top-line lights outside a theatre presenting a popular commercial success.

Toward the end of 1930, Alicia Markova had become resigned to the possibility that she might never dance professionally again. As she wrote in her memoir notes:

> The fact that had to be faced was that I was, by no stretch of the imagination, the sort of pretty young thing that managements would be willing to engage for revue musicals. Thin, dark, "exotic looking" as people still said, I was a complete misfit in the world of commercial theatre: it mattered not at all to anyone that I had worked with the greatest names in ballet, that I had laudatory notices from every major critic in Europe, that I had been hailed in every capital city. It mattered also very little to me: the past did not matter as much as the fact that I could not see any future at all for myself. That mattered enormously. . . .
>
> Then, one day, there came a letter. It was from a young man, Fred Ashton, who wondered if I would be interested in dancing with him.

5

Pioneering British Ballet

It has been remarked of Alicia Markova that she is "old enough to have had a share in the making of ballet history, and young enough, if fortune favors her, to play a large part in the future development of the dance." That she *will* ultimately play that "large part" seems predestined.

—"A Prima Ballerina: Alicia Markova, of the Russian Ballet, Delights European Capitals"
Gabrielle Costa, *The American Hebrew*, 1930

In 1930, Fredrick Ashton was a struggling, but promising, London dancer/choreographer. Though he would later be credited with defining classical 20th-century British ballet, the prolific artist was raised not in England, where he would first make his mark, but rather in the more exotic cultural landscape of Peru. "The thing that a choreographer really needs is an eye," Ashton is quoted as saying. "He has to do his training through his eye."

Lima, it turns out, was an eyeful. "Peru, with its 'particular interweaving of lightness, somberness and ritual,' formed Ashton's personality and permeates his art," writes Julie Kavanagh in her biography of the choreographer. A similar blend of lightness, somberness, and ritual colored the bravura classical dance performances of Alicia Markova, the choreographer's first significant muse. The pair was ideally suited in numerous ways and for a variety of reasons. And despite growing up on different continents, they experienced almost identical transformative events in their young lives.

~

Frederick Ashton was born in 1904 in Guayaquil, Ecuador, where his father George was vice-consul at the British embassy and a successful manager at the Central and South American Cable Company. A former postal worker in Dorset, England, George had begun a new life on a new continent after his first wife died. Frederick's mother was Charlotte Georgiana Fulcher, known to all as "Georgie," who had left England for what she thought would be an exciting life in South America with George. Though her marriage was not a happy one, she did enjoy the social position that came with having a diplomat for a husband. Frederick was the couple's fourth son, and after Georgie gave birth to their fifth and last child—a daughter—the family moved to the more cosmopolitan, up-and-coming city of Lima, Peru.

It was there, at the Teatro Municipal auditorium in 1917, that young Frederick would have a life-changing experience, one shared by Alicia Markova just two years later. The thirteen-year-old Ashton, who had no former interest in dance, was told to expect a most magical performance by a very famous ballerina. But when the curtain rose to reveal the 36-year-old Anna Pavlova, Frederick's initial hopes were dashed. As Kavanagh writes in *Secret Muses: The Life of Frederick Ashton:*

> [Ashton] felt cheated, and said so out loud: how ugly she looked with her pinkish wig and beaky nose, and how old. "Espera!" said the man sitting next to him. Wait. "And he was right." From the moment the ballerina descended the three steps on to the stage and began her variations—a delicate waltz, a sparkling, darting xylophone solo, and an adagio during which she balanced indefinitely in arabesque—the young Frederick Ashton's future was decided. Pavlova, he said years later, was the greatest theatrical genius he had ever seen.

A lifelong adoration of Pavlova would be responsible for bringing Ashton and Markova together some thirteen years later. Rather than being put off by the frail British dancer's unconventional looks, Ashton would be drawn to her strong resemblance, both physically and stylistically, to his Russian idol.

Margot Fonteyn wasn't as fortunate, reveals Kavanagh. Ashton's longtime muse after Markova, the exquisite Fonteyn opined, "I always felt that Fred was seeing Pavlova and that I wasn't living up to her by any means." Markova would fulfill "Pavlova fantasies" for many choreographers.

While Arthur Marks was delighted to indulge his young daughter's obsession with ballet, Ashton's father was anything but supportive. A taciturn, strict, and distant man, the well-to-do George Ashton thought a dance career completely unsuitable for his youngest son, whom he already felt was too effeminate.

"As a child, Freddie Ashton was considered special," writes Kavanagh. "He liked playing with dolls, 'but not in a motherly way,' more as if they were marionettes. He was sweet and gentle, rather pretty for a boy." And he was a blonde among mostly dark-haired children, making him a favorite altar boy at Lima's grand cathedral, despite the family's not being Catholic. The colorful pageantry of high mass, with its slow deliberate build to a symbolic crowning point, made a vivid impression on the young Ashton, later contributing to the exquisite timing and carefully planned climaxes of his beautifully costumed ballets.

Also under Ashton's watchful "eye" was the regal comportment of Lima's upper class socialites who attended Georgie's posh receptions. Their graceful, carefully controlled postures would be incorporated into his elegant, fluid choreography, with feminine allure becoming an Ashton ballerina trademark.

Not long after Pavlova cast her spell—"she injected me with her poison," Ashton would say wistfully—the fifteen-year-old was shipped off to England to complete his rather rudimentary education. Though he hated boarding school, its proximity to London enabled him to attend dance performances now and again featuring luminaries such as Isadora Duncan, a modernist whose free-flowing, improvisational movements would greatly influence his future work. ("The way she used her hands and her arms, the way she ran across the stage—these

I have adopted in my own ballets," Ashton later wrote to his friend Constant Lambert.) Ashton also watched Pavlova dance as often as he could, carefully studying her lightning-quick speed and boundless theatricality.

While George Ashton had no problem giving his son an allowance for ballet and theater tickets, funding dance lessons was completely out of the question. And Georgie was too preoccupied with her own social life to pay much attention to the needs of her children.

Adding to his parents' dismay, Ashton was a very poor student with no chance of attending a fine university and becoming a diplomat like his father. So after graduation, he moved in with friends of the family and took a job as an office boy.

What happened at his father's office one day in January 1924 would change Frederick's life forever. It began as usual, with George Ashton arriving at work and spending the morning at his desk. Then the short, brusque man suddenly walked down to the company's vault room, took out a gun, and blew his head clean off. Frederick's brother Charlie was in a nearby office when he heard the blast.

Few who knew George well were surprised, as the 61-year-old had suffered from severe melancholia and erratic behavior throughout his life. He also had a troubled marriage, with both spouses having engaged in serious extramarital love affairs.

Georgie quickly fled South America to join her son Fred in London (suicide was considered scandalous in Peru's religious society, and her latest affair might be blamed). George left the bulk of his small estate to the sons he was closest to, Charlie and Alex, with Georgie and Frederick essentially cut off. Though Charlie lent some financial support to his mother and brother early on, the inheritance would soon be gone through mismanagement and carelessness.

The death of his father seemed to free Frederick emotionally to pursue his dream. Living quite frugally, he managed to pay for weekly Saturday afternoon ballet lessons with the immensely talented dancer/choreographer Léonide Massine, whom Ashton worshipped as an ardent fan.

"Massine was very aloof and uncommunicative and you couldn't get near him at all but he was interested in teaching because he wanted to form a troupe," remembered Ashton. ". . . after I'd done five or six classes I said, 'Well, when are you going to teach me a dance?' and he said 'In three years time.' I was frightfully depressed about that. I hated classes."

Though Massine was an idiosyncratic innovator as a choreographer, he taught the rigorously disciplined Cecchetti method, which he had learned at the Ballets Russes from Maestro Enrico Cecchetti himself.

"Fred had a loose-jointed, delicate physique which seemed to look right in whatever position he assumed," wrote fellow dancer Leo Kersley, "so when practicing the Cecchetti eight directions his body seemed to fall into the correct placing quite naturally. This facility left him free to concentrate on the real object of these set positions—i.e. to be able to present yourself to the audience in a way which made your message clear to them—a message which at that time was not primarily concerned with 'getting your leg up' but with saying something about the character you were intended to portray."

The fact that Markova was also Cecchetti-trained aided the pair's early choreographic collaborations enormously.

"Cecchetti's training stayed with me my entire life," explained Markova. "I call it my compass. I could do anything modern after that."

In many ways, Frederick Ashton suffered a similar fate to Alicia Markova: both grew up in wealthy homes only to be left impoverished by their fathers' sudden deaths—coincidentally in the same year of 1924, and both probably by suicide. And of all the members in both families, it would be Frederick and Alicia who were counted upon to financially support their mothers.

"I was brought up with the idea, that well, if you're on the earth, you're here to earn your way. You're not meant to be taken care of," Markova would say matter-of-factly toward the end of her life.

At nineteen, Ashton "found himself thrust overnight into adulthood, responsible for the next twenty years [it was actually fifteen] for the welfare of his mother," writes Kavanagh. "The reputation for meanness he later acquired was a direct result of those early years of poverty; even at the height of prosperity, he would still *feel* poor."

Markova often felt the same way, with decades of primitive travel accommodations only adding to her ingrained sense of deprivation.

But at least Markova's family was always proud of her career and great success. Even with Ashton's father gone, his mother and brothers were vehemently opposed to his taking up ballet. Miserable in his office job—and not very good at it—Ashton had a nervous breakdown that finally persuaded them to give in. His brother Charlie offered to pay for dance lessons as long as Ashton agreed never to become anything as déclassé as a chorus boy, which would have been considered an egregious embarrassment to the family.

By this time Massine had left London to return to the Ballets Russes, recommending that Ashton continue his training with another teacher of the Cecchetti method, Marie Rambert.

Ashton's early relationship with Rambert was rather complicated. On the one hand, he found both the woman and her classes unprofessional, especially after the rigorously disciplined Massine. "She only had a part-time studio in Bedford Gardens when I met her and she shared it with a lady sculptor who used to chase us out after about an hour," he remembered. Then there were Rambert's well-known histrionics and personal inadequacies as a dancer, which Ashton enjoyed mimicking in public, often cruelly.

But intellectually, Rambert had a lot to offer the unsophisticated dancer, and emotionally, she was willing to connect with him outside the studio in a way Massine was not. Mim was, Ashton would say late in life, "an extraordinary cultured woman, well-read and . . . her presence alone was a constant source of stimulation." In addition to exposing Ashton to great literature and poetry, Rambert was also the first to identify and encourage his hidden talents as a choreographer, for which he was clearly in her debt.

And despite her lack of teaching finesse, Ashton did attend Mim's classes quite regularly for the simple reason that she taught him for free. She desperately needed male pupils to perform with her "girls," many of whom were the daughters of wealthy English socialites who could pay top dollar (or pounds, as it were) for lessons.

When he could afford it, however, Ashton supplemented Rambert's classes with lessons from Margaret Craske, who was considered one of the finest classical ballet teachers of her time, Nikolai Legat, and

Princess Seraphine Astafieva. It was at one of Astafieva's classes that Ashton first caught sight of the tiny Alicia Marks, who was then thirteen years old.

"I remember seeing her, this trim little figure with everybody fussing round her," Ashton recalled in an interview with Clement Crisp. "And she was already very much of a star and very assured, and of course in the class she took the front place and I was sort of fumbling away at the back.

"I think she was already on the road to fame. . . . She was you know very precise and very quiet and very well behaved and also very competent already."

Ashton would later see Markova perform professionally with the Ballets Russes, thanks in part to Marie Rambert, with whom he became very good friends. Yes, Mim could be a comical caricature at times; nevertheless, she was also extremely intelligent, supportive, and fluent in six different languages. Admittedly, her chatter was often non-stop—whatever language she was speaking—but Rambert had valuable dance connections and generously shared them with Ashton.

One of Mim's perks, courtesy of her former employer Sergei Diaghilev, was complimentary tickets to all the London performances of the Ballets Russes. Ashton was her frequent guest and was continually mesmerized by the tiny Markova.

"I saw her with Diaghilev in *La Chatte* and *Chant du Rossignol* and various other things that she did, including the little girl in *La Boutique Fantasque,* which she used to do so well," Ashton told Clement Crisp. "I remember her tremendous precision, tremendous chic and elegance which she had as a performer. And very strong technique."

And of course, there was Markova's uncanny resemblance to Pavlova. It was fortunate for the young British dancer that Ashton remembered her so well in 1930, when others seemed to forget all about her. Though the pair brought out the best in each other in their relationship as choreographer and muse, their personalities couldn't have been more different.

Raised primarily by an overbearing and isolating governess, Markova had never had a carefree childhood with friends her own age. With the added pressures of becoming a professional dancer at age ten, she reacted to life's uncertainties by pursuing adult approval and security through hard work and unblemished good behavior. Even as a grown-up, Markova remained quietly reserved, studious and single-minded about dance. Her closest supporters and confidantes were her mother and sisters.

Ashton, on the other hand, had been a pampered, social child with a loving, permissive nanny. Never enjoying the artistic approval of his family, he turned instead to his friends and peers for validation and stimulus. Ashton was witty, easily bored, and the life of the party. And even though ballet was his one true calling, he was "notoriously lazy about going to class and well aware of it," writes David Vaughan, who wrote the critical study.

Ninette de Valois, Ashton's future boss, also remembered him from those early days, describing the young dancer as "small, nervous and touchingly eager to please." And, as she wrote in her memoir, "Like so many artists, he was more in love with his second best talent; for at one time he appeared to want to dance more than anything else in the world."

That dream made him all the more enthralled with the technical prowess of the young Alicia Markova's performances, watching her again and again in the same Ballets Russes productions, just as he had studied Pavlova. But while Ashton was captivated by the "Baby Pavlova" on stage, he never would have understood her cloistered existence among such a wild, creative group.

"I never had time off, but I didn't seem to require it and never thought about it," Markova reminisced about her Ballets Russes days. "The only time that I wanted off was to sleep."

"Early to bed, early to rise" was never an Ashton motto, nor was "all work and no play." Writes Kavanagh, "Unlike his exact contemporary, George Balanchine, Ashton took delight in cultivating a dazzling life outside his profession."

In 1925, the gregarious dancer-in-training found himself among London's so-called "Bright Young People," a post-World War I Bohemian circle of pampered young socialites, Jazz Age aristocrats, and rule-breaking writers who enjoyed thumbing their noses at proper British Society. Their louche all-night revelries, lavish cross-dressing costume parties, and unfortunate addictions to absinthe and cocaine would be satirized in Evelyn Waugh's popular 1930 novel *Vile Bodies*.

Ashton first became acquainted with the eccentric group—which included photographer Cecil Beaton and the literary Sitwell siblings—through Sophie Fedorovitch, a struggling Polish artist who had previously painted scenery for the Ballets Russes. It was at Marie Rambert's studio that Ashton first met the exceptionally talented Fedorovitch, who would become a lifelong friend and artistic collaborator. She proved especially influential early on, not only introducing Ashton to London's youthful, artsy set, but also to Paris and the innovative jazz dance stylings of Josephine Baker in *La Revue Negre*.

Though Sophie and Frederick lived on meager incomes, their gay society friends had plenty of money to go around and welcomed the pair with open arms and pocketbooks. "Witty and well mannered, Ashton was the ideal escort for a modern girl," writes Julie Kavanagh. "Although his appearance was that of a languid exquisite [rather fancifully dressed] . . . Ashton was not so conspicuously effeminate . . . as to provoke parental disapproval."

Besides, everyone was highly amused by the dancer's comical, dead-on impersonations of the rich and famous, "whether imitating Garbo in a felt hat and raincoat, enacting Pavlova's *Dying Swan* in a swimming pool, or conjuring up what Cecil Beaton called 'the Parma-violet-scented aura' of Queen Alexandra."

British Vogue editor Madge Garland traveled in the same social circle and befriended Ashton at this time. In 1926, she would rave about his first choreographic outing, *A Tragedy of Fashion*, produced by the Rambert Ballet (it was at Mim's suggestion that Ashton first try his hand—and feet—at choreography) with splendid costumes and sets by Sophie Fedorovitch. The ballet's libretto, by Rambert's husband Ashley Dukes, centers around a couturier who is so despondent after one of his dresses is rejected by a rich patron that he commits suicide with a pair of his own dressmaking shears. Madge Garland called the modern work "a brilliant evocation of the period, reflecting not only the physical appearance, but the whole tonality of my youth"—a period of frivolous entertainment to be sure.

Though the ballet was derivative of works by Massine and Nijinska, something Ashton freely admitted, he still thought its success would launch his career. He became even more excited when the composer managed to get Diaghilev to attend—twice, in fact. "I thought I was made for life," Ashton later said wistfully. "I thought the offers would come pouring in. But nothing happened." Markova could undoubtedly relate to those sentiments.

Unlike Ashton, whose high-flying social life was as inspiring to him as his dance studio work, Markova was a veritable hermit after her Ballets Russes days came to their unfortunate, and sudden, end. After Diaghilev died, a French newspaper announced, "The puppet master is dead, the puppets must be put back in their boxes." That was sadly true for Markova, but certainly not by choice.

She spent most of her time at home simply because she had no money to go out. Though Markova would have been perfectly happy in the "cheap" gallery seats at the theater or grabbing a sandwich with a friend at the corner teashop, Anton Dolin—who was mostly performing in London's West End musicals at the time—warned her not to, as it would make her destitute circumstances too readily apparent.

She must keep up the front of still being a success. And how would it look if a ballet fan ended up seated next to her at the cinema? Markova "must never lose her essential mystery," Dolin reminded her.

A lack of funds didn't seem to bother Ashton, who was happy to let others treat him—especially Lydia Lopokova and Marie Rambert—for posh evenings out to parties, restaurants, and the theater. But Markova just wasn't comfortable accepting dinner invitations when she knew she couldn't afford to reciprocate.

The one exception was attending the theater when asked by the ever-generous Mrs. Emmy Haskell, who still looked upon Alicia like a daughter. Fortunately, Markova's new dressmaking skills kept her wardrobe fashionable and up-to-date despite her poor circumstances.

Mrs. Haskell's son Arnold was another frequent visitor to the Marks home, though he remained remarkably blind to Markova's great disappointment at not being invited into the Camargo ballet society he had co-founded, not to mention her need to make money. Earning a living was never a problem for Haskell, an only child, as family money had enabled him to dabble in dance criticism and self-publish books without worrying where his next meal would come from.

Arnold may also have felt Markova should just bide her time until Diaghilev's successor came on the scene. Despite his being an active participant in the formation of several British ballet concerns, Haskell believed in his heart that only the Russian companies truly mattered in those days. When one Colonel Wassily de Basil formed his own version of the Ballets Russes in 1933, Haskell was so enamored of the troupe that he joined them "without pay or well-defined position," as he related in his memoirs.

That action resulted in a serious conflict of interest for the British ballet critic, something that appeared to completely elude him, though not Anton Dolin. When Colonel de Basil first brought his company to London in the early 1930s, he had no local contacts, explained Dolin. So the dancer and the well-connected Haskell ushered de Basil into local society.

"Arnold saw the possibilities of many new books ahead and was in his element with this new Russian Ballet Company," according to Dolin. But that was not what disturbed the dancer the most:

> At the time, Arnold Haskell's criticisms carried great importance and were read and accepted as gospel truth. Alicia Markova was dancing with the Sadler's Wells Ballet at Roseberry Avenue, and because of the new Russian invasion of the de Basils' Company at the Alhambra, they were having a difficult time holding their own, even with Markova dancing. Arnold was at the Alhambra every night, enthusiastic and wonderfully generous to the Russian dancers, suppers at the Savoy, helping tremendously with his knowledge and encouragement to the young ballerinas.

Dolin, who often partnered Markova in her early dancing days in London, asked Haskell if he couldn't spare just one night to go see her perform with the Sadler's Wells Ballet. As Haskell was good friends with both Markova and the ballet company's founder—Ninette de Valois—wouldn't it be a great boon to English ballet if he would review their performances in his column?

"My dear Pat," Haskell answered Dolin, "she [Markova] has no right to be dancing in the suburbs of London. She should be here, as you are, dancing with the Russians. This is where she belongs. No, I have no time."

It was a shocking comment coming from the co-founder of the Camargo Society, whose sole purpose was to promote British ballet concerns.

For Markova's part, she never once demanded an explanation from her friend Arnold, or felt favoritism was her due. Haskell may have thought Markova should wait patiently for a Russian company to rescue her, but he managed to jump-start her career nonetheless when asked for advice by the Camargo Society's promising young *British* choreographer, Frederick Ashton.

By 1930, four years after his choreographic debut with *A Tragedy of Fashion,* Frederick Ashton was slowly making a name for himself, having briefly been engaged as a dancer with the Ida Rubinstein Company in Paris. The former flamboyant Ballets Russes star and stage actress founded her own troupe in 1928, ably funded by her considerable inherited wealth. Though Ashton was a "humble member" of the corps—"inexperienced, half-trained, and underpaid" according to Ninette de Valois—with Léonide Massine and Bronislava Nijinska as the company's chief choreographers, Ashton received an invaluable education in ballet conception and production.

He especially benefited from working with Nijinska, who recognized the inexperienced British dancer's creative gifts and devoted a great deal of time to tutoring him. "Nijinska, in particular, helped me tremendously," Ashton told his biographers Zöe Dominic and John Selwyn Gilbert. "I never took my eyes off her when I was with Rubinstein. I used to come and watch all her rehearsals, just to see her work. I used to sit in the corner all day long, just watching her."

But there was another comment Ashton made about Nijinska in a letter to his friend Mim Rambert. "She [Nijinska] is a beautiful dancer & a dancer above all her ugliness." It was the same type of comment that would be made about Pavlova and Markova throughout their careers—that their talents were so prodigious it made up for their not being conventionally pretty. Unlike those two dancers, however,

Nijinska was neither petite nor feminine, but rather muscular, with a very strong physique that made her jumps quite miraculous to behold. Though she had been considered a handsome woman when younger, Nijinska's features would appear more mannish as she aged. Fortunately, her often-disparaged looks would be of no consequence to her great success as a choreographer and teacher.

When Ashton returned to London after his educational stint with the Rubinstein company, his very close and conspiratorial friendship with Lydia Lopokova began. He met the fun-loving ballerina through Mim Rambert.

It was a perfect match—Ashton basking in the attention of a former (and wealthy) Diaghilev star, and Lopokova needing a more "frivolous" and approving alternative to the Bloomsbury bunch, still so clearly appalled at her marriage to their cohort John Maynard Keynes.

Lopokova had been entertaining as an amusing and idiosyncratic star of the stage, but no one had expected her to "steal" Keynes out from under their noses. Lytton Strachey called Lopokova "a half-witted canary," with Virginia Woolf writing to a friend, "Lydia's pranks put us all on edge." But Lopokova thought Keynes a god, and what man doesn't appreciate that?

As Marie Rambert recalled in her memoirs: "I asked her [Lopokova] whether she had read his *Economic Consequences of the Peace,* which had just appeared, and whether she understood it. She replied with ecstasy: 'Mim, there is no need to understand it, for me it is just like Bach.'"

When Keynes was off power-brokering his economic theories, Lopokova turned to Ashton for companionship. With him she could share her love of ballet, gossip, and occasionally shocking behavior. "Coming from a generation that considered itself to have a privileged monopoly on bad behavior, Ashton was both delighted and appalled to hear Lydia['s stories.]," writes Judith Mackrell.

Lopokova took Ashton everywhere—to late-night parties, theater openings, and Camargo committee meetings. Interestingly, they each perceived the other's failings when it came to ballet, but never their own. Lopokova saw herself as Ashton's choreographic muse—though she was too old and out of shape for that role—and Ashton wanted Lopokova to give him leading parts in Camargo Society ballets.

"'Poor Fred,' she would report to Maynard," writes Mackrell, "'he does not want to see his defects.' It took 'a long silence & tea & polite conversation' to talk him out of his delusions."

Nevertheless, Ashton was a frequent guest at the Keynes home, often bringing along his good friend, the equally charming young dancer William Chappell. Unfortunately, when Lydia was out of sight, Maynard was known to make unwanted and embarrassing passes at the handsome young men. Lopokova apparently knew of her husband's occasional "flirtations" and chose to ignore them.

Though Lopokova would have been happy to monopolize Ashton's time and creativity—she even befriended his mother, whom he was supporting financially—the budding choreographer couldn't live on the nominal wages paid by the Camargo Society and Ballet Rambert. Like many other British ballet dancers not from wealthy homes, he was forced to take commercial theater work to supplement his income.

Marie Rambert, who hoped to retain her best dancers by helping them find higher-paying outside engagements, introduced Ashton to Sir Nigel Playfair, the actor/manager of the Lyric Theatre in Hammersmith, London. Playfair's popular theatrical productions often featured ballet segments, much like the British pantomime shows little Lily Marks had performed in as a child.

In the fall of 1930, Playfair asked Ashton to work on a ballet for his new production of the Dryden comedy *Marriage à la Mode*. The choreographer's first thought for a partner was Vera Savina (the former Vera Clarke), as the two had met when she taught dance lessons with her then-husband Léonide Massine. His second thought seemed less realistic: the former rising star at the Ballets Russes, Alicia Markova.

"He had seen her perform on many occasions during the Diaghilev season at the Princess Theatre," writes Kavanagh in *Secret Muses*, "marveling at her poise and serenity, her instinct for phrasing, and her weightless descents. He was also attracted to her likeness to Pavlova, both dancers possessing the same fragility, rapidity, delicacy and lightness—the illusion of moving without preparation."

Though Ashton was infatuated with the very idea of working with Markova, he assumed that she wouldn't be keen on performing in a "commercial" Playfair production and that her salary demands would be too high. He couldn't have been more wrong.

Fortunately, Ashton decided to ask Arnold Haskell for guidance, and the ballet critic unhesitatingly recommended Markova—but not because of her precarious financial situation. Haskell's advice was based strictly on artistic reasoning, as he rightly believed that Markova's tiny, frail physique was ideally suited to Ashton's own thin, rather delicate frame. (As a dancer, Ashton was known for his grace and elegance rather than his athletic strength or elevations.)

Soon after consulting with Haskell, the choreographer sent Markova a letter offering her the role. The unemployed dancer was surprised, pleased, and eternally grateful. Throughout her life, whenever interviewed about this unsettling period in her career, Markova unfailingly responded warmly, "I was rescued by Sir Frederick Ashton. Dear Fred."

An arrangement was made for the pair to meet at the Hammersmith Tube station prior to their initial business appointment with Playfair. Markova asked Ashton what he would be wearing so she could find him in the crowd. He answered simply, "I'll know you."

When they met, Ashton told her, "When Sir Nigel gave me leave to choose my own dancers, I immediately thought of you, hardly daring to hope that you would accept so humble an engagement after the Diaghileff Ballet. But here you are, and I hope we are going to enjoy a long and happy association."

The partnership couldn't have started off on a better note. Not only was Markova delighted to work with Ashton, but she proved to be an excellent business negotiator as well. At the pair's first meeting with Playfair, the nineteen-year-old ballerina secured a fee of £10 per week for each of them, a great sum in those days. As Markova told her biographer Maurice Leonard, "I'd only just met Fred but soon learnt he could never negotiate for himself. He said, 'Will you see about my money, too?' So I fixed it up."

It seems Ninette de Valois's lessons in self-sufficiency had paid off. Markova also worked money miracles with the tight-fisted Marie Rambert, from whom she later extracted top fees for herself and Ashton, much to his amazement. But even more valuable to the choreographer was Markova's ability to immediately grasp and execute his creative vision. As David Vaughan explained in his critical study of Ashton:

> It is not Ashton's habit to demonstrate the actual steps and movements in any detail. . . . Very often Ashton asks the dancers to show him something . . . the kind of step they would like to do. Or he will give the dancers some indication of the idea behind a dance and ask them to improvise on that idea—it may be vaguely expressed . . . what seems to take place is a kind of joint creative act whose success depends very much on the existence of a deep rapport between Ashton and his dancers.

That method of creating ballets brought Margot Fonteyn to tears when she and Ashton first collaborated, but it was second nature to Markova, who from childhood had worked with the most innovative choreographers of her time. Ashton found his first muse in Markova—even under less than ideal circumstances, as was the case with *Marriage à la Mode*.

For one thing, the two were forced to rehearse in a very confined space on the Lyric Theatre stage, which they needed to share with other actors preparing their roles. For another, Playfair's penchant for cumbersome costuming presented a real impediment to quick movements. *Marriage à la Mode* was a restoration period comedy, so the theatrical producer outfitted Markova in an enormous red wig and full-length pouffy gown in the manner of 17th-century actress Nell Gwyn.

Ashton couldn't abide the wig, which he felt completely overwhelmed his partner's face. Markova's solution was to style her own dark hair, being true to the period while adhering to Diaghilev's dictum of ballerinas looking their best with neat, unadorned heads. And with her newfound dressmaking skills, Markova was able to shorten the voluminous costume skirt to a more manageable length for dancing without having to ask for "management" approval.

Markova was deliriously happy to be working again. She even dusted off her Ballets Russes autograph book for Ashton and the cast to sign.

Haskell had been absolutely correct in his assessment of the pair's onstage compatibility, and praised the ballet in a *Dancing Times* review: "Like all true artists, Markova and Ashton have not sought to shine at the expense of the ensemble. Their work fits in and rounds off an entirely artistic production."

Other critics agreed, as the reviewer for *Punch* who found the addition of a ballet to the musical comedy a delicious surprise:

> . . . And when to these were added a slip of a girl with apparently all the equipment of a *prima ballerina,* and a youth apparently just out of his teens [Ashton was twenty-six] who also knew how to move with ease and grace and intention, to complete this very pretty commentary on the betrothal of Prince and Princess, I could scarcely believe my eyes. The danseuse was Miss ALICIA MARKOVA (English also, as later inquiry established), the dancer and choreographer, Mr. FREDERICK ASHTON. Young Madam, young Sir. I offer you my most sincere congratulations on a very fine—not merely a promising—piece of work.
>
> —*Punch,* 10/22/30

Marriage á la Mode was a hit, leading to an extended run at the Royalty Theatre later in the season. Though Ashton's ballet was but a segment in Playfair's theatrical production, Markova was singled out for a great deal of press attention, even if they sometimes got their facts all wrong.

The *Glasgow Evening News* ran a caption under Markova's photo identifying her as "Miss Alicia *Markover,* the famous dancer"—well, perhaps not *that* famous. And a write-up in London's *Reynolds Weekly Newspaper* was a veritable fountain of misinformation:

> **Only a Russian Name**
>
> A delightful dancer in Diaghileff's [it was Dryden's] "Marriage a la Mode," at the Royalty Theatre, ALICIA MARKOVA, aged sixteen [she was nineteen], is an English girl whose real name is Alicia Marke [Marks]. She first studied dancing at the age of nine as a cure for knock knees [Correct!].

But by the time *Marriage à la Mode* ended its lengthy run, the press had gotten Markova's name right—and more important for the young dancer—was clamoring in print to see more of the captivating ballerina. The fact that she was "as English as Sir Nigel's hat," as the *London Evening News* reported, was becoming a source of local pride.

In December 1930, the *Dancing Times* ran a large photo of the gracefully posed Ashton and Markova in costume for *Swan Lake*, captioned:

> Alicia Markova and Frederick Ashton who have been the principal dancers in Nigel Playfair's production "Marriage a la Mode," recently transferred to the Royalty Theatre. It is hoped that Miss Markova will be dancing in the Tchaikovsky ballet at the next "Camargo" performance when Mr. Ashton will be responsible for the choreography of Façade.

The editor of *Dancing Times* magazine was Philip Richardson, also co-founder of the Camargo Society, so he certainly was in a position to see that Markova finally became involved with the organization. With all the positive publicity she had received, Richardson knew the young British ballerina would be an asset, perhaps bringing in a new audience to Camargo events.

But even before Richardson petitioned the still-resistant Lopokova on Markova's behalf, Ninette de Valois had begun thinking of her former charge to star in a new work she was choreographing based on the mythological Greek tale of *Cephalus and Procris*. Markova was elated to finally be thought of as a classical ballerina once again, and found that she got on splendidly with de Valois as a choreographer as well as a good friend.

The production debuted at the Apollo Theatre on January 25, 1931, just two days after Anna Pavlova unexpectedly died. It was a great shock to everyone in the ballet world, and in honor of her memory, the evening's program began with a solemn tribute. As all the dancers bowed their heads in the wings, the curtain rose to reveal an empty stage. After a moment of silence, the orchestra played Camille Saint-Saëns' music for the Russian star's signature ballet, *The Dying Swan*.

Markova took the news of Pavlova's death very hard, especially as it came so close on the heels of Diaghilev's passing. Her only comfort was in knowing she had made the right decision in turning down Pavlova's offer to dance with her company.

As she told Maurice Leonard, "I had thought at the time that maybe I had been wrong to turn down her offer, but I had already had ballets created for me. . . . Had I gone with her my life would have been in turmoil once again and delayed everything that was to happen to me in British ballet."

Though *Cephalus & Procris* got mixed reviews, Markova was highly praised, referred to as "slim and piquant" by one reviewer and a "delightful dancer" by another. From near oblivion during the past year, Markova suddenly shined:

> **Sadler's Wells Ballet**
>
> Ballet is a new undertaking for this company: it has begun well, and will probably improve if zeal is any indication. There is much to learn, and the principal thing is to dance. Only one of the company does that at present, Miss Markova, as Procris; the rest are busy with gymnastics, and varied and ingenious as these are, they are not dancing.
>
> —*Observer,* 1/31/31

Philip Richardson's review for *Dancing Times* seemed to speak directly to friend Arnold Haskell, with whom he disagreed about Markova's emotive abilities:

> As Procris in this ballet, Alicia Markova appealed very much to me. I like the extraordinary looseness of her limbs and her clean, finished movements, and I can well understand how such a far-seeing man as Diaghileff expected a brilliant future for her.
>
> Some say she lacks expression [referring to Haskell]. Possibly she does in her face—but she imbues her gestures and movements with so much meaning that she seemed to me to be the ideal person for a ballet of this nature.

Most important for Markova, people who mattered in the world of ballet were talking about her again. Lopokova now found herself in the awkward position of having to publicly speak fondly of the young Jewish dancer she so disliked (apparently for no reason other than her religion), as in this write-up in a society column following a performance of *Procris and Cephalus*:

> Lopokova, who was there with her husband Mr. J. M. Keynes, was very appreciative of the exquisite dancing of Alicia Markova, whom one remembers not so long ago as the little girl in Diaghilev's production of the *Boutique Fantasque*. Lady Oxford and Asquith, who never misses a performance of ballet if she can help it, was agreeing with her that Markova has a perfect balance.
>
> —*Birmingham Post*, 1/27/31

Even more unsettling for Lopokova, her own position as a leading light in British ballet had changed rather dramatically after the Camargo's premiere program the previous October. Though still admired for her energy and enthusiasm—on opening night she brashly proclaimed it to be "the birth of British ballet"—the former Russian star was no longer an electric stage presence.

Never a classically elegant dancer, Lopokova's magic was in her ability to surprise, soar, and charm. As fellow dancer Lydia Sokolova described her old friend in their Ballets Russes days: "If anyone could dart about the stage as swiftly or neatly as she [Lopokova] did, nobody could ever imitate the witty way she used her head and shoulders, or the zest with which she threw herself into the action, as if every step was improvised on the spur of the moment and every situation was occurring for the first time."

Now, that was all a distant memory. Looking anything but spontaneous, Lopokova's movements seemed affected and forced. No longer in shape to fly across the stage, she attempted to hold an audience by being coy or comical, and at her age, it often fell flat.

In his new ballets, Ashton tried to put his treasured friend in the best possible light; but his choreographic style was full of fluidity and grace rather than the character-driven theatricality of the Massine-type roles that had first made Lydia a star. To Ashton, Lopokova was now to be considered "a friend and mentor, rather than a muse," writes Kavanagh.

De Valois agreed. A talented choreographer herself, she too saw her friend Lydia as out of date and past her prime. Contemporary ballets were no longer personality-driven, with each dancer allowed to create his or her own distinct character. The choreographer's specific concept needed to be respected, and while the creative process allowed for a dancer's input and suggestions during rehearsals, once set, there was no room for spontaneous outbursts that would distract from the production as a whole.

Unfortunately for Lopokova, the time had come for a dancer like Alicia Markova—one with boundless technique, yet able, and willing, to submerge herself completely into another's vision. How ironic that the thing Markova was most criticized for—lacking a strong emotional core—made her the perfect blank canvas for budding choreographers in this new era of dance.

With Ashton, de Valois, and Richardson firmly in her corner, Markova would now become a Camargo fixture. Lopokova had no choice but to acquiesce, though not happily. She would be furious when Ashton gave Markova one of her former roles, dancing the "Tango" in *Façade* for Rambert's Ballet Club in May 1931.

As Judith Mackrell writes in *Bloomsbury Ballerina*,

> [Lopokova] suspected that Markova might outclass her in the "Tango," and she was right. Markova's precision-perfect style set up a comic tension with the debutante's naivety, and as Lydia registered the praise for her rival, she felt that she had been somehow made redundant. She might be happy to parade her age when there were loud voices to deny it, she might be happy to play the senior ballerina when that position gave her power. Direct, unflattering comparisons with a rising star like Markova were a different and humiliating issue.

Ironically, Markova was concerned she wouldn't live up to *Lopokova's* portrayal. As she explained to Maurice Leonard:

> Fred came over and asked me, "What about the Tango?" and I said, "Yes and no."
>
> "That's a funny answer," he said. "What's yes and no?"
>
> "Yes," I said. "If I can do it my way but I couldn't copy Lopokova. I couldn't do what she did, she was wonderful, but

> entirely different to me. It's up to you," I said. "If you let me do it my way then I'll do it."
>
> Well, he let me.

A review of her performance in the *New Statesman* read: "Markova brought the house down. She is the white hope of English ballet."

As co-founder of the Camargo Society, Philip Richardson couldn't have been more excited that a London-born dancer was now a leading light in his efforts to promote British ballet. And he made sure audiences realized that fact—Markova's name notwithstanding—as in this letter to the editor published in a London paper:

> MARKOVA IS BRITISH—Mr. Richardson, editor of the "Dancing Times" and one of the founders of the Camargo Society, writes: "Last Sunday, under the heading 'All Ready for a British Ballet,' appeared five paragraphs which all lovers of British dancing will welcome. You convey, however, the impression that Markova—whom you rightly refer to as being nearly the best dancer of the day—is not British. She is absolutely British and her Russian name was adopted, I believe, when she entered the Diaghileff Company some years ago."
>
> —*Sunday Pictorial*, 12/13/31

Things would get worse for Lopokova when the 39-year-old danced side by side with Markova in *Rio Grande* later that same year. Lydia wasn't convinced the bawdy role of "Queen of the Port" was right for her, but she had "boxed herself into a moral corner with this project," writes Judith Mackrell.

Rio Grande was ill-conceived from the start. Based on a poem by British writer Sacheverell Sitwell and set to jazz-influenced music by Constant Lambert, the steamy theme of prostitutes and wanton sailors in a sleazy Southern seaport was hardly ideal Ashton fare. The choreographer knew the project would be challenging for him, but had agreed because he was looking forward to working with close chums Sitwell and Lambert.

But when Rambert offered Ashton a more suitable commission around the same time—and to star Markova—he tried to back out of Lambert's production. Lopokova exploded.

It was under those circumstances that she issued one of her infamous anti-Semitic tirades to her husband: "A Bomb-shell. Fred under influence of Mim is behaving disgracefully, he refuses to do Rio-Grande for the first programme. . . . I am disgusted yet I know he is a nice boy & it is a matter of influence, the Jewess [Rambert] dominates him at present."

Adoring Lydia as he did, and willing to overlook the outburst, Ashton agreed to turn Rambert down and go back to work on *Rio Grande*. But now it was Lopokova who was stuck. She realized the role of Queen of the Port didn't play to her strengths, but since she had bullied Ashton into working on the ballet, she couldn't very well walk out herself.

Never known as a sultry dancer, Lopokova enacted the tawdry Madam with a coy innocence that was completely at odds with the character and mood of the production. Ashton knew she had been miscast, but he too was stuck.

As one of the Camargo Society co-founders—in addition to a respected ballet critic—Arnold Haskell was embarrassed by Lopokova's overacting, as was Ninette de Valois. Both thought their friend Lydia should consider retiring.

Pouring salt on the wound was Markova, surprisingly good in her role as the sexy Port tart. Writes Mackrell, "it was gall and wormwood that shining on stage beside her [Lopokova] was Markova, dancing the Creole Girl in Rio with a sure grasp of the role's witty perversities."

It was interesting how several dance critics avoided trouncing the beloved Lopokova in the press by not reviewing her at all:

> **The Camargo Society**
>
> . . . Lydia Lopokova, as Queen of the Port, had for her sailor in attendance Walter Gore, whose solo to the accompaniment of Angus Morrison's pianoforte cadenza was a thing to remember. It placed him among the leading male dancers of the day. Another dancer who takes foremost rank is Alicia Markova, the youngest member of the Diaghileff troupe. . . .
>
> —*Musica Times*, January 1932

But others were not so reticent to face facts:

> . . . There is some brilliant dancing by Mr. Walter Gore and Mr. William Chappell as two sailors, and by Miss Markova as a Creole girl. Mme. Lopokova gave one the impression that she simply could not bring herself to take the part of "The Queen of the Port" seriously.
>
> —*Morning Post*, 11/30/31

The press also began to take note of Markova's versatility and how easily she transitioned from the Russian classics to contemporary works in the same program:

> Alicia Markova is beginning to show a genuine versatility, not merely in her dancing but in her interpretation of rôles. Here she was all softness with a beautiful flowing line, and a subtle spirit of mischief. Her solo is the finest of the ballet. Half an hour later, in Rio Grande, she is disporting herself as the most vulgar and abandoned of women. The Swan, Terpsichore and a woman of the port.—Brava Markova!
>
> —*New England Weekly*, 6/23/32

Rio Grande (also called *A Day in a Southern Port*) was hardly a hit. As Ashton scholar David Vaughan explains, "Ashton attempted to create a genuinely louche and erotic atmosphere. It was not quite what people expected to see in a ballet, especially danced by classic ballerinas like Lopokova and Markova, supported by a corps de ballet of well-brought up English girls, some of them barely out of their teens."

But it wasn't a disaster either. Some reviewers found the production bold and exciting, and no one's career—save for Lopokova's—was really damaged in any way.

John Maynard Keynes made every effort to sing his wife's praises publicly and in print, reminding them how Lopokova could still be a crowd-pleaser in classical Russian ballets at the Camargo. This led to an interesting "letter to the editor" from Nigel Playfair of the Lyric Theatre:

> **Ballet in England**
>
> Sir,—Professor J.M. Keynes is quite right publicly to praise the Camargo Society, in whose performance his wife plays

> so ravishing and graceful a part, for continuing the never-to-be-forgotten work of the late M. Diaghileff for ballet in this country.
>
> But if he will forgive my saying so, he seems to me a little over-economical in his distribution of favours. There is a link which he has forgotten, a link necessarily on its surface not up to the gold standard, but nevertheless strongly forged, which connects the work of Diaghileff and the Camargo Society's present performances. I allude to the three little seasons of ballet presented by Mrs. Ashley Dukes [Marie Rambert] at this theatre.
>
> To the forging of that link were devoted services of Frederick Ashton, Markova, William Chappell, Woizikowsky, and above all, that great artist Karsavina, whose name he omits from his review.
>
> —*Observer*, 6/26/32

One can only imagine how enraged Keynes must have been at being publicly reprimanded for overlooking the fine work of Marie Rambert's Ballet Club, as well as Ballets Russes star Tamara Karsavina, unquestionably a stronger classical prima ballerina than his wife.

Further upsetting the Keyneses was the public perception that the Jewish Markova represented the future of ballet, clearly relegating Lopokova to the past, as in this article from the high-society fashion magazine *British Vogue*:

> . . . it is as a comedienne rather than as a dancer that she [Lopokova] captures our delight.
>
> Who then is the present occupant of the throne? . . .
>
> We wait expectantly for the night when the new Lopokova, the new Karsavina, the new Pavlova, the new Genée will be recognized by a delirious house.
>
> For my own part, it seems to me that there is one dancer in our midst who, given full scope for effulgence, might become what in the sphere of sport is called a world-beater. Alicia Markova, if I am not mistaken, has not only a more

> finished technique but a more responsive temperament than any of her comrades. It is a temperament capable of the most exquisite emotional inflexions. She is the only dancer of the moment who holds me spellbound, and to be held spellbound, common though the phrase may be, is the rarest of experiences, and one for which all lovers of art offer up daily, if unspoken, prayers.
>
> —Herbert Farjeon, *Vogue*, 6/8/32

The *Birmingham Post* put one more nail in Lopokova's professional coffin with this preview of the upcoming Camargo Society performance schedule, presumably offered by Philip Richardson:

> One of the ideas of this season is to give younger ballerinas the fullest opportunities. Madame Markova, for example, whose reputation has been growing steadily among connoisseurs will be prominent.

Ashton was caught in the middle. While thrilled that Markova—in contemporary roles he himself created for her—was receiving such wonderful press, he also felt guilty that Lopokova's reputation seemed to be suffering for it. The choreographer needed both dancers in his life, for very different reasons. Markova remained his artistic muse, but Lopokova had become his biggest supporter. Ashton was never much of a fighter when it came to getting paid work (a reason Markova often negotiated his salary), and Lopokova was a staunch, well-connected ally in that regard, at times almost acting as his agent. The pair also enjoyed frequent gossipy lunch dates.

But one gossipy rumor that didn't please Lopokova at all, according to Julie Kavanagh, was the suggestion that Markova was in love with Ashton. Considering that it was common knowledge that Ashton's current crush at the time was male ballet dancer Walter Gore, it seemed much ado about nothing. It's not like Markova wasn't aware that Ashton was predominantly homosexual.

Additionally, writes Kavanagh, "Markova insists that at the time, she was too intent on her career to take an emotional relationship seriously, and yet she admits that she found Ashton very attractive—handsome, elegant and beautifully mannered. 'I loved him but not in a physical way. I was more like another sister.'"

Markova had felt the same way toward the bisexual Anton Dolin. When the two dancers formed a ballet company together in 1935, the press often asked if the pair planned to marry. The very idea made Markova laugh.

But apparently it amused dancer William Chappell to spread tales of Markova's unrequited love, and just the thought of her and Ashton getting together romantically required immediate action on Lopokova's part. To prevent such an undesirable alliance, she invited Ashton's mother to lunch to discuss more suitable female matches, if her bisexual son was so inclined.

Homosexuality was still frowned upon in British society at the time, and was, in fact, against the law. That led to many odd public couplings of homosexuals and lesbians, which indeed defined Ashton's first physical relationship with a woman—Barbara Ker-Seymer, a bisexual photographer and fellow "Bright Young Thing."

There would also be frequent liaisons between handsome gay men in the arts—like Ashton and Dolin—and extremely wealthy women who enjoyed being in their company. Alice Astor, whose parents drowned on the Titanic, leaving her a great fortune, not only introduced Ashton to society's rich and famous, but also showered him with gifts. He in turn was charming, flattering, and entertaining. Married at the time, Astor found the talented choreographer's bisexuality merely an attractive challenge—as Lopokova had with John Maynard Keynes—but Ashton's long-term romantic relationships were always with men.

As far as Lopokova was concerned, since she had managed to turn Maynard Keynes "straight," might not Markova do the same to Ashton? It was bad enough that the Jewess was his creative muse. A romantic liaison would have been intolerable.

The fact is, Markova and Ashton were opposites socially and would hardly have clicked as a romantic couple. She was quiet and politely reserved, he more outgoing and flighty. And Markova was all work, needing to be coaxed out of her shell, while Ashton needed to be reined in.

As Arnold Haskell wrote of the choreographer, "[Ashton] went to Marie Rambert, who made him into a competent and interesting dancer, discovered and encouraged his gift, and turned him from a love of the chic to more serious things."

That close relationship with Rambert also did not sit well with Lopokova. She would rail about it to Keynes, grumbling that Mim's Ballet Club was just too small-time for her precious Ashton. When de Valois expressed interest in hiring the young choreographer for her own company, Lopokova jumped at the chance to encourage Ashton to move on and—in her estimation—up.

Neither Markova nor Rambert were anything but warm and respectful toward Lopokova, who managed to hide her true feelings from them. Her hatred for Markova in particular was born purely out of vehement anti-Semitism. When Lopokova briefly worked with Markova at the Ballets Russes, little Alicia was a cloistered obedient child who rarely opened her mouth. She clearly had done nothing personally to the Russian star to provoke such lifelong enmity—except to be Jewish and Diaghilev's favorite.

And Lopokova never expressed jealousy at *other* dancers' talents, as Anton Dolin attested in his book *Ballet Go Round*: "I do not remember in all my career and with all the knowledge I possess of my fellow artists that I have known anyone who has shown more love and open-hearted appreciation for the work of other dancers than Lydia Lopokova has."—except, it seems, for Alicia Markova, the only openly Jewish dancer.

In the Israeli magazine *Dance Today,* author Ruth Eshel explains why there were so few Jewish ballet dancers in Europe at the time:

> Since the laws in pre-revolutionary Russia and in Eastern Europe did not allow many Jews to live in the big cities, only a small percentage of them lived in the cities where they could study or view the ballet. Dance companies did not accept Jewish dancers, except in a few cases of dancers who concealed their Jewish origins. As is well known, Anna Pavlova, whose mother was Jewish, concealed this fact.

The most insidious part of this prejudice is that Markova was completely unaware of Lopokova's plotting against her, calling the Russian ballerina "an adorable and witty dancer" in her 1986 memoir.

Unfortunately, the "adorable dancer" took every opportunity to undermine Markova's relationship with Ashton and London's ballet community. If Markova hadn't been such a superb dancer, it might have ended her career aspirations in London.

Ironically, Lopokova's attempt at sabotaging Markova was completely at odds with her clearly heartfelt goal of establishing a world-class British ballet company with friend Ninette de Valois—something that would have been impossible without Markova's exceptional technique, artistry, and loyalty.

By 1932, Colonel de Basil and René Blum had re-formed the Ballets Russes and began touring England. British ballet fans were thrilled, and the theaters were packed. That made things even more difficult for de Valois, whose nascent company just couldn't compete. She would have been completely lost had Markova accepted de Basil's offer to join the Russian company rather than remain with de Valois and Rambert.

In light of the formidable Russian competition, de Valois and Lopokova put their heads together to plan a course of action that might keep British ballet afloat, as Judith Mackrell reports:

> [Lopokova] considered that the majority of her [de Valois's] company were still "puddings" by comparison with the Russians. She even had doubts about de Valois's new protégée, Margot Fonteyn, despite the beauty of her slanted dark eyes, elegant limbs and guileless smile. Whilst Lydia conceded rather viciously that "Fontaine [*sic*] has more possibilities than Markova as nature endowed her without a hookey nose and with strict unwobbly knees," she was not yet convinced that the sixteen-year-old was ballerina material.

Lopokova's stance was always anyone but Markova. Luckily, de Valois didn't share that opinion, realizing that the future of British ballet most surely rested on the tiny shoulders of the young, extraordinarily gifted dancer. In the near future, de Valois would give Markova the opportunity to be the first British-born ballerina to dance the full-length *Giselle*.

Mr. and Mrs. Keynes were in the audience on opening night in 1934. Lopokova watched the curtain rise, secretly hoping the newly anointed Giselle wouldn't compare with the exquisite Russian Olga Spessivtseva, who had taught Markova the role. The immature British dancer was too cold and reserved to pull it off, she thought.

But following Markova's unquestioned triumph that night, Lopokova quickly changed her tune—at least publicly—in order to get her name in the press and save face with friends, something she would do often in the future:

> Among the many friends who thronged Markova's dressing room after her brilliant interpretation of the name part in "Giselle" at the Sadler's Wells Theatre on Tuesday night, January 23rd, the most enthusiastic was Lydia Lopokova, who with her husband, Professor Maynard Keynes, had come specially to see this famous role danced for the first time by a British ballerina. A crowded audience gave Markova a big ovation at the end of the performance, for this exacting ballet had provided her with the biggest success of her career.
>
> —*Bayswater Chronicle*, January 1934

Giselle would indeed catapult Markova to worldwide fame, but that was several years off. The period from 1931 to 1934 would witness the true birth of British ballet, and much to Lopokova's dismay, Markova, and her new relationship with Frederick Ashton, would play enormous roles.

The professional partnership of Alicia Markova and Frederick Ashton was not unlike the pairing of Fred Astaire and Ginger Rogers, of whom Katharine Hepburn once said, "He gives her class. She gives him sex." But in the case of the two ballet dancers, the gender roles were reversed. Ashton brought out a previously unseen sense of humor and sensuality in Markova, and she in turn gave him the benefit of her invaluable experience with the most brilliant classical ballet teachers and innovative choreographers of their time.

For Ashton, "Working with Markova was an education in itself," writes Kavanagh. "Theirs was a genuine collaboration." As Markova told the author: "Fred was able to use me. I'd say, 'I don't think you can have that step.' 'Why not?' 'Well, because Massine or Balanchine has already done it.'"

"When I first worked with her I was rather alarmed by the fact that she had this kind of heritage behind her," Ashton admitted in an interview with Clement Crisp. "That she might consider me inadequate by comparison because she'd already worked with Massine and Balanchine and Nijinska and anybody who was there. . . . She was very helpful indeed, and enjoyable. It was very satisfactory after one had worked, to see the result and how she paid you back with it."

Ashton also benefited from Markova's mastery of anticipating music as she danced, a skill perfected under Igor Stravinsky's tutelage.

As dance writer Edwin Denby explained in the collection of his writing edited by Robert Confield, "Markova is a genius of phrasing, that signal aspect of the dancer's musical sense by which she plays with the relationship of the steps to the music and thus creates tension, surprise, and drama. . . . [She has a] remarkable freedom in attacking her steps a hair's breath before or after the beat, a freedom in which she shows a perfect musical instinct."

Ashton could neither read a score, nor play any musical instrument. As Ninette de Valois wrote of him, "When young, his weakness lay in a difficulty in keeping time with the music—and the clock. Eagerness and intense nervous energy (his natural reaction to movement) made him deaf to sound; one would hold him grimly and at the same time experience something of the trouble encountered by anyone involved in the capture of a wild Dartmoor pony."

Markova and Ashton had both studied under the Russian classicist Nikolai Legat. As Markova described the experience: "Legat, another great ballet master, was very different. He never left the piano while he taught you. He sat the whole time and played the piano himself. So he'd give you the combination, call it out, and then to whatever combination it was, he always composed the music to fit. So that was marvelous, but it wasn't too good for one musically, because often, you have to learn how to go over music, or through it and all kinds of things to syncopate it."

Ashton later learned to "familiarize himself thoroughly with the music," wrote David Vaughan, and then rely "on the collaboration of the arranger and/or rehearsal pianist to help him with such technical analysis as may be necessary, such as breaking the music down into counts for the dancers."

Markova never needed counts, an asset in Ashton's early choreographic efforts, as she had an immediate understanding of scores as few other dancers did, easily committing lengthy compositions to memory. "As far as I can remember—from two years of age—music has been my passion," Markova affirmed. "I couldn't imagine my life without music."

Ashton was in awe: "She was extremely musical and had such a large span of movement. She could do anything."

Their partnership really took off when Ashton persuaded Marie Rambert to hire Markova. "After we appeared in the *Marriage a la Mode*, I persuaded Rambert to take her at the Ballet Club, which was then forming," the choreographer remembered. "Rambert was rather reluctant to do this because she wanted to push her own girls, but I insisted. And I think to a very good advantage because she set a very high standard and she gave an example for all the girls to aim at."

Mim's reluctance had nothing to do with her personal feelings about Markova, whom she had admired even as a little girl:

> I first saw her dance when she was about twelve. She didn't know me at the time. It was at the pupils' matinee of Astafieva at the Albert Hall. She was described on the program in every number she danced as "Alicia Markova—The Miniature Pavlova," and it was true.
>
> Next, I saw her, she was already in service to Diaghilev. I was watching a rehearsal. She was rehearsing Stravinsky's Nightingale. And I was watching the rehearsal sitting between Diaghilev and Picasso. And the two of them were exchanging enthusiastic remarks all the time about her, and Diaghilev predicted greatness for her. And you know, the last interview he gave to the press before he died, he said, "Watch my little English girl." Wasn't he right?

While Rambert couldn't take credit for discovering Markova—as she could with Ashton as a choreographer—she certainly gave her the platform, albeit a tiny one, to become the first ballet star of a British company.

"The stage at the Mercury Theatre. It was very small," explained Rambert, "but she [Markova] turned it to her advantage. She developed a very effortless technique. You could stand quite close to her. You didn't hear her breathe. You didn't hear her move a step. She just floated on a cloud. It was really wonderful."

British dance writer Eric Johns found the Mercury "as intimate as dancing in a cabaret. She [Markova] could have shaken hands with people sitting in the front row."

But he too thought Rambert's theatre gave Markova the ideal training ground. "At once she realized any attempt to create illusion would be shattered unless she concealed all the strain and effort of dancing from her audience. She succeeded; that is why her ethereal roles were so utterly convincing."

That was especially true later on when Markova danced *Giselle*. As she told Marie Rambert, mastering the art of breathing control at the Mercury was invaluable in creating the disembodied spirit in the ballet's second act.

In later years, fellow dancers would also comment on Markova's never making a sound when she landed a jump and retaining an almost supernatural composure before, during, and after performances. "We would come offstage after we danced, hot, sweaty and breathless, and Alicia would be standing there waiting for her entrance, cool and serene," British ballerina Beryl Grey told Maurice Leonard. "She would then go on, execute the most intricate steps and bring the house to its feet, and then make her exit as coolly as she had gone on, not a hair out of place. I don't know how she did it."

Rambert and her playwright/theater producer husband Ashley Dukes were responsible for constructing the modest Mercury Theatre, an auditorium with just 150 seats. Since ballet was almost a religious experience for Rambert, it was only fitting that the building had been a former church vestry, as she explained in her autobiography:

> In 1927, Ashley bought the freehold of a large church hall in Notting Hill Gate. He saw at once that if the hall were divided in two it could provide not only a studio of my own for my

> rapidly growing school, but also a small theatre for both of us. When the theatre came to be built, he had the excellent idea of adding a dimension to the very small stage, with its proscenium opening of no more than eighteen feet, by putting an apron stage around part of the front and building a staircase in the back.

Most memorable to the dancers, however, was the Lilliputian-sized dressing room, so narrow, it required them to get ready all in a single line.

Years later, Markova was asked about her experience in the tight quarters of the Mercury after having performed in Europe's grandest theaters with the Ballets Russes:

> But don't you think that is life, what makes it very interesting? It never bothered me. The Mercury was like a little, well it was like a little corridor. And we all had to sit side by side. I remember, Diney—Diana Gould—of course Yehudi's wife today [famous violinist/composer Yehudi Menuhin]—she was next to me, and we used to sit, and sometimes, if they were doing a work on stage and doing the lighting, we had to have the lights off in the dressing room.
>
> So we would sit with a nightlight of a candle in the room, and if we had to get around out, often we used to have to go out through the window out into the street. Can you imagine anybody passing, and suddenly dancers seemed to be falling out of the sky?
>
> Ashton, after all, Sir Fred, started all his choreography there. He did wonderful works for us, and for me especially. And Antony Tudor also. It was really the birth of British ballet, wasn't it? I suppose it was.
>
> It was Mim, as we called her, Marie Rambert, at the Ballet Club every Sunday evening. She offered for the Sunday 6 and 6 pence. I'm afraid I had to decline because 6 and 6 just covered the price of my ballet shoes for the evening. And we were always terribly late, being a Sunday evening, and I missed the last bus home, which meant I had to have a taxi. And I think a taxi was 4 and 6 pence. So I told her I couldn't do the

> performance for less than 10 and 6 pence. Fred Ashton and myself had half a guinea—the top salaries.
>
> No one ever made a fortune in the ballet in those days. In those days, you had to make the decision whether you were going to stay with your art—I mean, today people don't talk like that—or whether you became commercial. And so I'm afraid, with me, I had lots of commercial offers, but it was to stay with the ballet and the dance that interested me. And also there was another reason. Because with Dame Ninette and Mim Rambert, we were trying to get ballet roots put down in this country.

In the context of that interview, Markova is defining "commercial work" as the many lucrative offers she received from music halls, West End theaters, and Hollywood film studios for full-time engagements throughout the 1930s, all of which she turned down in favor of her pioneering efforts to establish British ballet. (Apparently her burgeoning fame now outweighed any former aspersions cast on her ethnic looks.) But she and Ashton did continue to take on part-time commercial dance engagements in London, such as working for Sir Nigel Playfair, which had first brought them together. They had no choice, as they could never have supported themselves, let alone their mothers, on their "break-even" salaries.

"I had to live and I always had a great appetite," Markova later reminisced, laughing. "I love my food, so I was doing commercial work as well."

Ashton and Markova were careful, however, to only select jobs that wouldn't interfere with their more important—though intermittent—performance schedules for the Ballet Club, Camargo Society, and Ninette de Valois's Vic-Wells company at the Sadler's Wells Theatre.

"Nobody realizes what the situation was like then," de Valois explained years later. "It evolved very slowly. In 1931, we had a matinee about once a month, then gradually once or twice a week. It evolved slowly."

While Markova was turning down offers to appear *in* the movies, she gladly accepted an offer to appear *at* the movies. As she reminisced with Clement Crisp:

> One day, Fred, when I got to rehearsal, he said to me he'd had a phone call or something from the people at the Regal Cinema, Marble Arch—these American people who were over in London to try and stage a fantastic stage show like they had at the Roxy and Radio City in New York, which was three shows a day.
>
> And they'd got on to know if Fred would choreograph for them. So he suddenly said to me, how about you . . . would you like to dance there? So I said, well that's up to you. It depends what it will be and I'll leave it to you to see what they wish and whether it's possible.
>
> So anyway, the outcome of that meeting, Fred was contracted to choreograph "The Dance of the Hours" and I appeared in it with William Chappell. I think we were there for three weeks, and that was supposed to be it.

That performance at the Regal Cinema—much like the Rockettes shows at the Radio City Music Hall—took place three times a day between film showings. The pay was exorbitant for the times, £20 a week for Markova, and would subsidize her and Ashton's more serious creative collaborations for the budding British ballet community. It would be quite the culture shock, however.

Everything about the production was on a grand scale, especially when compared to the tiny, small-budgeted Mercury Theatre. The printed programs said it all: a single sheet of bright yellow paper folded in half at the Ballet Club, and a beautiful, oversized booklet bound with gold cord at the cinema. "The Regal" was elegantly embossed in scripted gold lettering on the handbill's shiny metallic jade-green cover, with the numerous inside pages filled with movie star photos, film information, and revenue-producing advertisements.

Smack dab in the middle was the program listing that "regally" spelled out the schedule of alternating film and live entertainments, from the REGAL NEWS and THE REGAL ORGAN playing to THE REGAL BALLET and REGAL FILM ATTRACTIONS.

Sandwiched between a performance of The Regal Symphony Orchestra and the Hollywood film *Illicit*—starring Barbara Stanwyck and Joan Blondell—Alicia Markova and William Chappell were to appear live on stage in *The Dance of the Hours*. The production was quite an extravaganza with the two leads amply surrounded by a large—though rather inexperienced—*corps de ballet*. The audience was wowed nonetheless, captivated by the two stars, elaborate sets, and fanciful costumes.

As in the best of the Ziegfeld Follies, Markova made her entrance gracefully perched on a "sky-high" crescent moon slowly lowered to the stage for her opening *pas de deux* with Chappell. The spotlights were so blinding, however, that the two dancers often couldn't find each other in the glare. But they figured it out in time and the show was a great success. (The live ballets at The Regal were reviewed in the press along with the films.)

"I just got an impression of being dazzled at what she was doing," Arnold Haskell remembered years later. "It was sandwiched between the selling of ice-creams and the film and all that, and you couldn't get into a ballet atmosphere, but you could admire the virtuosity, and it was a show of virtuosity for a popular public." In many ways, it could not have been a more effective tool for helping ballet trickle through all levels of society in England for the first time.

When The Regal invited Markova back as a regular, she made the condition that Ashton stay on as choreographer, feeling indebted to him for having gotten her the lucrative job in the first place. They were both very grateful for the money, but their working lives became extremely complicated, especially for the star ballerina.

The Cinema production numbers changed every three weeks, which meant Markova would be performing three shows a day in one ballet, while rehearsing the next one. It took a toll physically, especially in Ashton's *Foxhunting Ballet*, where Markova played the titled Fox "in all-over brown leotard, large bushy tail, a bonnet with little ears and paw-like gloves."

"I had to flee the pack by spinning as fast as possible across the stage, and this—interspersed with acrobatic tricks and falls on to one knee—meant within a couple of performances I was covered with bruises."

Markova's sister Doris served as her backstage dresser at the time. As she recalled:

> At the end of each show, Alicia appeared on the stage dressed as a fox in a hunting scene and sharing the stage with a pack of real foxhounds. She was padded to protect her from the climax of the scene, which was the kill.
>
> But when she came back to the dressing room and took off her costume, she was always black and blue with quite a few scratches. So I used to keep rushing down to the chemist for fresh supplies of liniment and disinfectant. And while the film was running in the cinema, I had to help Alicia with her first-aid, and before her performance at the next show, which was with real ballet dancers.

Doris's reference to "real" ballet dancers referred to Markova's having to leave the cinema after her 6:00 and 9:00 P.M. daily shows for her more "high-brow" performances at Marie Rambert's Ballet Club and Ninette de Valois's Vic-Wells company (later renamed Sadler's Wells, and eventually The Royal Ballet). It was extremely complicated, as Markova explained:

> Dame Ninette and Lilian Baylis were wonderful the way they cooperated. I used to take a taxi to Marble Arch to Sadler's Wells Theatre where they would let me dance the opening ballet, *Swan Lake*, Act 2.
>
> Then I would take the taxi back to The Regal to do my nine o'clock show, and after I finished that, I used to take the taxi then to go to the Ballet Club at Notting Hill Gate and usually I used to do Façade to close the evening, so that way I could accomplish all three.
>
> And that I did, oh, I think I did that for a couple of months.

Ashton was enormously impressed that Markova could charm the masses in the afternoon, and be equally affecting for the more discerning Ballet Club audience at night. "She was always successful in what she did. Always made an impact," Ashton recalled in a 1981 interview with Clement Crisp. Both conceded that this was in spite of Markova's not being "a fashionably pretty girl of the times," as Crisp put it.

Dancer/choreographer Agnes de Mille, who was a student at the Ballet Club when Markova was appearing in Ashton's ballets, was also amazed that a ballerina with such "odd" looks could be such a hypnotic performer. In one of her many memoirs, de Mille recalls watching a rehearsal of Ashton's ballet *Mercury*:

> One morning after class I heard music in the auditorium and stepped in. There were four or five of Mim's "lumpy, woolly" girls on the floor of the stage undulating, lifting, settling arms and legs. "It is the Adriatic," said Mim. "It is *Mercure* by Ashton." And by God, it was the Adriatic. "Watch," said Mim. "Venus will rise from the sea." And Venus did, in a yard-square space.

De Mille would never forget what she saw. There was no question Markova was the best and most experienced dancer at the Ballet Club, but that someone so painfully thin and fragile-looking could be so unforgettably magnetic was quite startling.

> Venus was Alicia Markova, the stringiest girl I ever saw, a darling little skeleton, with the great eyes of a moth at the top, and a butterfly blur at the bottom where normally feet would be, and in between shocks and flashes of electricity. When she paused there was the most beautifully surprising line I had ever looked at.
>
> She was twenty, although she looked much older because she was so thin. She didn't look any age when she moved. She became a delicate natural force. Ashton, who was lounging about, gave clipped instructions in his lazy voice.
>
> "Mim," I said, "this is extraordinary!"

Markova's own insecurity about her unconventional looks added to her appreciation of her newfound popularity at the Regal Cinema. She had been deemed not pretty enough for commercial music hall shows when she needed work after Diaghilev died; and that not only hurt her feelings, but also denied her an avenue to earn a living. Now she was in great demand, as big a draw to the movie house as the famous film stars on celluloid.

While dancer William Chappell called their cinema experience together completely "humiliating," as compared to performing in a "proper" theater with a trained ballet company, Markova didn't feel that way. It was well-paid work and introduced a whole new audience to ballet. The fact that cultured bluebloods thought those movie-house performances déclassé didn't bother her a bit.

It was much like photographers Richard Avedon and Irving Penn, who "drew a distinction between the pictures they took for fashion magazines and their art photography," as Judith Thurman pointed out in *The New Yorker*. "Fashion paid the bills, but they never looked down on it." And regularly appearing in the pages of *Vogue* and *Harper's Bazaar* made those photographers quite famous.

Markova also initially reached a much wider audience with her commercial work, which in turn helped popularize her purely artistic endeavors. Playing a scampering fox helped humanize the idea of ballet—and Markova—to many cinemagoers, who found her quite fun to watch and not at all elitist.

Partnering with Ashton, Markova would be equally amusing in his contemporary ballets, with the choreographer bringing out her sense of humor on stage while taking advantage of her phenomenal technique.

"I enjoy comedy," Markova told Maurice Leonard. "I can make an audience laugh as easily as I can make them cry. Ashton knew that but the 'Polka' was a shock to the audience. It was the first ballet striptease."

"I always look back with particular pleasure upon *Façade*," Ashton reminisced to his biographers Dominic and Gilbert. "[I] had a marvelous cast for it and it was the first ballet that I'd done bringing humour into a piece that was classically based. I still do regard it as a rather particular landmark in my work."

Façade's lead role was even more startling when Markova was the one performing it. "I was really thought of as a classical dancer," she explained. "And when I walked out for that first performance in those cotton bloomers with a boater hat—and walked out of my skirt!—there was such a gasp. Everyone thought I'd lost my skirt. They couldn't realize it was intended, and of course the type of polka—they expected me to do a classical polka on point. I had such a varied repertoire in those days."

ABOVE: Alicia Markova, 18, at Diaghilev's Ballets Russes.

LEFT: Anna Pavlova with her pet swan at Ivy House.

OPPOSITE: Anna Pavlova in her signature role, The Dying Swan, 1917.

ABOVE: Markova as Odette in *Swan Lake*, 1935.

ABOVE: Lilian Alicia Marks at 9 months with her father, grandfather, and great-grandfather, August 1911.

LEFT: "Conducting" a band concert at 18 months in her neighborhood park.

OPPOSITE TOP: On her second birthday, with mother Eileen.

OPPOSITE BOTTOM: Remedial dance lessons to cure wobbly, weak legs turned the 8-year-old, left, into the Thorne Academy's littlest prodigy.

ABOVE: A lively studio rehearsal with Princess Astafieva, far right, little Alicia in the middle (leg outstretched), and the ever-watchful governess Guggy sitting on the piano bench, 1922.

OPPOSITE TOP: Even at age 10, "The Child Pavlova" showed her flair for the dramatic.

OPPOSITE BOTTOM: The 9-year-old made quite an impression in her Thorne Academy *Arabian Nights* solo, 1920.

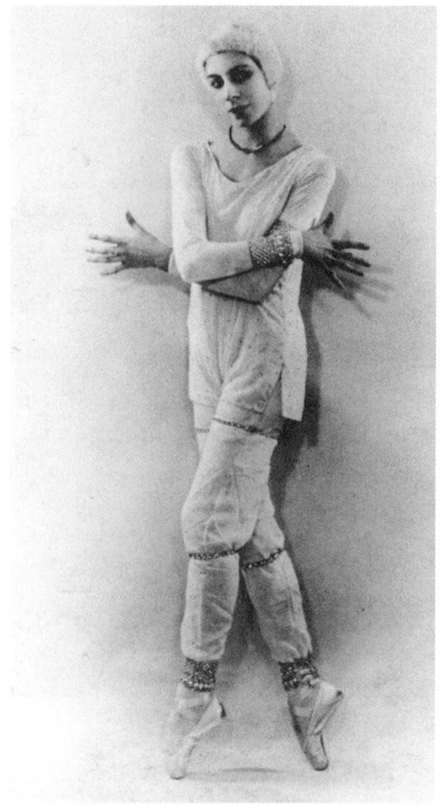

OPPOSITE: Alicia, age 13, walks with her first fashion role model, her mother. Coco Chanel would be her second.

TOP LEFT: As Papillon in a 1926 Ballets Russes production of *Carnaval*. Markova partnered with her famous teacher Nikolai Legat on stage.

BOTTOM LEFT: Adored by Sergei Diaghilev, the 14-year-old was whisked to sunny Monte Carlo in 1925, becoming the youngest-ever member of the Ballet Russes.

ABOVE: Markova starred in Balanchine's first work for the Ballets Russes, *Le Chant du Rossignol*. Henri Matisse designed her daring second-skin costume, but was asked to cover it up, as seen here, for more provincial London audiences in 1927.

TOP LEFT: After watching two ballerinas slip and fall on the slick black floor cloth for *La Chatte* (1928), Markova cleverly rubberized her ballet shoes for performances of Balanchine's difficult "Cat" choreography. TOP RIGHT: A fetching, high-hatted Markova floored audiences with her mastery of Léonide Massine's complicated choreography for *Cimarosiana*, 1927. BOTTOM: A more grown-up Markova (far left, next to her mother) poses with the Ballets Russes in Edinburgh, 1928. Dancers Alexandra Danilova and Serge Lifar are the second pair in from the right, with George Balanchine on the far right.

By 18, Markova fulfilled Sergei Diaghilev's dreams for her. Next season, the impresario promised, he would make her a true Ballets Russes star.

OPPOSITE TOP LEFT: In *Les Masques* (1933), Ashton created a tour-de-force role for Markova, with magnificent sets and costumes by Sophie Fedorovitch. OPPOSITE BOTTOM LEFT: Markova as a Creole prostitute (with dancer William Chappell) in Ashton's controversial *A Day in a Southern Port* (1931). OPPOSITE RIGHT: Markova was Frederick Ashton's first muse, here in *Façade* (1931), where the "classical" ballerina shocked audiences by stepping out of her skirt on stage. ABOVE: Markova's exquisite delicacy and vaporous stage presence made her the quintessential *Giselle*, a role she first performed in London on January 1, 1934.

OPPOSITE TOP LEFT: Ballet great Olga Spessivtseva taught Markova to drench her long hair following *Giselle's* Act I Mad Scene for the quick transformation into a ghostly spirit in Act II. OPPOSITE TOP RIGHT: Markova's precise preparation for each ballet was legendary, as was her immaculately laid-out dressing table. OPPOSITE BOTTOM: Markova was a favorite subject of artists throughout her career, here posing as Giselle for British painter Edward Seago (1938). ABOVE: When Markova's costume for Massine's Seventh Symphony arrived incomplete, designer Christian Bérard quickly created a bodice from her evening scarf and a headdress with paper, eyebrow pencil, and scissors (Ballet Russe de Monte Carlo, 1938).

TOP: Alicia Markova was America's first-ever Sugar Plum Fairy when *The Nutcracker* was revived by the Ballet Russe de Monte Carlo in 1939. BOTTOM: Massine's highly praised Rouge et Noir (1939) would give Markova one of her greatest modern roles. Henri Matisse drew the outlines of the flame appliqués directly on her body. *Both photos Copyright © Maurice Seymour, courtesy Ron Seymour Photography, Chicago.*

The press delighted in her performance, as in this review of *Façade*:

> It was danced by Miss Alicia Markova (who, by the way, is English, in spite of her Russian sounding name) and the Rambert Company. Shouts of laughter greeted the Yodeling episode [yes, Markova yodeled] and the Polka of Alicia Markova and the Tango danced by her and Frederick Ashton were particularly charming.
>
> —*Queen Charlottes Quarterly*, January 1932

"She is such an exquisite dancer," wrote another reviewer, "that one fears to miss a single one of her movements."

Ashton explained Markova's special gifts in that role to Clement Crisp.

> ASHTON: [Façade] was half based on classical dancing and half based on jazz dancing at the time. And she was able to combine this tremendous role. She had very strong rhythm for modern rhythm in those days.
>
> CRISP: You finished off with one diabolical step, which was the double tour en l'air.
>
> ASHTON: Yes, because she could do that you see—and which was supposedly reserved for males—but she was able to do it.
>
> CRISP: One doesn't see it anymore.
>
> ASHTON: No, because nobody can do it properly, quite. And so she had a very strong technique with a lot of the highlights of what she could do, people can't do now.
>
> . . . She was very helpful. She contributed a lot to me, sometimes even in the way of steps because she of course by then had trained with Cecchetti and everybody else. And she was also extremely musical and she also had a large span of movement.
>
> She could do anything really. I mean you know she could be witty, like Polka in Façade and she could be touching. She could do all these things.

Marie Rambert agreed: "Her most unusual role for the Club was without a doubt *La Goulue,* the can-can dancer of the *Folies Bergère.* She showed the most tremendous sense of humor and had the audience rocking with laughter. I think this helped very considerably in establishing her not only as a great ballerina, but as a great personality of the ballet."

Based on a Manet artwork in the National Gallery, *Bar Aux Folies-Bergere* was like the painting brought to life, with choreography by Ninette de Valois and striking set by William Chappell, who would become a successful stage and costume designer after his dance career had waned. Ballet Club performer Diana Gould was at first shocked when Rambert "cast Alicia as the chief lady of easy virtue—La Goulue." Many shared Gould's thoughts at the time:

> How would this limpid-pure, this creature of crystal and filigree, this delicate ice-maiden deal with anything so foreign to her whole quality and nature? How indeed? The answer is: gloriously. And with divine insolence that, catching everybody off-guard, floored them utterly. . . .
>
> This distant nymph was suddenly metamorphosed into a very tangible tart whose every glance was a beckon and whose couch was certainly not in the clouds. How she reveled in it, and with what wicked enjoyment she would catch my eye as I, one of her accompanying ladies, swung a wicked hip alongside her.
>
> . . . And what a lovely comedienne she was to play with—sensitive, responsive and always ready to improvise.

The *New Statesman* reviewer wrote, "Markova was as near perfection in this role as one could wish; her costume was delightful and she mimed and danced with a lightness and piquancy of allure which probably surpassed that of any can-can dancer."

Frederick Ashton also performed in the ballet, but was clearly less well known as a dancer than a choreographer. His only mention in one review was: "Cedric [*sic*] Ashton is the head waiter."

While a work by artist Édouard Manet had sparked Ninette de Valois's imagination, it was the intimate ballet scenes of Edgar Degas that caught Ashton's eye. He too would bring a painting to life in the splendid *Foyer de danse* set in a ballet school.

Ashton himself portrayed the imperious dance instructor (poking a bit of fun at Massine and Cecchetti in the part), with Markova as his self-obsessed prima ballerina *L'Étoile.* Markova's entrance in the ballet takes place when class is already in session. (Cecchetti would have thrown his cane at her!) Wearing an ostrich-feather hat and diamond bracelets, Markova's character is oblivious of the time and her tardiness, and more concerned with admiring her finery in the studio's expansive mirrored wall.

It was one of the dancer's favorite roles, as she fondly recalled in *Markova Remembers*:

> The joke was that Fred should set me diabolically difficult steps, but that I should be so fascinated with my reflection in the mirror that I would appear to pay only the slightest attention, while actually performing them with nonchalant ease. One variation ended with me so carried away with my own skill that I finished with my back to the audience; then, realizing that I was staring at myself, I registered, "That's strange!" and turned to bow sweetly to the public. It was great fun—and the Mercury audiences—loved it.

"I think her technical ability fascinated me," Ashton recalled of that time. "You see, all the dancers I'd worked with really didn't have much technique, and she had technique, and she had tremendous elegance and tremendous chic, and she was very exquisite.

"She was very small and very well proportioned. Also she was a tremendously hard worker and somehow, it was very nice to explore that."

The press enjoyed the ballet as much as the stars.

> [Foyer de dance] never degenerates into burlesque. Led by Alicia Markova, absurdly and appropriately sparkling as the star, and by the choreographer, who was also the ballet master, the company gave an excellent performance, and so, because it became a ballet which lacked neither imagination, execution nor production, the absence of which makes so many native

> ballets tawdry, "Foyer de Danse" could fittingly have taken its place in the Russian repertory.
>
> —*Manchester Guardian*, 10/10/32

Unbeknownst to that reviewer—and the audiences at the small Mercury Theatre—were the comical goings-on behind the scenes of *Foyer de danse*. In order to incorporate the backstage staircase into the set, the dancers were forced to enter and exit by way of a window. "It must have been something of a surprise for the passers-by in Notting Hill Gate to find fully costumed dancers dropping at their feet," joked Markova.

High Yellow gave Markova another opportunity to prove her willingness to master anything new, as she explained many years later to an audience of ballet students:

> I again was fortunate to work with all the—in my time—contemporary choreographers. Anybody who wanted to experiment, I was there, and did. Two weeks ago, maybe you noticed in the papers, Buddy Bradley died. In 1932 or '33 we had the Camargo season in London and Ashton had seen Buddy Bradley's work. He was a black dancer/director, the number one, who choreographed for all the great tap dancers and theater dancers of that time. And Ashton suddenly was interested in what he was doing and Buddy was very interested in the ballet.
>
> He had seen the beginnings of the Vic Wells. And for the Camargo season, they suddenly decided that they would combine, they would collaborate and do a ballet together. So I came into that.
>
> I had six weeks private lessons with Buddy. I used to stay over in the evening, under Sir Fred's direction, to learn how to dance . . . all the snake hips, the rhythms, everything, which I did. Then eventually they got together and did a ballet called *High Yellow*. . . .
>
> Bradley adored the same things we did, dance and the arts.

Working on the ballet was such a great learning experience for Ashton that he generously insisted Buddy Bradley be listed as the official choreographer in the program, as "*assisted* by Frederick Ashton." "[*High Yellow*] was very advanced in its day because it was really the first jazz ballet that was ever done," said Ashton. He especially enjoyed the opportunity to finally use the American jazz movements that first caught his eye in Paris when Sophie Fedorovitch took him to see *La Revue Negre* with Josephine Baker.

It was said that Ashton's "terror of boring people" accounted for the widely diverse themes of his ballets for Markova. A reviewer for *The Illustrated London News* decreed that "The dances derived by Frederick Ashton are so varied, ingenious and delightful that one overlooks the absence of a choreographic plot. From the technical point of view, the dancing was astonishing . . . maintaining the high standard set by Alicia Markova, the *première danseuse*."

Equally amazing, considering the limited budget and tiny Mercury stage, the sets and costumes were often quite spectacular. Vanessa Bell created the colorful Caribbean backdrops for *High Yellow*, with William Chappell's costumes so fanciful that Markova and Ashton were photographed wearing them for the fashion pages of *Harper's Bazaar*.

Ashton's great friend Sophie Fedorovitch was also frequently called upon to work her special design magic, and even Markova pitched in when it came to sewing costumes.

Marie Rambert was most appreciative: "Another lesson she [Markova] learned at the Club was to perfect her dressmaking. We could only afford to pay her 10 & 6 pence for her performance on a Sunday night. Remember, that was thirty years ago! And the dancers had to make many of their own costumes. Alicia was perfect at that and always looked wonderful."

Markova, Ashton, and Chappell had a grand time collaborating on the costume, makeup, and set designs for the exotic *La Péri*, which the choreographer created in 1931 for the Ballet Club's opening night. It started with Ashton walking into the studio one day, looking at Markova, and announcing, "*La Péri*, Persian, come along, we're going to the exhibition."

The "exhibition" was an enormously popular show of Persian Art at Burlington House (The Royal Academy) in London, with Ashton using it as a creative springboard, much as Diaghilev had done with the Egyptian mania of his time. Ashton, Markova, and Chappell spent many hours studying the Oriental paintings, furnishings, and *objet d'arts* for inspiration.

"Fred, Billy Chappell—also a Rambert dancer—and I were able to glean ideas about make-up, as well as about physical poses," Markova recalled. "So, in the ballet, Fred and I drew our eyebrows in straight lines across our foreheads, and I was able to indulge in purple nail-varnish."

Peri is a supernatural fairy in Persian mythology, and Ashton thought Markova's tiny frame and exotic looks were perfect for the role. Critics agreed.

"In La Péri the drama is interpreted essentially in movement in the female figure," wrote Arnold Haskell in *The Dancing Times.* "Ashton has created an inhuman figure, whose very charm lies in mystery and distance. . . . He has used Markova's restraint to quite extraordinary advantage and has also shown a new side of her as a dancer."

Another reviewer wrote, "Markova as La Péri is brilliant in the extreme."

Chappell truly was inspired while creating the sumptuous set and costumes, but he had a bit of unexpected help from Ashton. Since there was so little money to buy fabrics in those days, wealthy arts patrons were encouraged to donate their previous season's gowns, which could then be altered or cut up for the stage. While in the midst of working on *La Péri,* Ashton went to a Ballet Club event where he spotted a brocade evening coat—he remembers it being worn by Princess Galitzine, Markova thought it was Mim's own—but either way, Ashton pounced. He just had to have the Oriental fabric for his own costume and managed to abscond with it by evening's end. Chappell later cut it up and made a magnificent tunic for Ashton.

In writing about the paltry budget at the Ballet Club, British dance historian Mary Clarke explained some of Rambert's innovations:

> There was never any money to speak of and the work was guided by what Karsavina [Russian prima ballerina Tamara Karsavina] called "blessed poverty." Imagination and artistry made up for—rather, rendered unnecessary—elaborate trappings, and if the homemade costumes did not turn out quite right or were falling to pieces with age, Rambert would say, as

> she said once to Ashton, "Do not worry, they will be lost in your beautiful movements." When Ashton wanted a décor by Marie Laurençin [a famous artist who had worked with the Ballets Russes], she [Rambert] produced some old net curtains, dyed them in her bath, and persuaded him they would serve just as well.

Another one of Rambert's tricks was to buy the cheapest tarlatan material she could find for the underskirts of tutus, and then add a single top layer of the more expensive fabric. It looked wonderful, but itched like crazy.

The costumes and set for Ashton's *Les Masques* were an Art Deco *tour-de-force*, thanks to the surreal imaginings of Sophie Fedorovitch. It was all "in 'cinematic' black and white, incredibly chic," writes David Vaughan. Adding to the dramatic effect, all the dancers wore dark blue lipstick and elegant black eye masks. Markova was a Dada-esque vision in a transparent cellophane hat and hand muff.

Vaughan suggests that the minimal dimensions of the stage—just eighteen square feet—"forced Ashton into understatement: there was not a wasted movement in *Les Masques*," which was set to a sophisticated score by contemporary French composer Francis Poulenc.

Marie Rambert retained vivid memories of the striking production many years later, as she related to Clement Crisp:

> She [Markova] is on the stage when the thing started and she is wearing the most beautiful white dress . . . with an endless train, an enormous train, and practically at the beginning, she turns around and the train winds itself around her legs. And it was such a marvelous moment.
>
> And then two girls . . . they unwound it in a dance . . . the whole studio transformed suddenly into a place where the dancers have to dress . . . and she [Markova] went upstairs to the dressing room and left the door open. And there was a light from the auditorium flickering there . . . special effects invented by Sophie. When she [Markova] is up there, she arranged her train, lifts it up and pulls it together until it becomes sufficiently short for her to dance *en pointe*.

Markova looked spectacular in the publicity photos for *Les Masques*, which portrayed her as a mysterious masked *femme fatale*. In one pose she appears to be dancing with wild abandon, the long transparent train parted to reveal a short ruffled underskirt and her beautiful, long legs. This was not the shy, timid girl of her early Ballets Russes days.

In another photo, Markova is the most glamorous of fashion plates, unmasked and seated provocatively with one leg raised and crossed high above the other, once again splitting the diaphanous train. She wears elbow-length kid gloves and a saucy tilted hat dripping with feathers. The caption in one newspaper read: *Alicia Markova, the lovely Russian dancer, gives an idea of what we may be wearing in 1933. Well, if we have legs half as shapely as hers!*

The dramatic photos received a great deal of press coverage, with one even included in an art exhibition at London's Valenza Gallery. Having her appearance celebrated along with her talent was a surprising and pleasant novelty for Markova.

Dance critics were also swept away: "Alicia Markova surpasses her considerable best in the leading role of this ballet, which is beguiling in score, costume, and décor," wrote one.

And there was this newspaper scoop after another evening's performance:

> Mme. Markova danced well—and bravely—in the first ballet, the Poulenc "Masque": bravely for she had just had two teeth out and had a violent attack of hemorrhage in her dressing room before the performance. [And she was wearing all white!]
>
> —*London Daily Express*, 3/21/33

On the same programs she was performing in contemporary new works by Ashton and de Valois, Markova also appeared regularly in short scenes of classic ballet roles, such as from *Les Sylphides* and *Swan Lake*. Though she was not yet on a par with Russian stars like Olga Spessivtseva and Tamara Karsavina, Markova's technical and emotional range did not go unnoticed.

> Star Dancer—Alicia Markova, in the classical "Lac des Cygnes," was the triumph of the evening. She would now be a great star

> if Diaghileff were still alive. Her tremulous "swan" is a thing to be remembered. All who love dancing should support the Ballet Club, for it is infused with a spirit out of which true flowers of art may spring.
>
> —*Sunday Pictorial*, 11/15/31

> This has been very much a Markova season. She has, at the age of 21, made a new career and scored a real personal success, not only as a ballerina in "The Swan Lake," but in the lead of a variety of new works. She has always been a technical craftsman, now she is rapidly gaining a mature artistic expression.
>
> —*New English Weekly*, 7/7/32

> It is quite impossible to refer to the work done by the "Ballet Club" without mentioning Alicia Markova. Miss Markova is not a product of the Club, but on its stage for a long time now she has been given the opportunity for ripening her Art, increasing her already considerable reputation, and making her name a household word among the ballet-loving public of Britain.
>
> —*Dancing Times*, March 1933

Markova owed a great debt to Ashton and de Valois for recognizing her potential to enact more animated, personality-driven roles. In turn, the combination of Markova's technical prowess and pliability made her the perfect "tool" for an experimental choreographer.

"[Markova] is more responsive than any dancer I know," asserted de Valois. "Very responsive like that and consequently very inspiring. Because you feel you can do a movement as many times as you want to with her and she does it all in front of you, changing it, not saying that suits me, I prefer that one or something. None of that at all. I love working on her."

Marie Rambert said of her star ballerina, "She was always like a most beautiful picture painted. Everybody could judge the amount of technique that was hidden underneath this calm, because she has an astonishing technique. . . . That technique was so invisible, yet so felt, you know—a wonderful assurance of movement without any effort. She would do the most difficult things in the world—lovely. . . . I would say that she is perfection of dancing, as dancing without thinking of anything else."

Just three years after she thought her career was over, Alicia Markova was the most famous British dancer in London, but that was a small pond in the ballet world—with salaries to match. Though her financial situation had certainly improved, her home life changed little. True, she no longer had to rehearse at the bathroom towel bar, but she continued to share a modest flat with her mother and sisters. And with her demanding work schedule, her social activities were restricted to after-performance suppers and get-togethers with fellow dancers.

Nevertheless, Markova chose to turn down lucrative offers that came her way, partially as payback to Ashton, Rambert, and de Valois—the people who had "rescued" her after Diaghilev's death.

As the *Bayswater Chronicle* reported in October 1933:

> Alicia Markova, the famous English ballet dancer, has recently received two very enticing offers, one from Serge Lifar to accompany him as his partner on an American tour and another from Alexandre Levitoff, the late Pavlova's impresario, to join as prima ballerina a season he is organizing in Egypt this winter; but the dilemma is solved by her loyalty to Sadler's Wells, where she is under contract to appear in successive ballets until May, and where she is now regularly appearing in the successful "Vic-Wells" season. So London is not to lose for some time its foremost national artiste in the world of ballet.
>
> Besides her work at Islington, Miss Markova is to appear in the Degas ballet, "Foyer de Dance" at the Ballet Club, Notting Hill Gate, on October 20th, and on October 28th she is dancing the *pas de deux* from "Aurora" and "Les Sylphides" at Crane Hall, Liverpool.

Markova now shared the goal of Marie Rambert and Ninette de Valois: to put British ballet on the map. But Markova wanted to take that one step further. She felt ballet would never truly flourish in England until it was available to everyone, not just residents who could afford a trip to London. She made it her mission to bring ballet directly to them, traveling to the hinterlands of her country to build an ever-expanding audience of ballet "converts."

Markova accomplished those goals through re-invention, forward thinking, and an uncanny understanding of the media's power.

"Are we becoming ballet-minded?" That was a topic Markova brought up during an interview with the *Daily Sketch*. The reporter dutifully printed her answer:

> According to Alicia Markova, the new Alhambra ballerina, our audiences no longer look on ballet as "highbrow nonsense," but as an important item of popular entertainment, and what was once of interest to a few intellectual snobs has now become the delight of the ordinary theatre-goer.
>
> "British Ballet has had to work hard, but I think we have come through," Miss Markova told the *Daily Sketch*. "It is becoming so popular in theatres and cinema houses that thousands of British girls are going into training.
>
> "Soon we shall be able to leave off our 'Russian' names—and be just plain Jones and Smith," laughed Miss Markova. "I got all my early training with Diaghileff, and, of course, he wouldn't let us have any but Russian names."
>
> . . . It made all the difference, though, no doubt, the dancing was the same.

Markova would become the public face and most visible spokesperson for British ballet over the coming years, never passing up an opportunity to spread the word. A new-fangled medium called television? Not for the art of ballet, sniffed Ninette de Valois. "It will never catch on." Markova thought differently.

6

Becoming Giselle

Markova's unslaving devotion to her art, which has put the Vic-Wells Ballet on the level equal to that of any other company in Europe, makes her conversation as intriguing as her dancing. Quite apart from being a dancer, she is a ballet-fan, considering ballet the ideal entertainment:

"Ballet provides the perfect escape from the petty woes and cares of our daily routine. It transports us to another world where there are no motor cars, no ugly sounds and no adverse weather conditions. All is sheer beauty, in a fairyland peopled by ballerinas who do not even walk as we do, flitting on their pointes with arms that waft like soft music. What could be further removed from the din of cities?"

—"Markova—Our Only Prima Ballerina, An Interview by Eric Johns," *Theatre World,* 1934

Escapist entertainment is just what British citizens needed in the early 1930s. By 1932, unemployment hovered between twenty and thirty percent, hunger marches turned into riots throughout the country, and Hitler's fearsome National Socialist Party would come to power the next year in Germany.

Americans were faring no better, pinning their hopes on newly elected President Franklin Delano Roosevelt to lead them out of the Great Depression. Songwriter "Yip" Harburg's lyrics for "Brother, Can You Spare a Dime?" struck a national chord, but certainly not an uplifting one.

Hollywood had a better idea—one with a happy ending—and choreographer-turned-moviemaker Busby Berkeley proved just the ticket. His show-business-themed musicals featured scantily clad chorus girls, often filmed from above, producing Berkeley's signature kaleidoscopic shots. Though considered wholesome viewing, the movies had just enough sex appeal to entice men as well as women. (In *42nd Street,* Ginger Rogers's *Anytime Annie* "only said no once, and then she didn't hear the question!")

Dispirited Brits also flocked to comedies and musicals, both at movie houses and London theaters, with Beatrice Lillie and Noel Coward huge box office draws. Alicia Markova wanted the art of ballet to join those popular diversions. Filled with music, dancing—and yes, even shapely legs—didn't ballet have the same capacity to transport audiences? The varied repertoires had something for everyone, from breathtaking classics of unparalleled beauty to contemporary productions with wit and glamour. Evenings at the British ballet were true crowd-pleasers, if the masses would only give them a try.

Though Markova had signed on for cinema interval performances because she needed the money, the value of wowing new audiences every week quickly became apparent. People with little knowledge of the ballet were clearly becoming hooked. So when an experimental mass-media opportunity presented itself, the young dancer happily jumped on board.

-∞-

While Americans consider television a homegrown medium, Scotsman John Logie Baird is generally credited with inventing the first mechanical television system. (Admittedly, American Philo T. Farnsworth's electronic version a few years later would prove far more valuable.) Baird filed his first patent in 1923 after moving to England, and one year later actually transmitted an image—albeit only across a few feet.

According to a BBC recorded history of the inventor, Baird's early experimentation caused quite a stir:

> His first crude apparatus was made of odds and ends, but on 26 January 1926 he gave the world's first demonstration of true television before 50 scientists in an attic room in central London. In 1927, his television was demonstrated over 438 miles of telephone line between London and Glasgow, and he formed the Baird Television Development Company (BTDC). In 1928, the BTDC achieved the first transatlantic television transmission between London and New York.

That was all well and good—immensely exciting, in fact. But if no one could afford a home "televisor" set, as Baird called it, who would be watching? To drum up national interest, Baird presented a deluxe model as a gift to Britain's Prime Minister Ramsay MacDonald. Quite naturally, he was delighted. But a few people tuning in at No. 10 Downing Street hardly constituted Nielsen-size ratings.

Enter Selfridges department store, a London shopping institution since 1909. Not only did the company place a large-screen televisor set in their Oxford Street window, they also took out newspaper ads and bus display banners to promote scheduled performances and transmission times. The public was intrigued, and actually stood outside on the sidewalk long enough to watch a few short plays in their entirety. The first televised sporting event—the Epsom Derby horse race in 1931—was, needless to say, a real crowd-pleaser.

But despite the widespread fascination with the new medium, Selfridges needed compelling programs to draw queues of Londoners to their outdoor windows, presumably to be followed by a shopping trip inside.

Baird decided to approach London's most acclaimed ballerina, 21-year-old Alicia Markova. Although he warned her of the primitive and difficult conditions required for broadcast transmission, Markova literally leaped at the chance. She would be popularizing an art barely in its infancy in London, and get to experience an exciting new technological adventure to boot.

Luckily for Baird, Markova had as much stamina as pluck, because the rudimentary broadcast procedures in 1932 were both cumbersome and daunting. For starters, the entire production studio in Portland Place, Notting Hill Gate was a mere twelve by twelve feet, as Markova vividly recalled:

> It was the size of a postage stamp! The floor was covered in big black and white checks and we had to have a piano for musical accompaniment. Then there was this huge beam of light that used to flicker so it was very difficult to balance or focus.
>
> There wasn't room for a partner, so I had to dance alone. For everything, you had to stay in one place. You really couldn't move around because there wasn't anywhere to move.
>
> The costumes had to be brought in ahead of time and all outlined with black ribbons. And the make-up—dead white—with a black mouth and purple eyes. And when I finished the little variation, to get off camera, I had to duck down, bend, and crawl out under the piano. But I so wanted to be in [from] the beginning.

Markova chose two ballets that required little side-to-side movement: *Moods* by Balanchine and the "Polka" from Ashton's *Façade.* The black ribbon costume trim and startling makeup helped sharpen her image on the fuzzy black-and-white screen. Though the ballerina looked a bit like one of those string-pull puppets with static body and joyful arm and leg movements, Selfridge customers were entranced.

Markova continued to work with Baird as he slowly perfected the new medium. A slightly larger studio was soon built next door to the original broadcasting house, providing enough room for her to dance with partner Anton Dolin. The bizarre makeup evolved with the picture quality, going from a white mime face to a Halloween-like brick red. It was a form of the panchromatic makeup Max Factor created for black-and-white films in Hollywood, but the television transmissions weren't nearly the quality of celluloid, so the skin tones had to be greatly exaggerated.

When the BBC first began transmitting from Alexandra Palace in 1936, Markova was along for the ride. Fittingly "The People's Palace," as it was called, was near her childhood home in Muswell Hill. Though a full orchestra now accompanied Markova instead of a lone piano, the small size of the studios required the musicians be in a different room entirely. For some reason, the studios were not synched up for communication—no phone or visual monitors—so a "call-boy" ran between the two to tell the orchestra when to start playing, and Markova when to start dancing. And it was broadcast live!

"It's extraordinary what we went through," she remembered, laughing at the thought. "TV for me, I've never had any fears." And that was true in the United States as well. When Markova first visited New York in the late 1930s, her extensive experience was a great help to the National Broadcasting Company (NBC) in the early stages of their own televised dance trials. And in the 1950s, she would be the first ballerina to guest-host a variety show—Sid Caesar's comedic *Your Show of Shows*—a television appearance so popular, she was later given her own program.

"She could well have described herself as one of its [television's] pioneers," reported *Ballet Today* in a 1955 profile of Markova, "for she has made countless appearances on the screen, both in this country and in the United States. It is a medium in which she has expressed her faith by her very loyalty and devotion. She recognized it then as a suitable medium for ballet, which only recently has been universally accepted and appreciated. In the days before the war it was still treated in many quarters as a subject for derision and music-hall jokes."

Though many in the ballet world initially looked down on Markova's television work, she never shared their snobbery. The popularity of her Regal Cinema performances taught Markova the value of unorthodox venues as vehicles for attracting new audiences to ballet. And having been painfully forgotten and unemployed for lack of opportunities in England after the Ballets Russes disbanded, she was determined never to let that happen again.

Throughout the rest of her career, Markova maintained an adventurous spirit where new and mass media were concerned. Moreover, she instinctively understood how best to exploit each promotional prospect to make ballet more accessible. Peer approval mattered not a whit in that regard.

But even the disapproving Ninette de Valois soon came to recognize the value of the outsized publicity each of Markova's television appearances received, as in this widely read newspaper article from London's *The Evening News* on February 8, 1934:

When Radio Listeners Will Also See Television Is Making Progress

Markova has been broadcasting—in television! The fact that a ballerina of such importance was engaged by the BBC to appear (literally) on the air indicates how seriously this new art is already taken at Broadcasting House.

It revives the question the man-in-the-street is asking about it: "How long before we are all radio 'lookers' as well as 'listeners'?"

The Small Screen

In a darkened room at Broadcasting House I watched the image of Markova swirl and pirouette across a screen about one-sixth of the size of a page of this newspaper. She was dancing some movements from the "Faust" and "Coppelia" ballets.

Anything in the nature of a full ballet presentation is impracticable in the present stage of television's development, because the field of vision is so cramped and because the studio accommodation is so limited.

The modern "mirror-drum" television receiver goes much further than the old "rotating disc" televisor, which achieved a certain notoriety some years ago, with its amber-colored image about the size of a cigarette-card.

More Than "Close-ups"

It now gives a larger, black-and-white image, and best of all, the entertainment is not limited to "close-ups."

Most of Markova's broadcast consisted of a dance in "extended view," when poised on her toes and with arms held wide, she occupied the entire screen.

That's what I mean when I say the field of vision is still limited. To show a whole troupe of dancers at once is still a dream of television's future.

> And to perform any sort of dance in the narrow room which serves just now as a television studio is a feat of ingenuity.
>
> After her performance, Markova came from the half-darkened studio to the futuristic foyer outside, where I was introduced to her by Eustace Robb, the BBC television producer.
>
> **Care Needed**
>
> "One has to be so very careful in the choice of dances," she said. "The room is so small and in the darkness with only that bright beam of light thrown upon one, one feels so cramped. Of course, you can move about the room—the flickering beam follows you—but nevertheless, that feeling exists.
>
> "All the same, I like this work. It is an experience, to be in at the beginning of something that will grow—how big?" . . .
>
> Last night, at the end of Markova's dances, cartoons of the dances appeared on the screen, as a "curtain" to the act. . . . The sketches did not come out very clearly on the screen. It may be argued that much of this subtlety is wasted. But is it? Robb is creating a new art-form.

Unfortunately, it was an art form still few were able to witness, as noted by *News Chronicle* radio correspondent Geoffrey Edwards:

> Alicia Markova, in the television programme to-night, would be worth seeing—if you had a television receiver.
>
> She is the prima ballerina of the Vic-Wells ballet.
>
> It seems a pity to me that so much talent should be wasted on the television programmes. If only we all had the necessary television apparatus!
>
> As it is, I doubt whether more than a score or two "lookers in" will see her.
>
> But everyone can hear her.

Edwards was referring to the show's being simulcast on radio, as it included two popular singers of the day along with Markova dancing.

Though clearly the ballerina wouldn't be *heard* performing, her music accompaniment was quite lovely, encouraging listeners to *imagine* the ethereal dancer floating in the air. And of course one could *see* her by just buying a ticket.

Newspapers reported the BBC's progress every step of the way, even baby steps:

> **THE BBC**
>
> **Possible Transmission Changes Appeal to "Lookers-In"**
>
> . . . Late last night the television announcer asked those who were receiving the programme to send postcards immediately to Broadcasting House. He said the BBC were anxious to know the number of people actually seeing the programme, and added that the information desired was of "considerable importance."
>
> —*London Correspondent*, Fleet Street, 2/7/34

The new medium would also be of considerable importance to ballet, as another newspaper writer enthused:

> Television! The time is not far off when every listener will possess his own television set as a matter of course. As yet, the number of these sets in use in the country is not large. Television, as an industry, has yet to break down the many barriers before it can come into its own. But the experts are at work, perfecting and improving. One does not need to be blessed with unduly clear sight to see the writing on the wall. . . . The addition of vision has opened the door to artists who need, for the full appeal of their art, to be seen as well as heard.
>
> —*Daily Herald*, 2/7/34

And Markova *was* seen everywhere, whether people had television sets or not. The small number of actual viewers had little effect on the amount of publicity devoted to scheduled television programming in the print media of the day. As a result, Markova's name—accompanied by glamorous photographs of the dancer in various splendid costumes—appeared regularly in newspapers across the country. Alicia Markova was soon the toast of the town.

⁂

On December 5, 1933, Markova premiered in Frederick Ashton's exceptionally beautiful ballet, *Les Rendezvous*. It was his first major work for the Vic-Wells, and the star power of its leading lady—newly signed as the company's prima ballerina—helped lure Stanislas Idzikowski as guest artist. Often compared to the great Nijinsky, the renowned principal male dancer hadn't appeared in London since his Diaghilev days, having recently been on tour elsewhere in Europe with his own company.

One had only to look at the opening night audience to be convinced that British ballet had officially "arrived." There was interior decorator to the rich-and-famous Syrie Maugham, celebrated stage actress Constance Cummings, and trend-setting fashion designer Elsa Schiaparelli. Of particular note to Schiap, as she was called, were William Chappell's imaginatively festooned costumes, which, along with the daringly difficult footwork, presented a true feast for the eyes. The ballet had no plot per se, just a series of utterly charming vignettes in which frivolous philandering couples intertwined.

"It has no serious portent at all," said Ashton. "It is simply a vehicle for the exquisite dancing of Idzikowski and Markova." But oh, what a vehicle.

"[T]he leading role gave Markova her finest creation for the Wells," wrote British dance critic P. W. Manchester. "She was entrancing in her grey dress with the big red flowers on either side of her smooth head. No one who saw her will ever forget her exit at the end of her brilliant solo, head jauntily tilted, shoulders and arms delicately lifted, her narrow feet exquisitely placed. The whole ballet was designed as a showpiece to display her particular gifts of speed, precision, and lightness, and it was an uproarious success."

"It really brought out every gift she had with its speedy and stylish pyrotechnicalities," agreed British ballet photographer Gordon Anthony, whose lens immortalized many dancers of the day. "With her ballon amounting to levitation, her only difficulty appeared to be how to keep herself out of orbit!"

Years later Ashton said, "I think of all the ballets I did for her, that was the one she was the very best in, and nobody has come anywhere near her."

And that was exactly what Ashton was hired to do for the Vic-Wells. The 2000-seat Sadler's Wells Theatre had never been close to being filled until company director Ninette de Valois persuaded owner Lilian Baylis to engage Markova full-time, both on the basis of her unparalleled technique and her newfound place in British society as a household name. Showing their jewel off in the best possible light meant packed houses, a far cry from the company's early days, as recalled by Agnes de Mille:

> The Sadler's Wells company at this point was merely a troupe of students located way out to hell and gone, herded and driven by the implacable Ninette de Valois, who had vision and an iron nerve and took the brunt of long years of slogging. Margot Fonteyn and Moira Shearer were still in the classroom. The company's soloists were by no means first-rate until de Valois enticed Markova away from the music halls and Ballet Club, and until she commissioned Frederick Ashton to compose works for her.

Although Markova's power to sell tickets far outweighed her meager starting salary, the frugal Baylis struck an even smarter bargain, which she laid out in a letter to the dancer in June 1933:

"I have spoken to Ninette, and we agree to making the offer for next season ten pounds a week, this to cover your appearances in the ballet performances [and expenses such as costumes, tights, and ballet shoes!], and your help as choreographer when necessary."

Markova's phenomenal memory for choreography was a priceless commodity. She not only could recall every step she had ever danced, but also anything she had ever *seen*. That was especially valuable in restaging the classics at the Vic-Wells, as when she worked with de Valois on *Les Sylphides*.

"Alice did the main *corps de ballet* work for me," said de Valois. (She always called Markova Alice.) "She's got a wonderful memory, much better than mine, and she remembered the entire corps for me."

Markova was also a true choreographic collaborator when working on new ballets with Ashton. While she felt her first and foremost duty was to act as a compliant instrument for his creativity, Ashton asked for, and in those early days needed, her invaluable input. He was in awe of both her wide-ranging physical gifts and past experience with his idols: Balanchine, Massine, and Fokine. She helped Ashton develop his own personal style, pointing out when something seemed too derivative of his predecessors.

Ashton also admired Markova's intuitive knowledge of how to turn perceived personal weaknesses into strengths—the sign of a true artist. "It was wonderful, this extraordinary lightness that she had," he said. "And then in contrast to the other ballerinas who were sort of bigger and heavier, she'd cultivated this almost ethereal quality in opposition to their approaches. . . .

"In spite of her frailty and everything, her technique was extremely strong—steel-like, really—very strong feet and a very quick mover."

And unlike many dancers who prefer not to step out of their artistic or technical comfort zones when learning new ballets, Markova found it exhilarating:

> When the choreographer commences and the dancer says, "Oooh, I'm sorry that hurts me. I have a bad back here." Or "I really can't do this." Or "this shoulder—ooh." Or "this isn't my good side. Can it go on the other side?" you're restricting the choreographer right away. How can you expect him to do something inspired for you?
>
> I learned that in the beginning in the Diaghilev company. Being the baby of the company, I was willing to work on anything. So I had many choreographers experimenting on me, [starting with] Balanchine when I was fourteen.

That quality was especially appreciated by de Valois, who, unlike Ashton, knew exactly what she wanted when choreographing new ballets, as she explained when discussing her process for *The Rake's Progress* inspired by the British artist William Hogarth's paintings:

> Well, you know with me, I'm afraid I'm not really influenced by people. I do tend to bend them to what exactly I want done and she's [Markova] the most pliable person. . . . I mean

> I didn't look at her and think now what would suit Alice. I didn't do anything of the sort. I thought now she's got to be—give me what I think and feel—Hogarth movements here according to the pictures and their set. And she did, no trouble at all.

Markova's versatility was another undeniable asset, one that Ballet Club founder Marie Rambert thought quite extraordinary. "She had a very wide repertoire. She did tragic roles, like for instance Marguerite in *Mephisto Waltz*, Ashton's Marguerite, and then she was a brilliant comedy star when she was doing the can-can in *Bar aux Folies Bergère*. There she is doing the can-can! And for a really impeccable classical dancer, she had an astonishing variety and great range of emotion."

Because of her uncanny memory for choreography, Markova could easily jump back and forth in markedly different ballet roles on any given night. The *Notts Weekly Guardian* newspaper was quite impressed with that gift:

> **Her Busy Night**
>
> The life of a great ballet dancer is notoriously strenuous, but one usually supposes that the strenuousness is confined to the muscular exertion of the dancing itself. Recently the brilliant Markova not only had the exertion of dancing continually from early in the evening until late at night, but of nearly literally dancing all over London in order to do it.
>
> She performed in the ballet "Rendezvous" at the Sadler's Wells Theatre, an exacting performance of classical ballet under the baton of Constance [*sic*] Lambert with an orchestra of 30 players. Immediately after it she had to speed over London in a taxi to the Albert Hall to assume a quite different mood and style in the ballet of the Elijah production to an orchestra of 70, conducted by Albert Coates.
>
> After that she was due at Covent Garden Opera House to do a solo dance at the Annual Vic-Wells Costume Ball. Here she danced an invention of her own to the accompaniment of a jazz band playing a popular waltz tune. Despite her previous

> exertions she gave one of the most delightful performances of her career and got an overwhelming ovation.
>
> —*Notts Weekly Guardian*, 2/24/34

Markova's memory was a frequent topic of interest to many in the media, as in this 1940s interview with broadcaster Herman Brandschain:

> We asked Alicia Markova, the English girl who specializes in tragic and ethereal roles, how at a moment's notice she could dance any one of hundreds of roles—thousands of intricate movements all timed precisely.
>
> "I have a phenomenal memory," she admitted, "especially for muscular movements."
>
> Her brain, she said, is something like a moving picture camera, constantly recording images that never fade and which she can play back at will.
>
> "I make no special effort to remember," she said. "I just remember. It's something I inherited from my father."

And it was something Markova thought was quite normal for an artistic performer: "It's like an opera singer or a concert pianist. I suppose perhaps we have a gift in a certain direction. One must be very interested in what you do, and then you're so interested, you absorb."

Some felt Markova was *overly* absorbed, as her way of collaborating with choreographers drove several of them quite mad. In order to master new step combinations and emotional expressiveness, she sometimes needed to figure out what *not* to do in order to get it right.

Léonide Massine compared working with her to "Chinese water torture," but he was certainly thrilled with the end result.

"I used to get frightfully irritated," said Ashton. "I used to say, well, when am I going to see you do it properly? And one day, I got so angry I said no wonder you're called Markova—you're always marking everything you're not doing properly. She was. Anyhow she did a bit at the dress rehearsal and then came the first night. She exploded and it was wonderful."

Unhappily for the two choreographers, Markova was not a dance machine able to take effortless dictation.

Agnes de Mille, a student at the Ballet Club, was fascinated by Markova's process and single-mindedness, taking note of the dancer one day while waiting for a rehearsal to begin. As others chatted amiably about her, Markova sat silently on a bench, "doing finger-turns on Ashton's hand, six, eight, ten turns like a piano stool, round and round." She was rehearsing with the choreographer in her own head.

Female choreographers seemed far less bothered by Markova's painstakingly deliberate learning methods, perhaps because patience and a willingness to negotiate were part of their own work process as women struggling to succeed in a predominantly male profession.

The talented choreographer Bronislava Nijinska, a lifelong friend of Markova's, suffered from being both a woman in Diaghilev's all-boys club and the sister of Vaslav Nijinsky, the most celebrated male dancer in the world (and now tragically locked away in an insane asylum after succumbing to the crippling onset of schizophrenia).

"What a great choreographer Bronia would have been if only she were a man," Diaghilev once said. That didn't prevent him from hiring her, and the ballets Nijinska created for the Ballets Russes—*Le Train Bleu* and *Les Biches* among them—were extraordinary.

"She was an amazing woman," Markova said of Nijinska. "I adored working with her. While she was working with the Markova-Dolin Company [at Markova's behest], she and her husband [former ballet dancer Nicolas Singaevksy] and her daughter all traveled with us and you really get to know someone when it's not just steps in the studio. She'd be in the front row during rehearsals and really helped me perfect the classics. It was great to have someone to talk over interpretations—you'd call it stagecraft."

Nijinska was equally complimentary to Markova. In an interview with the *New York Post* in 1948, Nijinska—who lived and worked on the outskirts of Hollywood at the time—said her friend Alischka was "very, very great. . . . Markova has the SOUL!" But it should be noted that in the same article, Nijinska stated that the seven hundred lemon trees on her expansive California property also "have soul." They were "all in such even line, just like real ballet dancers," she explained.

Throughout her life, Nijinska continued to receive many prestigious choreographic commissions from ballet companies on both sides of the Atlantic. De Valois had solved her problem of securing work as a choreographer by simply founding her own dance company. Her exacting developmental process was completely in sync with Markova's, as described by Arnold Haskell:

"Her [de Valois's] success as a choreographer was obvious but what was equally striking was her complete professionalism. Many dabbled with brilliance at times, Ninette planned methodically. She looked ahead, her ideas were always on a vast scale but she was content to move step by step."

De Valois was happy to give Markova the necessary time and space to perfect her craft. It seemed a small price to pay, considering the ballerina's immense talent, work ethic, and pliability. As de Valois wrote about Markova in her memoir:

> I think of all the artists that I have ever encountered she is the most self-reliant. . . . Her dancing portrays the gentle but firm, precise yet fluid, lines of her character: effortless on the surface, yet submitted fundamentally to an iron control; she has a mind that is logical, and an outlook that is steadfast in its sincerity, integrity and loyalty to her art and her friends. She makes no enemies; in her difficult moments she can temporarily exasperate, or inspire good-humored ridicule; on all occasions, however, she commands everyone's affection, admiration and feeling of comradeship.

Even from her earliest days, Markova formed lifelong friendships with the people she worked with, including de Valois, Rambert, Nijinska, Danilova, Ashton, and Dolin, with whom she had the most complicated of relations. Markova would also have an unfortunate falling out with Ashton for a period, but the break was solely of his making, and over a small perceived slight. Major stumbling blocks between the choreographer and ballerina were their divergent goals and personalities. In the early years of both their careers, Ashton's main concern was understandably his own success and progress, while Markova saw herself as a prophet for ballet. Those lofty goals could be off-putting to anyone who didn't share her passion.

In the early 1930s, Alicia Markova's life was consumed with ballet and nothing but ballet, with a work ethic that precluded frivolous activities. "Dedicated and devoted, she wasted no time on giggle and gossip," recalled fellow dancer and friend Diana Gould. "We were all extremely young and she but a year or two older—but would arrive enveloped in the aura of the coming performance as a package delivered ready-wrapped for Christmas. She did not talk to us of Diaghilev—she might well have boasted a little of her great Maestro—rather did she prefer to remain completely immersed in her sacred duties: the head-girl of the Vestal Virgins and well on the way to becoming High Priestess."

Markova clearly wasn't a party person or amusing drinking companion, like Ashton and Dolin—though she did enjoy the camaraderie of intimate after-performance suppers with company members.

"She was friends with everybody," remembered Marie Rambert. "Wonderful manner most absolutely. Not in any way condescending." As a ballet worshiper herself, Rambert seemed to understand Markova's silences for what they really were. "She kept a lot to herself because I think she was thinking about dancing. I think it was inborn in her. She wasn't a talker, but she isn't a talker today either, but what she says is very intelligent."

Not having any extra spending money also became a barrier to Markova's socializing, though she never spoke of it at the time. When Dolin brought her home one evening after having treated her to an expensive late-night dinner, he was insulted that Markova merely thanked him graciously at the door and didn't invite him up for a nightcap. Years later, she told him why:

Despite her fame, Markova still lived in a tiny two-room flat plus kitchen with her widowed mother and three sisters, whom she was helping support. Had Dolin come up, there would have been family members asleep, no place to entertain, and piles of laundry waiting to be washed or ironed. Just because Markova was a ballet star didn't mean she was excused from household chores, which she continued to share with her sisters.

Though fellow dancers found Markova polite and friendly, her quiet demeanor could also be perceived as aloofness. It wasn't a matter of her being disinterested in the conversations around her; she just preferred listening and observing to talking, a trait she had displayed ever since she was a small child, when she didn't talk at all. Many beaus would later be captivated by that behavior, happy to dominate the conversation as Markova appeared to hang on their every word. But she also became much more fun-loving and outgoing as she matured.

At that time, "hers was a changeling personality," said Diana Gould. "Vague and undefined it was, as though she floated through us so lightly and with so little contact that her self, like her delicate foot, left no imprint to remember."

Markova was not unlike the soon-to-be-famous choreographer Antony Tudor, whom she first encountered at Marie Rambert's Ballet Club. Though Tudor began his career running the box office and operating the set lighting for Rambert, he eventually added choreographer to his duties, expanding that role after Ashton moved on to the Vic-Wells.

Unlike many of their peers, Markova related to Tudor's seriousness and was non-judgmental about his lengthy silences so similar to her own. "[T]he world was a difficult place for Antony," Markova told Tudor biographer Donna Perlmutter. "Even during the good times—those long evenings we spent together as a group with Hugh [Hugh Laing was a talented dancer and longtime lover/companion of Tudor] cooking something wonderful and all of us sitting around till two in the morning. He was outside the group, just observing. He related only one way. Some found it strange or arrogant or rude. But I thought he was just being Antony."

Markova and Tudor worked well together, both at the Ballet Club in his early days, and much later when he was a huge success in New York. She was always grateful for his creating the heartbreakingly exquisite role of Romeo's Juliet for her, a part that brought her great acclaim in America.

As a young dance student, Agnes de Mille studied alongside Tudor and Markova, noting that both seemed off in their own worlds of inner concentration, unlike their more gregarious and domineering peers. Tudor, de Mille wrote, "watched everything with remembering eyes and drank his tea quietly wrapped in dreams."

But at least Tudor had a love life. When she wasn't rehearsing or performing, Markova was either studying music or ballet history. It was just like when she had been a schoolgirl, with her nose buried in a history book while the other children merrily raced around the playground. She wanted to learn everything she could about her art, including studying up on the great classical prima ballerinas of the 19th century, Carlotta Grisi and Marie Taglioni.

It became a family joke that when Markova went missing, she was likely holed up in the back room of Cyril Beaumont's famous bookshop at No. 75 Charing Cross Road. Beaumont was an intellectual writer, bookseller, and publisher who, like countless others, first became interested in the ballet after seeing Anna Pavlova. It's hard to imagine what that fragile dancer must have communicated on stage to make instant ballet converts of so many. For Beaumont's part, soon after seeing the divine Russian work her magic, he dedicated the rest of his life to researching, critiquing, and writing about the ballet.

His dance-themed bookshop became so internationally well known that Nijinsky and Diaghilev stopped by when visiting London, as did numerous famous music composers, choreographers, and artists. Beaumont was especially fond of the young Markova. Of course, there was her astonishing likeness to Pavlova, but the pair also shared a similar temperament.

They were both quiet and studious—Beaumont often described as mole-like—becoming so totally absorbed in books that hours would go by before either moved or spoke. Knowing how much Markova revered the great Taglioni, Beaumont would set her up in a little corner chair by the shop's warm stove with a collection of rare volumes on the acclaimed dancer for her to read. That was especially generous considering that he ran a for-profit bookstore, not a library.

Though an engaging writer, Beaumont was shy—some said surprisingly boring—in person, but he shared Markova's dry sense of humor. Both were also kind and thoughtful, always remembering to send flowers to dancers on opening nights or if they were ill.

During World War II when Markova was performing throughout the United States, she knew Beaumont was hungry for ballet news from America. So the dancer would send him frequent care packages with playbills, reviews, and hard-to-obtain rationed goods she knew he could use.

When Markova returned to London in 1948, Beaumont had a special surprise waiting for her on opening night of *Giselle* at Covent Garden. It was a spool of mending silk from Taglioni's own workbox with instructions to: "Break off a piece and wear it in your shoe for luck tonight." Of course, Alicia did.

In later years when she could afford it, Markova amassed a stellar collection of rare books on Pavlova and Taglioni, now part of the Gotlieb Center archives at Boston University. Among her most treasured possessions was a letter written by Taglioni, Beaumont's gift to Markova the night she premiered in the full-length *Swan Lake.* Soon after, in 1935, the author/bookseller wrote a biography on Markova's early career.

As had been done for her, Markova felt it important to mentor younger dancers throughout her life. That included her sister Bunny, considered the beauty of the Marks family. Just like her actress sister Doris, Bunny took her mother's maiden name Barry for professional purposes. An Irish surname was better box office than a Jewish one.

But that didn't mean the family was any less religious. Since her father's death when she was thirteen, Markova had taken on the man's role in the Jewish family rituals, such as reciting the Kiddush on Shabbat. As Markova had become the family breadwinner, it seemed a natural order of things to her mother Eileen.

And Markova never hid her religion publicly out of any fear that it might hurt her professionally. In her early career, she was quite naïve about the prevalence of anti-Semitism in England. As previously discussed, she was completely unaware of Russian ballerina Lydia Lopokova's true feelings and insidious plotting against her at the Camargo Society. Markova considered Lydia a friend. But there was no escaping widespread anti-Semitism as Hitler rose to power. Even then, Markova made the conscious decision to speak openly, and proudly, about her Jewish heritage.

Anton Dolin, Markova's frequent partner, was more concerned with public perception. When he suggested she get her prominent "hook" nose surgically re-done, it wasn't just to make her more conventionally "pretty," but also so she'd appear less Jewish. Frederick Ashton agreed. But Markova rejected the suggestion out of hand. To quiet them both, she asserted that having to "look over" a differently shaped nose as she spun across the stage might affect her balance.

In shocking contrast is the story of Margot Fonteyn, an Irish/Brazilian (and Catholic) beauty, and her one-time lover, the celebrated French choreographer Roland Petit. The ballet critic Annabel Farjeon related the story to Fonteyn biographer Meredith Daneman:

> "I went to the ballet," said Annabel Farjeon, "and I saw Margot in the audience, and I thought, 'My God, what's happened to her face?' And she said, 'Oh, Roland Petit said, you're going to look very Jewish soon. You'd better have your nose done.' So she did, and there was a big blob on the end. She had it redone, and then it was this boring little thing. She had a lovely nose—elegant and sweet."

In light of such fears of "looking Jewish" and the measures some were willing to take to avoid it, it is understandable why Markova's openness about her religion and willingness to embrace her "ethnic" appearance was a major source of pride for London's *Jewish Chronicle* and *Jewish Daily Post* newspapers. When she was appearing in the religious-themed operatic work *Elijah* at Albert Hall, Markova told a reporter at the mainstream *Daily Mail* that "she was seeking in vain an answer to the query: 'Did Hebrew women of the period dance in bare feet?'" As a Jew, she felt the answer important. "She has now decided to make a reasonable compromise with Scriptural accuracy by dancing in her ballet sandals," was the conclusion.

Mainstream London newspapers also mentioned Markova's religion. It was as distinctive for a prima ballerina as not being Russian.

> **Ballet Ballyhoo**
>
> A Lot in a Name
>
> To compare with the two great Leningrad prime ballerine, Ulanova and Vassilieva, I have in the last few years seen only one dancer.
>
> She is a little Jewish girl called Marks, whose technique is as sure and exciting as Heifetz playing the fiddle. If she stretches a leg out, it stays out, and she doesn't have to hop about on the other foot in case she falls over.

> Nowadays Alice Marks is known as Alicia Markova. When she first appeared, at the age of 16 (or less) she was in the Diaghileff ballet, and Society applauded, duly impressed, thinking of course, that Alice was Russian. . . .
>
> I strongly object to this ridiculous prejudice that dancing is the national prerogative of the Russians.
>
> —*Daily Herald,* 12/27/35

Bunny idolized Alicia, who was eight years her senior, and faithfully kept detailed scrapbooks of all her sister's press coverage. On the opening page of each album was a very business-like handwritten inscription, such as "SECOND EDITION OF A BOOK ON THE FAMOUS BALLERINA 'ALICIA MARKOVA.' [COPYRIGHT, 1935, BY BERENICE BARRY, IN ENGLAND]." Most endearing, the keeper of the scrapbooks often took it upon herself to cross out reviewers' praise of other dancers—such as the beautiful Pearl Argyle—and highlight only the accolades for Markova.

It was not surprising that Bunny should have dreams of becoming another Markova herself, though that was not meant to be. While she was a winsome *corps de ballet* member and lead pantomime dancer, Bunny chose to marry and raise a family over a career. One of her close friends in ballet school was Peggy Hookham, soon to be known by the more mellifluous name Margot Fonteyn. Markova was always fond of Fonteyn, from their first meeting at Princess Astafieva's dance studio in 1933. At the time, the Russian teacher had been very ill with cancer, and had only taken Fonteyn on as a student because her overbearing mother had begged her.

Markova came to visit Astafieva one day, only to find the Princess too sick to teach. Markova offered to coach Fonteyn herself, later remembering "Peggy as a plump though beautifully proportioned child who giggled a lot in the dressing-room. . . . It's very difficult to think about potential, but at that time she really didn't seem too interested. It was Mrs. Hookham, you see, who was really interested. Margot was very good, you know, she went along with it. But at the beginning the mother was, I felt, more smitten, more ambitious than Margot was."

Mrs. Hookham was obsessed with Markova's talents and stage presence, which she so wanted for her own daughter. "Markova has exquisite feet," she told de Valois one day. "I love to watch the way she uses them like a bird taking off for flight, but I never watch Margot's feet." Ashton had referred to those offending appendages as "Margot's pats of butter," and both looked to de Valois to transform their shape. She did.

Even when Fonteyn began to share some of her mother's ambition, comparing herself to Markova made it seem all that more impossible. As Fonteyn recalled years later:

> When I first went to the then Vic-Wells ballet, I went as a student in the back row of the corps de ballet. Markova was the ballerina. She was the first person who showed me, inspired me to know what a ballerina was. Among the other effects she had, that I said to myself immediately of course, it's impossible for me ever to be like that. So I ruled myself out of the running at once.
>
> My conception of a ballerina was definitely based and inspired by Markova. That period in the early thirties, that was really the birth of British ballet as an independent national ballet force, and I think that Markova was an asset that one can't evaluate sufficiently highly.

Though later known for her grace and charm, Fonteyn was considered a bit of a brat at the Vic-Wells. Unlike Markova's early years when she barely said a word, the teenaged Fonteyn openly critiqued everyone. Dancer/designer William Chappell, on whom the young Margot had a serious crush despite his being gay, found Fonteyn quite correct in her assessments of others' talents—or lack thereof—but was also taken aback by her cattiness. He and Ashton could be brutal mimics, but that was their prerogative as established company stars.

Fonteyn, however, always had unwavering praise for Markova, who everyone felt was far superior to all the other dancers. That discrepancy would later become problematic.

Markova, in turn, looked upon Fonteyn as if she were a member of her family: "Margot was always rather like another sister for me because she was tagged on to my sister, Bunny. I was very busy with my life, my responsibilities, and my mother said, 'If you've got to attend receptions what are you going to do with Bunny?' And of course it was Mrs. Hookham who always used to say, 'Don't worry, I'll be with them.'"

Ashton initially didn't care for Fonteyn as a dancer, telling de Valois she was "obstinate" and "strangely lacking in warmth, charm, temperament and variety." When de Valois insisted that the teenager be cast in one of his ballets, Ashton only acquiesced on the condition that *Markova* teach the "stubborn" youngster the choreography, as he wanted nothing to do with her. Markova took pleasure in educating Fonteyn, as she later reminisced: "I remember her first performance, and she'd never had anything individual, you see, on the big stage. After we did it I said, 'We have to take a call,' and she sort of stood and looked at me, and I said, 'Come on, give me your hand.'"

Just prior to the premiere of *Les Rendezvous*, Frederick Ashton received his first job offer from the United States. American composer Virgil Thomson had scored an opera with libretto by, of all people, art connoisseur and author Gertrude Stein. Though completed in 1928, *Four Saints in Three Acts* had never been produced. Now that Stein had become famous for penning her *Autobiography of Alice B. Toklas*, a Hartford, Connecticut organization—amusingly titled "The Friends and Enemies of Modern Music"—consented to stage a production of the opera, with rehearsals to take place in New York.

The choreography was to be created by George Balanchine, director of the newly established School of American Ballet co-founded by Lincoln Kirstein in 1933. The school was originally located in Hartford, as the city's Wadsworth Atheneum (the oldest public art museum in the Untied States) had sponsored Balanchine's immigration to America. But after a year spent in Hartford, the Russian choreographer requested that the school, and ensuing dance company, move to the more cosmopolitan Manhattan, so by 1934 he was no longer available to work on *Four Saints*. It was then that Ashton was contacted in London.

The offer was almost laughable: third-class steerage boat passage to New York, a twin bed in a patron's guest room—quarters to be shared with Virgil Thomson—and $10 a week pocket money. But after close friends Lydia Lopokova and John Maynard Keynes agreed to take care of his mother, Ashton took the job. He had dreams of becoming a big success in the United States and looked upon *Four Saints* as his entrée.

Following the premiere of *Les Rendezvous*, "Ashton read the glowing reviews just before he sailed the next day on the Ile de France," recounted Steven Watson in his 1995 book about *Four Saints*. While on board, the choreographer "fantasized that he would be greeted by reporters and banks of orchids, but the Four Saints collaborators were too immersed in rehearsals and too poor for any such ceremony." Besides, Americans had never heard of Frederick Ashton.

Markova was also receiving offers to leave the confines of the fledgling British ballet companies—work that would have proven far more lucrative and prestigious than Ashton's non-paying engagement in America. In addition to being courted by Hollywood, the 23-year-old was invited to become a soloist with the re-formed Ballets Russes company, now under the aegis of Colonel Wassily de Basil. The wily and often bombastic de Basil had assembled a truly stellar group from the Diaghilev days, including the impresario's former director/managers Boris Kochno and Serge Grigoriev, brilliant choreographer Léonide Massine, and experienced dancers like Alexandra Danilova. (Balanchine was also originally involved but left in 1933 to form his own short-lived company, after which he received an offer he couldn't refuse from Lincoln Kirstein in the United States.) The renamed "Ballets Russes de Monte Carlo" quickly gained a reputation as one of the best touring ballet companies.

Arnold Haskell, who became very personally involved with the organization, believed the opportunity to join such a high-caliber company is what Markova should have been waiting patiently for all along. The undisputed Russian luminaries were back, and she should now join their ranks if she had any notion of becoming a world-class prima ballerina.

Haskell was therefore completely aghast when Alicia turned them down. While she would have loved to reunite with great friends like Danilova, Markova felt a strong loyalty to the people who had literally rescued her when her career seemed hopeless.

She was far and away the best female dancer in the Vic-Wells company at the time, and she feared it might not survive financially if she left. It was not hubris. Lilian Baylis often bemoaned the fact that the theater was more than half empty on any night Markova didn't perform.

Her name might have been changed to Markova, but Alicia Marks was British through and through. She now shared the patriotic goal of Ninette de Valois and Lilian Baylis: to permanently establish a first-class all-British ballet company. Despite the lack of funds, de Valois promised to find a way to produce the time-honored Russian classics in their entirety expressly for Markova to star in. Dancing the strenuous and difficult leading roles in *Giselle*, *Swan Lake*, and *The Nutcracker*, Alicia Marks of Finsbury Park hoped to prove herself a worthy successor to the great Pavlova to whom she was so often compared.

Arnold Haskell wasn't the only one who thought Markova was making a huge mistake in choosing the young Vic-Wells over the illustrious Ballets Russes de Monte Carlo. But it did come as a shock that her great friend since childhood then chose to professionally abandon her, along with British ballet, by going to work for, and extensively writing about, the Russian company. After all, Haskell was on the advisory boards of both the Ballet Club and Vic-Wells, not to mention having co-founded the Camargo Society with its expressed goal of creating a viable British ballet concern.

A London newspaper later commented that Cyril Beaumont's scholarly books and reviews of British ballet served as a complement to "the propaganda of Mr. Arnold Haskell." Perhaps fittingly, Haskell's defection to de Basil and the Russians coincided with the Camargo's disbanding.

"All those concerned with the Society were beginning to feel that its usefulness was coming to an end," explained British ballet historian Kathrine Sorley Walker. "They had done more or less exactly what they had set out to do, presenting regular programs and providing an incentive for British ballet artists to think positively about both the present and the future. The Vic-Wells Ballet and the Ballet Club were steadily developing. Choreographers, composers, designers, and dancers had become used to working together and had little need of special performances or coordinating committees. Money, never in great supply, was getting ever more difficult to raise."

To pay off all the Society's remaining debts and hopefully raise a surplus for the Ballet Club and Vic-Wells coffers, the Camargo's ongoing treasurer, economist John Maynard Keynes, suggested two fund-raising gala performances timed to take advantage of the international crowds attending the 1933 World Economic Conference in London. Not surprisingly, the gala programs would feature Keynes's wife Lydia Lopokova as the star of the opening ballet *Coppélia*, with Markova and Dolin dancing Act II from *Swan Lake* for the grand finale.

Coaching Lopokova for her leading role was the renowned ballet master Nicholas Sergeyev, whose claim to fame was his possession of the Russian Imperial Ballet's virtual bibles of classical dance movements. Painstakingly compiled by many talented hands over a twenty-year period, the notebooks were the Rosetta stone of ballet repertory notes. Beginning with Marius Petipa's glorious choreography for timeless works such as *Giselle*, *The Sleeping Beauty*, and *Swan Lake*, the collection contained analysis and deconstruction of every step and movement in relation to the musical accompaniment of each ballet.

Sergeyev had been a former dancer and director of The Imperial Ballet at the Maryinsky Theatre in St. Petersburg, at one time supervising the documentation project. Later, for political reasons, he was forced to flee his homeland following the Russian Revolution, but not before spiriting away the bulk of this invaluable choreographic material.

The Imperial Ballet (later renamed the Maryinsky) never got over the scandalous theft, which caused as much outrage in Russian culture circles as London's plundering of the Elgin Marbles elicited in Greece. (Renamed "The Sergeyev Collection," the historical ballet papers are now housed in the Harvard University Library Theatre Collection.)

This London newspaper story—written by a dance writer who sat in on a Sergeyev rehearsal at the Vic-Wells in 1934—explains the value of the choreographic documentation process:

> I fancy there would be points of resemblance between the shorthand of M. Sergeyeff and that of Walt Disney: each has to record briefly the movement of animate creatures, with stationary signs—Mr. Disney with drawings of Mickey Mouse

> and Company, Sergeyeff with signs that represent dancers, principals and corps de ballet.
>
> The choreographist divides a sheet of foolscap paper into eight squares, and from one square to another the dancers progress. But in each square they are in movement. This has to be indicated by curved and twisted arrows.
>
> But the choreographist shorthand writer has also to think of the music, so every now and then at the bottom of the square a few bars of music are scribbled.

By 1932, Lopokova learned that the 56-year-old Sergeyev—still in possession of those treasured notes—was poor, unemployed, and living in exile in Paris. Under the auspices of the Camargo Society, she brought him to London to re-stage the classics, later persuading Ninette de Valois to hire him at the Vic-Wells. Had Lopokova realized that this grand gesture would be of greatest future benefit to her bête-noir Markova, she might have reconsidered.

Sergeyev was the ideal ballet director for the Camargo Society's re-staging of the full-length *Giselle* with the marvelous Olga Spessivtseva as the doomed heroine and Anton Dolin as her partner Albrecht. Though the production budget was quite small, Victor Dandré generously offered to loan scenery and *corps de ballet* costumes from Pavlova's former company.

Interestingly, just months before Diaghilev passed away, he too had planned to feature Spessivtseva in *Giselle*, a role she was to alternate with Markova. Diaghilev intended for the Russian star to teach the extremely difficult part to his little English girl. While those plans had sadly died with the Ballets Russes founder, Spessivtseva was now in a position to honor the impresario's wishes. She had agreed with him that *Giselle* was ideally suited to the delicate, lighter-than-air Markova.

Considered one of the finest interpreters of *Giselle*, Spessivtseva had first danced the role in Russia in 1919, followed five years later by another acclaimed production in Paris under Sergeyev's direction. Perched night after night on a tiny wicker chair just offstage in the wings, Markova was able to study every step, mime, and expressive nuance.

One of the more difficult tasks to master, she learned, was showing no signs of breathing in the death scene at the end of Act I, despite having just furiously leaped around the stage acting out inconsolable madness. Markova thought Spessivtseva quite mad herself when she ran off the stage after the first act only to dunk her head in a bucket of water. It turns out that this was the quickest way to get her long black hair, now a tangled mess, slicked down for Act II. (This was before the days of hairspray.)

Spessivtseva's costume change was equally unexpected, as only the bodice was ready-made. Markova watched in amazement as "yards and yards of white tulle were somehow whipped around her waist in an instant, and sewn on by her dresser with lightning movements."

But that was all window-dressing. The most important lesson for Markova was the realization that taking on this full-length role would require a prodigious amount of preparation and energy. Spessivtseva was so zealous about her training for the demanding ballet that she refused to work on any other roles while in rehearsal for *Giselle,* and required an entire day before each performance for complete rest.

Markova tried to do the same, but intentionally broke that rule just once. It was when she was dancing *Giselle* nearly a decade later in the 1940s. Markova was performing in New York at the Metropolitan Opera House when news reached her that Olga Spessivtseva had been placed in a mental hospital upstate.

"A combination of sad circumstances and of loneliness had led to this breakdown of a fragile and rare person, and her sensitivity, which was naturally more than average, had failed to cope with ordinary life," Markova remembered sadly. She called ahead and asked if she might visit with Spessivtseva, and was told the Russian ballerina would be only too happy to see her.

On her one day off, Markova took the seventy-mile train trip from New York City to Poughkeepsie and had a touching reunion with Spessivtseva.

"Suddenly she remembered I was to dance *Giselle* soon. She had seen my picture in the New York papers. When I told her my performance was the next day, she was most distressed, and scolded me for making the journey. How could I dream of such a thing when I should be resting in bed!"

-∞-

After his great success with Spessivtseva in *Giselle,* Sergeyev was a natural choice to direct the classical ballet performances in the Camargo Society's farewell galas in 1933, coaching Lopokova in *Coppélia* and Markova in *Swan Lake.* An additional thrill for Markova was learning that her Swan Queen was to meet the British Queen. It would be the first time the dancer had performed before the reigning monarch, whom she would be presented to following the performance. There was no question that she needed a new costume for the special occasion, but the Camargo Society could ill afford to pay for one.

Though money and time were tight, the Marks women banded together on the project. Eileen went on a hunt for affordable transparent muslin—it takes eighteen yards of netting for a short tutu and thirty-four for a traditional ballet skirt—which Doris and Vivienne then cut, gathered, and stitched together. The fine finishing work, including sewing countless sequins and glittering paillettes to the underskirt, was left to Alicia. It was crucial that all ornamentation be fastened tight, as just one single loose sequin could cause a dancer to slip if it fell on the stage. The sewing process was quite lengthy, with the costume not completed until 4:30 in the morning the day of the performance.

To insure a perfectly fitted corset, Markova arranged to be sewn into the bodice at the theater. A seamstress arrived in her dressing room in plenty of time before curtain and began carefully stitching up the back. Suddenly there was a knock at the door. There had been a change of plans. Markova would be presented to Her Majesty *before,* rather than after the performance. Would she please come immediately?

Wearing a half-sewn corset, with needle and thread stuck in the fabric, Markova grabbed for her white gloves—a requirement for meeting the Queen—and raced out of her dressing room. As royal protocol forbids ever turning one's back to Her Majesty, it seemed unlikely that the half-open bodice would be noticed. More disturbing to Markova, she was covered in white powder to heighten the swan-like effect on stage, and she worried some of it might brush off in the Royal Box.

Queen Mary was completely charmed by the lissome Markova and couldn't get over her resplendent costume. After inquiring who designed it—and discovering it was actually homemade—Her Majesty asked Markova to turn around so she could see the back of the magnificent tutu. Markova had no choice but to comply. Graciously, Queen Mary never mentioned whether she noticed the needle and thread sticking out, but she did ask Markova to send her personal regards to Eileen, who was too sick to attend the performance. Eileen was thrilled that the Queen of England had sent her regards, and the "Royal" costume adventure became a favorite Marks family story ever after.

The Camargo galas would serve their purpose. All debts were cleared and the organization disbanded. Though he was now the Society's *ex*-treasurer, the wealthy Maynard Keynes offered to continue making personal financial and fund-raising contributions to the Vic-Wells, but on one condition: his wife remain in the spotlight. To make matters worse, the 41-year-old ballerina was retiring from dancing—the Camargo gala was to be her last performance—only to turn her attentions toward a new career as a thespian.

"What Baylis had to offer in return for Keynes's and Lopokova's generosity to the Vic-Wells ballet was an opportunity for Lopokova to act," disclosed Elizabeth Schafer, Baylis's biographer. "Baylis allowed the Vic-Wells's 1933 production of *Twelfth Night* to be, in effect, sabotaged by Lopokova's appearance in the role of Olivia. Lopokova's pronounced Russian accent was incomprehensible to most people and was much ridiculed by reviewers. Virginia Woolf, embarrassed at being asked by Lopokova to review the production, occupied as many column-inches as she could with a general meditation on the difference between reading and seeing a play by Shakespeare, thus delaying the moment when she would actually have to pass comment on Lopokova's performance."

While Lopokova was mangling Shakespeare at the Vic-Wells, Markova was preparing for the company's first full-length production of *Giselle*.

"We were lucky that from the beginning we could have a ballerina of her standing," acknowledged Ninette de Valois. "She was enormously popular and had a great adoring public. I think that she was lucky also because with us she was able from an early age to dance in all the important classical roles: in those days few companies mounted full-length classics.

"She had, and still has, a photographic mind and learned very quickly. She learnt *Giselle* from Olga Spessivtseva by watching her performances with the Camargo Society. She always studied very quietly and sometimes when one thought she had not taken something in, one always found she had mastered it completely. Her great musicality has always helped her to learn a role quickly."

Perfecting Giselle would become Markova's life work. She had always been fascinated by the acclaimed performances of the past, such as the Italian Carlotta Grisi, who originated the part in 1841. Then there was the lovely Tamara Karsavina, who had memorably been partnered in the role by Vaslav Nijinsky at the Ballets Russes. Luckily for Markova, Cyril Beaumont owned an extraordinary collection of pictures and writings on the subject for her to study.

Why all this fuss about *Giselle*? Equal parts skilled acting and technical bravura, Giselle is the Hamlet of roles for prima ballerinas. It requires a difficult, dramatic metamorphosis from one act to another.

In Act I, Giselle is a fragile young village maiden with a weak heart who becomes smitten with a handsome stranger. Though he pretends to be a peasant farmer while wooing her, Albrecht is actually a nobleman, betrothed to the daughter of a duke. Nevertheless, he and Giselle fall in love and Albrecht proposes to her. Despite her mother's warnings concerning her delicate health, Giselle dances joyfully in celebration with Albrecht. After his deception is revealed, Giselle goes mad and dances herself to death.

Act II opens on a dark and murky forest beside Giselle's grave. At midnight, she rises from her tomb to join the "Wilis"—the ghostly spirits of girls who died from broken hearts—and as a group they dance male trespassers to their deaths. When a repentant Albrecht comes to visit Giselle's grave, still in love with him, she valiantly saves his life.

Though many ballerinas tend to be stronger in one act or the other, the true greats are spellbinding in both. The role takes more than just technical virtuosity. At first, the ballerina must be able to convey the wide range of emotions of a love-struck young girl through dance, mime, and tiny gestures. Act II is completely at odds with that portrayal, requiring an otherworldly yet expressive ethereality. Not everyone thought the reserved Markova was up to the task. She desperately wanted to prove them wrong.

In addition to many months of reading up on *Giselle* in Beaumont's bookshop, Markova benefited greatly from her lengthy all-morning private sessions with Nicholas Sergeyev. Through his detailed notations of the historic productions—as well as photos from Russian choreographer Marius Petipa's revival at the Maryinsky—she was able to learn every dance movement as originally performed. And since Sergeyev's "stolen" manuals married the dance steps to the beautiful score, Markova was able to use her strong musicality to master the emotional choreography.

Sergeyev also emphasized the importance of making the role her own rather than trying to be a carbon copy of anyone else. Markova would indeed develop a distinctly different interpretation of the part, later considered the quintessential Giselle of her generation.

Opening night on January 1, 1934 was not only the first time Markova would dance the role, but also the first time any British-born ballet dancer had attempted the full-length *Giselle*. As the night before the premiere was New Year's Eve, rowdy revelers in Markova's apartment building eliminated any hopes of meaningful sleep. She had been invited to the party but thought rest more important. While that hadn't worked out as planned, the next day's weather proved even more troubling.

As she sleepily sipped her morning tea, Markova looked out the window at the gloomy fog enveloping London. Rather than dispersing, it only grew thicker and heavier throughout the day. Eventually, people caught up in it couldn't see their hands in front of their faces. How would Markova, or anyone else, find their way to the theater?

The weather was "threatening to cut me off from Giselle," Markova wrote in her memoir. But she refused to capitulate. "I had to grope my way to the tube station, feeling for railing and kerbstones, instead of driving off in a taxi, ballerina-style. But I had a horrible feeling it would cut off the audience."

She needn't have been concerned. The British pride in one of their own attempting such a famous role (with the Englishman Anton Dolin as her partner) had resulted in a sellout crowd. Though the weather naturally caused some late arrivals, every seat was taken by the time *Giselle*—second on the bill after a short *divertissement*—was set to begin.

Before going onstage, Markova had received a special gift in her dressing room. Marie Rambert sent her the white bodice Tamara Karsavina had worn in Diaghilev's production of *Giselle* in 1910, the year Markova was born. It was a wonderful omen.

Though Markova had not yet mastered the achingly beautiful performance she would be capable of delivering just a few years later, she was already quite wondrous in the role and the ballet was a triumph. The British prima ballerina received an astounding twenty curtain calls, while the audience steadily chanted "Markova! Markova! Markova!"

Reviews were universally glowing:

> In presenting Alicia Markova in the title-role of Giselle, the Vic-Wells Ballet has created a precedent. Never before has an English dancer been entrusted with this role. Technically flawless, Markova has at last been given the opportunity to show that her range of mime runs from gaiety to poignancy and includes both. In a ballet that is little more than a frame for the principal dancers, her village Ophelia was neither overweighted by tradition, nor overstylized by a lack of respect for tradition. She approached the role with simplicity and sincerity; and never can a great artist have tempered dancing cadenza less with personal showmanship. By her exquisite rising to the pointes—a lightness supremely her own—and a mastery of poise in developpé and arabesque sûr les pointes that admits her to the elect of great ballerinas, she was the perfect instrument through which the tragic tale was transmitted.
>
> —*Time and Tide*, 1/6/34

And to think, she wasn't even at the top of her game yet. Though Markova had a cascade of rave reviews to cheer her the next day, she kept remembering a single line from a write-up that didn't even spell her name correctly. Though she was mistakenly called Alice in his review—perhaps because it sounded all the more British—the *Telegraph* ballet critic expressed the sentiment Markova most wanted to read: "she is an actress as well as a delicious dancer."

Also won over was Madame Manya, Pavlova's former costume designer, dresser, and traveling companion. Manya had decided to retire after her beloved employer's death in 1931, as she felt no other contemporary ballerina could compare. But she changed her mind after seeing Markova dance the classics, offering to come work for her. Markova was touched and honored. The two became close friends, just as Manya had been with Pavlova, and traveled together quite often over the years. Manya was still designing costumes for Markova in 1958 shortly before retiring. (The brilliant costumier lived to be 100 years old.)

Markova was now as famous as any theater star in London. Marie Rambert enjoyed telling the following story, recounted in her memoir *Quicksilver.* It was about Markova's first meeting with acclaimed writer T. S. Eliot, whose plays were produced at the Mercury Theatre by Mim's husband Ashley Dukes.

> One night Ashley took a box to see Edwige Feuillière and invited Eliot and John Hayward [Eliot's editor] to come with us. In the interval I saw Markova in the stalls and asked Eliot whether he would like to meet her. When I brought her up, I said, "Here is the Taglioni of today." Thereupon Hayward said, "You should rather say 'Markova of today.'" But Eliot topped it by saying, "No, what you should say is 'Taglioni was the Markova of her day.'"

But even people who had never been to the ballet now knew the name of Markova. One evening, a taxi escorted the ballerina, her flowers, and costume/makeup cases home from the theater. As the driver helped unload all her belongings, he suddenly called, "Ere, Miss, you've left your wings in the cab." "My wings?" Markova asked.

The driver pointed to a single remaining case. "They tell me you're the dancer with invisible wings, so I suppose you take 'em round with you."

While in performances of *Giselle* (now partnered with Stanley Judson, as Dolin had become ill after opening night), Markova began rehearsals for *Casse-Noisette* (The Nutcracker Suite), a classical ballet that had never been performed outside of Russia. The lilting music was a national favorite, but now the bountiful choreography would be brought to life for the first time in England.

The Sugar Plum Fairy is but one of many crowd-pleasing roles in the ballet, but it is arguably the most difficult—especially when performed with the original choreography. "The actual classical Italian variation of the last act is very hard," Markova explained. "Some of us would call it a 'killer' under our breath. There are certain steps in that, which today are never done in the last movement, such as a double *gargouillade* [complex jump and rotation movement]."

"To most of us [Markova] was, is, and always will be the one and only Sugar Plum Fairy," wrote P. W. Manchester. "She was brittle and sparkling, like the frosted icing on a Christmas cake. There was a crystalline purity in every movement, and she made the beautiful adagio an unforgettable experience."

Happily for de Valois and Baylis, Markova's success led to more and more people discovering the Vic-Wells. *British Vogue* gushed:

> Markova. Say there is no dancer now dancing, male or female, to hold a candle to her. She is as classical as Mozart and as vertebrate in her liveliness as Scarlatti, achieving irresistible freedom without ever betraying the fundamental formalities. No one should miss her *Carnaval* and *Casse-Noisette*. For her miming, which is superb, see *Giselle*.
>
> But where may Markova be seen? My dear sir (or madam), at the Vic. or the Vic-Wells Ballet. And what, pray, is the Vic-Wells Ballet? My dear sir (or madam), go and see what it is for yourself, and don't waste much time over fifth-rate stars in sixth-rate talkies.
>
> —*Vogue*, 2/21/34

Markova was now a culture-minded man's pinup girl, as in this charming confession from newspaper feature writer Herbert Farjeon:

> When I was a youth, picture postcards of actresses devoured my pocket-money. Every week I would buy half a dozen of the

> most fascinating I could find. . . . No longer do I buy picture postcards of actresses. I don't even know whether they still cost twopence. . . .
>
> But I will have twelve of Markova. Her dancing in the last scene of "Casse-Noisette" at Sadler's Wells on Tuesday was as fine as any I have ever seen—highly traditional, highly individual, immaculately severe, profoundly delicate, responsive, controlled, strict, free, perfect. Here is supreme art—the one really great experience on our stage at the moment. Twelve pictures? No, twelve thousand—for if Markova is not filmed for posterity, the future will have a black mark against 1934.
>
> —*Sunday Pictorial*, 4/11/34

While Markova was galvanizing British audiences in the Russian classics, Frederick Ashton was having his own success in New York. The reviews for *Four Saints* were quite good, but as it was an opera rather than a full-length ballet, the choreographer received only partial credit for the production. Regrettably for the hopeful Ashton, no other job offers were forthcoming.

Feeling underappreciated in England, Ashton wished to remain in the United States, and asked *New York Times* dance critic John Martin for guidance. "He advised me against it," Ashton told David Vaughan. "[H]e said that there really was no place for me there, that the American dance wasn't classical, and indeed it wasn't in those days, it was before the full impact of the de Basil company, which changed everything."

So on March 22, 1934, Ashton sailed back home, hoping he would be offered another New York engagement in the near future. "But you know how it is in America," he later reminisced. "[Y]ou've got to be there, and if you're not, you're just forgotten. . . . It would be interesting to speculate what my future might have been if I had stayed there."

Though not thrilled with returning to London, Ashton was happy to be reunited with close friends. On an emotional high from his stimulating work experience in New York, he plunged into some hard partying, drinking, and even some drug use. It didn't take long, however, before he once again felt underappreciated and depressed.

Lopokova tried her best to console Ashton, inviting him to spend time with her in the country and once again lobbying to get him work. But when Marie Rambert offered Ashton a commission to create a new ballet to star Markova, he accepted quite reluctantly. As his friend, the painter and ballet scene designer Edward Burra said reprovingly, "I'm afraid our Ashton has grown too big for the little Ballet Club and nothing smaller than the Chiswick Empire [enormous London music hall] will do now."

Constant Lambert suggested Ashton consider Franz Liszt's *Mephisto Waltz* for Markova. It was a dark, somber ballet that matched Ashton's gloomy mood. Atypically, the choreographer did not play to his prima ballerina's strengths. As one critic commented, "Some people thought Markova miscast as Marguerite, presumably because she was given nothing to show off her technique." But he continued, "a dazzling piece of classical virtuosity would have shattered the illusion of the ballet." It was a short—only eleven minutes—emotionally austere work, requiring subtle acting, which Markova was indeed praised for.

Though she was now a huge box office draw for the Vic-Wells, Markova remained a team player. Following her star turns in *Giselle* and *The Nutcracker*, she took on a supporting role in de Valois's latest work, *The Haunted Ballroom*. The ballet was expressly designed to showcase the talents of Robert Helpmann, newly signed as the principal male dancer for the Vic-Wells.

The Australian-born Helpmann had shown great promise performing with the Pavlova company in the late 1920s. De Valois likened his athleticism to Massine's, and later made notations in her logbook of Helpmann's pros and cons. In his favor, she wrote: "talented, enthusiastic, extremely intelligent, great facility, witty, cute as a monkey, quick as a squirrel, a sense of theatre and his own possible achievements therein." On the flip side: "academically technically weak, lacking in concentration, too fond of a good time and too busy having it."

The latter description could just as easily have applied to Ashton. Helpmann would have ample opportunity to show off his powerhouse skills at the Vic-Wells in the coming years. At the end of their careers, Markova and Fonteyn both said he had been their all-time favorite partner.

The first work that brought Markova and Helpmann together was *The Haunted Ballroom*, described as "a grim story in the vein of *The Fall of the House of Usher*." De Valois was highly praised for her bewitching choreography, as was Markova for her unforgettable performance. From Cyril Beaumont's review in *Dance Journal*:

> When the young heir [Helpmann] told his women guests of the tragic legend associated with the ballroom, the spectator shared in that perceptible shiver with which Markova betrayed her dread of her surroundings, as trying to mask her feelings, she glided from the room. And in the second scene, when Markova represented a ghost, could any other dancer be more phantom-like in the way she seemed now to take shape, now to drift away, paradoxically ever present and yet never there, a yielding, elusive, fascinating, maddening phantom, remorselessly forcing the master to that final mad dance which was to take his life?

Markova's stage presence was enhanced further by the ravishing costumes. As a party guest in Act I, she is the epitome of chic in a sensuous black gown with white gardenias down her décolleté. A delicate lace fan—four times normal size—alternately conceals and reveals as she gracefully glides about the stage. But in Act II, Markova appears unnervingly ghostly, with the gown now completely transparent, nothing but a wispy gossamer illusion. Markova might have had a smaller role than Helpmann in the ballet, but her every moment on stage was unforgettable, with fashion photos of her in both dramatic costumes widely published.

In the fall of 1934, Markova was to complete her ballet trifecta of classical roles, starring in England's first full-length production of *Swan Lake*. Though she previously had performed Act II of the ballet to much acclaim, dancing all four acts was a far greater challenge.

For one thing, Sergeyev gave Markova the original strenuous choreography, which is no longer done today because of its high degree of difficulty. "It was a series of 32 of this, and 32 *fouettés* (quick whipping movements of a raised leg while pirouetting on the other foot), and followed by another series of 32," Markova recalled. "That is how you had to build up such an endurance physically to be able to express emotionally the story."

Paper-thin, Markova looked as if a soft breeze could blow her down, with the press often speculating that she needed to eat more to keep up her strength. When she appeared in *The Rake's Progress*, the *Daily Sketch* reviewer commented, "Markova, as the Betrayed Girl, was her exquisite self—a delight—but one wished for her art's sake that she would eat a dozen steaks a day." Little did he know about the dancer's legendary appetite, as Marie Rambert recalled quite vividly:

> Everyone who sees Markova, that exquisite ethereal creature, must imagine she lives exclusively on air. What was our staggered surprise when after our first matinée, in which she danced the most birdlike of Swans, she sent out for a large steak and kidney pie which she proceeded to consume with relish! We were even more staggered when, at the same evening's performance, her Sylphides was lighter than air! Not one ounce of what she absorbs ever turns to fat. It is all transmuted into the most subtle instrument of dancing.
>
> Happy Markova who can eat like a mortal and dance like an immortal!

Rambert also watched in amazement when Markova's mother popped by at lunchtime to bring her featherweight daughter large quantities of food with rich cream. Eileen would do the same thing at the Sadler's Wells where the dancers' standard lunch consisted of sandwiches filled with what Markova called "mouse trap cheese" and Heinz steak sauce. Markova ate pretty much everything put in front of her, astounding both fellow dancers—many of whom needed to carefully watch their own diets—and the press.

"I used to have my meal after every performance," Markova told a radio interviewer, "a good steak and potatoes and green vegetable, and I would have a Guinness. I was encouraged to drink it to keep fit." When a newspaper reporter asked what kind of potatoes she ate (guess he had run out of questions), she promptly offered up several of her personal recipes, which the paper printed. London's Potato Marketing Board took note and contacted Markova about becoming their official spokeswoman. She later posed for a lovely portrait photo caressing a potato as if it were a precious Fabergé egg.

Markova was also completely addicted to chocolates. At the Ballets Russes she had envied Diaghilev and his large, ever-present box of the rich sweets. But even when members of the company offered her chocolates, Alicia found them quickly snatched away and rationed by Guggy. Alicia could have just one each night, unless there was some perceived infraction of a rule, in which case she got none at all. As an adult, Markova never got enough, so much so that Cadbury chocolates came calling for an endorsement. "Cadbury chocolates keep you on your toes!" says famous ballerina.

But despite her bountiful meals and snacks, Markova was still having trouble getting through all four acts of *Swan Lake*. "Dame Ninette was very worried about me," Markova recalled. "She said, 'Are you eating enough?' And I said, 'Yes, I've always had a good appetite.' But I used to get such a cramp in my calf."

De Valois discussed Markova's cramping problems with Dame Adeline Genée, a retired Danish prima ballerina who served as an adviser to the Vic-Wells. Genée said, "Oh, I know. I have something I will send her." Markova would be eternally grateful, as she later recalled in a radio interview:

> I'll always remember at Sadler's Wells there arrived this funny little jar and in it was this note from Dame Adeline and she said that she thought I may find this very useful, that she had found it served remarkably well. It was raw meat beaten—concentrated raw meat!
>
> I always kept the note as one of my treasures. She said, "I always called it my rat poison. I think it should do the trick. I heard you had a cramp at rehearsal yesterday. I don't think you'll ever have another one after this."
>
> And she was right. So whenever I was dancing Swan Lake, these jars would arrive from her. She said, "You have to eat pounds of raw meat to get the strength," and I did. And after that, no cramps.

Twenty years later, Markova was in New York having lunch with actress Mary Martin who was then starring in *Peter Pan* on Broadway.

Martin chatted about the difficulties of keeping up her strength as she literally "flew" across the stage every night. Markova passed along Genée's "rat poison" remedy (better known in fine dining circles as raw steak tartare), and Martin's trip to Neverland was cramp-free ever after.

Raw meat wasn't the only "secret" to Markova's great success in *Swan Lake.* In preparation, she treated herself to private lessons with master teacher Nikolai Legat, who had danced the role of Siegfried in the acclaimed 1895 Maryinsky production choreographed by Marius Petipa and Lev Ivanov. Markova said Legat "knew the secrets of the *fouettés*!" Petipa had only added the extremely difficult moves because his star ballerina at the time—Italian Pierina Legnani—was famous for her mastery of the thirty-two rapid-fire turns. It would prove torturous for numerous Odette/Odile's ever after.

Opening night of *Swan Lake* was almost as foggy as for *Giselle,* but by now Markova took the inclement weather as a *good* omen. So did the press, dubbing it "real Markova weather." . . . "It is a singular coincidence that all the highlights in this famous dancer's career have been heralded by a 'London particular.'"

Manya gave the dancer another good-luck charm: the jewels Pavlova had worn on her own *Swan Lake* crown were now affixed to Markova's feathered headpiece. But it was Markova's dancing that brought Pavlova back to life for Robert Helpmann, who relished his role as her partner, the dashing Prince Siegfried. That night the Swan Queen achieved her third successive triumph in a full-length classical ballet, and all in a single year.

She might have been famous, but Markova was still woefully underpaid. The Vic-Wells was an expensive operation and Lilian Baylis a notoriously tough negotiator. Markova's eking out a five-pound weekly raise was considered miraculous. Fortunately, sister Doris was now also contributing to the family's living expenses as a crowd-pleasing performer in her own right

A popular child film star at age seven, Doris Barry, as she was called professionally, was a born entertainer—pretty, outgoing, and winsomely cheeky. Lacking her sister's exceptional balletic talent, Doris turned instead to musical comedy. By age fourteen, she had made it into the chorus of several shows as an ingénue dancer. Now twenty-two, she was a saucy soubrette—the young lead in musical, comedy, and dramatic sketches—at the famous Windmill Theatre.

The Windmill opened in 1931, the brainchild of the rather unconventional Mrs. Laura Henderson, a wealthy 68-year-old widow and social butterfly looking for a new lease on life. To make a go of her new business, the short, plump dynamo hired the equally colorful Vivian Van Damm, a theatrical impresario raised in a middle-class Dutch Jewish household. Though Van Damm's entertaining revues with leggy chorus girls were initially a hit for the Windmill, competition from other West End music halls soon put a dent in ticket sales.

The cigar-chomping producer needed a hot new attraction, and he came up with a doozy. Interspersed between the singing and dancing numbers, the consummate showman added an all-nude revue. There was one small problem: stage nudity was against the law in London. So Van Damm got around the regulations by persuading the righteous Lord Chamberlain Cromer that the act was art, not burlesque. The women may have been naked, Van Damm explained, but they didn't make a single risqué move.

The producer had created a provocative version of "tableaux vivants," a mid-Victorian merging of stage and art in which costumed models were carefully posed to create "living" pictures. But there was nothing proper or Victorian about Van Damm's still-life "paintings" of naked women. Themes varied widely, from the American Wild West (cowgirl hats and gun holsters, but no clothes) to Undersea Mermaids (use your imagination), with the curtain not rising until everyone was stock still in place. Surely that was artistic modeling, not lewd stripping, asserted Van Damm.

The Lord Chamberlain mulled this over and finally came up with a ruling. Van Damm's nude show could go on as long as there was subdued lighting, no smiling, and each model placed one leg carefully in front of the other. No exceptions.

It was a deal.

The "Revudeville" became a sensation, and, due to its ongoing popularity, The Windmill was the only London theater that never closed during the bombing blitz of World War II. Or, as Van Damm bragged, "We never clothed."

It should be noted that Doris was an acting-and-dancing "Windmill Girl," not one of the naked "Revudebelles." In fact, Doris went on strike with many of the other women in the show when they learned of the all-nude revues. But just as with the fusty Lord Chamberlain, Van Damm convinced his company that what they were seeing was just like "paintings in the National Gallery." Duly satisfied, everyone went back to work.

Doris's Windmill attire wasn't exactly wholesome either, amply revealing her shapely figure and legs. Photos of her in various sexy costumes were regularly sent to newspapers to promote the theater's productions. It wasn't lost on the press just who Doris was, with captions invariably mentioning that the perky showgirl's sister was the ethereal prima ballerina Alicia Markova. That notion was a bit incongruous printed alongside Doris wearing nothing but a large playing card.

Doris and Van Damm grew quite close and were rumored to be having an affair. (He was married.) The two were often seen around town together, with Doris repeatedly asking Van Damm to come see sister Alicia perform. He repeatedly said no. But Van Damm wasn't unaware of Markova's fame, often reading about her in the London *Sunday Times*:

> **WILD ENTHUSIASM FOR MARKOVA**
> Ballet That Would Make a Foreigner Gasp
> by Our Music Critic
>
> If you want to see a packed theatre and an audience beside itself, go to Sadler's Wells on any ballet night, especially a night on which the prima ballerina is Alicia Markova.
>
> Last night was typical. Markova had been on stage for only a minute or two, dancing with Harold Turner in "The Blue Bird," when the audience went mad. They had good reason. There may be, and there may have been, better dancers than Markova, but I for one don't believe it.
>
> —*Sunday Times*, 11/4/34

One night Doris finally dragged Van Damm to the ballet, but only on the condition that he could leave early if hopelessly bored. He wasn't. Rather, he was mightily impressed, both with Markova's ability to mesmerize an audience and their wildly enthusiastic response to her.

After the performance, Doris and Van Damm went backstage, and quite naturally they all started talking shop. Markova explained that she too had appeared in many London music halls in her career, and it was actually a necessity in the summer months, as the Vic-Wells ballet season only ran from September to early May. She also lamented that the rest of the company had to scramble for summer employment in order to pay their bills. That got Van Damm to thinking.

The next day, he asked Doris if she thought her sister might like to have her own ballet company as an extension of the Vic-Wells season, one that would do something no English ballet concern had tried up until that time—touring the provinces of Great Britain.

Markova loved the idea. Not only would it keep the company intact and able to work steadily all year long, but she would also be in a position to bring ballet directly to working-class people, one of her long-term goals. Most Brits had never seen any ballet, let alone a famous Russian classic, so a bill of fare combining *Giselle* and new contemporary works would be very appealing. But there was a catch. Markova told Van Damm she couldn't seriously consider such a venture unless Lilian Baylis approved, and that worried them both.

Baylis had always been "willing to fight hard, and dirty, in her campaign to establish the Vic-Wells as a serious force," explained Elizabeth Schafer. One example was Baylis launching "a series of very hard-hitting campaigns against any foreign dance companies wanting to visit London during the October to April season that the Vic-Wells operated, arguing that these companies should be denied work permits as they might take away the hard-won Vic-Wells audiences."

As it turned out, Baylis was only too happy to give her blessing to Markova and Van Damm, as long as they agreed the touring company would retain the Vic-Wells name. It was a shrewd move. Without Baylis spending any of her own money, the Vic-Wells would reap the benefit from all the attendant publicity.

The new business arrangement established Markova as a co-Director of Vivian Van Damm Productions Ltd., with Van Damm as managing director. Mrs. Henderson agreed to underwrite the rather substantial costs, leading Lilian Baylis to exclaim, "Good luck to you. I think you will do much good for British ballet but you will lose a fortune." Her words would prove prophetic on both counts.

As the company's chief box-office attraction, Markova saw her salary jump to £40 per week, which sounds like a fortune compared to the Vic-Wells until one realizes it also needed to cover hotel, meals, ballet shoes, tights, and costumes. For that fee, Markova was expected to give eight performances every week, or four thousand pirouettes a month, according to one newspaper's calculations.

Markova brought the talented Constant Lambert with her, also at top salary, accompanied by a 43-piece orchestra, eight dance soloists, a 24-member *corps de ballet*, and a truckload of costumes and set pieces. It was no wonder the venture would cost Mrs. Henderson dearly.

For the principal male dancer, everyone wanted Robert Helpmann. Unfortunately, he had already signed a contract to appear in the revue *Stop Press* at London's Adelphi Theatre, which the producers hoped would later tour America. Anton Dolin was eventually hired in his place, signing the same one-year contract with Van Damm as Markova.

Problems arose when Helpmann's play closed prematurely and the prodigal son returned hat in hand to the Vic-Wells, much to de Valois's delight. She was thrilled to have him back, but unfortunately she had already committed to Markova and Dolin as principal dancers for the 1935–36 season. While still anxious for Markova to return, de Valois no longer needed, or wanted, Dolin. Vivian Van Damm, however, had a year's contract with Markova and Dolin, not Helpmann.

Van Damm and Dolin put the hard press on Markova. Mrs. Henderson had already made a sizeable financial investment in the Vic-Wells touring company and its two stars. If Markova went back to partnering Helpmann, Van Damm's ballet company—and Dolin's career—would essentially be in limbo.

"I would have been happiest of all if our two Companies had remained under the Vic-Wells banner, one touring the provinces and one at 'home base' in London. But this was not meant to be," opined Markova.

Explained British ballet historian Mary Clarke, "It was obvious that no merger could take place as the policies of a repertory company and a commercial company headed by two famous stars were bound to be irreconcilable. Markova and Dolin consequently left the Wells to form their own company, which was to do much valuable pioneer work in showing British ballet to provincial and West End audiences, and the Vic-Wells Ballet had to learn to stand on its own two feet."

While the eventual outcome was a mutually agreed-upon split, the process wasn't without infighting, bitterness, and threats of legal action. It was especially painful for Markova, who had seriously divided loyalties between Dolin, Van Damm, and Mrs. Henderson on one side and de Valois and Baylis on the other.

Van Damm renamed his ballet troupe the Markova-Dolin Company after his two stars, with the express goal of touring throughout Great Britain. In that way they would work toward building a larger national audience for their art without directly competing with the London-based Vic-Wells.

Back in January 1935, when Van Damm made his original proposal to Markova, Ashton also had a job offer for his frequent muse. He had been engaged to create a new work for the Ballet Club and wanted Markova in the lead. The timing couldn't have been worse. She had just finished dancing the exhausting run of the strenuous four-act *Swan Lake,* was in rehearsals for the next Vic-Wells production, and needed to reserve time for business meetings with Van Damm and Mrs. Henderson. Not feeling she could give Ashton her full attention, Markova politely turned him down. He wasn't happy.

Ashton himself often turned down job offers from friends, such as when Constant Lambert asked him to create the choreography for *Rake's Progress* later in 1935. Ashton passed, saying it was a story he had little interest in and was just "not for him." (The ballet would prove a big success for Ninette de Valois.) But the choreographer felt Markova owed him. Things were about to get very ugly.

Ashton planned to revive *Rio Grande* (formerly *A Day in a Southern Port*), the controversial ballet he had created in 1931 starring Lydia

Lopokova as the Queen of the Port and Markova as the Creole prostitute. Denounced at that time for its "licentious" topic, choreography, and costumes, the original production was considered an ill-advised choice for any refined ballet company. When Ashton decided to restage it in 1934, many were surprised. "The rather exotic little ballet was of no great importance and some people disliked it intensely," wrote Mary Clarke.

Not surprisingly, when asked to revive her role in *Rio Grande,* Markova wasn't at all keen on the idea. In her biography of Ashton, author Julie Kavanagh presents the choreographer's version of Markova's answer:

> "Oh no, I can't," she said. "Not after Giselle." [Prissy, mock-refined impersonation.] She'd become frightfully grand and thought she couldn't stoop to do my little things. We were having dinner at the Café Royal and I don't know if under my breath I said, "Fuck you, that's the end," but that's what it was. It was the end. Her utter pretension . . . I cut her out of my life.

In that retelling, Ashton failed to mention that after Markova declined the role, she generously offered to teach it to Margot Fonteyn, something she would not be paid for, as the production was for Rambert's Ballet Club, not the Vic-Wells. And even if he did find Markova pretentious, did that warrant completely cutting her out of his life over *Rio Grande*? It's not like Ashton wasn't putting on airs himself at the time.

After returning from New York, he made it clear to many friends that he thought himself too good for the piddling British dance companies, especially Rambert's Ballet Club. Had a good offer come his way in America following *Four Saints,* Ashton might never have come back at all. And while he owed Marie Rambert everything for being the first to recognize and showcase his gifts as a choreographer, he had been actively plotting to abandon her and the tiny Mercury Theatre.

To that end, Ashton lobbied de Valois for a full-time contract with the Vic-Wells. She was receptive, but told him to be patient. (How Ashton would have managed working at the Vic-Wells while not on speaking terms with their prima ballerina remains a mystery.)

As time went by, Ashton was convinced de Valois was just stalling because she was jealous of his choreographic talents, but Lydia Lopokova assured him that was not the case. She was a good friend of de Valois, and offered to intercede on Ashton's behalf. As far as Lopokova was concerned, that arrangement would kill two birds with one stone: Ashton would get a new, secure job post and Marie Rambert would be pushed out of the picture. As Lydia told husband Maynard Keynes, "I believe Mim's [Marie Rambert's] atmosphere is destructive." The additional news of Ashton no longer speaking to Markova was like manna from heaven to Lopokova.

The break between Ashton and Markova was an unfortunate end to what had been a mutually beneficial partnership. In looking back on their relationship following Markova's death in 2004, London's *The Telegraph* noted:

> . . . At 19, Markova was far ahead of any dancer in Britain, both physically and intellectually. She already possessed a superlative knowledge of ballet steps and a fine sensibility; yet she was wholly obedient in the hands of a choreographer. Without such stimulation, Frederick Ashton might have remained a gifted but light choreographer in revue. Markova taught him to hone his ballets with a subtlety and technical virtuosity that might otherwise have been beyond him, given his sketchy ballet training.

While that is likely an overstatement, Ashton owed Markova as much as she did him. For her part, she remained eternally grateful. Despite his suddenly cutting her out of his life over such a seemingly small incident, Markova continued to make social and professional overtures, such as offering him a lucrative position with the new Markova-Dolin Company. While he turned her down flat, just the thought that Ashton might take a position elsewhere finally provoked de Valois to sign him to a full-time contract at the Vic-Wells.

But rather than be upset by that outcome, Markova was happy for Ashton, and despite his ongoing enmity (which would subside two years later), she continued to send him chatty correspondences and good-luck wishes. Markova considered them friends even if Ashton did not, and she never held his rude shunning of her against him. In interviews for the rest of her life, Markova unfailingly mentioned "Dear Fred" along with Diaghilev as the two greatest influences in launching her ballet career.

The chief beneficiary of the pair's initial break in 1935 was the young Margot Fonteyn, whom Ashton had formerly written off, and now turned to as a replacement for Markova. In a later interview, he told a revealing story about their early work relationship: "When I first made contact with her [Fonteyn], I didn't respond to her at all. I found her stubborn. I found her difficult to mold, and we had quite a sort of altercation. . . . 'That's no good at all, work much harder,' I said. And she was trying very hard, and she did it once more, and then she came and burst into tears on my shoulder, and then I knew that I'd won."

Markova never cried on Ashton's shoulder. She was his equal. And though he thought going to New York was his ticket to fame and fortune, it hadn't worked out that way. When Ashton returned to London, Markova had become the star of *Giselle* in his absence. Her success now eclipsed his—she aged twenty-three, he already thirty. No wonder his resentment began to build. There was no "winning" for him over Markova's refusal to do anything.

When Markova told Ashton that the controversial role of a Creole prostitute was no longer right for her—"Not after *Giselle*"—she was right, no matter what tone of voice she used. Markova was now considered not just the best British-born ballerina, but also a world-class dancer worthy of her Russian predecessors.

Though Ashton and Fonteyn would prove a magical partnership, Meredith Daneman concluded that "Ashton badly missed Markova and the artistic collaboration which he had enjoyed with her. Margot came to him uninitiated. He felt 'set back' by having to take his inspiration from a stubborn child who seemed to have pitted her exasperating will against his. Rehearsing with her, he admitted to 'a great frustration in being unable to mould her as precisely as I wanted.'"

Though not personally a pushover, Markova had always been malleable as a dancer. She felt that was her job. And no matter what Ashton said, she wasn't a snob on a star trip. After passing on the prostitute's role in *Rio Grande*, Markova had no problem taking a tiny part in *The Rake's Progress* for Ninette de Valois, even though it wasn't especially suited to her personality or capabilities. The work was the first major English-themed classic ballet, and therefore considered a breakthrough. Markova's name helped sell tickets, and she was all for anything that promoted the stature of British ballet.

When interviewed after *Rake's Progress* premiered, Markova playfully told the press: "I look forward to the day when Russian girls will assume English names because all the great ballerinas are English."

"Markova is, in my mind, one of the most remarkable cases in ballet," observed Ninette de Valois. "She has always been a very generous and loyal person. Like all great artists, her qualities are very personal. They are not easily defined, and one eventually accepts them as a part of 'Markova,' rather than a part of the classical tradition of ballet in general."

Ashton would eventually come to share that view. By 1939, he had forgiven Markova, who in her desire to reach ever-wider audiences had finally joined the Ballet Russe de Monte Carlo (no longer managed by Wassily de Basil). She would be an invaluable ally to Ashton when the company's artistic director, Léonide Massine, asked him to work on the choreography for a new ballet.

Just before the commission was to commence, Ashton's mother passed away, delaying the start date. Markova assured Ashton that Massine would understand and sent letters of sympathy and encouragement. After discovering that he was Massine's *third* choice for the assignment, Ashton became as insecure as he was depressed. Upon arriving in Monaco, he pleaded with Markova to attend all the rehearsals for his new ballet, even those where she was not dancing. He needed her strength and advice, and she didn't hesitate to help out.

The two would often send warm letters back and forth through the years, but the most touching came from Ashton just after the war. Markova was still performing in the United States and had tracked Ashton down in London to send birthday greetings and a gift.

"Darling Alicia," he replied, "Thank you so much for the cable of birthday wishes & for the parcel which has just arrived, it was most sweet of you to think of your old friend & I loved being remembered for it has been a cruel and frustrating war for me & during all these boon years I was in the R.A.F. & missed the fruits of my early pioneer labours. I suppose I was foolish not to come to America when I received the initial offer . . . I felt my place was here & I paid my price . . . perhaps I shall be all the better artist for it, even though I doubt [it].

"Ballet is such a rage now and the standards are so low, especially in male dancing & friend Helpmann is all the rage." (As an Australian, Robert Helpmann wasn't conscripted into Britain's armed forces and had taken Ashton's place at the Vic-Wells.) "[T]hey love him and the crowds at the stage door for him are phenomenal, he is now choreographer as well and his ballets are a great success, & he acts, makes films & the sun shines on him."

Ashton then talks about the ballets he has been working on and confesses that though "Margot Fonteyn is a really beautiful artist, now rather in the aloof Karsavina way," she is "slightly lacking—attack," a trait he had appreciated in Markova. "I always read with interest of your great success in America & people G.I.'s mostly who I have seen all rave over you. I do wish I could see you. I am now demobbed [discharged from military service] & I am getting on & have wasted 4 years of precious life & time to make money. Tudor I hear is also raved over. How I would give much to see a Balanchine Ballet again. To me he is the most satisfying & the real choreographic genius of the day, novel, inventive & the one who has carried the banner furthest forward."

After news about his current projects and upcoming engagements, Ashton mentions, "I saw Doris & Vivian the other day. They were both well & gave me all your news. I would love to see you dance again Giselle & Rendezvous. Perhaps you might come as a guest artist & dance at the Garden. I can't tell you how happy I am to be back at work again after my spiritual sacrifice.

"My darling my blessings on you, may you continue to flourish & to become a better & greater dancer & may you be happy in work & in love."

The closing is equally touching:

> "Remember your old friend. With love & affection.
> Fred X X X X"

7

Leaving the Nest

> Markova has the perfect hands of a great ballerina. They are white and delicately moulded, and she uses them as eloquently as a great actress uses words. But, as she sat with me last night, a charming soignée creature in silver-grey and scarlet, she did not seem to be wholly with me. Part of her was waiting for the moment to-night when she will flit into the white brilliance of the footlights.
>
> —"Markova Comes to Glasgow: Britain's Greatest Ballerina," *Glasgow Evening Times*, 8/5/35

Though temperamentally quite different, Sergei Diaghilev, Anna Pavlova, and Ninette de Valois all had an unwavering entrepreneurial zeal and personal artistic vision, as if creating a ballet company was their one true destiny.

Not Alicia Markova.

The prima ballerina had worked hard to become the reigning Queen of the Vic-Wells Ballet and she was very happy in that singular role. The younger dancers all looked up to her and she had a congenial, mutually beneficial relationship with de Valois and Lilian Baylis. All three women admired and respected each other for their particular skills, and were banded together in a common goal: to legitimize and popularize British ballet.

There was also a sense of belonging, something Markova would seek out—and often fail to find—her entire life. Family was everything. She had lost her loving father at a young age, quickly followed by a separation from her mother and three sisters when Diaghilev whisked her away to the greatest ballet show on earth. But for little Alicia, the Ballets Russes was initially a lonely and isolating experience in many ways, given that she was so much younger than everyone else, didn't speak their language, and was held a virtual prisoner by the unstable Guggy. Only after her "keeper's" death would Markova learn to fend for herself, come out of her shell, and earn the respect of her peers. It took almost five years, but the slow climb had been worth it.

Then, *poof*! Another death, another fall to earth. Diaghilev was gone, and so too was her whole world. It had all been just a house of cards.

It would take another four long years for Markova to stack the deck back in her favor, despite her "exotic" looks and the undercurrent of religious prejudices she encountered from the likes of Lopokova and Keynes.

Now her career was once again on the rise, this time with the added support system of her mother and three sisters to go home to each evening. Markova learned much too early that contentment was a precarious state, and she was in no great hurry to leave her hard-won security behind.

True, she wasn't earning a salary commensurate with her talents, but earning top dollar was never the driving force in the dancer's career decisions. She had enough to provide comfortably for herself and her family. That was enough. The Vic-Wells had mounted full-length productions of three of the most celebrated classical Russian ballets for her, and all in a single year. No other ballet company would have attempted such an undertaking for an untried novice in those roles, no matter how talented she appeared to be. De Valois and Baylis had gambled on Markova, and together they had all won.

Though Lilian Baylis couldn't reward her prima ballerina with great wealth, she was never stingy with her praise, and she encouraged Markova to take all the outside engagements she wished to earn extra money. "I want you to do lots of well paid work, but hope you'll manage to come to us in between with good enjoyment," she wrote Markova in January 1932. Baylis never tried to "control" her star, as many others had (and would), nor did she take her for granted. For that, Markova was eternally grateful. Though many offers came her way before and after her success in *Giselle*, the Vic-Wells prima ballerina made it clear that she wanted to sign on for another year.

"I am so happy that you want to return to us next season," Baylis wrote to Markova in May 1934, "and I hope that you will feel that you can do so for the weekly salary of £12 with an additional fiver to cover extra performances in the week. . . . It is such a happiness to me to have you with us, and I know that Ninette, too, rejoices not only in your lovely work, but in the help you give her generally. Thank you so much for it all."

Markova knew her worth (the Regal Cinema had paid her £20 four years earlier), but she countered with a figure she thought the Vic-Wells could afford: £15 per week. Uncharacteristically, Baylis capitulated right away, replying, "We just feel that we would hate to lose you, and that your presence in the company, and your general willingness to help in all sorts of ways, is invaluable, so we will make your weekly salary £15 with £5 for any extra performances. . . . I am so glad that you feel you want to stay with us."

Markova could have gotten much more money from another ballet company (Van Damm would soon offer her £40), but the raise was as much symbolic as it was necessary. Knowing how much she was needed and appreciated was a priceless commodity to the 23-year-old who had often been denied such good will and high regard in the recent past. Just five years earlier, Markova's ethnic looks had cost her jobs, the Camargo Society had snubbed her, and friend Arnold Haskell had compared her unfavorably to other more physically beautiful dancers. Then there was the fresh sting of Ashton's sudden and surprising shunning.

Markova's secure position and tremendous popularity at the Vic-Wells was one of the reasons she had spurned offers from prestigious ballet companies looking to introduce her *Giselle* to America. Would they welcome her as Londoners had? Would she again feel isolated in a new country?

Markova was a large fish in a small pond and she knew it. For now, she was willing to swim just so far.

When Vivian Van Damm offered Markova her own ballet company in the spring of 1935, her interest was piqued for just two reasons: it would give employment to members of the Vic-Wells company in their off-season, and they could introduce classics like *Giselle* to new audiences throughout the British Isles, rather than just in London. She had no burning desire to be out on her own or anyone's "boss," and she saw the new venture as merely the summer extension of her Vic-Wells home.

Underscoring that sentiment, Markova asked Ninette de Valois to be her co-director in Van Damm productions, but she had declined. De Valois was never keen on the idea of Markova and Van Damm taking what essentially was her own company on the road. It was a natural response. De Valois had done all the hard work in assembling and training the dancers, and felt proprietary about their future engagements. But Baylis overruled her, wishing to take advantage of all the free countrywide press and the infusion of cash.

De Valois also had other problems that demanded her immediate attention at the time. She became ill while choreographing *Rake's Progress*—set to premiere on opening night of the Vic-Wells off-season tour—and later required hospitalization. (She would recover both physically and emotionally, as she ended up marrying her doctor—a long and happy union.) On top of all that, Robert Helpmann was deserting her for the London stage. He had been the first star-wattage male principal she had groomed from her own ranks, and she was greatly distressed at his loss.

While it was common for Vic-Wells performers to take on more lucrative off-season engagements, Helpmann had signed on for a role in the West End musical *Stop Press,* which was scheduled to go on tour in the fall. The pay was much higher than the £3 per week he earned dancing for de Valois, so he decided to resign from the company.

If only he had learned of Van Damm's generous offer a month earlier for Markova's "summer" company, thought de Valois; but Helpmann might have signed on for the revue just the same. The musical included several production numbers from *The Band Wagon*, which had been a Broadway hit for Fred Astaire in 1931 (and a popular 1953 film he would star in). Helpmann shared the dance world's admiration for Astaire and was thrilled to be literally following in his footsteps. Helpmann had bigger plans for himself than just ballet.

Anton Dolin felt similarly. Throughout the early 1930s, the former Ballets Russes soloist had more jobs in vaudeville-type revues and musical comedies than in ballets. The work was steady, paid well, and reached a much larger audience than British ballet.

Arnold Haskell was appalled at Dolin's "denigration" of his talents:

> [H]e should have ruined his career time and time again through his flirtations with the commercial stage, with banality and bad taste. Few dancers can survive a season of music-hall appearances, certainly no young dancer. I have followed him carefully in the music hall, and it hurt me, both for his sake and for the art that he represents. . . . He has done dreadful things, vapid, meaningless, flashy things; he knows it, and so far he can always recover in time, and in the right surroundings.

Haskell was even more upset when Dolin announced that he was considering permanently leaving ballet and becoming a full-time stage actor. As he told his friend Haskell:

> I don't want people to say about me: "You should have seen him when he was young"—it has made me suffer too much for others. I know quite well that the big name I made had something to do with my youth and freshness. As Le Beau Gosse in Le Train Bleu I created a new type of dancing. It was the one Diaghilev ballet that was never revived for anyone else. That is something to remember, and I don't wish people to forget it by leaving it too far behind.

It was Dolin's curse that his most acclaimed balletic role, an athletic tour-de-force in Bronislava Nijinska's *Le Train Bleu*, occurred in 1924 when he was just twenty years old. At that time, Dolin was Diaghilev's first non-Russian male lover, a potentially risky liaison for the impresario. As Lydia Lopokova would anxiously write to John Maynard Keynes, it was "dangerous for Serge to be in sexual relations with a Britt. Shadow of Oscar Wilde." (The homosexual Wilde had been imprisoned in England for "gross indecency" with other men.)

Never a cautious man, Diaghilev pursued Dolin nonetheless, and presented him with the starring role that best displayed his singular acrobatic gifts. But as Sjeng Scheijen writes in his biography of Diaghilev, the impresario "also made an effort to tutor Dolin, as he had done before with Nijinsky and Massine, but his new protégé proved to be a less apt pupil"—and, according to Dolin, a reluctant lover. Soon Serge Lifar would replace Dolin in both Diaghilev's affection and key roles.

Anton Dolin was a very fine dancer, and the first international British male ballet star; but he would not prove to be a highly original and inspired performer in the mold of Nijinsky, Massine, or, later, Nureyev. The Brit's true strengths were in the classics, as an artistic director, choreographer, and superb partner to prima ballerinas. An often undervalued talent, partnering female dancers is a true art in and of itself. Many male principals—Lifar and Massine in particular—weren't willing to subordinate their own considerable technical abilities in order to showcase the female lead, a necessity in many scenes in the Russian classics. It is a credit to Dolin that he was entirely unselfish in that regard.

"[A]s a partner Dolin has always sought to put the ballerina in the limelight and to make of himself a fitting background," wrote Haskell. "The audience can feel the obvious admiration that he has for his partner and their pleasure grows with his."

A prolific writer of many ballet books (including *four* autobiographies), Dolin penned *Pas De Deux: The Art of Partnering* in 1949, a well-regarded work among fellow dancers that has been reprinted numerous times over the years. But as an immensely talented partner, by definition that meant Dolin needed an illustrious ballerina by his side.

When no longer Diaghilev's "favorite" at the Ballets Russes, Dolin chafed at being told what to do and which ballets to perform in. At the age of twenty-one, he returned to London, and with no British prima ballerinas yet on the scene for him to partner, he decided to pursue dance work in popular music-hall productions.

But Dolin never fully gave up classical ballet. In 1927, he approached the lovely Vera Nemtchinova to partner him in a new company. The celebrated Russian prima ballerina performed regularly with Massine and Pavlova's former partner Mikhail Mordkin. Though Dolin launched the Nemtchinova-Dolin Ballet Company in 1927, he would abandon it one year later to return to the far more successful Ballets Russes when George Balanchine called, leaving Nemtchinova to fend for herself.

Following Diaghilev's death, Dolin again returned to England, now thinking popular musicals might be his ticket to stardom. While pursuing that new course—performing in *Charlot's Masquerade* (1930) with comedienne Beatrice Lillie, and *Stand Up and Sing* (1931) with Jack Buchanan (who would later co-star with Astaire in *The Band Wagon*)—Dolin was asked to be on the advisory board for the newly formed Camargo Society. In that capacity, he danced in their quarterly productions, as well as guest-starring at the Vic-Wells—his name being a big box-office draw for Ninette de Valois's fledgling company—but ballet clearly played second fiddle to his West End career. As Dolin wrote in autobiography number three, "I danced many times for Lilian Baylis, often at great inconvenience to myself, dashing from the theatre at which I was appearing, to Sadler's Wells."

While performing in the West End show *Ballerina* (1933), Dolin decided to produce and star in a play based on his own life and experiences with the Ballets Russes—an enormous undertaking. The resulting *Precipice* (1934) was fraught with legal and production problems (an almost identical story about Nijinsky was being adapted at the same time), and Dolin wound up deeply in debt. To pay back his creditors, he took any job he could get in the commercial theatre. Some were quite dreadful, such as the aptly named *West End Scandals* (1934).

It was at this juncture that Alicia Markova told her dear friend Patte, as she always called Dolin, about Van Damm's need for a male principal dancer for their company, as Helpmann wasn't available. After having just spent over a year of his life recreating his Ballets Russes glory days for the stage, Dolin was undoubtedly nostalgic for what might have been. He also knew that his best chance at a secure future in ballet was as the partner of a truly great classical ballerina. Alicia Markova fit that bill perfectly.

Throughout the years, Dolin took more than his fair share of credit for Markova's early success, while failing to grasp what she did for him. As he was the more outspoken of the two, Dolin was also assumed to be the publicity and organizational mastermind for their various career triumphs together. But most of all, Dolin is forever praised as Markova's great protector and supporter, as if her needs were always his major concern.

Impresario Sol Hurok wrote in one of his memoirs, "Markova, if she is honest, and I have no reason to believe she is not, should be the first to admit her profound debt to three persons in ballet: Anton Dolin, who has projected her, protected her and occasionally pestered her; Frederick Ashton and Marie Rambert who, jointly and severally, encouraged, advised, and guided her." And indeed, in interviews throughout her life Markova did unfailingly thank all three (although Ashton and Dolin did not return the favor) in addition to Ninette de Valois, Lilian Baylis, and Diaghilev, among others.

Markova's physical frailty added to a sense of helplessness about her, as if she were a ballet Blanche DuBois dependent on the kindness of others. Markova fed into that image herself, not wishing the public to learn of her considerable managerial and business skills for fear that that might diminish her ethereal onstage persona. It was therefore easy for Dolin to publicly take credit for much of Markova's success, many of his claims dabbling in revisionist history.

In Dolin's biography of Markova, he immodestly writes: "Though Alicia has always said that Anna Pavlova was the object of her first hero worship, I like to feel that perhaps I was second. Not because of any attraction I might have had for her, but because of the glamour of my wonderful position, dancing in the great Diaghileff Ballet production of *The Sleeping Beauty*." In that production, as Dolin himself explains in a later autobiography, "all he [Diaghilev] really wanted was a few extras who looked good, moved well, and could adorn the stage in a magnificent Bakst costume."

At that time, Dolin was hired as a temporary, decorative corps dancer exclusively for the London run. (And had Markova not come down with diphtheria, she too would have danced in the production.) When little Lily Marks went to see *The Sleeping Beauty* as Diaghilev's special guest, she certainly did find her second ballet idol—prima ballerina Olga Spessivtseva—although the ten-year-old was extremely proud that her classmate Patte appeared in the production as "a royal page."

Dolin also pats himself on the back for trying—yet failing—to find Markova employment with him in musical comedies when she was destitute and unemployed after Diaghilev's death. Was it his fault she just wasn't deemed "pretty" enough for the popular stage, he asks? But Dolin was also on the founding board of the Camargo Society at that time; yet he never thought to suggest Markova be invited to participate in the planning or opening night gala performance. It was a real slap in the face that she was the only British ballet dancer of any standing who was not invited. In his biography of Markova, Dolin writes how hurt she was at the time, never mentioning that he had been in a position to have helped her.

Then there's the Markova-Dolin Company, the brainchild of Van Damm, where Dolin has been consistently credited as Markova's star-maker. Touring the British provinces did indeed turn her into a nationally known and celebrated artist, but it undoubtedly would have happened with or without Dolin. While he was truly a marvelous ballet partner to her, Markova had already won over London audiences dancing with many other male soloists, most recently Robert Helpmann—her first choice for the new venture. In the spring of 1935, it could be said that Dolin needed Markova more than she did him.

When Van Damm learned that Helpmann would be unavailable for his company with Markova, Dolin was appearing in the touring musical revue *King Folly*, where he danced the Cucaracha following a lewd comedy act and a snake charmer—a career low point to be sure. It was Markova who suggested that Dolin leave *King Folly* and come back to work full-time in the ballet with her—and, one might add, at a very considerable salary bump.

"Dolin was internationally known but by no means in Alicia's class as an artist," wrote the astute Agnes de Mille in 1953. "He was athletic, flamboyant, and unbridled, and produced narcissistic displays of egotism matched only by a few. With her, however, he curbed his more aggressive instincts, and he served her truly and well. They made a remarkable couple, the unleashed vulgarity of the one offsetting the purity of the other."

So on Markova's recommendation, Van Damm offered Dolin the same one-year contract his prima ballerina had signed. That included being part of a touring company from May to September, followed by Markova and Dolin returning to the Vic-Wells come fall, when Van Damm would make up the difference between the weekly salaries Baylis paid them and the £40 stipulated in their personal contracts with him. It would bring Dolin more job security and money than he'd had in the past five years.

Dolin quickly left *King Folly*, as he tellingly recalled in his autobiography:

> Saturday evening I finished dancing in Sunderland to Stanelli's accordion band, Monday evening I was dancing Tchaikovsky's Swan Lake with Markova for the first time. I was glad to be dancing with her again, with a fine orchestra conducted by Constance [*sic*] Lambert, surrounded by good dancers, and in front of an audience that appreciated Ballet. . . . I had had six months of another kind of work. It had been useful. I had paid my debts. I had enjoyed doing it. But now I was back in my right element.

In the end, it could be said Markova saved Dolin from himself.

All went well during the summer tour. Markova, Dolin and the other members of the Vic-Wells Ballet in their new guise were welcomed wherever they went. Theaters were full, audiences rapturous, and ten or more curtain calls the norm. That pioneering effort should not be underestimated.

As a Birmingham newspaper trumpeted: "This is the first time that a British ballet company has toured the provinces; and there is a great deal of significance—and romance—in the event, for it sets a seal of triumph on the first attempt that the art has made to win a place for itself in this country."

In addition to Markova and Dolin, the company featured many talented British dancers including Walter Gore, Harold Turner, William Chappell, Ursula Moreton, Beatrice Appleyard, and a very young Margot Fonteyn. Ninette de Valois traveled with them as technical adviser as well as a principal dancer.

Having a top-notch English company perform in their hometowns was a thrill for audiences throughout the British Isles, and they quickly fell under Markova's spell. People had never seen anything like her, and the fawning press couldn't stop waxing poetic and mixing metaphors in attempts to capture her allure. From a Blackpool newspaper review in the summer of 1934:

> Markova—she is moonlight on a rippling stream, she is the wind stirring the pine trees, ruffling the golden tops of corn; she is thistledown blown from the lips of a child.
>
> Or, if you like the metaphor better, she makes the average tap-dancer look like a centipede with sore feet.
>
> Markova—no wonder a Bank Holiday audience thundered applause upon you, upon your smile, upon the twin poems your flashing limbs, your little feet so full of quicksilver!

My goodness.

Dolin and the rest of the company also received excellent reviews, but the press clearly couldn't get enough of Markova. The provinces were not London. Newspaper readers wanted loads of "human interest" stories along with current events. Markova became more than just a celebrated dancer. People wanted to know everything about this exotic creature who so enthralled them on stage with her seeming ability to defy gravity. What was she really like?

The avalanche of personality profiles on Markova seemed to take Dolin by surprise. As he had already toured the provinces several times himself in musical-comedy revues, surely his name carried more weight than hers? While performing as a guest artist with Markova at the Vic-Wells several years earlier, he had insisted his name be twice the size of hers on all promotional material, even though she was the company's prima ballerina.

When the summer tour of the provinces began, Dolin fondly recalled a group of adolescent female fans waiting for him at the stage door one evening. As he wrote in his 1960 autobiography, "'Oh, Mr. Dolin,' they chorused, 'we didn't know you danced ballets like *Les Sylphides* and *Swan Lake.* We've seen you with Jack Buchanan in *Stand Up and Sing* and in *Ballerina,* but we didn't know you danced ballets like that.' Such is fame!" Dolin boasted.

But that familiarity seemed to work against him with the press, and though it didn't breed contempt, it didn't engender great interest either. In his 1953 biography of Markova (one of many attempts at co-opting her fame), Dolin tells the story of the Glasgow Theatre manager, who knew *him* well from a previous tour of *Stand Up and Sing,* but wondered aloud, "Who is this Markova? Is she good? What part of Russia does she come from?"

While the second question would be answered quite quickly, the first required a bit of digging. Markova was a mystery the press was eager to unspool, and their coverage of her would follow a similar trajectory from city to city.

First came the rave performance reviews, with headlines like "MARKOVA—THE SUPREME ARTIST," "DRAMATIC MARKOVA," and "MARKOVA'S GENIUS." Next came the biographical features of her early hardships, such as "MADAME MARKOVA, the famous ballerina of the Vic-Wells Ballet now in Glasgow, was almost a cripple when she was a child!"

Finally, there appeared the revealing, one-on-one interviews—very descriptive, and oh so "*intime*"!

I Meet Markova

A fascinating woman who is Queen of her Art

... Enormous dark eyes in a pale face, hair like black silk, and a wide red mouth. Markova matches her nails and her lipstick to the touches of scarlet in her dress. This day she wore a grey skirt and sweater with a wide scarlet belt, a scarlet bow at the throat, and a twist of scarlet on her flat, wide-brimmed hat of navy straw.

Her feet are so tiny that all her shoes, ballet shoes included, have to be built for her. . . . On her own confession, she is a superstitious little person, and always picks up pins!

—*Glasgow Evening News*, 8/10/35

Spend to-day with a Ballet Dancer

Like Napoleon (or a horse) Madame Markova can sleep twenty-four hours a day and standing up—but most days there's so much to do, she sleeps lying down and for only eight hours.

She would like to be a doctor; hates cold and cruelty to animals; loves children, flowers, and Tinker (large cat who loves Markova and eats flowers and bananas). Favourite breakfast is half grapefruit, thin brown bread and butter, honey and tea; golden hour: dinner after the show; golden rule: allows no one to touch her ballet shoes or to sew on their ribbons.

—*Daily Mirror*, 8/25/36

Secrets of a Dancer Markova Talks of Her Life

by a Special Correspondent

Famous people nearly always surprise us off stage. That was the way with Markova, premiere danseuse in the Vic-Wells company at the Leeds Grand Theatre—already whispered to be the second Pavlova.

She is quite a shy little person, with dark sad eyes and an unassuming manner. She dresses with astonishing simplicity—for morning wear, plain black with a touch of white at the collar. Her hair is quaintly and elaborately coiled on either side of her head and at the nape of the neck.

"I do it myself," she said. "It's past my waist. I believe lots of people think it's a wig."

She moves about the room like a little mouse, and when she speaks her voice seems to be coming from far away, and her thoughts to arise from the profound depths of a life of struggle.

—*Leeds Mercury*, 9/4/35

Eventually, Markova was asked to pen her own day-in-the-life feature stories that were published in British newspapers and magazines. While detailed descriptions of how often and how much she ate always amused, Markova also gave readers thought-provoking insight into her artistic process, as in the following passage describing her late-morning ritual after breakfast, deep-tissue massage, and *barre* practice:

> . . . Then, very often, I go to an exhibition of painting or sculpture, or sometimes the British Museum (most often to the Greek room) or a walk in the Park or round some quiet spot like London's Inn or the Temple. It is good to have a little while every day for exploration and adventure. All other art forms have something to give to dancing as has every aspect of Nature or of architecture, and it is surprising how often a shade of colour in some painting, a turn of the wrist or shoulder in some statue, the fall of a leaf in a London square, the light in an urchin's eyes, gives one a sudden understanding of a phrase of music or an elusive emotion which has hitherto been puzzling and difficult.
>
> —British magazine *The Lady,* 10/10/35

It was Diaghilev who taught Markova that the key to elevating her artistry was in the constant study of physical beauty beyond the world of ballet. She may have been his most apt pupil in that regard. As she told another newspaper reporter in 1935, all spare time should be given over to observing other art forms that might enhance one's own performance (except when other people were in need, which would sadly soon become the case for her country).

> When I met her [Markova] in her dressing-room at the Theatre Royal last night, I asked her if she had any recreations and hobbies apart from her work.
>
> **With Mme. Markova**
>
> She smiled her slightly wistful, April-like smile.
>
> "No, you see it requires so much of my time. In the comparatively small amount of leisure I have I visit museums and art

> galleries in order to get new ideas. For ballet work one needs new ideas all the time."
>
> . . . She has liquid brown eyes and gleaming black, smoothly braided hair. She is exquisitely dainty, and has an almost naively gentle manner for a person who has been so much written about and admired.
>
> She was extremely busy when I arrived preparing an appeal which she is making to the members of the company on behalf of the South Kirkby mining disaster.
>
> —*Birmingham Despatch*, 8/27/35

Though Dolin was happy that the press relentlessly covered Markova, a great boon to ticket sales, he also seemed a bit taken aback by the lack of interest in his own story. It's not as if his former Diaghilev days wouldn't have made compelling reading. Unfortunately, Dolin had already told that story himself in *Divertissement* (1931), the first of his four autobiographies. Quite literally, he was already an open book. Moreover, in the provinces outside of London, he was better known as a musical-comedy dancer, and one who played the second banana, not the leading role.

Dolin also suspected, quite rightly, that being a male ballet dancer was looked upon as an unmanly profession in the provinces, another reason the press was less interested in him. He took every public opportunity to counter that notion:

> **The Male Prejudice**
>
> . . . Mr. Dolin went on to explain that he was practically the first British male dancer who had become of any importance. The average Englishman, he said, is somewhat timid and shy. He is terrified that he will be thought effeminate, and there was for many years a prejudice against men dancing, because all dancing was considered effeminate. At last it was being overcome, and there were now several very fine young British male dancers, including Harold Turner and Walter Gore, who appear with the Vic-Wells Ballet.
>
> —*Edinburgh Evening News*, 8/12/35

Markkova and Anton Dolin

. . . Anton Dolin came in.

"Is it true," I asked him, "that you are seriously considering going on the straight stage eventually?"

"Perfectly true," he said. "When the time comes for me to give up the ballet I intend to try my hand at it."

Dolin is a man of great versatility. He is an extraordinarily fine athlete. Swimming and diving are his chief hobbies.

"It's the most absurd nonsense," he said, "to suppose—as many people do—that ballet dancers are effeminate people who follow a strict diet and never smoke or drink. You should see Markova eating! If she knows there's going to be roast duck for supper she performs twice as well!"

Markova laughed.

—*ISIS* magazine interview
by Walter Andrews, 12/4/35

If the press chose not to focus on him personally, Dolin made sure his name still got in print by discussing the state of ballet itself, its growing popularity throughout England, the company's high standards, and the huge costs involved in mounting a touring production—all topics of interest.

He also claimed the role of public spokesperson for himself—and Markova—whenever they made joint public appearances, a chore she gladly relinquished. As Agnes de Mille noted of the pair, "When the royal couple went out socially it was Pat [Dolin] with his Irish wit who talked; Alicia, looking exquisite, sat in a nimbus of attention and chirped."

"I dreaded being surrounded by a throng of people who expected me to give a lively discourse on 'My Favourite Rôle'!," Markova recalled of those days. "Time and an international career have changed all this."

Many people found it strange that Markova would sit so silently and attentively by Dolin's side. Some speculated she was in love with him, but that was never true in any romantic sense. Markova loved Dolin, but was never *in* love with him. He was like a member of her family. When an interviewer asked how she and Dolin matched temperamentally, Markova replied, "I wouldn't say we match at all. I think we're poles apart."

"Who's the practical one?"

"I'm afraid I am."

Dolin agreed: "On the stage we had a similar mental approach to our work, but away from the theatre no two people could be more dissimilar."

As with Frederick Ashton, Dolin was a preening party boy who adored being the center of attention, and with his devilishly entertaining banter, he was quite able to hold on to it. In his youth, he had the look of a handsome 1930s Hollywood film star: dramatic profile, slicked-back hair, cigarette dangling from the corner of his mouth. He was also a rather natty dresser in the Cary Grant mode of nonchalant elegance.

What Dolin lacked, however, was Grant's unspoken magnetism. The dancer's flamboyance and need to be noticed were just too obvious, though he could certainly charm a crowd. He was also publicly bisexual, something most performers attempted to hide in the 1930s. Dolin "never felt a need to be secretive," wrote Antony Tudor's biographer Donna Perlmutter. "Just the opposite. He was entirely candid about his many affairs with men."

While men would be the great loves of his life, Dolin had his fair share of dalliances with women, most of them famous or rich. As author/broadcaster John Drummond wrote in his book *Speaking of Diaghilev*, "I had always understood that Dolin was very fond of money, and spent most of his time in the company of rich older women who, though not exactly keeping him, certainly helped with the bills, and eventually left him quite large sums." The author also reveals that when he met up with Dolin to conduct an interview, the dancer took him to a scruffy gay bar in Cannes where he later sneaked out, leaving Drummond with a sizeable check he couldn't pay.

Markova may not have been aware of all the details of Dolin's complicated love life, but she certainly knew his proclivities and never considered him husband, or even boyfriend, material. As Dolin himself confesses in his biography of Markova, she liked quiet time after performances and took enormous care with her health habits; he liked all-night parties, drinking, and "smoking to excess." He says her personal life would have bored him silly, adding they nevertheless were completely tolerant of each other's disparate temperaments offstage.

Pat was one of Markova's best friends, despite those differences and frequent disagreements. He had known her since she was ten years old and was close to every member of her family. He adored her mother, and she his. Dolin was a jolly and gay presence, Markova more quietly amused. And both were capable of being tremendously annoying.

As partners, the pair spent more time together than practically any married couple, from rehearsals and performances to frequent gin rummy games in downtimes. When congratulatory crowds descended on Markova's dressing room after a performance, Dolin was there to divert attention from the exhausted ballerina, who would have preferred solitude to recuperate. He played host for both of them, and she was grateful. And on the stage, Markova trusted Dolin implicitly, and he her. They were completely attuned to each other's moves and moods—the perfect complement, and audiences marveled at their synchronicity.

But it suited Dolin to have people believe the two were a "real" couple. They acted it so convincingly onstage, why not offstage as well? Wouldn't that make for better box office?

In his biography of Markova, Dolin relishes his role as her partner in and out of the theater at that time: "Neither was seen without the other, and so we became associated in the minds of the public. One cannot think of Romeo without calling Juliet to mind. The mention of Tristan instantly conjures up Isolde."

Dolin actually proposed to Markova on two separate occasions, despite their never having been romantically involved. He also wrote her frequent love letters, most of the schoolboy crush variety though he was already in his thirties. But Markova was clearly uninterested, as in this letter from Dolin:

> *Alicia dearest,*
>
> *. . . I wonder dear if you will ever know my feelings about you. When I see you dance I want to rush round & clasp you to me. Yet when we meet dear you seem to resent any feelings of affection I want to express. And instead of saying all I want to my mind will*

> *not work. Little Alicia there is so very much I would say if I felt you wanted now to hear it. Take great care of yourself & try & think a little of me & about me. Three words!*
>
> *Pat.*

Of course only Dolin knew his true sentiments and motives, but there's no denying that their marriage would have solidified his career aspirations, as his future was far more secure *with* Markova than without her. The timing of many fawning letters is also a bit suspect, as they seem to coincide with his needing Markova's career help. After the Markova-Dolin Company disbanded in 1937, Markova chose to go off without Dolin, and her fame quickly soared even higher.

In August 1938, Dolin asks "Alicia Dearest" for a teeny-weeny favor, as he's almost finished with *Ballet Go Round,* autobiography number two:

> I wonder if you would write the forward to it. It would be nice to announce a book by Anton Dolin with a forward by Alicia Markova. You need only touch lightly if at all on the [recently disbanded] Markova-Dolin Ballet. . . . But you who have known me for so long, we also have worked so much together I feel sure it would be appreciated not only by me but by the public. What do you think. I should say about 3–5 thousand words.

In December 1938, Dolin was in Sydney, Australia performing with de Basil's company when he wrote the following to his "Alicia darling" in New York, where she was dancing with Léonide Massine and the Ballet Russe de Monte Carlo:

"I'm hoping this letter will arrive about Xmas to tell you that you are in my thoughts as always. I wish you all happiness for 1939, a year in which I hope we shall dance again together. . . . All my love and thoughts. I miss you so much & I will be so happy to see you again. Bless you and keep you safe. Ever Yours, Patte." At the bottom of the page is a postscript asking Markova to show the enclosed good reviews of his recent performances to Massine, who he hopes will hire him. Six days later, Dolin writes another affectionate letter asking Markova to also speak on his behalf to Ballet Russe impresario Sol Hurok.

Though effusive sentimentality and calling dear friends "darling" was probably typical of the extroverted and exuberant Dolin in his correspondences, he certainly lays it on thick to Markova when he wants something. In a January 1939 letter asking if she would meet with a director and lawyer from the de Basil company in New York—"do talk to him. He admires you so much."—Dolin makes it abundantly clear how much he wants to resume their professional and personal partnership. (He is in New Zealand.)

> *Alicia darling,*
>
> *How happy I was lately to get your very sweet & affectionate letter. You know sweet I love you so very much. My one desire is that we shall so soon come together. Who knows one day for life.*
>
> *. . . How proud & happy I [am] of you. And that you are speaking, exhibiting your own personality. That is what I want you to do. Dear sweet Alicia. And no one, no person, no dancer can be more dear, more loyal & loving than you.*
>
> *. . . I long to see you again. I hate the thought of you being without me but I know it was for the best. You will be yourself, but I can always help & guide you just as you can always help me. I want always to do that. And to be together again.*
>
> *My lovely Swan Princess & my own very dear to my heart Alicia. I long to see you dance again.*
>
> *Ever Yours, Patte*

Then before mailing that letter, Dolin decides to add another plea five days later:

> *Alicia darling,*
>
> *Opened letter to enclose this. Darling how I wish I could see you & talk to you about the future. I don't know what & how long your contract is & of course you can & must do nothing to jeopardize it or Hurok who is so very nice. I knew he would look after you for he is a really great man above all intrigues. My admiration for him has always been immense. Now it is even more so.*
>
> *. . . I long with all my heart to see you for I know that we shall find ourselves again. No stupid little battle around & I know so well*

how the American experience will have done you good. I mean that in the kindest way for Alicia my thoughts are, have always been for your good. For my love is one thing, but my admiration is another. To admire the supreme dancer & artiste you are was not difficult but allied to that was a being not as great & I always wanted you to find that being which I knew existed.

Write soon.
Better to Opera House
Wellington New Zealand postal address for Feb. & March
Ever Yours, Patte

If Dolin was madly in love with Markova at any time in his life, it seems to have completely slipped his mind in his 1960 and 1983 autobiographies, where he is nothing if not forthcoming about his seemingly endless list of paramours of both sexes.

Not only did Markova never consider marrying Dolin, she made sure the press was quite clear on that point, as in the following newspaper headline:

Dancers and a Rumour
"Marriage?—I Must Deny The Suggestion"—Markova
—*Edinburgh Sunday Referee*, 8/18/35

And when a journalist asked Markova if she was in love with Dolin, whose arm was around her shoulder at the time, she burst out laughing, much to her dance partner's chagrin. But Markova did love Patte as a brother, and he was an overly possessive big brother at that.

In a way, Dolin slipped into Guggy's former role as caretaker and guardian. But Guggy, unbalanced as she was, had no ulterior motive outside of protecting Markova, certainly never wishing to be in the spotlight herself. Dolin tried to build a wall around his leading lady so that he could become the all-powerful gatekeeper. If you wanted to communicate with Markova, you needed to go through him first.

To a great extent, it worked. Markova had a painstaking performance preparation and she always appreciated Dolin's keeping distractions at bay. She was dancing eight performances a week, a completely unheard-of workload for a prima ballerina in today's world.

In describing her typical workday, one newspaper actually created an illustrated Markova pie chart divided into 24 hours: "Sleep 8 hours; Breaking in new shoes 2½ hours; Photographs, fittings, interviews 2½ hours," etc. Not listed on the cartoon-like chart, however, was the considerable time Markova spent working as a company director, something she carefully kept hidden from the press.

"I didn't want to be recognized on the business side, though. I just wanted people to think of me as a prima ballerina," Markova explained. After all, she was known for her gossamer delicacy—or as one newspaper pointedly noted, none of those "bulging muscles that make most ballerinas look like female blacksmiths!"

It might have shattered some illusions if audiences pictured Markova behind a desk discussing production schedules, budgets, and travel details with Dolin and Van Damm. And no one outside the company knew how handy she was with a screwdriver and bathroom plumbing problems—a Markova specialty. But one of her true gifts was in stage lighting, something she had studied earnestly at the Ballets Russes. Electricians were always amazed at her ability to know within a fraction of an inch where spotlights should be placed.

Markova's many talents were put to great use on the road, as this was anything but a bare-bones touring company. It was a Van Damm extravaganza, including an astounding 1,600 costumes that needed to be loaded and unloaded at every venue. A gigantic, tricked-out truck was specially constructed for that purpose with a built-in organizational rack system, much like one would find in a modern-day dry cleaners. The state-of-the-art transportation vehicle became known as the "Markova-Dolin Noah's Ark."

The enormous company wardrobe was an endless source of fascination for the media:

> . . . All the girls have new shoes and new ballet skirts for every performance, and the average amount of net used for these skirts each week is 1,100 yards! The average number of pairs of shoes used each week is 370, while the 417 odd wigs used are doubled, in order that one lot may be returned to London to be remade while the others are being worn.
>
> —*Bristol Evening Post*, 12/9/35

. . . Silk tights cost 4 to 5 guineas per pair, and the mortality in tights which are put to such athletic uses is, not unexpectedly, very high. [The company won a very public lawsuit against the London Laundry Company for shrinking their tights—"TIGHTS MADE TOO TIGHT" read the headline.] . . .

There are 34 yards of net in each traditional ballet skirt. These skirts may just look bunches of frills to you; actually they are made on a definite plan. There are 6 skirts in each dress; the 2 underskirts have each 5 yards of material, the next double layer has 6 yards, and the top double layer has 7 yards. Look more respectfully on the next frilly skirt you see pirouetting behind the footlights.

—*Glasgow Bulletin*, 4/22/36

. . . The "dress allowance" for every ballet dancer runs into hundreds of pounds every year.

One of the designer's chief problems is finding suitable materials for dancing. Materials which stand up best to the continual movement are discovered to be cotton, rayons and heavy artificial silk. On one occasion, when pure silk was used, the girls complained that they couldn't hear the music for the rustling of their dresses.

For this reason taffeta is never used. . . .

The traditional ballet dress—the "uniform" of the corps de ballet . . . is made of tarlatan, a stiff net which can only be obtained on the Continent. . . . As soon as the dress loses its stiff silhouette it is useless, and consequently cannot be washed or cleaned. . . .

Fake jewellery is made from a piece of rope, gilded, and set with pieces of coloured glass. One particularly heavy piece I was shown had been constructed from pieces of an old brass fender, and short length of clothes-line.

The costume worn by Dolin in the ballet Bolero, played this week for the first time in Newcastle, was imported from Spain, and is worked with authentic Spanish embroidery. Such a costume costs from £14 to £15.

Among Markova's many lovely dresses, one of the most interesting is that which she wears in the Blue Danube ballet. It

> is made of net and sequins, and contains 18 yards of material. Another, which she wears in the Bluebird ballet, is accordian-pleated chiffon, appliquéd with diamante trimming, seven yards of material in the skirt alone.
>
> The head-dress with this costume is real ospreys died blue. . . .
>
> Mr. St. John Roper is responsible for the wardrobe of the Markova-Dolin ballet, and he began his career as a stage dress designer by "dressing" the *monkeys* in a Bertram Mills circus.
>
> —*North Mail & Newcastle Chronicle*, 11/19/36

Markova had so many elaborate costume changes that she hired a full-time dresser, Mrs. Silvia Mortimer. Known to all as "Morty," the kindly woman was a former silent-film actress who later took a job in the wardrobe department at the Windmill Theatre, where Markova's sister Doris performed. Doris introduced Mrs. Mortimer to Markova, and the pair worked together until Morty retired. Her daughter Edna then took over the position, and Markova remained close to both women throughout their lives.

Nothing escaped Markova's notice. She even traveled with a first-aid kit and medicines for company use. When a dancer playing one of the "Wilis" couldn't stifle a cough during Giselle's grave scene, Markova later instructed a staff member to give her some much-needed cough syrup rather than a scolding. And when the orchestra had a substitute musician, Markova could tell as soon as she heard them start to play, thanks to her amazing ear for music.

Despite all those responsibilities and interactions with performers and the crew, Markova was rather aloof and mentally off in her own world. Nevertheless, she was very protective of the young female *corps* members, such as the teenaged Margot Fonteyn and Wendy Toye. Looking back on that time, Toye compared Markova to Greta Garbo—untouchable, but not unfriendly. (Interestingly, when Garbo portrayed a prima ballerina in the 1932 film *Grand Hotel*, her most famous line was "I want to be left alone.") Toye said Markova never lost her temper or yelled, but it was clear when she wasn't happy with someone. "It was generally Dolin, the naughty boy," Toye added.

Marie Rambert knew Markova's silences for what they were: her mind was always on the next performance. "A friend who took her on a drive in Richmond Park said that Markova didn't say one word the entire drive," revealed a newspaper reporter. "It turned out that she has been thinking of her dance that evening and how she could improve it. 'The higher you are, the greater the responsibility,' she said. 'Other dancers can slip through, but people soon remark if I'm a little off colour.'"

Dancer Frederic Franklin was a company member who would eventually become good friends with Markova, but found her initially intimidating. She was the country's most famous classical ballerina and he had most recently performed in the burlesque *King Folly* with Dolin. When interviewed by Markova biographer Maurice Leonard, Franklin says he was scared stiff when asked to partner her. Both her incomparable technique and single-mindedness were off-putting. She was all work—only speaking in her quiet, polite way to make suggestions on dance steps. It was unnerving.

In her early touring days, Markova wasn't exactly the ideal playmate offstage either. She just had too many things to worry about: most of all, not disappointing an audience. It would be the biggest burden of her entire career. But she would lighten up considerably as she grew more comfortable in her role and more secure in her abilities. In the 1930s, however, perfecting her craft was still paramount, and she often needed to do that alone.

Rather than joining the rest of the company for group practice sessions, Markova preferred stretching and pirouetting by herself so nothing would break her concentration. "Dolin would take the company practice lessons when we were on tour," Wendy Toye told Maurice Leonard. "He used to do battle with everybody. Alicia never appeared for these."

Many dancers didn't realize Markova was working out by herself, giving rise to the oft-repeated myth that she never practiced at all. Markova also took one-on-one lessons with highly regarded master teachers at great personal expense.

Adding to the "Garbo" image, Markova never showed up in tatty rehearsal clothes like the rest of the dancers. She was always dressed immaculately, another substantial cost to her personal budget. Always taking pride in one's appearance was something she had learned from Diaghilev. Looking the part commanded respect, but it also made her seem less approachable.

Markova may have been all business when it came to the ballet, but she wasn't a heartless machine and showed great compassion for the world around her. While on tour, she made a point of visiting children in local hospitals and making contributions to worthy charities. Upon hearing of a horrific mining disaster in South Kirkby, Yorkshire, she immediately began to raise money for the victims' families.

Though Dolin liked the public to think he was the only one in charge of the Vic-Wells touring company, it was Markova who was an official director with a say in all decisions, not Dolin. Van Damm had only become interested in ballet as a vehicle for Britain's first prima ballerina, and originally wanted to name their new venture the Markova Ballet Company. That was a situation Anton Dolin aimed to rectify.

As would become the norm throughout their seven-decade relationship, Dolin attempted to manipulate Markova into doing what he wished by suggesting that any favor he might ask was only for her own benefit—a largely unnecessary ploy, as she was always happy to help him out in any way she could. One wonders if his effusive transparency amused her.

In a letter from the summer of 1935, Dolin asks for Markova's help to persuade Vivian Van Damm (who he called V.D.) to make him one of the company's directors:

> I think dear the suggestion should come from you about co-opting me on the board of the company. V.D.'s on it. Ninette is of course on it. [Not true.] And it is better you suggest it, that is, you wish it as I do. My interests are yours, & yours dear are most surely mine. Together we shall conquer the whole world. I predict this: Within three years Markova & Dolin will be known to the populace of the continent. De Basil, Nemtchinova & all the other co.'s cannot compete against a combination such as ours, I am sure.

And a follow-up letter added:

> The world is before us now. Both for each other's true, sincere & great success. My dear sweet child & my great wonderful dancing partner. Devotedly Yours, Pat.

Dolin's singling out Nemtchinova as a ballerina who won't be able to compare with Markova is typical of the egotistical dancer's ever-changing loyalties. Though starting the Nemtchinova-Dolin Company had been his idea, after just one year Dolin returned to the Ballets Russes when Balanchine offered him a great role, leaving the prima ballerina to fend for herself. Now he predicts Markova will be far more famous than the Russian ballerina ever was.

But when the steep financial costs of the Markova-Dolin Ballet resulted in its finally disbanding at the end of 1937, Dolin switched allegiances again when Markova went off without him. After reconnecting with Vera Nemtchinova (who fortunately for Dolin held no grudges), he asked the Russian ballerina to join him in yet another new company—and yes, presumably they would be even more famous together than he was with Markova. Every time Dolin and Markova split, he boasted of his next partner waiting in the wings bound for untold glories.

Dolin would turn on Markova many times throughout their long on-again, off-again work association. He was an indiscreet—and entertaining—gossip and she was often the subject of his none-too-flattering anecdotes. But Dolin really outdid himself on that score in 1960—and in print.

In 1959, Markova was forced to take time off from her career due to severe and painful colitis. Word got out that she was using her recuperation downtime to write a memoir titled *Giselle & I*. It would be filled with lovely and upbeat remembrances.

Dolin chose that moment to write his third autobiography, one that, in the most ungentlemanly-like fashion, revealed many behind-the-scenes incidents where Markova behaved badly in his estimation, especially in the very recent past. Particularly mean-spirited were his blow-by-blow accounts of all her temperamental outbursts in Israel in 1958.

While those histrionics concerned her unwillingness to perform on dangerous makeshift staging—which the other dancers found equally troubling—there's no question Markova could have handled the situation far more graciously. (It should be noted, however, that all her outbursts were directed at the company's managers and not in public settings.) But in the end, she performed magnificently in front of over thiry thousand Israeli citizens in Haifa alone. Audiences were overjoyed at seeing the first openly Jewish *prima ballerina assoluta* in her most acclaimed role of Giselle, and the press had been euphoric. Now Dolin was marring that very recent memory.

It seems especially spiteful since Dolin wasn't an equal opportunity reputation-basher in his book. While he criticizes Markova's selfishness for requiring a private dressing space in Israel, Dolin defends his old friend Spanish dancer La Argentinita for demanding not one, but two private—and carpeted—dressing rooms during a 1930 New York appearance. At that time, Argentinita was vilified in the local press as a prima donna, but Dolin explains that the two rooms were completely necessary "simply because her dresses had to be properly hung or they would have been spoiled," and naturally the carpet had to be dry-cleaned as well, he points out.

Dolin clearly had an ax to grind with Markova. Her fame continually rose in the 1950s, particularly after she ended their onstage partnership in 1952. (They wouldn't dance together again until 1958, and then only briefly.) Dolin seemed bitter and often resentful. As one book reviewer wrote:

> The Dolin-Markova partnership is unique in ballet history. It lasted for many years and made both dancers international stars.
>
> The idea that it was always an idyllic relationship is dispelled by Anton Dolin in *Autobiography* . . . it seems he was not always amused by his distinguished partner. . . .
>
> "The tour offered the highest salary ever paid to two stars of the ballet. After hours of incessant meetings and hours of needless discussions, Alicia signed the contract. You would have thought she was signing her death warrant." . . .
>
> This new book should have been much better than it is. I have an impression it has been hastily done.
>
> —*London Evening News*, Duncan Harrison, 11/17/60

Markova's balletic talents also seemed to have diminished in hindsight for Dolin. In his 1953 biography of her, he wrote that Markova "had a far wider range than Spessiva (Olga Spessivtseva) ever had" when performing *Giselle*. Yet just seven years later, he changes his tune in autobiography number three: "there is no one living whose performance can be compared with the sublime dancing and lovely interpretation that she [Spessivtseva] and she alone gave to the role of Giselle."

Of course, Dolin had every right to print his version of the truth, but as he still considered Markova a close friend, the timing smacked more of jealousy than a sudden need to set the record straight. Consider Dolin's reaction to Markova being feted on the popular UK television show *This is Your Life*, also in 1960. Shocking to the producers, the prima ballerina's most frequent partner refused to participate, expressing outrage that he was not honored before her. (When the show finally got around to featuring Dolin in 1978, Markova readily appeared.)

But true, false, or exaggerated, Dolin's unflattering stories of Markova were published in 1960 while she was still very much in the public eye performing around the world and hosting the BBC radio series *Markova's Ballet Call*. It was not only unkind, but also potentially damaging to her career. In the end, the book was so gossipy and poorly written that it had little effect on Markova's public image.

Inconceivable as it might seem, Dolin thought his much-publicized betrayal of Markova should in no way affect their longstanding friendship. He continued to write intimate letters to her throughout 1960 and '61, signed variously "All Love Dearest," "Love Ever," and "Devotedly." Though some reveal Markova's annoyance at his behavior—"Not a line from you. I hoped for some sort of line," Dolin implored in one, "Not a line from you. Did you not get my letter?" in another—it is also apparent that his poison pen somehow hadn't marked the end of their friendship.

In a letter from October 1960, Dolin thanks Markova for sending flowers and good-luck telegrams for his opening night in Cape Town, South Africa, adding how much he misses her and how being there is just not the same without her. (This on the eve of his book being published.) In other letters after the book came out, he expresses his appreciation for Markova's thoughtfulness throughout the period of his mother's long illness and eventual death. He even thanks her for remembering to send him a Valentine's Day card—the February after his book launch!

There obviously was a very strange bond between the two high-strung and strong-willed dancers that remained steadfast through thick and thin. On April 4, 1961, Dolin wrote a letter to Markova from the Hotel Caprice in Rome. They had recently seen each other on the French Riviera where Dolin had a home, and he references a spat that took place in Beaulieu-sur-Mer, not far from Monte Carlo:

"You were quite wonderful (except at Beaulieu)!! but forget that. I wish sometimes you would open up a bit & talk to me. You did for our last meeting after our nice evening with Princess Antoinette [of Monaco]. That made me very happy. Tho I wonder if I'll ever be really happy again."

Two months later came this note:

May 26, 61

Thank you my very dear, dear Alicia for today. Being with you, watching you dance, dancing with you. Talking with you, again quietly & with understanding, affection, & love.

You are very great & I shall always love you.

Bless you my dear & goodnight. Sleep well, & proudly on your achievements.

Ever Patté

The two dancers remained friends until Dolin's death in 1983. Markova never publicly held a grudge or retaliated with her own nasty revelations. But one myth that always prevailed was Dolin's being *forever* dedicated to and protective of Markova. If nothing else, his 1960 memoir readily belies that notion.

Dolin once told Vivian Van Damm, "Don't run away with the idea that all ballet dancers are nice, charming, human people, out to help their fellow artists. They're not."

One dancer who *was* charming and well liked was Frederic Franklin. As Dolin's understudy in the Markova-Dolin Company, he told the following story to Maurice Leonard. One week it was planned that Franklin would dance with Markova at a particular Saturday matinee, quite an honor for the up-and-coming soloist. The morning of performance day, Dolin invited Franklin to meet him for a game of tennis at 10:00 A.M. The younger dancer declined, explaining he needed to rest up for the afternoon show. As Franklin's boss, Dolin insisted that he come, and a rather long match was played. Franklin concedes that Dolin did it on purpose to sabotage his performance. "He was a terrible man, but I loved him."

The Markova-Dolin Company was officially formed after the initial Vic-Wells summer tour in 1935. It was Markova's generosity to Dolin that led to his name being joined with hers, as she was the star Van Damm and Laura Henderson were backing.

Though Helpmann's return to the Vic-Wells initiated the split of the two companies, de Valois had anticipated Markova's leaving for quite some time. The prima ballerina was just too talented to remain with them forever, and as she was so superior to the up-and-coming young dancers, it made them look far worse in comparison. De Valois also wanted to build a company free of "stars," as she often remarked, and groom principals from within her own ranks.

She remained friends with Markova for life (de Valois lived to be 102!) and wished her well in her new endeavor. When de Valois's brother, the dance photographer Gordon Anthony, published a book on Markova in 1935, he asked his sister to write the preface:

> The immediate years to come will certainly ask more of this amazing young dancer. The ballet is a hard taskmaster and Markova's rapid rise to fame in the last eighteen months demands a continuity of achievement. Too young to rest upon her hard-earned success, too ambitious to be content, and too tenacious to lose her hold, she will weight this question of continued progress with her strangely alert and penetrating mind.
>
> Markova is of Jewish-Irish extraction, the former has bestowed a foresight that amounts to second sight, whilst

> the latter has shown what an imaginative spirit in search of a Utopian adventure can find. May the blending of these two interesting nationalities manifest itself in the sagacity of her future plans, as it has in her past.

Markova would always be grateful to de Valois for her kindnesses during the Diaghilev days, as well as giving her the opportunity to master the Russian classics at the Vic-Wells. Those ballets would be part of the Markova-Dolin Company repertoire, along with lighthearted contemporary new works. As the company would primarily spend their time touring, they would not be competing with the Vic-Wells for London audiences.

Hundreds of British dancers auditioned—over six hundred, according to Dolin—as there was really no other English company besides the Vic-Wells at that time. An impressive group of thirty-eight was hired, including Frederic Franklin, Stanley Judson, Wendy Toye, Prudence Hyman, and Diana Gould. Nicholas Sergeyev proved invaluable in re-staging the Russian classics, and Bronislava Nijinska signed on as ballet master in the company's second year.

Nijinska was a perfect choreographer and adviser for Markova. As dancer Alexandra Danilova once explained, "It was always hard for me to remember Nijinska's choreography, and in the beginning, I couldn't understand why. Finally, I analyzed it and realized that it was because her dance phrase didn't finish with the musical phrase, as usual: sometimes the dance phrase would start in the middle of one musical phrase and finish in the middle of the next." Markova was known for that distinctive "between-the-notes" dance phrasing, which *New York Times* ballet critic John Martin found especially magical.

Frederic Franklin remembers that Nijinska was already going deaf when she joined the Markova-Dolin Company (she was only forty-six). "She would come over and give you the rhythm by [tapping her hand] on [your] shoulder," he explained.

Laura Henderson, who always traveled with her pugnacious Pekinese, looked upon everyone associated with the Markova-Dolin ballet as an extended family—one she was willing to indulge with her largess. At the company's one-year anniversary performance in Yorkshire, the 73-year-old *grande dame* sat in her box with a member of the press, watching Markova and Dolin perform. "Aren't they sweet children?" she asked, like a proud mother. Henderson then confided her one problem with the company: finding an anniversary cake big enough to feed them all, "from the principals to the dressers!"

But Markova was presented with a problem of her own, and it concerned her beloved *Giselle*. Though her dancing of the role always earned much critical praise—and many audience members were moved enough to write touching letters—it was not a big draw for advance ticket sales in the provinces, and was only performed once a week. Excerpts from other classical works, such as scenes from *The Nutcracker Suite* and *Swan Lake*, proved far more marketable. Van Damm felt the Markova-Dolin Company should only present popular, non-challenging ballets.

Markova explained the complicated process of choosing programs to a London reporter:

> You see, many things have to be taken into consideration. There must be one classical ballet, one popular one, and one modern. Then the same artist must not appear in all of them.
>
> Time has to be allowed for changing and all that sort of thing, I expect. And when you pay a return visit to a town, you have to remember what has already been given there. How do you come to the actual plan?
>
> Well, I draw up a specimen programme, so does Dolin, and generally my manager, also. Then the three of us get together and compare notes. All sorts of snags occur! In the end, we arrive at a kind of compromise.

When the prima ballerina discovered that Van Damm, Mrs. Henderson, and, more reluctantly, Dolin wished to drop *Giselle* from the repertoire—and they clearly had the voting majority—Markova was beside herself. She felt that her Giselle had grown enormously under Bronislava Nijinska's guidance.

"Mme. Nijinska really started me thinking about the role at the time of the Markova-Dolin Ballet," Markova recounted years later. "She said: 'You've got to have all that strength technically, but that isn't Giselle's character.' She said: 'When you do those leaps, you stay in the air.'

"The trouble with *Giselle* is that it's back to front. After pulling out every stop in the Mad Scene and tearing yourself to bits, you have to come back quiet and composed and belonging to another world. The second is the toughest act: it needs a man's strength."

Markova understood the company's financial concerns, but *Giselle* was her emotional touchstone. "It is the most complete ballet," she said. "I think it is perhaps that little human emotional element in *Giselle* that seems to reach people." But it was three against one. *Giselle* was out.

Often at a loss for words in those days, Markova took the only action she thought might win her case, and one completely out of character: threatening to jump off her first floor balcony, the door of which she flung open for added dramatic effect. It's doubtful the fall would have killed her, but a broken leg was a strong possibility. Either way, it was Markova *with Giselle*, or no Markova at all! The men were nonplussed.

Such an obvious bluff might not have worked if she were known for screaming scenes and histrionics; but coming from such a tiny, normally reserved woman, it carried a bit more weight. *Giselle* was back in the repertoire.

Markova later remembered the incident with great amusement—and some shame—admitting even she was surprised at her overplayed "balcony scene." Temperamental outbursts were for divas, which the contemplative ballerina certainly was not. Comparing her behavior to an outvoted corporation board member who threatens suicide to get his way, Markova admonished herself for such a high-handed course of action. She just couldn't think of anything else to do. Van Damm and Dolin may have acquiesced, but they also gave her a good talking-to, "declaring forcefully that I did not seem to know where *Giselle* ended and real life began—or *vice versa*, I forget now."

They may have had a point. Markova even slept like Giselle, as revealed by her good friend, the comedic actress Florence Desmond. Markova was often a guest at Desmond's country home, where the ballerina would go for a good rest. When her hostess checked in on her one day, Desmond noted:

"It's the first time I'd ever seen anybody sleep with their feet pointed as if they were on their points. She was sound asleep with her foot pointed as hard as it would go with her hands crossed over her breasts and she looked like the second act of *Giselle*. For a moment, I had to look to see if she was all right!"

Markova first met Desmond at Christmastime in 1936 when they appeared together in the pantomime *Mother Goose*. Not able to find a theater available for the Markova-Dolin Company during the holiday season, Markova and Dolin had agreed to perform a lovely Petipa *pas de deux* in the pantomime, artfully arranged for them by Bronislava Nijinska. The press was aghast that the classical Markova would stoop to appear in such a lowbrow venue. But she never looked down on music-hall shows, and loved being around talented comedians who made her roar with laughter in the wings. Anna Pavlova, it should be remembered, followed an acrobatic dog act on the London stage.

"That particular pantomime is one I shall always remember," Desmond reminisced years later. "You see, Alicia is such an excellent mixer and makes everyone so happy. We all thought it was such an honor to have her with us. I think the chief thing which made Alicia's appearance in pantomime so important was the fact that she brought ballet to the people who were probably seeing this type of dancing for the first time in their lives. And don't forget also that ballet in 1936 and '37 was by no means the popular entertainment it is today. I might say that Alicia definitely was one of the great pioneers of ballet in this country. And I'm more than honored to feel our friendship has grown over the years and I'm very proud to say that I know her so well."

Upon her retirement in 1963, Markova defended her past actions: "Ballet used to be a very closed world and many people wanted to keep it that way. I felt it should be expanded. Why shouldn't everybody be able to see and appreciate it? I wanted to see ballet introduced to a wider public."

She got her wish. The Markova-Dolin Company pioneered ballet throughout England, Scotland, and Ireland, proving that an all-British corps of dancers could compete with the Russians. And once again, that was a great source of local pride.

Going on tour and constantly meeting with the press in each new city was like immersion therapy for Markova's shyness. She learned how to charm, articulate her feelings, and anticipate what topics would interest readers most. Her natural reticence made interviewers feel like they alone were getting a real scoop, as Markova had that soft-spoken cultured persona of a young Jacqueline Kennedy. The ballerina learned when to be serious and when light-hearted, and she never gossiped in a manner that expressed an instant intimacy. That slight holding back was media catnip.

> This British-born dancer immediately struck one as being very sensitive, very sympathetic, very modest, and altogether very nice—attributes not always found together in those who have achieved such success!—so to meet her was a pleasure, and to leave her, a regret.
>
> —*Edinburgh Evening News*, 1936

But at the same time, Markova showed compassion and respect for the "everyman and woman." Famous prima ballerina or not, she was no snob, and her respect for her audiences endeared her to the public.

> **A Talk with Markova—and a Few Notes**
>
> "We were not too sure how we should go down in the provinces," said Markova, "but they liked us. . . .
>
> "I really believe—and I'm not saying this because I'm English—that the audiences here are more enthusiastic than any we have had."
>
> As she has danced in every capital on the Continent, her opinion shows no insular prejudice.
>
> —*Yorkshire Evening Post*, 9/2/35

Markova's ethnic, "exotic" looks, once considered a drawback for her career aspirations, were now her distinctive calling card, and women readers wanted to know everything about her diet, beauty, and fashion advice. Her flawless makeup application, something she had learned from Lydia Sokolova at the Ballets Russes all those years ago, would be written about and analyzed throughout her career. Before going onstage, Markova spent a full forty-five minutes on her face to achieve an effect dramatic enough for the back rows without appearing garish up close. For newspapers, she was happy to offer women her offstage makeup application tips, as well as some quite specific, and surprising, fashion advice:

Meet Madame Markova
Jewel of the British Ballet

... Before I rose to go, the conversation turned again to poise, this time in relation to dress. Mme. Markova has very decided views on clothes, and considers that new clothes usually tend to destroy that desirable possession unless their owner takes the precaution of wearing them once or twice in the privacy of her own room; so that when she ultimately appears in public she is quite at home in them; otherwise she becomes self-conscious, and that self-consciousness conveys itself to her companions, with disastrous results, from a social point of view.

For the same reason the famous dancer thinks that a woman should be very careful when she buys a hat, for if a too-persuasive saleswoman sells her a hat which she feels inwardly is not becoming, she will never be happy in it, and it will obtrude itself on her consciousness when she wears it, overshadowing the happiness of the occasion.

Most women will appreciate the truth of this, for have not we all, at one time or another, been beguiled into buying something we did not, in our hearts, really want, and which we never wore with pleasure? That is why, in so many houses, there are several cardboard boxes hidden away on the top shelf, each containing proofs or a shopwoman's blandishments and our own weaknesses! But we only have ourselves to blame!

—*Edinburgh Evening News*, 5/11/36

That commonsense (well, sort of) approach to fashion was completely at odds with the dramatic style and sumptuous wardrobe Anna Pavlova was known for.

Mme. Markova on Dress

Madame Markova, the lovely principal dancer of the Vic-Wells Ballet Company now visiting Scotland, tells me she prefers to dress in subdued colours—black, grey and white—as a contrast to the gorgeously bright colours she so often has to wear on the stage.

> When I asked her what she thought of the present fashions, she said, "Some of them are very attractive, but I think it is foolish to be a slave to fashion, and wear things that don't suit you just because everyone else is wearing them."
>
> Madame Markova certainly does not commit this foolishness herself. She has evolved a most distinguished and becoming style of her own.
>
> —*Glasgow Daily Record,* 8/7/35

Markova's sense of style was very particular and unerring. Once again Diaghilev had come through for her, offering none other than Coco Chanel as fashion exemplar. The two women shared a similar boyish, slim figure that looked sleek, modern, and undeniably chic in simple silhouettes in neutral colors. From Chanel, Markova also learned the importance of a few eye-catching accessories, and how to choose pieces that enhanced rather than detracted from her outfit. The ballerina's understated elegance was always remarked upon by the female press.

> **Markova in Edinburgh**
>
> . . . A lively, chic young person, this Markova of the everyday world, compared with the dreamy, withdrawn ballerina of the footlights. . . . My eye lingered admiringly, if discreetly, over the smart swathed black hat, her grey and white plaid woollen frock, and her long grey coat slung, Continental fashion, over her shoulders. It paused in its lingering on the tiny watch set into a diamond clip which she wore on her frock, and on the spray of orchids she had pinned on to the grey fur collar of her coat.
>
> —*Scotsman,* 4/26/37

Markova had always known the importance of looking the part. She'd just never had the budget for it before. When she was still dancing at the Vic-Wells and could ill afford an expansive wardrobe, the star ballerina confessed to a reporter how she tried to avoid being seen in public so as not to disappoint her fans:

> It is a little disconcerting to see a floating spiritual artiste emerge from the stage door in the form of an athletic, healthy

> young woman rushing to catch her last bus home. The public does not expect so rude a shock.
>
> Last summer, I was introduced by a friend to two ballet-fans at a seaside resort on the South Coast. When I had departed, one of them exclaimed, "That couldn't have been Markova!" "Why not?" enquired my friend. "Well, she had a pullover and skirt on," was the reply. Humorous as it is, the story carries a very strong moral for the dancer who would give her public what they expect of her.
>
> —*Theatre World,* January 1935

Diaghilev had told Markova the same thing; but unlike the perennially broke impresario, the young dancer wasn't willing to go into debt to dress the part. The Markova-Dolin Company changed all that. She now had enough money to buy new clothes—a good thing, as her rising fame made it almost impossible to avoid the public.

As Markova traveled on tour, the press would often snap her picture as she walked about their city or took in local entertainment. ["FAMOUS BALLERINA AT THE CIRCUS," boasted the *Lancashire Gazette,* which ran a photo of a rather elegantly dressed Markova chatting with "Doodles" the clown under the Big Top.] She was a visiting celebrity and everyone wanted to see what the acclaimed ballerina looked like offstage.

Being a whiz with a *Vogue* pattern, Markova supplemented her wardrobe with smart homemade suits and dresses, always perfectly tailored to her tiny physique. Each outfit was then accessorized with coordinating gloves, saucy hats, and an elegant fur piece effortlessly draped over one shoulder.

There was no missing Alicia Markova when she ran errands around any small town. A funny thing happened to the dancer while shopping in Leeds one day on tour, as recorded in the local newspaper:

> For over a week now, Madame Markova has been exploring Leeds, and giving a number of people pleasant surprises.
>
> One case in point was the lift girl in a large Leeds store—no names—who took Madame up to the top floor one morning last week.

> The girl gazed at the slender figure, the black coat with its cape trimmed in red fox, the little black hat, the sleek black hair, the long-lashed brown eyes, the vivid, smiling mouth. . . .
>
> Suddenly she guessed who the passenger was. Instead of opening the gates at the top floor, she sent the lift down to street level again.
>
> Then she sent it up again, down again, up again. . . .
>
> Madame became alarmed and demanded to be released.
>
> When she eventually escaped from the lift, Madame Markova went in to the café to recover. Her companion questioned the lift girl about her strange conduct.
>
> "It is her, isn't it?" she said breathlessly. "I wanted to keep her as long as I could."
>
> —*Yorkshire Post*, 4/16/36

Markova knew that entertaining stories about her local adventures helped sell tickets, and she found out just whom to contact to get them quickly into print. She also discovered the advantages of the perfect "photo op," often suggesting bucolic parks as an excellent place to meet. She remembered the photographs of Pavlova and her swans that had so delighted her as a child. Now it was Markova—impeccably dressed on a stroll—who was featured feeding the swans at parks throughout Britain, invariably with a caption mentioning her dancing a scene from *Swan Lake* the same evening.

Interestingly, Anton Dolin has always been credited as the media kingpin of the pair, with many—including Agnes de Mille, Frederic Franklin, and of course, Dolin himself—suggesting that Markova needed his knack for generating publicity. Thirty-odd boxes of news clippings say otherwise. Markova was a very quick study where the media was concerned, with a real gift for knowing exactly which topic would be of most interest to each outlet. (And the amount of her press coverage never diminished at times when she and Dolin were apart.)

Markova was also a surprisingly skilled writer, often penning her own feature stories on ballet and her life, which were widely printed in newspapers and magazines. And when it came to new media, it was Markova who first pioneered ballet on television, later using popular broadcasts as no ballet dancer had done before her.

Another myth was that Markova would have had no social life at all were it not for Dolin. As her fame grew, Markova became more comfortable in her own skin and realized that all work and no play made for an uninspired life. While she continued her demanding work schedule, she made time to socialize, often meeting friends for lunch, tea, or after evening performances. She also was now in a financial position to reciprocate invitations, easing her former guilt over never being able to pay her own way.

Markova documented each day's activities in her datebooks over the years. By 1937, the final year of the Markova-Dolin Company, it is evident that she had built up a wide circle of friends whom she socialized with on a regular basis. One thing about Markova: when she made a friend, it was for life.

Reggie and Jane Wright were a wealthy couple who started out as ardent fans—Reggie worshipped Markova onstage—but were soon escorting her to dinners and parties around town in their luxurious Rolls Royce. Fashion/portrait photographer Peter Fink met the willowy ballerina on assignment and, with his wife, dined with her often. The jovial "Freddie" Franklin obviously broke through Markova's "Garbo" aura at work, as the two regularly met for tea and afternoons out. (Along with the effervescent Alexandra Danilova, Franklin and Markova would spend the years of World War II performing together in the United States, cheering each other up and on.)

By 1937, Frederick Ashton had clearly forgiven Markova, as she records many dates at his London flat for tea or cocktails. On Sunday afternoons when she was in London, Alicia joined Doris at the cinema—they both loved Fred Astaire movies—followed by a rousing game of Monopoly at home with the family. (No one said her activities weren't wholesome.) And Markova so enjoyed having her warm and caring mother back by her side. Stanley Burton also came into Markova's life at this time, as perhaps her first serious love interest.

Dolin and Markova socialized often as well, especially when she dined with other couples. But Dolin preferred the company of "show people" who made entrances, got the best tables in restaurants, and enjoyed late-night partying. Throughout her life, Markova always preferred small gatherings of intimates. The following were typical days:

Tuesday, January 19, 1937
8:30 manicure
10-0 Rehearsal Sylphides & Biches till 1-0
Straight to Theatre for Matinee.
Went Shopping at Selfridges & home to tea & change
8-0 Show Hippodrome
Laura [Henderson] took Nijinska, Patte & myself to Wells to see first performance of Giselle with Peggy (Fonteyn)
John Gabriel and Jesse Lasky Junior [American screenwriter] took me to supper.
Patte came too.

Sunday, January 31, 1937
Slept late until 12-0
Lunch home. Rested in bed until tea.
7-30 Dinner with the Finks. Jane and Reggie were there & Derek Selby.
Went to show at the Gate Theatre. Saw Fred [Ashton] Billy [Chappell] & Bobby [Helpmann] for a few seconds. Back to the Finks for drinks. Very nice time.

Monday, February 8, 1937
12-0 Piccadilly Theatre.
Took Edris [de Valois] to lunch at Café Royal.
3-0 Orchestra rehearsal until 5-0. Home for tea and change.
8-0 Began show at Kings, rushed down to Piccadilly & danced for HRH Queen, presented during interval, dashed back & finished show at Kings.
Went back to Picadilly & to supper with Reggie & Jane at Berkeleys.
[Alongside each daily record was a list of ballets Markova danced that evening, such as: "*Swanlake Pas de 4, Snowflake Divert., Swanlake Adagio, Valse*"]

Markova also noted in her datebook when she wasn't feeling well or had painful foot injuries, and she made sure to record the number of any hotel room where she hadn't been able to sleep well for future reference. She also jotted down any special kindnesses people had shown her:

Sunday, July 7, 1937
Left on Golden Arrow 11-0
Very good crossing.
Met two very nice men who looked after me.
Arrived in Paris 6-0
Went to Astor Hotel, wrote letters & had a meal until 9-5 my train to Biarritz.
Good journey.

Monday, October 18, 1937
9-0 Manicure
12-0 Foot—Mme. Shackleton
12-30 Lunch Alice Nikitina [prima ballerina friend from Ballets Russes] at Cog d'Or
2-50 Train arrived
4-15 Tea hotel
8-0 Show. Lovely flowers
Supper alone. Developing cold.
Poisoned toe not too good.

Tuesday, October 19, 1937
Slept late. Awful cold.
Lunch hotel alone.
Drove to Birmingham to judge Beauty Contest, tea & drove back. Took Freddie.
8-0 Show
Went with Freddie to friends for supper.

Awful cold notwithstanding, Birmingham residents were thrilled at Markova's personal appearance:

> World famous ballerina—Alicia Markova—helping Varsity's bid for Hospitals by choosing Carnival Beauty Queen. Recognised successor to immortal Pavlova, has perfect technique,

> supple, expressive grace, translates movement into a lilting lyric, poise into beauty.
>
> —*Birmingham News*, 10/23/37

Also in her datebooks, Markova kept records of everyone's birthdays with notes to herself to send flowers. She ordered a special arrangement for the funeral of her cherished former teacher Nikolai Legat, and wrote of her resulting depression for weeks after his passing. She noted when people were ill, such as when Bunny had her tonsils out, sending get-well wishes and making time for hospital visits when possible.

And of course there were business meetings with Vivian Van Damm, Laura Henderson, and Dolin, as well as costume fittings with Manya. Markova even made time to attend the ice hockey finals at Wembley Stadium with a male friend.

Few days were filled exclusively with work activities. Socializing was now a very important and enjoyable part of Markova's life. She was invited to galas where she rubbed elbows with royalty and movie stars like Cary Grant and Douglas Fairbanks. And while she and Dolin remained close, Markova no longer depended on him for all her outside entertainment. He became a bit jealous, especially of Stanley Burton's affections.

By the end of 1937, Markova was ready for a change. When the Markova-Dolin Company was launched in 1935, she was quoted as saying, "We must have more fun in ballet," but she meant for the audiences. Eight performances a week were hardly "fun" for the prima ballerina. Markova wanted to work in a company with many alternating principal dancers and a chance to master more challenging modern ballets. Laura Henderson gave her an easy out. The heiress just couldn't sustain the cost of the ballet company any longer, as one newspaper enumerated:

> The weekly maintenance bill, including rent of whatever theatre they may be hiring, in London or the provinces, seldom comes to less than £1000, and sometime comes to more. . . . Then there is the buying of, on average, one hundred pairs of shoes a week. . . . Add to this the maintenance of scenery, the

> artists' and musicians' salaries, the paying of royalties (another £35 weekly), and the sum total can be realized.
>
> The company must, moreover, continually add new works to their programs, and the cost of new ballet varies, of course enormously, but is seldom less than £500 and often as much as £1000. Dresses, so important a part of this form of entertainment, are always a heavy expense.
>
> —*Southport Visiter*, 10/38/37

In his memoirs, Vivian Van Damm estimated that Mrs. Henderson had lost about £30,000 on the ballet. "But it was counted as money well spent," he added. The Markova-Dolin Company had successfully pioneered British ballet throughout the country, and Alicia Markova was considered a national treasure. That made it all the more difficult for her to decide what to do next.

~

By 1937, the Ballet Russe de Monte Carlo had split into two separate dance companies due to ongoing financial problems and management infighting. The autocratic Colonel de Basil headed one, with his more artistic ex-partner René Blum helming the other. The division was neither amicable nor productive, as everyone feared audiences wouldn't support two different Russian companies.

As if they were two competing sports team captains fighting for the best players, de Basil and Blum went back and forth choosing and losing various choreographers, dancers, and moneymen. In the end, Léonide Massine joined René Blum and Boris Kochno in a company named the Ballet Russe de Monte Carlo, backed financially by World Art, Inc. (later named Universal Art).

Based in the United States, the organization consisted of Sol Hurok as American manager, banker Serge Denham as vice-president/director, and wealthy industrialist/arts philanthropist Julius Fleischmann as the "bank" and titular president. Fleischmann was such a huge ballet fan that he named his diesel yacht "Camargo," after the famous 18th-century prima ballerina Marie Camargo. Built at a cost of $625,000 in 1928, "the 225-foot vessel was said at that time to be the largest and costliest pleasure craft ever built in the United States," according to the *New York Times*. The man had plenty of money to burn, and ballet was his new *cause célèbre*.

At that time, Léonide Massine was considered one of the most brilliantly creative choreographers in ballet—second only to Balanchine. He was also a stellar stage presence, not with a Nijinsky-like technical virtuosity, but rather a mesmerizing charisma in personality-driven character roles he created for himself. Massine had bowed legs, unfortunate for a dancer, but he cleverly concealed them with costumes that padded his calves.

As his most frequent partner, Alexandra Danilova, pointed out, "Massine always gave himself the best parts in his ballets. . . . He was a first-class dancer, very passionate, expressive, with a style of his own, in some ways more a modern dancer than a classical dancer."

And he knew exactly which talented dancers he wanted for his new company—though several others would be forced upon him by Denham. Plans were to take the re-formed Ballet Russe de Monte Carlo on tour throughout Europe and the United States, performing both the celebrated Russian classics and innovative modern ballets to be created by Massine. (A very controversial 1937 copyright lawsuit in London would award de Basil ownership of all of Massine's ballets the impresario had contracted and paid for during their association.)

Discovering that the Markova-Dolin Company was to disband in December 1937, Massine contacted Markova about signing on with him. It wasn't the first time. As an inventively experimental choreographer, Massine had been making overtures to Markova since 1932, anxious to work with so technically proficient and pliant a dancer. Then there was her resemblance to Pavlova, always an added bonus. Markova had said no in the past, preferring to help spearhead British ballet, but now she was torn.

Massine was persuasive: "You've danced for eight years in England. You've had your own company. It's time for you to expand. You must come to America."

It was true. Except for a single gala performance in Copenhagen in 1932, Markova hadn't performed outside of Great Britain and Ireland in the past eight years. But she wasn't sure if her pioneering efforts in that regard were complete.

For advice, Markova consulted Arnold Haskell and Ninette de Valois, half-hoping that de Valois would want her back at the Vic-Wells, which represented security and happy times. That would also allow her to stay close to her family and her new love interest, Stanley Burton.

But Margot Fonteyn was now the up-and-coming lead ballerina at the Vic-Wells, and de Valois never cared for "stars" in her company. She suggested it was time for Markova to show the world how talented a British-born ballerina could be. Naturally, Haskell agreed, as he always thought his friend belonged in a predominantly Russian company. Be a "British ambassador for dance," they urged her.

Markova also needed more artistic stimulus to raise her game. Though she had become a huge star in England, touring the provinces necessitated a certain sameness in the repertoire. There were no great choreographers challenging her with new roles, and her love of modern art movements like Surrealism was stymied by Britain's conservatism in that regard.

Joining Massine in France would allow Markova to combine her mastery of *Giselle* and other Russian classics with the new and avant-garde.

"I've been so fortunate," she told a radio interviewer in 1978. . . . "You begin with one choreographer and then you will move on to the next—and something else is added to one's artistry—that way, one can never be bored. It's always interesting and exciting. . . . Apart from working with all these great choreographers—who at the time I worked with them, each was the most modern choreographer of the day—I also had the classical, romantic side of my career, as in *Giselle, The Nutcracker, Swan Lake, The Sleeping Beauty.* So I always felt very lucky. I was rather a Jekyll & Hyde."

Markova was also heartened to learn that "Freddie" Franklin had signed on with Massine, as the two had become great friends. Equally enticing was the thought of reuniting with her surrogate "big sister," Alexandra Danilova.

To say the Russian-born ballerina was beloved would be an understatement. Onstage and off, Danilova was like just popped champagne—sparkling, bubbly, and lighter than air. Though her technique was clean and elegant, Choura, as everyone called her, was so much more than just a world-class dancer. She was positively magnetic, one of those performers whose appearance on stage you longingly anticipate, swoon over, then miss terribly when she's gone. Known for having the most beautiful legs in ballet—New York City ballet director Lincoln Kirstein likened them to "luminous wax"—Danilova could do almost anything, from emotive Russian classics to mischievous comedic roles where her fun-loving personality never failed to delight.

Influential American dance critic Edwin Denby wrote of her: "Danilova is not only a prodigious technician, but the way she points up a technical feat with a personal wit and distinction makes her the equal of any great actress." . . . and, "Where others look hasty she scintillates. But it is her feminine presence, her air of dancing for the delight of it, that captures the audience's heart."

Like Markova, Danilova was not classically pretty. Her features resembled those of a Modigliani carved stone head with large almond-shaped eyes, long nose, and small bowed mouth. But Danilova's face was heart-shaped, not elongated, giving her a sweet, rather than sad, countenance.

Nevertheless, her looks cost her a film role in a movie based on Massine's *Gaîté Parisienne,* one of Danilova's signature ballets. The director of *The Gay Parisian,* Jean Negulesco, said he didn't like the tilt of Danilova's nose. "My nose doesn't dance!" she snapped back. (Though Danilova was hurt—only exacerbated by her being asked to teach the role to the ballerina who was cast!—the movie was a big flop, so perhaps in the end she was better off.)

Danilova's outspoken playfulness and *joie de vivre* were like a tonic for Markova, who was very fortunate that the two became lifelong best friends. While Markova's early years had made her reticent and wary, coupled with an innately introspective personality, Danilova's harrowing upbringing had had the opposite effect—and it was quite an amazing story.

Choura's childhood was not unlike one of those Shirley Temple movies about the trials and tribulations of an orphaned mop top. Soon after she was born in St. Petersburg in 1903, Danilova lost both parents, to what illness she never knew. For the next several years, she and her older sister Elena lived with their stern grandmother. Then one morning, Choura discovered the old woman dead in her bed.

The children's wealthy godmother took them in next, but she was hardly a doting "Fairy Godmother." Though she didn't mistreat the little girls, they were shunted off Cinderella-like to a tiny room off the kitchen in the rather grand house. Danilova remembered never understanding why.

Apparently Choura's godmother had no interest in keeping the little girls, soon finding two different women to adopt each sister, cruelly separating them for life. Danilova's new guardian was "Aunt" Lidia, who had picked her over her sister because she was so tiny, just like her own recently deceased daughter whom the distraught mother eerily wished to "replace." In Aunt Lidia's elegant home—a butler took Choura's coat upon entrance—Danilova inexplicably was consigned to sleeping in the billiards room, though she was instructed never to touch the green felt or play with the colorful balls. Again, she was mystified by her sleeping arrangements.

Aunt Lidia divorced and remarried, frequently moving Danilova around, until one day the tiny girl was seen walking around on her tippy toes with ease. "She will be a great ballerina," Lidia thought, and within a year Danilova auditioned at the competitive Maryinsky Ballet School where Pavlova had trained. The talented young Choura was accepted, and the rest of her life would be dedicated to ballet.

One might think such an unstable upbringing would have resulted in permanent scarring and insecurity, but the opposite seemed true. Danilova had always been able to adapt to her new circumstances and learned early on how to charm others, take care of herself, and get her way when necessary. She also was mad about the ballet and felt lucky to have found such a wonderful creative outlet. Danilova was not only a perpetually cheerful person, but also able to make everyone around her happy. Diaghilev adored Choura, and that's saying something for a man who generally preferred the company of men.

Danilova may have been sweet-natured, but she was no pushover. She would fight tooth and nail for roles she thought "belonged" to her, a regular occurrence in the backstabbing, confrontational world of the Ballet Russe de Monte Carlo. Fortunately, those battles rarely included Markova, whose technical bravura was suited to different parts. For example, Danilova struggled to perform *Swan Lake's* thirty-two *fouettés,* which came so easily to Markova, whereas Markova often paled in comparison to Danilova in more playful roles, such as *La Boutique Fantasque's* can-can dancing doll, whose whimsical charm belies the complexity of the choreography.

Though Massine had not wanted Danilova for his new company—she was thirty-five years old!—Serge Denham overruled him. She was already enormously popular across the United States and would be a great asset at the box office.

The thought of reuniting with Danilova, and in Monte Carlo—her first ballet home—convinced Markova that she would be welcome in Massine's company. Little did she know how wrong she was and how much she would need Danilova's support in the very near future.

After Markova and Freddie Franklin signed on with Massine, Anton Dolin was the odd man out. Though he later claimed (in autobiography #3) that he had been asked to join the company but turned the offer down because he thought he and Markova needed a break from one another, everyone else involved said Dolin was never invited at all. In a later interview, Franklin said straight out that "Massine did not want Dolin in his new company," as the Russian artistic director anticipated a major clash of egos with the Brit.

Worse still, Dolin's former rival at the Ballets Russes, Serge Lifar, had been engaged as guest artist with the company to both restage *Giselle* and perform the male lead with Markova. Lifar was now the esteemed Director of Ballet at the Paris Opéra, with a much bigger following and more star power than Dolin. And though Massine didn't want Lifar any more than he wanted Dolin—Lifar was even more competitive and narcissistic—he was a great friend of Serge Denham's, who forced the vainglorious dancer on Massine.

Dolin was furious at Massine, Markova, and Franklin. In typical self-promoting fashion, he made a none-too-well-thought-out pronouncement to the press at the Markova-Dolin Company's farewell performance in Newcastle:

> Anton Dolin announced with regret that his famous partnership with Markova was to end at the end of the present tour.
>
> "We are hoping, however," he added, "to have another great Russian dancer to take her place."

> Mr. Dolin said how sorry they were to lose Markova, but he hoped she would be with them again in the future. He announced that they would have a Paris-Cannes Spring tour and a London season with Vera Nemtchinova as prima ballerina.
>
> —*Newcastle Evening Chronicle*, 1937

Dolin even sweet-talked Laura Henderson into loaning him the company's costumes and set designs for his new venture. Unfortunately, without Markova, no financial backers were forthcoming, and the planned company fizzled before it ever got off the ground. Dolin would later sign on with Massine's chief rival, Colonel de Basil, bound for a grand tour of Australia in the fall of 1938. But within a year, he would angle to rejoin Markova. During his downtime prior to the Australian tour, Dolin wrote his second autobiography, *Ballet Go Round*, to burnish his reputation. This excerpt from one of the book's press reviews says much about Dolin's state of mind:

> There is a big and not by any means exclusive public for ballet nowadays, and Anton Dolin's second book (the first was "Divertissement" in 1931) is the kind of gossipy literature which many of them read with avidity.
>
> When he refers in a preface to "this hectic life of the theatre and the jealousies of the ballet world" he seems to set the key for the "autobiography" which follows. Tales of jealousy we mind not, but much of his writing appeared to have been penned in a spirit of defence. Against what and against whom? Perhaps against people who have decried his achievements or have failed to recognize them.
>
> . . . "Alicia Markova," he says, "is the first English prima ballerina"; and Anton Dolin is "may I, without conceit, say the first English dancer of international reputation; and who knows, perhaps the last? . . . We shall dance again together and that day will be for me and I know for her a very happy one." . . .
>
> If Dolin could only write as well as he dances!
>
> —*The Nottingham Journal*, 12/8/38

Sadly, Markova was unable to dance in the final performance of the Markova-Dolin Company. She was suffering from synovitis, a recurring painful leg condition caused by her nonstop eight-shows-a-week schedule, and made worse by a recent fall while dancing *Giselle* at the King's Theatre in Hammersmith. Markova's doctor insisted that she rest for a few weeks lest she do any permanent damage. Vera Nemtchinova—who had been left behind by Dolin all those years before—kindly substituted for her.

As a going-away "present" to her dresser "Morty," Markova sang her praises to a newspaper reporter who wrote a lengthy feature article on the faithful employee. The headline amusingly read, "Markova's Dresser has never seen a Ballet."

The *Bristol Evening Post* reported on the prima ballerina's own plans:

> Mme. Markova, after a much-needed rest, will proceed to Monte Carlo to join Massine as his premier ballerina in a new company he is forming. She will break the journey "to take some lessons," she told me.
>
> When I expressed wonder at there being anyone who could teach her anything about the art of which she has such outstanding mastery, she said she is always learning. "You are finished when you think you have no more to learn," she told me.
>
> —*Bristol Evening Post,* 11/24/37

Whenever possible, Markova made time to take private lessons with a variety of celebrated ballet teachers in order to master diverse techniques. With her grueling schedule during the past 2½ years, that had not been easy.

Now, after a brief holiday in France—her first in a very long time—she returned to London and spent the next three months training intensely with Anna Pruzina, one of Pavlova's former teachers. Markova chose Pruzina because of her expertise in what is called "plasticity" in ballet, or a combination of pliancy and elasticity in modern dance movements, as in the free-flowing style of Isadora Duncan. Massine told Markova that he planned to create distinctive modern roles for her in his new ballets, and she wanted to make sure she was properly prepared to do them justice.

But even while on vacation, Markova practiced every day. "If you don't, you begin to wonder when you get back to dancing where to put your feet," she told an interviewer at the time. "With regular practice they just go where they ought to do, by themselves, as it were."

By spring, Markova felt ready to join Massine and the Ballet Russe de Monte Carlo. She would continue to take private lessons in Nice with the well-respected teacher Julia Sedova, who had been a former Maryinsky dancer.

The company's first season was set to begin in April with performances in Monte Carlo, Paris, and London, followed by a grand premiere in America. Though Markova was physically prepared, the fierce competitiveness within the company quite took her by surprise.

For starters, when all the dancers gathered in Monte Carlo to begin rehearsals in March 1938, close to forty of them were immediately let go by Massine, who had doubled down when extending contracts in case his first-choice performers weren't available. That made everyone skittish.

And even then, there were far too many top-tier soloists.

"There are so many stars that I cannot see how there will be enough ballets to go round," one dancer complained, according to ballet writer Kathrine Sorley Walker. "Those who got good roles were happy but there was considerable discontent and bickering over casting."

Markova had never thought she would retain the Queen Bee status she was afforded in England. One of the reasons she spent three full months in extensive pre-training was to put herself on surer footing—in every sense of the word—with all the multi-talented Russian dancers she would be joining. Markova looked forward to learning from them, as she had at the Ballets Russes.

Massine and Blum, however, were quite vocal about the company's great plans for their new "star." They planned to showcase her now-legendary *Giselle*, while also capitalizing on her gifts for mastering complicated modern choreography. Blum announced to the press, "an important addition to his company is in the person of Alicia Markova." The celebrated male dancers, including Igor Youskevitch and Michel Panaieff, were delighted; the Russian prima ballerinas, Tamara Toumanova and Mia Slavenska, not so much.

Their resentment was partially due to Markova's being British, but a contentious rivalry ran deep throughout the company no matter what the nationalities. (And there were many—including five Americans brought over from the United States.) In her autobiography, Danilova claims to have found few friends in her fellow Russian dancers, socializing instead with gregarious ballet fans she met on tour. She was very happy to have Markova and Freddie Franklin now joining her.

When it came to choreographing new ballets, Massine's methods were well suited to Markova. As Vicente Garcia-Márquez explained in his biography of Massine, many dancers couldn't cope with the choreographer's unusual process:

> Two aspects of Massine's method were especially disconcerting. One was his penchant for devising different choreography for the same musical phrase, then asking the dancers to perform all the versions, from which he would choose the one that he felt was most appropriate. The other was his routine lack of verbal communication with the dancers. As [dancer George] Skibine explained: "He would show the steps to you and then just sit and look. He wanted you to improvise; he showed you the steps so fast that you never really caught exactly what he did. You worked on it yourself—he let you create the parts."

Similar to Frederick Ashton, Massine's choreographic process required experimentation with his dancers; but the Russian was much more dictatorial. "If he [Massine] had an idea, he would absolutely break the dancer before he would change the step," explained Danilova. As Markova was willing to work endlessly on any variation, she and Massine got on well.

He also took advantage of her phenomenal memory for dance steps. When Markova was just a teenager with the Ballets Russes, Massine had used her as a human videographer. "He would say to me, 'Are you free tomorrow evening? There are a couple of wonderful Spanish dancers and I'd like you to take notice and tomorrow morning show me what you saw.'"

Markova was especially excited to be a part of *Seventh Symphony,* Massine's first new modern ballet for the company. It almost equaled her pleasure in coming "home" to the breathtaking cliffside paradise of Monte Carlo and reuniting with old Ballets Russes friends like Danilova and Boris Kochno.

With music by Beethoven, *Seventh Symphony's* four movements represented the grandiose themes of chaos as the earth and heavens were created, followed by its cataclysmic destruction. In the first act, Markova played the "Spirit of the Air and Sky" wearing a diaphanous costume that perfectly captured the pastel wonderland of Monte Carlo's sea and landscape.

French artist Christian Bérard was the set and costume designer, and an ideal choice for *Seventh Symphony*. The longtime lover of Boris Kochno—Diaghilev's former right-hand man and creator of the masterful chiaroscuro lighting for the production—Bérard understood the proper scale and dramatic integration of ballet backdrops, as well as how costumes should echo the movements of the dancers. As a popular fashion illustrator for *Vogue* magazine and surrealist couturier Elsa Schiaparelli, he also had a mastery of fantasy and the female form.

Markova thought Bérard outdid himself in her exquisite ensemble of all-over white silk leotard and tights topped by a layered transparent chiffon skirt. Horsehair was intermittently woven into the fabric so that when the skirt moved, it looked like clouds passing by. The silk chiffon was sky blue and appliquéd with almost imperceptible pale pink clouds. A larger cloud was appliquéd across Markova's breast and over one shoulder. She said it was not only a sublime work of art, but, unlike many of Picasso's all-too-structured ballet costumes, a pleasure to dance in.

Opening night in the Casino Theatre would be Markova's first of many backstage costume dramas with the Ballet Russe de Monte Carlo. Shortly before show time, she was wearing only her leotard and tights, still waiting for the company's perfectionist couturière, Barbara Karinska, to deliver the rest of the costume. When Karinska finally arrived just moments before curtain call, she had brought only the skirt, but no top or winged hair ornament.

Upon learning of the unfolding dilemma, Bérard rushed to Markova's dressing room, where he spotted a pale blue chiffon gown she had brought for the after-party. The designer grabbed its matching long scarf, which he quickly draped and stitched into a top. Next he took a pair of scissors and cut wings from a piece of white paper, decorating them with black eyebrow pencil from Markova's dressing table. The makeshift headpiece was fastened to her hair as Markova rushed on stage. Bérard was nothing if not resourceful.

But all was not yet well. When Markova came backstage to change costumes for the third movement, she realized that her flowered headdress was also missing. Fortunately, she had purchased a sculptural opalescent tiara earlier in the day, which was still in its bag in her dressing room. She now grabbed it and quickly popped it on her head.

Karinska was known to deliver her costumes at the very last minute, and in a rather piecemeal fashion, but everyone was quite willing to put up with her tardiness. She was one of the greatest ballet costumiers of her times—soon to be a much-in-demand designer at the New York City Ballet and in Hollywood—and one just couldn't rush genius. But there may have been a more calculating reason for Markova's missing wardrobe items, and one that had little to do with Karinska.

Many of the ballet seamstresses, who stitched and embroidered the costumes, had fierce loyalties only to their fellow Russian ballerinas and resented Markova's "stealing" their roles. That led to much spiteful costume sabotage of the British star, and at the most inopportune times.

One of the worst instances occurred on opening night of *Giselle* in July 1938 at London's Drury Lane Theatre. Problems actually started in Paris where Serge Lifar joined the company as guest artist and choreographer for *Giselle*. Lifar, whose ego knew no bounds, was decidedly a much bigger international star than Markova.

"For many years Lifar has been the darling of Paris," reported one entertainment magazine, partially because "he danced at the Opera with no first-rate dancers in his company who might show him up by comparison."

Rather than follow the classic Petipa *Giselle* choreography, which Sergeyev had painstakingly recreated for the celebrated productions with Spessivtseva and Markova, Lifar decided to greatly expand his own role as Prince Albrecht. So out went many of Giselle's beautifully emotive sequences, and in came Albrecht's overly dramatic spins and turns. A joke went around in Paris that they should rename the ballet *Albrecht*.

"[O]n his first entrance, Lifar ran around the stage like a witch aflame, his mouth open, eyes bulging," remembered Ballet Russe de Monte Carlo dancer George Zoritch. "If that were not grotesque enough, his fingers were spread to their widest and formed claws. I thought any minute he might start to claw Giselle when she finally appeared."

Markova wasn't happy about the bizarre new choreographic revisions, but she had little say in the matter. When she and Lifar danced *Giselle* together, it was as if they were in two completely different ballets. Danilova, who was the company's premier female dancer, would also dance the part of Giselle, which would subsequently be taught to Tamara Toumanova and Mia Slavenska so they could alternate later in the season. The famous Ballets Russes designer Alexandre Benois was engaged to create the costumes and sets, so the production promised to look decadently sumptuous.

When the company moved to London after Paris, Massine naturally selected Markova to dance *Giselle* on opening night, as British audiences assuredly would be clamoring to see her again, and in her most acclaimed role. As head dancer, Danilova really had "rights" to dance the lead at the premiere, but she agreed that Markova was the ideal choice, and generously offered to play the part of "Myrtha, Queen of the Wilis." (Danilova later said Giselle was never right for her because it went against her nature. "If Albrecht had left me, I would have suffered, but I would have worked myself out of it. I am not the type to give up on life, I would have fought back.")

Lifar wanted his good friend Toumanova as Giselle. The wardrobe mistresses agreed, thinking the beautiful young Russian far superior to the British interloper. But Massine relegated Toumanova to performances later in the run. The Russian seamstresses weren't happy.

Costumes were so expensive in those days that they were constantly being altered to fit each successive dancer in key roles. At the dress rehearsal the day before opening night, Markova arrived early, only to find all her costumes missing. The wardrobe department claimed to be taking special care to make them perfect, and they would of course be ready the next day. Markova was naturally rather nervous.

Though she never went to the theater before noon on performance day, Markova made an exception to check on her *Giselle* costumes. The wardrobers were indeed stitching madly away, and promised everything would be ready and waiting in Markova's dressing room when she arrived that evening. She had no choice but to go home.

As she became more and more worried about the situation, Markova remembered her wonderful Léon Bakst-designed *Giselle* costumes that she had worn for the Markova-Dolin Coronation Season for King George VI. As they were stored in London, Markova could easily get her hands on them and asked Manya to come by her flat to "freshen" them up. They still looked lovely, and Markova took them with her to the theater, feeling foolish at her nerves.

When she arrived in her dressing room several hours before performance time, the *new* costumes were still nowhere to be seen. Markova raced to the wardrobe department, only to find the door locked and no one answering. As few people were yet in the theater, she decided to stay calm and begin the long process of applying her makeup. One half hour before curtain, Markova apprehensively sent Morty to retrieve her Act One costume with instructions to "not return without it!"

At last it arrived. But when Markova put it on, the dress hung around her like a sheet. The wardrobe mistresses had intentionally used Toumanova's measurements instead of Markova's. Massine was summoned and told Markova he would simply make an announcement that she had suddenly taken ill and couldn't dance the part that evening, giving the role to Toumanova.

Absolutely not!, Markova shot back. Massine would have to tell the audience she was totally prepared to dance for them, but the costumes had been made for the wrong dancer. Needless to say, *that* wasn't going to happen.

Well, said Markova, if Massine tried to announce she was ill, she would run on stage in her dressing gown and tell them the truth! Just as the situation was getting really ridiculous, Markova remembered her backup costumes. Problem solved.

But, no. Upon hearing of the proposed wardrobe switch from one of the wardrobe mistresses, Lifar stormed into Markova's dressing room—already overflowing with an agitated crowd by this time—and screamed there was no way Markova would wear her old costumes and ruin the look of Benois's beautiful production design.

Markova started crying. Everyone was yelling. Finally, manager Sol Hurok was called in. As it was already well past curtain time and the audience was waiting none too patiently to see the great Markova, Hurok made a quick decision: Markova would indeed wear her old costumes and the show would go on as planned. End of conversation.

But now Markova, still hysterical, said she was too upset to perform. Hurok was beside himself, Lifar smug. Alexandra Danilova was the sole voice of reason. A little brandy was fetched for her friend as Choura managed to calm her down, prop her up, and repair her tear-stained makeup.

Markova took the stage and was a sensation.

Would that this were the end of the story. When the bedeviled performance was finally over, the audience jumped to its feet in unison and began applauding madly for one curtain call after another. As this was London, the thrilled British public kept screaming for their hometown prima ballerina to take the stage alone. But Lifar was having none of that. He refused to let Markova return to the stage without him.

Eight, nine, ten curtain calls. Still, Lifar wouldn't give Markova the spotlight to herself. The crowd got even louder: Markova! Markova! Markova! After an astounding twenty-four curtain calls, two sturdy stagehands physically restrained Lifar in the wings so Markova could take a solo bow. The audience exploded in cheers.

Furious, Lifar broke free and ran back on stage. The audience immediately booed. Lifar was incensed.

He became even angrier when he read the next day's newspaper reviews, like this one:

> Serge Lifar, specially imported from Paris, seemed more intent on advertising himself than Markova.
>
> Markova has been too little visible in this company. Her dancing last evening was so diamond bright and her acting so restrained that she emphasized, what London audiences already knew, that there is no finer classical dancer in the world.
>
> She did this against the heavy handicap of a partner whose intensive efforts at feats of elevation and display made anything but a satisfactory background.

> The performance ended with a campaign waged relentlessly by the gallery to separate Markova from her partner and to give her belated due. After ten ferocious minutes they succeeded.
>
> It was nice to be on their side.
>
> —*News Chronicle*, 7/22/38

Lifar wanted revenge. Toumanova too. Markova's American debut following London would be one for the books. Intrigues, jealousies, death threats—even a proposed duel! This wasn't ballet, it was a Wagnerian opera, and Markova was cast as the doomed heroine.

8

Only in America

> **Tragedies of War Temper Ballerina's Success in U.S.**
>
> Even English ballerinas have the charm of Old Russia. So it seemed today when Alicia Markova, born Alicia Marks of London, came to Boston and dazzled press-interviewers with her un-English accent, her chic American clothes, and a personality which would be a credit to any country. . . .
>
> "Only last week I had a cable saying my house near Marble Arch had been blown up by bombs. My mother and sisters are at Blackpool in the country. When I think of these things I just go down to the theater and rehearse and try hard to forget."
>
> —News report, Boston, Massachusetts 1941

"Jealousies," wrote Sol Hurok, "run high in the Ballet. The peak of a dancer's life is so brief that she must fight to get there as soon as she can and stay there as long as she can. Every potential rival holds a knife at her throat. Choreographers also have their pangs of jealousy, and managers too."

It's hard to believe in an art form as refined as ballet that competiveness could escalate to all-out war. Though some backbiting certainly existed in Diaghilev's days, the impresario's artistic vision was so comprehensive and his estimation of talent so unerring that few dared question his judgment.

"He [Diaghilev] taught the company to strive against petty-mindedness and jealousies, to create a masterpiece among themselves as a whole," said Markova. He was the iron hand in the velvet glove, and if you disagreed with any of his decisions, you were always free to leave the Ballets Russes. (And upon returning to your senses, you'd be cheerfully welcomed back, as was the case with Anton Dolin, and Lydia Lopokova on more than one occasion.)

Colonel Wassily de Basil, Léonide Massine, and Sol Hurok, by contrast, were too wrapped up in their own inflated egos and selfish maneuverings to garner unquestioning respect from their companies; and the sensitive, artistic René Blum was just too nice. Then there were the moneymen allowed to add their two cents (and pounds, and francs) concerning who should get hired and which dancer should perform what role. It was a recipe for disaster.

Diaghilev loved colorful press as much as the next impresario, but an audience rioting over Igor Stravinsky's music and Vaslav Nijinsky's choreography was a battle cry for the avant-garde, not the petty behavior of a puffed-up leading man refusing to bow to his leading lady. The encore-obsessed Serge Lifar embarrassed himself and the company on opening night of *Giselle* at the Drury Lane Theatre, and there was nothing anyone cared to do about it.

By the late 1930s, ballet had become an uncommonly cutthroat business. Even resigning from a company made dancers instant targets among their peers, especially if they were "defecting" to the competition. When Tamara Toumanova gave her notice to Colonel de Basil, announcing that she would be joining up with Massine at the end of the 1937 season, the eighteen-year-old was seen as a traitor. As she later told Sol Hurok, fellow dancers attempted to trip her during rehearsals, and "one night a hand came out under the canvas backdrop and caught her ankle, to make her fall as she was about to step forward. She managed, she said, to disentangle herself just in time."

But Toumanova could give as good as she got, as would soon be evident.

Adding to the rivalry between the de Basil and Massine camps was what would become known as London's "Battle of the Ballets." It happened in the summer of 1938. While Markova was knocking them dead in *Giselle* at the Drury Lane Theatre, de Basil's company was also performing in London, just down the road at the Royal Opera House in Covent Garden.

Though one would have thought the two ballet companies would siphon fans from one another and play to half-full houses, the opposite proved true. Londoners became completely ballet-mad, purchasing tickets from both organizations, often for the same evening!

Like sports fans studying player's stats, balletomanes carefully reviewed the planned programs for each performance, figuring how they could catch their favorite stars in their best roles. So one might begin the evening at Covent Garden watching Vera Nemtchinova in a scene from *Swan Lake*, then walk the few blocks to Drury Lane during intermission to catch Markova in *Giselle* or Alexandra Danilova in *Coppélia*.

The London press added to the furor for tickets. The prior year, daily news accounts of the choreography copyright lawsuit between Massine and Colonel de Basil had been a big boon to circulation. Fleet Street now took advantage of this trumped-up "ballet war" to sell papers.

The Colonel, who renamed his company with unfathomable regularity, had new financial backers for the London engagement, resulting in the awkward moniker "Russian Ballet presented by Educational Ballets, Ltd." So the press shortened the names of the two competing companies to the battle between Massine's "Ballet Russe" and "the Educational." It sounded more like a history lesson than a dance war.

But it did manage to turn ballet into a competitive sport. Double-ticket holders would meet up with friends during their interval marches from one theater to another, arguing about who was best in which role. Naturally they were imbibing alcohol along the way. Newspapers made lighthearted mention of the fact that the Bow Street police station was perfectly positioned between the two theater venues in case the amicable rivalries turned violent.

-ɷ-

After his company's successful 1938 summer season in London playing to packed houses, de Basil took the troupe on a long and popular tour of Australia. He had renamed the company in honor of his London success, now calling it the Covent Garden Russian Ballet presented by Educational Ballets Ltd. (Just one year later he would change it again to the even more awkward Original Ballet Russe Ltd's Col. W. De Basil's Ballet Company.) Massine et al. went back to Monte Carlo, planning a fall season in Europe prior to leaving for the United States.

While Markova was rehearsing with Lifar for the company's scheduled return to London in September—this time at Covent Garden's Royal Opera House—Lifar clumsily set her down on the stage, turning her ankle. It was doubtful he did it on purpose, but caring little for his partner's welfare certainly played a part.

The injury was serious enough that Markova was told she needed to rest throughout the entire London run so she would be strong enough to open in New York in October. It was a great disappointment for British ballet fans.

Markova's imposed rest gave her plenty of time to think. Was this company really right for her? She had never experienced so much turmoil among her fellow dancers. Diaghilev had protected her at the Ballets Russes and she had a congenial relationship with everyone at Marie Rambert's Ballet Club, Ninette de Valois's Vic-Wells, and the Markova-Dolin Company. This was something entirely new and unwelcome.

Massine wasn't helping matters. Where George Balanchine—the company's former artistic director and chief choreographer—had been patient and respectful with the dancers, Massine was more abrupt and authoritarian. "There was an immediate change of pace and mood," wrote Kathrine Sorley Walker. "Nothing was easy-going any longer."

"He was not gracious, neither was he unpleasant," observed Agnes de Mille. "He was totally, unattainably withdrawn from casual contact and you could place on this attitude any interpretation you chose."

Alexandra Danilova, who was Massine's most frequent onstage partner at that time, found him to be as selfish as Lifar in that regard.

"He considered lifting a ballerina or supporting her in pirouettes not part of his job and acted as if he were doing her a favor," she complained. "Like he preferred to dance by himself."

With no one looking out for her, and others out to get her, Markova was reconsidering traveling with the company all the way to America—over three thousand miles from her support group of family and friends. When she broached her concerns with Massine, he pooh-poohed the idea that the bad feelings would continue. It's just a "sticky" situation we'll all get through, he assured her, and New York audiences were already anxiously anticipating her *Giselle.* Not since Pavlova's *Giselle* fourteen years earlier had there been such excitement for the classic Russian ballet in the United States. Markova's opening at the Metropolitan Opera House was sure to be a sold-out event.

She, however, was not sold.

For one thing, Lifar had brought out all of Markova's insecurities about her ethnic looks by so publicly preferring the stunning Toumanova for a partner. Having never been abroad before, Markova imagined Americans favoring the pretty blonde-and-bubbly performers she had seen in the movies, like Ginger Rogers and Carole Lombard.

And there were far more important reasons to remain in London. While Markova was recuperating from her foot injury in September 1938, Czechoslovakia fell to the Germans. And how many Europeans really believed their fragile peace accord with Hitler would last? The British government began issuing gas masks as a precaution while digging trenches in London's bucolic parks as a place to duck and cover in case of air raids. This was not reassuring.

If war was imminent, Markova would prefer to remain home with her family.

But Sol Hurok had already heavily promoted Markova's *Giselle* to New York ballet fans. He wasn't about to disappoint them—or refund any money. ("His eyes used to click like cash register signs behind his glasses as he watched the crush of eager patrons," Margot Fonteyn wryly observed.) So the imperious manager (he talked about himself in the third person) invited Markova and her mother to tea with him and his wife at the splendid Savoy Hotel, Diaghilev's former London home.

Hurok could be very persuasive, despite his completely bizarre accent: a combination of his Russian Ukrainian roots and Brooklynese—not to mention switched "t's" and "th's." Margot Fonteyn thought Hurok talked like a character actor in a "B" movie, saying lines such as someone earned "toity tousand dollars," or he was "nervous about 'thicket' sales." But both Fonteyn and Markova also found the impresario eloquent and convincing in his own way. Hurok told Alicia and Eileen that he had adopted America as his home because it was the land of opportunity and optimism. She would be a huge success there, he guaranteed.

Markova was still unconvinced.

Finally, Hurok assured her that if she was miserable in New York, he would allow her to suspend her contract with him and return to London. That seemed highly unlikely in practice, but after further deliberation, Markova hesitantly agreed.

If she had only known what was to follow. . . .

Sailing into New York harbor was an awe-inspiring experience in the 1930s. Thanks to Elisha Otis and his invention of the elevator, skyscrapers dominated the view of Manhattan, with the Chrysler Building (completed in 1930) soaring over a thousand feet high, followed one year later by the completion of the 102-story Empire State Building. It would retain the title of world's tallest building for forty years.

Catching sight of the Statue of Liberty's torch, echoing the city's architectural reach for the heavens, gave visitors the feeling of a brave new world on the horizon. Equally startling for many Europeans were the cultural differences, large and small.

Alexandra Danilova recounted tales of the company's bewilderment on their first trip to America with Hurok in 1933. After being seasick aboard ship for seven days, everyone wearily checked into New York's Wellington Hotel. As was typical in Europe, all the dancers placed their shoes outside their doors before retiring so they could be cleaned and polished overnight. But the next morning, they were nowhere in sight. The hotel staff assumed the dirty footwear was trash and had thrown them all out!

Fortunately, Markova had Danilova to explain the ins and outs of local customs to her when the company returned in October 1938. But knowing what to expect in an American hotel was the least of Markova's worries. Internal ballet squabbles broke out almost immediately.

As Tamara Toumanova was a teenager, both her parents accompanied her to New York. Like Markova's former governess, they were fiercely protective; but unlike Guggy, they were also willing to do *anything* to promote their daughter. When Toumanova's stepfather—a former czarist army colonel—discovered that Markova had been chosen to star in the opening night performance of *Giselle,* he stormed in to see Massine and demanded that his precious Tamara be given that honor.

Massine said no, whereupon the colonel hauled off and punched the choreographer in the jaw, knocking him to the ground. While the fuming stage-father was quickly ejected from the theater, Markova—who had been a witness to the altercation—not surprisingly became unnerved. That was just the beginning.

After the final dress rehearsal at the Metropolitan Opera House, Danilova and Markova left the theater together to return to the Astor Hotel. As Danilova was hailing a cab, Markova found herself jostled in the rush hour crowd by a stranger who forced a piece of paper into her hand before vanishing from sight. The note read: "DON'T DANCE TOMORROW NIGHT, OR. . . ."

Markova turned as white as the paper. "I thought this—this—I've only seen this in the movies," she remembered thinking. "Don't tell me this country is really like this!" Then, she thought, maybe it's just a joke? Danilova wasn't the least bit amused and called Massine as soon as they were safely back at the hotel. Still smarting from being sucker-punched by Daddy Toumanova, Massine also took the note seriously.

Hurok was consulted and it was decided that his star British ballerina should not be left alone for one single minute prior to the opening night curtain. Danilova was to share her hotel room and the imposing male principal dancer Igor Youskevitch was sent over as their bodyguard whenever they went out.

Markova always sought solitude and quiet contemplation the evening before performing *Giselle,* but Hurok had other plans. To drum up publicity for the ballet, Markova, Danilova, Youskevitch, and Freddie

Franklin were given box seats for the rodeo at Madison Square Garden where newspaper photographers would snap their pictures. So instead of thoughts of the spiritual world, the ballerina found herself contemplating cattle-roping and bull-riding among peanut and popcorn sellers. On the bright side, if a sinister force was out to get Markova, the rodeo was probably the last place on earth anyone would look for the ballerina.

Safely back in her hotel room later that evening, Markova had time to think. Considering the costume fiasco in London and Lifar's dropping her during rehearsal, maybe her *Giselle* with this company really was cursed. The next day, she told Sol Hurok that it might be best all around if Toumanova did dance opening night. But the sold-out high-society audience expected to see the great Markova in her first New York appearance, and the impresario had no intention of letting them down.

Taking no chances, Hurok set about securing the theater, beginning with special identification badges issued to every Metropolitan Opera House employee—the first time that had ever been done. "A threat of possible violence caused me to take the precaution to have detectives, disguised as stage-hands, standing by," Hurok added. "I eliminated the trap-door and understage elevator used in this production as Giselle's grave, and gave instructions to have everything loose on the stage fastened down." It was like the first half of an Alfred Hitchcock movie. But what would be the denouement?

Hurok's final order caused its own set of problems. Already shaken by the sight of security guards in the wings watching her every move—not to mention making her American premiere!—Markova found herself equally agitated while *on* stage. A she tells the story:

> In Act II, Giselle has to pick two flowers from the ground row at the back of the stage during the *pas de deux* and toss them to Albrecht. It is beautifully timed musically: Giselle has to do a *glissade*, a *temps levé* and a run, plucking one lily and then the next.
>
> As I performed the step, I found the lilies had been nailed to the ground: battened down like everything else for security. They seemed immovable. The company later told me they had

> never seen anything like the way the ethereal spirit of Giselle gave one *wrench* and then another *wrench*, and tore the lilies from the ground with superhuman—perhaps supernatural—strength—and got back to center stage in time to carry on.
>
> I sometimes wonder why I never developed an ulcer!

That wasn't the only floral mishap of the evening. Lifar, none too happy about dancing *Giselle* with the British star who had shown him up in London, instigated his own onstage drama, as Markova continues the story:

> In Act II he [Lifar] insisted upon carrying real lilies when he came to Giselle's grave. I adore those huge Easter lilies, but if you tread on one they do make the most awful squelch.
>
> On opening night, Lifar was adamant that he should carry real lilies, a huge sheaf that he strewed all over the stage as he entered. For the rest of Act II, the *corps de ballet* and I spent our time trying to avoid stepping on these mushy, squashed flowers with their oozing stems. The corps slipped and fell, one after another. I fortunately managed to pick my way among them, but this carpet of flattened lilies played havoc with the lines of the dancers. Just as they—and I—were about to make a run or jump across the stage, there would be a patch of lilies in one's path, and one had to take evasive action, while hoping not to skid and fall down.

After all that, it's hard to believe the discerning New York audience was roundly enthusiastic. With gentlemen in top hats and tails and ladies in sumptuous jewels and furs, the grandiose crowd gave Markova one ovation after another.

Lifar was furious. Hurok was ecstatic. As the impresario wrote in his memoirs, "Markova triumphed that night in Giselle as she had in London. For the exquisite English girl it was not only a triumph. It was also a vindication. She had made her great name only in her own country, and her countrymen might have been forgiven if their appreciation of her gifts had been a little influenced by pride in a native ballerina.

"For New Yorkers there was no such public association. On stage of the Metropolitan that night she stood strictly on her own merits. She met the ordeal, and New York lay beside London at her feet."

"She [Markova] was described by the critics as 'breathtaking,' 'incomparable,' 'phenomenal,' and 'superb,'" recounted Barbara Heggie in *The New Yorker*. "John Martin of the Times called her 'visual poetry.'"

But Markova's relief and joy were to be short-lived. The very next evening in Act I of *Giselle*, Lifar seemed to lose his balance while lifting his leading lady, dropping her down so hard that he fractured her foot. While Markova felt it was an accident, others were doubtful. Lifar clearly had it in for her.

Somehow, Markova managed to finish the act. She later said the death scene didn't require any acting that evening, as she actually passed out from the excruciating pain. Mia Slavenska, a redhead, took over in Act II, much to the shock of the audience. *Giselle* apparently had been to the hairdresser before moving on to the spirit world.

Markova would have liked sufficient time to recuperate from her severe foot injury, but her *Giselle* had gotten such rave reviews that Hurok wanted her back as soon as possible. The fall 1938 Ballet Russe de Monte Carlo booking in New York was one of the first times the Metropolitan Opera House had been sold out for an entire ballet run.

Markova's doctors began an immediate intensive healing regimen, which would continue throughout the American tour. Despite lingering pain, she was back on stage just nine days later. While she wasn't up to dancing a full-length classical ballet like *Giselle* just yet, Markova could appear in less physically demanding roles, as in *Seventh Symphony* with her new partner (and former bodyguard), the immensely talented, and friendly, Igor Youskevitch.

But as if the foot pain weren't enough, Markova also developed an abscess in her tooth, requiring it to be pulled. While a replacement was being made, the dentist packed the open gap with gauze and prescribed ice packs to minimize the bleeding.

The next night, Markova was back on stage in *Seventh Symphony*. All was going well until the end of Act III. The choreography required Youskevitch and another dancer to flip Markova upside down, whereupon the gauze packing fell out. Instantly feeling that it had come loose, she carefully kept her mouth shut until the dance concluded with her dramatic one—two—three extended jumps offstage. But upon the third forceful leap into the wings, the tooth plug popped out of her mouth, and with it, a steady spurt of blood all over the floor. That was one accident no one could blame on Lifar.

In fact, Lifar was no longer a problem for anyone at the company. Not satisfied with just putting Markova out of commission, the vainglorious dancer had escalated his rants, complaints, and general disruption of the organization, resulting in a major public row. The New York (and later London) press reveled in all the juicy details, told here in successive press excerpts.

From *The New York Sun*:

Since the arrival of the company in this country, following the reorganization in London last summer, there have been reports of difficulties between the management and Mr. Lifar.

According to these rumors, Mr. Lifar objected to other members of the company appearing in roles with which he has been associated during his long career in ballet. He also was said to be displeased with the critical notices his own dancing received.

He danced the Opening night in the new production of "Giselle," and on that occasion most of the critical plaudits went to the English ballerina, Alicia Markova, who had the title role. Miss Markova was making her first appearance in America with the company.

—10/21/38

From the *New York Herald Tribune*:

. . . [Lifar] began to demand that he be accorded a voice in the selection of the casts in which he was to appear.

"I refused to permit him to have his way," Mr. Hurok said, "and on each occasion he sulked. We weren't pleased by his attitude, or his performances, and he knew it. He also knew that we had a dancer waiting in the wings, in costume and ready to go on in his place if he refused to perform. As a matter of fact, we have sixteen dancers in the company as good as he—or better," Mr. Hurok said, with some emphasis.

But nothing much happened until last Wednesday.

—10/23/38

From the *New York Times*:

[Lifar] said that he had challenged Massine in the wings after the first ballet, "Swan Lake," to a duel in Central Park at early dawn on Friday and had given him the choice of weapons, but his offer was declined. . . .

[Said Sol Hurok], "When he challenged Massine to a duel on Thursday night at the back of the stage the director waved his hand and said 'Don't talk such tommyrot, take an aspirin.' Then Lifar came to me and resigned."

Mr. Hurok added that the dancer had objected to the casting of the ballet "Swan Lake" because an American, Roland Guerard, had a solo dance which went well and Lifar insisted upon its being cut out before the curtain went up.

—10/23/38

And finally, from entertainment magazine *PIC*:

As was reported in the papers, Serge Lifar thought he was being badly treated, challenged Massine to a duel in Central Park, then quit the company in a huff in the middle of the New York engagement, and returned to Paris. As fine an exhibition of temperament as Broadway has been treated to in many a year! . . .

But temperament is phoney, and here is the joker behind Serge's spectacular antics. Lifar has had a soft job at the Paris Opera. He has grown fat and sloppy in his dancing from lack of practice and hard work. If he were acclaimed in America, he could return to his soft Paris job and grow fatter and sloppier. But if he were a complete flop in America (and there was every indication that he would have been) even the French might begin to wonder about their idol. They might decide that while he was gone they had found a better dancer to take his place. Lifar's temperament was phoney, but Lifar is smart.

> He has returned to Paris the victim of backstage politics—a great artist whose art was not (as was expected) appreciated by "vulgar, commercial Americans." He can't lose.
>
> —12/13/38

But Lifar *would* lose the French people's high regard, and in the very near future. After the Germans invaded France in World War II, the former Ballets Russes star kept the Paris Opera Ballet up and running by accepting favors from Nazi propaganda leader Joseph Goebbels. Though the dancer never joined the Nazi party, he did attend society functions with powerful German officials, a fact that became widespread public knowledge. The self-aggrandizing Lifar, who referred to himself as "*Le Dieu de la Danse*" (God of the Dance), just couldn't resist bragging about, and exaggerating, his connections with Hitler's hierarchy.

That led to formal charges of Nazi collaboration following the war, with Lifar disgraced and banned from the Paris Opera for life. He would flee to Monaco, where he later became director of the Nouveau Ballet de Monte Carlo.

Throughout the ordeal, many dancers stood up for Lifar, asserting that he had saved all their careers during the war. Respected dance critic and writer Clement Crisp expressed what many in the ballet world felt: "Lifar, like many people holding important posts in occupied Paris, accepted a fait-accompli: The Germans were there. A national theatre was also there, for whose ballet troupe Lifar had responsibility. Dancers must work. Dancers must eat. Ballet must survive, and serve as an immediate representation of French art. Lifar owed it to his artists and to his adopted nation to maintain dance activity."

Certainly not everyone shared that charitable view.

The once-superb Russian dancer mellowed as he aged and reconnected with many of his former "foes." Markova never held a grudge and the two often chatted amiably at social functions. Moreover, unlike Anton Dolin, Lifar was only too happy to appear on the 1960 U.K. television program *This Is Your Life* to help celebrate Markova's illustrious career.

But back in 1938, being rid of Lifar wouldn't be the end of Markova's troubles in America. There were still several envious Russian ballerinas gunning for her, especially since she was getting the lion's share of the publicity.

Markova was a great news story. She was the first ballet star born in Britain, not Russia, was already legendary for her *Giselle*, and was making her first appearance in the United States. She also had a fascinating backstory, that uncanny resemblance to Anna Pavlova, and spoke fluent English—a real advantage in the United States.

For many of the young Russian girls, the language barrier and resultant mangled English pronunciations presented problems in America. In New Orleans, one newspaper writer made unmerciful fun of the young Russian dancers:

> "Ay want to take a bathz."
> "Ay am in a hurry."
> "My beggege! My beggege!"
>
> Talking exactly like so many Ninotchkas, some 100 real Rooshians arrived by special train in New Orleans Saturday noon, collectively representing the Greater Ballet Russe de Monte Carlo.
>
> They are also, collectively speaking, the country's most baffling interviewees.

Worse still was an incident with ballerina Nathalie Krassovska. When bragging to the press "I am the best Fokine dancer," her heavy accent made the statement sound unprintably profane!

Markova was always "good" copy. When the Ballet Russe de Monte Carlo first arrived in Manhattan in October 1938, *The New Yorker* magazine did a brief write-up on the company for their "Talk of the Town" section. The article began by citing the Tower of Babel-like roster of "six American dancers, three English, one German, one French, two Italians, one Yugoslavian, one Czech, one Dutch, and a girl of Danish-Javanese parentage," in addition to the coterie of Russians. But the one dancer they chose to profile in depth was Alicia Markova, as in this tongue-in-cheek excerpt:

> . . . Some of Markova's enthusiasms are very un-Russian. Roast duckling, "black velvet," and ice hockey (purely as a spectator)

> are among these. She loves cats, too, but has restrained her tendency to make friends with theatre pussies since a big black Tom loyally followed her onstage when she was doing "Les Sylphides" in Birmingham. She says English love the ballet, that there you will find balletomanes among such lowly characters as cab drivers and tram conductors. When she said this, it reminded us that an Englishman, one Cyril Beaumont, had once written about her, "The manner in which the foot is attached to the leg compels admiration." We therefore took a gander at this attachment, and it seemed O.K. to us.

When the company moved on to Massachusetts, the *Boston Globe* also focused on Markova in the paper's feature story on the arrival of the Ballet Russe de Monte Carlo. She was the only dancer photographed:

> **Markova, Noted English Star,**
> **Arrives With Ballet Russe**
> Fragile-Looking Ballerina on First Visit
> Seen as Successor To Pavlova's Throne
>
> . . . Many new faces were noted among this reorganized company. Most important of the newcomers was the slight, fragile-looking Alicia Markova, first English ballerina of top rank to visit this country and said by some critics to be the most probable successor to the still vacant throne of Pavlova.
>
> Up at the Lenox, a Globe reporter and photographer found Markova, the English sensation, whose dancing last month won even the most blasé of the New York critics.
>
> Small and delicately built, her black hair drawn back severely in the traditional style of the classic ballerina, her immense black eyes seeming rather startled, she submitted courteously to the taking of pictures and the asking of questions. It is her first visit to America and she finds it all rather surprising, she admitted.
>
> But she likes it. American audiences, she said, in her clear, pretty English voice—she was born Alice Marks but followed the custom of taking a Russian name—surprised her by their warmth for she had been told they were cold and unresponsive

> compared with those in England. She was as astonished as pleased when the New Yorkers applauded so often and loudly, in the middle of a dance as well as at the conclusion. She'll never believe again that Americans are cold. . . .
>
> —*The Boston Globe,* 11/7/38

While remaining reserved and a bit shy, Markova had clearly mastered press interviews and would continue to do so throughout the American tour. Adding to her fame, and renown for the company, was the repertoire of classical *and* modern ballets, all lavishly produced.

The inclusion of Massine's avant-garde works like *Seventh Symphony* created buzz wherever they went, as did the extravagant sets.

"Magnificent scenery and costumes reminded one of a series of paintings in the modern Museum of Art," noted the *Boston Post,* referring to Fokine's *L'Epreuve d'Amour.* "[T]he reason was Andre Derain, who executed them." Diaghilev's legacy of collaborating with famous contemporary artists lived on.

Fortunately for Markova, her performances justified all the pre-press:

> . . . Markova's dancing in "L'Epreuve d'amour" on the opening night had already predicted the grace and exceptional lightness which would characterize her Giselle. But it was as nothing to the actual realization of last evening. . . . She seemed like a spirit in flight; when she met the floor, it was as if to sink into it or go through it.
>
> This marvelous lightness, so important in realizing the role of Giselle in the second act, was in addition to an exceptional mimetic and histrionic talent, similarly desirous in the first. It was possible to follow the almost absurd involvements of the story—as preposterous as anything in grand opera—with the greatest of ease because of Markova's genius for story-telling by gesture and facial expression. The high point of her characterization in this regard was her fit of madness, as unlike the conventional mad scene of opera or even of stage as day is to night. By the same token it was infinitely more convincing.
>
> —*Boston Evening Transcript,* 11/9/38

It seemed all of Boston was smitten with Markova, and she continued to receive extensive press coverage throughout the engagement. A photo spread in the *Boston Sunday Post* featured full-page portraits of the dancer's face and graceful hands, under the headline HANDS FROM THE BALLET TELL MANY TALES. The *Boston Herald* also ran a dramatic close-up photo, this time of Markova running her fingers through her long hair, as if from the mad scene in *Giselle*. The caption read "Lovely Alicia Markova." Words like those helped to lessen the dancer's insecurities about Americans not accepting her ethnic looks.

What had not diminished, however, were the behind-the-scenes jealousies within the company. Though Markova no longer feared any onstage antics or nailed-down props—now that the amiable Youskevitch was her Albrecht—she hadn't seen the last of the costume intrigues.

One evening while Markova was dancing Act I of *Giselle* in Boston, someone sneaked into her dressing room and completely slashed out the underskirt of her "Wili" tutu for Act II. At intermission, the dresser was aghast when she saw the frayed tatters. But ever since the costume drama in Europe, Markova had never traveled without a backup. Her trusty Bakst-inspired *Giselle* wardrobe was locked safely in a trunk. Massine extended the interval as the garment was steamed and pressed, and the ballet continued to wild applause.

Though it was never proven who had done the deed, everyone suspected the same perpetrators, as dancer Frederic Franklin explained: "Tamara was with us. And Mama Toumanova and Tamara Toumanova were very, very close. There was trouble. She protected her daughter from all kinds of things. I think it was getting back at Alicia. . . . We never knew who did it. But people surmised it was Tamara and her mother. . . . And Lifar and Toumanova were also very close. Very close."

Ironically, Toumanova had once looked up to Markova. When both were performing in London in 1933, Tamara, then fourteen, asked the British prima ballerina for a signed photo. "For Tamara Toumanova, Wishing her every success, Alicia Markova," wrote the gracious star, who thought the young dancer so very lovely and talented. Apparently, Toumanova's memory was short.

The remains of the ripped-out skirt were later found balled up in the corner of one of the Boston Opera House bathrooms.

If Markova thought joining a large company would make her work life less taxing than at the Markova-Dolin Company, she was dead wrong. Criss-crossing the United States—over a hundred different cities in just over six months—was far more punishing and time-consuming than the short hops required in Great Britain. With a greatly reduced salary, Markova also no longer had a private dresser or hotel accommodations, though she greatly enjoyed sharing a room with Danilova.

"It was in America that Alicia and I renewed the friendship we had begun at the Diaghilev company," Danilova reminisced. "We ate our meals together, went shopping together, we were always the last to leave the station together, stranded with our suitcases long after everybody else had gone, talking and dancing until morning."

And on they went, leaving Boston for Philadelphia, then Ohio, and then Chicago for Christmas. Critical praise also followed, despite some laughable moments.

One incident involved a corps member who had trouble napping on the noisy trains. To assure some much-needed rest after the performance, she decided to take a sleeping pill during the last act of *The Nutcracker.*

But it kicked in too soon.

While Markova was dancing the Sugar Plum Fairy's melodic solo, she suddenly heard a thud. The sleep-deprived dancer had dropped to the stage in a dead faint. As the show must go on, the ballerina's limp body was quickly—and gracefully—dragged offstage. Markova kept pirouetting like nothing was wrong, and a doctor was summoned.

The cause was assumed to be the high altitude, as the company was performing in mountainous Cheyenne, Wyoming; but when an oxygen mask didn't get a rise out of the poor girl, the real cause was discovered. Markova laughingly recalled, "From then on, Massine posted a notice: Please don't take any sleeping pills until after the performance!"

Company members really did need to stay sharp, especially when treading the boards in small towns. Hurok booked them into many rural locations without grand theaters; so performances were often held in college and high school gymnasiums, movie houses, or makeshift reception halls. The stage conditions were often unsuitable to dance.

"There was a marble floor in one auditorium in a Southern school," Markova remembered. "We arrived an hour before the performance and the floor wasn't only hard, it was polished! We tried to wet the floor and the male dancers danced in bare feet to get a grip on the floor. I was in my tights soaked in water because I couldn't wear my *pointe* shoes, and that's how we did our performance of *The Nutcracker*. We offered to cancel and give the money back, but they said, 'Oh, no—whatever you need to do.'"

In other towns, Markova recalled, "a board might give way and I'd go over, but I always had very good training and warmed up well, so I did pretty well."

A lopsided stage during a Texas one-night stand proved especially challenging when Markova was dancing the lead role in *Coppélia*. In the opening of the ballet's second act, the naughty Swanhilda plays a trick on Dr. Coppelius by taking the place of his mechanical doll. While the kindly old doctor faces the wall reading from one of his gigantic magic books, Markova as Swanhilda sits frozen in place in the doll's wheeled chair.

But the stage's tilt slowly set the wheels in motion, and the Markova "doll" began rolling toward the orchestra pit. Not wanting to break her pose, Markova stayed stock still as her eyes met those of the horrified conductor who she was about to collide with. Fortunately, a faint thumping of the wheels made Dr. Coppelius turn around just in time to catch the chair and turn it back upstage. But it wouldn't stay put, and the befuddled doctor kept spinning the chair in various spots in an attempt to stop it from moving. It didn't work, but the audience thought the scene hilarious, and as *Coppélia* is a comedy, everyone was amused.

Many of the mishaps went unnoticed, as rural audiences often had never seen any ballet before, let alone famous classics. American dance critic Jack Anderson explained how showman Sol Hurok drummed up interest:

> The company made efforts of several kinds to attract audiences. During its first tour in 1938 it almost brazenly billed itself as though it were an assemblage of Hollywood stars. Thus an advertisement in a Richmond paper informed Virginians

> that they were about to see "SEVEN MOST BEAUTIFUL BALLERINAS IN THE WORLD." . . . Each was described with a few provocative phrases. Krassovska, readers learned, "won a beauty contest in Paris," and when Danilova "stepped on the toe of the former Prince of Wales while waltzing . . . [he] deemed it an honor." Lest ballet still seem something remote, the advertisement told prospective ticket buyers not to be afraid of fancy names: "The ballet called Gaîté Parisienne [is] Gay Paree to you."

In a promotional advertisement for a Seattle, Washington performance, the announcement was similarly mass-marketed:

> **The Ballet Russe**
>
> A BOUNTIFUL BANQUET OF MUSIC, GLAMOUR AND BEAUTY
>
> THE BEST IN DANCING, MUSIC, SCENERY AND COSTUMES
>
> GRACE, COLOR, RHYTHM BRILLIANT ENTERTAINMENT
>
> AN EVENING OF THEATRE THRILLS FOR YOUNG AND OLD

The Seattle dance critics seemed willing to play along: "Like the frosting on your cake or the maraschino saved 'til the last in the bottom of a cocktail glass was the Ballet Russe de Monte Carlo's closing matinee yesterday."

Another gambit for generating pre-press was to offer up the ballerinas in "cheesecake" poses for newspaper photographers. Dressed in fancy suits and hats, dancers Nini Theilade, Mia Slavenska, Danilova, and Markova would sit in a group—often on their packing trunks—with their skirts hiked up to reveal their shapely crossed legs. Sometimes Massine was posed awkwardly standing behind them, looking decidedly uncomfortable.

Hurok wasn't the only one creatively promoting the ballet. "Sergei Denham courted high society and tried to make ballet performances social events in the same sense that opera performances were," noted Jack Anderson. "[N]ewspapers regularly sent society writers, as well as music or dance critics, to ballet openings, and syndicated columnists told readers from coast to coast what the rich and famous had worn to the Ballet Russe."

It worked.

SOCIETY GREETS BALLET OPENING, trumpeted one paper. "Opera House Presents Breath-Taking Array of Ermines and Sables—Every Seat Filled."

And in another: "In a crush of ermine, mink, orchids, gardenias and dressy clothes, with every right hand grasping opera glasses, and with glowing praise for dancers and orchestra sailing through the air, first-nighters ushered in a brilliant stay for the ballet."

The widespread popularity of ballet across the United States is illustrated in the following "Letter from Massine" that the artistic director wrote as an introduction to the company's programs. His words confirmed the audience's belief that they were indeed part of the "enlightened class," and attending frequent performances would make them even more so. There was also a wink toward the male ticketholders.

> . . . Proof of its potency as first rate entertainment and as cultural stimulation is the growing audiences for the Ballet Russe. Grown from fad to food, it is the cultural necessity of millions throughout the United States.
>
> When they can, audiences attend more than one performance, while many attend 4, 6 & ten performances. The repertoire can accommodate them. Changing casts afford new interest in the differing interpretations given to various roles.
>
> There are countless ballet fans in the US as there are sports-fans, circus-fans or theatre-fans. The ballet-fan or "balletomane" is ardent, informed and critical. He goes to ballet performances for fun as much as cultural satisfactions.
>
> —Léonide Massine, Ballet Theatre program, 1938–1939 season

While Danilova and Massine were already well-known, having performed together in many American cities on a previous Hurok-booked tour, Markova was new to audiences. Thanks to enthusiastic pre-press, anticipation to see her dance was high.

"You just must see Markova," a writer trilled in the *Seattle Daily Times*. "Alicia Markova, one of the stars of the ballet, is a real sensation. She has also amazed the dance world, as she is an English girl and not so many English girls have starred as ballerina. 'Her work is reminiscent of that of the great Pavlova,' commented Mr. Haas. And Mr. Haas should be able to make such comparisons for he was Madame Pavlova's agent for many years and managed her tours!"

A Milwaukee, Wisconsin paper was equally excited in this rather awkwardly worded preview:

> **Ballet Russe Coming to Pabst Theatre**
>
> . . . Outstanding among the stars of established reputation abroad who have joined the company this season, Alicia Markova, the adored idol of the ballet-minded English public, trained as a child under the exacting eye of Serge Diaghilev and since then the star of her own company in London. Miss Markova, admittedly a dancer whose technical brilliance is unexcelled in the ballet world today, has been accorded the laurels of the late Anna Pavlova for her sensitive emotional style as well.

An especially sophisticated and glamorous crowd greeted the company when they arrived for their Los Angeles engagement. It was the home of Hollywood film stars, including fellow Brits like Greer Garson, Laurence Olivier, and Charlie Chaplin, all of whom would become future friends of Markova's. But during her first appearance, the 27-year-old ballerina was completely star-struck, as she reminisced years later.

> The curtain came up and all the girls in the company kept running to tell me, "Did you see? Charlie Chaplin is in the front row and he's applauding you like mad!" And then suddenly, I had a chance to look and it was true! There was Charlie Chaplin and Paulette Goddard, and Greer Garson and Ramon Novarro, who at that time was a big heartthrob. Dorothy Lamour, you name it. Joan Crawford—they were all there.
>
> It was more or less a roll call, and I thought, I really have to pinch myself. These people who I've been spending my life in England sitting in the movie theater looking at—they're all seated here!

Markova would have to pinch herself even harder when she was invited to an after-party with all the Hollywood royalty. It was decided she should have a male escort, who she assumed would be one of the company dancers. But, no. Someone else came to pick her up—Ramon Novarro! How perfect that the quiet ballerina had been paired with an actor best known for his silent films. They got on famously.

But Markova was struck by more than just movie stars on opening night in Los Angeles. Another costume gremlin had been at work.

At the beginning of Act II, Giselle's spirit—in the form of a vaporous Markova wearing wispy layers of chiffon—rises from her grave and slowly glides across the stage to Myrtha, Queen of the Wilis. When Myrtha taps Giselle on her bowed head, the ballerina is to instantly spring to life again, whirling furiously across and off the stage.

But as Markova began her dramatic spins, she felt a sharp stabbing pain in her leg. A recurring injury? No, someone had hidden a very large steel packing needle in the costume's underskirt. Fortunately Massine was in the wings when Markova came off stage in pain. He saw the needle sticking out, quickly removed it, and sent "Giselle" floating back into the spirit world.

Another near-calamity occurred on opening night in San Diego, but this time, it had nothing to do with costumes. While the evening's first ballet was taking place on stage, dancers slated to go on next, including Markova and Massine, were waiting behind the set. As they all warmed up using the wood scenery supports for a practice *barre*, the backdrop suddenly gave way and began careening toward their heads. Luckily everyone—including the stagehands—noticed immediately and all worked silently together to prop it back up in place so it wouldn't fall on top of them—or the blissfully unaware dancers on the other side.

The next day, the *No sleeping pills during performances!* sign had company. *No warming up against the scenery!*

By spring, the company was back in New York, booked once again at the Metropolitan Opera House. With threats to life and limb a thing of the past—Toumanova and her crazed stage mother Eugenia had left the company when Broadway beckoned the young dancer—Markova was now able to enjoy the wonders of the robust, exciting city.

She discovered that the Radio City ice-skating rink of the previous winter had melted away (Rockefeller Center was in the midst of being built), with a lively outdoor restaurant taking its place. That was always fun for a light meal and people-watching. Another great spot was New York's expansive Central Park, lushly refurbished just a few years earlier thanks to celebrated urban planner Robert Moses. A short walk from the Opera House, the meandering gardens and greenery reminded the British dancer of home.

And the shopping! Markova and Danilova drooled over the windows at Bonwit Teller and Bergdorf Goodman, dreaming of the day they could afford the high-fashion offerings themselves.

One thing they could afford was food—and plenty of it. The Carnegie Deli on 7th Avenue between 54th and 55th streets had opened the previous year, serving its soon to be world-renowned gargantuan portions. Markova also delighted in drugstore soda counters where she could order ice cream sundaes with all the whipped cream and glorious sweet toppings she desired.

But she was a bit taken aback by sidewalk food carts. It wasn't that they sold cooked hot dogs and warm pretzels, but rather that customers ate those foods while walking down the street. And local bookstores sold "condensed novels." Was New York life so fast-paced that no one had time to read an entire book or sit down to eat properly?

At least they were willing to sit through an entire evening of ballet, especially when Markova performed. The New York dance critics saw to that. She was even able to win over the esteemed *New York Times* critic John Martin. Previously Martin had been unimpressed with the revival of Russian ballet classics, preferring more modern dance innovations as typified by Martha Graham.

When Arnold Haskell had first toured the United States with the de Basil Company in 1933, he was so incensed at Martin's off-hand dismissal of their Russian dancers that he tried to get him fired. (The Brit's complaints fell on deaf ears.)

Haskell later recalled, "She [Markova] really conquered the critics, especially Martin, John Martin who had been a bitter opponent of ballet. I tangled with him violently in the press when I came to America and he was converted by Markova. And there, critics have far more importance than we poor folk still do in England, because a critic can practically close a show. And Martin saying this was terrific really planted ballet in America, no question about it."

An example of Martin's praise:

> . . . Alicia Markova in Lac des Cygnes [Swan Lake] is pure poetry. Nor is it alone a matter of mood, for the fine, long line, the miraculously held arabesques, the completely unwavering verticality of her pirouettes in the adagios, and her incomparable lightness could belong only to a classical dancer of the greatest distinction.
>
> —*New York Times*, 3/14/39

Moreover, Martin appreciated Markova most for the qualities that differentiated the British prima ballerina from her beautiful Russian counterparts, as he explained in an article titled "Some First Impressions of Alicia Markova":

> There is in the company, to be sure, more captivating personalities, for Markova has nothing of the glamour girl about her. What she wins from her audiences is won by her intrinsic gifts as a dancer and not by Hollywood attributes or other subterfuges. To at least one habitué of the ballet, who is weary of the artificial eyelash type of allure, this comes as a blessed relief. Actually, it would be greatly to Markova's advantage if she were to capitalize upon it more, and to adopt a style of complete simplicity even to the point of plainness, for her dancing is most distinguished when it is most devoid of surface ornament and gratuitous charm. . . .
>
> If there was ever a dancer for whom rising upon her points was merely the preliminary step toward floating off into the air, she is it. Underneath is a steel-like strength and an unstudied precision, and the combination makes her sustained arabesques things of marvelous beauty, belonging far more to the air than to the earth.
>
> —*New York Times*, 3/19/39

Being praised for the physical attributes that had once held her back in England brought Markova a renewed sense of security and strength of purpose. Overjoyed at her success in America, she had great peace of mind while sailing back to Europe with the rest of the company on the Italian ocean liner S.S. *Rex*.

Dubbed "the Riviera afloat," the gargantuan S.S. *Rex* was too large to enter Cannes harbor, where the Ballet Russe de Monte Carlo was to disembark. That necessitated smaller boats being sent out to ferry the dancers, costumes, and cumbersome sets to the dock. As luck would have it, the Italian ocean liner was running late for its final destination, Genoa, so the captain decided to hurry things along.

In their haste, remembered Markova sadly, the overzealous crew ended up dumping several crates overboard. One was filled with André Derain's exquisite Chinoiserie costumes and sets for *L'Epreuve d'Amour*. The dancers watched horrified as the packing cases sank into the Mediterranean Sea and were quickly washed away. The company was never able to perform the ballet again.

Derain wasn't the only celebrated artist to work with the Ballet Russe de Monte Carlo. Fellow fauvist Henri Matisse also collaborated with Massine, and on his very next work, the abstractly modern *Rouge et Noir*.

Set to the music of Dmitri Shostakovich's First Symphony, it was to be an allegorical ballet along the lines of Massine's *Seventh Symphony*. Once again the themes were monumental: man and woman battling the spiritual and material worlds, with current political overtones.

There was also a battle between Massine and his dancers, as his choreography was tremendously difficult (and often physically painful) to master. "On the call-board the first day, were three names—Theilade, Slavenska, Markova," wrote dance critic Mary Mack of *The Music News*. "As the work progressed, two names were dropped, Markova remained."

In discussing the process of learning new choreography, Markova confessed, "I've rehearsed for a new ballet and haven't been able to walk for two days." She used Massine's *Rouge et Noir* as a case in point:

> He decided he wanted to blend the classical technique with [Isadora] Duncan from the waist up, with acrobatics and some [Martha] Graham. That's what I had to reproduce for him.

The first day, my legs were black and blue. I had two large black marks on my hips.

The second day, since my leggings had been splintered whenever I hit the wood floor, I came back wearing linen slacks. For the whole of the rehearsal for the ballet Rouge et Noir, I used to put cotton wool to pad my hip bones. I had kneecaps on, and I used to put this pair of linen slacks over the lot. I was well upholstered!

When it came time for the performance, all I had on was just white silk tights all over, no padding. I learned by that time where to put the strength, how to try to get the most effect and save myself. But even then, I used to have pads in the dressing room with witch hazel when I came off.

There again, you see, I was willing to be bruised black and blue for Massine to achieve choreographically something superb. Now, there were many dancers in the company who wouldn't do it.

This isn't really fair.

Dance writer Marya McAuliff reported on the collaborative process for *Rouge et Noir*:

> . . . Massine, sitting out in front worked along with Markova, but when she asked: "Who or what am I supposed to represent?" he would only answer: "You are just one, sweet little lady!" So Markova was left to interpret the role at will. After the final rehearsal Massine, who was watching out-front, called to her: "Alicia, come here!" She went, thinking he had some correction to make. Instead she found him, tears in his eyes, saying in wondering humility: "Did I do that? Did I really create that? It is beautiful, beautiful!"

Mary Mack found Markova's role nothing short of miraculous: "There are some remarkable feats—some lifts made possible only by her extremely small size and lightness—lifts that would not be feasible for other dancers. But what one always thinks when watching Markova is not: 'How difficult it is!' but rather 'How beautiful it is!'"

Adding to the poetry of her movements was the Matisse-designed all-over white bodysuit, specially made for the ballerina in Paris. The last time Markova had worked with the groundbreaking artist, she was just a teenager with Diaghilev's Ballets Russes. Coincidentally, the nightingale costume "Uncle Henri" created for her at that time was also a white silk unitard.

Markova often remarked that people didn't realize what a great sense of humor Matisse had. One day at the Ballets Russes, the fatherly Frenchman drew an amusing self-portrait for the young Alicia as they chatted amiably about the arts. Afterwards, the fourteen-year-old carefully folded the drawing in half and placed it inside a ballet program—perhaps hiding it away from Guggy. It was still there eighty-five years later, uncovered in Markova's archives.

Now, fifteen years after they worked together at the Ballets Russes, Matisse was no longer drawing *for* Markova, but rather *on* her. He had the idea of emphasizing the dancer's movements by cutting out geometric fabric appliqués to be stitched onto her tights. To make sure the shapes were in the exact right positions, Matisse studiously watched rehearsals while making notes. Afterwards, he had Markova don the second-skin white silk bodysuit so he could draw black outlines of the winged shapes directly on her body. The effect was aerodynamic.

In fact, Massine gave Matisse credit for more than just the design concept. His contribution "was as important as that of the composer or the choreographer," the dancer wrote in his memoirs. Several years earlier, when Massine was first thinking about the ballet, he had visited Matisse in the artist's Nice studio on the French Riviera. The choreographer was intrigued by the mock-ups of the gigantic site-specific "Dance" murals for the home of American arts patron Dr. Albert Barnes. Massine was especially taken with the tremendous rounded arches above each panel that echoed the undulating movements of the freeform, abstracted dancers.

Massine recalled, "I pointed out to him [Matisse] that they were very similar in conception to the ballet I was planning, which I visualized as a vast mural in motion, he became suddenly very interested." The high, vaulted arches would become the formative background element in the backdrops for *Rouge et Noir*.

Matisse then produced a series of boldly colored mockups of his proposed set and costume designs by combining gouache and cut paper shapes painstakingly adjusted until perfect, then thumbtacked in place. (It was a precursor to the artist's joyful paper cutout collages that would dominate the last years of his career—a creative outlet necessitated by illness that left Matisse wheelchair-bound and unable to paint.)

Massine explained their collaborative process:

> He [Matisse] suggested that Shostakovich's music could be interpreted in five basic colours, white, black, blue, yellow and red. Thinking this over, I realized the colours could be made to correspond, not only to the music but to the philosophic theme of the ballet, which was to be the conflict between the spiritual and material world. . . . With his unerring sense of decorative values, he designed for it an evocative background of abstract shapes of pure colour, and created tight-fitting costumes in the same colours decorated with white and black curvilinear patterns.

Matisse had told Markova when she was just fourteen that if it were up to him, he would only dress her in white. He kept his promise. As Massine noted, "The Man and Woman, danced by Markova with her usual delicacy, and Youskevitch with powerful spirituality, were in white."

Markova later revealed, "He [Matisse] was the first person to work with a white silver polish [outlining the appliqués] which he thought of for me for that ballet."

Massine was so taken with all of Matisse's work on the ballet that he had the artist boldly sign his name in large black lettering on the *Rouge et Noir* front curtain. The choreographer wanted the audience to know, even before the ballet began, who was responsible for the awe-inspiring design.

When Danilova asked Massine to explain the ballet to her, he said the "white was for Russia, black for fascists, and red for communists." Danilova thought the "most powerful part of the ballet was a solo for Alicia Markova, a cry—she bourréed all around the stage, changing the positions of her arms, or her body. She was weeping without tears, with her soul."

The symbolism was not lost on Europeans when the ballet premiered in May 1939 in Monte Carlo, and in Paris soon after. Many of the French thought Markova's painful solo represented the people of Czechoslovakia now oppressed by the Germans. "Markova's translation of Massine's conception was a revelation," wrote a reviewer who later saw the ballet in the United States.

Added Mary Mack:

> A fine musician, she [Markova] knows every note in the score she is dancing which accounts for the incomparable perfection of her timing. She is practically the only dancer with the exception of Massine who has such knowledge. . . . To Rouge et Noir as to all her other roles Markova brings that rare sincerity, perfection, and divine simplicity that belong intrinsically to great Art. No more striking monument will ever be erected to her as a dancer than this role that must take its place beside that of Giselle as one of the immortal roles of all Ballet History. Certainly it must be ranked as the greatest of our time.

When later asked to name her favorite ballets, Markova surprised many by listing *Rouge et Noir* along with *Giselle.* "The audiences today identify me as a romantic, but in my career I've done, well, every kind of dance, and every kind of ballet," she told a radio audience in 1959. "And I mean all the most modern works in the time that they were modern during the years that I've been performing. I adore the classical things and I'm a great one for tradition, but on the other hand, I've always been a person who's wanted to go forward too. I've had both together, and I always feel it's the modern thing that keeps my traditional work fresh."

One of Markova's "modern things" was her early understanding of television's potential to reach wider audiences. Back home in London on summer break in 1939, she continued to make great use of the soon-to-be-omnipresent medium. At a time when the most successful programming featured just one performer on camera, Markova made astute choices in her on-camera repertoire, leading several newspapers to place her in the pantheon of TV's most celebrated personalities. (Others were heartthrob actor Tyrone Power, comedienne Beatrice Lillie, and dramatic actor/singer Paul Robeson.)

When the fall season began, Markova was anxious to dance *Rouge et Noir* for her hometown fans. It was not to be. Three days before the scheduled London premiere on September 4, 1939, Hitler invaded Poland. On Sunday, September 3rd, Markova slept late, resting up for the next day's opening performance. At 11:15 A.M., British Prime Minister Neville Chamberlain came on the radio to address the British people. Hitler refused to withdraw his troops from Poland, and England was declaring war on Germany. France would follow suit shortly thereafter. World War II had begun.

What did the ballet matter now, thought Markova? She already possessed a copy of the pre-printed program for the two-week sold-out Covent Garden engagement. It was never to be seen. The dancer sadly placed the handbill in a box with other mementos. It is now part of her archives.

Just as Diaghilev's company had been on vacation and scattered about Europe when they learned of his shocking death ten years before almost to the day, Massine's troupe was also on holiday in various countries when the news of war reached them.

Markova and Danilova were in London. Since the ballet was of course cancelled, the two decided to volunteer for the war efforts, offering their services to assist nurses and government officials. But after just a few days, they were told the presence of two "famous" ballerinas just distracted the other workers and were asked politely not to return.

"Those first days of war were very dismal as even the cinemas were closed for fear of air raids," wrote A. E. Twysden (later Danilova's biographer), reporting on the Ballet Russe de Monte Carlo members adrift in London. "[B]ut at the end of the week these were reopened and were hailed with delight as affording a welcome diversion even though it involved returning through the 'blackout.'"

Danilova had already lived through the Russian Revolution, so was calmer than many others. She remembered her first air raid when she had foolishly packed a nightgown, only later realizing slacks were much more practical for an evening spent in the basement of a building. (Women had just begun wearing trousers in public.) Danilova also learned it was important to take key valuables along in case her apartment was destroyed by a bomb. She always kept a small suitcase packed with her passport and best jewelry so she could grab it—and her fur coat—on a moment's notice.

Danilova was disheartened to learn that while in London everyone was issued a gas mask, in Paris they were given only to French citizens. She thought that selfish and unpatriotic.

Paris and the South of France is where many of Massine's dancers were now stranded, as Sol Hurok fought desperately to have everyone in the company safely transported to the United States for their October booking in New York. Hurok was able to delay the American opening from October 10th to the 26th, but that was the final extension possible.

Most of the costumes and scenery went over first, and Massine was able to get out of France with his wife in early September. That had not been easy to do. Nearly all of the transatlantic ocean liners were operated by U.S. shipping companies, so priority bookings were offered to American passengers wishing to return home. Eight of the American dancers were therefore able to leave right away, but Massine wasn't sure who else in the company would make it to New York in time for the opening. As an insurance policy, he began training a second back-up company in Manhattan.

As for Markova, she had no wish to leave London at all. England was at war with Germany, and she felt her place was at home with her family and loved ones. But Hurok was playing hardball. Markova was now a star in the United States and her name sold tickets. He insisted she honor her contract.

While trying to find a legal loophole, Markova wrote a letter to her beloved beau Stanley Burton, with whom she had kept in touch during her months abroad. His family-owned clothing empire was frantically producing uniforms for Britain's Royal Air Force.

September 17, 1939

Stanley Darling,

I think it was very dear of you to find time to write me such a beautiful letter when I can imagine how tired and worn out you must be. If the strength that God willed me to have will help you through the trying days to come dear, please take it as I sit & wonder now why I am a dancer, as I find I am quite useless to the world under the present circumstances. My career is just in little pieces at my feet but I suppose I must still continue to fight. If you do have a spare moment you know I would love to hear from you. In the meantime, take great care of yourself for you are forever in my thoughts.

My love dearest,

Alicia

Markova consulted with her lawyer—and the British government at Whitehall—hoping an act of war invalidated her contract. But it was an American contract for a booking in the United States, and America was not at war. She received the following Western Union Telegram from Hurok's representatives on September 21, 1939:

MARKOVA ELEVEN MARBLE ARCH LDN.
AMERICAN TOUR UNCHANGED EXPECT YOU BE READY TO SAIL
WILL NOTIFY DATE SAILING LIKELY WASHINGTON STOP
ARE ARRANGING VISA
WORLD ART INC.

The solicitor also told Markova that if she chose to remain in England, Hurok could exercise an injunction that would prevent her from dancing anywhere. As her mother and sister Bunny still counted on her financial support, Markova needed to earn a living and had little choice but to leave.

Unfortunately, the British people wouldn't see it that way. They never knew of Markova's patriotic war efforts in the United States, and never quite forgave her for "deserting" the country in their time of need. She would become a much-loved ballet dancer again, but it would take her far longer than any other performer of her stature to be named a Dame of the British Empire.

Hurok finally managed to book passage for Markova and Danilova on one of the last ships to make the crossing before the London Blitz. The S.S. *Washington* was set to depart Southampton, England on September 29, 1939, and it was massively overcrowded.

Markova knew what to expect when she received the confirmation letter from the Northern Transport Travel Bureau. It not only listed her cabin assignment, but an individual cot number as well. She and Danilova were to share a tiny room with a family of four generations of Irish women—from the white-haired great-grandmother down to her infant great-granddaughter. As they all jostled for sitting room in their tight accommodations, Markova took comfort in the kindly Irish women, who reminded her of her own mother.

Markova later compared the accommodations to the hilarious stateroom scene in the Marx Brothers film *A Night at the Opera*, where Groucho needed to leave the cabin just to change his mind. But it didn't seem so funny at the time. Markova immediately began pouring her heart out in letters to Stanley. She didn't know how she would last until the following spring when the company would return to Europe and she would see him, and her family, again.

But they didn't return. Markova wouldn't be back in London or see Burton again for nine years. By then, he had married someone else.

Americans traveling to London are sometimes taken aback at arriving on one of the city's numerous "Bank Holiday" Mondays, with many institutions unexpectedly closed. Foreign passengers on the S.S. *Washington* found themselves similarly taken by surprise when the ocean liner docked in New York on Columbus Day, October 12, 1939. (The federal holiday had only been created two years earlier.) With a reduced skeleton crew of immigration officials, health officers, and baggage handlers, getting through customs and collecting one's luggage seemed interminable. With so many nationalities on board—the ship was filled with refugees fleeing war-torn Europe—everyone's papers needed to be carefully scrutinized.

Most of the weary travelers were relieved just to have arrived safely, so at least it was a civilized, if lengthy, disembarkation. "Nobody knew whether we would reach New York," remembered Markova. To avoid German submarines, "we zigzagged across the Atlantic."

For two of Markova's friends, the choreographer Antony Tudor and his lover, the dancer Hugh Laing, there was an added glitch. The pair, who had come to New York to join the newly established Ballet Theatre (today's American Ballet Theatre), booked passage under their real names of William Cook and Hugh Skinner. That didn't match up with their passports, so Tudor and Laing were detained overnight at Ellis Island to confirm they weren't actually spies.

Markova had worries of a very different nature. She arrived in the United States practically penniless. Great Britain had instituted wartime restrictions on the amount of money residents could take out of the country, which was a small percentage of one's bank balance. For Markova, that meant traveling over three thousand miles with just £10 (the equivalent of $100) to her name, and most of that had been spent on food and tips during the two-week ocean voyage. She was quite relieved that Hurok sent his business manager to meet her and Danilova at the dock, immediately giving each a $20 advance.

Though Markova's name was now a solid box-office draw in the United States, ballet was not big business compared to other forms of entertainment, so the salaries were relatively small. She and Danilova received just $150 per week for dancing eight or nine performances, with very few days off. Markova had received the equivalent salary (£15) five years earlier at the Vic-Wells for far less work and no travel—and she had been able to supplement that income with other engagements.

To save money, the two ballerinas roomed together and shared many expenses. That way, Markova could budget $100 weekly for her food, lodging, and ballet necessities, and send the rest of her salary home to her mother. (Fortunately, sending money *into* Britain was far easier than getting it out.) Markova also regularly mailed care packages home to family and friends throughout the war, a topic she discussed on the radio years later when being interviewed by her friend, the British ballerina Beryl Grey:

> MARKOVA: I would always ask what the shortages were and I remember the one time, they said lemons or something. You couldn't get lemons. I went out and bought a lot of lemons, and I thought how are we going to get them through? Customs will take them first, probably. So what we did, we got a whole lot of old sweaters that looked like awful old shabby things

> and filled the arms with the lemons and rolled them up . . . and we sent them over to the family.
>
> BERYL GREY: In the war, I was with Sadler's Wells School and you used to send us the most wonderful packages, parcels of food, and ballet shoe ribbons, and soap, and—hair things?
>
> MARKOVA: They called them bobby pins.
>
> GREY: Yes, bobby pins! We couldn't get anything like that. We were so excited and so grateful, and so touched that you were thinking of us.

Markova and Danilova arriving safely in New York was a great relief to Massine. He now had his two female stars. But much of the company was still stranded in Cannes, and Hurok had the Ballet Russe de Monte Carlo booked solid, from their opening at the Metropolitan Opera House to a tightly packed cross-country tour. The excitable impresario told Massine the show must go on, no matter what.

"Hastily I auditioned a number of young dancers, and began to rehearse them in our repertoire," wrote Massine in his memoir. "Although they were highly competent and learned quickly, it was a nightmare time for me . . . a week before the opening Hurok, who was as worried as I was, by dint of daily transatlantic calls managed to book passages for over thirty of the company on the *Rotterdam*. They arrived on the day of the performance, and after a hasty rehearsal went on as planned, with only a few replacements who later became permanent members of the company."

Adding to the drama was the "spookiness" of the Metropolitan's dark sepulchral rehearsal space. The Sunday before opening night, the *New York Times* ran a large photo of Markova under the headline "Backstage at the Ballet." Eerily dwarfed by an enormous gilded mirror, the tiny dancer was pictured stretching alone, looking for all the world like the doomed heroine in *Phantom of the Opera*. The *Times* seemed to agree, describing the troupe as "waking echoes in the dim backstage caverns in the Metropolitan Opera House."

But at least the dancers were able to return to their cozy hotel rooms every night. That comfortable situation was about to change, and would be the norm throughout the 1940–41 cross-country tours.

To traverse the vast United States (and into Canada), the company traveled by rail in six beat-up coach cars that were attached to transcontinental trains. One car was for the orchestra, two for the scenery and stage crew, one for the costumes, and another two for the dancers.

"We used to call it 'Hurok's Special,'" Markova explained years later, laughing heartily at the memory. "First class trains in America all had names. It was either 'Cheap' or the 'Supercheap' or the '20th Century.' I didn't realize, for a couple of years I think it was, the luxury of those trains, because we traveled on our 'Hurok Special.' And of course, we came to the conclusion that the coaches that we had on our 'Special' were the discards. Because it always seemed to us the springs were all gone and we used to shake along, miles and miles, from performance to performance."

Massine, it should be noted, had separate luxury accommodations for himself and his third wife, the dancer Tatiana Orlova. "I had bought a large Lincoln, with a trailer fitted with a modern kitchen and a comfortable bed-sitting room," he wrote in his memoirs. "This was driven by a Russian chauffeur George Labourinsky, who came of an old Cossack family. [Massine was also Russian. His real name was Miassin, but Diaghilev had thought it too hard to pronounce abroad and changed it.] Since Tatiana and I both disliked hotel cooking, we also engaged an Italian cook, who traveled with us, hundreds of miles, from one engagement to another, usually by night. It was not a very satisfactory way of living, but at least it spared us the monotony of long train journeys and the anonymity of a different hotel each night."

It's nice to be the boss.

"Because ballet was, in the late 1930s, still an uncertain commercial proposition outside the larger cities, we often played one-night stands, or short engagements, and traveling was an integral and often excruciating part of our life," Markova later recalled.

"Just before we were leaving the Metropolitan, the list—the tour list—went up, and I remember looking at the list and I couldn't understand it because for three whole weeks we never slept in a hotel. We were back on the train. That was my initiation to one-night stands."

It is one thing to be spending six-month stretches constantly moving from one town to another, but quite another when one has to sleep sitting up in the railcars because there's no time to check into a hotel.

"It all had to be down to the absolute minute to get the show unloaded, unpacked," Markova explained. "Wardrobe went in one direction and the crew in another to get it all hung. And then, because we traveled with everything, all our lighting equipment and the lot, that really was quite an experience to watch them—how they would get that show ready for eight o'clock."

It was like an artistic version of musical chairs: the dancers rehearsed while the sets were being built; then the crew slept during the actual performance. Afterwards, the stagehands came back to dismantle the scenery and transport it back to the train, while the dancers went out to eat. The entire company was thankful for that great American invention, the all-night drugstore with counter service. As everyone was ravenous after a performance, they would chow down on hearty breakfasts and copious amounts of coffee. That was the origin of what became known as "ham and eggs" tours.

But sometimes not even a drugstore was open, and the dancers would find themselves stranded on a train platform while the scenery was slowly being loaded onboard. To keep warm in the middle of the night in the middle of nowhere, they would often rehearse. Imagine a police watchman on a frigid winter's night as he stumbled across a large group of strangers pirouetting in their fur coats, hats, and boots at three in the morning. And when he approached, the group was speaking in four or five different languages!

Once on the train, Markova took out her inflatable rubber pillow, a constant companion throughout her entire career. Propped up against a window, it helped her nod off on the bumpy ride. But since "overnight" rest was generally limited to the four hours between 2:30 and 6:30 A.M., she probably would have slept anyway from sheer exhaustion.

When the train wasn't set to arrive at the company's next destination until late morning or early afternoon the following day, the male dancers gallantly created makeshift beds for their prima ballerinas by piling coats on top of luggage in the aisles. That way they could sleep lying flat.

Laundry quickly became an issue, as there were no easy-care fabrics like quick-drying nylon in those days. So the dancers would hand-wash their silk and cotton tights as soon as they arrived onboard, then hang them up to dry on a makeshift clothesline stretched across the length of the railcar. It was a good thing the company was separated from the rest of the train's passengers, as rail ticket holders would have been less than thrilled at having to navigate a sea of long wet tights to get to the lavatory.

Washing clothing wasn't the only concern. The dancers themselves needed to bathe. Markova remembers how she and Danilova would be elated when the train arrived early enough in the day for them to check into a hotel for the afternoon. They took advantage of the "day rates" offered at the time, booking just one suite and then generously tipping the maids to bring loads of extra towels. That way the dancers could take turns soaking in a hot tub.

If a performance venue was far away from the train station, the company frequently couldn't get back in time to depart until morning. In those situations, they would play what Markova dubbed the "Army Game," a tactical maneuver involving one dancer checking in to a single hotel suite, with six more sneaking up afterwards. They would all take turns bathing, eating, and sleeping. Once again, it was like a Marx Brothers movie—this time *Room Service.*

If possible, Markova would steal a moment—and hotel stationery—to write home. She wrote her mother, sisters, and Stanley as often as she could.

Deshler-Wallick Hotel
1000 ROOMS 1000 BATHS
Columbus Ohio

December 14, 1939

Stanley My Dearest,

Have been trying to write to you for the last two days but changing towns each day just couldn't find time. The last week has been quite hard with some trying journeys starting at 7:30 or 8:00 in the morning, so when I crawl out of bed early I think of your getting up also to work & try not to grumble. We shall be in Chicago on Sunday, where we stay until Jan. 3rd. Thanks so much darling for your last letter Nov. 22nd just received. Your letters give me so much pleasure.

Must rush off to the Theatre now.

My love to you dearest & take good care of yourself.

Alicia XX

A Happy Christmas & shall be thinking of you

When Markova arrived in Chicago, the bitter winter sent her in search of warmer gloves. Unfortunately, the local department store had nothing to fit her tiny size 5¾ hands. Always enterprising, the ballerina decided to check out the children's department, where she cheerfully selected an official pair of "Shirley Temple" embroidered gloves, which amused her no end.

A package from Stanley amused her even more, but she had sad news to send back:

The Curtis Hotel
Minneapolis Minnesota

January 13, 1940

Stanley Dearest,

I am so sorry I haven't written for such a long time but we had a very busy season in Chicago over Christmas and New Year & then this tour immediately. I received your Xmas card safely & yesterday I received Adolph in Blunderland which made me laugh so much. So whenever I am feeling a little blue I shall take a peep at Adolph. . . .

It is very cold here, 12 inches of snow & 6 below & just started snowing again now. I find my Scotch woolens & tweeds very useful. We leave tomorrow for Billings & Butte Montana. We shall travel all day & night more North & then Canada the end of the week, but I can just bear it with the thought of San Francisco & California to follow.

My present contract should have finished this March but the Company have taken up the option for a further year until February 1941, so I suppose I shall have to stay over here. I feel rather sad about it. I do wish you could fly over somehow as I long to see you my darling. I do hope you are keeping well & taking good care of yourself & that life isn't too dreary. I am enclosing a press cutting I thought you would like to have. Will send you later a souvenir programme & some more cuttings. Don't forget to send me a picture of yourself.

I have to rush to the Theatre now.

With my fondest love & thoughts always

Alicia

In February Markova wrote Stanley again, this time from New Orleans.

Dinkler Hotels
Written From St. Charles Hotel
New Orleans, LA.

Feb. 25, 1940

My Darling,

So happy to receive your picture yesterday which I like but don't think it does you justice. It is very serious & I like you when you smile. . . . We return to N.Y. March 17th. We tour until then & open another Met Season March 26th for about 3 weeks, then probably another 5 weeks tour & more places which I cannot write about yet.

Massine is doing a new ballet for me for the N.Y. season, a short one about 10 minutes to American music & based on the famous Krazy Kat comic strip. There will only be 6 men in it besides myself. Also revising Giselle & Coppelia. I sent Souvenir Programmes & some cuttings from Los Angeles last week as I thought they would interest you. Darling, I hope they arrive safely. I had some new pictures done so will send you one when they are ready.

This last week has been hectic, 4 nights on the train & one-night stands leaving at 8:00 in the morning which means rising at 6:30

& often we cannot get to bed before 1:30. I mustn't grumble as I am well, thank God & having great success. Write & tell me what you are working at & how you are my darling, as you know it interests me & I still think of you all the time.

My fondest love,
Alicia

Equally wearying were the various theater mishaps that invariably took place. Markova told biographer Maurice Leonard about two especially bizarre experiences during sequential Toronto, Canada bookings. On one occasion, the company was performing in a large auditorium where the changing areas were quite a distance from the stage. When Markova returned to her dressing room during intermission, she found a strange woman stone cold drunk in her bathroom, carrying on about a love affair gone wrong. Though unable to stand, the lovelorn intruder had no problem shouting at the top of her lungs. Markova gave her coffee and smelling salts to perk her up and get her out so she could change her costume in peace. Massine held the second-act curtain and prayed.

Toronto misadventure number two occurred when Markova was set to perform *Giselle*. The management decided to honor the great ballerina by waxing the stage to a glassy polish. As one might surmise, the dancers slip-slided their way through Act I. But the "fix" at intermission was just as bad. The stagehands heavily dusted the floor with some sort of powder that woke Giselle from her grave with an uncontrollable sneezing fit.

But Toronto was hardly alone when it came to on-the-road craziness. In another city the company was scheduled to perform in a movie theatre, with Markova set to open the evening's repertoire dancing a scene from *Swan Lake* with Mischa Paneyev. When the pair arrived to rehearse at 5:00 P.M., the theatre manager said they couldn't go on stage because there was still an audience watching the late afternoon movie.

Ballet Russe manager David Libidins, the American theatrical producer, was called in and insisted that the film be halted at 7:00 P.M.—finished or not—as the dancers absolutely had to rehearse. He offered to address the audience to explain and apologize. As

Libidins walked in front of the screen to do just that, the house-lights came up to reveal that all the seats were filled with his very own dancers!

The next morning, another sign went up: *No more movies on show nights!*

Markova thought every adventure just brought the company closer together, a camaraderie she never took for granted after those early days of petty jealousies and sabotage. The pay was low, the travel conditions poor, but they all took their jobs very seriously for the sake of the audiences. Wherever they went, people were so visibly grateful that such a high-caliber European ballet troupe had made the long trip to their city or town. In rural areas, fans were willing to drive several hours just to see Markova and Danilova perform. Neither wished to disappoint.

"I have never danced for an audience that I felt was unworthy of my performance," asserted Danilova. "In fact, never did an audience appreciate us more than in those small towns."

The newspaper coverage of those tours often spoke to the hardships the company endured in order to bring their art to the local citizens. Ballet patrons were also moved when reading of the dancers' fears for their relatives living in war-torn Europe.

Coughs in All Languages
Ballet Russe Sniffles Sleepily and Goes to Bed for the Day

> The Russian ballet has a cold in its head.
>
> While the mist still cluttered Vancouver's harbor, glamorous ladies with red noses and Apollo-like men with deep-throated coughs crept sleepily from their berths on the Victoria boat and went to bed.
>
> There were no dramatic entrances and no trumpet calls when the Ballet Russe de Monte Carlo arrived in the city this morning, just a lot of tired people who have been rushed across the continent through every extreme of temperature in a maze of strange stages and hotel rooms.
>
> . . . The English Alicia Markova has been hailed by authorities as the first child prodigy in Russian ballet who has

already played a major role in the history of the art in Great Britain.

This morning in spite of her exhausting twenty-four hours, her dark eyes were sparkling, and she ate her toast and marmalade with enthusiasm.

"Oh, it was such a lovely feeling last night to hear 'God Save the King,' after the performance," she said, shaking her snood-bound black hair. "It is so nice to be on British soil again."

—*The Daily Province*, Vancouver, British Columbia, 1/23/40

Ballet Their Escape From War Jitters
Markova and Franklin Believe It's a Relief to Audience, Too

. . . MARKOVA: Mr. Massine won't allow newspapers in the studio. And a good thing too. I was trying to take my mind off what I read at breakfast one morning. Suddenly one of the corps de ballet opened a paper. "London Bombed!" I felt quite sick. I forgot my entrances and things got pretty blue. . . .

The knowledge that your country is at war, that your family is in it, is always with you. While working you can get away from it for a few moments.

A Letter from Her Mother

Miss Markova's latest letter from her mother was dated August 31 and arrived early this week by clipper. She described it as "unbelievable."

Her mother wrote it in an air-raid shelter and dwelt on routine family matters. After being there six hours she remarked: "I hope soon the all-clear will come."

"It's a blessing to be able through the medium of art to help people forget, at least for a while," said Miss Markova. "Knowing what is going on over there one gets particularly impatient with people who grumble over petty annoyances like underdone steaks."

—*New York World Telegram*, 9/14/40

The news would get much worse for Markova:

> **Tragedies of War Temper Ballerina's Success in U.S.**
>
> Alicia Markova, pretty and England's most famous prima ballerina, has a country but no home to think about during the holidays.
>
> Here with the Ballet Russe de Monte Carlo, the world-famous dancer told how her apartment in London, Hyde Park, had been destroyed by a bomb. She received the news at a dramatic moment.
>
> "I picked up the newspapers the morning after my New York debut in The Nutcracker," she related. "In one hand I held most wonderful compliments from the critics—and in the other, a cable from my mother telling how a bomb had gone through our apartment.
>
> "Fortunately," went on the soft-voiced star of ballet, "my mother and three sisters were away at the time. They have taken a place by the sea and every week I send them a package of warm clothing."
>
> There were many things of sentimental value in the London home, Markova declared. "I don't know just how bad things are," she stated, "because when I get news from my family, the censor has clipped out everything but the good wishes." . . .
>
> Worry about her family's safety must be put aside as much as possible as she devotes herself to her work.
>
> "But when I am particularly successful and the audience applause is unusually great, at the moment I am taking my bows before the curtain, that is when I think of my mother," she said.
>
> "I just can't help it then. My success belongs to her."
>
> —*Victoria Times*, British Columbia, 1/17/41

In Markova's archives are detailed agenda books from her American tours during the war in which she noted the date of each package sent home and what was in it. She also carried a tiny photo of her mother and sisters with her everywhere, along with a swan charm her mother had given her when she first danced *Swan Lake*. Ballet not only supported the family financially but, for Markova, emotionally as well.

And Stanley was never out of Markova's thoughts.

150 W. 58th St.
N.Y.C.

May 15, 1940

Dearest,

How sweet of you to write so often to me when you must be awfully busy but I really do love receiving your letters as they help me to feel closer to you when there are so many things that divide us & thousands of miles. I sail the 18th for Rio, then Brazil, Buenos Aires, & Montevideo returning here the end of August. If you continue to write to the above address they will forward my mail, as I shall rent the same Apt. when I return. I had to be vaccinated against smallpox & have been at the Dentist every day the last week. Otherwise I am alright.

Your pictures were a lovely surprise for which many thanks. I have the large one in an ivory parchment frame on my dressing table to match my brushes. I thought you would like the enclosed pictures for your collection.

The news lately disturbs me very much & I try not to read the papers or listen to the radio as I feel quite sick & faint at the thought of all my dear ones being so near to this terrible reality.

How I long to see you Stanley darling. Do take great care of yourself.

With fond love,
Alicia
Must start to see about my packing

For Markova and her audiences, ballet was a great diversion and momentary escape from the war. Newspaper interviews with the British ballerina tended to combine entertaining frivolous details with patriotic praise for her fortitude:

English Ballerina to Dance Here

Has Smallest Foot in Ballet; Spends $1,000 a Year on Dancing Slippers, $25 A Pair for Tights.

Mlle. Alicia Markova, to give you a rapid portrait of probably the greatest English ballerina, is slight and dark looking; at size 2 1/2A, her feet are the smallest in the world of ballet; she is a hearty trencher-woman, being exceptionally fond of potatoes, any style, and steaks cut large and thick; she admits no peer in the preparation of a Spanish omelet and she is a reader of biographies, an expert rumba dancer and unlike most ladies of the ballet, who appear to dumpy disadvantage when not on the tips of their toes, she is grace itself. She has no time for hobbies, but would like to see a football game and at least one ice-hockey tilt a week. . . .

Right now, Mlle. Markova, or Miss Marks, as one thinks of her in this connection, doesn't know whether or not she still has a home back in London. She got a cable from her family a few weeks ago saying that their house had been hit by a bomb, and in the letter that followed the censor had been so active that she doesn't know if a few windows were broken or if there is one brick left on another. One thing she is sure of though; they'll never break the English spirit, no matter how many homes they cave in.

—*Cincinnati Times Star,* 12/6/40

But sometimes, it was just all in fun:

It's News To Me Herb Caen's Column
Memos to Myself:

5 P.M. Veddy funny a happening at the Ballet Russe Wednesday night. After the Matisse number, a character came trucking out from the wings and handed Alicia Markowa, premier ballerina, a heavy pot containing a gorgeous cyclamen. It was too heavy to handle, of course, so the flower was set on the stage while Miss Markowa took her bows. Then she exited and left the plant behind. Few seconds later, the curtain lifted—and lo, there was that huge 150-foot stage, empty save for the potted cyclamen, sitting smack in the center. The curtain

hastily lowered again while the hep ones roared mightily. First instance, I think of a potted plant ever taking a curtain call.

—*San Francisco Chronicle*, 2/2/40

When it came to the company's repertoire, Markova enjoyed alternating roles in classical and modern ballets, garnering excellent reviews in both. Massine's *Rouge et Noir* was especially well received coast-to-coast:

Massine Presents Symphonic Ballet

"Rouge et Noir," set to Music by Shostakovich, Has U.S. Premier at Metropolitan

. . . It reveals Alicia Markova in an entirely new light, and shows that if she is exquisite as the wistful Giselles and Odettes of the romantic repertory, she is also moving and beautiful in the stark and distorted medium of abstraction and what is sometimes known as modernism.

In Massine's perception of this hitherto undiscovered side of her art he has doubled her potentialities. . . . It is a taxing and even a perilous role and he has created for Markova, containing some of the most tortured adagio in the repertory. But she maintains through it a fine, clear emotional line, and sheds a kind of aura of tenderness and human implication over what might easily become sheer acrobatics.

—John Martin, *New York Times*, 10/29/39

New Russ ballet is a winner

. . . Alicia Markova, the slender British girl, cast as the Woman of "Rouge et Noir," surpassed herself in the role. Her bright grace and mimetic gifts have never appeared to better advantage in the memory of this reporter.

—Robert Pollak, *Chicago Daily Times*, 12/29/39

Markova Solo Wins Praise At Ballet Russe

If a prize were offered to the best solo performance in the Ballet Russe season, a very strong claimant would be Alicia Markova for her work in "Red and Black."

> For the second time, yesterday afternoon at the Memorial Opera House, Miss Markova was a chief reason why "Red and Black" has proved to be a top ranking addition to the Monte Carlo company's repertory. . . .
>
> Miss Markova danced with consummate precision and with wonderful soft fluidity. She delicately pervaded her role as well with expressive character.
>
> —Alexander Fried, *San Francisco Examiner*, 2/4/40

Markova relished all the contemporary roles created for her, as they gave her the opportunity to try something completely new and collaborative with the choreographer. She wrote to Stanley about two such ballets when the company was back in New York in September 1940:

> " . . . George Balanchine has just finished 'Card Party' music by Stravinsky. He has given me a very good part in it. Very modern. Massine has finished 'Concert in Europe' music by Weber. I have a Chinese dance with him, it will be the first time that we dance together. I was feeling so lonely last week, so one of my partners, Eglevsky, brought me a present of an adorable kitten to keep me company."

Balanchine's *Card Party* went by three names, the others being *Jeu de Cartes*—his first version performed by New York's American Ballet in April 1937—and *Poker Game*, as it became known in the 1940 revival for the Ballet Russe de Monte Carlo. Working on that ballet was like a Diaghilev reunion for Markova, with Balanchine doing the choreography to music by her "Uncle Igor" Stravinsky.

Humorously referred to as "a ballet in three deals," *Poker Game* was a highly entertaining, politically tinged work, with Balanchine taking the term "playing cards" quite literally. Adding to the audience's enjoyment were the fantastical sets and costumes by Irene Sharaff, who would go on to win numerous Academy Awards for her clothing designs in Hollywood films such as *An American in Paris* (1951), *The King and I* (1956), and *West Side Story* (1961).

Markova played the Queen of Hearts, wearing an elaborate crown headpiece with attached sculpted hair, and an open-necked fitted heart bodice accented by wide puffed-out cap sleeves. In a famous promotional photo from the ballet, Markova clasps her arms so tightly behind her back that they seem to disappear. With her alabaster skin and the floating "armless" sleeves, she looks like a dramatic surreal sculpted bust.

But when it came to surrealism in the ballet, no one could hold a melted candle to the Spanish artist Salvador Dalí. He had already made quite a name for himself in New York, and not just for a painting exhibition of his bizarre imagery. When attending a society masquerade party in 1934, Dalí "arrived wearing a pink brassiere in a glass case on his chest," recounted Julie L. Belcove in *Harper's Bazaar*. "Though provocative, it was prim compared with [his wife] Gala's headdress, which was ornamented with a model of an infant's corpse. It was reported that she was dressed as the Lindbergh baby, whose suspected murderer was then on trial. The ensuing uproar notwithstanding, the worlds of fashion and society were in his thrall."

Dalí would again make a notorious splash—literally—when he was asked to create window displays for the chi-chi Bonwit Teller store several years later. In the 1930s and '40s, New York retailers often partnered with artists and theater productions—including the Ballet Russe de Monte Carlo—promoting their shows in advertisements and store windows, along with related merchandise. (For example: a sign reading "Did 'Spectre de la Rose' make you want something in Victorian pink?" would be placed alongside mannequins in gowns similar to Markova's beautiful costumes in that ballet.)

Bonwit Teller hired Dalí in an attempt to capitalize on the publicity surrounding a controversial commission he executed for the 1939 New York World's Fair. The upscale retailer got more than it bargained for.

As *Time* magazine reported, "the dapper, delirious Catalonian placed in one window an old-fashioned bathtub lined with black Persian lamb and filled with water, from which three wax arms arose holding mirrors. Pensive before the tub stood a wax mannequin clothed in green feathers, with long bright red hair."

Dalí himself describes other additions: "On a table, a telephone transformed into a lobster; hanging on a chair, my famous 'aphrodisiac coat' consisting of a black dinner jacket to which were attached one beside another, so as entirely to cover it, eighty-eight liqueur glasses filled to the edge with green *crème de menthe*, with a dead fly and a cocktail straw in each glass."

Suffice it to say the second window was equally surreal—and puzzling. After all, these were windows in one of New York's most luxurious fashion stores. Both were completed in the wee hours of the morning, whereupon Dalí returned to his hotel for a restful night's sleep.

When the store opened the next morning, several well-heeled female customers complained about the "offensive" displays. Adjustments were dutifully made, including substituting a standard high-fashion mannequin for one of Dalí's quixotic waxworks.

Needless to say, that did not sit well with the artist when he came by for a look-see in the afternoon.

"Into the store to the company lawyer rocketed Salvador Dalí, sizzling in Spanish and French," reported *Time* magazine. "Next thing Bonwit's knew the Surrealissimo was in the window with the bathtub. 'Oomph' went the tub as he jerked it from the moorings. 'Crash' went Bonwit Teller's beautiful plate-glass window as the small struggling artist and his tub went though it and lit 'bang' on the sidewalk.

"Said Magistrate Louis B. Brodsky in night court later, freeing the artist with a suspended sentence: 'These are some of the privileges that an artist with temperament seems to enjoy.'"

Markova would have her own Dalí "experience" several years later.

Soon after the Bonwit's incident, Massine hired Dalí to design his upcoming ballet based on Richard Wagner's *Bacchanalia of Tannhäuser*.

"I got along quite well with Léonide Massine, who had been a hundred percent Dalínian for a long time," the artist modestly recorded in his autobiography. "I also had the good fortune to have Chanel take upon herself the designing of the costumes. Chanel worked on any show with a wholehearted enthusiasm and created the most luxurious costumes that have been conceived for the theatre. She used real ermine, real jewels, and the gloves of Ludwig II of Bavaria were so heavily embroidered that we felt some anxiety as to whether the dancer would be able to dance with them on."

That became a moot point, as the costumes never made it from Paris to the U.S. after the war broke out. So instead, Dalí's designs were re-created in New York by famous ballet costumier Barbara Karinska, who must have been astounded at the detailed sketches she received.

"Dalí centered the décor on an enormous swan, wings spread, with a large hole in its breast through which the dancers made their entrances," wrote Massine biographer Garcia-Márquez. "The costumes, with highly-charged sexual overtones, were a riot of imagination: one female dancer had a large rose-colored fish head; Lola Montez wore a hoop skirt [decorated with a double row of teeth] over harem trousers; some male dancers' tights were festooned with large red lobsters symbolizing their sexual organs; Venus wore a long blond wig as well as full-body pink tights to give the illusion of nudity; and the three Graces wore absurdly large breasts."

The ballet was clearly to taste. "The only section of the audience that was seriously upset by *Bacchanale* were the devoted adherents of Wagner," wrote dance critic Grace Robert, who added, "The ballet enjoyed a *succès de scandale*."

But that was in New York. When the costumes were toned down for future engagements on the road, the production lost much of its shock value and was simply disliked.

Bacchanale would surely have been a hit in Europe, thought Massine, but the company was prevented from returning home throughout the war. So Hurok suggested the choreographer instead focus on what American audiences might like.

For example, performances of *The Nutcracker* always received popular and critical acclaim. Though the ballet is now a holiday staple throughout the United States, it had rarely, if ever, been performed there until the Ballet Russe de Monte Carlo revived it in 1939. Alicia Markova was America's first and foremost Sugar Plum Fairy.

Hurok was all for anything that would bring new audiences to the ballet. To that end, the impresario called upon his friend Irving Deakin, a former publicity manager for the Ballet Russe de Monte Carlo. The British-born Deakin was now Markova's business manager, a freelance ballet critic, and host of a New York radio program called *Music and Ballet* from 1937 to 1943.

Deakin knew how to promote dance to the masses. Typical of his handiwork was the following event held at Gimbels department store—actually the first retailer to hold a Thanksgiving Day Parade in New York—and Macy's biggest competitor:

> **"How to Enjoy the Ballet"**
> 6 p.m. tomorrow
> *With* Alicia Markova, *prima ballerina* of the Ballet Russe de Monte Carlo; with Irving Deakin ballet critic, lecturer and writer.
>
> The fabulous Ballet Russe de Monte Carlo flashes across New York's theatrical sky next week. Will you be there? Or will you be sitting at home because you think ballet is for long-haired men and short-haired women and just a little too esoteric for you? That's pretty silly. Irving Deakin author of "To the Ballet!" and "Ballet Profile," will tell you why. He'll show you that even your husband will find ballet as much fun as baseball. Having converted you into a thorough-going balletomane, Mr. Deakin will introduce Markova, exquisite prima ballerina of the Ballet Russe de Monte Carlo. New York will be cheering her Monday night. It is our very great privilege to bring her to Gimbels tomorrow.
> Gimbels 11th floor

And if those adventurous men in attendance did indeed buy tickets for the ballet the following Monday—or were dragged by their wives—they would be rewarded with Markova dancing in Balanchine's *Poker Game*, both a crowd-pleaser and appropriately "manly-themed" work.

Hurok wanted the same from Massine and told the choreographer to sideline his allegorical symphonic set pieces in favor of what the impresario termed more "box-office friendly" fare, such as American-themed ballets. Massine wasn't happy, and it showed.

His *Saratoga* (1941), based on the chic racing resort at the turn of the last century, was considered pretentious and lacking in the sophisticated humor that made Nijinska's *Le Train Bleu* so successful; and his production of *The New Yorker* (1940)—curiously inspired by the famous cartoon characters in the cosmopolitan magazine—lacked a jazzy all-American quality, despite its musical score by George Gershwin.

Invited to a company rehearsal of *The New Yorker*, esteemed dance critic Walter Terry of the *New York Herald Tribune* found it problematic: "[T]hese dancers would execute a shuffle and wind up with their toe pointed in the best ballet manner, so that anything resembling a tap was out of the question. Alexandra Danilova assured me beforehand that she would probably resemble 'a cow on ice' and although she didn't live up to her promise I must admit that some of her steps were completely new to the vocabulary of tap dancing, and to all other kinds of dancing for that matter."

More successful was an American-themed ballet Massine handed off to one of his Ballet Russe de Monte Carlo dancers who had choreographic aspirations. Born in Seattle, Washington, Marc Platoff (later Marc Platt) was just right for *Ghost Town* (1939), a ballet about the American Gold Rush. It was a hit despite the production's having lost its first choice composer, Cole Porter. Platoff wanted to know who this Richard Rodgers was who eventually signed on. He had never heard of the Broadway team Rodgers and Hart.

But if Sol Hurok had wanted a true American choreographer for his company, he shouldn't have been so dismissive of Agnes de Mille. In 1942 when Hurok was managing Lucia Chase's Ballet Theatre, he rejected de Mille's western-themed ballet *Rodeo*, with music by the soon-to-be legendary American composer Aaron Copland. She sold it instead to the competing Ballet Russe de Monte Carlo, dancing the lead herself. Hurok was sure the "vulgar" work would be a miserable flop.

Not only was *Rodeo* a triumph, but de Mille would also go down in Broadway history the following year for her spectacularly original choreography for *Oklahoma!*. Richard Rodgers worked on the music for that production too, with Oscar Hammerstein II writing the lyrics, in what would become known as a landmark American musical.

Afterwards, Hurok tried to hire de Mille back, but with this less-than-irresistible offer: "I want you should be Hurok attraction. You have earned the privilege." This time it was de Mille who found Hurok "vulgar."

"It was an adventure," Markova mused about her Ballet Russe de Monte Carlo experience. "It was very hard and very serious, but it was more a family in those days, so we did have fun."

Markova had the most fun of all with the effervescent Danilova. The two were inseparable and had a grand time wherever they went. Choura brought out the best in Markova. She made her laugh and look on the sunny side of life. Danilova was also calming and reassuring when necessary, helping Markova temporarily forget the perils of war back home.

"We used to room together, and we sat on the train together," Danilova cheerfully recalled of those early days. "I always consider Alicia like my younger sister. And it used to tickle us to death, because nobody could understand Alicia's British accent and I would say, 'Oh, let me translate.'" (Choura, don't forget, was Queen of the Russianized English malaprop.)

One of Danilova's favorite on-the-road stories with Markova happened in Los Angeles:

> It was in Hollywood when both of us stayed in a very swanky hotel and one evening we came in after the performance and there on the table were two baskets of fruit and two bottles of very good wine. We thought, "Oh, we have an admirer," and it's wonderful, he admired both of us. And we carry on. And it reminded us of Europe where people sent us flowers. And we had a marvelous supper and enjoyed the wine and ate the fruits.
>
> A man knocked on the door the next morning and said he had left two baskets of food and wine there by mistake. They were for a wine convention and he wanted them back! You can imagine how we felt.

On Danilova's first American cross-country tour in 1933, she had found the other Russian dancers too competitive and unfriendly to spend time with. So instead, she chose to accept dinner invitations from ballet patrons in each new city. "I was exposed to a broad range of ideas and interests, to the world beyond ballet," she explained.

Danilova continued that tradition with Markova, who also found those nights out with "real" people a welcome diversion. There was a war on. Ballet had its place as escapist entertainment, but there were so many other issues the dancers wished to discuss. Markova was also fascinated by the differences in people's daily lives in various parts of the United States. The country was so much less homogeneous than England.

Most gratifying, Markova made friends everywhere she went, so when the company returned to a city to perform the following year, there were people she already knew who were looking forward to seeing her again.

Markova and Danilova also loved to dance—not just ballet, but popular dances. In Mississippi, the local newspaper ran a photo of Markova dressed in a tailored skirted suit while merrily square-dancing. The caption read:

> "Tain't art but it shore is fun," says caller Myrl Frazier (left) of the square dance, and Alicia Markova (facing camera) agrees. "Hoot" Roane (right) refers to his plaid jacket as an "atomic tux." And dang if Markova wasn't good at it!

Dance contests were popular entertainment in those days, and even when ballet wasn't involved, Markova shined. In one city she won a local "swing" contest, but gave her prize away to the second-place finisher. Where would she find the time for three free lessons from the Arthur Murray Dance Studios?

In her autobiography, Danilova tells many humorous stories of her adventures with Markova. On a 1941 tour to South America, the two were sharing a boat cabin when they met a group of naval officers one night at dinner. Danilova couldn't believe the sailors were drinking milk with their meal and sent over a more "appropriate" bottle of Russian vodka. They all became fast friends and the two ballerinas would sneak back on deck after everyone else was asleep to join the sailors—still on duty—for impromptu parties. One stood guard as the rest of the naval personnel kept Markova and Danilova rocking with laughter at their tall tales of 'round-the-world travel adventures.

Another night onboard, everyone was asked to dress up for a costume ball. Markova decided to go as a "blackout," wearing a full-length gown with wrist-length sleeves and a high neck. "On her head she wore a balloon, like the ones that filled the sky in London during the war," remembered Danilova. Markova won first prize.

Alicia adored Choura and would do anything for her. After Massine disparaged Danilova for being too "old" for his company, she spent years battling with much younger Russian "baby ballerinas" and their pushy stage mothers. Choura was grateful that the seven-years-younger Markova was an ally, not a competitor. The two often rehearsed together, helping one another master complicated choreography by dissecting the steps analytically. They called the most troublesome dance sequences their "Waterloos," battles no less decisive than Napoleon's own, they joked.

The two would also cover for each other when one fell ill. Theater contracts required that specific soloists appear at each performance (though Massine tried to "save" his principal dancers by alternating full-length starring roles with supporting ones). Since Markova and Danilova were two of the biggest names, they were generally permitted to substitute for one another when necessary.

It was often a Godsend, as dancers frequently were called upon to perform when sick or in pain. While traveling in the frigid cold, Danilova was prone to bouts of bronchitis, and Markova's substituting for her gave Choura a chance to recuperate before it got much worse. Danilova returned the favor, as when Markova's toe became infected when dye from her colorful costume tights seeped into an open cut.

"The rule was: You may die, but you must not be ill," Markova quipped many years later. "In those days, you see, dancers lived a very different, a very much more rigorous life. The theory was that there was always a replacement for a dead dancer, but if you were ill, you were a nuisance."

Choura also came to depend on Markova's fashion advice, having been struck by her friend's newfound elegance since their Ballets Russes days. In an interview in 1941, Danilova amusingly announced that she had "named" one of her favorite entrance-making gowns "'Alicia Markova' for the two were shopping together and Danilova was afraid that the dress, which has lemon flowers on an orange ground, was too bright for her, but Markova persuaded her to buy it and now she finds it very becoming."

Like Markova, Choura had experienced unkind remarks about her looks in her early dancing days. Though later known for her exceptionally beautiful legs, Danilova was considered quite chubby when she first joined the Ballets Russes. (Dolin unkindly compared partnering her to being a "piano mover.") She had lost that baby fat long ago, but was now quite conscious of showing off her face and figure to the best advantage. Alicia taught her which clothing styles and colors best flattered her.

There was one especially kind gesture Markova managed to keep secret from Danilova. Choura was keenly superstitious about the color purple, thinking it bad luck. She would never dance in a mauve costume, and didn't want anything that color in her dressing room.

She wouldn't even accept mauve flowers if presented to her onstage, unless it would hurt someone's feelings. In that case she would just hand them off as quickly as possible. Danilova thought it remarkably good luck that for several years the offending color never appeared in any of her bouquets. She didn't learn until much later that Markova watched over the floral deliveries and always switched out Danilova's lilac blooms for different colors from her own bouquets. As a bonus for her good intentions, mauve just happened to be Markova's favorite color and a pleasant reminder of Pavlova.

Danilova was truly like another of Markova's sisters. Alicia never needed to be guarded with Choura and could tell her anything. They enjoyed intimate "girl talk," confiding in each other about their romantic entanglements and dreams. While on tour, Danilova became involved with another dancer in the company five years her junior, the handsome Kazimir Kokic. They would marry in a small civil ceremony in Los Angeles on Valentine's Day, 1941. Markova stood beaming by her friend's side, always supportive, non-judgmental, and the soul of discretion.

Unfortunately, the marriage wouldn't last, and Markova's romance with Stanley Burton would also fade away due to time and distance apart. Danilova and Markova commiserated about their love lives always taking a back seat to their dancing careers. Sadly, happy marriages with children were just not in the cards for either one of them.

While performing together with the Ballet Russe de Monte Carlo, Danilova had watched as Markova's fame in the United States exploded. Rather than become jealous, Choura was delighted for her friend, and it's not like Danilova wasn't getting rave reviews herself. The two were very different on stage—one a bubble of champagne, the other a fragile otherworldly sprite—but were equally adored by audiences.

Someone who *was* jealous of Markova's burgeoning fame was her ex-partner Anton Dolin. He certainly didn't wish her ill—like Lifar or Toumanova. He just wished he were the one dancing by her side.

After the war broke out, Dolin had traveled to New York on the S.S. *Washington* with Markova. (Unlike Markova, he freely chose to leave London during the war.) Sol Hurok had facilitated Dolin's passage in case the company's principal dancer Igor Youskevitch couldn't get out of France, and Markova needed a backup partner. Youskevitch was able to make it to New York after all, so Dolin's services were no longer needed.

Dolin had his own plans. He and the vivacious Russian ballerina Irina Baronova were successful dance partners with the de Basil company. Now on break, the two intended to perform together in Manhattan prior to returning for the Colonel's next Australian tour. But Baronova suddenly received an offer from a Hollywood film studio, abruptly leaving Dolin for the West Coast.

Not wishing to return to the unpleasant and ruthless de Basil, especially without Baronova, Dolin accepted an offer from the newly formed Ballet Theatre in New York. (He was able to get out of his contract with de Basil because of a proposed reduction in his salary.) Ballet Theatre featured Pavlova's talented former partner Mikhail Mordkin and was backed financially by the philanthropist/dancer Lucia Chase.

Antony Tudor was the company's chief choreographer of contemporary works, with Dolin hired as a dancer and choreographer for the staging of Russian classics like *Giselle* and *Les Sylphides*. He was very excited about the opportunity to make his New York stage debut; but as Dolin writes in autobiography number three:

"I had no star billing with the Company and had not asked for it. I had no publicity agent, nor had I asked for one."

Though his production of *Giselle* was lovely, and far superior to Lifar's pompously altered version, Dolin lacked one essential ingredient: the quintessential Giselle, Alicia Markova. She was performing down the street at the Metropolitan Opera House with the Ballet Russe de Monte Carlo.

When Dolin picked up the papers to read the latest ballet news, it was his former partner who was the city's reigning star. The all-powerful dance critic for *The New York Times* told his readers that seeing Markova perform *Giselle* was a once-in-a-generation experience:

> **The Dance: Miss Markova**
>
> A Word of Appreciation for a Memorable Artist—
>
> Events of the Week
>
> by John Martin
>
> The Ballet Russe has enlivened its Spring season with more than the usual number of special events—new works and new personalities—but now that all the novelties are over, the crowning achievement of the season, in the mind of at least one observer, remains the performance of Alicia Markova in "Giselle." To allow the engagement to close without a paragraph or two of appreciation would be the rankest of ingratitude.
>
> Those who saw her last week in her first performance of the role here since last Spring may congratulate themselves on having been present at a memorable occasion. After such testimony as she gave then, there can be no doubt that Markova is a classical dancer without peer.
>
> Of the qualities that make an artist it is always difficult to speak specifically, for art lives in an unrationalized world and refuses to be pinned down and described. Ultimately Markova is an artist because she touches this intangible realm and communicates its essence to those who sit before her. . . .
>
> Markova's arabesques are beautiful not because the lines of her body are symbolic of meanings, or because they are difficult to sustain, but because they capture a purely choreographic quality that is self-contained as a musical tone. The technical acrobat can assume the same posture and achieve nothing. Similarly the exquisite quality of suspension that pervades all her aerial movements is no more a matter of

> technical prowess than is the timbre of a musical voice. Here is simply a great and unique talent developed to the top of its form, inimitable and unapproachable.
>
> —*The New York Times,* 4/14/40

Unlike in England, Dolin wasn't a big name in the United States, and now Markova clearly was. She was not only being exalted by the critics, but also appeared to be the talk of the town.

"I was thrilled to see this transformation taking place," Dolin wrote in his biography of Markova, "as in no small measure I was responsible for it."

Nifty trick, as the two weren't even working together at the time and hadn't been for the past three years. But Dolin's delusion of being Markova's Svengali reached far beyond their partnership onstage, as he often enumerated in print. And since Markova never made a point of correcting him publicly, Dolin has often mistakenly been credited with much of her early success, to the detriment of Markova's own hard-earned personal growth and achievements.

According to Dolin's biography of Markova, she was considered a "dull and ordinary" person when they went out together, as she "scarcely opened her mouth." He was determined to do something about that sad state of affairs, so he begged his friend, the affable British actress Constance Collier, to take the socially backward Markova in hand. The two women met in New York and hit it off.

Dolin contends that because of his generous introduction to Collier, Markova suddenly became a sparkling conversationalist. It's such a strange thing to boast about. Why hadn't he taken on that role himself if he felt so strongly about it?

It *was* true that when Markova accompanied Dolin to celebrity parties she often sat quiet and composed in a corner; but that was due both to Dolin's expansive personality and the company he chose to keep. Markova wasn't a one-upmanship type of raconteur looking to be the most entertaining person in the room, as Dolin and Frederick Ashton liked to be—and usually were. She preferred small intimate dinner parties with close friends.

It didn't help that Dolin would often greet Markova for an evening out by picking apart her appearance and wardrobe, which he rarely thought glamorous enough. He probably thought he was doing her a favor.

"He was Irish, extrovert and temperamental," Markova told a reporter many years after Dolin's death, when she finally began to open up a bit more. "He knew I had very little self-confidence [in those days] and he wore me away constantly with criticism. He usually made comments like: 'Your hair looks terrible,' or 'Why are you wearing that?'"

In contrast, Danilova always complimented Markova on her appearance and counted on *her* fashion advice when they went shopping together. Choura was a confidence builder, not deflator, and she shared Markova's love of smaller gatherings with non-celebrities.

Dolin's garrulous society friends overwhelmed the reticent ballerina, who said she would have preferred resting in her room after a performance, reading a book. Dolin couldn't think of anything more dreary. Markova thought it restorative. Neither was right or wrong. They were simply personality opposites. Unfortunately, the extrovert of the pair just couldn't let that stand.

Dolin concluded that Markova was a recluse because she didn't know how to talk to people. That's why he says he enlisted the 61-year-old Collier's help.

But that was not true when Danilova was around. The two ballerinas loved to go out together on the road, frequently dining with ballet patrons and accepting invitations to attend local dances and events. (They both loved the circus, of all things.) Markova looked forward to talking about everything and anything with a variety of interesting people, none of them famous. And she felt especially secure with Danilova by her side, unlike with Dolin, who was generally off somewhere being the life of the party.

Dolin actually appears to be jealous of Markova's friendship with Danilova. He writes that Choura only wanted to talk about "dancers and slippers," rather than important topics of the day. But as Dolin never traveled with the two ballerinas, how would he know what they did or didn't discuss? And since the two women made conscious efforts to meet new people quite different from themselves, one can only assume that they talked about a wide array of topics, not just ballet.

As early as January 1939, Dolin was already aware that Markova had become a well-spoken, popular celebrity. After some of her widely circulated New York press interviews reached him in Australia (where he was performing with de Basil's company), he had written her: "How proud & happy I [am] of you. And that you are speaking, exhibiting your own personality. That is what I want you to do. Dear sweet Alicia."

But since he was on the opposite side of the world at the time, Dolin's taking credit for Markova's "personality makeover" is all the more bizarre. Without his dominance or influence, Markova had become a worldly thirty-year-old woman who clearly enjoyed participating in fun-filled nights out. It was just that her definition of "fun" was very different from Dolin's. And unlike many performers, Markova was a great listener. New acquaintances on tour found her delightful, if a bit shy. And she clearly could be an engaging conversationalist one-on-one—as her lively press interviews surely confirm.

As one interviewer wrote that year:

> What is she like offstage, this ethereal being? Markova is as charming a lady as she is magnificent as a dancer. Small and black-haired she looks more Russian than the Russians in the company. Exquisitely groomed, there is nothing theatrical about her appearance. She wears her lovely clothes with quiet chic. Her voice is soft and bears faint traces of a continental accent. Her conversation is gay and witty.
>
> —"Alicia Markova, Greatest Classical Dancer of Modern Times Creates Sensational New Role," Marya McAuliff, 1940

Markova did indeed benefit greatly from meeting Constance Collier, who would become a close and wonderful friend. But the quick-witted Collier didn't give the reserved ballerina lessons on how to behave in public. She just helped build her self-confidence and welcomed her into her inner circle.

A former British stage actress, Collier had come to the United States for a successful Hollywood career playing character roles in films starring everyone from John Barrymore and James Stewart to Shirley Temple and Katharine Hepburn. With the advent of "talkies," Collier's impeccable diction became her calling card for part-time speech coaching, which she offered actors in both Hollywood and New York in the 1940s. She was beloved by many, many celebrities, particularly ex-pat British actors, who visited her often.

Collier introduced Markova to this group, which included Laurence Olivier, Vivien Leigh, Charlie Chaplin, and Ethel Barrymore, most of whom became her good friends. But the dancer didn't meet those people at the type of star-studded, late-night cocktail parties Dolin and many other celebrities of the day were so fond of. Collier held intimate afternoon teas in her lovely New York apartment drawing room, encouraging lively conversations without press flashbulbs and prying eyes. That was Markova's favorite milieu.

Dolin just felt that wasn't enough. He insisted Markova go out with him to late night soirées to enjoy "basking in her fame" (and where Markova would generously split Dolin's ample bar bills). Many others felt it was Dolin who needed Markova by his side to enhance *his* stature.

In her book *Portrait Gallery*, Agnes de Mille writes of Dolin's holding court in his dressing room, with Markova a tiny quiet figure seated off in the corner. Dolin's supposed "charms" were lost on de Mille who found him pompous and rude.

"He was very grand at these séances, lounging about in his expensive dressing gown. He was ducal, even royal, languidly receiving homage and never rising. At one interview I stood in his dressing room for ten minutes discussing problems about the current production . . . Elsa Maxwell was in the other chair, but he didn't bother to introduce us. He also didn't bother to offer me a seat."

That incident occurred in New York. By the end of 1941, Dolin and Markova were dancing together again, reunited at the Ballet Theatre. Danilova stayed with the Ballet Russe de Monte Carlo. Markova's star would rise even higher, but she would greatly miss Choura's companionship. While on the road, the women wrote back and forth as frequently as possible, still vacationed together, and remained best friends. For the next decade, it would be Dolin by Markova's side as they traveled the world together. Their onstage partnership was magical, their close friendship enormously complex and volatile.

Dolin was thrilled to once again have his quintessential Giselle. So too was Sol Hurok.

9

Spreading Wings

> . . . Rather on the introspective and intellectual side, Markova has lots of things to say to those girls who intend to enter the ballet. Said she:
>
> "I think it should be instilled into every dancer, that she must be interested in everything—art, politics, music, the theater, literature. To know the technique and to practice is not enough. You must mix with people and get to know them. You must discuss things and know the world until you develop your sense of judgment. This is all part of being a good dancer."
>
> —"Markova, Famed Ballerina, Found Health in Dancing," *Berkeley Daily Gazette*, California, 1943

Sol Hurok may have been the hardest-working impresario on the American ballet scene in the early 1940s, but, unfortunately, loyalty wasn't one of his strong suits. His own managing director German Sevastianov claimed Hurok "was absolutely void of any idealism" and loved "only two things—his wife and money." Nice for his wife (Hurok's second—he had abandoned his first), but not so much for his business associates.

As Hurok biographer Harlow Robinson explains: "Comfortably and advantageously positioned as an independent presenter operating within the security of NBC's National Broadcasting and Concert Bureau, Hurok loved to exercise his power by pitting his various rivals against each other." Those "rivals," it turns out, were often his very own clients.

Why would competing ballet companies put up with such an arrangement? They basically had no choice, as they each needed both the impresario's connections—he alone could deliver café-society glitterati on opening nights—and his extensive bookings network throughout the United States. (Hurok held the exclusive lease for ballet performances at New York's Metropolitan Opera House, for example.) And with the war on, returning to Europe was not an option.

Staying in Hurok's good graces required just one thing—a willingness to do whatever the impresario wanted. The Ballet Russe de Monte Carlo's Director, Serge Denham, and financial backer, Julius Fleischmann, were hardly pushovers, and they paid the price. Between 1940 and 1942, Hurok would end up managing not one, not two, but three competing ballet companies in the United States, giving preferential bookings to whichever was most compliant. Apparently the term "conflict of interest" was not in the Russian's vocabulary.

So in the summer of 1940, Colonel Wassily de Basil's re-born company, now laughably called the "*Original* Ballet Russe," became a Hurok concern. The impresario had been kept abreast of the troupe's highly successful Australian tour by Anton Dolin, who had been angling for Hurok to reunite him with Markova at the Ballet Russe de Monte Carlo.

Thinking de Basil might be easier to control than Serge Denham, Hurok decided to put the latter in his place by forcing the two ballet companies to compete head-to-head in New York. It worked.

From a publicity standpoint, de Basil had the obvious advantage of re-presenting his teenage dance prodigies from the 1930s. Previously widely promoted as the beautiful "Baby Ballerinas," Tamara Toumanova, Irina Baronova, and Tatiana Riabouchinska hadn't performed together for many years, so their reunion was considered "an event." De Basil also won out as far as the critics were concerned. They preferred his company's classical Russian repertoire to Denham's program of predominantly contemporary American works, such as Massine's half-baked comedic *The New Yorker.* Of course, the choice of presenting those uninspired ballets at this time was Hurok's.

As *Time* magazine reported on November 25, 1940:

> Whereas Diaghilev was imaginative, ahead of his time, and not above shocking his audiences, Mr. Hurok's two troupes make little effort at even keeping up to date. Massine's ballet, St. Francis, whose music by Paul Hindemith is among the best in the modern theatre, has slipped from the repertory; Sol Hurok does not like it.

But despite Hurok's efforts to undermine Denham, the competition continued unabated. "By 1941," writes Robinson, "the hostility between the Original Ballet Russe and the Ballet Russe de Monte Carlo had become so intense and litigious that local managers were afraid to book either company."

Even Hurok recognized the folly of that. He also didn't want to sink the Ballet Russe de Monte Carlo without first extricating his golden girl, Alicia Markova. To set that goal in motion, the impresario approached his friend Irving Deakin, who was the business manager not only for Markova, but for Dolin as well. Hurok was conniving to sign both dancers to personal service contracts, giving him the power to reunite the duo sometime in the future at the company of his choosing.

Dolin knew being "owned" by Hurok was a risky proposition, as he and Markova might be forced to work for de Basil, like it or not; so both dancers turned the offer down. Hurok was furious at the decision, but unleashed his anger—and vitriol—only on Deakin. After all, the impresario couldn't afford to make enemies of Markova and Dolin. They were much too valuable.

Besides, Hurok had another scheme cooking. If Markova and Dolin refused to work for de Basil (Markova's contract with Denham was up at the end of the spring 1941 season), Hurok could still reunite the pair at Ballet Theatre, the third company he would take over. But booking three ballet troupes simultaneously would be a nightmare. One of them had to go.

Opportunity knocked in the spring of 1941 when de Basil's Original Ballet Russe was set to go on tour in Mexico City, Cuba, and South America. In an effort to increase profitability, Hurok decided to reduce everyone's contracted salaries by a whopping 40%, commensurate, he said, with the lower living costs south of the border. The impresario sent German Sevastianov to deliver the unwelcome news to de Basil, who, in turn, informed the dancers. Shocked, many of them decided to fight back.

In Mexico City, a group of eighteen dancers threatened to strike, but de Basil's purse strings were tied. (Hurok had seen to that.) When the company arrived in Cuba, there was a mutiny. The "strikers" walked out on opening night, leaving the troupe in shambles.

The Cubans—who had a very specific contract as to program requirements for each performance—were justifiably displeased and reneged on payment. Hurok then cited de Basil for his own breach of contract and promptly cancelled all the company's future South American bookings, as well as transportation reservations. They were left virtually stranded in Cuba.

Prima ballerina Irina Baronova, however, was given immediate passage back to New York, as she was under personal contract to Hurok, not de Basil. And, oh yes, her husband was German Sevastianov, who many claim had urged the dance strike all along just to facilitate the impresario's coup. Sevastianov had supposedly promised the "strikers" future employment with Ballet Theatre in New York, and indeed many, like George Skibine, would wind up there.

But even if that story is exaggerated or inaccurate, Hurok certainly took advantage of a bad situation that he had personally precipitated. Unbeknownst to any of his ballet concerns, the impresario quickly contacted the U.S. theaters where de Basil's troupe had been pre-booked for 1941–42, informing each manager that the Original Ballet Russe would be replaced by Ballet Theatre in the coming season. It was his "patriotic" duty, Hurok said, to rescue the only American-based ballet company during the war. (Years of lawsuits between de Basil and Hurok would ensue, with constant delays and motions insuring no one ever saw the inside of a courtroom. Most incredibly, de Basil signed on with Hurok again five years later.)

It should be noted that management at Ballet Theatre was neither aware of Hurok's negotiations on their behalf, nor thrilled at the prospect of working with him when he first proposed a merger. His reputation as a powerful bully was well known, as was his belief that the only good ballet was a Russian ballet—claims of patriotism notwithstanding. Richard Pleasant had founded Ballet Theatre to encourage innovative dancers and choreographers of many nationalities, Americans and British chief among them.

But once again, the impresario's business and social connections—"S. Hurok Presents" was like a seal of approval—gave him negotiating leverage, especially since Ballet Theatre was hemorrhaging money. As it was her personal wealth being squandered, Lucia Chase carefully weighed her options, one of which was to fold the company altogether.

Tipping the scale in Hurok's favor was Chase's trusted classical star dancer/choreographer Anton Dolin. "He admired Hurok, agreed with his judgment of what the public wanted, and, as his advocate, succeeded in impressing both Mr. Zuckert [Lucia Chase's lawyer and head of the dance company's Board of Directors] and Miss Chase," explained Charles Payne, Ballet Theatre's managing director. "He also proposed as business manager a former associate whose experience in ballet management had equipped him not only to solve Ballet Theatre's fiscal problems but also, should it prove necessary, to outsharp Hurok. His candidate was German Sevastianov."

Dolin had become friendly with the devilishly persuasive Sevastianov—and Irina Baronova—when they all worked together for de Basil. When meeting with Chase and her board, Dolin was like a "marriage broker," according to Payne, personally vouching for the integrity of both Sevastianov and Hurok. But it was the dancer's own integrity that should have been called into question, as Dolin had negotiated a side deal with Sevastianov to deliver Markova as his leading lady.

Richard Pleasant rightly felt that his artistic vision would be compromised under Hurok and reluctantly resigned (or was fired, depending on whom you believe). Not wishing to be loaded down with overwhelming management responsibilities, Chase (who was a dancer in the company as well as its financial backer) acquiesced to signing with the Russian impresario. Sevastianov took over the day-to-day operations, and the ballet musical chairs began again. Unfortunately, talent wasn't the chief criterion for ascendancy.

It was like the "Russian Occupation," remembered Payne, with former Diaghilev choreographers Mikhail Fokine and Bronislava Nijinska soon hired. It was all part of Hurok's master plan for billing the American company as "The Greatest in Russian Ballet."

Both the impresario and Sevastianov cared little for the so-called "English Wing" of the company, headed by Antony Tudor, but they did consider Dolin a key player, both for his loyalty and his choreography of exclusively Russian-themed ballets. Though Tudor's influence was initially diminished, Lucia Chase stood by him—and her money talked.

The cast changes, however, were like a military coup. "Sevastianov saw to it that dancers who were formerly principals would now be demoted to soloists," writes Tudor biographer Donna Perlmutter. "He cast a jaundiced eye on the likes of Miriam Golden, Nora Kaye, Muriel Bentley, David Nillo, and more—most of them Jews—and brought in dancers, along with Baronova, from the Ballet Russe [de Monte Carlo]. It was said that he was anti-American, anti-Jewish, and anti-Tudor."

But when it came to Markova, Sevastianov had no choice. The "Jewess" was to share the limelight as principal ballerina with his wife, Irina. Markova was not only a huge box-office draw, but also Dolin's promised reward. At least her name was Russian.

As in the case of so many powerful men with anti-Semitic leanings, exceptions were made where business was concerned. From Markova's personal diaries, it is clear that Sevastianov was never anything but cordial to her, and she liked, and got on well with, Baronova. And according to Charles Payne, Sevastianov felt "Markova's style of dancing was so different from his wife's that she would be a complementary rather than a rival talent."

Markova, it should be noted, was blissfully unaware of all the backroom wrangling over her future. She was carefully weighing all her options, as she wrote to Stanley Burton:

The Biltmore Hotel
Los Angeles

Feb. 15th 1941

Stanley darling,

Just received your photo safely for which many thanks. I like it very much. I haven't had a letter from you since before Xmas. I hope things are alright & try not to worry. We have had a hectic time here. Amazing success but it keeps me so busy. My contract finishes with this Co: Feb 28th but I have agreed to finish the tour until March 16th when we return to N.Y. Then I shall have to decide which contract to sign. I have three definite ones at the moment besides other things in the wind. Take good care of yourself & write to me if you can to the N.Y. address 150 W. 58th St.

My love & thoughts dear—Alicia

Though Harlow Robinson claims Hurok "took full advantage of the fact that dancers, especially Russian ones, had virtually no legal protection or rights, and treated them like pieces of furniture to be placed where he wanted them," that was not the case with Markova. She was one of the two most famous ballerinas in America (Alexandra Danilova being the other) and, as Markova wasn't under personal contract to Hurok, he couldn't order her to do anything.

Despite the harrowing touring conditions at the Ballet Russe de Monte Carlo, Markova's close friendship with Danilova was the happiest personal work relationship of her life, and she was loath to leave her and the company. Markova was also content on the artistic front, enjoying the challenge of being a choreographic muse to the multi-talented Massine, even if his last few works had been less than stellar. (Unbeknownst to her, Hurok was plotting to bring Massine to Ballet Theatre as well.)

Like an army general, Hurok plotted tactical maneuvers for luring Markova to Ballet Theatre. His plan of attack began with sending Dolin as an emissary, and he couldn't have had a more stalwart representative. From almost the moment they split up at the end of 1937, Dolin had been scheming to reunite with Markova. He was initially angry she had left him for the Ballet Russe de Monte Carlo, but he couldn't afford to stay mad.

While on tour with de Basil in Australia, Dolin began a letter-writing campaign to renew their friendship. At first, he just wanted Markova to know he had no hard feelings, but she was enjoying the break from her former controlling partner and didn't respond. Dolin wouldn't give up, as in this excerpt from a letter he wrote on Valentine's Day, February 14, 1938:

> *Alicia dear,*
>
> *I wonder if you ever got my letter. I have waited to hear from you in answer. I now can only think you have not written because you have not heard from me.*
>
> *From my side, there is no reason for such a long silence & I cannot think there is from yours.*
>
> *. . . I hope now all is well with you & it would be nice to hear.*
>
> *My love Patte*
>
> *I want an exclusive photo for the book*

As soon as detente had been reached, Dolin started asking Markova to speak on his behalf to Denham, Massine, and Hurok, always attaching press clippings of his splendid Australian reviews for her to pass on. (He would send similar—though certainly less personally effusive—letters to Hurok.) But probably most persuasive for a proposed reunion were Dolin's condolence letters to Markova after she was injured on stage.

In a letter written from His Majesty's Theater, Melbourne, Australia, dated November 7, 1938, Dolin commiserates with his ex-partner:

> *Alicia darling,*
>
> *Today I have had the [Markova's] American press. I am happy & sad dear. Happy for your success but sad & disgusted at the apparent lack of support that is yours to command. I should have been with you & you with me. And now this filthy Lifar publicity. Really Serge should know better.*
>
> *But now I read again that you have hurt your foot & that Slavenska had to finish Giselle. So all my thoughts are on that &*

> *you. Write me please dear at once to Sydney c/o Russian Ballet how you are & everything. I am so worried & distressed.*
>
> *. . . I want & can arrange for you to come here for the 1940 season. Darling you & we could have an enormous success & they would adore you. . . . I have made a wonderful personal success & am the only one who gets a reception. What we could have done together & how many people here ask me to bring Markova & Dolin perfection in the dance duet as they call us.*

Needless to say, Markova declined Dolin's offer to leave the prestigious Ballet Russe de Monte Carlo in America to join him at a less-than-stellar company in Australia. But now that he too had moved to New York, signing on with Ballet Theatre, Dolin was more anxious than ever to reunite with Markova as his dance partner. He could just taste their shared fame. Markova's name was everywhere, and not just as a critical darling.

As had been the case in England, American fans wanted to know all about her, from her early years with Diaghilev to what she ate, wore, and did in her spare time. Markova was not only featured in society columns, but also asked to model for fashion magazines. Imagine, the plain little Jewish girl from Finsbury Park in the pages of *Vogue*!

In one of the fashion magazine's spreads, two glamorous gowned models stand on either side of the ethereal ballerina, who looks equally resplendent in a diaphanous, off-the-shoulder costume of layered tulle. The caption read:

> "Alicia Markova, première ballerina of the Ballet Russe de Monte Carlo—being congratulated backstage by two first-nighters. The scene is New York—but the scene and the clothes and the furs and the jewels might be the same in any city of America when the ballet comes to town."
>
> —*Vogue*, November 1940

And it was.

Though Markova would have been pleased to dance with Dolin again, it wasn't a strong enough inducement to get her to jump ship from her current position. For that, Hurok would have to bring out the big guns.

He fired his first shot at her bank account, with the offer of a tremendous leap in weekly salary from $150 to $400. Think of all the extra money and much-needed rations she could send home to her family and friends in England! After a bomb destroyed their Marble Arch apartment, Eileen and the girls had retrieved what they could from the rubble and moved out to Blackpool, where Vivienne was working for the Civil Service. With such a substantial raise, Markova would be far better able to support them.

But the prima ballerina was so valuable to the Ballet Russe de Monte Carlo that Denham offered to match Hurok's proposed salary. It would make Markova the highest-paid prima ballerina in the country.

Hurok's shot number two was at Markova's artistic heart. Mikhail Fokine, Diaghilev's celebrated choreographer from the Ballets Russes days, was now working at Ballet Theatre. He was interested in staging a new production of *Romeo & Juliet* to music by Sergei Prokofiev, one of Markova's favorite composers. Fokine wanted Markova for Juliet. As the brilliant choreographer was now sixty-one years old, an opportunity like that might not come around again.

Markova waved the white flag and signed with Ballet Theatre. Though more famous in the U.S. than Baronova, she generously agreed to share top billing with the Russian dancer in all advertising and publicity, but Sevastianov clearly favored his wife, according to Charles Payne:

> [T]he souvenir program would be printed so that Markova's picture appeared first in half the copies, Baronova's first in the other half. Everyone praised Sevastianov for his Solomon-wise solution and everyone lost patience with Markova for her constantly voiced suspicion that every souvenir book offered for her to autograph had Baronova's picture in first place. (This may well have been because the printer of the program, an old and dear friend of the Sevastianovs', had interpreted the sharing agreement to mean that Markova's picture should appear first in one third of the copies and that in the other two thirds it should be preceded by Baronova.)

Sevastianov also made sure Dolin's name and picture always came before the more inventive choreographer Antony Tudor.

At the Ballet Russe de Monte Carlo, Danilova may have lost Markova, but she gained George Balanchine as a choreographer when he joined the company in 1944. Though the two ballerinas would miss each other terribly, Markova's move was probably best for both of their careers.

As dance critic Edwin Denby explained:

> The difference between the two companies added to the pleasure. Ballet Theatre's aesthetics under its English choreographer Tudor, tended to dramatic pantomime; the Monte Carlo's under Balanchine, toward a classic dance grace. They had different repertoires, though both included 19th Century classics, Diaghileff, and pre-war pieces. . . . And each had a very great artist as its star ballerina. The Monte Carlo was the witty warm-hearted Alexandra Danilova. Delighted by the fresh stimulus around her she reached in 1944–45 a new magnificence in strict classicism. Ballet Theatre's ballerina, on the other hand, was the frail English classicist, Alicia Markova; but Ballet Theatre's tendency toward pantomime developed her latent genius as an actress. For several seasons she showed us a shyly dazzling spirituality of expression, the secret force of which captivated alike warworkers, housewives, and intellectuals. Her "Giselle" became New York's big ballet night.

But what Markova would gain in fame, she lost in personal contentment. The close bond she had formed with Danilova helped her deal with the forced separation from Stanley, her mother, and her sisters. Communications in the early 1940s were predominantly by letter and telegram. You couldn't just pick up the phone and chat for hours to catch up. In fact, during the war, the still-rudimentary AT&T network couldn't handle the increased telephone volume and actually took out ads requesting customers not make *any* long-distance calls—and that included within the United States.

So Markova and Danilova wrote letters and compared schedules, arranging to meet whenever their bookings landed them both in the same city at the same time. They also spent many summer vacations in each other's company. But with the joyful and supportive Choura gone from her everyday life, Markova became more prone to depression. Not all the time, but enough that she would suffer larger and larger mood swings.

For many women, close contact with a best girlfriend can be as life-affirming as the true love of a man. For the foreseeable future, Markova would have neither.

As was true in Markova's Vic-Wells days, the Ballet Theatre members had to fend for themselves during the summer months until the new season—and their new contracts—began in September. Some landed jobs. Some went on unemployment. Most were scattered.

Markova and Dolin had a better idea.

Located in the bucolic Berkshires of Massachusetts, Jacob's Pillow is a name now synonymous with dance. That historic association began in 1930 when modern dance pioneer Ted Shawn purchased the sprawling 150-acre mountaintop farm as a retreat and rehearsal space. Far less well known is the role Alicia Markova played in the establishment of the first international dance festival on the grounds in 1941. The success of that venture—and Markova's personal connections—saved Jacob's Pillow from being sold off as vacation or development property for some wealthy landowner.

Long before buying the Jacob's Pillow farm, nearly three decades before, Ted Shawn formed an avant-garde modern dance troupe with his like-minded dancer wife Ruth St. Denis. Founded in 1915, the Denishawn Dance Company and School were very progressive for their time and would prove to be an invaluable training ground for many cutting-edge choreographers, including Martha Graham and Doris Humphrey.

Shawn and St. Denis had what might be called today an "open marriage." In 1930, according to Shawn's biographer Walter Terry, both husband and wife ended up having separate affairs with their handsome young business manager. "This was not a new experience for St. Denis," wrote Terry, "but for Shawn, if his words to me and to others are to be believed, it was the first time he had established a more than casual physical relationship with another man. The rivalry became intense." And ugly.

St. Denis threatened to divorce Shawn and go public, which would have effectively ended his teaching career, as in those days no parents would trust their child to an admitted homosexual. But she later changed her mind, and though the couple split up, they never officially divorced.

In 1933, Shawn took the innovative step of founding a new all-male company, appropriately—if not imaginatively—named "The Men Dancers." A sturdy, athletic figure, Shawn wanted to promote dance as a fittingly masculine profession. He succeeded. Shawn's testosterone-fueled choreography—a blend of sharp gymnastic and methodical modern dance movements—was kinetic and dynamic, often with themes concerning manual labor.

Shawn also teamed up with the innovative Société Anonyme Inc, an organization founded by artists Katherine S. Dreier, Marcel Duchamp, and Man Ray to "promote contemporary art among American audiences." In the spirit of a Diaghilev collaboration, Shawn choreographed pieces inspired by modern abstract drawings, paintings, or sculpture, with the artwork duplicated on a grand scale as a backdrop. For many years, The Men Dancers profitably toured throughout the United States, Cuba, Canada, and Germany.

"The first performances were held in the summer of 1933 at Jacob's Pillow," Walter Terry explained. "Shawn didn't think anyone would come, but he tried it and about fifty people showed up at seventy-five cents apiece. He talked about dance and his goals, the boys served tea and danced, the audience sat on the floor at one end of the barn converted into studio. For some of the heftier Berkshire dowagers who adored Shawn . . . and appreciated the nearly nude boys, camp chairs were provided. These were the modest antecedents of what was to become the most famous dance festival in the world."

By 1940, most of the men in Shawn's dance troupe had enlisted in the army. "Creatively and artistically," wrote Shawn in his 1943 memoir of Jacob's Pillow, "the seven years' achievement of the men dancers gave me a deep inner satisfaction. But financially, since I never had a cent given me outright as an endowment, or underwriting, I went deeper and deeper in debt."

At the brink of bankruptcy, Shawn leased the farm to a dance teacher from New York, Mary Washington Ball, who hoped to establish a school and yearly summer dance festival on the grounds. That had enormous appeal for Shawn—who Ball hired as a teacher—so she was also given an option to buy the property outright with her profits.

Unfortunately, that never happened, as Ball's first festival lost so much money that she was forced to abandon the project altogether. "Again, I listed Jacob's Pillow with the real estate dealers," explained Shawn, "and spent the winter in New York to be near in the event of a buyer showing up."

That could have been the end of the story—with a "Jacob's Pillow Condo Resort" on the property today—had it not been for Alicia Markova and Anton Dolin. Shawn and Dolin were acquainted, as they both shared a desire to popularize dance as a manly pursuit. Upon learning of the financial difficulties with Jacob's Pillow, Dolin visited the expansive property and thought it perfect as a place he and Markova could start practicing together again, while teaching a summer school to raise money.

When he suggested the plan to Markova, the idea got bigger. After the petty jealousies she had encountered at the Ballet Russe de Monte Carlo when first joining the company in 1938, Markova thought it would be advantageous for her to "bond" with the Ballet Theatre dancers prior to the official start of her new contract in September. And what better way to get to know one another than in the verdant farmlands of the Berkshires?

So just as she had formed an off-season Vic-Wells dance company with Vivian Van Damm, Markova worked up a plan with Dolin for the Ballet Theatre dancers to spend the summer at Jacob's Pillow, with everyone exchanging free living quarters and a place to rehearse for teaching and performing.

Of course, that plan required some serious money.

Markova's exceedingly wealthy British friend Reginald Wright—who she had become quite close to during her early London dancing days—was now living in Palm Beach, Florida with his American wife. The millionaire had previously told his favorite ballerina that he would be happy to fund a future dance project for her should she ever be interested. Now she was interested. Wright was delighted with Markova's plan and contacted Shawn.

"As it was late in the season, and no outright buyer had appeared on the scene, I thought it wise to rent Jacob's Pillow again," explained Shawn. "Alicia Markova made an arrangement with her former partner in the Dolin-Markova Ballet, Mr. Anton Dolin, to act as artistic director, and they planned to conduct a school and a festival series along the general lines established by Miss Ball. I was asked to be on their faculty for four weeks and to give one of the weekly festival programs—which I accepted."

Wright not only leased the property from Shawn for June, July, and August, but he also moved to the Berkshires himself to share in the festivities and spend time with Markova.

The hordes of dancers descended. Most of the corps members were quartered in rustic log cabins throughout the property, but Antony Tudor, Hugh Laing, Irina Baronova, and Sevastianov stayed in a large converted barn nearby owned by the welcoming Ruth Derby. (Derby House is still used by Jacob's Pillow houseguests today.) Also joining the group were Lucia Chase and Markova's great friend Bronislava Nijinska, with her husband and daughter in tow.

There was just one additional problem. They all needed to eat.

Since the dancers wouldn't actually be paid any salary for the summer, they were able to collect unemployment—all of ten dollars per week. Of that less-than-princely sum, they were asked to contribute one dollar per day for food.

In addition to rehearsing new ballets and giving master classes and performances, Markova was responsible for the none-too-easy task of planning all the meals with those meager funds. Dancers ate a lot. But as would be true throughout her career, Markova was a mastermind at budgets for everything from food and travel accommodations to costumes and toe shoes. Each morning, she would get together with the on-site hired cook to plot out carefully cost-controlled menus. Kapp, as he was called, was an ex-army man well versed in food rationing. But Markova thought Sunday meals should always be special—something to look forward to. So on that day, she asked Kapp to serve ribs of beef, Yorkshire pudding, and apple pie, a little something for everyone, as it were.

Markova also found a solution to the rudimentary plumbing issues—no running water or showers—as she explained to Maurice Leonard. While many of the dancers bathed in the stream, Markova wanted a bit more privacy. Ever resourceful, she consulted a New York camping shop for advice, and they had just the thing: a portable zip-up rubber bath, lightweight enough for her to tote around. With water from the outdoor pump, the ballerina managed to bathe in her own room, the only one available in the main house.

That top-floor master bedroom—formerly Shawn's—had its advantages and disadvantages. While it was spacious and gave Markova easy access to the downstairs kitchen and cook—who cheerfully brought her breakfast in bed each morning when he arrived—after dark, she was quite alone.

One night, Markova was awakened by a huge racket on the roof that sounded like someone trying to break in. She thought the best thing to do was pretend to be asleep. Soon she was.

The next morning, Markova was relieved to wake up safe and sound with the sun shining. But then she heard the thundering noise again. She had to laugh when she found out what it was.

Much like a Walt Disney cartoon, little chipmunks were rolling their nuts down the ridged wood roof beams with a constant ca-chunk, ca-chunk noise echoing loudly in her bedroom just beneath. While Markova had no trouble sleeping sitting up on a bumpy train, Chip and Dale were another story.

Throughout the summer, everyone pitched in, from the dancers and company management to students and their mothers. It was like a 1940s Andy Hardy movie starring Mickey Rooney and Judy Garland where someone suddenly shouts, "Hey, kids. Let's put on a show!"

In archival photos of the farm, Markova and Dolin can be seen rehearsing on backyard rocks and ledges, as well as dusting and sweeping out the huge barn. While pushing a large broom, Markova is dressed in a rather fetching pantsuit with fitted jacket and wide-leg trousers. The outfit would be the envy of any fashionable woman of today.

Dolin may have chided Markova for dressing too casually, but she was actually a frontrunner in establishing a modern comfortable chic that was widely copied. Three years before Lauren Bacall taught Humphrey Bogart to whistle in *To Have and Have Not* (1944), Markova was photographed at a restaurant wearing an almost identical wide-shouldered herringbone fitted suit and jaunty beret. (Bacall was another nice Jewish girl who made good.) Markova was also one of the first female celebrities to wear pants out in public.

The fashion magazines loved her, and that got Jacob's Pillow some much-needed attention and publicity. Markova's presence drew the most famous photographers from *Vogue* and *Harper's Bazaar*—including Horst P. Horst and George Hoyningen-Huene—who despite strict gas rationing made the trip to the Berkshires from New York to take photos of the willowy ballerina in the great outdoors. Of course they stayed to watch her dance.

As a reporter from *The Berkshire Eagle* later rhapsodized about Markova:

> Her artistry was akin in spirit to that of a violinist or pianist playing gentle and lyrical passages to chamber music. . . . Diminutive and delicate, her paleness enhanced by jet-black hair, her features suggesting Anna Pavlova, Markova smiled subtly her Mona Lisa smile and virtually floated across the open dancing space.

Someone else who saw Markova perform that summer was dancer/choreographer Agnes de Mille. In her book *Portrait Gallery*, she tells a rather lengthy and disturbing story about arriving at Jacob's Pillow only to find Markova alone in her bed, sobbing uncontrollably for hours at a time. Admitting to "unkindly" spying on the frail ballerina through a crack in her bedroom door, de Mille was shocked at Markova's alternately catatonic and hysterical state. Not feeling personally close enough to intervene, de Mille went to Dolin to express her concern.

As Irina Baronova and Nina Strogonova were also experiencing off-and-on crying jags, Dolin simply pooh-poohed the histrionics of all the "weeping women" in his midst, suggesting that they seemed to enjoy their tears and could stop any time they wanted. But de Mille felt Markova's case was far more serious than the other ballerinas' behavior, which she agreed was quite typical of emotional, high-strung performers. Markova hadn't left her room for two days and was turning away food—the signs of severe depression, de Mille warned Dolin.

If Danilova had still been around, she undoubtedly would have been able to talk her friend through the melancholic state. Dolin couldn't be bothered (and many thought his antics were the root cause). Though he "was devoted to her [Markova], even dependent on her," writes de Mille, "he could never resist wicked Irish mockery." But in fairness, she adds that despite his "naughtiness, capriciousness, and flamboyance, Anton Dolin was one of the kindest-hearted men in the dance world," as when he lent aid to Nijinsky and Spessivtseva when they became seriously mentally ill. Clearly, Markova wasn't headed for an asylum, and Dolin was being thoughtless rather than intentionally mean-spirited.

Markova's depressions would worsen over the years.

Yet as de Mille explains in amazed wonderment, when it came time for Markova to perform on stage, she was "transcendent." Even her fellow dancers couldn't believe their eyes. Afterwards, Markova's mood immediately brightened and all seemed well again. When de Mille congratulated the ballerina on reaching perfection, she brightly replied, "It was all right." Never in her entire career would Markova feel she had attained perfection. Reaching for the stars gave her a reason to dance.

Though the cost of performances at Jacob's Pillow was eminently affordable—the top price was $1.50, and that included afternoon tea—the publicity surrounding Markova's summer performances in the rural town (not to mention the official premiere of her re-partnering with Dolin) was invaluable. There was also the added cachet of prominent guest lecturers, including John Martin from *The New York Times* and Walter Terry of the *New York Herald Tribune*.

With all the talented Russian and European company dancers, the festival was considered an international event, helping to raise $50,000 in donations. Leading the formation of that funding committee, and acting as its first president, was Markova's benefactor Reginald Wright.

Shawn explained, their "plan was that a new, non-profit-making, artistic and educational corporation be formed by them which would buy the property from me, and build a proper dance festival theater so that dance artists could have ideal conditions in which to show their work, and audiences have ideal conditions in which to see it. They asked me whether, if this was done, and the corporation engaged me as managing director, would I consent to stay on and conduct school and festivals at Jacob's Pillow. . . . I consented."

Ted Shawn would forever be grateful to Markova, whom he called "Adored Alicia" in his frequent letters over the years. They always remained great friends, and Markova returned to dance at Jacob's Pillow in the 1950s at the pinnacle of her career.

Markova and Dolin had indeed "put on a show!" and Jacob's Pillow flourished ever after.

While Ted Shawn was the chief beneficiary of that summer of '41 at Jacob's Pillow, it was also transformative for the Ballet Theatre members in attendance. After Hurok's major personnel shake-up, spending several months working and playing together made them seem more like a family. Odd man out, however, was German Sevastianov, who continued to instill fear—and some loathing—in many of the dancers and choreographers by wielding his power to promote favorites (mostly Russian) and cast aside Americans (mostly Jewish) and Brits. Legally changing his first name from German to Gerald so as not to be associated with the Nazis didn't help his cause.

Back in New York in September, Markova was thrilled at the opportunity to work with Mikhail Fokine. Though he was known to be difficult and often cruelly critical, Markova was so compliant and technically proficient that she soon won him over.

Their first project together was Fokine's restaging of his own Russian classic *Les Sylphides*, which had debuted at the Ballets Russes in 1909 starring Vaslav Nijinsky, Anna Pavlova, and Tamara Karsavina. In preparation for this new production, Fokine insisted that Markova learn all three past versions in their entirety before he chose which he thought best. Another dancer might have balked at such a burdensome task, but Markova found it exhilarating.

Most often described as a romantic reverie, *Les Sylphides* is an exquisite one-act ballet Fokine choreographed to evocative music by Frédéric Chopin. With no plot per se, it is more a lovely mood piece—perhaps a poetic man's dream—of walking in a moonlit forest and coming upon a suite of ethereal dancing "sylphs" or wood nymphs. Dressed in the most diaphanous long white tutus, the young women are thought to be spirits of the air, and the leading man revels in joining them.

As Grace Robert explains, "The *pas de deux* danced to the Valse, Opus 64, No. 2 opens with one of the loveliest lifts in all ballets. The mechanics of support are reduced to a minimum and in a first-rate performance are not visible. The partner appears merely to restrain his lady's flight rather than aid it. In this *pas de deux* Alicia Markova's thistle-down lightness is unforgettable."

Though ideally suited to the lead role, Markova felt that the emotional context of the ballet had eluded her prior to working one on one with Fokine. But after mastering each interpretation under his tutelage, the meaning suddenly became crystal clear: it was like a poet who pulls inspiration from the air in the form of the sylph. *Les Sylphide's* gasp-inducing *pas de deux* would become one of Markova's most memorable performances throughout her career, especially when partnered with Dolin.

For his part, Fokine found her technical skills a marvel and perfectly suited to the choreography. "There are no preparations for the steps; they just happen," explained Markova. It was what she did best. As the *Boston Post* reported in January 1942: "Alicia Markova shone brightly at the Boston Opera House last night. Her 'Les Sylphides' was exquisite—the lifts in the Pas de Deux airy and drifting."

Les Sylphides would become a permanent favorite of Markova's, and was one of the first ballets she re-staged as a choreographer after retiring from dancing.

On a more comical note, Fokine created the crowd-pleasing ballet *Bluebeard* the same season, with Dolin in the title role and Markova as the banished princess. Here Fokine had his leading lady play against type, much like Frederick Ashton had done in *Façade* and Ninette de

Valois in *Bar aux Folies-Bergère*. Rather than choreographing classical ballet steps for his prima ballerina, Fokine had her dancing the can-can and executing pratfalls while madly kicking her legs.

Markova once again suffered some serious bumps and bruises—especially when she had to fall to the stage on her back—but unlike in *Rouge et Noir*, her *Bluebeard* costumes left enough room for extra padding to cushion the blows.

Fokine never did choreograph his planned version of *Romeo & Juliet*, finding the Prokofiev score uninspiring in the long run. But he did teach Markova a great deal in the short time they worked together. He would die unexpectedly in August 1942, just eight months after *Les Sylphides* debuted.

Arts writer Eric Johns tells of one rather unexpected lesson Fokine passed on:

> Make-up is another aspect of the dancer's profession to which Markova has devoted infinite study. She always looked so fresh. No one ever saw her with a hair out of place or a stain on her ballet shoes and she always took great pains to effect the ideal make-up for the rôle in question. She was bewildered while making-up for the puppet Ballerina in *Petrouschka*, in a production of the ballet supervised by Fokine himself. The great choreographer happened to enter Markova's dressing-room while she was wondering how to make red blobs on her doll-like cheeks. Fokine took the lid off the rouge box on her dressing table and pressed it against her cheek, leaving the outline of a circle. "Now fill that in!" he smiled.
>
> —*Theatre World*, 1963

Perhaps the greatest gift Fokine and Markova gave to each other was the rebirth of Anna Pavlova's signature ballet *The Dying Swan*, set to Camille Saint-Saëns's painfully forlorn cello solo *Le Cygne* (The Swan). Markova had been asked many, many times to perform the role but had always turned it down.

This, however, was Fokine asking. He had created the original choreography for Pavlova, whom he too thought Markova so closely resembled. "I gave in, but only with some misgivings," she said later.

And Markova had a firm condition: "In the program, it was always dedicated to her memory."

Markova had never actually seen Pavlova dance *The Dying Swan*, so her interpretation could never be viewed as a carbon copy. As she would teach many students in her later years, one should never imitate another dancer, but rather make each role your own.

Though Pavlova had favored a black velvet curtain as a backdrop for her dying swan, with a bright spotlight outlining her body, Markova had a very different conception. She imagined a wide bare stage with a sky-blue floodlight to emphasize the bird's tragic attempts to flutter and fly off as life left its body. It was both heartbreaking and profound.

Markova's *Dying Swan* premiered on the anniversary of Pavlova's death, January 23, 1942, at the Boston Opera House. As was true with the Russian ballerina, it would become one of Markova's signature roles ever after.

"Having seen Pavlova dance her immortal version of The Dying Swan several times, I would say that Markova is the nearest in perfection," wrote one reviewer. It was "so beautifully and movingly danced that I wished that all applause could be forbidden, and a minute's silence kept instead at the end."

But there never was any silence—just thunderous, explosive applause. Afterwards, excitement over Markova's uncanny likeness to Pavlova again reached a fever pitch in the press. Perhaps that was another reason she had been so reluctant to take on the role. Even before Markova danced *The Dying Swan*, the American papers often highlighted the two ballerinas' similarities.

> "Pavlova faced Markova" was the description used by European ballet audiences when they spoke of Markova. . . . She is described as looking enough like the late Anna Pavlova to have been her daughter, and she dances in the classic style of the great Pavlova.
>
> —*Fresno (California) Bee*, 1/24/41

Eventually, Markova made peace with the comparisons, as her bringing Pavlova somehow "back to life" seemed to give everyone so much pleasure. Letters from friends and peers expressed such warmth and gratitude.

Constance Collier wrote to Markova that not since Pavlova had she been so moved by any ballerina. "I didn't think I would ever see the replica of that moment of magic again."

Also mesmerized was Russian music conductor Efrem Kurtz, who had traveled on tour with Pavlova until her death in 1931. When conducting for Markova in New York, Kurtz thanked the British ballerina for bringing the Russian star back to him in spirit. In some ways, he even thought Markova superior. "The music followed Pavlova," Kurtz explained. "Markova follows the music."

One of her biggest fans was the renowned music and dance critic Carl Van Vechten, who became an accomplished photographer later in his career. He and Markova met when she first arrived in New York with the Ballet Russe de Monte Carlo, becoming fast friends. Van Vechten's letters to Markova are delightfully unrestrained with praise: "Since Pavlova, there has been no one else with such lightness and grace, such skill and ease, such facility of execution, such distinction and LINE. That's it, LINE!"

If anyone had the opportunity to study Markova's balletic line up close, it was Van Vechten. The two spent many hours together in his photographic studio, with Van Vechten creating beautiful costumed portrait studies of Markova, along with step-by-step records of her movements in various roles. (He would take more than a thousand photos of Markova.) Many of those images were later projected on a large screen so that students could study her precise technique and the way she held her arms and legs through each pirouette, leap, and spin (some of those images are now in the Carl Van Vechten Photographs Collection at The Library of Congress).

There were many other dancers who posed for Van Vechten, but he claimed that only Markova's positioning was perfect in every single frame. Ballet critic/historian P. W. Manchester reminisced many years later, "Carl Van Vechten took a series of color photographs of Markova which would be a revelation if they could be shown today."

The photographer was in awe not only of Markova's talents, but also of her astonishing work ethic. She always arrived at his studio one hour before their scheduled appointment so that he would never have to wait for her to be properly costumed, made up, and exercised.

She would then give Van Vechten all the time he needed for each laborious setup, unlike many other sitters who quickly lost patience.

Van Vechten never forgot one especially lengthy session where Markova didn't leave his studio until four in the morning. As always, she had been an absolute professional, never mentioning the acute pain she was experiencing from a ruptured hernia—so severe that she had already scheduled surgery for the following morning. Markova didn't wish to spoil the session.

The perfect technique Van Vechten captured on film was the end result of Markova's continued training with Vincenzo Celli in the late 1930s. Celli was an Italian dance teacher extraordinaire who, like Markova, had initially studied with the peerless Enrico Cecchetti. Celli had first seen Markova dance when she was a mere teenager with the Ballets Russes and they had taken classes together.

They would meet again in New York when Léonide Massine appointed Celli ballet master of the Ballet Russe de Monte Carlo. As Markova always preferred one-on-one lessons, she budgeted a sizable amount of her limited salary to pay Celli for private tutoring, and she would continue to do so throughout the rest of her career.

In 1939, Markova learned that the semi-retired Olga Spessivtseva was in New York, and invited her to share Celli's private class with her. Markova would always feel indebted to the lovely Russian ballerina who had first taught her the role of Giselle. Not long after, the fragile Spessivtseva had a mental breakdown and was confined to an institution. Markova was glad she had those last memories of chatting away with Olga as Celli put them through their paces. At forty-four, Spessivtseva had still been a marvelous dancer.

In Celli, Markova found a fellow perfectionist, and one who was willing and able to criticize even the tiniest mistakes she made.

"The most important thing of all is the training," Markova later explained. "The training to prepare the dancer is really to serve the choreographer. That's really what we're there for. At least that's the way I felt always." In contrast, a star prima ballerina like Pavlova viewed training as a way to perfect what she already did best rather than mastering new movements to inspire choreographers. They were there to serve her, rather than the other way around.

Celli would write of Markova:

> One could buy a Stradivarius but a dancer's body must be created. Sacrifice and a conformity to an ideal Alicia Markova carries within herself, and, this no teacher has taught her. . . .
>
> During her class Alicia Markova is an eager, hardworking student; on stage she is not learning but giving of her innermost self. Something the world needs. A miracle of art in a mystery of a person. How can one explain that in words?

How, indeed.

The New York premiere of Ballet Theatre's *Giselle* starring Alicia Markova and Anton Dolin took place on November 27, 1941. As Carl Van Vechten commented, rather than lifting her up, "Dolin actually seemed to PULL his partner out of the air. Apparently Alicia Markova had elected to remain in her native element, the ether."

Dance critic and photographer Arthur Todd was also a witness. "The great Markova boom did not really get under way until 1941. All of us will always remember those wonderful years in the early forties when Markova was dancing Giselle at the Met. On those nights the house was always sold out to capacity, and the atmosphere was electric. I well remember one of those evenings, when there were thirty-six curtain calls for Markova."

Though Markova's *Giselle* would be considered an "event" throughout the rest of her career, a much bigger event took place ten days after that New York premiere. At 7:55 A.M. on December 7, 1941, the Japanese began bombing the United States Pacific Fleet at Pearl Harbor on Oahu, Hawaii. Over 2,400 people were killed—sailors, soldiers, civilians—and nearly 1,200 wounded. The United States was now at war.

At the very moment Pearl Harbor was under attack, Markova was dancing her matinee performance of *Giselle* at the 44th Street Theatre in Manhattan. The audience would learn of the horrific Japanese raid during the intermission. Suddenly the poignancy of Markova's performance would be a never-to-be-forgotten moment.

Markova saved a letter she received from an acquaintance who was there:

> I always speak of you on Pearl Harbor Day. . . . Why? Because we were at the matinee on the Sunday in 1941 in New York City when you danced Giselle. To us it was the definitive performance.
>
> I have never forgotten your kindness in writing to me while in hospital, in the Army, in Africa. Far from theatre dance as you well knew. . . .
>
> You come often to our minds—but on this day, with a special poignancy.

The war had been a daily reality for Markova long before Pearl Harbor. She was terrified for the safety of her family and loved ones, especially after a bombing raid destroyed her London home. She also had been on tour in countries where the people's sympathies were emphatically with Germany, a completely unsettling experience.

"In Rio, we'd gone to the cinema to relax, and suddenly news came up that Paris had fallen and everyone got up and cheered," Markova remembered. "I was with Freddie Franklin and some of the other members of the company and we were just in shock."

Franklin whispered that none of them should speak so the animated crowd wouldn't realize they were English. Just days before, British war vessels had sunk the German battleship *Admiral Graf Spee* off the coast of South America, and the dancers were worried that their nationality might cause a riot.

When the U.S. entered the war, the American Theatre Wing in New York started the Stage Door Canteen, a warm and hospitable environment for servicemen to visit and relax between deployments. Though the Bette Davis-sponsored Hollywood canteen became the most famous outpost, the organization had branches in many cities throughout the country.

To keep the atmosphere wholesome, alcohol was forbidden, but there was plenty of coffee and doughnuts, as well as pretty female volunteers happy to take a spin on the dance floor. Alicia Markova was one of those amiable volunteers in whatever city the company visited on tour.

"When we used to go to the Stage Door Canteen in New York, where of course we all went when possible, sometimes you danced, other times you served coffee or just chatted with the servicemen," she recalled. "And I enjoyed that."

Markova was also a frequent volunteer in Los Angeles. "I shan't forget those days. Bette Davis was in charge of the Hollywood Canteen. I was the dishwasher. And, oh, yes; I learned to dance the jitterbug. A huge Coastguard (man) taught me. His name was 'Killer' Joe."

According to *My New York* newspaper columnist Mel Heimer, "He got the name 'Killer Joe' during World War II when his jitter-bugging at the Stage Door Canteen—with such as Judy Garland, Bette Davis, June Havoc, and even ballerina Alicia Markova—was so violent that people were afraid he'd knock himself out, but good." Markova thought Joe resembled Massine in that regard.

While Markova learned the jitterbug (and later danced it with Mickey Rooney for everyone's enjoyment), she in turn taught the servicemen how to ballroom dance, which they surprisingly enjoyed. "Why is it they always think we need pop stuff?" several G.I.'s asked Markova. "They said, you know, we'd like some classical things. So eventually, I think one Sunday afternoon, it was decided we would try a different plan . . . a classical afternoon. So that consisted of [Jascha] Heifetz and Arthur Rubinstein—he said he would play the piano, Heifetz naturally played his violin—and Pat Dolin and myself were to dance."

Joining the illustrious group were opera singers Lauritz Melchior and Helen Traubel. To accommodate as many soldiers as possible, Bette Davis commandeered an empty airport hangar near a San Diego military hospital. Inside the cavernous concrete building were placed row upon row of evenly spaced white stretchers. Though the setup was unsettlingly like a military cemetery—with its perfect grid of white headstones—the soldiers in attendance were very much alive and enthusiastic, despite the sea of white bandages.

Markova and Dolin decided to perform the beautiful *Grand Valse pas de deux* from *Les Sylphides*, ably accompanied on the piano by Arthur Rubinstein. As Markova began to dance between the stretchers, Dolin lifted her high into the air. She said she would never forget the sight of peering down on the seemingly endless expanse of bandaged bodies, their battered and bruised faces looking up at her from the ground, entranced.

Bette Davis sent Markova a thank-you letter of gratitude for her efforts: "We thought you should know how very happy you made the service men when you visited with them at the Canteen recently. Although these men can never express their pleasure and gratitude individually, we all know how truly grateful they are to see in person the individuals known to them only on the stage."

Davis was wrong on one count. Markova's archives are filled with sentimental thank-you notes from G.I.'s who took the time to write her from army bases all over the world.

"This letter comes from a G.I. Joe whom you won't recall, but let me refresh your memory," began a typical note. But Markova always did recall, as another G.I. recounted in his letter.

It seems the serviceman had been bragging about dancing with Markova at a Stage Door Canteen, but his army buddies didn't believe him. To embarrass the poor fellow, they insisted on waiting for the ballerina to exit the theater one evening. When Markova came out, her Canteen dance partner caught her eye, and she went right up to him and asked how he was doing. His pals almost fell over. The elated G.I. thanked her for a story he could dine out on the rest of his life.

Markova also got requests for signed photos that were posted in army lockers—"You'll be up there with Gene Tierney!" wrote one—and the ballerina always enthusiastically obliged. She couldn't believe anyone would consider *her* "pin-up girl" material.

Throughout the war years, Markova accepted any fundraising or volunteer opportunity that came her way, from gala benefits for the Red Cross to being photographed promoting clothing drives:

> **Shoes for Drive**
>
> Ballerina Alicia Markova contributes her ballet shoes to the Clothing Collection Drive. They'll be used as hospital slippers. Have you sorted out the clothes you don't need?
>
> —*New York Post*, 1945

Markova personally organized the donation of goods from the Ballet Theatre employees, which she carefully packed up and sent on to England. She joined the American Women's Voluntary Service to sell war bonds and, when performing at the Los Angeles Opera House one winter, appeared in the "Victory Window" of I. Magnin's department store.

The local newspaper advertised Markova's appearance, letting readers know the lovely ballerina would be sitting inside the fashionable retailer's window at 10:45 A.M., being interviewed on the radio about the importance of supporting the troops. Afterwards she would be happy to sign personalized photos for anyone willing to contribute.

A letter from the Headquarters of the Commandant, Third Naval District in New York thanks Markova for her "kindness and enthusiastic cooperation" when she "so willingly met and chatted with the group of sailors and the marines blinded in action." She felt it was an honor to have been asked.

The popularity of ballet actually increased during the war years. As Edwin Denby explained, "Wartime, here as abroad, made everyone more eager for the civilized and peaceful excitement of ballet. More people could also afford tickets. And in wartime the fact that no word was spoken on the stage was in itself a relief. Suddenly the theaters all over the country were packed."

Dancing Intrigues 2,200 Lucky Enough To See It

Alicia Markova Leading Feminine Star in Ballet

Some 2,200 ballet-hungry Miamians forgot war and ration worries for a few hours Saturday night as they watched featherlight dancers of the ballet theatre troupe, foremost dancing group in the United States today.

—*Miami Herald,* 12/12/42

Ballet Too Ritzy for Soldiers?

Dancers Say It Would Wow 'Em

. . . Little 96-pound Alicia Markova, who admits her heart is tangled up with an Englishman now making uniforms for the R.A.F., thinks the ballet has a definite war mission. "Escape," she says. "Ballet is a dream—and a peaceful one."

—*Philadelphia Record,* 1943

Ballet Hailed as War Outlet

Markova Here for Guest Artist Appearance

Servicemen everywhere are enthusiastically accepting the ballet as an outlet from the sordidness of war.

In fact most persons today, in the opinion of Alicia Markova, are desperately in search of simple, finer things. "They want beauty . . . they want to relax . . . and ballet seems to be one of the answers."

—*San Francisco Examiner,* 7/29/44

Sol Hurok went so far as to suggest that attending the ballet was downright patriotic, as he explained at great length in press releases and the Ballet Theatre's lavishly printed programs:

Communiqué from S. Hurok

Ballet in time of war is not merely a form of amusement. Combining the arts of dance, music, drama, and painting, it mirrors and at the same time influences the free exercise of these artforms. In a world threatened with a forced return to the dark ages, the ballet spotlights the future and the reward of victory.

It is not an accident that Russia, our steadfast ally, has been for centuries the home of the ballet. . . . What was once caviar for the Czars is now the spiritual diet of the Russian people. On the eastern front ballet troops from Moscow and Leningrad dance for the soldiers as they rest momentarily behind the lines. To the rhythm of field artillery the dancers pirouette and leap delighting the weary warriors who thus refreshed return to the front to continue their courageous counter offensive.

The company, a composite of America, England, and Russia represents the finest dance talent of the united Nations: Irina Baronova, Alicia Markova, Anton Dolin, Nora Kaye, Lucia Chase. . . . America and Russia, allies in the world conflict, are today also sharing honors in the dance world. The Ballet Theatre represents America on the ballet front.

—*The Ballet Theatre Program,* 1942–43 Season

Walter Terry served in the armed forces abroad, and upon returning home told Sol Hurok that American soldiers were actually quite jealous that ballet—"full companies and full orchestras, complete with costumes and stage sets"—was regularly performed for the Russian troops on the war front, despite the dangers involved.

Compared to that, one would think hauling costumes and scenery around the United States would be a piece of cake, but that was not always the case. Unlike the old days, when the ballet had its own railcars—albeit the beat-up "Hurok Specials"—the war necessitated travel by public rail. Sometimes trains were commandeered for emergency army transport and all the ballet's sets and luggage needed to be quickly unloaded onto the nearest platform awaiting the next available railcar.

The dancers were also frequently delayed, and the hardships of touring got exponentially worse. As Ballet Theatre managing director Charles Payne recalled, "The dancers hurried to the railroad station only to wait, sometimes for hours, for a civilian train that had been sidetracked by troop movements. After a ride in a crowded, often unheated coach (to which a diner was almost never attached), they arrived late and stood in long lines for transportation to their hotels, where they were told they must wait until the priority-occupants of their rooms moved out and their beds could be made up (there was no promise that the rooms would be cleaned)."

The *Arkansas Gazette* ran an amusing photo of Markova, Irina Baronova, Nora Kaye, and two other forlorn-looking ballerinas sitting dejectedly on the steps of the local theater, accompanied by the following article:

> **Ballet Bows to Needs of War When Loss of Baggage Delays Performance Until 3 P.M. Today.**
>
> Some of the best-known figures of the ballet stage were halted in Little Rock yesterday after eight weeks of performances throughout the country.
>
> Scheduled to give a performance at 8:30 P.M. at the Auditorium yesterday, the troupe was unable to appear for the first time in 50 scheduled performances.

> Coming from Columbus, Missouri, scenery, props and wardrobes were sidetracked at Memphis to allow passage of troop trains.
>
> "Our performances have run late before due to delay of wardrobes, but we have never had to cancel a performance until now," Leon Spachner company manager said.
>
> —*Arkansas Gazette*, 12/12/42

When Markova was asked to comment, she put a cheerful spin on the situation: "Alicia Markova, dark-haired, attractive prima ballerina, said she regretted the delay, but that Little Rock seemed a nice place to be held over. 'It is all because of the war effort,' she said, 'and none of us can become too angry about that.'"

As transportation problems multiplied, the company management did the best they could to avoid financial losses:

> **Audience Thrilled**
>
> **Ballet Stars to Give Extra Performance This Evening**
>
> Owing to transportation difficulties that interfered with a scheduled appearance in Seattle today, the Ballet Theatre, which has been delighting audiences at the Strand Theatre, will present an extra performance this evening.
>
> —*The Vancouver Daily Province*, 1/20/43

Coast-to-coast ballet tours were grueling under any circumstances, but the war took an extra toll on everyone, both physically and emotionally. No matter how harried her schedule, however, Markova made time for the press, as she felt it her duty to serve as an emissary for ballet—certainly needed now more than ever.

"The Mayor Gets Snubbed" read a headline in a Springfield, Massachusetts newspaper in 1941. Underneath was a photo of a smiling Alicia Markova shaking the mayor's hand. The caption read:

> Though a bevy of beauties from the Ballet . . . was scheduled to meet the mayor this morning at the city hall, only one showed up. She was Alicia Markova, revered as one of England's greatest ballerinas. . . . Anyway, Markova kept the date and

> got a promise from Roger L. that he'd be at the Court Square theatre tonight to see the entire company.

That last line says it all. Unlike most celebrities, Markova used her carefully honed media skills not for self-aggrandizement, but rather to sell tickets and promote an appreciation of her art. She also realized that thousand-word platitudes on the sublime beauty of dance wouldn't make for very good copy, nor appeal to the average newspaper reader.

Markova thought if average Americans could relate to her personally, they might give ballet a chance. And she was able to do that because she could so easily relate to them. It was a singular gift for one so famous.

Dolin, for all his wit and easy banter, did not have Markova's emotional connection with everyday people. His snobbish attitude toward anyone he considered unimportant—as attested to by Agnes de Mille and many others—makes the notion that he was personally responsible for the successful marketing of Markova all the more far-fetched.

It was Markova's common touch that endeared her to the public.

> **Ballerina Doesn't Have to Reduce;**
> **Keeps Her Weight Up with Sweets**
>
> . . . "Nothing relaxes me so much as a circus," she [Markova] said. "In my world of ballet, which started when I was eight, there is so much shop talk I must get away from it or be bored to death." . . .
>
> The ballerina changes costumes six times, but they are all done while she is on the run behind the backdrops and she climbs up and down a ladder several times.
>
> "I am so good on the ladder I think I should be an auxiliary fireman," she said.
>
> —*Minneapolis Star and Tribune*, 1943

The combination of Markova's down-to-earth manner and the undivided attention she showered on each journalist was as unexpected as it was beguiling. And when news photographers came to take pictures, her approachability was downright refreshing.

One New York reporter and photographer were pleasantly surprised when brought back to Markova's dressing room at the Metropolitan Opera House. There was the world's most celebrated ballerina lounging about in a simple blouse and skirt—one leg tucked under the other—laughing away while playing gin rummy with friends.

Appearing in the next day's paper was a photo of Markova smiling craftily while carefully guarding her hand of cards. The caption, and excerpted article, read:

> **Alicia Markova, leading classic dancer of the Ballet Theatre, likes to play gin rummy in her Met dressing-room. She usually wins.**
>
> . . . Miss Markova is not, she insists, a glamour girl. She's a simple, quiet English girl who happens to be a good dancer. Her press agents have asked her to dress more snakily, let down her hair and throw off her natural reticence. But Miss Markova insists that being herself and a good dancer into the bargain is Quite Enough.
>
> —"Necessity Is the Mother of Markova,"
> *New York World-Telegram,* 10/26/42

Markova dressed for the times. She understood—even if Hurok's press agents did not—that a period of self-sacrifice and rationing called for simple attire, not the fancy furs and gowns that had been Pavlova's signature. Markova adopted the fashion uniform of American working women in the 1940s: a broad-shouldered fitted suit with knee-length skirt. It was what Hollywood actresses like Rosalind Russell, Greer Garson, and Joan Crawford wore in their popular "real women" movie roles.

That attitude won Markova many female fans. She was willing and able to put herself in the place of average American women whose lives had changed drastically after the United States entered the war. Not only were their loved ones drafted, but in a way they were too.

Women who had never held jobs in their lives were needed as factory workers and fill-in employees for all the men now overseas. Many were scared, tired, and feeling neglected. Markova was a Jewish woman at a time when her religion had horrific consequences. She knew what it was like to feel insecure and afraid.

Her interviews were filled with practical beauty and health tips to make women feel better in those tough times. It was hard to feel attractive while doing factory work. Markova knew how happy her sisters were to receive her care packages of lipsticks and nail polish, which they were unable to get in war-torn England.

Ballerina Tells Secret of Her Lovely Hands

> Women war workers may have hands as beautiful as anyone, according to Alicia Markova, dainty ballerina of the Ballet Theatre. . . .
>
> "Every night before I go to bed," she says, "I soak my hands about ten minutes in some warm milk. I drink a pint of milk every day and during rehearsal periods when I am working extra hard, I drink a quart of milk. I think it is good for the skin and the nails."
>
> Markova knits, sews, and washes her own stockings. "Idle hands," she believes, "are not often attractive."
>
> —*Seattle Times,* January, 1943

Exercise Feet, Advises Markova

> . . . To women whose feet feel the strain of war work Markova advises hot Epsom salts foot baths and exercises.
>
> "This may sound paradoxical," continued the ballerina, "exercises for tired feet, but it turns the trick. Feet that ache from continued standing or sitting need limbering up and relaxation that muscle workouts give. For best results, pick up marbles with your curled toes—master the trick and find how good it makes your feet feel."
>
> —*Detroit Evening Times,* 1943

Women readers saw Markova not just as a star, but as someone they could picture as a girlfriend, and they came to see her perform in droves.

"A Russian girl I know who works in a defense plant brought along her whole swing shift on Sunday into standing room," wrote Edwin Denby of a Markova performance. "They had never seen ballet, and they unanimously fell in love with Markova. Markova has the authority of a star, but her glamour comes from what the English so well call a genuine spiritual refinement."

At times, that "genuine spiritual refinement" took a back seat to a sly sense of humor:

> **The Lyons Den, By Leonard Lyons**
>
> Sports Depts: Alicia Markova went to a fashionable shop to buy stockings. She asked for size 8. The salesgirl told her the smallest size in stock was a 9. . . . "I could wear 8½," Miss Markova pleaded. . . . "Nine's the smallest we have," said the salesgirl. "You'll find it difficult to get stockings smaller than 9. If you don't mind my making a suggestion," she told Markova, who spends five hours a day practicing to maintain her position as the world's greatest ballet dancer, "do a lot of feet exercises. That'll make them larger."
>
> —*Pittsburgh Post Gazette,* 2/19/45

Of course no one would have known about that amusing encounter if Markova hadn't made the effort to pass it along to the press herself. And despite her reputation for being serious and reserved, she was quite a lively storyteller, as revealed in the following newspaper article:

> **Markova—Lady With Twinkling Toes**
>
> . . . Once, in a small town in Oregon during the war, she [Markova] arrived late and disheveled, and felt it essential to visit the local beauty parlor before the evening's performance.
>
> "I had no appointment," she recalls, "but the girl said she would try to fit me in. Well, I read every magazine they had and meanwhile, it appeared to me that every woman in town had gone in ahead of me, while I was sitting there, waiting.
>
> "It was getting close to time to go to the theater so I asked the girl if she couldn't squeeze me in soon. 'I'm sorry miss,' she said, 'but there's a ballet tonight and we have to take care of these other women first. They're all going.'"

And what American woman couldn't relate to that story?

-∾-

But all was not harmonious that year, even with the retreat in the Berkshires and the unified sentiments brought out by the war effort. While Ballet Theatre's Lucia Chase was a huge fan of Antony Tudor's, Sol Hurok was not. The impresario had always felt ballet, by definition, meant Russian, and the British choreographer's works were far too experimental for his tastes. However, it was the heiress Chase who kept the company afloat financially, so Tudor wasn't going anywhere. Hurok would find other ways to get what he wanted.

Hoping he could inject some Russian magic in the Ballet Theatre's programs, the impresario decided to go after Russian choreographer Léonide Massine. Just one problem: Serge Denham had Massine under contract at the Ballet Russe de Monte Carlo until 1948. The ensuing negotiations for the artistic director were chock-full of ironies that seemed to elude everyone involved.

By the end of the 1941 season, Denham was dissatisfied with Massine because his recent American-themed ballets had been critical flops. Of course, it was Hurok who had forced Massine in that unsuccessful direction in the first place. Making matters worse, the art director's sky-high salary was costing the company a fortune. So when Hurok approached Massine about doing freelance work for Ballet Theatre, Denham was delighted to lend him out and save several months' wages.

Meantime—in a Sol Hurok-type move—Denham and his moneyman/partner Julius Fleischmann re-examined Massine's contract and discovered a loophole that voided the agreement. Rather than "fire" Massine, Denham said the company was just choosing not to renew his contract. Whatever the semantics, Massine was both furious and unemployed.

Ah, but there was a white knight waiting in the wings. It was none other than Sol Hurok, who galloped to Massine's artistic rescue by inviting him to join Ballet Theatre. And what types of ballets was Mr. Hurok interested in? The very Russian-themed symphonic works that he had prohibited the choreographer from creating just two years earlier at the Ballet Russe de Monte Carlo—and which eventually led to Massine's being fired. The outcome?

Massine was happy. Sol Hurok was happy. And Denham and Fleishmann were happy. In the ballet wars, it was a rare occurrence indeed.

As a bonus for Massine's joining Ballet Theatre, he would be reunited with Markova and able to rekindle their creative partnership. She starred in the first Ballet Theatre work he created while "on loan" from Denham. It was the theatrical *Aleko*, based on the passionate poem "Gypsies" by Alexander Pushkin.

"It was a subject close to his heart and to mine," explained Hurok, "the poetic Pushkin tale of the lad from the city and the tragic love for the daughter of a gypsy chieftain, a love that brings him two murders and a banishment."

Aleko's musical score was set to Tchaikovsky's Trio in A Minor, so Hurok got exactly what he asked for: an all Russian-inspired creation. And the best was yet to come.

As he had done in the past with Henri Matisse and Salvador Dalí, Massine was anxious to collaborate with an innovative modern artist on the production. His first choice was the allegorically expressive Russian painter Marc Chagall, whom *Time* magazine art critic Robert Hughes later called "the quintessential Jewish artist of the 20th century." This was the man who first immortalized the "fiddler on the roof."

Chagall had his own connection with the Ballets Russes. From 1908 to 1910 he studied under the company's brilliant colorist and designer Léon Bakst at the Zvantseva School of Drawing and Painting in St. Petersburg. Chagall enrolled in the art academy because Jews were not permitted to attend Russian public schools or universities at that time. Also Jewish, Bakst served as a teacher, mentor, and role model for the young Chagall, encouraging him to further his painting studies in Paris.

In 1942, the 55-year-old Chagall was a recent émigré to the United States. He and his adored wife Bella had loved their life in Paris—"No word sounded sweeter to me!" he wrote in his autobiography—but as Jews, they were forced to flee the German atrocities. Chagall would decry the Nazi persecution in his art before taking refuge with his family in New York, propitiously invited by the Museum of Modern Art.

According to Massine biographer Vicente Garcia-Márquez, as "two Russians in exile," Massine and Chagall forged an immediate bond "that would rise to a special level of intimacy." Massine recalled that as soon as he approached Chagall about *Aleko*, the artist was "so intrigued by the theme that he immediately offered to design the costumes and scenery. When he showed me his preliminary sketches, I realized how well his particular blend of realism and fantasy would enhance the atmosphere."

Markova also found a kindred spirit in Chagall, with whom she would develop a very close relationship over the years. They both shared immense joy in their art, as well as the life experiences of Jews in horrific times. Though Chagall had come to New York to escape Hitler's religious persecution, anti-Semitism was also on the rise in the United States during the 1930s and '40s. In his book *The Jews and the Nation*, author Frederic Cople Jaher cites a 1938 survey of Americans in which "approximately 60 percent of the respondents held a low opinion of Jews, labeling them 'greedy,' 'dishonest,' and 'pushy.'. . . excoriation and exclusion of Jews escalated throughout World War II and peaked in 1946."

Large numbers of Americans blamed "the Jews" for the country's entrance into the war, denying them job opportunities, housing, and hotel rooms; or worse still, perpetrating violent physical attacks and desecrating Jewish cemeteries and synagogues. Markova and Chagall experienced those troubling times in a way non-Jewish artists never could, no matter how sympathetic.

Closely bound both emotionally and artistically, Markova, Chagall, and Massine delighted in collaborating on *Aleko* during the late spring and summer of 1942. Those five months were spent in Mexico City where the Ballet Theatre was booked at the *Palacio des Bellas Artes* as guests of the Mexican government. Hurok's plans were for the company to use that time to not only perform (and earn money), but also create and rehearse all the new choreography for the 1942/43 American cross-country tour—one that would begin and end in New York. The foreign locale was the perfect backdrop for creative work on the tantalizingly exotic *Aleko*.

Chagall brought Bella and their daughter along, and Markova fondly remembered them all as one big happy family. The dancer really needed a supportive family at that time, as she was simultaneously rehearsing five different ballets, a crushing workload. Roaming the picturesque city for design inspiration with Chagall and his wife—who helped with the ballet costumes—was a welcome break from the backbreaking practice studio.

"I used to go to the market with Chagall often, and in Mexico at that time, it was very primitive," Markova later recalled. "You could go to the market and buy all the wonderful cotton materials, and they were all dyed—by the Indians you see—in these fantastic colors. Well, they were almost psychedelic colors: the marvelous candy pinks, and yellows, and oranges. You could choose your materials and choose the lace and everything, and the braids, design your own, what you had in mind, and then you bought it and you took it to the other end of the market."

There, a "little lady in black" sat at a Singer sewing machine, and Markova would show her what she had bought and present her design ideas. Since the fabrics were so cool and lightweight, the ballerina thought them ideal to wear while on tour in stifling hot climates.

Rather than shop for themselves, the Chagalls used the outdoor marketplace as an inspiration laboratory for costume design; and they too would buy fabrics, intricately cut lace, and decorative trim for the elderly seamstress to stitch up to their specifications.

"She'd say come back in two hours," Markova recalled. "There would be a little café there, with the musicians strumming away, and you went and had a drink and chattered and talked, and in two hours you went back and everything was ready."

Markova got her chic peasant blouses and skirts for traveling, and Chagall got his costume samples. The finished products, with spectacular appliqué and embroidery work, were a sight to behold.

Like Matisse, Chagall chose a pristine white for Markova's first costume, but he covered it in elaborate colorful decoration befitting a wild gypsy girl. On the bodice, the artist hand-painted a red heart just below Markova's own, with a "tree of life" supporting it from underneath. "Chagall adored fantasy," Markova said, "and whenever he sent me messages he signed them with a heart and his name inside it—saying he gave me his heart each time, which was a typically happy idea."

Adding to the dazzle of her ravishing costumes, Markova made her own glittering necklaces and armlets from gold coins she found in the local marketplace. On stage, they jangled seductively with her every undulating movement. Though it was not easy to create bold, eye-catching jewelry without substantial weight, that task was a snap compared to mastering Massine's choreography.

Alexandra Danilova had been Massine's most frequent dance partner for many years, and often commented on his brutal creative process: "Massine was unmerciful, and he couldn't have cared less. He had no qualms about making extreme physical demands on the dancers for the sake of his choreographic vision."

Markova was always willing to try whatever a choreographer had up his sleeve, but many of Massine's steps for the gypsy role of Zemphira were downright dangerous, including some agonizingly twisted backbends.

"I knew that the pain was part of the artistic satisfaction of the work, and it had not only to be endured but to be conquered," Markova stated emphatically. "The result, I'm sure, meant that I always had new and exciting roles throughout my career, because of my willingness."

That willingness came with a price: Markova's painstaking process for mastering new choreography, which often drove Massine and Frederick Ashton crazy. Massine described it as "Chinese water torture," because of all the time involved. As Danilova attested, Massine was a bully as a choreographer and wanted what he wanted—right now!

Anton Dolin found Massine's process unsupportable. Originally cast to star opposite Markova as *Aleko*, he quickly became incensed at the choreographer's demanding and unorthodox working methods, walking out in a huff during rehearsals.

That was no great loss as far as Massine was concerned. He had never cared for Dolin to begin with, and gladly replaced him with Yura (George) Skibine. (Massine's "murderous lifts" would later cause Skibine to withdraw with a back injury, and Dolin would dance *Aleko* after all.) Hugh Laing was cast as the "Young Gypsy," and Antony Tudor as "Zemphira's Father" (with a great deal of makeup, as Tudor was only two years older than Markova).

However difficult the choreography may have been to master, the intensity and fury of the ballet proved unforgettable. "The double murder of the gypsy girl and her lover by Aleko is one of the most shattering experiences not only in the dance, but in the whole world of theatre," wrote Robert Lawrence in the *New York Herald Tribune.*

From the day it premiered in Mexico City on September 8, 1942, *Aleko* electrified audiences, with Chagall's décor playing a crucial role in the work's impact. The Russian artist's tireless and inspired efforts had resulted in four magnificent hand-painted backdrops (30 by 48 feet each) and close to 70 costumes. "Extraordinarily colorful and dramatic," wrote Grace Robert, "they are among the most distinguished ballet settings since Diaghilev employed the finest easel painters of his period to work for his company."

It was lucky the ballet was created in Mexico City, because the American stage painters' union would not have permitted Chagall to do the work himself in New York. The completed designs were so glorious that the "sale of the Chagall backdrops in 1977 when the company faced a financial crisis consigned the ballet to history," reported dance historian Leland Windreich.

On opening night in Mexico City, artists Diego Rivera, Frida Kahlo, and José Orozco were all in the audience, having heard of Chagall's spectacular murals. Unusual for any ballet, the artist was asked to join the dancers on stage for the nineteen curtain calls.

As was the custom in those days, Chagall sent Markova a congratulatory telegram even though he had seen her right after the performance. It was marked "URGENTE," and the strange phrasing explains why the pair always spoke French together. (As Chagall explained: "It took me thirty years to learn bad French. Why should I try to learn English?")

> Not knowing enough English to tell you my dear and poetic Semphira our sincerly admiration. Thanks for your tender and warm creation. Kiss your wonderful hands and feet.
>
> —Marc Chagall

Though the explosive *Aleko* received a few mixed reviews when it later opened in New York—some finding the choreography overwrought and disjointed—most were unqualified raves, and everyone thought Markova's performance a revelation. Carl Van Vechten called her the embodiment of a "priestess of evil," and Grace Robert concurred:

> The great surprise of *Aleko* was the superb Zemphira of Alicia Markova that reminded those aware of her career before coming to America that not always had she dwelt on the remote heights of the *ballet blanc*. . . . Her exquisite *Swan Lake* and matchless *Giselle* contained no hint of the fire and quite different sort of dramatic intensity of her gypsy. With sunburnt make-up, wild hair, and a vivid red costume, her very appearance was a shock, though a delightful one. Nothing was left of the familiar Markova but the thistledown lightness, and authoritative dancing style, now turned to the uses of *demi-caractère*.

At the same time that Markova was contorting her body into Massine's twisted *Aleko* moves, she was rehearsing another role of equal complexity, but opposite temperament. It was Antony Tudor's *Romeo & Juliet*, and the lovesick, blushing teenager was the antithesis of the wild seductress Zemphira.

One of the reasons Markova had joined Ballet Theatre was to work on *Romeo & Juliet* with Fokine. "When I transferred," she recalled, "suddenly the management said they were very sorry, but they had rather sad news. That Fokine had received the score—they had to get it from Russia, this was the early '40s—and he didn't care for it. He didn't feel he could choreograph to it. He didn't wish to use it." She was disappointed, but moved on.

Not long afterwards, Antony Tudor approached Markova asking if she was still interested in the role. "I said, yes, very much. I'd like to do Juliet," Markova chirped. "So he said, 'Would you like me to listen to the score?' I said, please. So, anyway, he listened to the score and the same thing—he didn't feel he wished to do it. So I thought, oh, dear me."

Though a magnificent piece of music, Prokofiev's score was just too full-bodied and grand for the more intimate staging Tudor had in mind. (Choreographer Kenneth MacMillan disagreed and in 1965 created a magnificent *Romeo & Juliet* ballet to Prokofiev's music, immortalized by Rudolf Nureyev and Margot Fonteyn and still performed today.)

Once again, Markova gave up on the project. "So the months went by, and then suddenly whilst we were in Mexico, [musical conductor] Tony Dorati came. He said, 'Can you and Antony come to dinner tomorrow evening? I think I have found the music for *Romeo and Juliet*.' And when we went there he had the idea for Delius."

Frederick Delius's beautiful opera "A Village Romeo and Juliet" had been written at the turn of the last century and embodied more of the innocence of young love Tudor had envisioned. As a side benefit, Delius was British, as were the ballet's choreographer, conductor (Thomas Beecham), and lead dancers (Markova and Hugh Laing). That sense of national pride pleased Tudor no end, as it flew in the face of Hurok's definition of all great ballets being created by Russians.

Too bad Tudor didn't think to consult a British scenic designer. Inexplicably—considering the intimate setting the choreographer had in mind—he approached larger-than-life surrealist Salvador Dalí for the job. (The artist once famously said, "I don't do drugs. I am drugs!") Never lacking in imagination, Dalí proposed a rather distinctive visual for dramatizing the theme of doomed love: making the famous balcony as a great big set of false teeth, ably supported by sky-high crutches.

"I said to Antony, I don't think I could get Juliet across with that," Markova remembered, laughing. "The management agreed. So that went out."

A surrealist artist with more of a romantic streak was approached next, the Russian modernist Eugene Berman. When Berman met with Tudor and Markova, the ballerina made a suggestion that would be the springboard for the production's design.

Following Diaghilev's advice, Markova had spent many hours studying Renaissance art at the Uffizi Museum in Florence, Italy. The way the female figures in the paintings held their hands in repose, and the subtle, graceful tilt of their heads were poses Markova later incorporated into her own delicate dance movements.

Her favorite Renaissance artist was Sandro Botticelli, especially his euphoric *Primavera*. A rapturous work of tremendous scale, the well-known painting provided endless inspiration for the ballet's saturated color palette, costume detailing, and floral motifs.

In fact, Berman's magnificent Botticelli-influenced designs were among the most sumptuous of the early war years. Markova's gold-braided empire-waist costumes were so lushly romantic that they set fashion trends in many cities where the ballet was performed. Published photos of the leading lady as Juliet sent couturiers scrambling for ballet tickets so they could make sketches and take notes.

To let their female readers know all about the opulent period costumes, newspapers sent fashion writers along with dance critics to report on the ballet:

> **Ballet Is Inspiration for Fashions**
>
> . . . Her [Markova's] jewel colored velvet robes de style and flowing, ingénue gowns are truly inspirations for modern fashions. "I find it so much easier to dance and act my roles when my costumes are inspiring," explained the ballerina. "My favorite costume in this ballet is one that is reminiscent of a Botticelli painting. A rose pink lamé foundation has an ice blue overskirt appliquéd with darker blue flowers. Shocking pink, velvet bands outline the bodice . . . and the cuffs are a band of aqua velvet." . . .
>
> "For the potion scene, I wear a gold lamé wedding dress bejeweled with topaz stones. The skirt is designed to represent the petals of a lily, and is very beautiful for the dancing and acting movements of the scene," says the romantic danseuse, with a wave of her slim graceful hands.
>
> —*Detroit Free Press*, 1943

To prepare for her role, Markova read and memorized the entire Shakespeare play. (Apparently, committing words to memory came as easily to her as music.) She told Tudor she wanted to have Juliet's thoughts, words, and actions in her head as she danced.

And Markova had another visual idea. As a 32-year-old ballerina portraying a fourteen-year-old naïf, she decided her dramatic black hair—so right for *Aleko*'s wild gypsy—was totally wrong for Juliet. Instead, Markova asked a wigmaker to duplicate the flowing russet waves of Botticelli's heavenly Venus.

Commented P. W. Manchester: "In the golden dress with its heavy pleats which Eugene Berman designed for her, and the long, red-gold curls which were her own idea, Markova looked like a Botticelli angel, but an angel with a passionate human love and one who was not afraid to show us the ugliness of violent death. There was no favor and no prettiness in her Juliet's death. With her back to the audience, the dagger struck, and her body convulsed, and her limbs contorted in a final agony."

The production—both design and choreography—was extremely labor-intensive, and Tudor wasn't nearly finished when the company returned to the United States from Mexico in the fall of 1942. Markova remembered practicing new steps on every break during the 1942/43 coast-to-coast tour, from train station waiting rooms to the Metropolitan Opera House studio. She even slept in her dressing room to accommodate last-minute rehearsals of Tudor's latest revisions.

Despite all that, nine months after Tudor had begun work on *Romeo & Juliet*, the ballet still wasn't finished. The production seemed as star-crossed as its lovers. Finally, Hurok laid down the law. *Romeo & Juliet* had already been announced for the April 1943 season at the Met in New York, and it was going on—no matter what. With the sets and costumes incomplete and Tudor still toying with the staging, the choreographer decided to present only part of the ballet on opening night.

Hurok was exasperated, but in his inimitably manipulative fashion, planned to tell the audience that the shortened ballet was the result of "concessions to the war effort"—an all-purpose, hard-to-argue-with excuse. But as Donna Perlmutter recounts, the choreographer "wouldn't hear of such a lie." Tudor insisted on addressing the opening night crowd himself, which he did, already costumed and made up as Juliet's hot-headed cousin, Tybalt.

But quite unlike the combative Capulet, the soft-spoken Tudor politely apologized for that evening's abbreviated performance. He also reminded the chi-chi crowd that even at its current 45-minute length, the production was still longer than the average ballet, which generally clocked in at just half an hour.

Tudor then cheerfully invited everyone back to see the finalized version four nights later. That olive branch must have sent Hurok into a complete state of apoplexy, lest the crowd think tickets to that later performance would be compliments of the house. They most certainly were not!

For her part, Markova loved the entire production, especially being reunited with the celebrated British conductor Thomas Beecham.

"Oh, I adored when he conducted, because it was renewing the acquaintance of earlier years in London," she reminisced. "And of course, Beecham and Delius—what more could one ask for? Sol Hurok used to tear his hair out sometimes, because when Sir Thomas became inspired and carried away, we would go maybe ten or fifteen minutes overtime because of the beautiful *legatos*, which *I* enjoyed, but the management didn't. Hugh Laing used to say, 'I don't know if I can hold you up that long!'"

The Delius music was less popular than the revered conductor. Critics disliked it for the very reason it had appealed to Tudor—it just wasn't grand enough for the Shakespearean tragedy.

Dancing Juliet was one of Markova's all-time favorite roles. Critics agreed. "Her new Juliet," wrote Edwin Denby of the *New York Herald Tribune*, "is extraordinary. One doesn't think of it as Markova in a Tudor part; you see only Juliet. She is like no girl one has ever seen before, and she is completely real. One doesn't take one's eyes off her, and one doesn't forget a single move. It doesn't occur to you that she is dancing for an audience, she is so quiet. Juliet doesn't try to move you. She appears, she lives her life, and dies."

Added Grace Roberts: "For once, there was a Juliet who made Romeo's quick reactions believable. Her light darting steps barely seemed to touch the ground. . . . Markova's deerlike shyness in the first scene, her tragic controlled despair, the exquisite movement of her hand as she wakes up in the tomb scene, are all unforgettable in their subtlety."

When the ballet premiered in New York, Markova's dance teacher Vincenzo Celli was in the audience with his wife. The production brought them both to tears, and Celli later told Markova it was like they were back in Verona, Italy, and he could even smell the flowers.

Throughout the 1942–43 season, Markova had expended a herculean effort for Ballet Theatre. Mexico City may have been a rebirth as far as artistic creativity was concerned, but the five months of nonstop work left the dancer in a physically weakened state. Not only had she been performing nearly every night, but she was also tasked with mastering *five* new ballets: Massine's *Aleko* and *Don Domingo*, Tudor's *Romeo & Juliet*, Dolin's *Romantic Age*, and Fokine's *Helen of Troy*.

Though normally a healthy eater, Markova had problems with the Mexican food and her weight dropped to an alarming 89 pounds. Adding to the strain was the high altitude and unusually thin air. Many of the dancers experienced breathing difficulties and dizziness as a result.

Back in the United States, the coast-to-coast tour only added to Markova's health issues. In addition to arduous travel conditions, she had to take on additional roles, as Irina Baronova decided to divorce Sevastianov and leave the company. (The Russian prima ballerina later confessed she had only married the twice-her-age Sevastianov to get away from her abusive mother.) Markova was scheduled to dance every performance of *Giselle*, and only missed one—the curious reason why related in the 1978 memoir book *American Ballet Theatre*:

> . . . On February 9, 1942, the company arrived in Toronto, Canada to discover that Markova and Dolin had been assigned rooms on the thirteenth floor. They refused to remain on the floor with so ominous a number. Payne, who was then the executive director, shamed Markova out of her subservience to superstition, but the Irish Dolin was adamant. Eventually another room was found for him, but Markova remained on the thirteenth floor. That evening in PAS DE QUATRE she sprained her ankle.

Superstitions aside, Markova was exhausted all the time and twice fainted on stage during a performance. While waiting for a bus early one morning in Miami, she placed several overcoats down on the pavement and, with a hatbox for a pillow, lay down and went to sleep. The other dancers looked on in amazement.

Markova so loved what she was doing, she never complained about her workload. She just noted her various aches and pains in her daily agenda book and continued to dance through them. But on Christmas Day 1942, Markova recorded the following in her diary:

> Not better. Doctor came.
> In bed all day. Lunch alone.
> Hugh [Laing] John [Taras] Antony [Tudor] came to see me.
> Had a strange feeling I may die.

Markova may have been a sensation in Massine's *Aleko* and Tudor's *Romeo & Juliet*, but that was all icing on the cake as far as audiences were concerned. When they came to see Alicia Markova, they wanted her to dance the classics, and she continued to mesmerize fans in scenes from *The Nutcracker*, *Swan Lake*, and *Sleeping Beauty*.

Then, of course, there was *Giselle*. The role and the ballerina were inextricably linked. No one thought of one without the other.

"Anyone who has seen Markova's transcendent performance of the Wili has witnessed one of the greatest re-creations the contemporary theater has to offer and certainly one of the greatest interpretations of the role in all its period of existence," wrote Grace Robert.

Markova was to Giselle what Judy Garland was to "Over the Rainbow." When you read that song title, Garland's voice pops into your head. In her day, Alicia Markova was as beloved and iconic as Judy Garland—or Maria Callas, for that matter. But because ballet is so ephemeral, Markova is less well remembered today. There are few video recordings—and even then, one really needed to see her on stage to appreciate her extraordinary gifts.

In 1943, critics across the country declared Alicia Markova the best in the world.

"Alicia Markova is, by practically unanimous consensus, the greatest ballerina alive," wrote *Time* magazine. "She has a combination of flawless classical technique and an ability to project emotion that bowls over even the uninitiates in the audience. Balletomanes may discuss the superb qualities of her sustained Arabesques (balancing on one toe) and battements de gages (kicks from a tiptoe position), but even the man from the street can tell that Markova is a sensation in tights."

John Martin of *The New York Times* upped the ante: "We recognize in her the greatest ballerina of history. . . . 'What!' cries the careful conservative, involuntarily dodging the lightning, 'Greater than Pavlova?' Yes, greater than Pavlova."

It was a lot to live up to.

The famous choreographer Jerome Robbins was a young dancer with the Ballet Theatre when Markova was there. He tells a funny story about the pressure he was under when Markova performed *Giselle*, as he had a rather unusual "supporting" role:

> **Ballerina Catcher**
>
> Ballet Theater Dancer Earned His Position the Hard Way
>
> Twenty-three-year-old Jerome Robbins is the "catcher" of the Ballet theater [*sic*], meaning that it is his particular function to catch ballerinas as they come leaping from the stage into the wings where a jungle of cables and equipment is a hazard to life and limb.
>
> Most important is his job of catching the great classical ballerina, Alicia Markova, as she vanishes from Giselle's tomb and into the darkness of the wings.
>
> "It's a very great responsibility," admits young Robbins. "Miss Markova is the greatest classic dancer of our generation and if I miss my catch, the history of ballet might be substantially altered!"
>
> —*St. Petersburg Times*, Florida, 12/7/42

In July 1943, a record crowd of thirty-five thousand bought tickets to see Markova perform at the Hollywood Bowl in Los Angeles. The conditions were less than ideal. "Dancing in the humid air five nights a week, after rehearsing through a hot, sunny day at the Hollywood Bowl, or in one of the airless dance studios, was having its effect," recalled Dolin.

Several days before opening night, the ballerina noted in her appointment diary: "felt ill, bad hemorrhage, no time for good rest."

The afternoon of the Hollywood premiere, Markova had to forgo her usual nap to attend rehearsals for Massine's latest work, *Mam'zelle Angot*. While attempting an especially difficult spinning backbend in mid-air, she so severely pulled a muscle that she passed out cold. She was helped back to her hotel to recover, but there was no way she could disappoint such an enormous crowd that evening. Making matters worse, Markova was set to dance *Aleko*, with equally tortuous acrobatics. (Hurok insisted the "all-Russian" *Aleko* be continually featured in the company's repertoire. It appeared "to confirm his contention that, when given a choice, Americans preferred their wine French and their ballet Russian," wryly commented Charles Payne.)

The program went on as scheduled and Markova gave her normally fiery performance until almost the end of the ballet. Suddenly she felt a stabbing pain that she just couldn't dance through and dropped to the stage. Co-star Hugh Laing immediately carried her into the wings and an ambulance was called. Another ballerina quickly took Markova's place to finish the ballet, which at that point, required only that she be stabbed to death by Laing's Aleko. But the audience barely paid attention. They were all murmuring about what had happened to Markova.

The pain was so acute that the ballerina thought it was a burst appendix, but the doctors told her she was just suffering from severe muscle strain. Markova would need to rest throughout the summer so she'd be well enough to start the New York season at the Met in the fall. Hurok was beside himself.

Though Markova had always been perfectly content to do absolutely nothing while on her infrequent mini-vacations, the imposed downtime was anything but restful. She was justifiably worried and depressed. But soon her dance coach Vincenzo Celli helped her get back into shape, and she began to cheer up.

While recuperating that summer, Markova's contract was in negotiations for the upcoming year. Rather than being less valued for her injury—as would be true for a baseball player—Markova's absence made her immense worth plain as the nose on Hurok's face.

The *New York Daily Mirror* got the inside scoop:

Markova and Dolin Are Signed by Ballet Theatre

Ballet Theatre has signed Alicia Markova and Anton Dolin to contracts for 1943–44, starting in September. Ballet Theatre

> management sent the dance stars contracts last month, but the terms, financial and scheduling, were not acceptable and they turned them down.
>
> Markova and Dolin went to Florida for a vacation after the Ballet Theatre's spring season at the Metropolitan Opera House and the management conducted negotiations by phone. The stars won all their demands for bigger salaries, top billing and rest periods between major engagements.
>
> Markova is rated by critics the greatest ballerina since Pavlova. Dolin is best of the partners and an excellent soloist. They are not replaceable.

Markova and Dolin were both represented by manager Irving Deakin, and Dolin never would have received such a favorable offer without Markova. She was the golden goose, as theater critic for the *New York Daily Mirror* Robert Coleman made abundantly clear:

> Don't miss Markova, no matter what she dances. She always comes through with a thrilling performance. This marvelous technician will go into the book of the dance along with Taglioni, Elssler and Pavlova. She's making history and it's a privilege to sit in at the writing. You'll tell your children about it some day.

Dolin and Markova also had different sticking points in contract negotiations, he demanding top money and billing, she just wanting a less strenuous schedule. She was rightly worried about her physical stamina.

Fortunately, when Markova finally returned to the Ballet Theatre in September, her dancing hadn't lost any of its enchantment:

> **Markova is Tops in 'Swan Lake' Ballet**
>
> High spot of the Ballet Theatre's program last evening at the Metropolitan Opera House was "Swan Lake," in which the incomparable Alicia Markova danced the Swan Queen with such perfection of style as to be breath-taking.

> But recently recovered from a serious injury, Markova showed no ill effects. Her dancing was marked by amazing precision, stunning equilibrium and beauty of line.
>
> She held her positions so long as to defy the impossible and every figure was executed flawlessly. It was justification of those reviewers who have proclaimed her the finest artist since Pavlova.
>
> Anton Dolin was an admirable Prince Siegfried.
>
> —*New York Daily Mirror*, October 1943

A few days later, Markova was on stage performing for another sold-out crowd, but the repertory was more demanding, including Massine's diabolically difficult *Aleko*.

> **Markova Felled by Fatigue, but Not Till Ballet's Last Curtain**
>
> Already acclaimed as the greatest ballerina of all time, Alicia Markova last night proved she was also one of the best little troupers in show business when she fought off a ravishing fatigue after dancing two successive arduous ballets. She finally collapsed, but not until the final curtain.
>
> Markova danced the opening ballet, "Romantic Age," in flawless style, but then she had to rush upstairs and change her costume for a still more exacting chore in "Aleko." . . .
>
> Then, midway through the ballet, Markova was seen to falter and sag in the arms of Hugh Laing, her partner. But she doggedly kept on until the curtain. Most of the audience was quite unaware of the incident because the final scene is a tableau on which the character portrayed by Markova lies dead.
>
> Later in the dressing room, Markova said, between sips of champagne given to her by a doctor, that come what may she'll dance "Les Sylphides" tonight. That's a great medicine, champagne.
>
> —*New York Daily Mirror*, October 1943

Despite lingering pain, Markova did go on the following evening. *The New York Times's* John Martin was in the audience.

> **Markova is Cheered on Return to Ballet**
> Welcomed by Audience After Illness
> of Previous Showing
>
> Alicia Markova received a most affectionate welcome last night from the Ballet Theatre's audience at the Metropolitan Opera House, where everybody was apparently anxious to show her how glad they were that she had recovered from her indisposition of the night before. The applause after "Les Sylphides" persisted until Anton Dolin brought her before the curtain to receive a personal tribute which included cheering.
>
> The performance of "Sylphides" itself was a beautiful one, and Miss Markova outdanced even her own self.

Markova's recovery wouldn't last. Soon the pain was just too great to ignore, and she learned that she had a ruptured hernia requiring immediate surgery. Massine's somewhat sadistic choreography had done her in.

But Markova wouldn't agree to enter the hospital until she had helped teach her roles to the Ballet Theatre dancers who would be filling in for her. Though the doctors said that was ill-advised, she insisted.

They would have been equally disapproving of Markova's keeping a longstanding appointment at Carl Van Vechten's photography studio the night before her scheduled surgery. She never let him know throughout the lengthy session that she was checking into the hospital the following morning.

Markova was told that the earliest she would be able to go back to work was late in the Christmas season, but there was a frightening caveat. There was a chance that she might never dance again. That was not something the ballerina was even willing to contemplate. Vincenzo Celli had been a principal ballet dancer at La Scala in Milan before a herniated disc cut his career short. While Markova was convalescing alone in her small hotel apartment, Celli visited often, assuring her he would never let his fate be hers.

As the days went by, Markova sank into a deeper and deeper depression. She knew there were rumors in the papers that she'd never dance again, or if she did, she'd never be as good. Dolin called her faithfully every evening at 11:00 P.M. after the curtain went down, giving her

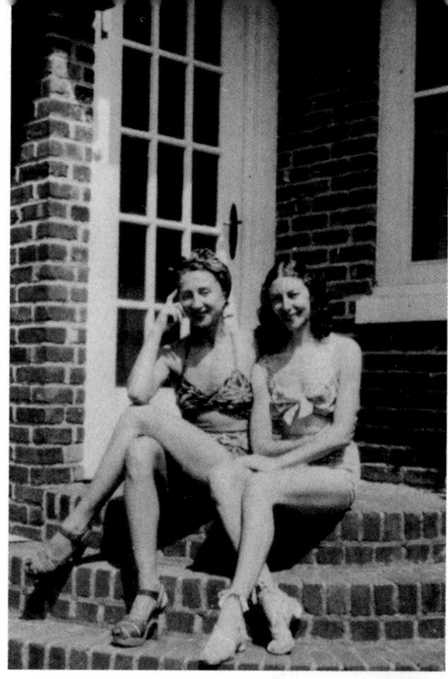

LEFT: Showing off their best assets, Markova and Danilova enjoy a weekend together at Choura's New Jersey country home, 1940.

CENTER: Criss-crossing America and Canada during the war years, Markova spent more time on trains than on stage.

BOTTOM: Markova and her lifelong best friend Alexandra (Choura) Danilova dine *al fresco* in Monte Carlo, 1938.

A. DANILOVA

OPPOSITE TOP: While vacationing with friends in Biarritz, Markova cheerfully posed outdoors with Serge Lifar (1936). Two years later, the egotistical Russian dancer would ruin her Giselle.

OPPOSITE BOTTOM: Dancer Freddie Franklin, a great friend to Danilova and Markova, standing with Choura at her country home in the 1940s.

ABOVE: The delightfully costumed Markova and Massine in the choreographer's *Vienna 1814* for the Ballet Russe de Monte Carlo, 1940. *This page's photo only: Copyright © Maurice Seymour, courtesy Ron Seymour Photography, Chicago.*

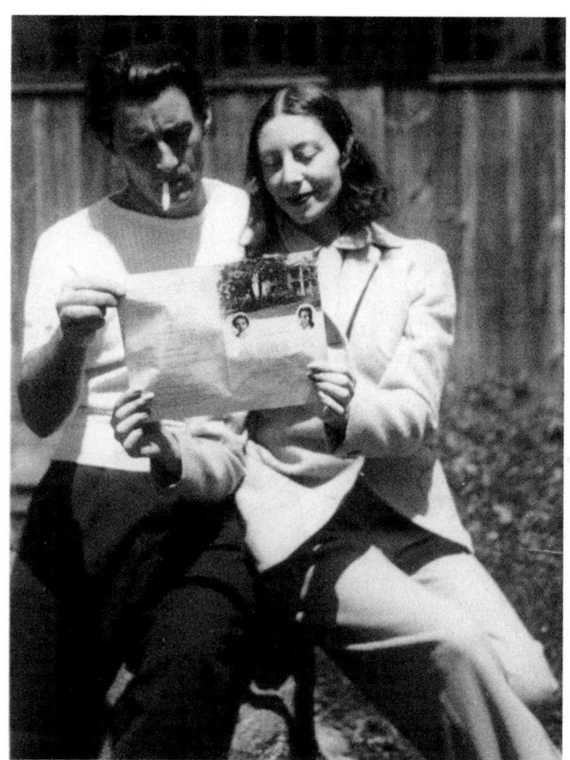

LEFT: Before formally reteaming at New York's Ballet Theatre, Anton Dolin and Markova spent the summer of 1941 supervising a summer school/dance troupe at Jacob's Pillow.

BELOW: Markova and Dolin practicing outdoors at Jacob's Pillow.

OPPOSITE: Balanchine suggested this surreal "armless" publicity pose for Markova as the Queen of Hearts in his production of *Poker Game* (1940) for the Ballet Russe de Monte Carlo.

OPPOSITE TOP: Ted Shawn, longtime director of Jacob's Pillow, credited Markova (shown performing there in 1941) with "saving" the Massachusetts dance enclave from certain financial ruin.

OPPOSITE BOTTOM: The dancers' "jobs" included teaching, performing, and housekeeping, such as sweeping the studio. Markova was one of the first female celebrities to wear pants in public.

ABOVE: Three years after Markova was photographed in this chic fitted checked suit and beret, Lauren Becall wore an almost identical outfit in *To Have and Have Not* (1944). Photo from a 1941 Ballet Theatre tour in New Orleans with Lucia Chase center right, and Dolin far right.

OPPOSITE TOP AND CENTER: Whenever possible, Markova volunteered to serve and entertain American troops at Stage Door Canteens across the country. Countless soldiers sent her thank you notes and fan mail.

OPPOSITE BOTTOM: Markova and Dolin backstage in Los Angeles with the notoriously controlling impresario Sol Hurok, 1944.

ABOVE: Onstage, Markova and Dolin were magic together in *Giselle*, 1940.

LEFT: Markova danced with wild abandon in Massine's *Aleko* (1942) in costumes hand-painted by her great friend, the Russian modern artist Marc Chagall. RIGHT: While working for New York's Ballet Theatre, Markova lived in toe shoes, rehearsing new ballets every day and performing nearly every night.

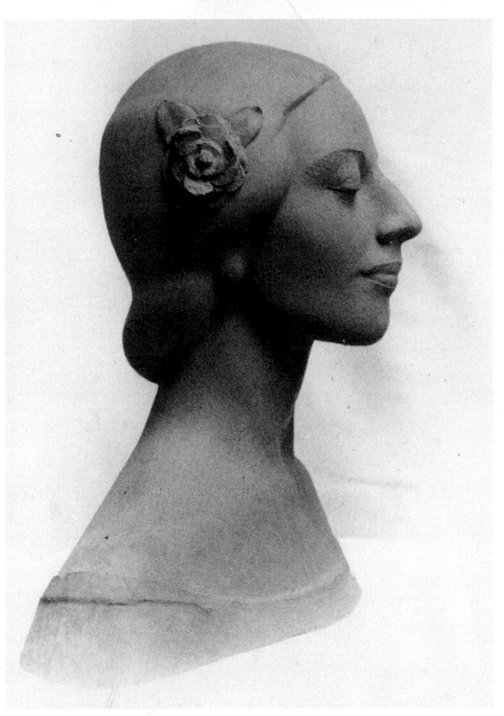

TOP AND BOTTOM: Though Markova was urged to have her "Jewish" nose fixed by male partners and choreographers, photographers and artists found her exotic beauty compelling. (Unkown photographer and sculptor.)

LEFT: Wearing a beautiful native gown presented by the people of Manila, Markova poses in the war-ravaged city where she danced in 100-degree heat with Dolin, 1948.

RIGHT: Markova became the most widely traveled ballerina of her generation, volunteering to tour remote locales all over the globe. Here with Dolin in the Philippines, 1948.

TOP: While on tour with Dolin in South Africa, Kenya, and Mozambique, Markova sat enthralled throughout a five-hour Zulu tribal dance ceremony, just as Anna Pavlova had done 25 years earlier. Here with Dolin and local tribesmen in Johannesburg, 1949.
BOTTOM: In Cape Town, resident Russian artist Vladimir Tretchikoff begged Markova to pose for him between performances, 1949.

ABOVE: Though The Festival Ballet (today's English National Ballet) couldn't get off the ground without Markova's talents and fame, she was treated shabbily by company artistic director Anton Dolin, putting an end to their famous partnership, 1951.

OPPOSITE TOP: When Markova appeared on the popular television variety program *Your Show of Shows*, 30 million American viewers tuned in. Here rehearsing with show choreographer James Starbuck, 1952.

OPPOSITE BOTTOM: The press couldn't get enough of Markova in the 1940s and '50s, here being interviewed about Agnes de Mille's profile of her in *The Atlantic Monthly*, January 1953.

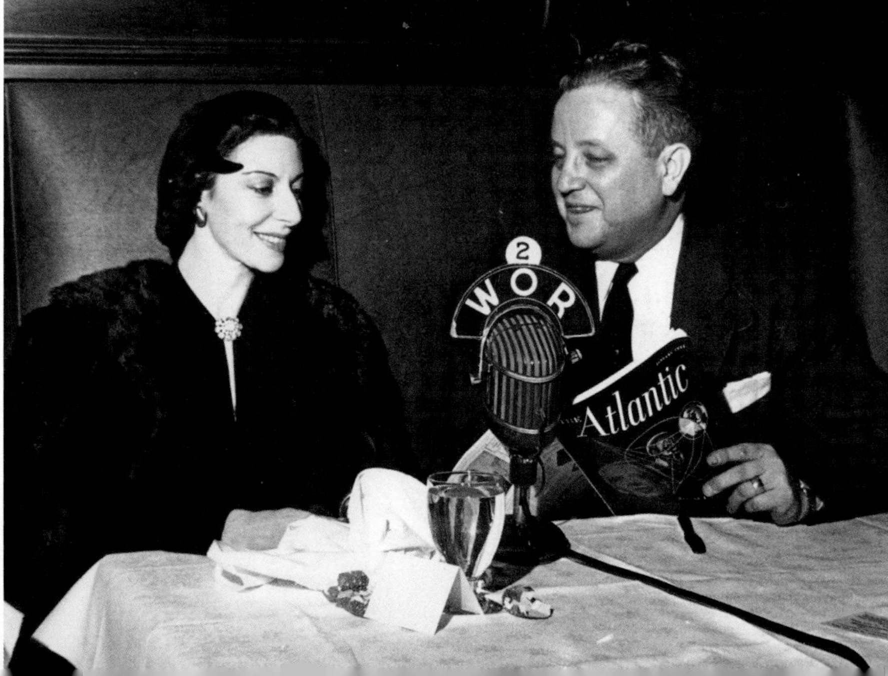
2
WOR
Atlantic

ABOVE: A soulful Markova in rehearsal for Ruth Page's *Revenge* with the Chicago Opera Company in 1955.

RIGHT: British news photographers never missed Markova's comings and goings at Heathrow Airport throughout her career. The ever-chic ballerina had a surprise for them on New Year's Day 1963.

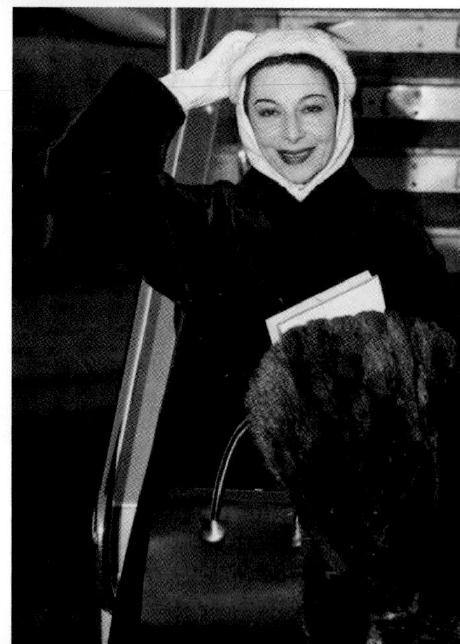

all the latest gossip and encouraging her to start practicing again as soon as possible.

Not to detract from Dolin's thoughtfulness, but he must have been as worried as Markova about her future. He didn't receive such a huge salary for being the world's greatest soloist or choreographer (though he was excellent at both). He was being paid top dollar because he was the world's greatest partner for Alicia Markova.

While still undergoing bed rest, Markova received a phone call from Agnes de Mille, whose choreography for *Oklahoma!* was the talk of the 1943 Broadway season. De Mille told her she had recently run into the colorful New York showman Billy Rose, who was planning a new theatrical extravaganza titled *The Seven Lively Arts*. Rose was interested in featuring top performers in a variety of art forms in one show, and had already lined up Benny Goodman and his orchestra, comedians Beatrice Lillie and Bert Lahr, and composer Cole Porter. In his typical hyperbolic manner, Rose asked de Mille who the best ballet dancer in the world was, and she unhesitatingly answered, Alicia Markova.

De Mille called Markova to "warn" her Rose might be getting in touch, and indeed he did. The impresario wasn't the least bit discouraged that she was currently indisposed, as *The Seven Lively Arts* was planned for the 1944–45 season—a year away. Rose offered to take the recuperating ballerina out to dinner to tell her all about his plans.

"That was supposed to be the show of all shows," Markova remembers. "He had bought what had been the Ziegfeld Theater—it was built by Ziegfeld and it had become a cinema—then Billy Rose bought it back again and had it all put into condition. . . . Dalí did the decoration for the bar. Oh, it was amazing what he had in mind."

Billy Rose never did anything by half. He was a scrappy "slum kid" from the lower East Side of New York who had become a self-made multi-millionaire in the entertainment business. And he was constantly reinventing himself.

First it was writing song lyrics, with hits such as "Me and My Shadow" and "It's Only a Paper Moon." Next it was producing, beginning with shows starring his first wife, Jewish burlesque queen Fanny Brice (later immortalized by Barbra Streisand in the movie *Funny Girl* and subsequent *Funny Lady*, about her life with Rose). Proud of his Jewish heritage at a time when most were trying to hide it, Rose persuaded

Brice to go back to her previously successful Yiddish humor after she had abandoned it—and had surgery to bob her famous hook nose—in an attempt to become a "mainstream" actress. Rose reinvigorated her career, boasting "She stood out like a bagel in a loaf of white bread."

He would go on to produce Oscar Hammerstein II's operetta *Carmen Jones* in 1943, a risky commercial proposition as it featured an all-African American cast. It was Broadway's greatest success story of the season.

Rose alternated between the high- and lowbrow—like "The Billy Rose Aquacade," a water ballet starring ex-Olympic swimmers Johnny Weissmuller (of *Tarzan* movie fame) and Rose's second wife, Eleanor Holm. It was the biggest thing going at the 1937 New York World's Fair, personally netting Rose $80,000 per week. He used those profits to begin building what would become a world-class art collection of Old Master paintings and sculpture, much of it later donated to the National Museum in Jerusalem.

The impresario once famously said, "All it takes to make a lot of money is a lot of money. Money is like a forest fire; it sort of feeds on itself." Money bought the best—and Alicia Markova, he'd been told, was the best.

It was hard not to be swayed by the larger-than-life Billy Rose (who was actually quite short). His enthusiastic belief that classical ballet should be showcased on Broadway was certainly appealing to Markova. Moreover, the two really hit it off. The ballerina was still recuperating and deeply worried about her future, yet here was Rose, pooh-poohing the idea that she wouldn't come back better than ever. She felt stronger just listening to his plans.

But Markova also told Rose that a formal commitment to him was out of the question until she was fully recovered and back performing with the Ballet Theatre. That was fine with Rose. He was a man used to making things happen and wasn't the least bit worried. (They didn't call him "the Little Napoleon of Showmanship" for nothing.)

That might have been the end of discussions for quite a while had the famous pair not been dining out in New York. Heads turned when Alicia Markova and Billy Rose were spotted head-to-head in a see-and-be-seen swank restaurant, and the gossip columns had fun speculating on what possible business interest the Broadway producer might have in the wraithlike ballerina. A squib in the papers caught Hurok's eye. The hotheaded impresario decided to shoot first and ask questions later.

Without ever contacting Markova, Hurok had his lawyers fire off an injunction forbidding her to appear in *any* Billy Rose show. She was rather taken aback, as she had always planned to speak to Hurok before entering into any potential negotiations with Rose—but now her own lawyers stepped in.

Hurok's hasty—and legally unsupportable—actions caused the courts to side with Markova. As her Ballet Theatre contract was up at the end of the 1944 spring season, it was a foolish gambit on Hurok's part.

Dolin was also concerned. If Markova joined Billy Rose without him, his salary and status within the company would undoubtedly diminish. Dolin sent an urgent telegram to Markova from the company's layover in Kansas City, Missouri:

> DARLING FEEL NOTHING SHOULD BREAK OUR PARTNERSHIP NOW WHEN WE HAVE SUCH CONTROL OVER OUR BALLET CONTRACT OUR FUTURE HAPPINESS AND PROSPERITY TOGETHER THIS IS WHAT WE HAVE BOTH BEEN FIGHTING FOR THESE YEARS LONGING SEE YOU ALL LOVE PATTE

Markova, for her part, just wanted to be able to dance again. Beginning with baby steps under Celli's supervision, she was finally well enough to rejoin the company at the end of January. But there were doctors' caveats: no Massine ballets, no eight performances a week, and no full-length *Giselle* until she got stronger. Audiences were quite happy with her Juliet, always achingly rendered and bringing everyone to tears.

Antony Tudor was most anxious for Markova's return as Juliet. In an amusing letter sent from Kansas City on January 17, 1944, he writes of various goings-on at the company, and how much they all look forward to seeing her again. And though he expresses envy at her being able to rest and enjoy time off in New York, he also recognizes her undoubted longing "to get back in harness, or should I say tights and toeshoes, since you are a ballerina and not a mule. Not that there is anything particularly wrong in being a mule on the right occasion."

Tudor's letter is also a reminder of the continued ration situation, despite the war's end in sight. The company's biggest problem, apparently, was the lack of Kleenex. When someone found a supply in a drugstore in Tulsa, the entire company descended and bought out the lot. "Now we are all starting a conservation of Kleenex movement," Tudor stated emphatically.

With or without a sufficient tissue supply, Markova was thrilled to be back dancing with Ballet Theatre. While she was on the road, Billy Rose found a way to irritate Sol Hurok just for the fun of it. Close to curtain time wherever Markova was performing, Rose would telephone the theater and ask to speak with her. "Long distance call from Billy Rose for Miss Markova," echoed loudly backstage for all to hear. When the ballerina picked up the phone, the Broadway showman would simply say, "How are you, honey? Eleanor sends love. Keep well. This is just to make them Goddammed *mad*!" Markova had to laugh. Hurok—not so much.

When Ballet Theatre returned to New York in the spring, Markova decided the time was right to attempt *Giselle* again. She hadn't danced her signature role in over six months. Hurok was ecstatic.

Another "Battle of the Ballets" was brewing with the Ballet Russe de Monte Carlo opening in New York the same evening as Ballet Theatre. The impresario knew Markova dancing *Giselle* meant a sold-out house.

The first performance was scheduled for Easter Sunday, April 9, 1944. That morning, Markova remembers watching from her hotel window as crowds exited St. Patrick's Cathedral. On the street below, the women were modeling their finest bonnets for the Easter parade. Markova had always been a "hat" person, and she greatly enjoyed the show.

When she got to the theater that evening, it was like a dream, she recalled. Markova was more excited than nervous. The audience and critics erupted.

Elsa Maxwell's Party Line

> . . . The opening at the Met was all the more thrilling. You couldn't have squeezed a balletomaniac eel into that ancient edifice, and the standees, packed like tuna fish, had the hypnotic absorption of people watching a fire. And they WERE

> watching a fire—a conflagration of such beauty and talent rarely seen on a single stage before.
>
> Markova, who has been off the stage for six months since her operation, told me afterward that she hadn't the slightest idea of what would happen when she made her entrance in that fascinating and strange two-act ballet. But never has she danced more wonderfully. In her performance I believe this little London girl from the East Side, who was born Alice Marks, reached the apotheosis of her entire career.
>
> —*New York Post*, 4/12/44

> **Ballet Theater Opens Its Season**
>
> . . . The prima ballerina, who had been taken ill shortly after the opening of the last New York fall season, was greeted with long applause at her entrance. In the middle of the second act a demonstration held up the show for an even longer period. This time, however, it was not merely a gesture of sentiment, but one of those rare unanimous and spontaneous responses to accomplishments which are perfect in so many respects that it is difficult to know where to begin analysis. One element among the many is Miss Markova's ability to do the most difficult things so naturally, and in such a way that they merge into one another. Each gesture is not projected as something separately bargaining for its own applause, which is so often the case with Anton Dolin, who danced opposite her with his customary fine technic. He indulged somewhat less in posturing last night, perhaps because he was infused by the general atmosphere of humility established by Markova.
>
> —Arthur V. Berger, *New York Herald Tribune*, 4/10/44

Arthur Berger was a music critic for the *Herald Tribune*. The paper's dance critic, Edwin Denby, was asked to cover both Ballet Theatre and the Ballet Russe de Monte Carlo openings on the same night:

> A trustworthy spy of mine reported that Markova far exceeded any of her previous performances, and that she received at the end the greatest ovation ever heard at the Met. . . . I saw the

> opening of the first act, and found Miss Markova airier in her motions, more delicate and more natural than ever in the past.
>
> —*New York Herald Tribune*, 4/10/44

Billy Rose was also in the audience on opening night. Unbeknownst to Markova, he had never even been to the ballet when they first talked, much less seen her perform. After witnessing the thunderous and relentless ovations for her *Giselle*, he was desperate to have her dance the role with Dolin in *The Seven Lively Arts*. But Markova wouldn't hear of it. *Giselle* wasn't meant to be chopped up and served to the public in popular bite-size pieces.

She did agree to perform in Rose's show, however, for no other reason than that she needed a rest. Needless to say, only Alicia Markova would consider fourteen performances a week (twice nightly) a vacation. But compared to her arduous workload at Ballet Theatre, dancing two *pas de deuxs* each show (without daily rehearsals of any other new ballets) would be like a walk in the park—Central Park, to be exact.

Living in New York for a six-month stretch would give Markova the opportunity to make the city her true home. She would grow to love Manhattan almost as much as London, and kept a "flat" there for the next twenty-five years. But for a ballet star of her stature, her living quarters were surprisingly unglamorous.

Markova's longtime apartment was conveniently located in the Hotel Windsor at 100 West 58th Street. (The Ziegfeld Theatre was at 54th and 6th and the Stage Door Canteen at West 44th in Times Square.) It was a favorite residence of many British expatriate dancers. She had just two rooms—a small, furnished bedroom and a sitting room—plus a bathroom and kitchenette. There was a refrigerator, but no stove, so she was never able to cook, something she was rather good at. But since the apartment was in a hotel, she did have access to room and maid service.

Markova may have been the highest paid ballet dancer of her time, but ballet wasn't nearly as popular as other forms of entertainment, and the salaries were commensurate.

In March 1944, *Life* magazine ran a photo-filled feature on the life of a dancer at the Ballet Theatre. As the reigning star, Markova was singled out in both the photographs and copy:

> Almost every ballerina of any importance is dancing leading roles by the age of 20. Only the best ones are still dancing after 30.
>
> One of these is Alicia Markova—born Lilian Alicia Marks in England—who, at 33, is considered the best of living ballerinas. Like all good ballerinas, she never stops working and studying (see opposite page). For all her greatness, Markova gets only $350 a week, which is considered fabulously high pay for a ballet dancer.

For the year 1943, Markova made less than $15,000. Compare that to dancing film star Ginger Rogers, who earned $219,500 in 1938 alone. And Rogers undoubtedly never had to pay for her own hotel rooms on location or meals on set, or buy the shoes and costumes she wore in the movies.

At any one time, Markova always had six pairs of new toe shoes in her dressing room, all of which she had paid for, and each of which lasted for only a single performance. In the same way a professional tennis player chooses a racquet with just the right tension before each match, Markova carefully selected her toe shoes—all with ribbons she personally hand-stitched—based on the type of ballet, technical moves required, and stage conditions.

She also spent her own money on costumes when she felt it warranted. Ballet Theatre often used rayon during the war years because it was cheaper and more readily available than the rationed natural fabrics. Markova thought that was "cheating" the audience, as her second-act Giselle would look far more dreamlike in satin silk. So Markova paid to have the costumes duplicated in the finer fabric.

And after sending a large portion of her salary home to support her mother and sisters, Markova was hardly a wealthy woman. But she wasn't complaining. She loved to dance, and the opportunity to bring ballet to as many new audiences as possible was reward enough. Besides—there was a war on. As Markova said many times, how can any of us who aren't in battle or constant danger grumble?

After Pearl Harbor, there actually *were* fears that New York might come under attack. "When the United States entered the war, New York was the largest city in the world, with more than seven million residents in the five boroughs and another four million in the nearby suburbs," writes historian Kenneth T. Jackson in his book *WWII & NYC*. ". . . New York's harbor was the busiest, its skyscrapers the tallest, its land values the highest, and its industrial output the greatest. . . . Once war was declared, residents of the city faced the unknown. They had read in newspapers and listened on radios about the Luftwaffle blitz on London in the fall of 1940. Would American coastal cities—New York chief among them—become targets for bombing?"

Although that never occurred, very visible precautions kept everyone on edge. "Eastern Defense Command ordered all lights above 15 stories doused after sunset," writes Jackson. "Coastal streets and parkways were lit just enough to permit safe driving. Bright beachside attractions like Coney Island went black from sunset to sunrise to prevent Nazi U-boats from easily locating transport ships in New York harbors and sinking them."

New Yorkers even experienced air raid drills, with "in case of emergency" signs popping up everywhere. In the *Seven Lively Arts* playbill, the following warning came before the marquee stars' names:

> Emergency Notice: In the event of an alert, remain in your seats. A competent staff has been trained for this emergency. Keep calm. You will receive information and instructions from the stage.
>
> F. H. La Guardia, Mayor

In August 1944, there was good war news to celebrate for a change. Paris had been liberated. The famous gossip columnist Elsa Maxwell—dubbed "The Hostess with the Mostest" for her not-to-be missed celebrity parties—sent out a telegram to all her friends:

> WILL YOU COME TO MY VICTORY PARTY TO CELEBRATE THE LIBERATION OF FRANCE SATURDAY EVENING SEPTEMBER 9
>
> DINNER PROMPTLY AT 8:30 O'CLOCK. BLACK TIE. BRING YOUR COATS FOR ANTON DOLIN, ALICIA MARKOVA WILL DANCE AND ARTHUR RUBINSTEIN WILL PLAY IN THE GARDEN. STOP. ALSO MISS CLAUDETTE COLBERT, MISS GENE

TIERNEY, MR LAURITZ MELCHIOR, MR CHARLES BOYER, MR FRANK SINATRA, MR DANNY KAYE, MR RAY BOLGER WILL APPEAR

R.S.V.P. IMMEDIATELY BY TELEGRAM TO 913 NORTH BEDFORD DRIVE BEVERLY HILLS

ELSA MAXWELL

It was heady company, but most of those stars were already Markova's friends, as was Elsa Maxwell, who she frequently dined with on both coasts. With the Hollywood community chock-full of avid ballet fans, cross-country American ballet tours always included extended runs in Los Angeles. Through various social invitations, Markova had met many people in the film world, bonding immediately with other British expats who she would regularly spend time with on her days off, as she later discussed in an interview with Clement Crisp:

> Greer Garson always, being English, Sunday lunch it was recognized [was] the roast beef and Yorkshire pudding. We'd spend the day with her and her mother or Paulette Goddard—but after she divorced Charlie Chaplin, when she married Burgess Meredith. And they had the house at the beach. The same thing always—Alicia on Sunday—Sunday roast.
>
> And that was because one was so homesick. I felt so cut off. You know it was wartime and so somehow we all used to get together.
>
> I remember we used to go for a picnic sometimes to the beach on our free day and it would be Gladys Cooper . . . and Lillian Gish and Constance Cummings, Merle Oberon and Greer maybe would come along. We all used to gather and take our picnic and sit on the beach there and talk about friends at home. And everybody, we were all trying to do so much, and everybody was trying to earn as much money as possible to send it back home. It was an extraordinary period.

Markova also became pals with contemporary film dancers, many of whom she met at intimate house parties thrown by another of her new Hollywood friends, director George Cukor of *Gone with the Wind* fame.

"I played charades with Gene Kelly in 1943, when I was invited with some friends to his home in Hollywood," Markova later reminisced. "Now, that was an evening of complete relaxation. Inevitably, Gene and I talked shop, but it was all gloriously informal."

In a birthday tribute to Markova many years later, Gene Kelly talked about having been a huge fan from the moment he first saw the ballerina dance. She returned the sentiments. She loved watching Kelly and Ray Bolger rehearse on the film sound stages. "They are such very great artists in their own medium," Markova explained. As a fellow artist, "you could always learn something."

Markova also made a point of keeping up with the latest in modern dance movements. "Very good friends of mine were Ted Shawn and Ruth St. Denis and Martha Graham and Katherine Dunham," she reminisced years later. "When I was dancing in America, it was the beginning of modern American dance. Katherine Dunham used to perform on Sunday nights because modern dance wasn't a big enough draw, so they danced on Sundays. I used to attend their performances and they mine."

Though Markova had told Billy Rose that she wouldn't perform a scene from *Giselle* in *The Seven Lively Arts*, she was happy that he had liked her *pas de deux* with Dolin, and suggested Rose hire him as well. (Rose had originally wanted to feature Markova in a bigger role with a speaking part in the production, but she turned him down. "I have no desire to be an actress or anything other than a ballerina," she told him.)

Dolin jumped at the chance to maintain his partnership with Markova—not to mention the higher salary he would receive for far less work—a bump from $400 to $750 per week! Sol Hurok agreed that Dolin should take a leave from Ballet Theatre, asking him to watch over their "valuable property" by staying close to Markova and making sure she eventually came back "home" to Ballet Theatre.

In July, Billy Rose had dollar signs in his eyes while watching Markova and Dolin perform in front of twenty-two thousand fans at Lewisohn Stadium on the campus of City College of New York. As the *New York World Telegram* reported, "A turn-out of 22,000 ballet-hungry fans, eager to see two dancers in five short numbers, was one more sign of vast changes in the native art world. Ballet is on the best-selling list here and New York wants and is ready for more."

Rose was convinced his new production would be a beneficiary. He asked Dolin to choreograph the two *pas de deux* he would dance with Markova in *Seven Lively Arts* ("The" was eventually dropped from the show's title). For the lengthier, featured ballet, Markova recommended that Igor Stravinsky compose the music. But rather than tell Rose that "Uncle Igor" was a longtime friend, Markova simply said, "He's the best." Rose was all about bests.

George Balanchine was staying with Stravinsky at his home in California during the time he composed the beautiful *Scènes de ballet* score for *Seven Lively Arts.* In Bernard Taper's biography of Balanchine, the choreographer tells the following story about Dolin and Stravinsky:

> The pas de deux was beautiful. The melody was played by a trumpet—a beautiful silver sound, like something you might hear in the woods. But dancers, ballerinas—they really don't believe anything sounds as beautiful as a violin. That's what they really love to dance to—all that heartthrob, you know. So the morning after the first performance a telegram arrives from Dolin, saying, "Ballet great success but if you would allow violin to play pas de deux instead of trumpet it would be a triumph." Stravinsky immediately writes a telegram in reply: "Satisfied with great success."

Scènes de ballet would inspire other choreographers over the years. One was Frederick Ashton, and he came upon the music purely by accident. It was while taking a bath, of all things.

As he humorously related to David Vaughan, Ashton was lounging in the tub one day in his London flat when he heard *Scènes de ballet* on the radio. Intrigued, he called the BBC to find out what it was. He had to laugh upon discovering the music was a Stravinsky piece created specially for his ex-muse, Alicia Markova, who had been faithfully sending him care packages during the war. Ashton would choreograph his own successful ballet to the rhythmic modern score in 1947, danced beautifully by Margot Fonteyn.

For Markova's closing *pas de deux* in *Seven Lively Arts*, Billy Rose asked her to consult with the show's multi-talented music director, the incomparable Cole Porter. The ballerina had a swell afternoon with the composer in his lavish Waldorf Tower living room, as he played song after song on his grand piano.

Porter was surprised Markova turned down *Night and Day*, one of his biggest hits. But the song had been featured in the Fred Astaire/Ginger Rogers movie *The Gay Divorcee* in 1934, and Markova had found the duo's highly romantic "cat and mouse" choreography too deliciously memorable. She thought it best to try something less well known.

Porter then recalled that he had once created a never-used symphonic version of *Easy to Love* for a movie musical several years earlier. Markova loved it, and it became her second orchestration.

As if a private piano concert in Cole Porter's apartment wasn't a special enough memory of her Broadway premiere, Markova also found herself serenaded by the "King of Swing," Benny Goodman.

"Oh, he was wonderful," she recalled fondly. The two met under rather unusual circumstances.

Unlike the tightfisted Sol Hurok, Billy Rose knew how to take care of his stars, giving each not just a private dressing room, but an entire private *floor*—each decorated with its occupant in mind by top interior designer Dorothy Hammerstein (wife of famed composer Oscar). Markova's was like the inside of a ballerina-themed jewelry box—all pale pink and white with *broderie anglaise* (delicate white lace patterning) as accents. On her door was painted a pair of toe shoes. (Benny Goodman got a clarinet.)

"The lift would come up, and then the doors opened, and you had this ante space," Markova explained, "and then it led into your dressing room, your costume room, your bathroom, and your receiving room. So the first floor was Bea [Lillie], and then Bert [Lahr], and then I came, and then Benny and Pat."

As there was a balustrade in the anteroom of Markova's floor, she used it as a *barre* to warm-up. "This one evening," she continued, "apparently Benny was coming down in the lift and pressed the wrong button, and the doors opened. And there was Benny with his clarinet and I was doing my little *entrechats* and everything, so we both looked very surprised."

Markova was amused when Goodman said, "Oh, you're tuning up!" "Yes, I have to," she replied. Goodman then suggested the two "tune up" together. "So from then on, I used to do my warm-up to Benny Goodman playing Mozart or the classics for me," Markova delightedly recalled.

Performing in *Seven Lively Arts* provided Markova with her most tranquil schedule of the past eight years, despite the fact that she worked seven days a week. (Her choice.)

On Sundays off from the Ziegfeld Theatre, she offered to dance *Romeo & Juliet* or *Giselle* with the Ballet Theatre at the Metropolitan Opera House. Markova said it was "a little tedious" performing the same two ballets twice a day every day, "so it was very nice to go over and keep the repertoire going also." Sol Hurok was quite pleased.

Also quite pleased were all the wounded soldiers at a New York Army camp hospital where Markova arranged to perform two or three times every week. The shows were her way of saying "thank you" for their immense bravery. She explained, "To me dancing should be beauty. And there is so little of beauty now in the world" for our men in uniforms. And she was extremely grateful for all the beauty in her own life.

Markova loved living in New York, and New York loved having her there. She was asked to model beautiful clothes in the city's most glamorous magazines, such as a "Snow Bound" layout in *Town & Country*. The caption read:

> Fur below zero, Alicia Markova keeps fair and warm in a mink cape and muff from Jaeckel. Miss Markova enlivens the holiday season with her interpretation of one of "The Seven Lively Arts" in a ballet written for her by Igor Stravinsky for the new Billy Rose revue.

Macy's department store created a Markova-inspired "Celebrity Room" in their home design department, and *Harper's Bazaar* ran a photo of Markova in her quite fashionable practice attire: a fitted hand-knit sweater with peplum, short tulle tutu, knit tights, satin toe shoes, and pearl sunburst earrings. Today, she could wear that same outfit (minus the toe shoes) on the streets of any fashion capital in the world and be considered modern and chic.

Seven Lively Arts was a modest hit with the critics, but was popular with the public. More Ed Sullivan-type variety show than Broadway musical, it was quite an extravaganza. "Stripped of its fancy wrappings, The Seven Lively Arts is oversized and overstuffed," reported a reviewer in *Time Magazine* (12/18/44). "The big names frantically jostle one another. . . . For all that, The Seven Lively Arts is quite a show."

Lewis Nichols of *The New York Times* felt similarly (12/8/44): ". . . Billy Rose has piled a little bit of everything but the kitchen sink—and if that could dance or were pretty, it probably would be there too. . . . It is big and rambling, and sometimes it is top-heavy, but there is no getting away from the fact that as a Broadway show it is right in the groove, like Benny Goodman, who is part of it."

Critics thought Dolin's choreography for himself and Markova was pleasing enough, if uninspired; but ballet neophytes were completely charmed. Performing on Broadway introduced Markova to a whole new audience, and her fame grew—especially in New York. (A local gossip columnist spotted "Jose Greco, a famous dancer himself, lining up with other worshippers at the Ziegfeld Theater to get Alicia Markova's autograph.") Balletomanes, however, were concerned that she had permanently "defected," especially those in England.

While Markova was on Broadway, Anna Pavlova's jewelry collection was being auctioned at Christie's in London. Victor Dandré passed away in February 1944, and everything he had saved from his former great love was up for sale. The *London Daily Express* sadly reported on the story of Pavlova's things being undervalued:

> . . . Last memento of the Dying Swan: A gold swan brooch with a pearl body. It fetched £32. Said an onlooker: "Maybe it's only worth that, but as a Pavlova relic, it will sell for ten times its value. What are the dealers thinking of?"
>
> Somebody else wondered whether any present-day ballerinas have anything of Pavlova's ethereal glamour. Well, Markova (Alice Marks to her London parents) is the nearest

> thing. But she is not in a ballet company any longer. She is pirouetting in a Broadway musical called "The Seven Lively Arts." No dying swans for her.

They needn't have worried. Markova was just "on vacation." And she quite enjoyed it. The regularity of her schedule and six-month break from grinding tours was a huge boost to her well-being, both physically and mentally. For one thing, she got to spend far more time with Danilova, which brought great joy to them both. As Markova told a local newspaper when interviewed about her first turn on Broadway:

> . . . A ballerina with no aspirations to be anything other than a ballerina is the petite black-haired, black-eyed Alicia Markova, who is here to guest star with the Ballet Theatre during its week engagement at the Opera House starting tomorrow night.
>
> Speaking as lightly, facilely, and pointedly as she dances, the English-born star of Monte Carlo and Ballet Theater companies will tell you Alexandra Danilova is her dearest friend. . . .
>
> Her friendship with Danilova dates back to that early association with Diaghilev when Danilova was ballet mistress. The famous star took the little English girl in charge and was a regular big sister to her, and, although they have since been costars and rival stars on the same stage, the professional rivalry has in no way affected their friendship.
>
> —*New York News*, 5/22/44

Danilova got her own press coverage on the pair's great friendship:

> BALLET NOTE: After the Ballet Russe finished at the New York Center of Drama and Music the other evening, Danilova, the dancer, hastily brushed off her make up and practically flew from her dressing room to the street. Crossing Sixth avenue on Fifty-fifth street, she was almost hit by a motor car. But she continued on down Sixth until she reached the Ziegfeld

> Theater stage entrance. The doorman tried to stop her but without wasting a moment on him, she whizzed upstairs and almost onto the stage just before the final number of "The Seven Lively Arts." Danilova had almost broken her neck and arches to see a ballet sequence danced by her very good friend, Alicia Markova.

While Danilova was like a tonic, Billy Rose's star treatment came in a close second. His generosity went beyond giving Markova an entire floor at the Ziegfeld Theater. Rose genuinely liked the ballerina. (And not as a conquest for the legendary philanderer.) During summer rehearsals, Rose and his wife Eleanor liked to play host to Markova at their Mount Kisco country retreat in tony Westchester. (It was "the best"—a Georgian red brick mansion filled with art and 18th-century antiques.)

And there was no hidden agenda. Rose hadn't invited Markova with a large crowd just to show her off. He just wanted her to be able to relax and get a nice break from the hot city. And it was.

Back in Manhattan, Markova's social life picked up.

By 1944, Markova and Stanley Burton had been forced to admit that it was impossible to maintain any kind of romantic relationship without seeing each other for five whole years. Even communicating by mail had been difficult due to the war, as excerpts from Markova's letters to her beloved illustrate:

> *Darling,*
>
> *For two months I didn't hear from you & was a little worried until yesterday when I received two letters & a card altogether. So glad that you are well but life must be so tense & wearing on one's nerves. . . .*

> *My darling,*
>
> *I couldn't understand why I hadn't heard from you for so long & now I have received five letters all together. They made me very happy except for the one where you said you hadn't received a letter from me for a long time. That distressed me very much as I wrote quite often. I suppose one cannot grumble about the mail these days*

> *but just be thankful that the letters get there somehow. My mother also cabled me that she hadn't received a letter for 3 months & I had written every week without fail. . . .*

It was an understandable split, but one that Markova never seemed to completely get over. Her heart was truly broken. In later years, she would often reminisce about what might have been, and she maintained a great friendship with Burton and his future wife Audrey.

From Markova's diaries in the mid-1940s, she appears to have become a serial monogamist after her breakup with Burton, avoiding getting too serious with anyone. A man's first name—Alvin, Jerry, David—would appear regularly on her calendar for several months, with a notation where and when they went out together. Then the name would disappear, perhaps after a note like the following:

> August 27, 1946
> Slept until 11.
> Lunch Jerry at Longchamps, then shopping.
> He gave me a gold compact & asked me to marry him.
> Tea home. Rested. Dinner home. Helen B. came.

The men really couldn't complain when Markova eventually turned them all down, as she never led them on in the first place. The ballerina made it quite clear to everyone—and in newspaper and magazine interviews—that marriage was out of the question while she was still dancing. As one headline read:

> **I Can't Ask a Man to**
> **Take Second Place, Says Markova**
>
> "Leading the life I do . . . that would please few husbands.
>
> "That is why, adoring my work as I do, I have always felt it would be grossly unfair to expect any man to take second place to my dancing.
>
> "To those men who have been kind enough to suggest I should take their name, I have steeled myself and said no.

"But life is full of surprises and I am usually ready for the next one.

"One day I may decide to hang up my dancing shoes for the last time—frankly I don't visualize that day at the moment—but when it does eventually arrive, who knows?

"I'm a very adaptable sort of person and could, I think, adjust myself to a cosy, homelike life."

Life doesn't always go as planned.

10

Taking Flight

Many Happy Returns to Ballerina

There is cause for celebration. . . . For it is the birthday of Alicia Markova, the first she has celebrated in this country for 12 years.

This time last year she was in San Francisco, the year before somewhere else. Which should give you an idea of the life of a ballerina of international reputation.

"It's certainly a gipsy [*sic*] life," she said, when I met her in Bristol hotel. She has a flat in New York and "roots" in London too, for her sisters have a flat there.

But most of the time she is on the move, and as far as I can gather she has danced in every country except India and Australia.

—*Bristol Evening Post*, England, 12/1/49

When *Seven Lively Arts* finished its almost-six-month run in the spring of 1945, Alicia Markova was rejuvenated and restless to get back to what she liked best—bringing ballet to new audiences everywhere. Having conquered Broadway—and mingled with celebrated thespians like Katharine Cornell and Helen Hayes at New York theater parties and events—she was now more famous than ever.

Before rejoining Ballet Theatre, Markova and Dolin went on holiday to California. It would be Markova's last vacation for a very long time. She made the most of the social whirl. On one Saturday, as she recorded in her diary, it was: "Lunch at Rubinstein's" [pianist Arthur] and "Basil Rathbone dinner party. Lovely time;" followed by Sunday's "Lunch at Paulette Goddards," "Tea at George Cukor's," and evening at "Hurok's party."

Dolin could certainly no longer claim that Markova was an unsociable mouse. She was one of the most stylish and popular women in Beverly Hills.

Alexandra Danilova had often commented on the lack of sophistication in film stars' wardrobes. It was always "slightly exaggerated," she said. "[I]f it was a narrow skirt, it would be a little too narrow, a wider skirt, a little too wide." Hollywood was larger than life and prone to exaggeration in so many things.

In contrast, Markova was the epitome of chic. Never flashy, and not one for dripping jewels, she had a quiet elegance, favoring subtle neutral colors or basic black, accented with a single gold brooch or pearls. Combined with her enviable lithe physique, natural grace, and reserve, the ballerina always turned heads—even in Hollywood.

At thirty-four years old, Markova had never looked more attractive, making the most of her unconventional beauty with flawless makeup and understated designer clothes. And she made her appearance look effortless, just like her dancing.

Markova's one evident extravagance was her mink coat. Every star and socialite had one, but in the ballerina's case, it was her travel necessity. If she was cold, the fur was her blanket; if tired, her mattress; and whenever she arrived at her destination, putting it on gave her instant glamour for the press.

Thanks to Billy Rose's generous salary, Markova was no longer the nose-pressed-against-the-glass window shopper from her early New York days alongside Danilova. She could now afford luxurious fashions, her one lifelong indulgence. Fortunately for Markova—and fine stores everywhere—Ballet Theatre was willing to match Rose's $750 per week wages (more than doubling her former salary of $350) when she returned to the company in 1945. It was an unheard-of amount for a ballet dancer in those times, and one also paid to Anton Dolin. He would continue to partner Markova and choreograph the company's classical productions. They were a team, after all.

There were several reasons those astronomical wages made any kind of economic sense. First was the country's newfound love affair with ballet, as touted by *Life* magazine, one of the most popular publications of its day:

The Ballet

It Fills America's New-Found Liking for Classical Dance and Spills Over Into Musical Comedy

> To most Americans, the ballet for years meant a hammy kind of culture which was danced on tiptoe by dainty men and women, was enjoyed only by fancy people and was patronized heavily by kings and dukes who liked ballerinas for reasons other than their dancing. Except when they suffered through stage presentations in movie houses, Americans were aware of the ballet mainly when Pavlova toured the country in the 1920s and was followed wherever she went by vaudeville parodies of dying swans. Americans unashamedly enjoyed the parodies more than the original. . . .
>
> [T]he ballet has become a huge popular success in the U.S., far outdoing any success it ever knew before. . . . This year the Ballet Theatre, whose dancers are shown in photographs and paintings on these pages, and another top-notch troupe, the Ballet Russe de Monte Carlo, have made successful tours of 82 and 80 U.S. cities respectively.
>
> —*Life*, March 20, 1944

Life was known for its spectacular photography, and the article above featured Markova in stop-motion freeze frames to illustrate one of her astounding leaps. Equally intriguing was a full-page photo of Markova and Antony Tudor standing precariously atop chairs, with the choreographer bending dangerously backward, one foot on each of two chairs. The caption read: "Antony Tudor demonstrates a difficult gesture to Alicia Markova in rehearsing balcony scene in 'Romeo and Juliet' ballet." Readers ate it up.

The *Life* magazine article ran in the spring of 1944 before Markova had left the company for *Seven Lively Arts*. Sol Hurok wanted her back.

According to the company's executive director Charles Payne, in 1945, "Hurok still maintained that it was impossible to sell Ballet Theatre without billing it as 'The Greatest in Russian Ballet.' As for stars, he refused to accept Nora Kaye [American] and Hugh Laing [British] as substitutes for Markova and Dolin and demanded that the latter pair be re-engaged (they had withdrawn to appear in Billy Rose's *Seven Lively Arts*) regardless of the cost to Ballet Theatre."

Never mind that neither Markova nor Dolin was Russian. Their renown in classical Russian ballets was all that mattered, and at least Markova's name fit the bill.

Hurok had several other reasons to quickly sign Markova to a new contract, whatever the cost. Ballet scenes had become very popular in the movies in the early 1940s, luring beautiful ballerinas like Irina Baronova and Tamara Toumanova away from their respective dance companies to take up residence in Hollywood. Dance magazines bemoaned this fact:

> **The Boom in Ballet**
>
> . . . The high salaries offered strongly tempt girls to desert the rigorous life of the touring ballerina committed to ballet repertory. . . .
>
> Artistry usually suffers when ballet dancers leave the ballet proper. There are many reasons for this. The Broadway or Hollywood ballet number is sometimes a disconnected pastiche of ballet passages, hardly stimulating to the performers. . . . Further, the constant exercise required in full ballet repertory work can often be skimped in less exacting fields, and the dancers are likely to lose top condition and style. Nor is there the steady goad of competition from younger ballet dancers in the corps. All in all, while it may be sensible for ballerinas of great personal charm but not superlative talent—girls like Vera Zorina—to seek careers in show business generally, an

> absolutely top-rank ballerina like Markova or Danilova seems to require persistent challenge of the ballet discipline in order to maintain her preeminence. Ballet dancers, like other artists, cannot flirt with the entertainment world without seriously risking quality.
>
> —*Dance Magazine*, December 1945

Unbeknownst to Hurok, Markova quite agreed with that assessment. While performing in California with Ballet Theatre, she had unexpectedly gotten her own taste of moviemaking, as explained later that year in the *New York Sun*:

> Alicia Markova's movie debut was unexpected. She had not thought of pictures when she danced with the ballet in Los Angeles. It was Richard Rowland who realized this slim, dark young woman should be photogenic. Mr. Rowland was making "A Song for Miss Julie" at the time. He promptly asked Miss Markova and her dancing partner, Anton Dolin, to appear in the film.
>
> It was well that he acted promptly. The ballet troupe was leaving that week. Miss Markova and Mr. Dolin conferred, decided on a classical style and selected some Mendelssohn music. They had only one day in which to make their sequence. Miss Markova, who has seen the picture at a preview, chuckled a little as she remarked:
>
> "We had taken such pains to arrange the dance with the music. They had already recorded the sound, of course. We danced to the playback of the records. Then, when we saw our sequence, we found they had reversed the order of the music. The first part came last, the last first."
>
> —Eileen Creelman, *The New York Sun*, 1945

It's not surprising that Markova later said she felt dancing in the movies was "cheating," as the cutting, editing, and special effects could completely alter the mood and original step sequences. She was quite happy to leave Hollywood behind and become a full-time touring prima ballerina once again.

But even if Hurok was aware of Markova's negative attitude toward dance films (or returning to Broadway for that matter), he had one additional reason to lock her and Dolin into long-term contracts. With the war winding down (victory in Europe would be declared on May 8, 1945), America's biggest ballet box-office draws would be able to return home to England.

Markova's family certainly wanted her back. In June 1945, she received a letter from a law office in London informing her that Mrs. Laura Henderson (sponsor of the Markova-Dolin Company) had passed away the previous year, bequeathing a beautiful diamond brooch to her favorite ballerina. The solicitor added, "I got your address from your sister, who said that she was hoping you might be coming back to this country soon." The English ballet-going public shared those sentiments.

Hurok spared no expense to keep Markova under contract to him, and she wouldn't return to England for another three years. His faith in her moneymaking ability was well founded. When dancing *Giselle*, Markova always sold out the house.

One of her fans was Liberace, who started his career as a struggling classical pianist in New York where he befriended Markova and Dolin. In 1945, the three performers were all in Chicago at the same time—the dancers on stage with Ballet Theatre and Liberace opening at the Empire Room in the Palmer House Hotel. Liberace planned to change his traditional concert performance and go "commercial" in Chicago, for the first time topping the grand piano with what would become his signature glitzy candelabra.

When he learned Markova and Dolin were in town, Liberace begged them to come to his opening to calm his nerves. He dedicated his first Chopin waltz to Markova, as a tribute to her magical performance in *Les Sylphides*. Markova also became friends with Liberace's mother and brother George, often getting together with all three in New York, and later Europe. The flamboyant pianist and reticent ballerina may seem an odd couple, but they bonded over a shared love of music.

Victory over Japan was declared on September 2, 1945. While it would take a very long time for England to recover emotionally and financially from the brutal war, Americans didn't face bombed-out buildings as a constant reminder like their counterparts across the pond. Though returning American soldiers and their families needed time to readjust to a changed society, war rationing and feelings of deprivation would soon be a thing of the past in the United States.

Just one year earlier, programs at Broadway shows and concert and dance performances included the following message:

> Because of governmental restrictions, The Playbill, in common with all publications, will have to curtail its consumption of paper. During this emergency it will not be possible to furnish a copy of The Playbill to every person. With your cooperation this regulation can be met without hardship if you will share your copy of The Playbill with your companion.

It was a small thing, certainly, but a reminder that all was not well. Now life would be getting back to "normal."

For Markova, that meant continuing to wow audiences, as John Martin confirmed when Ballet Theatre returned to Manhattan for the fall 1945 season—the first since the war officially ended:

> **Ballet Theatre Opens in 'Giselle'**
>
> . . . What remains to be said of Markova's "Giselle" at this late date? It is one of the established masterpieces of the repertoire, and its fluctuations are so slight as to be generally negligible. Last night, if it varied at all from precedent, it was only to seem more brilliant, more touching, more a triumph of style. The little interpolated solo in the first act, the mad scene, the entrance in the second act and the great solo of that act were all magnificent. Not only technically but dramatically and poetically it was a superb performance.
>
> Anton Dolin has quite apparently given time and care to rehearsing the production and it has rarely moved with more authority. His own playing of Albrecht was finely subdued on the dramatic side, neatly danced and altogether cooperative.
>
> —John Martin, *The New York Times*, 10/8/45

Unlike Serge Lifar's *Giselle,* Dolin's critically praised choreography of the Russian classic was truer to the original Petipa version, showing the prima ballerina to the best advantage. And Dolin's coaching also drew more emotionally satisfying performances from the other dancers. Despite his personal love of the limelight, Dolin was completely unselfish on stage, the opposite of many male dancer/choreographers, such as the self-centered Lifar and Léonide Massine. It can't have been easy to have one's performance called "altogether cooperative" by the country's preeminent dance critic. Yet Dolin continued to be the most generous onstage partner Markova would ever have. Consciously or unconsciously, he seemed to feel she owed him for that professional generosity. The financial rewards of their partnership apparently weren't enough. Dolin wanted to be the offstage boss of the pair as well, and it would result in increased friction between them in the years to come.

But in 1945, Markova was quite content. Though at the peak of her dancing career, she remained very approachable and down to earth. When featured in a lengthy profile for the *New York Post,* the prima ballerina was photographed not as "Giselle" floating in a diaphanous tutu, but rather in street clothes while spiritedly chomping on an apple.

Twinkletoes of the Met

> There is probably no dressing room in any theatre anywhere that is more loaded with flowers than No. 12 of the Metropolitan Opera House during Alicia Markova's tenancy.
>
> "It's funny," says the little prima ballerina of the Ballet Theatre, "different ballets bring different flowers. 'Giselle' always brings lilies—white Easter lilies." . . .
>
> Markova accepts her flowers simply and easily, just as she does the applause of her audiences and the ecstasies of the critics, who call her a "miracle" and "greater than Pavlova." And she sits in No. 12 unaffected, relaxed and seemingly untired after four hours of steady rehearsing, munching a big red apple and answering questions in her light, childlike voice. Her inflection is British, for she was born Lillian Alicia Marks in a suburb of London.
>
> —Mary Braggiotti, *New York Post,* 10/31/45

In addition to *Giselle*, Markova also starred in the title role of Ballet Theatre's *Firebird*, the first restaging of Mikhail Fokine's work since the Ballets Russes. Hurok had been lobbying for the Russian fairytale ballet for quite some time. It seemed a natural for the company, as the dancer who played the lead in Fokine's original production, Adolph Bolm, was now a choreographer at Ballet Theatre. Hurok also enlisted Igor Stravinsky to revise his original score.

But Ballet Theatre management wasn't sold on producing *Firebird*—an expensive undertaking—and used it as leverage in contract negotiations with Hurok.

As Charles Payne recalled, the impresario let his enthusiasm for the Russian ballet cloud his business judgment, eventually signing an agreement to personally pay for any of the ballet's production costs exceeding $15,000. Worse still, revealed Payne, Hurok "had not retained any control over such costs."

Trouble arose when the Ballet Theatre appointed Oliver Smith co-director in 1945. Smith was a brilliant set designer, previously having worked on ballets with Massine and Agnes de Mille. (Later, Smith would also create sets for the legendary Broadway shows *West Side Story*, *My Fair Lady*, and *Camelot*.) Smith took one look at the proposed *Firebird* costume sketches—and already *completed* scenery—and declared them far too conventional and uninspired for Ballet Theatre. Despite the sizeable initial monetary investment, they were all immediately scrapped.

Few, however, would argue with Smith's choice of a new designer, least of all Hurok. It was the impresario's fellow Russian—modern folk artist Marc Chagall, who had already proved himself an innovative ballet set designer on *Aleko* three years earlier. Too bad Hurok never thought to ask about the revised budget.

As had been true with *Aleko*, Chagall's *Firebird* sets and costumes were bold, breathtaking, and a joy to behold. John Martin thought them a bit too spectacular:

> **Décor by Chagall Dominates Ballet**
>
> . . . There is no use even pretending that it [Firebird] is much of a ballet, but it is an excitingly beautiful spectacle. Ballet Theatre apparently did not learn from its first experience with Chagall in "Aleko" that no ballet can stand up against his designs. They

> are overwhelming, and in front of them the conventional human being looks insignificant. He creates a naïve and irresponsible world without gravity or function, in which only creatures of similar mold can move without being rank intruders. . . .
>
> Naturally enough, Mr. Bolm's choreography is not in such an idiom, and though Alicia Markova in the title role dances brilliantly, not even the two of them can succeed in taking the eye and mind from Chagall.
>
> —*The New York Times,* 10/25/45

But many other reviewers disagreed, finding Markova's *Firebird* as spellbinding as Chagall's scenery.

> **The "Firebird" Is Presented**
>
> Triumph for Markova In Last Night's Ballet
>
> . . . As presented last night the ballet served more as a vehicle for the brilliant art of Alicia Markova than anything else. But this in itself was enough. The ballerina's Firebird was a thing of beauty and passion, magnificent skill and inimitable grace. The figure of this dancer dominated the scene, and her exhibition was one of the most rewarding spectacles Montreal balletomanes have seen in this city.
>
> She was at once the glittering and unearthly supernatural being, flitting and darting in the transports of joy, and a tragic figure, wounded by her love for mortal man. Partnered by Anton Dolin, she danced with conviction and a haunting and an exquisite grace and passion whose memory will remain long with her audience.
>
> —*The Gazette, Montreal,* 3/20/46

For Markova, costume fittings and rehearsals for *Firebird* meant a chance to spend more time with her great friend Marc Chagall. As had been true with Matisse, the Russian artist created Markova's costume directly on her body, as she explained:

> For this we met in the studio of Edith Lutyens, the costumier, to discuss my costume. Chagall had asked Edith to make me

> a leotard of gold lamé, as there was no design, and he would then create the costume on me. Pieces of net in all colours were chosen and cut into feather-like shapes. With the leotard complete, I stood while Chagall used these fragments like paint, placing them on my body, at which moment Edith pinned them to the leotard.

The headdress was highly dramatic, with a large beak on one side and a crown made from bird of paradise feathers. But it was the makeup that really astounded. It began with a dark brown all-over body wash. When that was dry, patches of a greasy substance were applied to the ballerina's back, legs, arms, and shoulders. Next, gold dust was sprinkled—or rather thrown at her—by the dresser, sticking only to the grease. The result was that Markova seemed to shimmer on stage, just like a bird's glistening feathers in the sun. While performing *Firebird*, Markova bought gold dust by the pound.

It was quite a spectacular effect, and one that took a great deal of time to both apply and remove. Markova quickly learned that the gold dust was so rough, it couldn't be wiped off without severely scratching her skin. The only way to remove it painlessly was to soak it off slowly in a warm tub or shower.

Because of the complicated body makeup, *Firebird* was always the last ballet of the evening, as Markova never would have had time to change for any other roles. But that still meant leaving the theater covered in gold dust, which she would later painstakingly soak off in her apartment or hotel. In order to be able to join friends for an after-show supper, Markova covered her arms and shoulders in a soft black cashmere turtleneck to avoid looking like a glittering Vegas showgirl.

Touring presented its own set of problems. As usual, Markova frequently was required to quickly exit the theater after her final performance to make a bus, train, or plane connection to the next scheduled venue. She certainly didn't have time to take a hot bath. But even with the turtleneck as cover, the ballerina spent many an uncomfortable night trying to sleep sitting up while covered in itchy gold dust.

Sometimes the next booking was a one-night stand, generally in a smaller town where the company performed in a school gymnasium rather than a proper theater. That required Markova's going straight from the train to the school's rehearsal stage, rather than checking into a hotel. The local athletic team must have wondered why their locker room appeared to be paved with gold the day after the ballet had been in town. Markova's first stop was always the shower stall, and she tended to leave some rather tiny gold footprints.

Unions would later demand higher fees for performers who had to endure complicated makeup applications, but those regulations came too late for Markova—something she used to joke about. Actually, she enjoyed the challenge of dancing the *Firebird* and became quite fond of choreographer Adolph Bolm. In addition to collaborating with her on the ballet, Bolm gave Markova a helpful survival tip for life on the road.

It happened when the company was traveling in the frigid Dakotas and Markova became quite ill. Due to tight scheduling, she needed to leave the comfort of her hotel bed for a rough train ride with the rest of the company. Underfed, chilled, and feverish, the stuffed-up ballerina was miserable.

At the first stop, Bolm ran out to the nearest drugstore and bought her several cans of baby food. Heated up, it was soothing, easy to digest, and nourishing, making her feel stronger, if not well. Markova was always grateful to Bolm for his kindness, and "thereafter I never traveled without such emergency rations."

Firebird would prove problematic for Sol Hurok for very different reasons than scratchy gold dust. Chagall's elaborate set designs and costumes ended up costing the impresario a whopping $19,000 surcharge. Ballet Theatre held his feet to the fire for payment, refusing to present the ballet on opening night until all the bills had been paid. Hurok reluctantly wrote the checks.

When Hurok and Ballet Theatre parted ways six months later, the impresario got to keep the glorious *Firebird* scenery as part of his "divorce" settlement. Uncharacteristically, he generously donated it back to Ballet Theatre in 1949 for a new, and highly praised, production of the ballet choreographed by George Balanchine.

The official breakup between Hurok and Ballet Theatre in April 1946 was a long time coming, according to Charles Payne. The final straws for both parties were accusations of Ballet Theatre's "conspiring with local managers to undermine Hurok"—which was true; and

Hurok's violating his management contract by both creating a separate Markova-Dolin Company, and agreeing to manage modern dance sensation Martha Graham—also true.

Markova's last *Giselle* for Ballet Theatre was in April of that year in New York.

> **'Gizelle' [*sic*] at Met Holds Audience Spellbound**
>
> Alicia Markova, Anton Dolin, and Nora Kaye gave an amazing demonstration of mass hypnotism at the Metropolitan Opera House last evening. Dancing "Giselle" superbly, they held a capacity audience spellbound for two acts and one hour.
>
> The spell was finally broken by the curtain's fall, which was the signal for the more than 3,000 present to snap out of their trance and give the trio of artists the most enthusiastic ovation of the Ballet Theatre's current season.
>
> The marvelous Markova surpassed herself in the title role. Her dancing was magnificent and her acting wonderful. In the mad and death scenes, she had handkerchiefs dabbing moist eyes throughout the house. And there were audible sobs.
>
> Were Newton alive today he would restate his laws of gravity, or charge Markova with being an enchantress. Never have we seen a ballerina so buoyant. By comparison a feather becomes heavy as lead, a fleecy cloud a wing of steel.
>
> —Robert Coleman, *New York Mirror*, 4/25/46

Added Edwin Denby of the *Herald Tribune*, "Alicia Markova in 'Giselle' is Ballet Theatre's greatest glory."

She would certainly be missed.

The new Markova-Dolin Company under Hurok management was the antithesis of the original British incarnation, this one streamlined and built for ease of touring. There were only twelve dancers including the two principals, but they were all experienced performers, such as the winning American ballerina Rosella Hightower (who had previously worked with Markova at the Ballet Russe de Monte Carlo and Ballet Theatre) and leading Russian male soloist George Skibine (who had just returned to the U.S. from serving in the Army). Unlike Anna Pavlova, Markova wasn't looking to be the one and only star among an inexperienced *corps de ballet*.

While the company was too small to mount a full-length production of *Giselle*, they could easily handle Act II alone. Markova had always thought dancing anything less than the entire *Giselle* cheated the audience, whom she felt needed to take the entire emotionally complex journey with her to truly appreciate the work. It was no problem to dance a *pas de deux* or excerpt from *The Nutcracker Suite* or *Swan Lake*, but *Giselle* was quite different.

And indeed, it was rarely done. But in the 19th century, one of the first and most highly praised Giselles, prima ballerina Carlotta Grisi, frequently danced the second act alone. That somehow reassured Markova. Hurok was also pressuring her to do it. Audiences everywhere had heard of the great Markova and her *Giselle*, a guaranteed major box-office draw as the Markova-Dolin Company toured cities throughout America. The ballerina acquiesced.

While in Detroit on their first tour, Anton Dolin badly hurt his knee, requiring George Skibine to take his place as Albrecht with just a few hours' notice. Skibine had been dancing the role of the second male lead Hilarion (Giselle's rejected suitor) to great acclaim, and had spent enough time watching Dolin that he had learned the part. While Dolin was superb in the role, audiences truly came to see Markova, and discerning critics found Skibine equal to the task.

Sol Hurok, meanwhile, had reconnected with Colonel Wassily de Basil, whose absurdly named Original Ballet Russe had managed to stay afloat during the war years by touring South America. Remember, it was Hurok who had left the company stranded there in 1941.

Apparently both sides were willing to let bygones be bygones, especially in light of Hurok's enticing offer: Markova and Dolin as guest artists, and first-class American theatre bookings that were formerly promised to Ballet Theatre.

Markova and Dolin were reluctant to work with the less than scrupulous de Basil—who cared more for the bottom line than artistic integrity—but had little choice, as they were now under personal service contracts to Hurok. On the plus side, there was also some quite wonderful news for both dancers at that time.

After a lengthy visa process, their mothers had finally secured boat passage from London to New York. Reservations had been in great demand and hard to come by since the war's end. Markova hadn't seen Eileen for seven long years. Mrs. Marks had moved many times throughout the war, most recently settling in Birmingham with Vivienne, who had a civil service job in that industrial city.

Though Arthur Marks had been to America many times, his wife had never made the trip. Spending time with Alicia in New York was a revelation on numerous levels. First and foremost was the emotional catharsis of their reunion, with mother and daughter having missed each other terribly for far too long. Eileen understood what Alicia had given up—the closeness of her family and lover—in order to financially support the Marks women throughout the war. And she had so thoughtfully and conscientiously sent care packages of impossible-to-get rationed goods. For Markova, it seemed like an eternity since she had her mother's warm, enveloping arms wrapped around her. There were many tears shed.

Markova took great pride in being her mother's tour guide all over Manhattan, a place she now called home. For Eileen, it was like being on another planet compared to the bombed-out city she had just left. New York was so modern, sophisticated, and exciting. The same could be said for Alicia.

The last time Eileen had seen her eldest daughter, she'd been a frightened 28-year-old reluctant to leave home. Now she was a strikingly poised woman, whose close friends included movie and theater stars. Eileen could hardly believe it.

Sol Hurok reserved a box seat for Mrs. Marks at every performance, so she could see for herself what all New York had known for years: Alicia Markova was the most magically engaging ballerina of her generation—just as Eileen's idol Anna Pavlova had been before her. In the unlikeliest of scenarios, everything Mrs. Marks had once dreamed of for her daughter had come true.

While Markova delighted in her mother's visit, Sol Hurok was busily plotting ways to newly burnish his own image after the public fallout with Ballet Theatre. First on the agenda was the 1946 publication of his self-aggrandizing autobiography *Impresario*. In addition to running full-page newspaper ads filled with gossipy tidbits, Hurok asked Markova to help publicize his book by posing with him in promotional photos. Ravishingly costumed in a feathered tutu and headdress from *Swan Lake*, Markova certainly upped Hurok's glamour quotient.

Equally important to the impresario was his desire to make a splash with the New York premiere of de Basil's Original Ballet Russe, which would be going head-to-head with Ballet Theatre for the first time. But rather than play to the Ballet Russe's strength in classical ballet—a grand production of *Giselle* with guest artists Markova and Dolin was a guaranteed crowd-pleaser—Hurok wanted to wow audiences and critics with something completely new.

He settled on *Camille*, the Alexandre Dumas doomed love story between a courtesan and a gentleman, perhaps in the belief that it might duplicate the passionate intensity of *Romeo & Juliet*. But Antony Tudor was under contract with the competition as lead choreographer at Ballet Theatre. So the commission fell instead to a talented soloist from the Markova-Dolin Company, John Taras. Though he very much wanted the job, Taras had little experience in choreography at that time, and it showed.

Hurok did score big, however, with his choice of set and costume designer: Cecil Beaton. Markova had known the designer/portrait photographer from her early dancing days in London. Now living in New York, Beaton was a society darling and frequent contributor to upper-crust magazines like *Vogue* and *Vanity Fair*. In addition to shooting glamorous fashion spreads, Beaton produced iconic portraits of Hollywood and Broadway theater stars, including Marlene Dietrich, Fred Astaire, and Greta Garbo (the reclusive, bisexual actress with whom the openly gay Beaton had a much-publicized affair).

Beaton was also known for his ebullient interior and costume designs (he would win an Academy Award in 1964 for his unforgettable *My Fair Lady* gowns, which dazzled on Audrey Hepburn). A longtime balletomane and former party pal of Frederick Ashton's, Beaton frequently entertained Jerome Robbins, Agnes de Mille, and

Lucia Chase in his seductive rose-print-covered suite at New York's Plaza Hotel. The bon vivant seemed perfect for *Camille*.

With Diaghilev-like finesse, Beaton convinced cosmetic tycoon Elizabeth Arden to underwrite the sizeable budget for his sumptuously romantic costumes. The designer's obvious knowledge of current fashion trends infused Markova's stage gowns with a couture-like luxury. Beaton's photos of her modeling the enchanting dresses were reprinted everywhere.

As glorious as those ballet costumes were, they couldn't compare with the over-the-top splendor of Greta Garbo's Gilbert Adrian-designed wardrobe for the 1936 film *Camille*. It was lost on no one that Garbo was Beaton's date for Markova's opening night.

According to biographer Maurice Leonard, the equally reticent prima ballerina and film star had met at a party when Markova was performing on Broadway. They would often bump into each other in the city, Garbo appreciating Markova's reserve and understanding of her desire for privacy. Ironically, when Beaton was called on stage to take a curtain call for his beautiful *Camille* sets at the ballet's premiere, Garbo was incensed to *be left alone*.

Unfortunately for Hurok—and all the dancers involved—Beaton's creations were the best thing about the ballet. "Whatever honors the work has belong to Mr. Beaton, who has designed a decorative and ingenious setting, together with some fetching costumes which Karinska has executed as only Karinska can," wrote *New York Times* dance critic John Martin. More from his review:

> **'Camille' Ballet in World Premiere**
>
> . . . In spite of all this impressive array of names, the work turns out to be a veritable nothing, a perfectly harmless and inoffensive little bodiless wisp of a ballet, without dramatic line or choreographic continuity. . . .
>
> Miss Markova dances what little comes her way with her customary skill and exquisiteness, and makes a valiant effort to give the work some dramatic entity. But the cards are stacked against her. Mr. Dolin danced his bit on this occasion quite badly; a series of entrechats, indeed with unpointed toes, smacked almost of travesty. In general, the performance by the corps de ballet was a good one.

> Virtually the entire cast, incidentally, consists of "guest artists" and not of regular members of the Original Ballet Russe, for it was rehearsed here while the parent company was still in South America.
>
> —*The New York Times*, 10/2/46

As Agnes de Mille often said, Hurok's primal instincts—"greed and vanity"—were too often confused with "discernment." In his desire to one-up Ballet Theatre, Hurok had blundered badly with *Camille.* While Markova had enjoyed reconnecting with Beaton—and the costumes were truly breathtaking—she was dismayed by both the production and its reviews.

Moreover, neither Lucia Chase nor Sol Hurok had benefited from their split—Hurok losing a much more accomplished dance troupe, and Chase unable to match her ex-partner's U.S. booking connections. As *Time* magazine weighed in:

> **Feather Feud**
>
> In a flurry of ruffled tutu feathers, a battle was joined last week. At the Metropolitan Opera House the Original Ballet Russe opened to a predominantly male first-night audience (including a young man with sequin dust in his hair). The next night Manhattanites scurried to a Broadway Theater for the opening of the America-style Ballet Theater.
>
> The two ballet companies were dancing out a personal feud between two former partners: American Ballerina Lucia Chase and Russian-born Sol Hurok, the Little White Father of ballet in America. Last spring Miss Chase canceled her contract with Hurok and took her troupe to London, where they packed Covent Garden for two months. Thereupon Manager Hurok imported the Russian troupe from South America and bolstered it up with the peerless Alicia Markova (born Alice Marks of London) and other favorites. Then the two companies booked parallel autumn seasons.
>
> —*Time* magazine, 10/14/46

Added Edwin Denby, ballet audiences were the real losers:

Original Ballet Russe and Ballet Theatre Openings

The current exceptionally full New York ballet season has not yet shown any exceptional lustre.

One might have hoped to see it as a lively competition between a pre-war and a post-war style of dancing, as represented the first by the Original Ballet Russe of Col. de Basil, and the second by Ballet Theatre. Instead, it has taken on the gloomy appearance of a war of attrition between Ballet Theatre and S. Hurok, the impresario. . . .

Both openings were crowded and demonstrative; the Original had the dressier, and the Ballet Theatre the livelier crowd. But by the third night the weather prophets were foreseeing that by next fall Ballet Theatre would be back at the Metropolitan, and that faced with their respective deficits, Ballet Theatre and Mr. Hurok would soon find themselves in overwhelming artistic agreement. [It was not to be.]

People go to the Original out of curiosity and because it appears at the Metropolitan; but despite the extra attractions they find the troupe as a whole depressingly second rate. Ballet Theatre, on the other hand, has not the money either for the bold new productions or for the enlargement of the company that it needs to keep its spirit and its vitality at their best. It is, of course, clearly much the better ballet.

The best part of the Original's season so far has been the individual work of the dancers newly added to it—notably Markova and Eglevsky. But such isolated moments of brilliance do not blend with the rest, and the American dancers already look uncomfortable.

—*Ballet Today*, November 1946

Though Markova's association with the Original Ballet Russe did no serious harm to her prestige or reputation at this time, it put her on notice. Sol Hurok had been good to her in the past, but his priorities had shifted. He now seemed more concerned with avenging his bruised ego than what was best for his stars.

Frederick Ashton thoughtfully weighed in on what he perceived as this sad state of affairs in a letter to Markova from London:

27th November 1946,

Darling Alicia,

. . . I hear from Cecil that "Camille" was, alas, not the success you had anticipated. I must say that on paper it seemed a wonderful idea; but I am sure that you yourself were exquisite.

Are you still dancing at the Met.? It is such a pity, it seems to me, that Ballet companies have to indulge in such rivalry; it is my firm belief that in the end, through our own behaviour, we will destroy the great interest that exists in Ballet today. I think all these little companies everywhere, and even big companies battling against each other, are a great mistake. It seems to me to come from lack of generosity on the part of artists.

Hurok's fallout with Ballet Theatre took Markova away from fine talents like Antony Tudor and Jerome Robbins and allied her instead with the disreputable de Basil. This was not what she had signed on for.

Markova had health issues to worry about as well. Hurok was working the entire troupe like farm animals, sending them on non-stop cross-country tours for six months at a time. At thirty-six, Markova may have been at the peak of her dancing abilities, but she was more vulnerable to flus and muscle strains. Her daily diaries from this time are filled with notations of ongoing sore throats and severe menstrual pain, as well as wrenched ankles and torn ligaments. "Not feeling well" was a phrase she recorded with great frequency, along with more alarming notations, such as "Swollen ovarie [*sic*] very painful," and "fainted during show."

Markova had difficulty keeping her weight up, which wreaked havoc with her endurance. When it dropped to a skeletal ninety-two pounds, she would seek medical attention. It wasn't that she didn't eat regularly; she just burned calories faster than she could replace them. One doctor recommended that she drink large chocolate milkshakes in her dressing room as soon as she came offstage. It seemed to help, and she made it part of her routine along with popping chocolates in her mouth, which allowed her to eat while changing.

But there was one cure-all that no doctor could prescribe. When Markova was performing in New York and had an especially stressful week, she often retreated to Danilova's country home in New Jersey for rest and relaxation with her very best friend. On those Saturdays, she would always record "Lovely Day" in her diary, followed by "Wonderful time!" on Sunday evening.

Unlike Danilova and Dolin, Markova never owned a vacation home. Her mind didn't work that way. She was all about work, not play. But she had reconsidered when Eileen visited her in New York. They fantasized about a time in the near future when Markova would be back in England and the family would once again be together. Perhaps Alicia would buy them a country home just outside London where she could visit whenever she had any time off. It would be like Pavlova's Ivy House, but on a more modest scale.

In actuality, it had been decades since the Marks women had all vacationed together. Even when Markova was on summer break from the Ballets Russes, the teenager spent more time with family friends the Crewleys than her own sisters. When little, Markova had always been closer to her father than her mother, and there was something unnatural about Eileen's taking the three other girls on vacation without her eldest daughter. Markova was looking forward to becoming a real family again.

But that was in the future. For now, she was excited about bringing ballet to people who rarely or never had the opportunity to see it. The modest-sized Markova-Dolin Company was ideal for that purpose, and its reigning star informed Hurok that she wanted to venture beyond the United States. Their first tour would be Central America—and considering Markova's previous trip to the region, it's surprising she wanted to go back.

In 1940, Markova and Danilova had traveled to South America with the Ballet Russe de Monte Carlo. While they greatly enjoyed each other's company, dancing in 120-degree heat—with no air-conditioning in the theaters—was far less fun. For Markova, the trip had been problematic from the start.

The day before departure from New York, a doctor was sent to vaccinate the entire company at their last rehearsal. Massine thought everyone should take their shots in the leg, so that if there was an unsightly skin reaction, it could be covered with tights. Markova wasn't keen on the idea of a needle in her left leg, as she had experienced bad reactions to vaccinations before, and her legs were her livelihood. Massine prevailed. *Every* dancer was vaccinated in the leg. Many hobbled around for a day or two, but all seemed fine when they boarded the ship for the three-week cruise to Rio.

Danilova and Markova were booked in a "first class" cabin, which they soon discovered was "the size of an average broom-cupboard." The close quarters would seem even more so as the boat went farther and farther south and the weather got increasingly hot and humid.

About ten days into the trip, Markova's leg began to swell, eventually ballooning to twice its normal size. The ship's doctor insisted that she lie still the entire trip with her leg elevated while he attempted to treat the inflammation with various dressings. But the swelling only got worse, hardened, and eventually went numb. "I had a left wooden leg. It was like a piano leg," Markova remembered all too well.

Massine was more in a panic than the stricken ballerina. At least she had the entertaining Danilova to keep her spirits up, as well as the equally amusing classical pianist Arthur Rubinstein, another Hurok performer who was on board traveling with his family.

As the ship got closer to landing in Rio de Janeiro, a long list of warnings was issued to the company prior to disembarking. Markova's stiff leg seemed to pale in comparison.

Drinking plenty of bottled water with salt tablets was standard enough advice, but they were also told to avoid alcohol at bars, as local café glasses were known to spread syphilis of the mouth. If that wasn't dismaying enough, the pretty young corps members were cautioned never to go out alone, as white slavery was a thriving business.

Welcome to Rio!

When they docked, Markova almost didn't make it off the boat, but not because of her leg. No one could leave the ship until matched to his or her passport. While waiting to hear her name called, Markova sat patiently reading a book. Suddenly she felt a poke in her ribs. It was Danilova. "Marks. That's you!" she kept repeating. Markova had completely forgotten that her British passport listed her birth name, and would never have looked up had Danilova not been there. Miss Marks managed to hobble down the gangplank leaning on her great Russian friend.

There was just one day to practice before opening night when Markova was scheduled to perform an excerpt from *Swan Lake*. Wouldn't you know—that particular scene was danced almost entirely on the left leg.

"[T]he heat, it was agony," she remembered quite clearly. "I suffered really quite a few days after we were there with that leg." Though the tights masked her wound, they only made her feel hotter.

The rest of the company wasn't faring much better. Despite all the health warnings, one after another the dancers fell ill from dysentery, heat prostration, and various other ailments. It became hugely problematic.

As had been true when de Basil experienced his infamous dancer mutiny in Cuba, the contracts in Rio stipulated that a certain number of principal soloists and corps members appear in each performance. There were now so many in the corps too sick to dance that Hurok was afraid they would have to default and not get paid.

Markova and Danilova volunteered to take on corps roles when not soloing themselves, and prima ballerina Mia Slavenska agreed to do the same. Massine was the hardest to convince. As Danilova had often said, he was a selfish dancer, and even though he was the company's artistic director, Massine never paid attention to ballets he wasn't in.

His filling in for corps members made even serious ballets a bit comical, as Massine never quite knew what direction he should be turning in. He quite startled soloist Freddie Franklin on a number of occasions, almost bumping into him. One evening Markova had to dance the demanding leads in two lengthy ballets and, upon leaving the stage after the final curtain, fainted from exhaustion in the wings.

Local customs also presented some unwanted surprises.

Danilova and Markova were hugely popular with Brazilian audiences. As the two dancers exited the theater one day, they heard shots ring out. Terrified that they would be caught in gun crossfire—not a farfetched notion in a country with frequent revolutions—they scurried back to the theater for cover.

The stage door keeper immediately calmed them down. They were actually being serenaded, he explained. "When the public love you, they set off firecrackers in your honor." That wasn't completely comforting. Instead of taxis, open horse-drawn carriages transported the dancers back and forth to their hotel. Markova had visions of a firecracker exploding on top of them or frightening the horses into rearing up. Sometimes there was such a thing as too much love.

The rest of the trip—including visits to São Paulo and Santos, Brazil; Buenos Aires, Argentina; and Montevideo, Uruguay—presented one set of difficulties after another, with wild swings in the weather, from winter temperatures in the mountains to unbearable heat and humidity in the tropical flatlands. Then there were all the bugs. Makeup left exposed in a dressing room would quickly become infested with insects. They were everywhere.

"On the way back I think we stopped at Trinidad, and of course I was very excited because Trinidad at that time was the nearest thing to home," Markova later reminisced about the island then part of the British Empire. "I found a little shop there that still had some Crosse & Blackwell jam and . . . one of these large tins of English biscuits, so of course I bought everything they had and took it back to the ship and thought, 'I'm taking this back to New York.'"

Markova's food parcels remained in her cabin for the three-week return trip and one day while rehearsing back home she decided to fetch her cookie tin. "And I opened it up, there wasn't a biscuit, it was alive with ants! . . . I had to ring for help and to get these things out before the hotel was alive with them. But the disappointment in carefully carrying all these things back!"

For Markova, the trip must have been like childbirth—you selectively remember only the joy left behind—because she couldn't wait to travel to the tropics again. She always looked forward to bringing ballet to new audiences, and that would be the case in many of the Central American cities. And there was a new wrinkle in ballet tours by 1947. For the first time, dance companies often traveled by air.

Unlike the rest of the company, Markova was an experienced plane traveler, and not just because "I fly on stage!" as she once joked.

"Dolin and I were the first dancers to fly everywhere. We'd done it since 1931—Imperial Airways, Croydon [London] to Paris. How that came about—we'd been doing three shows a day in the new movie theatre in Leicester Square. We finished Saturday evening and were due to open in Madrid on Monday. Pat said that if we flew to Paris Sunday morning and caught the overnight train, we could be in

Madrid Monday morning, which we did, and danced that night. Can you imagine? Murder."

If plane travelers are squeamish about boarding "puddle jumpers" today, imagine what tiny planes were like in the early 1930s. Markova's trip from Croydon to Paris was in an aircraft so small, the seats were actually basket chairs. And forget refreshments. The only thing passengers received on board, according to Markova, were "big wads of cotton wool to stuff in your ears to blank out the deafening noise."

By the late 1940s, Hurok was thrilled with the speed of air travel. It allowed him to double the company's bookings and make more money on every tour.

"[A]t the pace we were now working, this simply meant the packing in of more and more concerts," Markova lamented. "I was beginning to feel a certain strain in it all, a fear perhaps that the whole enterprise of the Markova-Dolin group, which was drawing such huge attendances, stood in danger of becoming too commercialized. Beauty and elegance and spiritual refreshment, those essentials of classical ballet, seemed to be fighting for life against the demands of our crowded schedule."

There was quite another type of fighting going on when the Markova-Dolin Company departed on their first foreign tour—eight weeks in eight different countries. They were scheduled to start in the Caribbean islands and Cuba, followed by Guatemala, El Salvador, Costa Rica, Venezuela, and Colombia. To say the region was politically unstable would be an understatement.

In Bogota, the British consulate left word that the company was not to leave their hotel, as "there is going to be shooting today." Only one matinee and evening performance were cancelled. Apparently they were all done shooting by the next morning.

A sudden revolution also prevented Markova and Dolin from a quick stopover in Nicaragua to dine with an old friend. "So we missed luncheon and the possibility of a bullet in the hors d'oeuvre," Markova humorously recalled.

But it was in Cuba that Markova danced on the worst stage of her career—and that's saying something. She had already maneuvered around holes, slippery marble, sharp tilts, and squished flowers, but the Cuban floorboards were a veritable roller coaster. Due to the incessant heat and humidity, the wood was so warped that it looked more like a Mediterranean tile roof than flooring. To avoid getting her foot caught in one of the furrows, for the first time Markova danced *Les Sylphides* without going *en pointe*. Dolin also managed his solo as best he could.

Unfortunately, Markova's scheduled performance of *The Dying Swan* necessitated her rising on toe, and the Cubans were quite anxious to see it. As the ballerina didn't want to die in real life, she asked if it might be possible to locate a large smooth strip of linoleum she could dance on.

During the intermission following *Les Sylphides*, workmen miraculously showed up with the new material and began hammering it onto the uneven stage boards in front of the audience. This was met with cheers and singing.

While the surface was smooth, there were still bumps underneath as Markova danced. Oddly, it added to the illusion of a bird's wings going up and down. The audience gave the ballerina a standing ovation.

Though Markova always enjoyed winning over new ballet converts, she was as happy as everyone else to return to the United States in late spring to resume performances in traditional American theaters.

Eileen had returned to England prior to Markova's south-of-the-border engagement, and now sister Doris was coming to visit. As was true with Eileen, Doris had never been to America and was astonished at the sophistication of New York City life. And the shopping! After so many years of not being able to buy even a lipstick, she equated department stores with Disneyland.

Then there was Alicia. The two had always been close, and they wrote constantly during the war, but they hadn't seen each other in eight years. Even Eileen's gushing about the success of her eldest daughter didn't prepare Doris for Alicia's American celebrity.

One afternoon, the two went to tea at Constance Collier's ritzy Manhattan apartment. Doris almost fainted when she walked in and saw Charlie Chaplin, who clearly adored her sister. Not one to disappoint, Chaplin chatted animatedly about his next film, including jumping up on a table with an impromptu performance that entertained one and all.

London was still shell-shocked after the war, making Markova's life all the more enticing to Doris. She had only recently left her longtime dancing job with the Windmill Theatre and had no desire to hurry back. Soon enough, Doris would finagle a job as the Markova-Dolin Company stage manager, later becoming Markova's personal manager. It was the start of a whole new life.

After an arduous tour of the United States—Milwaukee, Chicago, Memphis, Decatur, St. Louis, Mobile, Shreveport, Athens, Miami, Jacksonville, Fayetteville, Norfolk, Cleveland, Pittsburgh, and beyond—the Markova-Dolin Company was booked in Mexico for a good portion of the summer in 1947. Markova genuinely looked forward to being in one location for six uninterrupted weeks.

She was also delighted that Mexico now had its own ballet company, which hadn't existed five years earlier when she roamed the local marketplace with Marc Chagall and his wife. As a joint artistic endeavor, the Markova-Dolin Company and government-sponsored Ballet of the City of Mexico would be performing as one, with a combined repertoire of Russian classics and new works by local Mexican choreographers.

It was a collaborative process that Markova found especially rewarding. She was always gratified when a young dancer she had tutored became a future success, such as Lupe Serrano of the Mexican ballet. Years later the two would work together in New York, Serrano starring as Queen of the Wilis to Markova's Giselle. In the coming years, Markova would make a concerted effort to help many fledgling ballet companies get off the ground.

Performances in Mexico City were held at the magnificent old-world Palacio des Bellas Artes. The schedule was restricted to four days a week, because the visiting dancers suffered endurance and breathing problems due to the especially high altitude.

Dolin decided to create his own ballet for the occasion, a fresh interpretation of *Camille.* Regrettably, his *The Lady of the Camillias* wasn't any more successful than the John Taras version several years earlier.

As the new company stage manager, Doris accompanied Markova to Mexico. She quickly learned about the perils of foreign customs.

One evening while performing *Giselle,* Markova finished her "mad scene" at the end of Act I only to find another one waiting for her in the wings. As she tried to scurry to her dressing room, the ballerina's path was blocked by a rowdy, though friendly, group of Mexican peasants.

Alarmingly, each held a pair of steel scissors. As soon as their favorite dancer was in reach, they merrily began snipping away at her long, disheveled hair. Doris heard the commotion and helped fend them of, whereupon Markova discerned that they just wanted a memento of her immortal performance. She promised to give each one some personal souvenir at the end of the ballet if they would just let her change for Act II. The crowd peacefully retreated.

When they all returned after the final bows—as Markova had no doubts they would—she started handing out every small thing she could find in her dressing room, from hair nets and pins to powder puffs and empty makeup tubes. When everyone had gone, she sat back in her chair and finally got a glimpse of the locals' handiwork in the mirror. She could only laugh at her impromptu choppy haircut. "I could not look on it as anything but a most touching compliment," she mused.

Back in New York for the fall season, the Markova-Dolin Company had their first major flop in hometown New York. It was actually a disaster.

"I take the entire blame for it because Markova was against the proposition from the first," Dolin later admitted. The "it" he refers to was a booking of three special performances at the Metropolitan Opera House arranged by Sol Hurok. The Markova-Dolin Company was just too small for such a venue, and Markova knew it. As Dolin further explained:

> To add importance to the Company and repertoire, Hurok engaged André Eglevsky to dance and Jerome Robbins to choreograph a new pas de trois for Markova, André and me. It turned out to be an amusing trifle, a typical Robbins skit on the classical ballet, in which Markova excelled. . . .
>
> Exaggerated Hurok advertising saying the public would see "Markova, Dolin and their Ballet" instead of twelve dancers, including André and Rosella Hightower, only tended to make things worse, and the critics, rightly so in this case, were far from our side of the fence.

Imagine how Markova felt when she read John Martin's savage review in *The New York Times*:

THE DANCE: FAUX PAS
Some Sad Thoughts About Markova
at the Metropolitan—Coming Events

If Alicia Markova has no Dutch uncle handy, somebody else should step forward and talk to her like one about the sorry goings-on of which she was a part at the Metropolitan Opera House last week-end. The series of performances in which she and Anton Dolin were stars and André Eglevsky was guest artist would be hard to match for artistic shoddiness, and there was about them a disturbing suspicion of cynicism which seemed to imply that it was quite legitimate to cash in on big names and let the customers make the best of it.

Nobody who has watched Miss Markova through the nearly ten years that she has been dancing in this country and has come to know her meticulousness and her impeccable standards can believe that she subscribes in any such theory, yet she has allowed appearances to bear strong superficial witness against her. In the entire repertoire she appeared in five numbers, not one of which exhibited her art at even its second best or caused her to extend herself in any way. . . .

The two new works which called for Miss Markova's services were frankly poor. Rosella Hightower's "Henry VIII," her first excursion into choreography . . . is without merit of any kind. In addition, Miss Markova's role is brief and thankless.

The other novelty, Mr. Dolin's version of "The Lady of the Camellias," is more irritating because he can certainly not claim inexperience as an alibi. . . .

Greatness entails responsibility. Both in these columns and elsewhere Miss Markova had been called the greatest of all classical ballerinas. If she accepts the designation (and she can scarcely otherwise) it is incumbent upon her to keep faith. . . . It is rather appalling to realize that this kind of repertoire and this kind of roles are what the rest of the country is seeing on tour these seasons as representative of the great Alicia Markova.

—*The New York Times*, 10/26/47

Markova was aghast.

Dolin put most of the blame on Hurok, who clearly only saw dollar signs in the engagement. "With all his vast experience, he [Hurok] must have known that bad notices—and they were very bad, devastatingly so—would damage and have a bad effect on the long tour that still lay ahead," asserted Dolin. "*The New York Times* is read from coast to coast, and local managers and sponsors pay attention to its critical words."

But of everyone who read Martin's review, Markova reacted the worst. He was absolutely correct in everything he had written, and she knew it. She felt she had let him down—someone who had always been one of her most ardent supporters. And she could do nothing to correct the situation in the near future. After New York, the company was booked on another of Hurok's brutal five-month cross-country tours—more humiliation.

In some ways the disaster emboldened Markova. She needed to take more control of and responsibility for her career. It's not as if Hurok and Dolin had coddled her, with the men taking on all the work responsibilities and the frail ballerina required only to dance. Markova was also involved in overseeing company budgets, costume design, and travel accommodations. Her archives are filled with handwritten accounting notes for each production on the road.

As the company's new stage manager, Doris could now help in that capacity, but the ultimate responsibility was still Markova's. Doris also gave her sister the moral support she needed to eventually break free. A witness to all the backstage machinations and goings-on, Doris warned Alicia not only about Hurok, but the dangers of Dolin's dominance as well. She urged Markova to be more independent.

Earlier that year, the photographer John Gabriel published a book titled *Ballet School*. *Dance and Dancers* magazine was intrigued with his shots in which "several leading dancers performed *enchainements* in front of a high-speed camera. The resulting sequences revealed how steps and phrases were performed—but they also showed up the less graceful links which ordinarily the eye just does not see. These occurred in everyone's dancing—even Fonteyn's, even Danilova's—everyone's, that is except Markova's. Throughout a solo from *Les*

Sylphides, the camera never once caught her in a shape that was less than beautiful."

Markova knew she needed to win back the critics and preserve her legacy. Though she would have liked nothing better than an immediate triumphant return to *Giselle,* she had the rest of Hurok's contract to fulfill and she would honor every commitment.

After the scathing New York reviews, everyone anticipated a dispiriting five-month tour; but with a revised repertoire, they were generally well received. *The Sleeping Beauty Suite* and Jerome Robbins *Pas de trois* proved especially popular.

Since the company was booked in a different city every few nights—often performing in venues like high school gymnasiums, municipal auditoriums, and American Legion halls—there were many ongoing mishaps. In a Dallas, Texas high school, for example, overzealous students worked overtime to wax and polish the auditorium stage until it was smooth as glass for their honored guests, not realizing how slippery it would be for satin toe shoes.

Despite attempts to roughen the surface again—with the use of kerosene oil and rosin—it was touch and go at the rehearsal. (And the kerosene fumes didn't help.) Before the start of the performance, Dolin apologized to the audience in a curtain speech: "We are doing our best and trying to stand up, but neither Miss Markova nor I nor our groups are billed to appear as *The Ice Capades.*"

In contrast, things couldn't have gone better in California where Markova and Dolin danced *Giselle* with the San Francisco Ballet Company. The production received universal rave reviews, restoring the prima ballerina's confidence.

As had been true in Mexico, the small Markova-Dolin troupe was shown to best advantage as guest artists of a large established company. Performing by themselves, the twelve dancers were overworked to the point of collapse. It wasn't fair to them or the audiences.

At least there was a sliver of a silver lining ahead.

While performing in Mexico, Markova and Dolin were invited to be guest artists with the Sadler's Wells Company at London's Royal Opera House in the summer of 1948. It wasn't the first offer the two had received from England since the war's end, but it was the most prestigious. The other proposals—though far more lucrative—were for commercial productions that Dolin was eager to accept, but Markova not at all. Money was never the driving force in her decision-making, and she felt her return to London after all these years should be quite special. Since the previous offers were strictly for the *two* dancers in their acclaimed partnership, Dolin had been forced to pass as well.

Now the thought of performing at Covent Garden, and reuniting with Ninette de Valois, was the best possible news for Markova. When Sol Hurok heard of the Sadler's Wells invitation, he told Markova she'd be a fool to accept such low wages for a three-month booking when she could be earning so much more working for him. Her current salary was $1,000 per week, making her the highest-paid ballerina in the world. She would take a big cut in London.

But few people realized how much of Markova's salary went to company expenses. Hurok of course knew, so he upped the ante if she would just sign on for one more cross-country American tour. As usual, the impresario had ulterior motives. He was working on his own deal with the Sadler's Wells Ballet to bring them to the United States, a tour that would eventually make Margot Fonteyn a huge star. Hurok didn't want Markova's name associated with the company until *he* was ready.

Markova's personal physician voiced his own concerns about Hurok's offer: "Are you trying to be the richest girl in the cemetery?" he asked. "That's what you'll be if you accept these offers from Mr. Hurok. You're not a machine." Markova had to agree.

While in the midst of their last, exhaustive tour across America, Markova and Dolin informed their manager Irving Deakin that they would not be renewing their contracts with Hurok. Deakin would soon be out as well. But those contracts weren't set to expire until halfway into the London booking, and the impresario played hardball, according to Dolin. It would cost the dancers a combined $35,000 to break their agreement early. Both thought it was well worth it. They were going home.

If Markova had wished to be well rested prior to returning to London, she might have reconsidered a commitment she soon made to her new manager, Alfred Katz. She and Doris met the effervescent Katz at a cocktail party hosted by mutual friends, the lawyers Fanny and David Holtzmann (who had represented Markova and Dolin since they first arrived in the United States).

Katz had recently handled a tour to the Philippines for the world-renowned American violinist Yehudi Menuhin. (Coincidentally, the musician had just married Markova's friend, the great beauty and former Sadler's Wells dancer Diana Gould.) Menuhin had a history of visiting war-torn countries, having once given an emotional performance for the surviving inmates of Nazi concentration camp Bergen-Belsen following its liberation.

Apparently in far worse shape than Great Britain and Germany after the war, Manila remained a city in ruins after the Japanese bombing and shelling raids during the Battle of Manila in early 1945. Menuhin found the enormously appreciative audiences an inspiration.

Listening to Katz talk of the experience, Markova immediately volunteered to make the trip herself. No dance company had visited the Philippines since Anna Pavlova in 1924. As the journey would be both long and arduous, it was decided that only five people should go—Katz, Markova, Dolin, Doris, and a concert pianist. (Claude Jean Chiasson was later chosen.) Dolin initially wasn't all that keen on the trip, but Markova talked him into it.

"Whenever people would say to me, 'Oh, you can't go to a certain place because there is no theater there or there isn't any public,' I would always say to Pat [Dolin], that's where we're going because it must be opened up," she explained.

Katz arranged that the group break up the seemingly interminable plane flights by accepting a week's booking in Honolulu on the way. (It would take four days just to fly from Hawaii to Manila.) The stopover in Hawaii proved quite fortuitous for Markova, as she would soon be in need of an emergency shipment from New York.

The ballerina hadn't realized how much her feet would be affected by the combined heat and humidity. It's not as if she hadn't traveled to hot-weather destinations before; but this time her feet swelled so badly she could barely fit into her ballet shoes. Worse still, the blocking in the toe turned to complete mush.

A panicked telegram was immediately dispatched to Capezio in New York, where all Markova's ballet shoes were hand-made, requesting that the company quickly send a dozen new pairs a half-size larger, lighter weight, and with sturdier toe blocks. The shipment arrived well before the departure for the Philippines. Never again would Markova attempt such a trip without a supply of what she now called her "tropical" toe shoes.

There were no complaints on the multiple-day plane trip to Manila, as mattresses were thoughtfully provided so the group could sleep lying down. They were also well fed, although Markova said everyone got a bit tired of chicken salad, the only menu "selection" available for lunch and dinner every day.

When Manila's airport finally came into view, nothing had quite prepared the travelers for the awaiting devastation. Even from the air they could see miles of strewn rubble, bombed-out buildings, and a strong military presence. The only way one could determine actual streets, Markova recalled, was by the rows of empty gas canisters strung together as demarcation.

Upon landing, the visitors were treated like visiting dignitaries—covered in sweet-smelling gardenia garlands, and presented with various ceremonial gifts. Markova received two lovely, lace-trimmed gowns, which she gladly wore—and was photographed in—at all the social events thrown in their honor. The Filipinos could not have been more gracious.

Markova and Dolin were set to perform at the Manila Opera House, which amazingly was still standing from the days when Pavlova had danced there over two decades earlier. But many isolated locations with rather makeshift staging were also on the itinerary. No worries. As John Martin had written of Markova, she could perform a ballet "in an abandoned warehouse and give it elegance and poignance."

First on the agenda was checking into the Manila hotel—or half a hotel, as it turned out. "I remember opening a door next to my suite, which led directly and terrifyingly on to nothingness; the rest of the building had been sheared away by bombing," Markova wrote in her memoirs.

At the hotel's front desk was the sign PARK YOUR FIRE-ARMS HERE—a none-too-reassuring reminder of daily shootings. Also unsettling was the news that the mayor of Manila had suddenly passed away. That delayed all performances in the city for a short period of mourning.

In the meantime, the troupe ventured out to explore the various islands and jungle settings for their upcoming three-week itinerary.

Many locations seemed highly unlikely spots for any kind of performance, as they were almost completely deserted. But no sooner had the dancers appeared than so did the crowds—some having driven most of the day to see their first ballet.

When Markova arrived in Cebu, she was taken to the barren outdoor cinema where she and Dolin would dance that evening. The locals were transforming the site right before her eyes.

For a stage, dozens of upturned lemonade cases were lashed together and covered with a canvas. Off to one side sat a group of Filipino women, who one by one were cutting open old military grain sacks. The flattened fabric was then stitched together and painstakingly decorated with hundreds of wild tuberoses. It was a unique and quite beautiful scenic backdrop.

On the other side of the makeshift stage were placed several drained gasoline drums, now filled with fragrant flowers. The scent was overwhelming, Markova remembered, as if someone had spilled bottles of expensive perfume everywhere.

The ballerina had brought her own scenic magic: various colored gels for the spotlights. Doris taught several local workers—young male volunteers—how and when to switch colors. It was a simple way to create distinctive dramatic moods for the different ballets.

During the performance, the first color shone bright—but then never changed. Having never seen a ballet before, the boys entrusted with the job were so captivated they completely forgot about the gels. Later, Markova and Doris had to laugh.

It hardly mattered. The entire audience seemed hypnotized. Every time Markova rose up on her toes, there was an audible gasp. No one could imagine how that was humanly possible.

The rapturous reception was the same all over the Philippines, bringing as much joy to the dancers as the worshipful crowds. Markova and Dolin also made the time to visit one of the local ballet teachers, helping her develop easy-to-master lesson plans for her newly starstruck dance students.

Before they returned home, Markova decided there should be one additional performance for the army soldiers and poorer Filipinos who previously hadn't been able to afford tickets. The fee would be just one dollar. Markova and Dolin would dance for free and donate all proceeds to the local symphony orchestra, which was desperately in need of new instruments.

So many tickets were sold that the only venue big enough to hold them all was the local baseball stadium. Someone had the bright idea of bringing a boxing ring to the arena for a stage, and Doris went to work on lighting. With a large contingent of U.S. Army soldiers in attendance, several officers volunteered their searchlights as follow spots. The evening was completely magical.

In the spring of 1948, Alicia Markova hadn't been back to London in nine years. When asked the difference between New York and her hometown, she thoughtfully replied: "New York is a pair of evening shoes—stylish, glittering and gay. But London—and I hope London won't mind this—is a pair of old slippers. So warm, so comfortable and, for me, so familiar. I suppose that's why I love it."

To the world-famous ballerina, London first and foremost represented family. Though Eileen and Doris had visited her in New York, Alicia hadn't seen her sisters Vivienne and Bunny in almost a decade. Bunny was now married to John North, a former RAF captain, and had a two-year-old daughter. When in Manila just prior to reuniting with her family, Markova bubbled over to a reporter about her niece: "They tell me that it's almost impossible to keep her feet flat on the ground—she's always on her toes." Little Susie was just like her Auntie Alicia.

Markova was also looking forward to reuniting with Ninette de Valois and Frederick Ashton. She had kept in touch with both throughout the war, frequently sending them care packages of difficult-to-obtain supplies. Ashton was especially touched, as many of his ballet "friends" seemed to forget all about him after he was drafted into the military. He wrote many letters of thanks for Markova's continued concern and thoughtfulness, as in this letter from November 1946:

Darling Alicia,

I don't know whether you owe me a letter or if I owe you one, or whether I ought to thank you for a parcel or not. But if I haven't

> *done so, you must know how gratefully I receive them and how sweet I think it is of you to remember us over here in starving Europe. . . .*
>
> *I do hope that you will soon come over and dance in Europe. How lovely it would be to see you. I should feel a particular pride, knowing how I encouraged you in the old days. Please always hold me in your thoughts, darling Alicia, and perhaps in the not too distant future we may work together.*

That time had finally come.

After the physically demanding trip to the Philippines, Markova was tired, weak, and underweight. A leisurely cruise from New York to London was just what the doctor ordered to rest up in preparation for her much-ballyhooed return to the London stage. The only things on her agenda for the six-day trip were eating and sleeping. Doris would be joining her sister on board the *Queen Elizabeth*. They would arrive in plenty of time for a family reunion and adequate rehearsals prior to opening night.

But just before departure, Ninette de Valois sent a frantic cable to Markova and Dolin, asking if they would make a special appearance at the Sadler's Wells Benevolent Fund Gala. It was to take place the night immediately after Markova's boat docked.

The ballerina knew that being on the ocean for so long would affect her equilibrium, and it usually took several days to be able to dance comfortably without any dizziness. The Gala was quite a to-do, however. Princess Elizabeth, a few years prior to her coronation, and the young Princess Margaret would be in attendance. The dancers felt they couldn't say no.

Dolin was flying to Europe well in advance, so preparation was less of an issue for him; but Markova was naturally concerned. Yes, they would only be dancing a single divertissement, but it would also be their first performance in England in over nine years. She suggested the Valse from *Les Sylphides*, a scene they had danced together hundreds of times and always to great acclaim. But Dolin had other ideas:

"I disagreed, being of the opinion that, facing as I was, a new generation, the comments would have been something like 'Poor old Dolin! Of course he's too old now, and doesn't dance—just supports.' So we chose the flashy Don Quixote pas de deux, solos and codas."

"We" wasn't exactly the right pronoun. Markova thought the choice ill-conceived from the start, as neither role played to the dancers' strengths and they had so little experience performing it together. But she also understood why Dolin was drawn to the flamboyant male solo. It was a part that would later make Rudolf Nureyev a star, the perfect showcase for his stupendous leaps and impossibly graceful athleticism.

Markova argued that *Les Sylphides* was a much better, and safer, choice in light of the limited rehearsal time. Dolin, however, was so set on proving himself a still-vital dancer that she reluctantly agreed.

Though the ship crossing from New York to Southampton was uneventful, there were minor delays along the route, putting the docking time way behind schedule. Markova didn't arrive in London until the wee hours of the morning on the very day of the Gala.

After an abbreviated night's sleep, she rebounded for a tearful homecoming party with her entire family at the hotel. It was heartbreaking to have to leave them again so soon, as she needed to attend her one and only *Don Quixote* rehearsal with Dolin.

Markova was in no shape to dance, physically or emotionally. She barely walked through it.

The Gala performance did not go well for either dancer.

Afterwards, according to Dolin, Arnold Haskell was in the theater lobby overheard loudly proclaiming, "Well, *he* has gained in vulgarity, and *she* has lost everything."

Had it been just another evening at the ballet, all would have been forgotten quickly; but British audiences hadn't seen Markova and Dolin perform in almost a decade. "So this is how they dance now," thought many in the audience. How very sad.

And there was another disappointment. The future Queen Elizabeth hadn't been in attendance after all. Princess Margaret had come down with the measles.

Markova was surprisingly resilient, perhaps too tired to be upset. She knew she could win everyone back with her Giselle the following week; but now de Valois and Ashton were concerned. Had her American press reviews been overstated?

Also giving them pause was the fact that "Madame Markova is not a great believer in too much rehearsal," as a London magazine revealed. "An hour of practice a day at most, and special rehearsal of her work only when necessary, as she prefers to retain her energies for her performances."

No one would see Markova's Giselle until opening night.

But she must have allayed most doubts while learning *The Sleeping Beauty* from her old friend Nicholas Sergeyev. De Valois had asked Markova and Dolin to star in the full-length Russian classic, now in the company's repertoire. It was a ballet Markova had never danced in its entirety before. She shocked everyone by mastering the difficult role of Aurora in less than two weeks.

Markova had a distinct history with *The Sleeping Beauty* that only she remembered. In the very same London Royal Opera House where she now practiced, the ten-year-old Lily Marks had sat night after night with Sergei Diaghilev. Together they watched the Ballets Russes perform *The Sleeping Princess,* as it was then called. The impresario encouraged his Douchka to study each prima ballerina's interpretation of Aurora, and Lily was an apt pupil. Diphtheria had prevented her from being up on stage with the illustrious Russian company all those years ago, but now she would make up for it.

In Markova's dressing room at the Royal Opera House was a framed photo of Diaghilev, something she carried with her everywhere. Wouldn't he be delighted at what "his little English girl" had achieved?

Reconnecting with old friends at the Sadler's Wells was a special treat for Markova. She was exceedingly proud of Margot Fonteyn, now herself a huge star. And Constant Lambert was still the invaluable company orchestra conductor, as he had been at the Vic-Wells and Markova-Dolin Company all those years ago. It made practice sessions so much more enjoyable.

During an orchestration rehearsal for *Swan Lake,* Markova stood in the wings waiting for Lambert's cue. Time passed—no music. She waited a bit longer. Still no music.

Finally Markova walked over to Lambert in the orchestra pit and asked if there was a problem. The conductor smiled and held up his score. It was the same sheet music he had been using since their time together at the Vic-Wells. Lambert pointed to a handwritten note in red. "Wait for Markova," it said, as Lambert had been instructed to follow the ballerina's cue rather than the other way around.

"And I've been waiting for a very long time!" he joked.

Lambert was not alone. The British people had also waited nine long years to see their Alicia again—and in *Giselle*! Despite the poor *Don Quixote* reviews from the week before, there was still much anticipation for the official opening night.

Theatre World dance critic Eric Johns was in the audience:

> Barely has Covent Garden experienced so electric a first night as that which recently welcomed Alicia Markova and Anton Dolin back to this country in Giselle after an absence of nine years in America. Could they hold their own with the new generation of dancers that had arisen in their absence? . . .
>
> Though there were loyal friends in the house, reputations were at stake, making the occasion a major ordeal such as few dancers have been called upon to face.
>
> Frenzied applause greeted their final curtain—that thunder only heard on historic occasions at the opera house. Both Markova and Dolin had never been seen to better advantage. It was not necessary to make excuses for them or to wish the younger generation had seen them ten years earlier. They were obviously two of the greatest dancers of our time, now at the peak of their careers. . . .
>
> Markova's Giselle is still one of the great balletic characterizations within living memory.

The British public fell in love with Alicia Markova all over again. Each night, fans waited for hours outside the stage door at Covent Garden as the ballerina patiently smiled, signed autographs, and gave out flowers from her countless bouquets.

Though comparisons to Pavlova were never-ending throughout Markova's career, in this one regard the two couldn't have been more different. Markova was grateful to her public, and their joy in her work sustained her. Pavlova danced for herself. Her carefully orchestrated theater exits—always above and distant from the waiting throngs—were designed to bolster her public image as a star, not endear her to fans.

After the London season with the Sadler's Wells, Markova and Dolin would be heading back to New York as guest artists with the

Ballet Russe de Monte Carlo. For Markova, working with Danilova again would take the sting out of having to leave her family. There was another sting that would soon be soothed. While still in England, Markova received a newspaper clipping written by John Martin of *The New York Times*.

THE DANCE: MARKOVA

Return to Ballet Russe—Current Programs

From London comes the excellent news that Alicia Markova, together with Anton Dolin, will be a member of the Ballet Russe de Monte Carlo in September when that company returns to the Metropolitan Opera House after an absence of six years. It was with this company, when it was newly organized, that she made her American debut ten years ago in "Giselle" and gave us the standard for classic style which we had not seen for many a year, if ever.

That ballet, which provides her with her greatest role, will again be in the repertoire; of course, so will Leonide Massine's "Rouge et Noir," in which she originated the leading role. . . .

With luck, this should end the aimless free-lancing, barnstorming, small-company road-show interlude which has occupied Miss Markova since she left Ballet Theatre. She is not an artist for the music halls and the lyceum circuits; her place is in a major company which boasts a sound and sensitive artistic director. . . .

Both Miss Markova and Mr. Dolin, absent from their native England for a decade, have just closed an engagement as guest artists with the Sadler's Wells Ballet at Covent Garden, and covered themselves with glory. Their first appearance in London in May was an unfortunate one in which they danced, of all things, the "Don Quixote" pas de deux at a benefit performance and were politely berated for it. It was a different story, however, when they opened in "Giselle at Covent Garden. Both the audience and press were highly enthusiastic. Q.E.D.

—*The New York Times*, 7/4/48

Markova was relieved that Martin had finally forgiven her, but it was also a reminder that Dolin, like Sol Hurok, often had poor artistic judgment. She and Dolin were wonderful ballet partners, but Markova needed to be more independent in decisions of where, what, and when she performed.

While the esteemed John Martin seemed back in her corner, there was one British critic Markova had never been able to win over. Arnold Haskell, such a great friend for so many years, had always thought Alicia a talented ballet technician rather than a world-class prima ballerina.

But that was finally about to change. When she returned for a second London engagement in January 1949, Haskell sent her the following letter:

> *My Darling Alicia,*
>
> *This is a love letter. You know I never pay compliments and am always completely sincere. I never dreamed you could dance with such a depth of feeling and the effortless simplicity that I have seen in no one since Pavlova. I have certainly never seen you dance like that before. You were always a considerable ballerina but never before a class completely by yourself. In "Autumn"* [a new ballet Nijinska created for Markova] *you made us all cry and I was with a very hard-boiled & critical crowd. Petit* [the famous French choreographer] *& his ballerinas said you were the greatest dancer they had ever seen.*
>
> *This has made me very happy as I always wanted to believe you were great myself and not to feel that though everyone else thought so I still knew it was not the case.*
>
> *Now I have not the slightest doubt. I might be able to add a very exciting chapter to the autobiography I have in preparation, the sequel to "Balletomania." You are now in your artistic prime. Be careful. Don't overwork because I want to enjoy such beauty for a very long time to come.*
>
> *Much Love,*
> *Arnold*

Perhaps the most surprising thing about that letter was not that Haskell had fallen in love with Markova's dancing at long last, but that he had done so after seeing her perform in a cavernous sporting arena.

London's Empress Hall at Earls Court could seat over 6,000, compared to approximately 2,250 at Covent Garden. "The proposition came up that we do performances where we could get many people in at reasonable prices," Markova recalled, "which is what I enjoyed doing throughout my career, so we could reach as many people as possible."

Though it was huge, Empress Hall had been cleverly constructed on a single level with not one obstructed view. There was just one problem. Home to ice-dancing musical extravaganzas and ice-hockey sporting matches, the Hall had one very frozen stage.

As one newspaper explained, "Two stalwarts of British ballet, Alicia Markova and Anton Dolin, put on the show at the Empress Stadium and as an experiment it was quite successful. The dancing was done on a wooden sprung platform raised above the ice-hockey rink, the whole being an imitation Italian garden. It took 125 tons of turf, bushes, and flowers to make the garden."

The stage may have looked like summer, but it felt like winter, with the dancers constantly feeling the effects of the frigid ice below.

"It was *cold*," remembered Markova, who only took her woolen practice tights off for performances. "I lost my voice. But it didn't matter, because I didn't need to talk."

Booking such a large arena for entertainment as esoteric as ballet was unprecedented in London, and some thought foolhardy. They were wrong. Every seat would be filled for all five scheduled performances, with over 32,000 people watching Markova and Dolin dance in a single week—the largest ever for ballet in England at that time.

Audiences *and* critics were thrilled. "An experiment in ballet presentation was staged at the Empress Hall last night when Alicia Markova and Anton Dolin returned to London to give five special performances of famous solos and excerpts," wrote the *Daily Telegraph*. "The floodlighting of a rectangular stage in the stadium for the corps de ballet and spotlighting for the soloists produced some remarkable effects." Even ticketholders in the back rows were awed.

Of course there were some detractors of the mass marketing of ballet. One couldn't escape Markova's picture plastered all over London's red double-decker buses, offending several highbrow critics. But even those who looked down their noses at the "experiment" begrudgingly admitted Markova's power to entrance despite her performing in the unhallowed sporting arena.

> **All for Markova**
>
> To see Alicia Markova dance Pavlova's Dying Swan—the beautiful bird-like flutterings and the incredible grace and expressiveness of her arms—it was worthwhile braving the crude spotlights, the micro-phoney orchestra and even the strange gambollings of the corps de ballet at the Empress Hall last night.
>
> —*Daily Herald*, 1/4/49

The event was such a huge success that Markova and Dolin were asked to add another week's performances. Dolin was roundly enthusiastic, but Markova turned it down. She had a sore throat and laryngitis due to the frigid stage conditions and didn't want to push her luck.

The pair had already committed to future bookings in Puerto Rico and New York, followed by their first tour of South Africa and Kenya. Markova needed to be healthy. Dolin pushed again for just one more week at Empress Hall, as it would have been a highly lucrative engagement. But this time Markova stood firm. The answer was no.

Markova was in top form, once again performing in the U.S. After the final New York show, she was scheduled to fly directly to South Africa. But suddenly, she decided to make a detour to London and visit briefly with her mother and sisters. South Africa was the country where Arthur Marks had spent much of his youth, and family was very much on the ballerina's mind. A stopover in England was out of the way and Markova's booking agents were not happy, but she insisted.

It was a wonderful visit. Alexandra Danilova and Freddie Franklin were currently guest artists with the Sadler's Wells Company at Covent Garden, and Markova enjoyed being in the audience for a change, sitting with Eileen. They all had a celebratory dinner afterwards.

Looking ahead to the future, Markova wanted to spend more time with her mother. They discussed Eileen's moving from Birmingham to a cottage in Brighton—perhaps near their friends the Crewleys. Markova knew her mother loved the area, and she wanted to buy her a place of her own. It could be a second home for Alicia as well.

The ballerina planned to take some time off around Christmas and spend a month or two with Eileen. Dolin had already mentioned wanting to appear in a stage play during the holiday season, something he liked to do off and on. Markova told Eileen they would go house-hunting together when she returned.

It was a small group that made the trip to South Africa: Markova, Dolin, Alfred Katz, and the concert pianist Leon Kushner. Doris remained in Europe, as she was now managing a tour for the American dancer Katherine Dunham and her company. (The two had met through Markova in New York.)

Unlike with the Philippines tour, Markova came well prepared for the heat and humidity. As a local newspaper reported, "Madame Markova has reduced the necessity for 'travelling light' to a fine art. She has brought with her to South Africa about two dozen costumes, all of which have been made in New York to her own designs. As she usually travels by air, specially light fibre cases have had to be made to carry this precious freight with safety and without bulk."

And of course Markova had placed a large order for "tropical" ballet shoes. She would need every single pair, as their performances proved so popular that the trip was extended from twelve appearances to forty-eight. A four-week booking turned into four months.

> **12 Girls Go 1,000 Miles to See Ballerina**
>
> Johannesburg, Saturday
>
> Alicia Markova, world-famous ballerina, was breathless after two hours of enthralling dancing at Johannesburg's high altitude, before a full house on the opening night of the Markova-Dolin South African tour.
>
> But she was not nearly as breathless as the dozen little Rhodesian dancing students who motored 1,000 miles in two days to see the ballet—and were enchanted when asked to go backstage to meet the ballerina.
>
> For all but one of them, it was their first visit to Johannesburg.
>
> —*Sunday Tribune*, Durban, 4/10/49

After every performance, Markova was besieged by autograph-seekers. She accommodated every single one, often spending between one and two hours with pen and papers in hand. But a local masseuse had a unique request. Following a session of therapeutic muscle treatment, he asked to make a plaster cast of Markova's foot in lieu of payment. It was the most beautiful he had ever seen, she was told.

Even the local bars shared in "ballet fever," serving what they called "Markova-Dolin cocktails." Generally a teetotaler, Markova never learned the recipe.

There was indeed cause for all the hoopla. It had been over twenty-five years since a prima ballerina had danced in South Africa—it was of course Anna Pavlova—and once again Markova was following in her idol's footsteps.

While in Johannesburg, both ballerinas had taken the time to attend the traditional Zulu tribal dance ceremony. It lasted a full five hours. The time-honored ritual featured tribesmen draped in animal skins and elaborate feathered headdresses waving their spears and shields in sync to the ever-changing drumbeats.

Alfred Katz had vivid memories of the event, which he later passed along to British dance writer Peter Simon:

> Watching a massed dancing display by ten African tribes, Markova half-rose from her seat and let out an involuntary cry of sheer excitement upon their first entrance into the arena. The manager of the Crown Consolidated Mines, sitting next to her, remarked that some twenty years earlier, Pavlova had seen the same display, and reacted in precisely a similar fashion.
>
> Markova was so thrilled by the rhythmic precision and artistry of the native dancing, that she asked to meet the Zulu chief. Her host made the introduction, adding the gallant compliment that she was the greatest dancer in the world. At this, the chief drew himself up to his full six feet four and shook his head. "No," he said. "She is not the greatest dancer in the world. I am!"
>
> Markova, though she is inclined to agree with the chief, tells the story against herself with great delight.
>
> —*Pas De Deux*, Peter Simon, 1949

Markova was enthralled with South Africa—the people, the culture, the landscape, even the food, all as her father had described. She shared her childhood memories with a local reporter:

> **Childhood Dream of Ballerina Comes True—She's in S.A.**
>
> Years ago, a mining engineer from the Rand took a little girl on his knee in their English home and showed her a book of fading sepia snapshots of dusty Johannesburg streets, tin shanties, and men in old-fashioned clothes. The man was Arthur Marks and the child was Alicia Marks—later to become Alicia Markova, world-famous ballerina.
>
> Arthur Marks loved South Africa, and knew the country intimately in its early days. He trekked from Johannesburg to Barberton, Bulawayo and Nairobi, and when he was weary of the wilds, traveled down to the "civilized" Durban to live.
>
> This was years before Alicia was born, but Arthur Marks absorbed sufficient of South Africa to pass his love of the country on to his daughter, who recently looked down from an aeroplane on the wilds through which her father trekked.
>
> In their English home, the Marks spoke of sweet corn as "mealies," and threepence was always a "tickey."
>
> "Since my father give me mealies to eat as a child at home I've been asking for them all over the world, and they never seemed the same to me until I tasted them here," Madame Markova told me yesterday.
>
> One of the most pleasant experiences she has had in South Africa was meeting Mrs. Thelma Raymond of Johannesburg, again. Mrs. Raymond, then Thelma Henderson, stayed with Alicia Marks's family in England and the girls went to the same school. Madame Markova was delighted to discover that Mrs. Raymond's daughter has been christened Alicia, in memory of the childhood friendship.
>
> With a South African background to her childhood, Madame Markova does not feel that she is entirely a stranger in this country. Her manager, Alfred Katz, of New York, commented to me: "She is strangely happy here."

> He cannot say why, but he supposes it may have something to do with the ballerina's early associations, her father's snapshot album, and because her child imagination was stirred by the tales of early days on the brawling Rand.
>
> —*Sunday Times*, Johannesburg, 4/10/49

The day after that article appeared in the local paper, a cable arrived from Markova's sister Vivienne. Their mother was dead.

Mrs. Marks had been in London lunching with family friend Vivian Van Damm when she suddenly collapsed and was rushed to the hospital. It was a stroke. Eileen died without ever regaining consciousness.

Markova was completely shattered. She couldn't even go to the funeral, as it would have taken her almost ten days to get back to England. Everyone told her to stay in South Africa and keep dancing. It was what she needed to do.

"Now I had to carry on with our tour, and the social round of parties and receptions that went inescapably with it, with scarcely a pause to allow for the effect of the blow," Markova sadly recalled. "Looking back on such experiences, I sometimes wonder about their influence on me. The artist whose work lies in the theatre, is always compelled to throw a bridge across gaps opened by private grief, and this must sometimes be done with what seems inhuman swiftness. Yet, long afterwards, it may be seen that such griefs are distilled into the art itself, and help to purify it."

Dolin, who knew Eileen and the entire Marks family so well, was an enormous comfort. He understood exactly what Markova was going through—being so close to his own mother—and how guilty she had been feeling about not spending enough time with her.

Eileen had recently expressed concerns of her own when the family reconnected in London the previous year. She could not have been prouder of her unimaginably successful daughter, but at what cost? Her eldest child had no personal life, no husband, no children. Mrs. Marks asked Alicia to consider slowing down, and a new country home for the pair was to be a first step in that direction. What point was there now?

When Markova went back on stage after the dreadful news, she was performing the second act of *Giselle*. It takes place in a graveyard. She enters rising from her own tomb. The symbolism practically choked her.

As the tour progressed, Markova found South Africa deeply consoling. She was too busy to dwell on her personal tragedy, and each new place was a reminder of happy childhood days with her father. The worshipful audiences also provided solace. Their immense gratitude sustained her. There were breathing problems when the altitudes were high, and staging difficulties in the most rural areas, but Markova didn't seem to mind.

In Mozambique, a stage was so decrepit that one of the piano legs fell right through it when the instrument was wheeled on stage during the intermission. Markova and Dolin spent the second act making spur-of-the-moment adjustments to avoid getting caught by the jagged hole opening.

The mortified local manager profusely apologized afterward, explaining it had been a very long time since anyone had performed on the stage. It was back in 1924. And yes, the performer had been Anna Pavlova.

The lengthy booking in Cape Town was especially rewarding for both Markova and Dolin. They decided to produce the full-length *Giselle* with dancers from the South African National Ballet and Cape Town University. The locals had never attempted anything nearly as complicated as the Russian classic before, and there was great excitement throughout the city.

Auditions were held, roles were cast, and the construction of scenery began. The dancers were in awe of their famous teachers, who coached and trained them in both technique and acting. It was the type of collaboration Markova always relished.

A local newspaper writer was as surprised as the young cast at her approachability.

> **Markova weighs 97 lb.**
>
> I have in my time, interviewed many celebrities. There was, I remember, an actress who received the Press lying in a glass coffin and a Prima Donna who shouted her life story at me through the bathroom door, as she splashed and soaped within.
>
> It was therefore with considerable relief that I discovered that Alicia Markova, perhaps the most famous ballerina

> to-day, is modest, charming and helpful. Our interview took place in her dressing-room which, unlike that of many stars, was a model of neatness and order.
>
> Markova is a tiny, fragile creature with exquisite hands and the skin of a child. She weighs 97 lb. and loses an average of a pound after every performance. . . .
>
> When she is not on tour, Markova lives in New York where she has had her headquarters for the past ten years.
>
> —*Cape Town Times*, 5/20/49

The first full-length *Giselle* at Cape Town's Alhambra theatre was exceptionally moving to the city's residents. The joint production of two reigning ballet stars and their own local dancers was a source of great civic pride.

Before leaving the continent, Markova and Dolin would return to Johannesburg for another week, followed by a previously unscheduled stop in Nairobi—much to the locals' surprise. The news was like a "bombshell," wrote a Londoner living there at the time. "With bookings coming in from all over the colony by letter and telegram, the house was immediately sold out."

On the long trip home, Markova had time to think. She would later take stock of her life when asked to write about her career for a British magazine. Her mother had been right. She had given up everything to bring the beauty of ballet to others. She had to feel it was worth it.

Alicia Markova Tells Her Own Story

> . . . A ballerina's life, of course, isn't always spent in the radiance of footlights and applause. A great deal of it is lived in the unromantic glare of rehearsal, in characterless hotel bedrooms and thundering express trains. So, like every other artist, I have had to learn to adapt myself to a wanderer's life. . . .
>
> It's difficult for someone like me to achieve anything approaching a balanced life. Work can so easily swamp one's days—and even seep into one's nights! If I want to go to a concert, for example, I have to plan and scheme to fit it into my engagements. For me, music is the perfect relaxation. My idea

> of luxury is to sit perfectly still and listen to a fine orchestra playing anything from Bach to Britten. . . .
>
> Living nowadays has not become so serious that there is no place for light-hearted pleasures. The more we have to concentrate on matters of great significance, the more essential it is to refresh our minds with moments of relaxation. There are millions who find that relaxation in the ballet. And I am proud to contribute to their delight.

Upon returning to London, one of the first things Markova did was to visit Eileen's grave at the Jewish cemetery in East Sussex near Brighton. Dolin went with her. Twelve years later, his own mother would be buried in the Christian cemetery next door.

Eileen and the dream of a country cottage may have passed out of her life, but Markova was determined not to let that happen with her sisters. She had leased an apartment in New York and would do the same in London.

Markova found just what she was looking for at 43 Park Mansions in Knightsbridge. "The flat belonged to [film actress] Constance Cummings's father-in-law. And he was American, which is why it has two bathrooms," Markova explained. (Wealthy Americans demanded, and were willing to pay for, their creature comforts.) The apartment also had central heating, an uncommon London amenity in those days.

It was the ideal flat for three women: Vivienne, Doris, and Alicia, when she was in town. "It came up for rent in 1949 and we took it because it had been decorated and we didn't have to do a thing," said the time-strapped ballerina.

No one could have imagined that Doris and Markova would still be living together in that apartment fifty-five years later.

After great success at cavernous venues like the Hollywood Bowl in California and the Empress Hall in London, Markova jokingly referred to herself and Dolin as "pioneers of arena ballet." She refused to let dance snobs deter her. The larger the venue, the lower the ticket price, and Markova wanted to reach as many new people as possible in her hometown.

Next on their agenda was the 9,000-seat Harringay Stadium in North London—home to boxing matches, greyhound racing, and the circus. Markova laughingly recalled the smell of horses and elephants greeting her around every corner.

As they would be performing with Marie Rambert's talented ballet company, Markova very much wanted to produce the full-length *Giselle*; but the combination of Harringay's theater-in-the-round and unwieldy audience size made others doubtful. Markova was convinced she could pull it off, having already done so at Manhattan's Lewisohn Stadium. That arena, she pointed out, took up two square city blocks, was inspired by Rome's Coliseum, and had a seating capacity of 25,000!

Harringay's producer Tom Arnold agreed and spent £10,000 upfront to transform the space.

> **Ballet will cost £10,000**
>
> A £3,000 sound-absorbing ceiling in thirty sections, each weighing a ton, has been suspended over the stage to cut the echo and exclude noises from outside, and all the windows have been covered with special paint.
>
> A large stage open on three sides with a pit for the London Symphony Orchestra has been installed and accommodation behind the stage cut out in order to give it a theatre atmosphere.
>
> —*London Star*, 8/23/49

As was true with Empress Hall, Markova's *Giselle* played to sold-out houses at Harringay and turned a tidy profit. Many in the audience had never seen a ballet performance before and were completely enchanted. It didn't matter a whit to Markova that they dined on hot dogs and orangeade during intermission rather than the pricey cocktails and vanilla ice cream sold at the Royal Opera House. British balletomanes could tsk-tsk all they wanted.

Surprisingly, the dance critic who had originally coined the term "balletomane"—Arnold Haskell—was completely won over. He even wrote the introduction for the Harringay program, as excerpted here:

> **An Appreciation by Arnold Haskell**
> Our foremost Authority of the ballet
> Alicia Markova
>
> Markova belongs to the Royal Family of the Dance. A true descendant of Taglioni and Pavlova, her name is already a household word on both sides of the Atlantic. . . .
>
> Hers is the strong fragility of an aristocrat of ballet. To quote a great poet on Taglioni, "She flies like a spirit in the midst of transparent clouds of white muslin . . . she resembles a joyous angel who scarcely bends the petals of heavenly flowers with the tips of her pink toes."

Sadler's Wells ballerina Beryl Grey visited Markova backstage at Harringay, the two having become friends the previous year when dancing together at Covent Garden. As Grey told Maurice Leonard, she couldn't get over the comfy seating area Markova had pulled together in her dressing room, utilizing old furniture found lying about the arena. Markova brought her own roll-up pink carpet for the floor and even hung a pair of makeshift curtains. It wasn't remotely fancy, but Grey found it quite an amazing transformation considering the booking was for less than a week. Markova "always created this aura of serenity," she recalled.

For Markova, each new dressing room became an integral part of her physical and emotional preparation before going on stage, with her efforts to transform the space more than just a matter of aesthetics. Anton Dolin outlined his partner's painstaking ritual in his 1952 biography of her. He had never seen anything like it with any other dancer.

As Dolin explained, Markova always came to the theatre a minimum of two hours before curtain. She wanted time to prepare *everything* just right without any hurry or worries.

First on the agenda, in light of her history with costume disasters, was making sure all necessary stage attire was on the premises—properly steamed and pressed. Though many costumes in ballet companies are shared, Markova often had her own bodices, tutus, and headpieces made to order by Manya, Pavlova's former designer, who had now been working with Markova for over fifteen years. Those items would be brought to the dressing room at the beginning of an engagement, then carefully wrapped and unwrapped in tissue paper before and after each stage appearance.

Next came the selection of ballet shoes. Markova had at least six pairs available for any given performance, each with ribbons she had sewn on herself, and she chose a pair based on the ballet she would be dancing and the condition of the stage flooring. As toe shoes were completely hand-made, each felt slightly different on the foot.

A full forty-five minutes were allotted for makeup application, producing one of the most flawless faces in ballet. Markova was unnaturally orderly and precise. In contrast to a typical star's dressing table haphazardly strewn with cosmetics and dirty brushes, she carefully laid out every makeup tool, jar, and hair accessory, always arranged the same way. More than one person likened it to a surgical tray in an operating room. It was a manic neatness, and one of the reasons she needed privacy while preparing.

"I never like to see people in my dressing room during a performance," Markova confessed in a newspaper article. "I even won't have my maid in the room while I am making up. So for forty minutes she has to sit outside my door. I prefer and nearly always do unpack and repack my theatrical clothes, shoes, tights and make up. No wonder I am often asked, 'Why do you have a maid when you do it all yourself!' I suppose I have never forgotten the days when I could not afford one."

When her makeup was finished, Markova would carefully affix her headdress. Ever since the Diaghilev days when her tiara had spun off during a performance, she pinned and even glued all hair ornaments to her head if necessary.

"At seven," noted a reporter shadowing Markova's pre-show ritual, "she makes her way to the stage, a tiny figure with Pavlova's glittering diamond crown on her head—a Swan Princess. She wears practice costume . . . grasps the frame of the onstage door and begins to bend, stretch, flex, kick. She works silently, diligently. She does not stop even when she talks."

When warmed up, and secure in the knowledge that her headpiece would stay perfectly in place while dancing, Markova returned to her dressing room, where she put on her costume. Once sewn in, she would not sit or lean to prevent rumpling.

In 1944, a writer from *The New Yorker* magazine had been allowed to quietly observe Markova backstage at the Metropolitan Opera House. She reported the following:

> She [Markova] has her changes figured out to the second, and she clocks herself by a watch which is set in the exact centre of her dressing table. Of the twenty-minute intermission between the first and second sets of "Giselle," the first five minutes are all allotted to her maid's peeling off the dancer's damp costumes, wiping off her makeup, and sponging down her hair. The next five minutes are devoted to changing her shoes and the remaining ten to rearranging her headdress, sewing her into her second-act costume, and putting on fresh makeup which transforms her from a healthy peasant girl into a corpse.
>
> —*The New Yorker*, Barbara Heggie, 4/15/44

After performances, Markova was a different person, cheerfully greeting press and well-wishers in the same dressing room that had previously been a private citadel.

"My friends often laugh at me for taking bits and pieces of my own with me to create a home wherever I go, but they have to admit that I succeed," said Markova. "Give me half an hour and I can make any four walls feel like home."

In 1949, the 51-year-old impresario Julian Braunsweg came into Markova's life. It would not be a pleasant association.

Born in Warsaw, Poland, Braunsweg first became interested in the ballet when he moved with his wealthy Jewish family to Moscow. After later resettling in Berlin, he made a connection that led to a freelance job for the Ballets Russes: the supervision of local booking arrangements and publicity for the company. When the Berlin ballet engagement was over, Braunsweg was taken aback when no payment was forthcoming. "Never become a ballet impresario, young man," Diaghilev told him with a smile. "It never pays."

Braunsweg was undeterred, perhaps even emboldened by the experience. He would eventually manage the Russian Romantic Ballet with Tamara Karsavina in Berlin, and handle a few tours for Anna Pavlova and La Argentinita toward the end of their careers. During World War II, the diminutive impresario moved to England, where he brought Colonel de Basil's Original Ballet Russe to Covent Garden, and Serge Lifar's Monte Carlo Ballet to the Cambridge Theatre.

In 1948, all of London was buzzing about Alicia Markova's *Giselle* with the Sadler's Wells Ballet at Covent Garden. Critics played "Can you top this?" with superlatives, and Markova and Dolin performed to sellout crowds. Julian Braunsweg wanted a piece of that success.

Realizing that de Basil's Original Ballet Russe was never going to bring him the blockbuster status he craved, Braunsweg approached Anton Dolin about representing him and Markova on a tour of the British provinces. While very interested in the proposal, Dolin felt the timing all wrong for approaching Markova. They had only recently ended a problematic long-term contract with Sol Hurok and she would be disinclined to sign another, he explained. Dolin advised patience.

Six months later, Braunsweg was in the audience at Empress Hall when Markova and Dolin broke all previous attendance records for ballet bookings in England. In his autobiography *Braunsweg's Ballet Scandals*, the impresario claims to have been so excited by one of those performances that he ran backstage as soon as it was over and offered Markova and Dolin the most generous salaries in the history of ballet for a 2½-month tour of the British provinces.

Braunsweg condenses what transpired over the next several months into two short paragraphs:

> Dolin was very excited about the offer. Markova wasn't. She did not particularly want to tour the provinces and thought it might be detrimental to her image to make such a tour with me—a foreigner she had never heard of.
>
> Dolin exerted a tremendous influence over Markova and began his gentle art of persuasion. Hurok, who had been their impresario in America, also urged her to sign with me. But she continued to hesitate. Eventually, her indecision infuriated Dolin [and Braunsweg].

That passage fairly sums up Julian Braunsweg's feelings toward Markova throughout their working relationship. How *dare* she not immediately capitulate to his and Dolin's plans for *her* future? As the impresario makes abundantly clear in his memoirs, Markova's personal opinions, concerns, and career goals had no place in his universe, where money—his money—should have done all the talking. (He felt the same way about Margot Fonteyn, whom he also later worked with, and who came under even harsher personal attack in his book.)

Like Sol Hurok, Braunsweg thought Markova should have been grateful for his generous offer, sign on the dotted line, and do what she was told like a good little girl. Also like Hurok, Braunsweg enlisted Anton Dolin's help in "landing" and managing Markova.

In 1949, Alicia Markova was still at the peak of her career, and if history was to be her guide, she had roughly six years left to dance professionally. (In a magazine interview at the time, she talked about dancing "for a few more years" before permanently settling down.) She was receiving a steady stream of offers from the most prestigious ballet companies in the world, as well as invitations to dance in countries she had always dreamed of exploring. Markova needed to carefully consider her options for the dancing years she had left.

At present, she and Dolin had a great thing going. As valued guest artists in top-tier ballet companies, they could parachute in for limited runs, enjoy the fame and fortune of performing in the best theaters with the finest dancers, and move on to the next enticing offer without any legal entanglements.

When the spirit moved them, they could fly thousands of miles to the middle of nowhere—just the two of them and a pianist—exposing hungry new audiences to ballet while enjoying the stimulation of foreign cultures and people. No other ballet partnership at that time had the star power or repertoire to pull off such a feat and make money in the process. Even Pavlova almost always traveled with a full *corps de ballet*.

Braunsweg was interested in creating what Markova and Dolin had happily left behind: another touring company—once again based in England—presenting the best of ballet at mass-market ticket prices. That had been the goal of Vivian Van Damm and Mrs. Laura Henderson in the 1930s, an extravagant venture that had cost the wealthy widow a small fortune.

The second Markova-Dolin Company—this time in America—did turn a profit, but mainly for Sol Hurok, who reduced the number of dancers and increased the backbreaking workload to make that happen. The day-to-day business headaches of both companies had fallen to Dolin and Markova. Why would they want to go through all that again?

In the beginning, Braunsweg was pushing for just one season—the fall of 1949—and the salaries he was proposing were awfully good. That got Dolin excited.

Though Markova was still hesitant, she was well aware that many large theaters throughout England were publicly clamoring for the two dancers to perform there. It would be their first time back in the provinces since the mid-1930s. Sentimentally, Markova was inclined to say yes. And with Eileen's recent death, remaining in England would allow her to spend more time bonding with her sisters.

Besides, Markova thought, she and Dolin had already committed to a winter tour of Puerto Rico, Havana, Jamaica, and the Caribbean, followed by engagements in Miami and New York. Since the contract with Braunsweg was just for four months, she agreed.

The impresario started small: curtain backdrops instead of elaborate sets, a portable stage, and a small symphony orchestra. As one newspaper noted, the musicians "more than redeem a certain thinness of tone by the extreme delicacy and taste of their playing."

Braunsweg asked Dolin to book the youngest, prettiest ballerinas he could find—fourteen of them, to be exact—and two youthful male dancers. "Markova thought the corps were too pretty and far too young," wrote Braunsweg; but he reminded his leading lady: "A diamond shines better in a good quality setting."

In Markova's defense, she found the male dancers too young as well.

The new Markova-Dolin Company gave their first performance on September 12, 1949 in Newcastle, continuing on to Leeds, Birmingham, Edinburgh, and numerous other cities before finishing up in Bristol on November 28. Braunsweg billed the pair as "The World's Greatest Ballet Stars," and the tour was a smash.

Regional newspapers picked up right where they had left off in 1936, photographing Markova wherever she went, writing glowing feature stories about what she ate and wore, and taking enormous pride in the celebrity of the two British dancing stars.

Parents who had first seen Markova and Dolin in the 1930s now brought their children to share in the experience. Every seat was filled and stage-door crowds were almost frighteningly overzealous.

> **Police 'Rescue' Dancers**
>
> After their premiere performance at the City Hall, Newcastle last night, ballet stars Anton Dolin and Alicia Markova were mobbed by ballet lovers as they left the hall.
>
> The dancers were held at bay by the mob of more than 100 enthusiasts for half an hour and police had to assist to get them through the crowd.
>
> —*Journal and Northern Mail*, 9/13/49

> **Ballet does the "impossible"**
>
> The Markova-Dolin ballet in Edinburgh last night confounded some experts—it filled the Usher Hall, a feat which in weeks immediately following previous festivals has been considered impossible. . . .
>
> Markova's dancing of "The Dying Swan" alone was worth going to see.
>
> —*News Chronicle*, Edinburgh 9/16/49

Braunsweg licked his lips. "I began discussions with Markova and Dolin about establishing a full-time company," he explained. "Neither of them was very enthusiastic despite the phenomenal success of their tour, which clearly demonstrated that there was a big demand for popular ballet at popular prices."

Markova and Dolin pointed out that Mrs. Henderson had felt the same way in the 1930s, only to lose a considerable sum. But the dancers hadn't shared in that loss, being well paid for all their work, Braunsweg reminded them.

That argument fell on deaf ears, as the dancers' arrangement with Braunsweg would be completely different. He was proposing a joint venture with Dolin and Markova each having a personal financial stake. They would be taking a big risk with someone they hardly knew.

Making matters worse, when Dolin asked Braunsweg if he had the substantial funding needed to start a new ballet company, the impresario was hardly reassuring: "No, but with your names I can get money." Markova wasn't interested. She didn't need or want the aggravation.

So Braunsweg went to work on Dolin.

There was his future to consider, the impresario warned. Dolin was forty-six years old. How much longer would he be able to dance? Braunsweg was offering him a permanent position as artistic director of his own company. Dolin would be choosing the corps, the soloists, the repertoire—just as his rival Massine had done in the past. Naturally, Dolin would also continue his starring role as partner to Markova.

It was a pretty picture of his future, but none of it would be possible if Markova didn't sign on. Braunsweg and Dolin needed her name and prestige to obtain financial backing. No Markova, no company.

Unfortunately, she didn't need them. Alicia Markova could dance wherever and with whomever she chose. It was her name that sold tickets.

That couldn't have been made clearer to Dolin than in June 1950, when the two dancers were booked to perform together at London's Royal Albert Hall. The historic theater may have been more exclusive than Harringay Stadium, but it was close to the same capacity with 8,000 seats. At top-tier ticket prices, that was a tall order to fill. But Markova's name sold out the house.

Then, just a few weeks before the scheduled opening, Markova had an attack of appendicitis necessitating emergency surgery. The Albert Hall appearance was immediately cancelled, and 20,000 tickets were refunded.

Dolin protested, as he made clear in his autobiography: "I wasn't ill and I had the choice of two other ballerinas, who would have flown over from America to replace Markova."

But producer Victor Hochhauser released the following statement to the press: "Anton Dolin was willing to carry on with a substitute for Markova, but we do not think it would be the same thing. It was the first time ballet was to be produced at Albert Hall."

Hochhauser was just anticipating the inevitable avalanche of ticket returns that would have erased all his profits. If Dolin had been indisposed, another fine partner could have been found for Markova—perhaps Eglevsky or Skibine—but not the other way around.

Dolin was feeling undervalued—through no fault of Markova's—and as had been true in 1941, he wanted to have control over their future partnership to ensure his own professional value. As art director of the Braunsweg-sponsored ballet company, he most certainly would.

Now it was Dolin's turn to work on Markova.

First he convinced Braunsweg that a magnificent production of the full-length *Giselle* was the perfect enticement to get Markova on board. It was the ballet she loved above all others, and the one that was synonymous with her gossamer artistry. The impresario promised funding for sensational new backdrops, scenery, and costumes, including a jewel box of a setting—the splendid Stoll Theatre. Second only to the Royal Opera House in grandeur and prestige, the Stoll had dramatic entrance foyers, an opulent auditorium, expansive rehearsal space on the upper floors, and elegant dressing rooms. It would be the company's permanent London home.

And in addition to mounting a sumptuous new *Giselle*, other Russian classics would also be added to the permanent repertoire, including *The Nutcracker*, *Swan Lake*, and *Les Sylphides*.

Though excited at the prospect, Markova was concerned that a corps filled with young, inexperienced dancers wouldn't be up to the task. Dolin guaranteed her that accomplished soloists would also be engaged, as well as world-famous guest artists, including Léonide Massine, Mia Slavenska, and her beloved Alexandra Danilova.

Markova was finally convinced, but made one last request. She was willing to trade money for a bit of freedom, a concept totally foreign to Braunsweg. As she consistently received exciting offers for ballet engagements outside of London, she asked for written assurances that she could accept those bookings, providing the dates didn't conflict with the company's schedule. She also wanted to be able to travel wherever she liked during the off-season. There was a limit to how much Giselle was willing to have her wings clipped.

Braunsweg agreed to Markova's terms, but the lengthy contract negotiations made him resentful of his prima ballerina even before their formal working relationship began. She had never been rude, demanding, or confrontational—just slow to acquiesce. It was a perfectly normal give-and-take process for a dancer of her stature, but Braunsweg still fumed.

In his book *Braunsweg's Ballet Scandals*, the impresario describes Markova as "indecisive, temperamental, inclined to be lazy and one of the greatest Romantic ballerinas of the century, particularly in *Giselle*."

To him she was a necessary evil—a sublime and beautiful dancer, but a real pain in the neck. It is true Markova would give Braunsweg some serious trouble throughout their association, but the reasons for that will shortly be made clear. He also never gave her credit for all the hard work she put in in training and coaching the younger dancers.

Braunsweg's Ballet Scandals was published in 1974. Though most of the dancers maligned in the text had retired (Fonteyn being a notable exception), many were still actively involved in the ballet world. Braunsweg relished dishing dirt on each and every one of them, as the book's title suggests.

The memoir got quite a bit of attention. It was well written by ghost-writer James Kelsey—its authorship is listed "as told to"—since the Polish Braunsweg had trouble *speaking* English, let alone writing it. (Commenting on the impresario, dance critic Clive Barnes wrote that he "talks in an almost impenetrable accent, which is charming but difficult. Also when he doesn't want you to know something the accent deepens as the smile broadens.")

In his review, Clive Barnes found the book entertaining. Who wouldn't? "Some of the stories listed herein are horrific and definitely anti-Romantic. Alicia Markova, eating Black Magic chocolates and complaining, Anton Dolin, miffed at receiving a smaller Brazilian decoration than Braunsweg. . . . But without them, there would be no Festival Ballet. . . . Braunsweg's story of having Dolin approve, as artistic director, a cast of highly distinguished but extraordinarily dead dancers is hilarious—yet at the beginning both he, and originally Markova, provide the company with its momentum."

And that is the main problem with the memoir. Braunsweg overlooks everyone's contribution to the company but his own. Like Sol Hurok and so many other impresarios, Braunsweg is manipulative, egomaniacal, and a serial exaggerator.

Let's assume most of the stories are true—though Clive Barnes writes amusingly that in the one instance where he is mentioned, almost every fact was wrong, "perhaps resulting from the transcription, Julian's accent and Julian's memory," he adds charitably—they are also one-sided. Naturally, that is the case in most autobiographies. Looking at the founding of the British ballet company from Markova's point of view—something she never endeavored to do in her lifetime, though she had many opportunities—offers a far more balanced picture.

The story begins not with Markova being temperamental, but rather in a great deal of pain. She was bedridden in London's St. John and St. Elizabeth Hospital (fondly known as "John & Lizzie's"), recovering from emergency appendix surgery. Dolin and Alfred Katz paid her a visit to discuss the planning progress of the new ballet company and come up with a name.

In a barely audible voice, Markova told them she couldn't bear the thought of yet another "Markova-Dolin" ballet. Dolin quite agreed—too much past baggage.

The ailing ballerina had thought of an alternative.

Plans were under way for a national "Festival of Britain" to be held in the summer of 1951. It was to be a major celebration of the country's vast contributions to the arts, architecture, science, and technology. So Markova suggested calling their new venture "The Festival Ballet." Dolin and Katz thought it a splendid suggestion, and hurried off to tell Braunsweg they had their new name.

Markova couldn't hurry off anywhere. She would be confined to her hospital bed for an entire month, having developed severe liver problems and dysentery following surgery. Daily liver injections were administered and would continue throughout the summer, which was spent recuperating at home. Doctors told the dancer not to even consider practicing again until sometime in September.

When she felt up to it, Markova went to the Stoll Theatre to meet with the talented set designer Hugh Stevenson, or watch rehearsals. Otherwise she took it easy and visited with family, often taking in a movie with Vivienne or Doris. One of her favorite activities was lunching with Bunny and her three-year-old daughter Susie, who Markova absolutely adored.

"Susan—she's three—is just like Alicia, small and very dainty," wrote Doris at that time. "I think she will be a dancer too. We all dote on her, especially Alicia."

Bunny's husband had been an officer in the RAF. So was Markova's former love, Stanley Burton. When she performed in Leeds the previous spring, Markova had visited with Burton and his wife Audrey in Harrogate. They were a very happy couple with much in common. Together, they developed various charitable trusts, particularly for the arts. They were animated and cheerful, and had an enviable life. Markova couldn't have been more pleased for them both, and always enjoyed their company. But while there's no doubt she would have made the same choice of career over marriage again, her sacrifice had clearly been great.

Markova had a lot of time on her hands in that summer of 1950. Her daily diary, normally overflowing with commitments, was quite sparse. Each morning the same activity was penciled in: "Garden." As she walked alone among the beautiful flowers, for the first time, they brought her no joy. She mourned Eileen's death and what might have been.

And what of her future? She was weak, had serious liver problems, and was aging in an unforgiving profession. Markova was about to turn forty, a traumatic age for many women, but especially so for a world-famous ballerina whose technical skills weren't what they used to be.

As she became more fretful and depressed, Markova could no longer sleep peacefully through the night. That was a natural gift she had always counted on. Her hopes were that this new Festival Ballet—and perhaps the greatest production of *Giselle* in modern times—would turn everything around for her. It would not.

11

Taking Charge

Alicia Markova, the ballet dancer, is one of many famous people I consulted who believe that the happiness you find in your work depends almost entirely on yourself—on how to adjust yourselves to your colleagues, to your superiors and above all to your surroundings. . . .

"In any kind of work, you must find out by trial and error the conditions that suit you best," she stresses. "Friendly advice is all very well, but only *you* can decide the conditions under which you work best."

—*Everybody's Weekly*, London, 7/31/54

The Festival Ballet's London debut of *Giselle* starring Alicia Markova was scheduled for November 2, 1950. As Julian Braunsweg had promised, no expense was spared.

Hugh Stevenson—noted for his memorable work with Antony Tudor and the Ballet Rambert—created sets so astonishingly opulent that the audience would breathlessly "ooh and ah" when the curtain rose. Markova's trusted costumier Manya worked closely with Stevenson, echoing his richly saturated color palette in the lavish Act I peasant costume. Even noted ballet historian Cyril Beaumont was called in as a consultant to make sure the production was true to its Russian roots.

While Markova was home recovering from surgery, Dolin spent the summer hastily auditioning and hiring a corps of forty dancers, with the beautiful Russian Nathalie Krassovska—formerly with the Ballet Russe de Monte Carlo—engaged as prima ballerina.

Prior to the inaugural London season, Braunsweg booked the company on a tour of the British provinces. It would serve as both moneymaker and out-of-town training ground. Since Markova was indisposed, Léonide Massine was engaged as the chief box-office draw.

At fifty-five, the multi-talented dancer/choreographer was still wildly popular with audiences. In 1948, he had co-starred with Moira Shearer in the now-classic ballet movie *The Red Shoes*, adding to his celebrity. For Braunsweg's nascent dance troupe, Massine staged and starred in two charming ballets: Fokine's *Petrouchka*, and his own Viennese-themed *Le Beau Danube*. The lively productions delighted audiences and critics alike.

Markova came to the theater to watch rehearsals, cheer on the young dancers, and reconnect with her old friend Massine. By October, she would be well enough to perform with him in *Petrouchka*. Meanwhile, she watched the role danced by the 31-year-old Krassovska. Markova thought her quite lovely.

Margot Fonteyn was also thirty-one. As the *prima ballerina assoluta* of London's preeminent Sadler's Wells Ballet, Fonteyn would now be considered Markova's rival as far as the press was concerned. Comparisons were inevitable. The older ballerina wasn't jealous, as she had always admired and wished the best for her friend Margot, but Markova was beginning to feel old and vulnerable.

Following her surgery, she hadn't been able to dance for three months. The last time that had happened, Markova was five years younger. How much longer would it take her to bounce back this time? Making matters worse, her trusted coach Vincenzo Celli was over three thousand miles away in New York.

Markova once told Eric Johns, "If I took a month's holiday, I would need two months solid practice before regaining my normal working pitch. Leisure to the dancer simply means a waste of time and a slipping back in art. She cannot afford such a luxury."

That interview had been fifteen years earlier. Could she really be in shape by October?

British theatre critic Caryl Brahms was invited to watch Massine's summer rehearsal for a feature story that would run in *Modern* magazine after the London opening of The Festival Ballet. Despite Markova's not yet being well enough to dance, she was the focal point of the article.

> **Caryl Brahms takes you behind the enchanted stage, to the bare bleak classroom where a Ballet was born**
>
> . . . Britain's newest ballet is called The Festival Ballet and it has been brought into being to support the two great British exponents of Classical Dance, Alicia Markova and Anton Dolin; British dancers whom I never consciously think of as being British at all, so closely have they identified themselves with Russian Ballet.
>
> Markova is like a living Taglioni—a ballerina who has stepped down from a Victorian print. And Anton Dolin supports the exquisite lightness of her dance with his distinguished offices as Cavalier.
>
> The Ballet which they have newly gathered around them is basically a young company, one which may promise more than it can at first achieve. . . . [T]heir own beloved Assoluta, Alicia Markova was convalescing (in the stage-box—she couldn't keep away!) and had been forbidden to appear with them for the first few weeks of their tour. . . . [T]hough a young company can be buoyant and pliant, and pleasing and loyal, the soul of the ballet is its ballerina, whether like Margot Fonteyn she shines like a diamond at a woman's throat, or, like Markova, is the white camellia at the breast of the Spirit of the Dance.
>
> As I write this The Festival Ballet has not yet opened in London, but when it does it will be with its full complement of soloists with Alicia Markova, its own exquisite Assoluta.
>
> —*Modern* magazine, January 1951

Markova knew the future success of The Festival Ballet depended entirely on her. It was her name that would draw nightly crowds to

London's Stoll Theatre, and her *Giselle* had better deliver. Normally, she could count on Dolin to prop her up in such times of stress, but as art director, he was now too busy. He also had just hired a young male dancer who would become his closest confidante and companion for the next thirty years. Dolin's mind and attentions were elsewhere, and his priorities had changed. Markova and Dolin were soon to do battle, but for now the prima ballerina rose to the challenge as the press followed her progress.

> **Markova Steps Out**
>
> Practising daily in a bare first-floor room in Mayfair, Alicia Markova is preparing for her reappearance with Anton Dolin next month, after a long illness.
>
> Her first public appearance with the Festival ballet will be in Edinburgh on October 9, then on to Glasgow, followed by an eight-weeks season at the Stoll before Christmas.
>
> Thousands were disappointed when appendicitis laid Markova low just before an Albert Hall opening with Dolin. . . . A month in hospital was followed by a long rest, and now she has been practising for just three weeks. It is probably one of the longest breaks from work she has ever had.
>
> —*London Evening News*, 9/30/50

Markova's daily diaries from this time show a full schedule of solitary studio practices, doctor's visits, costume and wig fittings, and publicity interviews. After a month, she had worked her way up to daily rehearsals with the company, but she continued to practice alone each morning in her rented studio space. Braunsweg thought her lazy, not realizing she wasn't in the theater because she always did her *barre* exercises alone.

November 2 came quickly. It seems Markova was ready.

> **Markova-Dolin Festival**
>
> One night last week I left the Stoll Theatre in the state of exhilaration that can only be created by a deep spiritual experience. Markova had been dancing Giselle, but with such perfection of artistry as I never remember having seen brought to the role, even by Markova herself.
>
> —*Spectator*, 11/10/50

She is top of the town

There is one great performance to be seen in London. Just one—and not in a play.

Alicia Markova's Giselle, in the season of the Festival Ballet at the Stoll, communicates a sense of effortless wonder. She has danced it hundreds of times—but never better than now.

The production is also graced with a haunting décor from Hugh Stevenson, the panache of Anton Dolin, and an able corps de ballet. Its worst enemy is the orchestra, which battered its way through the score, without style or accurate intonation.

—*Sunday Graphic*, 11/12/50

Ballet

It was Markova as much as anybody who made it possible for English ballet to exist. These days this fact is too often forgotten. Markova it was who helped to pollinate the young Sadler's Wells with the Russian tradition brought from the Diaghileff company; Markova who made an English revival of the great classical ballets worthwhile, and popularized them; Markova who was an inspiration and an incalculable help to the young choreographers who created ballets for her, to Ashton for instance, and to the young dancers who worked with her. (One need look no further than Margot Fonteyn for an example of her influence.) Her tradition continues. So much so that foreign dancers complain of its tyranny. . . .

Markova may have decorated the part of Giselle with more technical virtuosity in the past, but I doubt whether she has ever given a more beautifully modulated or more finished performance of it than she does now. Certainly no ballerina to-day can approach it.

—*The New Statesman and Nation*, 11/18/50

Markova was a sensation. So great was her acclaim that the 84-year-old Queen Mary, the wife of the late King George V, asked to meet her in the Royal Box while attending a performance. It was reported in the newspapers the next day that Her Majesty was quite taken with Markova's ballet shoes and tiny feet. The *Overseas Daily Mail* got an additional scoop from an eyewitness:

> After chatting for several minutes Queen Mary glanced down at Alicia's ballet shoes and remarked, "When you dance, do your feet hurt?"
>
> "No," replied Alicia.
>
> "How difficult it must be; I can't imagine how I could do it," said Queen Mary, raising her heels slightly.

Photographs of Markova and Queen Mary—the ballerina in costume and the elderly HRH in black brocade—were published in newspapers throughout England. Dolin in white tie and tails had escorted Markova to the Royal Box and was standing next to her. The newspapers cropped him out.

Eric Johns was another respected journalist given access to The Festival Ballet rehearsals, having known Markova and Dolin for over twenty years. But unlike Caryl Brahms, Johns came on the scene after Markova was back with the company, rather than sitting anxiously on the sidelines. As Markova worked to get her own strength back, Johns was fascinated by her generosity in coaching and training the younger dancers:

> **Markova's Heritage**
>
> Eric Johns discusses Alicia Markova and the new Festival Ballet Company
>
> . . . Markova feels that it is the duty of the mature ballerina to take youngsters under her wing and pass on the priceless heritage received from the great dancers of yesterday. . . .
>
> Markova has talked to them about the significance of the roles they are called upon to dance. When they staged *Les Sylphides* she explained the ideas in Fokine's mind at the time he created this most poetical of ballets. The work took on a new meaning for them, and once they grasped the significance of their roles they were never guilty of a purely mechanical interpretation. They were obviously inspired by Markova's

> presence in the cast and conveyed to the audience something of the delicate grace and loveliness of the ballet.
>
> Never for a moment does Markova lose sight of the fact that a ballet is a theatrical performance and not an academic display of fine dancing. The stage picture is a vital factor, and on that account she insists upon young dancers paying special attention to the wearing of costume. She gave them instruction in managing a crinoline when rehearsing. . . . The girls were taught to walk differently and shown how to sit down and rise from a chair gracefully when wearing a Victorian dress. Such points, all vital to a stage production, are not taught in class by the ballet master. Markova is constantly impressing upon young artists the importance of *being* a role, rather than a dancer in fancy costume.
>
> Markova, a past-mistress in the art of stage make-up, is severely critical of those dancers who conceal their faces behind a grotesque mask of greasepaint in the belief that such application makes their presence felt at the back of the gallery. She maintains that no one beyond the tenth row of the stalls can see a dancer's face in any detail, so the entire body has to be used as an instrument of expression if she wishes to impress the whole audience. Nothing can be attained by excessive and unnatural painting of the face. She gave the company useful tips concerning quick-change in make-up, from the dark Italian colouring of *Capriccioso* to the moonlit pallor of *Les Sylphides*. . . .
>
> It is gratifying to hear that the boys and girls of the Festival Ballet are more than appreciative of all that is being done for them. They are fully conscious of their good fortune in having such expert supervision. The love and devotion of the company were, in fact, a source of great consolation to Markova last Summer when she was away from the ballet for some months on account of illness. The youngsters left her in no two minds about being wanted back. They longed for her gentle guidance and encouragement.

That lengthy passage illustrates Markova's significant contribution to the formation of The Festival Ballet. In their future autobiographies,

Braunsweg and Dolin reduce Markova's role to one of a skilled and famous dancer able to sell tickets—nothing more. The only stories they bother to tell are ones of her temperamental outbursts—directed solely at Dolin. Unfortunately, those are the narratives that have received the most attention over the years.

Dancer Malcolm Goddard was with the company from the first provincial Braunsweg tour in 1949. He found Markova an inspiration, and the two became friends. "I learned economy on stage from Alicia," Goddard told biographer Maurice Leonard. "When she was learning anything she pared it down to basics. Nothing was wasted and no movement was unnecessary."

In a radio tribute to Markova in later years, Goddard recalled, "I was always aware of the enormous responsibility one had toward someone like this because whenever Markova danced, there was always the extra tingle of expectation from the audience. I remember the enormous Stoll Theatre packed to capacity for the *Giselle* performance and the feeling backstage was incredible. For a ballerina to dance *Giselle* was an enormous responsibility to the audience and consequently one felt an enormous responsibility to your ballerina—Markova."

Goddard played the key role of Hilarion to Markova's Giselle at the Stoll. He told Leonard of one evening when the ventilation system broke down, making ungodly noises throughout the performance and forcing the dancers to perform in unbearable heat. Markova was cool as a cucumber. "There was never any foot stamping from her," Goddard recalled. And he wished more people realized what a great sense of humor she had.

During the London season, Markova and Dolin were asked to record *Giselle* for American television. The production would be filmed at Riverside Studios in Hammersmith, so the dancers could rehearse there during the day and perform at the Stoll Theatre at night. Festival Ballet company members would also participate. No one would be paid.

Earlier that year, Charlie Chaplin had asked Markova and Dolin to perform in his upcoming film *Limelight*, but they had been forced to turn him down due to scheduling difficulties. They were now inclined to make the sacrifices necessary to record *Giselle* for posterity, even if the production was less than ideal.

Because it was for television, the ballet would be reduced to two thirteen-minute acts with commercial advertising as intermission. To accommodate such a short time frame, *Giselle* would need to be "pared to the core," as Markova described it.

But the show also had an impressive roster of participants, including a score recorded by Sir Malcolm Sargent conducting the London Symphony Orchestra, and an introduction written by *New York Times* dance critic John Martin. That commentary was delivered by Markova's good friend, the British actor Jack Buchanan, perhaps best known to American audiences for playing the flamboyant producer in the 1953 film *The Band Wagon*, starring Fred Astaire and Cyd Charisse.

The filming schedule was a nightmare. After having danced the full-length *Giselle* at the Stoll Theatre in the evening—and not getting to bed until two A.M.—Markova needed to rise again at five the next morning and travel in the bitter December chill to the recording studio. She would work there all day until it was time to return to the Stoll for her next performance. That routine continued for one entire week. It was just six months since Markova's surgery.

The completed program was quite popular on television, so much so that the producers decided to release *Giselle* as a thirty-minute short film in American cinemas paired with a feature-length movie. But the sets had been cheap, designed to be viewed on the small screen only, and couldn't compare with the typical movie musicals of the day. While the public found the ballet interesting, dance critics were less kind.

> **Would it Were Not Dep't . . .**
>
> A 30 minute British film "Giselle" just appeared in American movie houses as a short and we would happily support such a large scale viewing of one of our favorite ballets if we could, especially when it boasts Markova at her best in the title role. But the uninspired postured partnering of Anton Dolin, the insipid (in this chopped up version at least) corps of the Festival Ballet, the horrid sets, bad lighting and merciless cutting of the ballet weigh the balance deep in the negative.
>
> —*Dance Magazine*, May 1953

Even though Markova's performance was widely praised in all the reviews, she was upset with both the unfortunate editing and ill-suited oversized format. Several years later, her comments on the subject were recorded at a London Ballet Circle lecture:

> Regarding ballet on film, which question followed the television discussion, Madame Markova said that she disliked fake of any kind, and had a deep distrust of the filming process. In the Giselle film, for instance, which she did not regard as good, she had insisted that her two solo dances be filmed straight through and un-interrupted by the "cut and begin again" process, which destroyed all feeling, as she likes to have perfect control over whatever she is doing and when filming, this is obviously impossible. Madame Markova left no doubt as to her feelings on dancing in films, and said that she would not easily be enticed into the film world and the audience nodded its unanimous approval.

Markova was exhausted after her double workload of performing *Giselle* on stage and in the studio day after day. She had just turned forty on December 1, and post-surgery, her endurance wasn't what it used to be. Within a week of completing the film commitment, she came down with severe gastric flu. She would have ongoing intestinal problems throughout the decade, which eventually developed into severe and painful colitis.

Following doctor's orders, Markova sipped high-caloric milkshakes—known in London as "chocolate frosteds"—as soon as she came offstage at the end of every performance, and popped milk chocolates during intermission for an instant blood sugar boost. As she had once said of taking dancing lessons instead of wearing leg braces as a little girl, "It was the best kind of medicine."

The spring of 1951 brought more than just warmer weather. The Festival Ballet left the security of England for the first time to dance in France. The booking was in Monte Carlo, and for Markova, it was a reminder of Diaghilev and the Ballets Russes days. She had not danced in France since before the war, and her *Giselle* was considered an "event."

Markova Honoured

A singular tribute has been paid to a British ballerina by the French ballet critics. When Alicia Markova danced Giselle with the Festival Ballet in Monte Carlo earlier in the month, all the leading Paris critics traveled south to see her, and declared in their newspapers and on the radio that she gave the finest performance of the part ever seen in France.

—*Performer* magazine, 4/26/51

Packing Them In

I hear that the Markova-Dolin Festival Ballet Company are playing to packed houses at Monte Carlo. They are the first British ballet company ever to be invited for a season at this famous resort.

The Queen of Spain, the Prince of Monaco and many other distinguished people from Britain and the Continent have been present.

—*London Star*, 5/7/51

When the company returned to London, the Festival of Britain was in full force. The celebratory spirit was everywhere, except between Dolin and Markova. Their relationship had been getting frostier by the minute.

As artistic director of The Festival Ballet, Dolin thought he would acquire a similar stature to Léonide Massine. But Massine was a dominant character-driven dancer, not a supportive partner, and his choreography was original and modern, not merely a beautiful rendering of an established classic.

Within ballet circles, Dolin was being praised for his stewardship of the young company, but all the public wanted to know about was Markova, and it was beginning to grate on him more than ever.

What were her travel wardrobe secrets? "I buy all my clothes by weight." How does she transport her hats? "Distinctive and elegant, these call for no cumbersome boxes but fold flat and go into an ordinary case." And "What does a ballerina do when she is not occupied with her all-absorbing art? 'I sleep,' she smiled, 'but I like symphonic concerts, and an occasional good film.'"

When she had a spare moment, Markova consented to pose for the numerous artists requesting to paint her picture, produce life-size drawings, or sculpt her torso.

> Ballet dancer Alicia Markova will have no hands unless 2s. 6d. worth of clay arrives at the Savoy within the next few days. Italian sculptor Vaccarino sat in his room last night and said, "Without the clay I can't finish a model of Markova properly.
>
> "I have almost completed the head—but I haven't enough for her hands." . . .
>
> He thinks Markova a perfect model—"She is never still, talks the whole time, and takes an interest in the work."
>
> —*London Evening Standard*, 11/28/50

Markova mania was in full force. A photo of the glamorous ballerina in a full-length mink coat ran next to one of Rita Hayworth; Markova and actress Vivien Leigh were declared the best-dressed women at a summer garden-party gala; and shoe designer-to-the-stars Salvatore Ferragamo told the national media that Markova had the "most perfect feet in the world." The Italians were jealous, and so was Dolin.

If the artistic director wanted his picture in the paper, he needed to be standing arm and arm with Markova—and that was the last place Dolin wanted to be these days.

Julian Braunsweg had a ringside seat to the meltdown, offering the following observations of his two leading dancers:

> [Dolin] was an extrovert, happy at parties, witty, charming, conceited and a lively conversationalist. He was forty-six when he began working with me and although a superb partner, past his prime as a dancer. . . .
>
> At forty Markova was still beautiful. She had the classical grace of a ballerina and was always immaculately groomed and gowned. When she was animated and happy she had a luminous attraction. She was unhappy frequently and then her high-pitched voice took on a nasal tone. . . .

> [T]heir relationship was temperamental and tempestuous and eventually Markova could no longer endure it.
>
> —*Braunsweg's Ballet Scandals*, 1974

What Markova couldn't endure was being ill-treated and publicly disrespected by Dolin.

Markova and Dolin had known each other since childhood. From their many decades dancing together, there came an ease and comfort. They understood each other's moods, fought and forgave like siblings, and, up until The Festival Ballet, had appreciated the life of exciting travel that their partnership made possible.

In the early days of The Festival Ballet, Markova spent her time regaining her strength and coaching the other dancers, while Dolin was stretched thin as artistic director, businessman, and dancer.

And then there was John Gilpin. If there's such a thing as a *coup de foudre*, Dolin experienced it with Gilpin. It would be a loving, if unorthodox, lifelong relationship.

Gilpin looked even younger than his nineteen years when he first met Dolin, then aged forty-five. Very handsome and clearly talented, Gilpin was initially discovered by Marie Rambert, with the press suggesting that he was "perhaps the next Anton Dolin of England." That statement certainly intrigued Dolin, who soon hired Gilpin for The Festival Ballet, planning to pair him with Nathalie Krassovska.

The two men grew increasingly close and accompanied one another to high-society soirées and supper parties. They shared an elegance of manner and a fastidiousness of dress and appearance.

Dolin made it his mission to give Gilpin career-making roles. They would live together off and on for the next thirty-three years, and were devoted to each other.

Marie Rambert playfully accused Dolin of "being a Diaghilev to my John Gilpin," but Dolin denied the relationship as ever being sexual. The two men were publicly bisexual, with Gilpin actually marrying twice and Dolin once courting a wealthy widow who left him a considerable fortune when she died.

In his fourth and last autobiography, completed in 1983 just a few months before his death, Dolin claimed that his relationship with Gilpin was one of love, but never physical:

> For thirty-three years, since 1950, he was my friend, loyal, affectionate, and more than anyone, understanding my faults—my abominable Leo aggressiveness and ego. I have known all those he loved. Maybe only two in that long period did I despise, not—as so many thought and said—because I was jealous. I have never been jealous of anyone, men or women. We were never lovers, Now it can be said, though there are many—too many—who would believe otherwise.

The editor of Dolin's last book added the following postscript:

> Sir Anton Dolin died on November 25, 1983, yet his close friends knew that his personal raison d'être had been extinguished some ten weeks previously, on September 5, the date of John Gilpin's sudden and untimely death.

Whatever the truth behind the complicated life-long relationship of the two men, one fact was abundantly clear: Dolin's priority at The Festival Ballet was now John Gilpin, not Alicia Markova.

When the ballet company first opened at the Stoll Theatre, Dolin complained to Braunsweg that the only photos in the lobby were of him and Markova together. Where was Gilpin and the rest of the company? The impresario brushed Dolin aside. "It's you and Alicia the public will buy tickets for, not the Festival Ballet," he told him.

The reviews most assuredly supported Braunsweg's statement. Dolin had gotten used to Markova receiving the lion's share of the critical praise; and in the past, that had always benefited him as well. She sold tickets and made them both a great deal of money. But he now found her fame a distraction from his protégé.

Making matters worse, Markova had been a firm believer in stressing the Russian classics in the new company—something she was promised from the start—while Dolin insisted on introducing contemporary works to the repertoire, as he knew Massine would have done. They often fell flat with the critics. As a soloist and art director, Dolin was found lacking.

The following review was typical of The Festival Ballet critiques. The opening spoke to Dolin's choice of the *Don Quixote pas de deux* for Markova, a role that had never suited her talents, further casting doubts on his judgment.

> . . . From such a company one does not expect to see new ballets or ballets of direct expression at all. One expects that very virtuosity which is the company's *raison d'être*, paraded in those immediate pre-Diaghilev works which are the apex of classical dancing. . . . Just a trace of this was provided in Monday's performance by Mme. Markova's Odette and by the Don Quixote *pas de deux*.
>
> This latter, however, is not ideally suited to Mme. Markova's style. It needs keen attack, hard excitement; every step should be incised home. Mme. Markova's style can be described as feather. Effort disappears. The most demanding technics dissolve into something as unsubstantial as floating down. It is this quality which makes Mme. Markova's Odette supreme. She is always (the only Odette I have seen in this) half bird, and further half spellbound. She achieves a strange pathos by the suggestion of conflict and complexity that her heart is already maimed by the magician. Combined with this lightness she has brittle, slender, almost—like Pavlova—angular arms, which become something very beautiful like frost patterns on a window. Above all she is the incarnation of Tchaikovsky's music, cold, lovely, almost vicious and shot with changing colours. As a partner, Mr. Dolin had all the skill and efficiency of an expert glass blower handling the frailest, most intricate creation. Otherwise he is inclined to be mannered and rather stagily sweet in facial expression and his Bolero proved the most disappointing item, a caricature of the Spanish dances one performs in one's bath.
>
> It was, in fact, in this insistent departure from classical tradition that the company came off the worst. . . . The American influence generally was for the bad. Especially in Mr. Puppet and in the evening as a whole there was not simply enough Markova.
>
> —*The Isis*, 4/26/50

Markova knew *Don Quixote* was not ideally suited to her, but Dolin was the art director and she performed the *pas de deux* as asked. She was more upset that he insisted that she partner with Gilpin, a dancer half her age and one she felt looked like her "son" rather than a romantic interest.

"He's too young and inexperienced," Markova told Dolin, according to Braunsweg. "I will not dance with him. He makes me look very old."

Dolin ignored her protestations and announced the partnership of Markova and Gilpin to the papers. In his autobiography, Dolin coolly describes informing Markova that if she refused to dance with Gilpin, the audience would be told she was indisposed and Nathalie Krassovska would take her place.

"Quite a few people have bought seats to see Gilpin dance tonight, and this is a chance you cannot take from him," Dolin told her. One had to assume far more people had bought tickets to see Markova.

That is not the way a ballet company treats its *prima ballerina assoluta*. Markova danced with Gilpin, but she wasn't happy.

Lest one think Markova was being unreasonable, Alexandra Danilova—one of the first guest artists with the company—was also taken aback by Gilpin's baby-face. "My God, he is young!" she said upon first meeting him. "You know he best put on a moustache or I look like his grandmother."

No one was more delighted than Markova when Danilova was asked to appear with The Festival Ballet. As Braunsweg described Choura's arrival:

> She was a great friend of Markova's from the days of the Diaghilev company. . . . Markova was eternally grateful for her kindness. However, there were one or two problems. Danilova who had created the role of the Street Dancer in the original production of Le Beau Danube in 1933, was cast in her old role, a decision that made Krassovska cry. "But it is her part," I said to Tata as she sat sobbing in my office.

It was commonplace, and common courtesy, in established ballet companies that world-famous prima ballerinas "owned," for lack of a better word, certain roles. There had always been a proper hierarchy, and the most experienced dancers were treated with the utmost respect.

In the spring of 1952, for example, Markova was asked if she would dance *The Sleeping Beauty* with the Sadler's Wells Ballet. "I feel that is Fonteyn's ballet," Markova replied quickly. "She has danced it so beautifully and made it her own so completely that I think I'd rather watch her do it than dance it myself!"

"What about Balanchine's Swan Lake, had Miss Markova seen that?" the interviewer continued. "'Yes, I did—it's very different, isn't it?' Yes, very different. Would she like to dance it? Miss Markova smiled and said, 'I can't visualize myself doing it. It's wonderful when Maria Tallchief dances it. . . . When a ballet's created for a dancer, it's created for *that* person, and it never enters my head that I should dance it."

Choura "owned" the role of The Street Dancer in *Le Beau Danube*, just as Markova owned *Giselle* at The Festival Ballet. That did not mean other ballerinas didn't perform *Giselle* at the Festival Ballet, but only on nights when Markova wasn't dancing, and never on an opening night. Mia Slavenska and Yvette Chauviré would later be brought in as guest artists for that purpose.

Prior to their meeting with Danilova to discuss the planned repertoire, Markova asked Dolin—as art director—to tell her dear friend that she could dance any role she wanted but *Giselle*. When discussions began, Danilova asked to perform The Street Dancer, the Black Swan, and the lead in *The Nutcracker*. She said "no" to *Don Quixote*, "I do not feel hot enough for that." Imagine how Markova felt.

Then Danilova did something she must have realized was inappropriate. She asked to dance *Giselle* with Dolin. Danilova had always fought tooth and nail to protect roles she thought belonged to her. After first seeing Massine's *Gâité Parisienne*, she claimed the lead of the Glove Seller for her own—even though the part had already been danced successfully by another ballerina—and threatened to walk out on the Ballet Russe de Monte Carlo if not given that starring role on opening night in New York. (She won.)

Danilova now assured Markova that her interpretation of *Giselle* was very different from Alicia's own, as if another ballet entirely. Then Choura threw in the kicker: dancing the role, she said, "That make me very happy."

Dolin said not a word. Nor did Braunsweg. When Nathalie Krassovska came crying to the impresario, not understanding why she should have to give up her starring role as The Street Dancer to Danilova, Braunsweg gently, but firmly, explained the rules of ballet hierarchy. But he wasn't willing to stand up for his own *prima ballerina assoluta*.

Markova would never say no to her oldest and dearest friend, who couldn't understand why Alicia was so continually overwrought. In her autobiography, Choura mentions that she thought Markova had become "a little bit swollen-headed" at The Festival Ballet—not with her, of course, but with others with whom she could be quite demanding. Those "others" were her co-managers—Dolin and Braunsweg—rather than subordinates, to whom Markova remained gracious and helpful. Choura was unaware of the behind-the-scenes battles that had turned Dolin and Markova from close partners and friends to feuding adversaries.

Danilova danced *Giselle* with Dolin. At the final curtain, she was presented with a magnificent bouquet sent by Markova—no purple flowers in sight.

Ironically, Dolin and Markova were enacting their own *Giselle* roles in real life. Dolin as the duplicitous Albrecht pretends to be in love with Giselle, while he is engaged to another. He flirts and charms the innocent peasant girl, knowing full well he will soon abandon her. The following review was like foreshadowing.

> **The Stoll "Giselle"**
>
> Not since Olga Spessivtseva wrung our hearts as Giselle nearly 20 years ago has the tragic role been more movingly danced in London than by Markova at the Stoll on November 2, when Anton Dolin produced the classic masterpiece for the Festival Ballet company, with décor and costumes by Hugh Stevenson.
>
> Markova gave an inspired performance. With such wide-eyed innocence and such complete faith in mankind, she is earmarked for tragedy from the outset. She hardly deserves the fate so cruelly awaiting her.
>
> —*Stage*, 11/9/50

There *was* a cruel fate awaiting Markova. Dolin turned almost vicious at times, issuing edicts as to what she was to dance and with whom. He knew exactly what to say and do to anger her and baited her in front of the company. In his 1960 autobiography, Dolin even admitted that many of their fights were his fault, but that didn't stop him.

It all came to a head when Dolin engaged as guest artist the radiant Yvette Chauviré, considered the greatest French ballerina of her generation. One of Chauviré's most acclaimed roles was as *Giselle*, in a very different interpretation from Markova's. As one critic compared them, Chauviré had "the impeccable style and sense of period," while Markova emphasized "lightness and spirituality."

Markova wasn't anxious for the comparisons between herself and the seven-years-younger Chauviré. Worse still, Dolin decided that as the ballerinas would be dancing the same role on alternating nights, he would partner Chauviré, while Markova would be mismatched with the boyish, far less experienced Gilpin.

For quite a while, Markova had been begging Dolin to engage older, more experienced male guest artists for her to partner, but he claimed no one was ever available, or they were too expensive. He had no problem, however, in booking established prima ballerinas such as Danilova, Mia Slavenska (who insisted on bringing her own male dance partner—Milorad Miskovitch), and Chauviré, for himself, and Gilpin.

Markova was honest and up front about her fears of appearing old, but her entreaties fell on deaf ears. Dolin was supposed to be her ally, not to mention in a similar position himself as an aging dancer. That was the main reason he had accepted Braunsweg's offer to be art director of The Festival Ballet in the first place.

When Dolin insisted that Markova dance with the youthful Gilpin while Chauviré would have the benefit of Dolin's masterful support, Markova cracked. She knew a formal full-company rehearsal with the orchestra had been arranged for Dolin and Chauviré. As it was about to begin, Markova walked on to the stage "still in her sable coat and high-heeled shoes," according to Dolin, and began to give the orchestra instructions as to the correct tempo to follow.

But it was not the tempo Chauviré required, and the French ballerina complained to Dolin that this was supposed to be *her* rehearsal.

Dolin was embarrassed, but didn't have the nerve to order Markova off the stage in front of everyone. The *prima ballerina assoluta* accomplished what she wanted—making Dolin experience the same powerless and helpless feelings she had been forced to endure. In the process, she had been unforgivably rude to Chauviré.

Mentally, Markova was at the breaking point. The outside world was at her feet, but internally, the male managers of her own company ignored or tormented her. Markova was so miserable at work that she couldn't sleep at night. She got on fine with the young company dancers, many of whom she took out to lunch and dinner on a regular basis, but Dolin, Braunsweg, and even second-in-command Benn Toff often treated her like a temperamental employee. Markova's name was not only on the marquee, but she was also a co-founder of the company with a financial stake in its success or failure. She should have been consulted on major decisions and respected by her co-directors.

In his autobiography, Braunsweg seemed obsessed with the fact that Markova was never without a large box of Black Magic chocolates in her dressing room. "She had a voracious appetite and was addicted to them. She ate them by the box and ate them all herself. Benn Toff used to take great handfuls and give them to the stage staff.

"'My chocolates seem to vanish,' Markova told him.

"'It's because you have such an enormous appetite,' Benn replied."

Braunsweg and Toff thought that quite amusing, but this wasn't high school where you raid someone's locker as a joke. Markova needed those chocolates for energy to dance. They were stored in her private dressing room. Moreover, the sweets bizarrely represented success to her. Only when she was "perfect" had Guggy permitted her to have a chocolate. Now they had become a physical necessity and Markova's reward to herself.

A week after the embarrassing Chauviré rehearsal, Dolin remembers Markova coming to his dressing room to discuss upcoming roles and casting decisions. The two got into an awful row and Markova ended up slapping him across the face. Dolin compared the incident to Anna Pavlova's notorious slap of partner Mikhail Mordkin. Never mind that Pavlova had attacked Mordkin on stage and in front of an audience. Dolin and Markova were alone in his dressing room at the time, and he promptly threw her out.

No one could claim Markova was blameless in the situation, but as Dolin's longtime friend—and the undisputed star of The Festival Ballet—she couldn't understand why he had become so dismissive of her needs and suggestions when she was in such obvious distress. Fortunately, the dressing room blow-up came at the end of the season and Markova and Dolin soon went off on very separate vacations.

The Festival Ballet was back on tour in the provinces in the fall of 1951. One night in Glasgow, Markova and Dolin were scheduled to dance together in *The Nutcracker*, preceded by a short ballet featuring John Gilpin. As happened all too often, Gilpin didn't show up. He was known to disappear for days and weeks at a time without warning. The company referred to his absences as "John's affairs of the heart," according to Braunsweg. "We all got used to them."

While Markova was warming up backstage, Dolin made an announcement that Gilpin had taken ill and would not be performing that evening. Markova was still stretching at the *barre* when she tripped on a slippery board, badly wrenching her ankle. In a great deal of pain, she knew right away it was not a minor injury.

Normally Markova would have asked Dolin to have a backup dancer take her place, but since Gilpin hadn't shown up, she felt it would be completely unfair to the audience to announce another major substitution. While ably supporting Markova on stage, Dolin could tell she was badly hurt, and her ankle continued to swell. The next morning, she flew back to London to consult her foot specialist, Dr. William Tucker. There were no broken bones, but she had torn several ligaments.

Markova didn't want to stop dancing altogether, afraid it would set her back once again, so she worked out a combination of daily treatments with Dr. Tucker followed by light *barre* work. Luckily for her, the company was on break. Markova planned to rejoin them for the Christmas season in Monte Carlo.

During his time off, Dolin flew to New York for a meeting with Sol Hurok, hoping the Russian impresario would represent The Festival Ballet for their first U.S. tour. (No one held grudges for long in the ballet world.) Dolin hobnobbed with celebrity friends and attended many dance performances and hit stage plays. Due to his overbooked schedule—and some inclement weather—he arrived late to Monte Carlo, just one day before the company's opening night.

Dolin told Markova he was just too tired to perform *The Nutcracker* with her as scheduled, and she would have to dance with Gilpin instead. But the weary artistic director felt he would be fine to dance *Swan Lake* with Krassovska the following day.

There are various accounts of what happened next. Everyone agreed Markova appeared hurt when dancing *The Nutcracker* with Gilpin and barely made it through the performance. She mustered polite audience applause at best. Afterwards she told Dolin she was in great pain.

The other undisputed fact is that Markova packed her things and flew to London with Doris the next day to see her foot specialist. Dolin and Braunsweg claimed Markova had exaggerated her injury on stage to punish Dolin for not dancing with her; but it's hard to imagine her intentionally performing badly in front of an audience just to spite Dolin.

Whatever they might have thought, Markova was seriously injured, as physicians' letters in her personal medical files document. Dr. Tucker found that the inflammation of her ankle had indeed worsened, and was convinced she had gone back to dancing too soon. (He had previously recommended complete rest, advice she had ignored.)

But far more troubling were the letters *to* Dr. Tucker from a neurology specialist Markova had consulted about her balance issues and continuing sleep disorders, excerpted here:

> In going into the causes of her present nervous upset, I was impressed by the amount of tension which had developed between Madame Markova and others with whom she worked. It is quite clear that whereas previously she was able to handle the emotional difficulties to which this gave rise, since her abdominal operation and particularly since the damaged ankle, her capacity to do this has been reduced, that it is now giving rise to the early symptoms of a neurosis. It is my view that if Madame Markova continues in her present difficulty she may well have a serious breakdown. . . .
>
> She is not sleeping well, she is worried and tense, and she has for the present lost confidence in her capacity to undertake

> first class dancing. My impression was that she was more distressed about this last point than she was prepared to admit and that it should be taken seriously. With reasonably good fortune Madame Markova should make an entirely full recovery and get back to her former skill and composure, but this is going to take time.

The letter goes on to recommend that Markova take a minimum six-month vacation from dancing. Shockingly, she was more than willing to agree. Markova had six months left on her contract with The Festival Ballet and the very thought of returning to the company made her physically ill. Her hurt ankle allowed her contractually to leave the company as long as she didn't dance anywhere else, which she was certainly in no condition to do.

Markova's lawyer sent a letter informing Braunsweg of her need to withdraw, accompanied by medical records confirming her injury and doctor's orders that she stop dancing. Braunsweg doubted the veracity of the documents and was convinced Markova was just behaving like a diva.

When Dolin heard the news, he realized he had gone too far. A flurry of anxious letters to Markova followed, all full of concern and pleas.

He was as upset as she about her hurt foot, and promised to ease up her schedule. The only reason he had signed on as art director in the first place was "*because* of you & because of us." He realizes how much she has lost financially in The Festival Ballet—but so has he and Julian, don't forget.

Dolin now promises no program will be announced without her "knowledge and sanction." She needs to return not for his sake—"I ask nothing for myself"—but for the sake of the company. Their future is uncertain without her.

Just a few years later, Dolin would leave The Festival Ballet high and dry just three weeks prior to a scheduled tour by accepting a lucrative foreign engagement and taking the company's prima ballerina and principal male dancer John Gilpin with him.

"What about the corps, the soloists, the company, what will happen to them?" Braunsweg asked his art director. "I argued and pleaded, but Dolin was adamant. He did not tell the company he was leaving."

Markova did not return to The Festival Ballet.

~

Though still not feeling at all well, Markova enjoyed spending Christmas with her family. She also attended the premiere of a new Massine ballet at Covent Garden. At the after-party she was photographed dressed in an exquisite gown and fur wrap, alongside an equally glamorous Beryl Grey. Braunsweg was annoyed.

After the holidays, Doris and Alicia flew to New York, the energizing city Markova had once likened to "a pair of evening shoes—stylish, glittering, and gay." Hopefully that's how the ballerina would feel in the near future. Even in the snow, New York was dazzling.

But the two sisters wouldn't stay long. Soon they were off for a long, leisurely vacation in California—just as the doctor ordered. Markova's West Coast friend, the wealthy society hostess Eleanor Peters, generously offered a guest suite in her grand Sherman Oaks estate for their stay.

As Markova later told Maurice Leonard, luncheon guests at the Peters home often included famous actors such as Dame Judith Anderson, Roger Moore, and Leslie Caron, who had recently starred in *An American in Paris* (1951) with Markova's friend Gene Kelly. The two women enjoyed swapping ballet stories while washing dishes together after supper parties. No one could say Markova was an ungrateful guest. She actually enjoyed household chores.

While in California, Markova was deluged with invitations from friends in the film community. Though she went out sparingly—careful to rest her ankle—distractions were always welcome. In private, Markova was prone to melancholy and weeping. She had experienced serious bouts of depression before, but usually there were performances, rehearsals, or, most recently, family reunions to cheer her up. Now, her future seemed so uncertain—the one thing she loved more than anything else, on the verge of disappearing. She was increasingly despondent, but in public she hid those feelings well.

She certainly looked on top of the world in the widely circulated newspaper photos taken on movie sets where "the internationally famous English ballerina" mixed and mingled with Hollywood stars.

There was the lovely Alicia Markova on the Metro-Goldwyn-Mayer soundstage of *Hans Christian Andersen*—chatting away with actor Danny Kaye, smiling up at the beautifully costumed French ballerina Zizi Jeanmaire, and in a private tête-à-tête with the handsome and talented French choreographer Roland Petit. At the Warner Brothers lot, Markova was photographed talking shop with actor/dancer Ray Bolger and singer Doris Day as they filmed *April in Paris*.

When those Hollywood photos of Markova made the London papers, Dolin and Braunsweg were not amused. They felt their still-under-contract prima ballerina seemed to be having a gay old time when she should be back at work with them. Even more annoying, gossip columns were rife with rumored lucrative job offers coming Markova's way. Sol Hurok, for one, was very interested in his former client, and he now represented the Sadler's Wells Company in the U.S.—The Festival Ballet's chief competition. But it was all just speculation, as Markova was still very much out of commission.

That didn't matter to Braunsweg. He was incensed. And just as Hurok had jumped the gun when Billy Rose initially contacted Markova, Braunsweg immediately fired off threatening legal notices to Hurok and Markova. If she took one step on any stage prior to the official end of her contract in June, he would sue both of them.

Markova was unconcerned. She had no intention of dancing before the summertime at the earliest.

In March, the top-rated national television variety program *Your Show of Shows*—starring the versatile comedians Sid Caesar and Imogene Coca—invited Markova to make a guest appearance. In a newspaper interview, the show's dance director James Starbuck mentioned how excited he would be to choreograph a ballet for the world-famous Markova. Starbuck's background was in the classics as a former dancer with Massine's Ballet Russe de Monte Carlo.

No date for the show had been set, but that didn't stop Dolin from exploding at the thought. Gossip columnist Dorothy Kilgallen got the scoop in her column *Smart Set*:

> Big gab in the dance world is Anton Dolin's threat to slap a lawsuit on TV choreographer James Starbuck if he creates a six-minute ballet for Alicia Markova's American TV debut on

"Your Show of Shows." Dolin, estranged partner of the famed ballerina, claims an exclusive contract with her that is valid until June.

—*New York Journal-American*, 3/16/52

Prior to the threatened legal actions on the part of Braunsweg and Dolin, Markova had taken the high road in all press interviews, explaining that her hurt foot was the reason she had left The Festival Ballet. She assured everyone it was on the friendliest terms, and she was in the United States to see her doctors in New York and recuperate in California.

Now the gloves were off.

Ballet Partnership Ends After 20 Years
Markova breaks with Dolin

The world-famous British ballet partnership of Anton Dolin and Alicia Markova is at an end—after nearly 20 years.

Fragile, seven-stone Alicia Markova—born Alice Marks in Finsbury 41 years ago—admitted it in New York last night.

"I am not going back to his ballet company in London," she said. "And I don't think I shall ever be dancing with him again.

"A row? Just a matter of Mr. Dolin wanting what he wants—and I wanting something else." . . .

Her sister and manager, Mrs. Doris Barry, explained that Markova is nursing a foot injury—her fourth in ten years.

"Her contract with Dolin expires in June," she added. "In July, when the foot is healed, she will go to South America."

Dolin sitting in a box at Stoll Theatre where his Festival Ballet opened this week—did not mention a break-up. But he said:

"I don't know when we shall dance together again. Or if she will return to my company."

Forty-seven-year-old half-Irish "Pat" Dolin—Patrick Healy Kay is his real name—was silent for a moment.

Then he went on: "Markova is one of the great ballerinas.

> "But in a company everyone must have a chance. My company is fresh and eager.
>
> "I am sorry that Markova is not dancing. But the ballet must continue."
>
> —*London Daily Graphic*, 3/20/52

Dolin had hired Tamara Toumanova, Markova's former rival from her early Ballet Russe de Monte Carlo days, to take her place as prima ballerina at The Festival Ballet. The same day he was interviewed for the above story concerning Markova, the following review of his company's new fall program appeared in the London press.

> **Festival Ballet**
>
> The Festival Ballet (Stoll: 18th March) presented five items plus guest-artist Toumanova, all supported by the company as before, excepting the departed Markova. . . .
>
> The programme was badly balanced and far too long; when will directors and artists learn what the public has known for a long time?—to paraphrase Miss Gertrude Stein, "Enough is enough is enough." . . . On this night's showing, Markova is the biggest single loss *any* contemporary Ballet Company could face; none of the other female dancers has her sheer ability as a dancer, her suitability to this repertoire, or her combination of reserve, assurance and humility towards the *art of dancing.*
>
> —*London Theatre Newsletter*, 3/19/52

Braunsweg was far less sanguine than Dolin. He was losing a fortune, and now had the still-crazed, overbearing Mama Toumanova to contend with. Maybe Markova and her Black Magic chocolates hadn't been so bad after all.

By mid-May, Markova was ready to start practicing again. She had rested for six months, and though extremely nervous about regaining her ability to dance well, was feeling much better about herself now that she was legally free from Dolin, Braunsweg, and the Festival Ballet. She had been among people who adored her, took care of her, and chatted about everything and anything but ballet. It had been the longest break from dancing in her life.

Fortunately, Vincenzo Celli was once again available to get Markova back into shape. The trusted dance instructor knew exactly how Markova should proceed and was able to keep her spirits up as she ever so slowly regained her strength and confidence.

Markova sent a polite letter to Dolin asking for the return of music scores she had left behind. Considering that he had threatened legal action two months earlier, Dolin now seemed contrite and a bit forlorn in his reply, as in this excerpt:

". . . You are always missed by me. Don't let it be for always. . . . Don't forget Patte—for all our years together cannot be cut apart so. Let's think one day we'll dance again. Perhaps with happiness & toleration on my behalf. I shall always love you."

Dolin also tells Markova how lucky she is to be going to South America in July and wishes her every success. When first invited to perform in Buenos Aries, Markova intended to ask Dolin to partner her, but that was before their professional relationship fell apart.

According to a letter from manager Alfred Katz, the two dancers would each have earned $10,000 for the six-week summer booking. Dolin regretted the loss.

The beneficiary of that salary was no longer Dolin, but the acclaimed Polish soloist Roman Jasinsky. Three years older than Markova, Jasinsky had danced with Ida Rubinstein, George Balanchine, and the Ballet Russe de Monte Carlo, where he had partnered Markova in *Rouge et Noir.* Jasinsky (known as Jasha) had been a winning partner with Danilova as well, and Markova felt lucky to have him with her.

The Argentina contingent would be small, just the two dancers, Doris as manager, and music conductor Robert Zeller, who had also worked for The Festival Ballet. It was arranged that Markova and Jasinsky be guest stars with the Buenos Aires ballet company in a production of *Swan Lake* at the Teatro Colon Opera House, followed by a series of classical dance concerts in several other cities.

The tour was sure to test Markova's strength and abilities after her long convalescence. She had already accepted another booking for the fall season as guest artist with Ballet Theatre in New York. Argentina was a test run.

Just before the group was set to leave for South America, Eva Peron—wife of Argentina's President Juan Peron and the "Spiritual Leader of the Nation"—passed away at age 33. The country was plunged into such a period of grief-stricken mourning that many citizens were injured or crushed to death in the massive crowds flocking to see their beloved Evita's body lying in state.

The Teatro Colon Theatre managers asked Markova to delay her trip during the official mourning period, but as the ballerina was much loved in Argentina, people still wanted her to come perform.

Markova realized the trip would not be an easy one. The American embassy in New York informed her of the precarious political situation she was flying into, and instructed her to be careful and compliant with any government requests or restrictions. That was made quite clear from the second she stepped off the plane.

Before passing through customs, Markova and her small entourage were required to pay their respects to the First Lady of Argentina. A flower-filled makeshift chapel had been set up for that purpose. Markova would soon learn that similar temporary chapels had been constructed all over the capital. One could not enter or exit the hotel, rehearsal hall, theater, or practically any other building without first stopping in a chapel and kneeling before a portrait of Eva Peron. Her image was mounted high on an altar, always surrounded by mountains of floral arrangements and wreaths.

To maintain the spectacle, everyone was asked to contribute. Markova learned that lesson the first evening she danced. After being presented with numerous beautiful bouquets at the final curtain, the ballerina returned to her dressing room to find they had mysteriously disappeared. It seems Argentina now had a "flower tax," with a large portion of all arrangements designated for one of Evita's chapels.

Could she just have the cards, Markova asked meekly? She wanted to write thank-you notes to the senders.

Flowers weren't the only things that went missing in Buenos Aires. Musicians often disappeared during orchestra rehearsals when suddenly called away to perform in another of the many Requiem Masses. And valuables left in one's hotel room or unsecured theater locker also had a way of vanishing into thin air.

Markova and Doris remained composed and unruffled through it all. In fact Markova's only complaint was the "command performance" designated for the union workers—a government policy for all visiting entertainers. It wasn't the extra show she objected to, just the timing, which required her arriving at the theatre at 8:30 A.M. Markova was never awake, let alone onstage dancing, at that hour. Once again, she graciously complied.

At least they didn't have to deal with insufferable heat and humidity. The temperatures had been close to 100 degrees when Markova left New York City in early August, but it was winter in Argentina and the cold was refreshing. When Doris wrote to their sisters Vivienne and Bunny back in London, she mentioned how strange it was to suddenly be wearing a fur coat again.

The news the sisters most wanted to hear, however, was how Alicia was holding up. This was her first performance since the six-month recuperative period. Was she still experiencing pain? Was she dancing well? Doris gave them the news.

> *Viv darling & Bun too,*
>
> *This will have to be another joint letter as I will not have time to write to each of you separately. . . .*
>
> *I knew you would both be anxious to know—Alicia really danced beautifully, Sylphides pas-de-deux—then Swan Lake. She had a big ovation. . . . Just everyone is talking about her, her pure classic style, technique with no tricks. It is really gratifying. Thursday's programme was Suite from Sylphides—opening Nocturne Jasha's solo, Prelude & Valse pas de deux. Then her Giselle solo 1st act which literally brought the house down. They rose & cheered & cheered, then Dying Swan which left them speechless with emotion & finishing with Nutcracker. So you see it was a hard programme for Alicia to get through but she did & really danced better than she has for a long time. Jasha looked excellent & partnered her very well. . . .*
>
> *Next week only 2 shows—Wed & Sat Sylphides & Swan Lake, but Alicia has interviews & sittings for photographer & a famous Hollywood painter who is here wants to paint her so she has to sit for him too.*
>
> *Her foot held up marvelously which was a great relief to her as it was a hard programme.*
>
> *All our love darlings to you both & Suzy.*
>
> *God Bless, Doris*

In her next letter, Doris wrote Vivienne about ongoing legal wrangling with Sol Hurok concerning Markova's upcoming New York engagement. It was apparently business as usual with the slippery impresario.

> . . . In brief, Hurok tried to stop Alicia appearing with Ballet Theatre at the Met—he has stopped Bob [Zeller] conducting for her but as things turned out here, that does not matter. [According to Doris, Zeller had become as manipulative as Dolin.] Hurok thinks she should return to Sadler's Wells & England & stay with them. Then again he gets the honor and glory (& Box Office) when he brings her back with them next year to N.Y. 1953. . . . She naturally will do B.T. as contract was signed & all N.Y. is waiting for her.
>
> After her terrific success here & in Montevideo she has nothing to worry about. She is dancing wonderfully & hard programmes too, but also has gained a new quality to her work & personality & everyone is raving about her.

Markova headed "home" to America greatly relieved.

Before departing for Argentina in July, Markova had sent flowers and fond birthday wishes to Dolin. It was something she did every single year, no matter what their current personal relationship. In writing to thank her, Dolin added a postscript: "I long for the day when you will return happily to 'guest.' You can decide on your billing & your ballets. When & where & with whom you dance. Me I hope. I think it will be a happy night for us & for the thousands here who will acclaim us."

Markova was praying for acclaim in New York. She was terrified of what John Martin at *The New York Times* would think of her after all these years. His former admonitions still stung. And now she was older and recently injured. Her technique certainly wasn't what it used to be, even if she had danced well in Argentina.

Martin's review of her Ballet Theatre engagement would be read throughout the United States, and even London. It would have a big impact on Markova's comeback and future career.

After two days' rehearsal with her old friend and former dancing partner, the celebrated Igor Youskevitch, Markova opened at the Metropolitan Opera House in *Giselle.*

THE DANCE: MARKOVA

A Luminous Manifestation of a Great Ballerina

by John Martin

After all these years, Alicia Markova has worked another miracle. She came to New York first in 1938 with Massine's newly formed Ballet Russe de Monte Carlo, and during the war years in this country, with this company and later with Ballet Theatre, we saw her reach such a point of perfection that she was justifiably declared to be the greatest of all classic ballerinas. That this was the peak of her career seemed obvious, and such a judgment was strengthened by later seasons in which she made only run-of-the-mill guest appearances here and there, toured with a mediocre concert unit and eventually went back to England and disappeared from the local scene altogether.

Her recent return, however, puts everything in a different light, for astonishingly enough, she has shown herself to be an even greater artist than ever. To claim that she is at the height of her technical form would be impossible, but it was never as a technician that she overtopped the field. Now she has restudied once more her major roles (always in a process of restudy, anyhow), editing them, as it were, so that no detail is allowed to remain which might put a shadow of strain upon the spirit of the whole. If there are minor elisions and adjustments here and there, the compensations are more than generous, and the result, instead of being a lessening of value, is an enormous enrichment.

Realizing that her strength lies in evocation rather than in spectacle, in spirit rather than in body, in the distillation of essences rather than in propulsions of force, she has concentrated with the intensity of a mystic upon these magic processes and eliminated every element that would deny or diminish them. . . . Happily, Markova is so strikingly unique

> that not many young dancers will try to imitate her; it would be appalling to see them try. . . . There has been nothing like her in our time.
>
> —*The New York Times*, 10/12/52

Many years later, a radio interviewer said to Markova, "You've danced Giselle for over 25 years. How on earth can you do something for that long and still find something new in it over time?"

"Every time changes," the ballerina replied. "I didn't wear the same things. . . . The partner that was with me was different. The audience had changed, the approach to the performance. After all, time goes on, you know. It doesn't stay the same."

John Martin's review was meaningful on many levels. First, it heralded Markova's return to the American ballet scene in glorious form. Second, it renewed her personal confidence following such a long break from dancing. And third, by analyzing how completely different Markova was from other dancers—such as Ballet Theatre's fiery prima ballerina Alicia Alonso—Martin's words lessened the competition within the company. The attention paid to Markova as a guest artist benefited them all, as explained in this British theater magazine column:

> As for Alicia Markova on her return from England and her appearances with Ballet Theatre, she is being acclaimed "an even greater artist than ever" by critic John Martin of the *New York Times*, which is just about the highest praise possible. . . . That this is not just one man's opinion is testified by the fact that every performance in which she danced was sold out and a new enthusiasm swept through the Ballet Theatre company, once considered America's finest, but in recent seasons diminished in stature with the rise of the New York City Ballet Company. Nor did Alicia Alonso, Ballet Theatre's own prima ballerina, have to settle for second honours, for her dazzling, bravura style, diametrically opposed to Markova's, was equally acclaimed, applauded and attended.
>
> —"Echoes from Broadway," *Theatre World*, November 1952

Markova traveled with Ballet Theatre to several other American and Canadian cities, where she was also welcomed with universally effusive praise. But in Chicago, the old "Giselle curse" made a brief reappearance. During the ballet's second act, Markova—as the deceased spirit of Giselle—dances ever so slowly and poignantly in the middle of a ghostly gathering of Wilis.

Markova explained what happened next in *Giselle & I*:

> The music reaches its quiet climax—and in that moment of stillness, when the last note has died away, you should be able to hear a feather fall.
>
> What I did hear, at this precise moment, was the "Poofh!" of the main electric bulb exploding in the flies [theater ceiling storage space] directly above my head, to shower me, hair, nylon dress and all, with fragments of splintered glass, as fine as candy floss.

She and Youskevitch finished the entire second act dancing on glass.

To close out the New York ballet season in November, Markova took center stage in a one-night Gala performance celebrating the thirty-fifth anniversary of the Federation of Jewish Philanthropies. The sold-out event at Madison Square Garden featured many of Markova's old friends: the violinist Yehudi Menuhin, choreographer George Balanchine and his New York City Ballet, and that company's leading principal male dancer, André Eglevsky.

Markova and Eglevsky hadn't danced together in years and greatly enjoyed the renewed partnership. The press enjoyed their rehearsal, finding the pair quite humorous, as Eglevsky expressed his doubts about the strange choice of venue:

"'How will it be—dancing in Madison Square Garden? All sandy? . . . I was there twice. Once I took my three kids—two boys, 10 and 6, and my little girl, 4—to the circus and another time to the rodeo. Both times it was sandy—and smelly,' he grimaced."

Markova laughingly assured Eglevsky it would be "beautiful" with a specially built, very large and sand-free stage. She had quite a bit of experience dancing in sporting arenas, she told him, as the newspaper story elaborated.

> She has performed in a baseball stadium in the Philippines, in an ice rink in London and was the first to dance on the outdoor stage of Lewisohn Stadium here.
>
> As a result of the mob scene which followed her Stadium appearance (she had to be carried by cops to her car), Miss Markova lost one of her specially made size-four shoes to an enthusiastic fan. But the experience served to confirm her belief that: "Ballet should give pleasure to anyone. People don't have to know about it or study it. If it gives people pleasure—or makes them forget their problems for even two hours—that is my goal."
>
> —"Ballet Will Ride Into Garden on Wings of Markova's Swan," *New York World-Telegram & Sun*, 10/30/52

The event was not intended as a fundraiser, but rather to build awareness of the Jewish Federation, so ticket prices were on a sliding scale, which greatly pleased Markova. The program began with the reading of a congratulatory telegram from President Dwight D. Eisenhower, soon followed by stars Markova and Eglevsky. The ballerina's *Dying Swan* received a standing ovation from the fifteen thousand in attendance.

But that crowd was small potatoes compared with the number of people who watched Markova on October 18, 1952. On that Saturday night—from 9:00 to 10:30 P.M.—she appeared before thirty million viewers, the weekly audience for the musical/comedy television program *Your Show of Shows*, starring Sid Caesar and Imogene Coca.

NBC thought the timing perfect. Markova was back dancing in the United States better than ever and had received a great deal of positive buzz in the national press. Her performing a six-minute ballet on the show was sure to be a big ratings draw.

But the program's pioneering producer Max Liebman had an even better idea. Why not have Alicia Markova guest-host the show? No one had ever heard her speak!

Audiences surely assumed Markova was Russian. Her clipped British accent would be the first surprise. And a ballerina delivering lines written by funnymen/show writers Mel Brooks, Neil Simon, and Woody Allen? Intriguing, to say the least.

Liebman had a surprise coming himself. He had no idea Markova was blessed with such a phenomenal memory. After the dress rehearsal, she was able to deliver all of her lines without cue cards. And the show was live.

For her dance number, Markova chose the dreamy classical *pas de deux* from *Les Sylphides* and asked show choreographer James Starbuck to partner her. Though he was thrilled at the offer, the NBC censors were a bit nervous. How would a man in tights play across America?

As *Dance Magazine* later reported, "We presume Starbuck's substitution of trousers for the white tights of 'Sylphides' was a concession to male America's intolerance towards the accoutrements of classic ballet. (And don't think he doesn't know what he is up against. Just visualize the audience—farmhands in North Dakota, miners in West Virginia, cowboys in Colorado—getting a view of the 'Sylphides' pas de deux for the first time!)."

The magazine was wrong. Markova and *Les Sylphides* were a huge hit with Middle America—so huge, in fact, that she was invited back throughout the season to dance other ballets. The lively snowflake scene from *The Nutcracker* was a natural choice for a popular comedy/musical program, but Markova's achingly moving *Dying Swan* caught viewers off guard.

Commented one newspaper, Starbuck's "imaginative production of 'The Dying Swan' faded out on a close-up of the final convulsive flutter of Markova's exquisite hands, a shot which brought tears to the eyes of many viewers."

When Alicia Markova first appeared in television viewers' living rooms across America, she was not swathed in tulle, tights, and toe shoes as everyone imagined her. The raven-haired dancer walked out in a magnificent couture gown with intricately draped full skirt and tiny wasp waist. The dramatic drop earrings and elbow-length black gloves made her look like royalty. Women were glued to their sets.

Would she speak like the daughter of a Russian Tsar?

That Markova was British was less unexpected than her disarming delivery. The fine-boned ballerina was endearingly humorous and self-deprecating. Millions of Americans were enchanted with both the woman and her dancing.

"Fan mail poured in by the thousands," reported one newspaper. Another added, Markova's *Your Show of Shows* "fan mail was so huge, a special room was given over to it." The charming and soft-spoken British ballerina was now an American sweetheart, and her instant—and widespread—popularity didn't go unnoticed by other television networks:

> **Alicia Markova to have Her Own New York TV Show in Fall**
>
> Alicia Markova, who made three very successful television appearances in New York on Your Show of Shows before she left for London to rejoin Sadler's Wells Ballet as guest ballerina for the Coronation Season, will become a television star of her own show when she returns to New York late in June.
>
> Charles Kebbe, producer of the Lili Palmer series on CBS-TV, has signed a contract with Markova to star in 13 15-minute television films. . . .
>
> All subjects will deal with ballet and Markova will narrate as well as do a four-or-five minute dance. Each program will be divided into three sections: a commentary on the historical background of the ballet, making full use of stories and anecdotes; information in story form, on the subject of the program; and the dance.
>
> —*Dance News*, April 1953

Just as she had during the war years, Markova connected with the American public. She made ballet seem accessible to one and all and was suddenly in great demand for public speaking engagements in cities where she was performing.

> **In New York**
>
> The first of a dance laboratory series conducted by Walter Terry at the 92nd St. "Y," on October 26th, was a small miracle of give-and-take between Mr. Terry and Alicia Markova.

> **In Chicago**
>
> Ballerina Markova Will Outline Her Career in Talk at Arts Club

For a woman whose lifelong goal was to spread the gospel of ballet, it was a marvelous opportunity. Women's groups in particular were hugely interested in Markova's talks, as ballet schools for young girls were cropping up everywhere. Any advice she could provide on little Debbie's possible future as a dancer would be greatly appreciated. (Markova received an average of seventy letters a week from young girls asking for advice on ballet careers. She read and answered every one.)

There was another aspect of Markova's personality that made her a much sought-after celebrity: she always held something back. She was honest and forthcoming when questioned, but not your chatty new best friend. Americans tended to over-share. Markova was more reserved and elusive. It made everyone wish they could know her better.

Markova's reclaimed popularity in the fall of 1952 initiated a new, and daring, phase in her career. She would never again sign a personal service contract with any impresario, and she would personally take charge of all her own business affairs.

That meant a prodigious additional workload, as all contract negotiations, travel, music, and costume arrangements became Markova's responsibility. She was willing to make that trade-off for her freedom. The ballerina did have business managers and lawyers on her payroll, but *they* worked for *her*, not the other way around. They were often completely dumbfounded at her career choices.

Markova was now in a position to command the highest fees for her services of any ballerina in the world. She could simply have racked up a big bank account and retired rich. But money was a means, not an end, to her. She chose a working life of great variety, constant travel, and generosity of time and spirit. Her expenses were considerable (no more roughing it on the road—and she paid for her own hotels and airfares), so she never accumulated great wealth—no mansion, no country house, no servants. Markova's only homes were the two rental apartments she maintained, one in New York and one shared with her sisters in London.

"I have just a room," Markova explained to a Danish journalist. "We are three sisters who live together in Knightsbridge and when I am in London, I have a room which I can call my own. It is my only home, but it is very cozy especially when our fourth sister calls on us. She is the only one who is married and has children."

While outwardly claiming to love her living situation, in private Markova sometimes expressed bitterness at having to support her sisters. At various times both Doris and Vivienne were on Markova's payroll, but they worked hard for their salaries. If the ballerina felt any pressure to support them, it came from herself. She never outgrew feeling responsible for being the family breadwinner following her father's death.

But Markova did seem to feed off helping others. If she was able to pass on her knowledge to younger dancers, or to bring ballet to the uninitiated, then maybe her life of sacrifice was worthwhile. She flitted back and forth between engagements at the Metropolitan Opera House in New York and Town Halls throughout the British provinces; one day dancing with a prestigious ballet company, the next a fledgling or struggling troupe.

Canada's Royal Winnipeg Ballet was a case in point, a company that found itself deep in debt and practically broke in 1953. The board of directors came up with the idea of asking Alicia Markova to be a guest artist in hopes that ticket sales from her appearance would raise desperately needed funds. Markova agreed and flew from New York to Winnipeg in January 1954.

"Why did you step from your pinnacle of fame to accept an invitation to appear with the Royal Winnipeg Ballet?" a reporter with the *Winnipeg Tribune* asked Markova.

"At heart, I have a pioneer spirit and I derive most enjoyment from helping others," she replied.

Markova explained further the philosophy that governed her final dancing years: "I feel it is not only my duty, but a great privilege, to hand on what I can to young hopefuls and young companies. I have been associated with so many companies in the starting stages and have probably done more than any other ballerina in the formation of ballet companies. You can derive so much happiness when you are helping a lot of people gain something which you alone can offer."

When Markova left Manhattan for Winnipeg, it was cold. But Manitoba was a new level of cold—25 degrees below zero. Markova later said she never forgot that bone-chilling feeling every time she stepped outside, but the warmth and good will from the dancers more than made up for it. Markova returned the favor, as company member Betty Farrally later recalled:

> She [Markova] took time to teach and coach the dancers and, when the costumes for LES SYLPHIDES failed to meet with her approval, she dug into her own pocket and paid for new top layers. The show turned a profit of almost $2000. The board asked Markova to join the Company in February in Washington. She agreed.
>
> The Company departed for Washington at the end of January, their first major American appearance. Markova's presence in three performances at the end of a week-long run played a critical factor in drawing crowds for the "unknown" dance company from Winnipeg. The engagement was a success.

Markova's appearance in Washington, D.C. in February required her to fly back to the United States from London—at her own expense. To an outsider, there was no rhyme or reason to her career choices. But if there was ever an ambassadress of ballet, Alicia Markova was it. The rapidity with which she criss-crossed the globe was mind-boggling.

"I want to dance for everyone in the world," Anna Pavlova once said, and Markova picked up where her idol left off. The two dancers, so often compared stylistically, were the most traveled ballerinas in history. Pavlova perhaps had the more difficult path, covering vast distances prior to plane travel. But Markova was far more generous with her talents, teaching and coaching others wherever she went.

The year 1953 was typical in terms of the variety of engagements Markova accepted. She was the celebrated guest artist for the Queen's Coronation Season with the Sadler's Wells Ballet at the Royal Opera House in London, and the ballet sensation of *tout de Paris* at the Palais de Chaillot. She danced for Ted Shawn's Student's Summer College at Jacob's Pillow in the Berkshires of Massachusetts and performed in a huge open-air Greek Theatre in Hollywood, California.

That summer, Markova broke all attendance records in Philadelphia, Pennsylvania when twenty-three thousand people attended a free concert at Robin Hood Dell in Fairmount Park. As a local newspaper reported:

23,000 See Classic Ballet in Dell Dance Program

Statistics were not available at this writing, but it surely must have been a tossup whether Robin Roberts, burning sliders past the Brooklyn Dodgers at Connie Mack Stadium, packed them in in greater numbers than Alicia Markova, famed ballerina, and her partner Oleg Tupine, at Robin Hood Dell.

Last night was blessed by perfect weather, so that one of the largest crowds ever to enter the Dell, a crowd estimated at 23,000 or more, attested [to] the popularity of classic ballet as a form of entertainment.

The vast throng quite covered all available space, meadows and adjacent hills, providing an imposing spectacle, if one took the trouble to turn around in one's seat and look.

Enthusiasm for the fine and varied program quite matched the robust appearance of the audience.

—*The Philadelphia Bulletin*, 7/10/53

Markova ended 1953 with sold-out performances at the Met in November and a return to Paris in December to dance with the Grand Ballet du Marquis de Cuevas. As columnist Art Buchwald wrote of her at the time:

Markova Rounding Out 33 Years on Her Toes

PARIS—We had the rare and rewarding experience the other day of watching Alicia Markova rehearsing a scene from "Les Sylphides." Miss Markova, considered by many as the greatest living ballerina, and by others as the greatest ballerina who ever lived, flew to Paris to appear in six ballets with the Marquis de Cuevas' famed ballet company. Because of her fame, experience, and talent, she is one of the few ballerinas in the world who can free-lance, go where she wishes, do what she wants and demand the salary she believes she justly deserves.

—*New York Herald Tribune*, 11/22/53

12

The People's Ballerina

> Markova floated around and above the melting pots of criticism with that quaint little smile and far away look in her large expressive eyes. Herself a wraith, she danced when and how she liked, but with all her apparent intangibility she was intensely practical. She remained faithful to her public as they were to her, giving them their fill of their beloved romantic ballets of yesterday and today, of which she remained Queen for over thirty years.
>
> —"Pioneers of the Royal Ballet: Alicia Markova," Gordon Anthony

Throughout the 1950s, the diversity of Markova's work engagements was matched only by her social life, a truly improbable mix of activities for a classical ballerina.

She enjoyed American baseball games, circuses, and movies—sometimes seeing two or three films a day when she had the time (which wasn't often)—and was completely taken with slot machines on her first visit to Las Vegas. "I worked a fruit-machine for over three hours," she confessed to a London newspaper just after her trip. "That's how I got the blisters."

"Did you win anything?" she was asked.

"'Oh, yes,' said Markova brightly. 'A couple of cowboys took me in tow and showed me how to beat the machines.'"

In Markova's parallel, more rarefied universe, she attended countless black-tie fundraising galas—co-hosting several high-profile events with Sir Laurence Olivier—and frequented society luncheons with the likes of good friend Cecil Beaton (who often accompanied her to the movies), Elsa Schiaparelli, and Noel Coward. And for a woman who preferred reading in bed to attending parties, she managed to meet every boldface name of her era. (Marilyn Monroe once shyly asked Markova, "Do you remember me?")

Though the British ballerina enjoyed life in New York, in her heart London was always home—warm and comfy as a "pair of old slippers." The city meant family reunions, with Bunny and niece Susie close by, and sister Vivienne great company in the Knightsbridge flat. Markova's cat Moey was also in residence, quite fond of sleeping on his mistress's tutus and curling up in her lap whenever she sat down to read.

Markova was never without a pet cat throughout her life. She was often seen in photographs with one of her feline friends, and was once even compared to one.

> When I meet Alicia Markova, I think of my Russian Blue cat. Alicia has bold brown eyes of remarkable size and limpidity, a soft—yes—almost a purring voice; behind the statuesque way she sits, behind the assured manner, the slow gentle smile, there lurks, one feels, a sense of mischief. She teases just a little—and oh so delicately! There, I hasten to add, the resemblance to my Russian Blue ends.
>
> —*Woman and Beauty*, 1955

After the mischievous Tinker passed on—the banana-eating cat's antics had been a big hit with the British press many years earlier—Moey came into Markova's life, named after niece Susie's imaginary friend.

"Before the kitten arrived, my young niece—she was three then—had developed quite a thing about a mysterious person called Moey," Markova later explained. "It was always 'Moey says I may stay up late tonight,' or 'It wasn't me—Moey did it.'

"I decided if Moey were to become a reality, it might cure her. When next she came to see me, I said 'Moey is here.' She looked quite staggered and wouldn't believe me. However, I introduced her to Moey—and she never mentioned the name again!"

The cat shared Markova's celebrity at one point by falling out a window and dropping six floors. Moey used up just one of his nine lives thanks to "The People's Dispensary for Sick Animals." A regular contributor to animal charities, Markova used Moey's successful treatment to publicize the organization's exceptional work. The ballerina had founded her own animal charity in the 1930s—The Honourable Company of Cats—with all donations helping to offset veterinary bills for those in need.

Markova was very much part of her Knightsbridge neighborhood, and was extremely "well liked locally," as a reporter for the *West London Times* discovered. Even at the height of her fame, she was known "for her frequent openings of charity fairs and bazaars, and this expresses her philosophy of life," he continued.

Also appreciated by fellow Brits was Markova's resumption of ballet tours in far-flung cities and towns throughout Great Britain—this despite the much higher fees she could have commanded elsewhere. In December 1953, Markova received £30,000 for ten performances with the Grand Ballet du Marquis de Cuevas in Paris. She could have made a fortune in 1954, but chose instead to spend March through June touring the countryside of England, Ireland, Scotland, and Wales. That ongoing mission to pioneer ballet outside of world capitals was Markova's generous and heartfelt gift to her countrymen, and her mother's place of birth.

To make such a tour feasible—she visited fourteen cities in the first month alone—Markova decided to travel just as she had with Dolin in the old days: two dancers with piano accompaniment. There would be no corps, no scenery, and no orchestra.

Markova personally looked after the costumes, music arrangements, and repertoire, engaging the exceptional Yugoslav dancer Milorad Miskovitch as her partner.

"For the first time since the days of Pavlova, a ballerina is to tour Britain accompanied only by her partner," heralded one newspaper. It was considered important and historic in the provinces, and each engagement received a great deal of publicity.

> **Brought Ballet First to Provinces**
>
> . . . A month ago, Markova was dancing in the Metropolitan Opera House, New York, which, she admitted, was a little different from the Albert Hall, Nottingham, where she will be dancing this evening.
>
> "But," she declared, "all that matters to me really is the audience. If I can give a little pleasure, that is all that matters."
>
> —*The Guardian Journal*, 3/1/54

Accustomed to performing with large companies in major city theaters, Miskovitch was overwhelmed by audience responses in the provinces. He quickly came to understand Markova's sense of purpose. It didn't matter if ticketholders were knowledgeable about ballet. They were captivated, appreciative, and enthusiastic. Ten to twenty curtain calls were the norm.

Miskovitch also couldn't have imagined the amount of worldwide publicity their performances would receive, thanks to Markova's playful marketing skills. It started at the very beginning of the tour when Markova was being interviewed over breakfast at the Manchester Hotel.

The reporter, who clearly knew nothing about ballet, asked how she managed to balance on her toes. Another prima ballerina might have scoffed at such a silly question, but Markova thought for a moment, walked over to the waiter's serving station, picked up a large tray topped with a coffee pot, and placed it carefully on her head. She then stood on one foot explaining balance skills.

The photographer immediately snapped her picture and the amusing photo was later picked up by the news wire services, appearing in papers as far away as San Antonio, Texas and Bethlehem, Pennsylvania. The astonished hotel waiter was in the background of the photo and made it into the captions as well: "'If I could do that,' thinks Ernest, 'I could carry three trays at once, and save no end of time, exertion, and shoe-leather.'"

But it was not all fun and games. Shortly after beginning the provincial tour, Markova took a bad fall. While she broke no bones, the doctor's report revealed, "She has obviously bruised herself badly, strained the ext. lateral ligaments of left ankle and wrist, and the muscles of left buttock and shoulder." Markova refused to cancel any bookings and asked the doctor for whatever treatment he could suggest. He provided her with the following letter:

> She [Markova] has had some diathermy today and this will be given again tomorrow before she leaves for Bristol.
>
> In addition she has had gentle massage.
>
> I understand that she always arranges to have general "toning up" massage wherever she is staying.
>
> Would you mind, therefore, putting this into an envelope for her to give to a Masseur in the next City she visits, as I think she should continue therapy until she is free from ill effects.

Liverpool provided Markova with her next media master stroke. She and Miskovitch were set to perform at the Liverpool Philharmonic Hall, but the Philharmonic Society suddenly cancelled her engagement:

> **"She might harm machinery"**
>
> 7 st. Alicia 'must not dance on our stage'
>
> Seven-stone Alicia Markova, "the ballerina who lands like a snowflake," has been refused permission to dance at the Liverpool Philharmonic Hall—because her dainty movement might damage delicate machinery under the stage.
>
> The stage holds the weight of the 72-strong Philharmonic Orchestra. School choirs use the stage and hundreds of boys scurry across it to receive their prizes at school speech days.
>
> But Markova—she drinks a bottle of stout every night to keep her weight from dropping below seven stone—has been told: "Sorry, but we can't allow you to dance on the stage."
>
> Critics have said Markova defies the law of gravity. Anton Dolin, her former partner, once said: "I have to pluck her out of the air."
>
> Mr. W. C. Stiff, secretary of the Philharmonic Society, said yesterday: "Delicate machinery which operates the 25ft.-high screen is housed under the stage. The corporation put a ban on dancing because of the risk of damaging the machinery.

> **No exception**
>
> "It might cost thousands of pounds to repair any damage, and we cannot take the risk.
>
> "A request from Markova's agent was considered, but we could not make an exception in her case. It is a matter of principle."
>
> Mr. Stiff added: "Although the stage is used for a variety of purposes the people do not dance. Markova dances."
>
> —*London Daily Express*, 4/12/54

Markova knew a good story when she saw one. The next day she called a press conference at the Hall.

> Feather-weight (7-stone) ballerina Alicia Markova—banned from dancing at Liverpool Philharmonic Hall because her weight might damage the delicate machinery—stepped on to the forbidden stage yesterday.
>
> Mink-coated and in high heels, she danced a few steps "just to prove a point."
>
> Then she said, "I am willing to have my dance vibrations compared with those of the percussion player in the orchestra."
>
> —*Liverpool Evening Express*, 4/13/54

> **Chocolate-box ballerina**
>
> Men? I can eat them all under the table—says Markova
>
> My life has been one long battle . . . to stop myself just fading away.
>
> Chocolates, starch, stout, five-course meals—I've tried the lot.
>
> And I'm STILL The Snowflake. I STILL have a 20-inch waist and take size 2½ shoes. I STILL weigh under 7 stone.
>
> It's comic that I should have been refused permission to dance at Liverpool Philharmonic Hall last week "because I might damage the delicate mechanism under the stage."
>
> I'D BE MUCH MORE LIKELY TO FLOAT STRAIGHT UP AND DAMAGE THE CEILING!
>
> —*London Sunday Graphic*, 4/18/54

The story once again made it to the international news wires, but that wasn't the end of the press coverage. Markova still needed a venue to dance in Liverpool, and the local boxing ring—getting in on all the publicity—offered their arena, probably assuming the ballerina would say no. They were wrong.

> **Markova: weight 98 pounds**
>
> Liverpool, May 30 (Reuters)
>
> Alicia Markova, the elfin-like British ballerina who weighs 98 pounds, rehearsed tonight—in a boxing ring.
>
> Miss Markova was earlier refused permission to dance on the stage of the Liverpool Philharmonic Hall because "she might damage the delicate machinery under the stage." So tomorrow night, accompanied by the Liverpool Philharmonic Orchestra, she will dance at the boxing stadium.

The reviews were excellent.

> **The Brilliant Markova**
>
> Alicia Markova's brilliance sparkled and shone last night even amid the tawdriness of the setting of Liverpool STADIUM. This was dancing such as the city has not seen for a long time—the greatest ballerina that England has given the world of dancing at her incomparable best.
>
> —*Liverpool Evening Express*, 6/1/54

Markova continued to milk the story at her next venue, where she posed on a large scale for photographers. Once again the picture was sent out via the AP newswires. The caption read as follows:

> BALLERINAS TOO?—Ballerinas as well as boxers have to be weighed in now, it seems. Alicia Markova weighs in at London's Royal Albert Hall to make sure she's not over 104 pounds. The Liverpool Philharmonic Hall recently refused to let the ballerina dance there on grounds that her dancing might affect delicate machinery housed under the stage.

Following the successful tour, Markova returned to London for an engagement with the Sadler's Wells Ballet, where she had become a seasonal guest artist. Members of the company's *corps de ballet* were threatening to strike over a wage dispute, and Markova was asked her opinion on the matter.

A Girl Must Eat, Says Alicia Markova

Thirty members of the Sadler's Wells Theatre Ballet have refused to sign new contracts. They want an extra 30s. a week all round.

What does a girl who has got to the top think about it? I spoke last night to Alicia Markova.

She said she could not take sides in the dispute.

Then said:

"I don't think any ballet dancer is ever paid too much. It is a hard profession. The training is very demanding and the work more so.

"Any money that comes the dancer's way is usually earmarked for food and equipment—ballet shoes, tights, practice clothes. They are very expensive."

But Sadler's Wells dancers are now provided most of those things. And with the security of regular employment and free medical attention.

When Markova started, work was on a day-to-day basis. Five guineas a week was the standard rate. She danced three times a day in a cinema programme to augment the budget.

She says: "While commercial ballet companies sometimes pay three times as much as the Wells, they often don't live as long."

And she stresses that, with a dancer, Art should be the thing.

"It's no use anyone undertaking ballet as a career with the idea of making a fortune," she says. "I haven't."

—*London Daily Herald*, 8/18/54

Milorad Miskovitch was one of many talented partners Markova danced with in the last decade of her career. Parting with Anton Dolin seemed to free her up creatively, encouraging more experimentation with each new collaboration. As John Martin had written, Markova made "adjustments here and there" as she got older, and "the compensations are more than generous." Other dance critics were equally impressed.

> **Markova The Astonishing**
>
> Back with Sadler's Wells Ballet. . . . Her performance is quite astonishing. It sounds ridiculous to say that an artist in her forties dances as lightly as dandelion down, yet she seems to do so. . . .
>
> There is at times a sudden and surprising agility in her dancing, but this mature and understanding dancer gives more delight just by the serene beauty of her apparently effortless movements.
>
> She has an admirable partner in Michael Somes.
>
> —*London Star*, 3/17/53

Having experienced so much personal turmoil concerning jealousies and competition within ballet companies, Markova made an effort to be fair and respectful as a guest artist. Prior to her arrival for the Paris engagement with the Grand Ballet du Marquis de Cuevas, she received the following telegram:

> PLEASE WIRE IMMEDIATELY IF YOU CHOOSE SKIBINE OR SKOURATOFF AS PARTNER GISELLE LOVE MARQUIS DE CUEVAS

Markova replied:

> TO AVOID HURT FEELINGS SUGGEST FIRST GISELLE SKIBINE SECOND SKOURATOFF LOVE MARKOVA

While George Skibine and Vladimir Skouratoff were both established luminaries of the ballet, that was not always the case with Markova's partners. Considering her stature, she could have demanded dancing only with the male principals of each company, but she thought that selfish. Markova knew her fame would call attention to talented, lesser-known male artists who danced with her, and she offered to coach those would-be Albrechts on the fine points of *Giselle*. As the director of London's Royal Ballet (formerly the Sadler's Wells), Ninette de Valois was taken aback by Markova's generosity. As the *London Daily Chronicle* reported:

> **Markova passes on tradition**
>
> Markova's insistence on dancing with the two young male stars of the Royal Ballet is typical of her. It would possibly have been easier for her to bring her own partner, but she felt, and rightly, that she could be of far more use to the company if she appeared with their own dancers. If you remember how much she did to help Michael Somes with his interpretation of Albrecht in Giselle when she appeared with the company a few years ago, it is indeed heartening to think that she will again be passing on her great knowledge to the most promising of today's male dancers.
>
> Incidentally, Markova has also insisted that, during her month with the Royal Ballet, she gives two matinee performances. Her reason for this is so that the children will get a chance of seeing her, and also those who live at longer distances from the centre of London.

One of the chief beneficiaries of Markova's coaching was the 27-year-old Danish dancer Erik Bruhn, who Markova is credited with catapulting into overnight stardom.

It was in 1955, the fifteenth anniversary year of Ballet Theatre. Company founder Lucia Chase decided to celebrate that achievement with what was billed as:

> THE GREATEST CAST EVER ASSEMBLED FOR ONE SEASON
> 24 MEMORABLE PERFORMANCES, 30 FAMOUS BALLETS

Many fine dancers who had previously performed with the company were invited back for the gala three-week booking—April 12 through May 1—at the Metropolitan Opera House in New York. Alicia Markova, Anton Dolin, and Hugh Laing were among those asked to return.

Markova was looking forward to reprising her original role of Juliet to Laing's Romeo, and once again partnering Igor Youskevitch in *Giselle*. Her third ballet was to be *Les Sylphides* danced with company newcomer Erik Bruhn, formerly of the Royal Danish Ballet.

As is proper with ballet hierarchical etiquette, the opening week's performance of *Giselle* was reserved for the company's two resident principal dancers, Alicia Alonso and Igor Youskevitch. Markova was to dance *Giselle* with Youskevitch once each in weeks two and three.

But there was a problem. Markova's second *Giselle* was reserved for the final performance of the Gala celebration—the Sunday matinee on May 1. When Youskevitch learned of the schedule, he informed Lucia Chase that dancing matinees was in violation of his contract, and he wouldn't make an exception.

Chase went to Markova with what she thought the perfect solution. Wouldn't it be wonderful if Markova were to close the Gala 15th Anniversary season dancing *Giselle* with Anton Dolin? Markova thought it not wonderful at all. Her relationship with Dolin had been frosty since The Festival Ballet, and she had no intention of feeding any media frenzy about their reuniting.

Chase then offered Erik Bruhn, but warned that he had never danced the role of Albrecht before. If she thought the suggestion of the less-experienced Bruhn would encourage Markova to dance with Dolin, Chase was mistaken. Markova had found the Danish soloist an accomplished classicist when they danced together in rehearsals of *Les Sylphides*. Bruhn would be just fine. (And, as Markova surmised, he was soon to be famous not only as a true "dancer's dancer" with brilliant technique, but also as one of the most talented and generous partners of his time.)

For his part, Bruhn was both flattered and extremely nervous. After all, this was Alicia Markova, considered the greatest Giselle of her generation. Though he hadn't performed the role of Albrecht before, Bruhn had studied Youskevitch in the part, watching him nightly from the wings. But that only made him more fearful. Bruhn idolized Youskevitch, who he thought had the perfect build, technique, and manner of a classic romantic ballet dancer. Critics agreed.

Interestingly, Bruhn had never liked Dolin's partnering of Markova in *Giselle*, which he compared unfavorably to Youskevitch:

> Though Dolin's technique was less brilliant, he, too, had these qualities to a degree, but his attitude toward the character Giselle was very different, influenced perhaps by his personal feelings for the ballerina who performed the role. He appeared to regard Markova as his protégé; he was the Svengali who had instructed her and was now presenting her to the public. Throughout the ballet he was her protective mentor, a relationship that was made even more evident during the final curtain calls, when with his arms about her he seemed to say to the audience, "Isn't this a lovely Giselle I have created?"
>
> —*American Ballet Theatre,* Charles Payne

Markova had indeed received some of her best-ever reviews in *Giselle* when partnered with Youskevitch. Nevertheless, Lucia Chase asked Dolin to stop by the studio where Markova and Bruhn were rehearsing and give the Danish dancer coaching tips.

In her autobiography *Giselle & I,* Markova writes that it was "lucky" Dolin stopped by to "instruct Bruhn in some of the finer points of partnering the second act." She was taking the high road, as usual.

"Dolin did, as Markova says in her account, attend one rehearsal," Bruhn counters, "but instead of coaching me, he criticized Markova so indelicately that he was asked not to return."

Alicia Markova hardly needed coaching in *Giselle,* but she never disparaged Dolin in print. Quite the contrary—she tried to put a positive spin on his inappropriate behavior.

Markova was in the process of writing *Giselle & I* at the same time Dolin was working on autobiography number three. Both books were published in 1960. But while Dolin appeared to relish revealing numerous stories of "how infuriating Alicia could be"—the only parts of his book that received press attention—Markova went out of her way to offer him only praise.

Markova had just two days to coach Bruhn in *Giselle,* and he found her work process fascinating. First, Bruhn was perplexed at Markova's teaching him a different interpretation of Albrecht than the one favored by Youskevitch, with whom she danced so beautifully. When he asked, she explained why.

"When Markova danced as a guest of Ballet Theatre, with her contemporary Youskevitch, he was in control. She did it his way," Bruhn learned. "When she danced with me, her junior and newfound protégé, *she* was in control. We did it her way."

Markova was old-school. There were unwritten rules one was to follow out of respect. But she didn't stand on ceremony when teaching and coaching dancers. As Bruhn later explained:

"Markova was so clear in what she told me about the ballet that I felt ready to go on stage that night after only one rehearsal. She never had to repeat herself and she said once, 'We seem to speak the same language.' Thanks to her, it worked out just right."

Numerous dance critics present for that matinee declared the performance a once-in-a-lifetime event.

The Matinee That Made History

Ever since January 1, 1934, a select group of ballet goers have been able to boast that they were present at the Old Vic Theatre, London, when Alicia Markova danced Giselle for the first time. It is highly probable that from May 1, 1955, a somewhat larger group will be boasting that they saw the first performance of Erik Bruhn as Albrecht in the same ballet. And his Giselle was Alicia Markova. . . .

Alicia Markova's name in an announcement of a performance of Giselle is sufficient on its own to sell out a house anywhere in the world, and there was little advance publicity beyond the bare fact that on this occasion Erik Bruhn would be her partner instead of Igor Youskevitch, the great Albrecht for many years of this company's productions. . . .

It was immediately recognizable that Bruhn was giving the role a quality such as no one could recall having seen for years. It was the perfect masculine counterpart of Markova's interpretation. . . . If his dancing was magnificent, and it was, his partnering of and playing to Markova were no less so.

The result was one of those electrifying performances when everyone both in the audience and on the stage is aware that something extraordinary is happening. . . .

> [Markova] not only consented most gladly to accept an untried newcomer to the role as a partner, but out of her humility as a great artist she found within herself the strength to teach him the part, to coach him with the utmost patience, to talk to him about all she had learned and felt and knew about the ballet in the years since she herself had first danced it. She gave him all her experience, and between them they shaped a performance as only they themselves, dancing again together in this ballet, will be able to match and surpass perhaps in our time.
>
> —P. W. Manchester, *Dance News*, June 1955

Added John Martin of *The New York Times*, "It may well be a date to write down in the history books, for it was as if the greatest Giselle of today were handing over a sacred trust to what is probably their greatest Albrecht of tomorrow."

Markova would dance with Bruhn throughout the fall 1955 season, but not just in New York and not exclusively. She had already made "several" commitments:

> **Alicia Markova Begins Busy Season on Tight Schedule**
>
> LONDON, Aug. 17—It is usually believed that guest ballerinas invited to appear with major companies have an easy time in comparison with the day after day performance of the regular stars of those companies. But just take a look at Alicia Markova's schedule for the next two months and see what she has lined up for herself.
>
> On Sept. 11 she will appear here on a special TV programme. She will dance Giselle Act 2, with Erik Bruhn as Albrecht and Ballet Rambert in support. She will appear in Copenhagen on Sept. 23 and 25 with the Royal Danish Ballet in Giselle, again with Erik Bruhn.
>
> The Royal Opera House, Stockholm, wants her to dance Giselle there also, and she will do this, if possible on Oct. 1 and then go straight to Paris in time for the gala opening of the Grand Ballet du Marquis de Cuevas, Oct. 7, when she will dance the title role in La Sylphide, the famous Bournoville

> ballet which Harold Lander, formerly ballet master of the Royal Danish Ballet, set for the Grand Ballet two years ago.
>
> **Fly to Chicago**
>
> She will dance with the company three weeks, to Oct. 26, and then will fly to Chicago to appear in the special opera season there, as announced elsewhere in this issue.
>
> Because of her other commitments, Markova has had to refuse other offers from Helsinki, Amsterdam and Brussels. In the last two cities she was wanted to dance Giselle in productions by Anton Dolin.
>
> In addition to all this, she is dancing Aug. 28 in Deauville for the big children's hospitals charity Bal des Petits Lits Blancs at which Maurice Chevalier, Gene Kelly and his wife, Betsy Blair, will also appear.
>
> —*Dance News*, September 1955

Of that exhausting schedule, Markova's performances with Bruhn in *Giselle* would get the most press attention. Their extraordinary partnership left every audience spellbound, including millions of British ballet fans who watched the performance televised by the BBC that same season.

A similar delirium swept the ballet world when Margot Fonteyn first danced with Rudolf Nureyev seven years later. But while that magical partnership lasted seventeen years, Markova disappeared from Bruhn's life as quickly as she had materialized—just like Giselle.

Markova was thrilled at having played a part in helping to launch what would become a brilliant career for Bruhn, and was delighted to dance with him again in the future, but now it was time to move on.

In 1957, Doris Barry was asked to write an article about her famous ballerina sister, and the following is an excerpt:

> We come from a family of inventors and pioneers and this spirit seems embodied in Markova. As often when she could accept a lucrative engagement in London or New York, an offer comes from a new national company struggling to establish itself, and though she knows it means physical discomfort

> from climate, hotels, etc., we find ourselves in a plane and my sister turns to me and says, "Well, here we go again—another new country to conquer!" . . .
>
> She has danced with Russian, British, American, Canadian, South African, Danish, French, Italian, Brazilian, Argentinean, Mexican, Cuban, and Philippino Companies, and even this year danced her classical solos with a traditional Spanish Company. . . .
>
> [Doris also stressed that young dance students should take note of Markova's vast knowledge outside ballet.]
>
> [W]hen one visits these foreign countries it is essential to know something of their geographical, historical and political facts. One also needs a mathematical brain to cope with the different currencies. Another asset is to be able to understand and speak the different languages; of course in the world of ballet, mime is universal and can always bridge the gap!
>
> I hope this short insight into a great ballerina's personality shows the unique and wonderful person she is and that all her hard work and devotion to her Art has been well worthwhile.
>
> —"My Sister . . . The Ballerina," by Doris Barry

Alicia Markova's hard work and devotion to her art also made her a worldwide celebrity. She was the subject of comic books, crossword puzzles, and trading cards (along with Winston Churchill). Her portrait was painted and sculpted by celebrated artists, and etched onto highball glasses and commemorative plates. She was asked to judge the Miss World contest held in Paris, create a "supper club" act for Las Vegas, and appear with Bob Hope and Buddy Holly and the Crickets at the Palladium Theatre in London.

Advertising agencies besieged Markova with requests for product endorsements. Some made sense: footwear, elegant stationery, and nail polish. Others not so much: Readers Digest and the unfortunately named Craven "A" cigarettes.

Markova didn't smoke, but she was told that wasn't a problem. The company just wanted to use an eye-catching photo of her flying "smoothly" through the air with the headline: "'Smooth' is the key word, says Markova, Internationally Famous Ballerina."

It must have made sense to someone.

More suited to Markova's own personal tastes was an ad for Cadbury chocolates.

> **TOO FAMOUS TO EAT**
> —yet lovely MARKOVA,
> Britain's own prima ballerina,
> dances with tireless energy.
> **HERE SHE TELLS YOU HER SECRET**
> "A ballerina's life is very strenuous," she says. "With hours of rehearsals as well as the actual performances I am kept very much 'on my toes.' Being in the theatre frequently from 9 A.M. until midnight, and unable to find time for a substantial meal, I find a bar of Cadburys Milk Chocolate an excellent way of keeping my energy."
> **CADBURY'S MILK CHOCOLATE**
> **"FEEDS YOU ON YOUR FEET"**

When Markova was quoted in a London newspaper explaining that she ate a steak and potatoes after every performance to get her energy back, England's "Potato Council" pounced. Would the ballerina consent to being a spokesperson to benefit the ailing local agricultural industry? Markova was more than happy to oblige: "I love potatoes and I eat them with every meal," read the brochure's headline.

A lovely photo of the ballerina in *au courant* hat and pearls shared honors with a drawing of "Potato Pete"—a cartoon character of a dancing spud—and many of the ballerina's favorite recipes.

In 1955, Markova appeared on American television as a guest on Edward R. Murrow's *Person to Person*. The talk show was appointment television for millions of viewers. Every Friday night, the legendary newsman could be seen chain-smoking on air in his CBS studio easy chair while chatting amiably with a variety of international celebrities.

Famous guests weren't the only draw for the popular half-hour program, which was credited with launching the TV talk show format. Unheard of for the times, Murrow lobbed softball questions from his

New York City stage set, while celebrities responded from the comfort of their very own living rooms—live!

Prior to the days of satellite transmission and videotape, live location feeds were quite a technological achievement. It required two to six enormous cameras at stars' homes—as far away as Hollywood—along with elaborate cable wiring, lighting, and prep rehearsals. That was the only way subjects could be followed smoothly from room to room as they gave intimate tours of their homes and family life. Once again, it was a live transmission—no do-overs or editing out mistakes.

Pairing segments of guests in different professions was a signature of the show, such as performer Sammy Davis Jr. with French couturier Christian Dior, or playwright Noel Coward with former First Lady Eleanor Roosevelt. So when viewers checked their newspaper TV listings for March 4, 1955, the *Person to Person* write-up wouldn't have struck them as at all odd:

> It's too late for the kids, but grownups can have a look at Roy Rogers, wife Dale Evans, and their five kids on Rogers' ranch in Encino, Calif. Expected also on the scene is Trigger. Murrow also visits ballerina Alicia Markova one of the world's best in her New York apartment. Talk will include discussion of new popularity of ballet and Miss Markova's brilliant career.

Luckily for Markova, Trigger failed to make an appearance with the crooning cowboy. The beloved horse would have been a tough act to follow. As it was, she had been a last-minute substitute for ex-President Harry Truman, who had needed to reschedule. "It isn't every day a ballet dancer can stand in for an ex-President," joked the *San Francisco Chronicle*.

But as was typical for the always-engaging Alicia Markova, her television performance got boffo reviews:

> Miss Markova, generally acceded to be one of the all-time greats of the ballet, was a charming, voluble and intelligent guest and her descriptions, reminiscences and words of advice made good viewing and good sense. . . .

> This—whether by intent or indirection—was one of the most penetrating of the "Personcasts." In mood and in direction, it went beyond the customary "this is our playroom" bit and provided a little bit of insight into the real makings of people.
>
> —*Variety New York*, 3/9/55

The contrast between the large and loving Roy Rogers/Dale Evans clan—all warmth and humanity—with the single (and singularly career-minded) British ballet star was part of what made the show a compelling half-hour. But many also found the 44-year-old dancer a far more complicated individual than they might have initially supposed.

As a writer commented in the next day's *T.V. News*, "With the best of intentions I brought home a full briefcase from the office. But my wife wanted to watch Markova. That was the end of me and my work. I tried hard to concentrate, but Markova won. What a fascinator she is!"

Markova had plenty of practice with public appearances. She looked effortlessly glamorous, yet came across as open and sincere. Women viewers watched intently as she carefully sewed ribbons on her ballet shoes while chatting with Murrow. And she had a "wow" finish, demonstrating how she actually glued her toe inside prior to dancing. The ballerina also hand-knit her own practice tights, as she showed the camera. Who would have thought?

Men laughed at Markova's conceding that she ate like a truck driver—though she made that point far more delicately on air. And when Murrow asked if she worried about living up to her reputation as "probably the greatest ballerina of all time," Markova responded earnestly, "Yes, before every performance."

When Murrow inquired about Markova's lack of a real childhood, it was hard not to feel sorry for the frail little figure. She'd been dancing professionally since age ten. While she never complained of her own life, Markova advised mothers watching the show not to rush their daughters into serious ballet lessons too young. Let them enjoy their life first, she said softly.

Throughout the fourteen-minute live interview, cameras followed Markova about her apartment, but they obviously didn't have far to go.

The world-famous ballerina lived in just two tiny rooms—and alone. In contrast, Roy Rogers called a sprawling ranch home, one he joyfully shared with a loving wife, five children, and a singularly devoted horse.

Making Markova's tastefully decorated living room seem even smaller was the large open trunk in the center, waiting to be packed or unpacked for the next scheduled venue.

Alicia Markova may have been wildly successful and talented, but few watching that interview envied her life.

Throughout the 1950s, the media seemed as obsessed with Markova's single marital status as they were with her dancing. The topic came up at practically every major interview. The older she got, the more she was quizzed about it. And it got worse after 1956, when Margot Fonteyn married (albeit to a philandering Panamanian diplomat) yet kept on dancing. What about Markova?

> **Home is Where You Hang Slippers**
>
> Alicia Markova, prima ballerina and Commander of the British Empire, is that mid-20th century rarity: a woman married to her art with no regrets, no complaints.
>
> No matter how present-day social thinkers may frown on the single woman's single-mindedness, the dancer who often has been called the "Pavlova of this generation" sees no other solution for the sincere and unselfish artist.
>
> "If God has given me a gift I think it is my duty to share it with as many people as possible by constant work and travel. It would be too much to expect such dedication in a husband," the simply dressed, meticulously groomed great lady of the dance explained last week in her Metropolitan Opera dressing room, lined with the frothy costumes little girls dream someday of wearing.
>
> **24-Hour Job**
>
> "My life has been one long series of pirouettes from city to city. And for me, ballet is a 24-hour a day job. All plans

> for costumes, tours, even the orchestration of my music stem from me.
>
> "A prima ballerina has terrific responsibility. Like the general of an army, she must know how to get the best out of her troupe. And if they are tired, she must make them forget their tiredness.
>
> "Let's put it this way," Miss Markova continued. "I definitely hope to marry when I retire. I don't want to be alone. But when I marry I want it to be to someone I can respect. Not a martyr. He would have to come first, not me. But while I am still dancing, dancing must come first. So marriage is impossible."
>
> The world's most famous Giselle, the gracious and graceful Miss Markova thinks her life might have been different had she been born nine years later [a reference to Margot Fonteyn].
>
> "As a dancer, I was alone in my generation. When I started training with Diaghileff, the whole outlook was to give your life to your art. This generation [now] includes marriage. Maybe they are right."
>
> —*The World Telegram*, 10/7/58

Markova may have been single, but she was rarely without a man—or men—in her life. A very private person, she never publicly discussed whom she was dating. She was far too classy to kiss and tell. But squibs in gossip columns over the years revealed some of her wealthier beaus.

In February 1955, "John Hammell, Canadian gold mine magnate of Oakville, Ontario" was very much in the picture, according to the *Nassau Guardian.* (Numerous amorous letters from Hammell are in Markova's archives.) But by May, the ballerina seemed to have moved on, as Cholly Knickerbocker revealed in his popular *New York Journal-American* column:

> INTERNATIONAL JEWELER Louis Arpels [of Van Cleef & Arpels] and ballerina Alicia Markova are the latest pas de deux. Louis even changed his sailing date to embark on the same ship with Alicia. And if you've tried that in this tourist jammed season you'll realize it must be love.

For close to a decade, Markova dated Theodore (Ted) Rousseau Jr., the very handsome and urbane curator of paintings at the Metropolitan Museum of Art. From letters between Alicia and Doris, Rousseau was the one Markova hoped to wind up with one day.

It's easy to see what attracted her. Rousseau was highly educated, well traveled, and had been actively involved with identifying and returning looted Nazi art after the war. He appreciated the arts as much as Markova did, and the two often attended gallery exhibits and the theater together when she was in New York. Markova was completely smitten.

Unfortunately, Rousseau was also a notorious ladies' man—though incredibly discreet—and many women had set their sights on him. He never married.

But Markova wasn't exactly sitting by the phone:

> **Society Today**
> **Overseas Mailbag:**
> Slim Greek shipping heir Perry Embiricos, in Monte Carlo for the gay season, isn't very salubrious himself these days. Parental objections to his long courtship of prima ballerina Alicia Markova has cast a gloom over the usually congenial Perry.
> —*New York World-Telegram and Sun*, 8/5/57

Doris remarked that Alicia could have married one of several millionaires who proposed to her over the years and retired rich and well cared for. But Markova would never have married for money or security, and who knows what those men might have demanded of her time and freedom in exchange? She needed to be deeply in love and for the moment to be right. While still dancing, she felt marriage was just out of the question.

Between 1955 and 1958, Markova continued her arduous schedule, thinking nothing of traveling vast distances for even short engagements.

> 6,000 miles to the Eisteddfod—then no salmon
> MARKOVA DANCES FOR SUPPER
> They promised prima ballerina Alicia Markova fresh Dee salmon for supper if she would fly 6,000 miles to dance in a tent in the Welsh hills.

> Markova thought of that tasty reward as she danced in the heat of Rio de Janeiro—and accepted.
>
> She came home specially to star tonight at the opening concert of the 10th International Eisteddfod here.
>
> A cosmopolitan audience of 8,000 saw her dance with gossamer lightness on the wooden platform. It was a performance worthy of an international star.
>
> But although Markova danced with such superb skill for her supper, the Eisteddfod committee had to tell her they had fallen down on their part of the bargain. The fishermen's nets were empty. . . .
>
> **No red carpet**
>
> She came by train from London with five costume boxes, but there was no brass band, red carpet, or reception committee at the station to greet her as she stepped on to the platform.
>
> She said, "I don't mind. Why should anyone make a fuss? I have come here to dance and it is the audience that matters.
>
> "But I am disappointed about that salmon."
>
> —*London Daily Mail*, 7/11/56

What the Eisteddfod committee didn't know was Markova had become seriously ill with ptomaine poisoning in Rio, eventually requiring intravenous feeding. They were lucky she made the trip at all.

In 1958, Markova flew six thousand miles to dance for three minutes. She was among the first passengers to fly on the super-speed British Airways jetliner *Comet 4*. It was "the most wonderful experience," she wrote to Stanley Burton, "so smooth & exciting and easy."

The occasion was a Royal Gala matinee at the London Coliseum. The Queen Mother, Princess Margaret, and eight-year-old Princess Anne were to attend. Markova flew from New York to London on a Wednesday, danced Thursday (Princess Anne asked to shake her hand), and flew back to New York on Friday.

A smiling and impeccably dressed Alicia Markova was frequently photographed daintily walking down the plane exit stairs at Heathrow. Representatives of the London press were always waiting for her at the airport. Markova would give a slight royal wave—then snap—and her picture appeared in all the papers with a caption as to where she was coming from and where she was going next.

Though she couldn't have looked happier or more glamorous in the photographs, non-stop travel had taken a huge toll on Markova's health. She frequently suffered from intestinal and bronchial problems, as well as prolonged menstrual bleeding. And then there were all the aches and strains from various stage falls. Markova was now in almost constant pain of one form or another, often performing against doctors' orders.

Slowing down and only accepting prestigious engagements with renowned companies would have given her body more time to heal. But while she was still able to dance, Markova just couldn't give up her single-minded mission to bring ballet to the world and inspire the next generation of young dancers. It was like a mania.

When Markova traveled to Madrid, Spain to perform in November 1957, Doris went along and wrote to their sister Vivienne about the daily grind:

> *Viv darling—*
>
> *. . . She had a great success & good press yesterday. Change of plans though—big discussion last night, as they can not give the matinee performances without her. I believe there was quite a to-do yesterday—so they wanted her to do extra perfs! to make up the 12. This is impossible as her poor feet already are bruised as they have put down a special wood floor for their Spanish heel work & it is murder for Alicia. So Touras asked her if she could release them from their agreement & only do one week 6 perfs. This actually Alicia had rather been planning how to achieve—so actually she is glad. This means less money but as it rests I don't know what is happening anyway about the money so it is just as well. . . . Alicia had asked me to stay till the Sunday anyway, as frankly, I don't know what she would have done. She is completely left on her own! All we do is eat & go to the theatre so far. . . .*
>
> *Life is so different. Imagine the show starts 11:15 p.m. (& she does not go on until 12:30 a.m.) finishes 2 a.m. & before we leave Theatre with autographs etc. it is 3 a.m. Too tired to go out to nightclubs. So*

eat at Hotel & to bed at 5 a.m. . . . Food is excellent, though until yesterday she really wasn't hungry. She is still full of the flu aches but is trying her best to keep going. She danced beautifully I must say, but oh the music—never mind if only she can get through the six and finish Wednesday. Today she is doing a matinee too (this starts at 7 p.m.)

The shops here are terribly expensive, all Dior things & like Hermes in Paris, so I shall have to mooch near the Theatre.

What is your news dear? Hope you are all right & everything going on all right at the Office. How's Moey?

Alicia is still sleeping, but I know she would send her love. God Bless.

Fondest Love, Dods [family nickname for Doris]

In the spring of 1958, Markova was sitting alone in her dressing room at The Royal Opera House in Covent Garden. She was exhausted, in pain, and deeply depressed. On theater stationery, she wrote the following letter.

March 24, 1958

Dear God,

I offer you my heartfelt thanks for giving me the power & strength to live and dance through the last two years. Since Rio, I have suffered such constant pain at times it has been almost unbearable. No one will ever know how much I have suffered mentally & physically. Only due to my faith in thee and the feeling that I must try & accomplish as much as possible to help people and make them happy (as time is limited for me) has kept me going.

Thank you dear God for helping me to live a good life and one that I could be proud of. I only regret that all the truth & knowledge I have acquired in my art & otherwise will be of little use as so few people seem to want it. Those that do are strangers not close to me. I am so tired of being Father, Mother, sister, husband and not being understood and thanked. Just everything expected and taken for granted.

There is nothing here on earth to make me feel I want to stay so I am ready to leave at anytime.

Ever since she was a teenager, Markova sought approval not as a needy emotional crutch, but as an acknowledgement of a life well spent. Applause wasn't about ego, she told a newspaper reporter in 1955. "I need the applause as a stimulus. If I should ever be satisfied with myself, the day has come to leave the scene." Just one year later, Markova felt painfully rejected by her own country on the most public stage of all.

In 1956, Margot Fonteyn was named a Dame of the British Empire at age thirty-seven. It was an honor rarely bestowed upon someone so young, and many in and out of the British ballet community were shocked that Markova hadn't received the country's highest award before Fonteyn.

That same year, respected dance authority A. H. Franks had written: "ALICIA MARKOVA: She does not dance; she IS the dance." Few disagreed.

Markova was England's first *prima ballerina assoluta* and the dancer credited with pioneering British ballet in the 1930s. She was instrumental in the creation and early success of every ballet company born in England: Ballet Rambert, Vic-Wells (later Sadler's Wells and currently The Royal Ballet), Markova-Dolin, and The Festival Ballet (currently the English National Ballet).

Fonteyn had spent her entire career working for Ninette de Valois, the woman who had desperately needed the immensely talented young Markova to turn her rag-tag corps into a worthy competitor in the world of ballet. It was Markova who danced the country's first full-length *Giselle*, and *Swan Lake*, and *Nutcracker Suite*. It was also Alicia Markova who brought ballet to the provinces for the first time.

Some thought working in America during the war years was being held against her. Others assumed it was just anti-Semitism. Whatever the reason, Markova was crushed. She felt she had given up so much for ballet—and specifically British ballet—and had been very publicly snubbed.

Making matters worse, in January 1958 Markova was awarded the lesser honor of C.B.E., or Commander rather than Dame of the British Empire, as if being thrown a bone. While she greatly valued that title, it was clearly second best.

Considering her debilitated physical and mental state in 1958, it is a wonder she didn't just retire. Markova was forty-seven years old, and most prima ballerinas stopped dancing fulltime before age forty-five. But it was as if she still needed to prove something to her countrymen.

That was one of the reasons Markova did something truly bewildering in the spring of 1958. She accepted an offer to star as guest artist with The Festival Ballet, now called London Festival Ballet.

It meant returning to a company where Julian Braunsweg and Anton Dolin were in charge, two men who had made her life miserable seven years earlier. John Gilpin was still there, and so was Benn Toff, the company manager who had enjoyed making fun of her and stealing her chocolates for a laugh.

Markova was invited to join the London Festival Ballet as guest artist for an international tour co-sponsored by the British government, which regarded the company as an official cultural ambassador. Perhaps Markova wished to remind the powers that be that she too was a British cultural ambassador. London was her true home.

There were also other inducements for Markova's signing on for the May-through-August tour. Doris had recently taken a job working in the press office for the Festival Ballet and would be accompanying her on the trip. Then there was Markova's burdensome workload. Doris suggested that this "mini-vacation" from all booking and logistical arrangements would be a relief. The company had two staff stage managers, Benn Toff and Tony Gilpin, who was dancer John Gilpin's brother. For a change, all Markova would need to do was dance.

Another plus was the opportunity to perform in Israel. Markova had never danced there before, having been forced to cancel her one previous planned engagement in 1956 due to illness. It would be even more special now—the Tenth Anniversary Year of the State of Israel.

When negotiating with the Jewish state, the Festival Ballet was asked if there was any way Markova could take part. The Israelis so wanted to see the legendary Jewish prima ballerina perform. She was such a great source of national pride. Markova felt honored. What's more, she took comfort in the fact that the company had performed in Israel before, hopefully minimizing logistical surprises.

Everything started out amiably enough on the Festival Ballet's first stop in Paris. There was a glittering opening night crowd at the Théâtre

Sarah Bernhardt, with much audience buzz about film legend Charlie Chaplin in the audience. After the performance, "The Little Tramp" was the first person backstage in Markova's dressing room, where the two old friends were photographed along with Chaplin's wife Oona and Markova's sister Doris. The photo appeared in the press media all over Europe.

Dolin and Braunsweg decided not to open their tour with Markova in *Giselle,* choosing instead *Les Sylphides* starring resident prima ballerina Nathalie Krassovska. The company had invited all of the top British dance critics to attend the Paris opening—a highly unusual thing to do—flying them in for the occasion. London ballet critic Peter Williams wrote the following review:

> . . . The *Valse* was well given by Krassovska, though she seemed rather heavy and while obviously realizing Fokine's intentions lacked the fluidity and ethereal quality one imagines to be the especial perogative [*sic*] of *Sylphs*. . . . Then on came Markova, as a guest *Sylph*, to dance *Prélude* and upset the balance of the whole ballet. Obviously it was not intentional and obviously it was the right thing that she should dance something on the opening night of the season, but she just cannot help making everyone else, with the exception of Gilpin, and he is not supposed to be an ethereal creature anyway, look earthbound. In rôles of this kind, no living dancer can match up to her sense of style and artistry. Her Prélude is the most evocative poetic sigh that ever attempted to enter a young poet's dreams. After that the ballet appeared to go clumping to its conclusion.
>
> —*Dance and Dancers* magazine, June 1958

Following that performance, Markova brought every critic to his or her knees with *Giselle,* alternately danced with John Gilpin and Dolin. Doris later commented that Markova and Dolin hadn't lost any of their magic together, even after seven long years.

From Paris the company toured the South of France before moving on to Lisbon, Portugal. Many of the corps dancers weren't happy with the various travel arrangements and complained constantly. It was not a cheerful group.

As had been true in the early days of The Festival Ballet, Braunsweg and company manager Benn Toff did little to make Markova—now their "guest" artist—feel welcome, comfortable, or valued. There were numerous problems, especially with unsafe stages.

Doris wrote sister Vivienne about the various daily goings-on. Alicia had caught an intestinal bug in Lisbon, and the theater conditions weren't helping matters, as Doris reported.

> *May 12, 1958*
>
> *Viv darling,*
>
> *. . . Had big success here, all billing and advertising wrong, but Julian insists the Theatre's fault. Alicia thought of coming back* [to London], *but then thought about the money, & also every one would crow & think she & Pat had quarreled—when actually he is simply wonderful to her! . . . phones her all the time & sees her, etc. etc. (Damn clever—but it is really the same with both of them.)*
>
> *Anyway we stayed, & such a terrible stage she tripped in Sylphides & I thought that's that—but anyway she did Swan, & though her foot is bruised, she thinks it's O.K., so we are staying on. . . . Weather is nice here, sunny. But as I say, you can not go out & just walk & see the shops. Such characters around, like a "B" movie.*

The next day Doris wrote of arguments with Festival Ballet manager Benn Toff and stage manager Tony Gilpin.

> *Alicia thank goodness got over her "flu attack," thanks to the romycine, what a good job I put them in. She did Giselle last night & danced very well. Unfortunately an awful "to-do" with Benn, all over the lights & long interval. He was so rude & Tony Gilpin too. So I don't know quite what is going to happen unless he apologizes, but he was rude again this morning. To me too. Pat has been really marvelous to Alicia. Naturally, he's clever, he wants to continue dancing Giselle with her everywhere, but meantime, at least it is nice to have him on her side & attentive. I do not know what the outcome will be of last night's episode, as Alicia certainly can not*

> *have such treatment. If it sorts itself out & he apologizes, I expect she will continue.*

Toff and Gilpin seemed completely unperturbed by the fact that the theater stage floor was in such poor shape that Markova tripped. If she had been in charge, Markova would have asked that linoleum be laid down on top, something she often had done on past tours. Toff and Gilpin did nothing.

Markova was now forty-seven years old. A serious accident could have ended her career. After her intestinal flu, Markova developed a severe head cold. If Israel hadn't been the next stop, it's likely she would have withdrawn.

From Lisbon the company flew to Marseille, where they were to meet a boat for the trip to Israel. It was a money-saving plan, and extra time had been built in between booking dates.

But Marseille was completely chaotic when they arrived, with an active local French resistance aiding Algeria's war for independence. Boat transportation was cancelled, and the company was stranded in the dangerous port city for almost a week until plane travel could be arranged. Doris again wrote to Vivienne.

> *. . . Things have been very uncomfortable here with the political tension & not knowing quite what was going to happen hour to hour. I shall be so glad when we finally get off tomorrow. Tonight we were going to spend quietly in as we had been told to keep off the streets at 5:00 & there was a demonstration then. But then Randolph Churchill walked in, from Corsica, & Pat knows him & so we had drinks with the newspaper men & then Churchill took us for dinner. It was his Birthday & we had a nice gay little party—how funny life is—never thought to be dining with him! . . .*
>
> *[T]hings are very unsettled everywhere that it really makes one stop & think a little before rushing away. People joke but it is not a very nice feeling not knowing if one is going to be free to leave & get a plane. There was nothing the other day—no trains, planes, mail, newspapers or anything. Maybe it would be nice to go to Ireland for a change. . . .*

Things have been better here, but she really isn't O.K. Still has this cough etc. Hope maybe the change in Israel will help.

Still suffering from earaches and sinus problems, Markova was advised by doctors not to fly, as the cabin pressure was sure to be immensely painful. She had little choice if she wanted to dance in Israel. Markova had been forced to cancel two years earlier due to illness. She was loath to do it again.

No direct flights were available to Tel Aviv, so the trip required a long layover in Greece. By the time the London Festival Ballet arrived in Israel, it was the wee hours of the morning. Everyone was tired, grumpy, and out of sorts.

All the company passports were collected together and handed over to authorities, as asked. One by one each person's name was called out and each passed through customs. Eventually everyone but Markova had been called. She was told her passport was missing.

That was not actually the case. She would later learn that the Israeli officials were so taken with the arrival of the world's first openly Jewish classical prima ballerina that they "borrowed" her passport and put it on display in a secured area for all to see. Airport personnel began clustering in droves, each taking the time to closely examine the prized document. As more and more time passed without a word, poor Markova waited in the uncomfortable deplaning chamber, tired, concerned, and woefully ill.

She was eventually allowed to leave the gate, but was quite worried about having to get a new passport. Doris was furious. When the passport was finally returned, Markova was less than thrilled to learn the true story. Couldn't they have just asked for autographs? She would have been happy to oblige.

But Markova was too excited about her first trip to Israel to dwell on the misadventure—and for reasons beyond just her religion. She had a very personal connection to Tel Aviv, specifically the ballet company's first performance venue, the Fredric R. Mann Auditorium.

Markova was a friend of the concert hall's namesake, and through charity events had helped him raise building funds for the theater. The two had first worked together at the Robin Hood Dell Stadium in Philadelphia, Pennsylvania, where Fredric Mann served as director.

The wealthy arts philanthropist had a passion for music and for Israel, and was close to many famous Jewish musicians such as Arthur Rubinstein, Jascha Heifetz, and Itzhak Perlman. Mann helped found the Israeli Symphony Orchestra, with the Auditorium bearing his name their official home.

Because the theater was a concert hall and not a proper theater, a production of *Giselle* with scenery was impossible. Markova had been asked to dance it anyway, but she really wanted her first *Giselle* in Israel to be perfect. Though disappointed, the audience roared its approval for her *Dying Swan*.

The next theater, in Haifa, was in horrendous shape, and once again, *Giselle* was out of the question.

Braunsweg, Dolin, and Toff all admitted that the stage was rickety and unsafe, but they wanted Markova to dance *Giselle* anyway. Since she had tripped badly on Lisbon's uneven boards, she was terrified it might happen again.

It was finally determined that the only place Markova could possibly dance *Giselle* in Haifa was in their huge outdoor amphitheater. With its seating for twenty thousand, the tickets could be sold at reasonable prices—always a plus as far as Markova was concerned. And whether management approved or not, there would be plenty of "free" seating as well, since anyone who lived in the surrounding neighborhood could easily watch the performance from a balcony or hillside vantage point.

But they were not out of the woods yet. Proper staging was still very much a concern. Markova was assured that a large group of workmen would be placed at Benn Toff's disposal to construct a proper platform and dressing rooms for all the dancers. She was elated at finally being able to "give" her *Giselle* to Israel.

The morning of the performance, Markova visited the site. It was a disaster. The stage had been constructed of splintered boards placed directly on top of the uneven ground—doubly dangerous, as it was both wobbly and rough. There were no dressing rooms, just a single curtained-off area on gravel that would have given the surrounding residents quite an eyeful.

In the small time remaining, Markova pleaded for portable tents to be set up with old rugs covering the ground so the dancers' ballet shoes wouldn't get filthy. And since there were no bathrooms, she asked for a bucket of water in her tent so she could wash up after Act I and smooth her hair back after the frantic mad scene. She was assured it would all be taken care of.

Two hours before showtime, practically nothing had been done. The changing areas had no rugs and were in clear view of anyone in the surrounding hillside. Already, the hills were packed solid with people and vehicles as far as the eye could see.

Markova and Nathalie Krassovska—Queen of the Wilis—were appalled.

In his autobiography, Braunsweg admits the dance floor and dressing areas were "terrible," but his annoyance was not with Toff—who was responsible for all the staging—but rather Markova for complaining about it. The impresario claimed that any problems were the fault of the Israelis, and that the only company member who fell down on the job was Markova for making such a scene.

Dolin was equally unsympathetic, writing that he and Markova had danced on worse stages before. What was her problem? Of course, those stages were part of a concert tour with just the two dancers and a piano. This was a full production of *Giselle* in front of over thirty thousand people.

Despite Markova's protestations, nothing was done to improve the conditions. She just couldn't disappoint such a huge crowd. She danced.

There were insects in her make-up, crawling on her feet, and swarming about the lights on stage. The rock-solid boards made jumps much more difficult, but Markova managed. She was relieved when Act I was coming to a close without incident. All that was left was the conclusion of her famous mad scene when she takes the final fall to her death. Unfortunately, the wood flooring was so hard that when her head hit the stage, she was knocked unconscious.

The audience thought Markova's acting outstanding and gave her thunderous applause. They didn't realize she was actually out cold. Dancers carried her limp body offstage, as if she was staying in character, and someone fetched water to revive her. Though groggy and in pain, Markova picked through the bugs to refresh her makeup, drenched her hair and pulled it back, and changed into her second-act costume. The show went on, and it was a sensation.

"Again and again the public gasped with admiration," wrote an Israeli dance critic. "Again and again you think that Markova has no bones. Her elasticity is a wonder and so is her dramatic ability. Now we too are able to see why Markova has been named the greatest Giselle of them all. . . .

"It is an honour and a great privilege to see this famous Daughter of Israel dancing for the Israeli public."

After the Haifa reviews, fans in Tel Aviv were even more disappointed they hadn't seen Markova dance her signature role of *Giselle*. City officials offered her their outdoor Ramat Gan Stadium if she would just consent to add one more performance. Markova was more than happy to oblige. She also found it reassuring to read in the next day's newspaper that "[u]nlike the primitive Haifa Amphitheatre, the Ramat Gan Stadium is ideal for a ballet performance. The 16,000 people who saw London Festival Ballet perform at the Stadium two years ago have never forgotten their wonderful experience."

One must ask, if the Festival Ballet had already performed in the Ramat Gan Stadium and knew it ideally suited to *Giselle*, why hadn't they booked it in the first place?

Of that final performance in Israel, Braunsweg wrote:

> I don't think, in the last fifty years, that any artist in the world has received such acclaim as Markova did that night. Again and again she was recalled by name to the stage. Flowers were piled high all around her and a continuous hail of bouquets landed at her feet, finally carpeting the stage. . . .
>
> [W]atching her, I thought that despite all the frustrating problems that surrounded Markova, it was all worthwhile.

Markova continued on with the Festival Ballet to engagements in Zurich and Munich, where she was quite nervous about anti-Semitic sentiments. But German audiences cheered her loudly. The tour ended successfully in London.

It was a relief to part company with Braunsweg and Toff and return to the welcoming arms of Erik Bruhn and New York's Ballet Theatre (now the American Ballet Theatre). It had been three years since the two dancers had "made history" together in *Giselle*. Would the old magic still be there?

Ballet Theatre: "Giselle"
Alicia Markova Takes Lead Role at "Met"
by John Martin

Alicia Markova gave her first New York performance of "Giselle" in three years as guest artist with the American Ballet Theatre at the Metropolitan Opera House last night. Familiar though it is by now, it still remains something of a miracle.

Markova has danced the role so many times that she could undoubtedly do it in her sleep; what is so notable is that she never does. She is as fresh, as sensitive, as creatively alert as if she had never done it before; but what a wealth of background she has accumulated for it!

—*The New York Times*, 9/25/58

A few days after that triumph, Markova wrote to Stanley Burton. She had stayed very close to her first true love and his family.

New York
Sept. 28th 1958

Stanley darling,

Many thanks for your letter. I do hope you received mine as I haven't had an answer yet to the questions on the R.A.D. [Royal Academy of Dancing Gala] matinee. I hope you & the family are all well and over the holidays.

I know you will be happy to receive the enclosed press from the New York Times. It has really been very hectic and lots of hard work as so many rehearsals, etc., so I shall be very glad to return to London and maybe retire on these notices. I will have to give it some thought, what do you think. I think I would like to stay put longer than I have been doing and have a home for a change.

The weather here has been very trying, the temperature up in the 80's and humidity just like the tropics.

Keep well and happy.

Write soon.

With My Love,

Alicia

Alicia Markova did not retire. She performed regularly in New York and London and at important festivals in Dublin and Edinburgh. She danced in Cuba in 1959 when Fidel Castro announced his revolution, and starred in—as well as choreographed—ballets for the Metropolitan and Italian Opera companies.

Markova produced and starred in numerous ballets for television and, when suffering from severe colitis and shingles in 1960, took a two-month break from dancing to produce twelve half-hour radio programs for the BBC titled *Markova's Ballet Call*.

"I had a half an hour program once a week and I wrote my own script because it was something really where they wanted my personal feelings about certain music and different ballet music," she later explained. "I would talk about the composer if I happened to have worked with him personally and tell stories for people about what the ballet was like."

Though not yet named a Dame, Markova and her illustrious career were feted on the popular British television program *This Is Your Life* in January 1960. Toward the end of the show, the host turned to his honored guest—who was overcome with emotion—and pointed out that with her childhood infirmities, there was "no one less likely to become the first British ballerina than you!" He then asked Doris what profession she thought Markova might have gone into instead.

"Well, I think she might have made a very good plumber, because when we're traveling in foreign countries and in all sorts of strange theaters when drips go wrong, Alicia always dashes off and fixes it.

"Actually, I think she really wanted to become a doctor. And I think with her great sensitivity, she'd have made a wonderful one."

The show was a big hit and was re-aired. Many wondered out loud at Dolin's absence from the festivities.

In America, Markova was honored as "Woman of the Year" for her achievements in the field of art; after that she received the prestigious "Spirit of Achievement Award" at New York's Waldorf-Astoria. (Fellow recipients were cosmetic tycoon and philanthropist Helena Rubinstein, playwright Lillian Hellman, and legendary theater musical-comedy writer Betty Comden.)

When back in London performing, Markova ran into the popular British writer Beverley Nichols at a party. He told the following anecdote about that meeting in one of his monthly magazine columns.

My World, by Beverley Nichols

A dancer's discipline

. . . It was a very crowded party—the sort of party where you are so wedged together that while you are talking to one girl you are staring at the neck of another.

That was precisely what was happening at this moment. I was staring at the back of an elegant head, and it looked strangely familiar.

Where had I seen her before? And when?

Then it came back to me in a flash.

Her name was Markova. . . .

Well, all this is rather a long preamble to a single remark Markova made at the party round about midnight. . . .

It was very simple, and she made it just as she was leaving the party . . . though she longed to stay.

"It's silly to go yet," I said, "just as you're beginning to enjoy yourself."

"I know," she answered. "But I have to choose."

She sighed, and waved away a glass of champagne with an exquisite gesture of the wrist.

"Between being a dancer and enjoying yourself?"

"Between being a dancer and . . . everything. You've got to go on choosing, every day of your life, every hour of your life. You can't ever 'let up,' can you? I think that if you did you'd

> be lost. You'd . . . you'd . . ." she searched for a phrase, "you'd have broken a rhythm."
>
> "But wouldn't it do you good, once in a while?"
>
> "Would it?" She shrugged her shoulders. "I don't know. I've never tried. Whenever I've had a choice, I've chosen the hard one. And now," with a firm little frown, "I choose to go to bed."
>
> With which Markova left the party—a star who will always remain a star.

In 1962, Markova was finally forced to slow down due to illness. She had suffered so often from throat problems that she was forced to have her tonsils removed—a very painful operation for an adult—and her recuperation was lengthy. After spending a happy Christmas with her family in London, she headed to Heathrow, bound for New York to visit friends. It was New Year's Day.

"Reporters asked me at the airport if I had any New Year's Resolutions," she recalled, "and I don't know why I said it, but I just blurted out, I don't think I'll ever dance in public again."

And she never did.

Postscript

Markova was on her toes in the snow . . .
but never again in ballet

As a great actress grows old, she changes her roles. Instead of Juliet, she plays Hedda Gabler.

But for the prima ballerina there is no valid release. She must dance Giselle, then when she has doubts she must bow herself off the stage.

Last year was not a good year for Markova. Her tonsil operation in the spring was more serious than was thought at the time. She had to cancel her season at the Metropolitan Opera House. She has passed her 52nd birthday.

And now, nonchalantly, as she gets on to a plane for New York, where she has done perhaps more than anyone to foster interest in ballet, she announces her retirement from active dancing.

Those near to her were surprised at the timing of the announcement, but not surprised at the way she did it. Yesterday's casual statement in an airport lounge made it easy for this shy little woman to avoid the many questions she didn't want to answer.

—*London Daily Mail*, 1/2/63

That the news came as a complete surprise to sisters Doris, Vivienne, and Bunny was one thing. But it also surprised Markova herself. Sure, she had thought of retiring in recent years, especially during several prolonged illnesses. But she had always come back.

Suddenly—there at the cold, snowy airport on New Year's Day—the time just seemed right.

She wasn't one to do the grand farewell tour and milk it for all it was worth. She didn't even want to dance just "one" final performance. Better that everyone should remember her at her peak.

Needless to say, the announcement made headlines on both sides of the Atlantic. The news was greeted with admiration, fond memories, and sadness.

> **Dancing no more—the infinitely graceful Markova**
>
> It is hard to become a great dancer. It is harder still to stop. But Alicia Markova, who became a dancing legend in her own lifetime, made the decision yesterday. . . .
>
> She is 52, has been dancing for 42 years. . . .
>
> Markova was always a pioneer. She helped found all the major British dance companies—Ballet Rambert, the Sadler's Wells Ballet, and Festival Ballet—and the American Ballet Theatre.
>
> Markova, indeed, set standards by which other dancers are judged.
>
> She opened windows of delight for millions. It is hard to accept that we shall never see her dance again.
>
> —*Daily Express*, 1/2/63

Just a few days after Markova arrived in New York, the phone rang. It was Rudolph Bing, the general manager of the Metropolitan Opera Company. "Come and visit with all your friends at the Met," he cheerily suggested. The invitation was to attend a full dress rehearsal of *La Sonnambula* starring Markova's close chum Joan Sutherland. No press. No crowds. Just friends. How could she say no?

Bing had an ulterior motive. He wanted to ask Markova a teensy favor. Before retiring for the rest of her life, how about staging two ballets for the Metropolitan Opera Ballet School? Her old pal

Antony Tudor was the school's director. Markova didn't hesitate to say yes.

She was an extraordinary producer and teacher.

"I don't believe you have to raise your voice and yell to make people do things," Markova explained in an interview. "If people yelled at me it would paralyse me and I would not be able to do anything at all. It's best to be straightforward and simple. Treat people like human beings. You need to have respect for people."

The young dancers at the Met adored Markova, so much so that they petitioned Rudolf Bing to hire her full-time.

And that's what he did.

In March 1963 it was announced to the press that Alicia Markova would become the new Director of the Metropolitan Opera Ballet. Her "retirement" barely lasted a month.

The London papers were full of effusive praise, both for Markova's pioneering career in British ballet, and her decision to pass on her great knowledge of dance to others.

Ballet is such an ephemeral art. It requires one-on-one training from masters and choreographers to flourish. Markova, with her uncanny memory for steps, and her legendary creative partnerships with Balanchine, Fokine, Ashton, Massine, Nijinska, and Tudor, was like a walking (and dancing) encyclopedia of early 20th-century ballet.

"It's marvelous to be a dancer," Markova announced joyfully to an impressionable audience of London Royal Ballet School students in 1972. "To think the command you have over your hands, your feet, anything, just that alone—to be able to give pleasure to people. I think that's very important. . . .

"Try to enjoy it. You'll have problems. But think what a heritage you have."

A Tribute to Markova, C.B.E.

Miss Markova, who made her United States debut at the Metropolitan Opera House in 1938 as Giselle, the role which she set a standard for our age, has been directly associated with the Metropolitan Opera Company in recent years as prima ballerina in *Die Fledermaus* and *Orfeo ed Euridice*, but now, for the first time, will be completely responsible for the Ballet Company as a whole.

In accepting her new responsibility, Miss Markova is now fulfilling the second of the two goals of a great dancer: first to dance, and then to pass on the heritage of her art to succeeding generations.

The renowned ballerina, who began her career when still a child as the youngest ballerina of the famed Diaghilev Ballet, is justly proud of her history of "firsts" in the ballet world. She has started more ballet companies than any other ballerina, was the first ballerina televised, the first prima ballerina of the Old Vic-Sadler's Wells Ballet (today The Royal Ballet), the first English prima ballerina ever, and the first English dancer to star in a full evening ballet.

—*New Daily,* London, 1963

That was one of dozens of similar articles. Several must have made their way to Buckingham Palace, as Markova again made all the London newspapers in June.

Markova Honoured

Alicia Markova's great work for the ballet and her rare distinction as a dancer have at last been officially recognized. In the Queen's Birthday Honours last Saturday she was awarded a D.B.E. When she has received the honour from the hands of the Queen we shall be able to address her as Dame Alicia. And about time, too!

—*Stage & Television Today,* London, 6/13/63

Clive Barnes

Great satisfaction is felt in London dance circles by the announcement in the Queen's Birthday Honors that Alicia Markova, the 1st British ballerina, had at last been suitably recognized by the State and promoted to the rank of Dame of the British Empire. The fact that it was over-due made it no less welcome.

—*The London Spectator,* July 1963

Clearly, many thought the award too long in coming, and Markova herself never got over it.

Almost thirty years later, British journalist Louette Harding interviewed her on the occasion of her ninety-second birthday. Harding once again brought up the topic of Markova's having had to wait so long for the official honor. The public slight still seemed fresh.

> . . . She [Markova] had been made to wait while her one-time protégé at the Vic-Wells ballet, Margot Fonteyn, and her old friend, Dame Ninette de Valois, had been honoured years previously. She says that the British ballet world regarded her as an interloper, perhaps because she spent so much time working abroad—or perhaps she discerned covert anti-Semitism. She made a great point of stressing her Britishness to me, which suggests she still bears scars.
>
> She was once accused of bailing out of Britain at the outbreak of the war to dance in the safety of America; in fact, she had a contract with the Ballet Russes in New York.
>
> —*Daily Mail*, London, 12/1/2002

After the Queen's Birthday Honours list was made public, the *Manchester Evening News* sent a photographer to Markova's London home. He snapped the smartly dressed ballerina with her head looking heavenward, a beatific smile across her face, and a letterbox full of congratulatory telegrams clasped to her breast. She was now and forever more *Dame* Alicia Markova. It meant the world to her.

Markova's position at the Metropolitan Opera wasn't scheduled to begin until August, as she had previously committed to many speaking engagements across the United States. She explained to a reporter, "Not long ago I had an audience of ten thousand students at Brigham Young University in Utah. At other times, my audiences are club women. Yes, I like them too, for I know I'm talking to parents, many of whom may be apprehensive about letting their children become involved with ballet. I try to be a reassuring influence."

She would continue public speaking to groups large and small for the rest of her life. Her lectures were sellouts wherever she went.

When Markova returned to New York to begin her new full-time job in August, she was staying once again at the Windsor Hotel apartments. In all of her worldwide travels, the frail ballerina had never experienced the terror that awaited her in the early evening of August 14.

> **Markova Tied Up, Robbed of Jewels**
>
> by Nora Ephron
>
> Alicia Markova, one of ballet's all-time greats, was robbed and manhandled in her hotel apartment by a pair of gun-wielding thugs who tied her up and escaped with more than $4,000 in jewelry and $70 in cash, police revealed today.
>
> The retired prima ballerina told police two men surprised her as she was entering her 15th floor suite at the Hotel Manger Windsor, 100 W. 58th St., at about 5:30 P.M. yesterday.
>
> Near hysteria, she related that one of the burglars thrust a pistol in her back and commanded: "You better tell us where everything is and you won't get hurt."
>
> One gunman kept her covered while his accomplice bound her hands and feet with venetian blind cord.
>
> Miss Markova, 53, directed the bandits to a bedroom drawer containing $70 in cash. They then tore away a bracelet, ring and necklace she was wearing, and threw her on the bed.
>
> The bandits systematically ransacked the two-room suite and fled.
>
> —*New York Post*, 8/15/63

What that story didn't reveal was that while one robber held a gun to Markova's head, the other had a knife pointed at her stomach. The cord was tied so tight, it cut off her circulation and she passed out. When she awoke, the robbers—who had worn handkerchiefs to cover their faces—were gone, and she was able to knock the phone off the bedside table and alert the operator she needed help.

Markova suffered severe bruising around her wrists and ankles where she had been bound, but was grateful to be alive, as she told the press the next day:

> . . . Looking regal in a brown dress with gold-leaf trim, Miss Markova told reporters of her five-minute ordeal today.
>
> "It's been awful," she said. "Thank God, physically, I'm all right."
>
> Miss Markova, who has been under sedation since the robbery, apologized to reporters for being "quite unadorned, because, you see, I have no jewelry."
>
> —*New York Post*, 8/15/63

Though it was an inauspicious beginning to her new career, Markova enjoyed the new opportunity to "pioneer" ballet at the Met, as she explained to a London newspaper:

> **My New Career at 53—by Markova**
>
> Alicia Markova looks good at 53. Life in the executive Suite suits her. The former Alice Marks from Finsbury Park was in London this week on her way back to New York where she is now Director of Ballet at the Metropolitan Opera.
>
> We sat in the park and talked about teaching Birgit Nilsson the Dance of the Seven Veils.
>
> Turning a great Wagnerian soprano into a seductive dancer for Salome is just one of the jobs Dame Alicia now tackles at the Met.
>
> Gone are the days of Giselle. Instead she works with Sutherland on her performance in Lucia or trains her company for large-scale ballet scenes for operas like Samson or Manon.
>
> After 26 years through the Stage Door, she now goes in through the Executive's entrance. Her colleagues are Messrs Bing, Bernstein and Schippers and her collaborators are opera producers like Franco Zeffirelli, Gunther Rennert and Margherita Wallmann.
>
> Almost immediately after she announced her retirement from dancing—"not even time for a come-back farewell tour!"—the Met snapped her up. She has a great chance there now to lay the foundations for an American national ballet company.
>
> "It's the second time around for me," she said.

Markova was ideally suited for her new position, not only a master in ballet but an expert in music as well. She and Joan Sutherland had become friends in London when the coloratura soprano was first performing at the Royal Opera House. Sutherland was in awe of Markova, as she later explained in an interview:

> When I first went to London in 1951, it was one of my first great experiences to see Dame Alicia dance *Giselle*. And for me she became Giselle. She was Giselle. And it was the beginning of a wonderful association with this almost unreal creature, for me. Alicia was Giselle and every other character that she undertook to portray on the stage. I couldn't see enough performances of hers and for me personally, she was a great inspiration, because I felt very awkward in my younger days and I was able to watch her and gain some knowledge of the intensity with which one has to perform to come across to an audience.

In addition to getting on well with the most famous male and female opera singers of the day (typically not an easy task), Markova inspired the ballet dancers by giving them their own spotlight as a performing solo company outside of the opera.

"Opera ballet is a real challenge," she explained. "You often haven't had the best dancers. Who wants to be just an appendage to something else? Now, with the additional chance to perform on their own right, the company's morale is high."

Markova's "retirement" hadn't worked out as planned. Though the job was far less physically demanding than in her dancing days, the hours were far longer. The ex-ballerina remained calm and unflustered. Unlike her early British cohorts Marie Rambert and Ninette de Valois, Markova was known for her warmth, encouragement, and lack of temperament.

"I had everything . . . now I want to help other young dancers"
Speaking, DAME ALICIA MARKOVA

> . . . She told me: "I have had my career. Anything I am doing now is a bonus." . . .
>
> Her tranquility, the result of the long years of a dancer's discipline, is almost unnerving.

> She said: "Now, two years after what I believed to be my retirement day, I am working 16 or 18 hours a day. "If one is doing creative work, creating a company, which is what I have begun to do, one does not work to a schedule.
>
> "Last season, the Met mounted 19 operas. Since I am in charge of the ballet it means that I must know the scores of all those operas.
>
> "Often I am up until two o'clock in the morning studying the music.". . . "I am firm when it is required," she said. "My company know that when I ask for something I mean it."
>
> "But I always explain exactly what I want and always give my dancers the utmost respect.
>
> "I think they know that I am considerate and try to protect them."
>
> —*London newspaper,* Margaret Horrigan, 1965

Markova conducted many interviews in her office at the Met—the first three years in the original location at 1411 Broadway—the rest at the Opera House's new home in Lincoln Center Plaza, where it remains today. Every reporter commented on her grace, composure, and looking fifteen years younger than her age, "even at ten paces!"

The tasteful office décor always made a lasting impression—equaling the understated elegance of its occupant—as did the two framed accent pieces: one a photograph of Diaghilev, the other Markova's certificate naming her a Dame of the British Empire. They were bookends to her career.

Markova was quite content in her new role. A reporter from *Women's Wear Daily* asked if there was one thing she wished were different about her life. She thought for a moment and then answered,

"One wish? I wish my day could start later—I am at my peak at night—I hate to get up."

Markova was a true New Yorker. She even did the choreography for the Opera Ballet's performance on a float in the Macy's Thanksgiving Day parade. She loved it all.

But there were difficult times as well. Markova would suffer two very serious accidents at the Met, the first when her heel got caught in a metal grate. As she was falling, what popped into her head? If she broke her nose, Hurok, Ashton, and Dolin would finally get their wish—she would have to have her nose fixed. Still defiant, she swiftly turned her face to the side and fractured her cheekbone instead, along with several ribs. Her recuperation was lengthy.

Markova fell again two years later when her knee buckled under, just as it had when she was a child. Perhaps now that she was no longer dancing, the muscles and ligaments gave way. It would require more surgery.

In 1969, the Metropolitan Opera was involved in a protracted strike/lockout that lasted nine months. While Markova had been stimulated by the work, management never gave her their full support in making the ballet a viable separate performing company. She asked to be let out of her contract during the strike, and terminated her directorship.

But once again, her retirement didn't last long. Markova would spend the rest of her life teaching, producing, and assisting in the management of various ballet companies and schools—as always, both large and small.

British ballet critic Eric Johns had been a firsthand witness to Markova's coaching of young dancers over the years, and praised her willingness to pass on her vast knowledge, rather than spend her later years sunning herself on the Riviera.

Markova's New Career

by Eric Johns

> Great ballet performances in the classics are handed down from one generation to the next. . . .
>
> Now it is Markova's turn to be a link in the chain and hand on her priceless knowledge and interpretation to younger dancers, so that Giselle continues to remain immortal upon the international stage. . . .
>
> Markova's approach to ballet is essentially logical. When she has directed productions in the past she has always impressed upon dancers never to take a step or move an arm unless they know why they are doing so. She is likely to call out suddenly to any dancer in class. Why are you doing that? And she expects a sensible answer! It is amazing how much more interesting a

> ballet looks from the front when the dancers know exactly what they are doing and why they are doing it.
>
> Markova is the most approachable person. No one in class need be nervous about asking questions, to which they will receive practical and authoritative replies. Her retirement heralds the beginning of a new career in the life of one of the beloved dancers of all time.
>
> —*Theatre World*, 1963

After Markova left the Met, she gave a speech at the University of Cincinnati and spent some time with the local Civic Ballet Company. When asked, she consented to an appointment as Distinguished Lecturer on Ballet at the University's College-Conservatory of Music. Why would the legendary ballerina move to Cincinnati? As dance critic Walter Terry explained, it was "where David McLain heads one of the most vital dance departments to be found on the university scene." Markova was a phenomenal instructor, and was quickly promoted to a full professorship.

And she didn't limit her teaching to ballet students. Markova also worked wonders with the University of Cincinnati basketball team. If there was anyone who knew how to jump and soar, it was Alicia Markova. As noted American choreographer Merce Cunningham said of her, she gave "the illusion of moving without a preparation—as if she had no weight to get off the ground." She appeared "on top of her jump, like an animal," he added.

Markova taught the ball players how to invisibly redistribute their weight in preparation for a jump to conceal their intended moves. She thought their height a great advantage that she never had.

The University signed another famous professor while Markova was there—the astronaut Neil Armstrong. Upon meeting the ex-ballerina he confessed to her, "My little dance on the moon wasn't so good."

After three years, Markova was offered tenure at the University. That was probably a mistake on their part. Any career permanence was anathema to the ballerina.

"I was there with a full professorship for three years to help them set up their new ballet department in a beautiful new building and form their own ballet company," she explained upon her return to

London. "Last year, when I thought the department and the company was running perfectly, I felt my work was done."

~

Though Markova had always said she would consider marriage after retirement, she never truly retired. "She remained married to her art," suggested a London newspaper, "her phenomenal memory making her an illuminating coach, her personal history offering a reservoir of important souvenirs."

But the woman who so adored children found it a joy to always be among young dancers, helping them find their way.

> "I find it very exciting if one can find young talent and help them to achieve. Because otherwise, I've always felt it's very stupid for someone like myself who spent a whole lifetime trying to perfect something to suddenly perhaps disappear and it would all disappear with one.
>
> "It was an understood fact that everything had to be passed on. In the training I received, and again I was very lucky, I had the finest Italian training with Cecchetti, I had the finest Russian training with Astafieva and Legat, and many other great teachers. It went without any question that this would be passed along. You would hold onto it as long as you could and then find somebody else to pass it on to.
>
> "There isn't anything in my mind to touch the human element of passing from one human being to another, the expression, the interpretation, the real—if one could say flesh—of a role.
>
> "It's a matter of listening to the music. The most important thing when I'm teaching or coaching, you have to see that the tradition is still kept, but it has to be kept alive and vital, so you have to find a way to bring it in line with the way the young think today.
>
> "While teaching a young ballet dancer the Sugar Plum Fairy, 'When you're dancing this, this is your kingdom. This is your whole domain. You own all of this. It has to have a freedom,

a happy freedom, because of all the children. That's why you are the Sugar Plum fairy every child sort of idolizes.'

"I would try to pass on and convey the feelings of the Sugar Plum Fairy and it will be up to our young dancers and ballerinas, for them. I can't dance it for them, they have to find their way of keeping it alive and passing it on."

Markova never stopped traveling. Throughout the ensuing decades, many reporters interviewed the ballerina when she was back in London in her Knightsbridge flat—the one she had rented in 1949 and still shared with Doris. They invariably commented on its looking more like "temporary" living quarters than a true home. There were always trunks about, either being packed or unpacked, and piles of ballet books, files, and papers everywhere—including stacked high on the delicate white chairs she had inherited from Anna Pavlova.

Markova was continually intrigued by new experiences. She flew halfway around the world to work with her old friend Robert Helpmann, the co-director of the Australian Ballet Company. She went to Buffalo, New York to train the Niagara Frontier Ballet for their upcoming European tour with guest artist Rudolf Nureyev. And she returned to coach the Royal Winnipeg Ballet in Canada.

In London, Markova became president of the English National Ballet, a company she co-founded as The Festival Ballet back in 1951. And she was appointed governor of The Royal School of Ballet. Those were not ceremonial titles. Markova actively worked at both right up until the time of her passing.

Perhaps the most touching thing in Markova's archives are the boxes and boxes of letters from everyday people who felt their lives transformed by her dancing. The following is typical. It is an unsigned fan letter sent to Markova when she finally returned to perform in London in 1948—after having been away in America for nine long years.

Dear Markova,

I am going to try to convey to you what your visit to London has meant to at least a handful of your admirers of some years standing, so that when this Season is over you will not be sorry that you came and that you will not stay away too long before you dance for us again.

First of all I have to go back quite a while when we saw you with Diaghileff and have followed you around, finance permitting, to The Wells, Hammersmith, Wimbledon, Streatham, Bournemouth and Brighton, etc. We none of us had very much money but we loved Ballet and worshipped you as the perfect interpretation of all it stood for, for us.

Then came the War with all its horrors and separated our small clique, when we did manage to meet occasionally it was to talk of the end of the War and return to our Darling which with all due respect, was how we referred to you. I hope this does not sound like the hysterical ravings of a silly young girl. Believe me we are none of us very young but we are very sincere in our admiration of you.

When we heard that you were coming back to London we were very happy and excited and wondered what the new and younger generation would think of you, poor things they had never really had any sort of standards to judge by.

At long last came the 7th, The Day, for which we had waited so long. There we sat, six of us together and others dotted about the House, all clutching our handkerchiefs, believe me there was not a dry eye amongst us before the evening was over. To have gone through all we had for nine long years and to have lived through it all, then to have it all slip away as soon as you set foot on the Stage. No wonder we were overcome. I have no doubt you know your own value but I think it is nice to be told how good one is. We thought you were the perfect Dancer before you went away but if such a thing is possible, you have added perfection to perfection and it is positively breathtaking to watch you.

I'm sorry I have gone into so much detail, I am not used to writing this sort of letter but how else would you know what your public think, although I do not think you could have doubted our feelings after your reception of Monday evening. We just can't bear the thought that you are here for so short a time and beg you to come back to us soon. The American public cannot love you more than we do and we have remained faithful, so do please come back again very soon.

There is no need to wish you a successful season, that seems assured but we do wish you lots and lots of good luck.

Dame Alicia Markova passed away on December 2, 2004, one day after her ninety-fourth birthday. A few years earlier she was in a taxicab with friends when they drove past Westminster Abbey. She joked that she would never get a Royal send-off in Britain's famed cathedral because she was Jewish. She was wrong.

Alicia Markova got her wished-for Westminster memorial service on March 8, 2005. As had been true throughout her career, it was standing room only.

The pioneer of ballet also achieved another of her many "firsts" when the Abbey allowed dancing at a service. The English National Ballet performed tribute scenes from *Giselle* and *Les Sylphides*.

Dancer Freddie Franklin attended the ceremony. He told biographer Leslie Norton he "had mixed emotions. While saddened, he was gratified to see Alicia so richly honored by the British people. He found it 'a wonderful thing, really.'"

Yes, it was.

Acknowledgments

The person who introduced me to the extraordinary life and world of Alicia Markova is Vita Paladino, the Director of the Howard Gotlieb Archival Research Center at Boston University. Vita knew Dame Alicia personally and was instrumental in the Markova collection's being entrusted to the Gotlieb Center.

Vita not only encouraged me to write this biography of her friend, but also enumerated all the reasons I was perfectly suited to the task, giving me the confidence to pursue such a labor-intensive and ultimately rewarding project. Throughout the lengthy research phase, Vita granted me unfettered access to the entire Markova collection—which was vast, to say the least—as well as providing temporary office space, the assistance of her able staff, and a personal introduction to Dame Alicia's sister Vivienne Haskell, without whose permission and approval this book would not have been possible. I am grateful to Vita for her fine judgment, assistance, and immense support throughout the project.

Also of enormous help at the Gotlieb Center was Assistant Director Sean Noel, an unflappable problem-solver with a great sense of humor who went above and beyond in facilitating my on-site work space, while generously offering his time and expertise throughout the multi-year project. Alex Rankin, assistant director for acquisitions, along with Katelynn Vance and Sarah Pratt, archivists for acquisitions, made sure

I always had access to the Markova materials I needed at any given time. My thanks go to them as well.

A highlight of writing the book was meeting Dame Markova's sister, Mrs. Vivienne Haskell, in her lovely home in Bath, England. The widow of Arnold Haskell, a prolific British author of ballet books and dance criticism, Vivienne spent her life surrounded by ballet, though she was the only one of the four "Marks girls" never to perform on stage. Now in her nineties, Mrs. Haskell is a still-beautiful and gracious woman who cheerfully shared many personal remembrances. I am grateful that she has trusted me to tell her sister's astonishing life story utilizing Markova's own diaries, memoirs, correspondence, and photos.

As to the many photographs throughout the book, all were part of Dame Markova's personal archives, and extensive research was conducted to trace potential copyright holders. Please note that any credit omissions were inadvertent and will gladly be acknowledged in subsequent editions.

Some of the most iconic images of Alicia Markova—including the emotive cover shot—were taken by the Chicago-based photographer Maurice Seymour, who was legendary for his ballet and theatrical portraits. Mr. Seymour's son Ron Seymour is also a talented photographer and generously consented to the reproduction of several of his father's arresting photos in the book. More of Maurice Seymour's portrait photography can be seen on his son's Web site at ronseymour.com.

Thanks also to the Frederick Ashton Foundation and Anton Dolin's genial nephew Philip Kay, the estate heirs of Frederick Ashton and Anton Dolin respectively, who kindly gave permission to reprint the personal letters of those two great ballet talents.

This book would never have seen the light of day were it not for my insightful agent Laura Gross, head of the Laura Gross Literary Agency, who gave me encouragement from the very beginning of the project. Laura recognized early on that this was not a "ballet" book per se, but rather an inspirational tale of a woman overcoming personal and physical hardships—not to mention the prejudices of her time—to become a superstar in her chosen field. It was Laura's perseverance in representing this book that resulted in finding the perfect publisher and editor, Jessica Case at Pegasus Books, who has been a thoughtful, perceptive, and enthusiastic editor.

And thanks also to those closest to me: my attorney sister Pamela Sutton for her astute legal advice, my computer engineer brother Jonathon Sutton for his technical expertise, and last, but certainly not least, my delightful husband of thirty years, John Carroll. As a brilliant writer, editor, teacher, and media commentator, John has always been an invaluable adviser, sounding board, and in-house grammarian.

Moreover, John never let me lose sight of the big picture, something one tends to do while immersed in the minutiae of another person's life. His endless fascination with my research—"And what did you learn about Markova today?" was John's nightly greeting—made me realize even men with no interest whatsoever in dance could be captivated by a ballerina's travails through extraordinary historical periods of social change, war, and unprecedented creativity in the arts. And as John kept reminding me, who wouldn't want to read about an intelligent, talented woman who shared her life with the greatest choreographers, dancers, artists, music composers, film stars, and media personalities of her day?

My advice to future biographers: it helps if you choose your subject and spouse wisely.

Source Notes

All personal letters, memoir notes, newspaper clippings, radio interviews, and transcripts referenced in *The Making of Markova* are part of the Dame Alicia Markova Collection at the Howard Gotlieb Archival Research Center at Boston University, Boston, Massachusetts. Director Vita Paladino, Associate Director Sean Noel, and the entire Gotlieb staff provided immeasurable help and consideration during the lengthy research process.

Chapter 1: Another Pavlova

2. "If Markova springs like a winged fairy," "Alicia Markova", by Cyril Beaumont, *The Ballet Annual* (1963) Mary Clarke and Arnold Haskell.
2. "The risk was too great," "Markova in Edinburgh," *Scotsman*, 4/26/37.
2. "Her weight had to be poised with absolute," AP Newsfeatures Writer, Trudi McCullough, dateline New York.
2. "I saw her in *Les Sylphides*," *Ballet Magazine*, 9/30/77, Jane Simpson.
3. "The more you see her the more you value her," *Modern Music*, January–February 1942, Edwin Denby.
3. "Who Markova is, nobody knows," *New York Herald Tribune*, 10/18/43, Edwin Denby.
3. "the perfect epitome of the classical ballerina," "Concerning Art and Alicia Markova," John Martin, *The New York Times*, 4/11/43.
3. "I once asked the great Russian-American prima ballerina," *Ted Shawn: Father of American Dance* (1976), Walter Terry.
4. "both my inspiration and my despair," BBC Television program: "This is Your Life, Alicia Markova", 1/11/60.
4. "Always about her there was an aroma," *Portrait Gallery: Artists, Impresarios, Intimates* (1990), Agnes de Mille.
5. "her name was synonymous with the art," *Dance to the Piper* (1980), Agnes De Mille.
5. "I have seen two dancers," Ibid.
7. "The lithe, slim figure danced across the stage," "How a Mother's Prayer was Answered", *Everybody's Weekly*, London, 1/12/35.
8. "Mother was quite a talented singer." "Alicia Markova's Sister Looks Back," by Doris Barry, *Birmingham Gazette*, 10/18/49.
9. "You are going to enter fairyland," *Nijinsky, Pavlova, Duncan: Three Lives in Dance* (1977), Paul Magriel.
10. "The child certainly danced well," *The Diaghilev Ballet: 1909–1929* (1953), S.L.Grigoriev translated by Vera Bowen.
10. "I was interested in most things around me. I just didn't speak much," BBC Radio interview: "Myself When Young," with Claire Rayner (unknown year).

11. "silent, but not unsociable." Memoir notes from Markova's archives.
11. "I didn't even look a typically English little girl of the period," Ibid.
11. "Everyone laughed, but I wore a little black satin dress," "Britain's No. 1 Ballerina Sets the record Straight," Lois Lehrman, *New York Journal-American*, 5/30/59.
12. "I also earned another nickname at this time," Memoir notes from Markova's archives.
12. "I was trotting along the beach when I was about maybe seven," Radio interview: John Dunne Show, 12/5/84.
12. "Thank God that man was interested in the ballet," Ibid.
13. "I rather enjoyed it because I met other children," BBC Radio program: "Markova Birthday Tribute," December, 1970.
13. "as fragile as Venetian glass." *Portrait Gallery*, Agnes de Mille.
14. "My mother thought it was a dodge to get more fees out of her." Memoir notes from Markova's archives.
14. "When you watch Markova, the music seems to come *from* her," "Alicia Markova," by D.P. Daniels, *Ballet Today*, 1959.
15. "Alicia would produce, design, choreograph, and teach," "My Sister . . . The Ballerina," Doris Barry, 1957.
16. "I was very attached to my father," Memoir notes from Markova's archives.
17. "Her manager, Alfred Katz, of New York," *Johannesburg Sunday Times*, 4/10/49.
17. "One of our favorite games was traveling," "My Sister . . .The Ballerina," Doris Barry, 1957.
17. "Mother, to me, always seemed to be waiting," interview with Louette Harding, *Daily Mail*, 12/1/02.
18. "One doesn't expect Princess Aurora or the Sugar Plum Fairy," "Why I Love London," Alicia Markova, *The Star*, London, 12/2/57.
18. "First my father had a Buick." LBC Radio interview: Steve Allen show, 7/1/96.
18. "She was a wizard at mental arithmetic," "My Sister . . . The Ballerina," Doris Barry, 1957.
19. "How little the daily life of a ballet dancer," *Pavlova: Portrait of a Dancer* (1984), presented by Margot Fonteyn.
19. "At week-ends my father," "Why I Love London, Alicia Markova," *The Star*, 12/2/57.
20. "I envy people who have had serious education," Memoir notes from Markova's archives.
20. "I often wondered what the Cinema audience must have thought," Ibid.
20. "I shall never forget the thrill I had when I literally," Ibid.
22. "presumably contributed towards the large flat in which Pavlova lived," *Anna Pavlova* (1973), Oleg Kerensky.
23. "how they came to live at the tranquilly situated Ivy House." *Anna Pavlova* (1972), Victor Dandré.
24. "I love London best of all," *Home Chat*, London, 1924.
24. "Pavlova herself was allergic to cats," *Anna Pavlova: Her Life and Art*, Keith Mooney.
25. "I myself married her off in the press," *Impresario* (1946), Sol Hurok.
27. "When it was a case of parents," *Anna Pavlova in Art and Life* (1932), Victor E. Dandré.
28. "Nobody dreamed of daring to ask for her autograph," *Pavlova: Portrait of a Dancer* (1984), presented by Margot Fonteyn.
29. "What ordinary ballet-goer had the chance," *Ballet Today*, January/February 1957.
29. "when efforts were being made to engage," *Anna Pavlova* (1973), Oleg Kerensky.
29. "I have a tremendous admiration for Markova," *Ballet* (1951), Cecil Beaton.
30. "It was a beautiful summer day," BBC Radio interview to celebrate the opening of the Pavlova Museum at ivy House, June 3, 1975.
32. "Your life will be all work and unless you're prepared to give," BBC Radio program: *The Alicia Markova Story*, 10/3/60.

33. "Pavlova was Miss Markova's ideal," interview with Markova and Dolin, *Winnipeg Free Press*, 12/12/47.
33. "I recalled Pavlova telling me," "Markova Pays Penalty of Fame, by John Bolton, *Yorkshire Evening Post*, 5/27/50.
34. "As a student, Pavlova was talented and also different." *Anna Pavlova: Her Life and Art* (1982), Keith Money.
35. "When you talk to her you forget," "The Dancer Who Thinks," *The Strand Magazine*, London, October 1924.
35. "I chatted with her for a short while in her dressing room," *Newcastle Journal*, 5/28/34.
36. "And what of another now-retired ballerina," "Ballet Stars Without the Body Beautiful", *New York Herald Tribune*, Walter Terry, 9/15/63.
37. "I was stirred by this comparison," *Giselle and I* (1960), Alicia Markova.
39. "Markova's 'Swan' is a lovely, ethereal creature," Unknown newspaper, 1942.
39. "During the Diaghilev season at the Princess Theatre," BBC Radio program: *The Alicia Markova Story*, 10/3/60.
41. "She was sitting in the box at the Sarah Bernhardt Theatre," Radio interview: Round Midnight with Brian Matthew, 1986.
41. "her undeveloped androgynous body and fearless," "Alicia Markova Queen of British ballet dies at 94," Ismene Brown, *The Telegraph*, London, 12/3/2004.
41. "appetite for modernity," "Dame Alicia Markova," Nadine Meisner, *The Independent*, London 12/3/04.
42. "Whenever Markova dances in London," *Bristol Evening World*, December 1937.
42. "What can I recall of her gestures?" *Sheffield Telegraph*, 1/12/56.
42. "If I had a daughter, she," *Everybody's Weekly*, January 12, 1935.
43. "It was funny," Memoir notes from Markova's archives.
43. "The spirit of Pavlova has entered Markova." *Manchester Evening News*, 5/8/35.
44. "People said all sorts of things because," *Markova: The Legend* (1995), Maurice Leonard.
44. "dancing appeared spontaneous and elusive," *Apollo's Angels* (2010), Jennifer Homans.
45. "She wore only the soft slippers," AP Newsfeatures Writer, Trudi McCullough, dateline New York.
45. "frailty turned out to be her greatest asset." *Apollo's Angels* (2010), Jennifer Homans.
45. "Pavlova at that time hardly realized," *Theatre Street* (1961), Tamara Karsavina.
46. "Every country, of course, has its admirable born dancers," *Anna Pavlova in Art and Life*, Victor E. Dandré.
46. "You have a Russian soul!" interview with Nijinska, *New York Post*, 1/5/48.

Chapter 2: Diaghilev's Prodigy

49. "I think perhaps, she missed a lot of the fun," "Alicia Markova's Sister Looks Back," Doris Barry, *Birmingham Gazette*, 10/18/49.
51. "I think the ermine caused these orange-sucking youngsters," *Markova: Her Life and Art* (1953), Anton Dolin.
51. "the very shy little girl with big sad eyes." BBC Radio program: *The Alicia Markova Story*, 10/3/60.
52. "[Markova] did this little dance," Ibid.
53. "My secret fear all through the rehearsals for Dick Whittington," Memoir notes from Markova's archives.
54. "It was my very big number which used to stop the show," interview for BBC Television documentary "Markova" (1981).
54. "I can remember that at the end I finished," Memoir notes from Markova's archives.

54. "You remember how in Giselle at the end of the Mad Scene," *London Sunday Times*, unknown year.
54. "I loved it because I learned," Ibid.
56. "There, in a circle of flame," *Markova: Her Life and Art*, Anton Dolin.
56. "I was extremely impressed with this little girl." BBC Radio program: *The Alicia Markova Story*, 10/3/60.
56. "a secret passage led from the Grand Duke's box directly," "How Ballet Fell for Flower-Giving," Judith Mackrell, *The Guardian*, 12/18/12.
57. "Sima [Astafieva], a dancer from the Imperial Theatre," *Bronislava Nijinska: Early Memoires* (1981), translated and edited by Irina Nijinska and Jean Rawlinson.
57. "carrying a peacock on her shoulder," Ibid.
58. "vultures waiting for the tired and weary bodies to emerge from class." Memoir notes from Markova's archives.
58. "Fearfully, I rang the bell." Doreen Young's remembrances of Princess Astafieva, part of the Alicia Markova archives.
59. "Occasionally, Astafieva took me," Ibid.
59. "not really dirty, just near-white." *Balletomania Then and Now*, Arnold Haskell.
60. "Tallish, aged about 60, worldly and elegant," *Margot Fonteyn: Autobiography* (1977), Margot Fonteyn.
64. "[H]er classes were a revelation," *Balletomania Then and Now*, Arnold Haskell.
64. "a pair of brown velvet knickers," *Anton Dolin: Autobiography* (1960), Anton Dolin.
65. "Madame adored him as a son," Doreen Young's remembrances of Princess Astafieva, part of the Alicia Markova archives.
65. "always the first to arrive and the last to leave," BBC Radio program: *The Alicia Markova Story*, 10/3/60.
65. "Her technique was really quite extraordinary," Ibid.
65. "After class I would rehearse with Alicia." interview for BBC Television documentary "Markova" (1981).
65. "extraordinary fondness of cats." BBC Radio program: *The Alicia Markova Story*, 10/3/60.
66. "At that time, he treated me like a very small sister," interview for BBC Television documentary "Markova" (1981).
66. "The early years of training I had," Memoir notes from Markova's archives.
67. "One morning there was great excitement." Memoir notes from Markova's archives.
69. "bizarre, very quiet, very reserved," BBC Television program: "This is Your Life, Alicia Markova," 1/11/60.
70. "Olga Spessivtseva and Anna Pavlova are like two halves," "Sergei Diaghilev," by Arnold L. Haskell, *Ballet Review*, Summer 1996 (written in 1990).
70. "That was where I think I started to acquire all the knowledge," "My Life as a Dancer," Markova's recorded talk at the Royal Ballet School, London, 9/27/72.
71. "Arthur was without work again," *Markova: The Legend*, Maurice Leonard.
71. "suddenly found himself penniless." *Markova: Her Life and Art*, Anton Dolin.
71. "While we were still in London," *Choura: The Memoirs of Alexandra Danilova* (1987), Alexandra Danilova.
74. "When she was a little girl," Speech "Preparation for Ballet," given by Nadine Nicholaeva-Legat.
76. "He [Diaghilev] said he would come back," "My Life as a Dancer," Markova's recorded talk at the Royal Ballet School, London, 9/27/72.
77. "I met Alicia at a Christmas party," *Balletomania Then & Now*, Arnold Haskell.
77. "I saw a great deal of Alicia," Ibid.
78. "I met her and her three sisters," interview for BBC Television documentary "Markova" (1981).

78. "Her legs were like arrows," *Balletomania Then & Now*, Arnold Haskell.
80. "I had visions of being Olga Tredova," BBC Radio program: "Markova Reminiscences" (circa 1990s).

Chapter 3: The Ballets Russes

82. "People said I appeared 'foreign,'" Memoir notes from Markova's archives.
82. "No one ever knew what Diaghilev looked like." "Ballerina's Career in Retrospect," Scott Cain, *Columbia Record*, South Carolina, 11/14/83.
83. "He was a monster in a way," "Dancing For Diaghilev," interview with Henry Fenwick, *Radio Times Magazine*, August 1979.
83. "force the family into bankruptcy," *Diaghilev: A Life* (2009), Sjeng Scheijen.
83. "I had learned very early on," Memoir notes from Markova's archives.
84. "There were no unions," Ibid.
84. "I knew he was the greatest man in ballet," "Alice's Wonderland," *The Sunday Times*, London, 7/7/68.
85. "He was my artistic father," *Jewish Chronicle*, 12/2/60.
86. "The dream and purpose of my life are to work creatively," *Diaghilev: A Life* (2009), Sjeng Scheijen.
86. "never to utter the words 'I can't,'": New York Times Book Review of Sjeng Scheijen's *Diaghilev: A Life*, Jennifer B. McDonald, 9/22/10.
86. "I am first a great charlatan," "Letter from London—exhibit honoring Sergei Pavlovich Diaghilev" by Margaret Willis, *Dance Magazine*, September 1996.
87. "Only a fighter and an absolute autocrat could have succeeded," "Sergei Diaghilev," by Arnold L. Haskell, *Ballet Review*, Summer 1996 (written in 1990).
87. "maintained that Diaghilev's Ballets Russes," "The Divine Vision of Diana Veeland," Laura Jacobs, *The Wall Street Journal*, 12/29-30/2012.
88. "The theory of art for art's sake never enjoyed a clear victory," *Diaghilev: A Life* (2009), Sjeng Scheijen.
89. "had the most tremendous influence," Charles Spencer being interviewed on BBC Radio program "Woman's Hour" (1994), on the occasion of his museum exhibit "Designers and Dancers of the Ballets Russes" held at Pallant House in Chichester, England.
89. "The era 1909–1929 was the Diaghilev era," "Sergei Diaghilev," by Arnold L. Haskell, *Ballet Review*, Summer 1996 (written in 1990).
90. "All eyes were on Diaghilev." *Bronislava Nijinska: Early Memoirs* (1981), translated and edited by Irina Nijinska and Jean Rawlinson.
91. "I was a very shy, timid person," BBC Radio interview: "Frankly Speaking," 2002.
91. "I did not dance with the Company that season," Memoir notes from Markova's archives.
92. "admired him; it almost amounted to worship;" "Sergei Diaghilev," by Arnold L. Haskell, *Ballet Review*, Summer 1996 (written in 1990).
92. "'Frightening' is a word used over and over," "The Master of Motion," Robert Gottlieb reviewing John Drummond's *Speaking of Diaghilev*, *The New York Times*, 8/1/99.
93. "He was crazy about her," interview for BBC Television documentary "Markova" (1981).
94. "Who is this man Basket," *Balletomania Then & Now* (1977), Arnold Haskell.
95. "I would spend hours thinking up all sort," Memoir notes from Markova's archives.
96. "I was saying Good-bye to my dear Mother," Ibid.
96. "I was one of those sorts of adopted aunts." interview for BBC Television documentary "Markova" (1981).
97. "the deal would give Monaco the world's most prestigious dance," *Diaghilev: A Life* (2009), Sjeng Scheijen.

98. "he found common or unsuitable for the Russian Ballet," "Sergei Diaghilev," by Arnold L. Haskell, *Ballet Review*, Summer 1996 (written in 1990).
98. "He advised me," Memoir notes from Markova's archives.
99. "I don't suppose many people think," Radio program: "The Alicia Markova Story," 10/3/60.
99. "with Guggy it was a grim ritual without a scrap of pleasure," *Markova Her Life and Art*, Anton Dolin.
100. "Everything had to be done her way," *London Jewish Chronicle*, 12/2/60.
100. "I was bathed, dressed, changed, as if I were a doll," Memoir notes from Markova's archives.
100. "She sat and watched everything," interview with Jane Kelly, London *Daily Mail*, 5/21/96.
102. "That first year at Monte Carlo was," Ibid.
103. "Every penny went into his dreams." "Sergei Diaghilev," by Arnold L. Haskell, *Ballet Review*, Summer 1996 (written in 1990).
103. "I was so delighted when I heard," Memoir notes from Markova's archives.
104. "an unpardonable affront to the family name." Memoir notes from Markova's archives.
106. "Lydia Sokolova, Paris, June 1926" From Markova's personal autograph book in her archives.
108. "It seemed a very precarious business to me," Memoir notes from Markova's archives.
108. "The thing that Diaghilev adored," BBC Radio program: "Markova Reminiscences," (unknown year).
108. "Thank God I danced impeccably," Ibid.
108. "From that day on, I never moved without adhesive," Ibid.
110. "I was thought particularly suitable for roles," Radio interview: John Dunne Show, 12/5/84.
110. "In the first scene I had to emerge," Ibid.
111. "In the morning I would have my classes," *Speaking of Diaghilev* (1997), John Drummond.
112. "There were several acrobatic steps," Memoir notes from Markova's archives.
112. "more, more, more!" explained Peter Martins, *60 Minutes* interview with Lesley Stahl, November 2012.
113. "Alicia's incredible virtuosity thrilled Balanchine." *The Independent*, 12/3/04.
113. "He planned that she," *George Balanchine: Ballet Master* (1988), Richard Buckle.
113. "I remember the very first rehearsal," Radio program: "Myself When Young" with Claire Raynor (unknown year).
114. "He was very kind," *The Birmingham Post Weekend*, 11/24/90.
115. "Henri Matisse in particular was going through a brief critical slump," "Matisse: In Search of True Painting," 2012/13 exhibit at the Metropolitan Museum of Art, New York.
115. "Just after we arrived in Paris," Memoir notes from Markova's archives.
117. "I'm very amused," BBC Radio program: "Markova Reminiscences" (circa 1990s).
117. "Honors go to the 'baby' of the ballet," London Press, 7/20/27.
118. "Again, my size seemed to fit me," 1963 talk shortly after Markova's retirement and subsequent directorship appointment at the Metropolitan Opera Company in New York.
119. "I didn't know that," Radio interview: John Dunne Show, 12/5/84.
119. "I was pirouetting quite alone across the stage," "Markova in Edinburgh," *Scotsman*, 4/26/37.
119. "I found it totally absorbing and deeply exciting," Memoir notes from Markova's archives.
120. "He believed in, and encouraged," Markova's speech at Forbes House, 1/16/55, in honor of the current Diaghilev Exhibition.

121. "Alichka, you are to go to the Maestro himself," Memoir notes from Markova's archives.
121. "Spotlessly clean and tidy," "Alicia Markova Reminisces About Cecchetti," *Dance News*, September 1953.
122. "Now I don't think we're allowed," "My Life as a Dancer," Markova's recorded talk at the Royal Ballet School, London, 9/27/72.
122. "My Russian training," Memoir notes from Markova's archives.
123. "With Cecchetti we had to wear," Ibid.
124. "Sometimes they would go on for four," Ibid.
125. "How old was I?" Ibid.
125. "She used to sit beside me," *Dance and Dancers*, January 1955.
127. "She had no one." interview for BBC Television documentary "Markova" (1981).
127. "I was put in your care," BBC Radio tribute to Ninette de Valois, 1998.
128. "From the very beginning," *Dance and Dancers*, January 1955.
128. "For the first time someone treated me as an equal," Memoir notes from Markova's archives.
129. "Diaghileff said to me," *Berlingske Aftenavsi*, Denmark, 9/24/55.
130. "One can truly say that he was a genius," "Ballerina's Career in Retrospect," Scott Cain, *Columbia Record*, South Carolina, 11/14/83.
130. "He used to have a trick," *London Observer*, 11/13/32.
130. "Grigoriev takes pride in recording," *Hampshire Telegraph*, 11/18/60.
131. "I was so shy and wooden in my dancing," Unidentified London newspaper clipping, Markova archives.
131. "[A]t that time it had just come out," *Herald Scotland*, unknown year.
132. "Go shop!" *Markova Remembers*, Alicia Markova.
132. "Spessivtseva created it and had an accident," *Speaking of Diaghilev*, John Drummond.
132. "I thought, I don't want to hurt my foot," Ibid.
133. "The Cat of Alicia Markova was flawless," *Liepsig Zeitung*, Berlin, 11/26/29.
133. "Mlle. Markova has shown herself," *L'ami du Peuple*, Paris, 12/21/28.
133. "Sergypop explained to me" BBC Radio interview: "Myself When Young," with Claire Rayner (unknown year).
133. "He genuinely loved 'his English girl,'" *Balletomania Then & Now*, Arnold Haskell.

Chapter 4: Starting Over

137. "I remembered the last time I saw him," *Choura: The Memoirs of Alexandra Danilova*, Alexandra Danilova.
138. "When Serge Diaghileff died in 1929," *World Book of Modern Ballet* (1952), John Martin.
138. "Now, to all intents and purposes," Ibid.
139. "For the second time in my 18 years," Memoir notes from Markova's archives.
139. "My home and my roots were in the physical structure," Ibid.
139. "I was surrounded with people so much older," BBC Radio program: Parkinson Show, 1/11/75.
140. "The following season, as he put it," Memoir notes from Markova's archives.
140. "The first time one noticed her," BBC Radio interview: "Myself When Young," with Claire Rayner (unknown year).
141. "The 'real' end of the season each year," Memoir notes from Markova's archives.
143. "I must inform you," From Markova's archives.
144. "He was an old devil," Markova's speech "My Life as a Dancer," to the Royal Ballet School, 9/27/72.
145. "I lived in a waking nightmare," Memoir notes from Markova's archives.
146. "high minded planning for a better world," Juliet Gardiner, author of *The Thirties: An Intimate History* (2009), writing on the topic in the London culture blog *The Dabbler*.
146. "The 'dream palaces'—the massive fantastical cinemas," Ibid.

147. "At that time, I hate to say," Forces Radio interview with Tommy Vance, 12/12/78.
147. "English Ballet an odd sense of release," *Come Dance With Me* (1980), Ninette de Valois.
148. "My mother gave me the name," Ibid.
149. "a woman of high religious fervour," *Margot Fonteyn* (2004), Meredith Daneman.
149. "Staff asking for a pay rise," *Lilian Baylis: A Biography* (2007), Elizabeth Schafer.
150. "I don't care. It will have to go back to Berts." Ibid.
150. "I have no wish to join the ranks of those," *Come Dance With Me*, Ninette de Valois.
150. "Where de Valois and Baylis," *Lilian Baylis: A Biography* (2007), Elizabeth Schafer.
150. "wooden hand," Ibid.
151. "The Polish-born Marie Rambert," *No Intermissions: The Life of Agnes de Mille* (2000), Carol Easton.
151. "Sometimes, Mim merited a scolding," *Dance to the Piper* (1951), Agnes de Mille.
153. "The actors made great friends," *Quicksilver: An Autobiography* (1972), Marie Rambert.
153. *"annus mirabilis," Sadler's Wells Ballet: A History and an Appreciation* (1955), Mary Clarke.
154. "With Diaghileff alive, such competition," *Balletomania: The Story of an Obsession* (1934), by Arnold Haskell.
154. "Both Richardson and Haskell believed," *Sadler's Wells Ballet: A History and an Appreciation* (1955), Mary Clarke.
154. "It is significant that when the Camargo Society." *Markova: Her Life and Art*, Anton Dolin.
155. "The aim of the society was production." "The Camargo Society," Kathrine Sorley Walker, *Dance Chronicle*, 1995.
155. "These people are idiots in business." Shaw's postcard was re-printed in several newspapers at the time.
156. "This was read out and got us a lot of publicity," interview for BBC Television documentary "Markova" (1981).
156. "The Camargo Society was my first experience," *Balletomane at Large* (1972), Arnold Haskell.
156. "Lydia Lopokova was full of surprises," *Dancing For Diaghilev: The Memoirs of Lydia Sokolova* (1960), edited by Richard Buckle.
157. "She [Lopokova] was so gay and feckless," Ibid.
157. "Lydia had a remarkable sense of sincerity," Ibid.
157. "She should have been content with this," *Balletomania* (1934), Arnold Haskell.
158. "drawn to the promise of security and power," *Bloomsbury Ballerina* (2009), Judith Mackrell.
159. "I am no judge of his," *Balletomane At Large*, Arnold Haskell.
159. "Bloomsbury made much of personal relationships," Ibid.
160. "almost the only attitude the two," "Was Keynes Anti-Semitic?" Anand Chandarkar, *Economic and Political Weekly*, 5/6/2000.
160. "On all occasions, Lydia Keynes," *Come Dance With Me*, Ninette de Valois.
160. "Lydia rapidly found herself," *Bloomsbury Ballerina*, Judith Mackrell.
160. "lubricated by Maynard's claret," Ibid.
161. "Lydia had never liked the younger ballerina," Ibid.
161. "Lydia may have initially been fond of Marie," Ibid.
161. "A Bomb-shell. Fred under influence of Mim," Lydia Lopokova letter to John Maynard Keynes, 11/14/31.
162. "a delicious little person of irresistible charm." *Quicksilver: An Autobiography* (1972), Marie Rambert.
163. "When Diaghileff died Alicia began a new and very difficult career," *In His True Centre* (1951), Arnold Haskell.
163. "Naturally, I was pleased at this success," Ibid.
163. "*Cephalus and Procris* [1931] was Alicia Markova's," "The Camargo Society," Kathrine Sorley Walker, *Dance Chronicle*, 1995.

164. "I can say that I have known Alicia," *Dancing Times*, June 1931.
164. "Imagine what it must be like to," *Come Dance With Me*, Ninette de Valois.
165. "At that time her beauty had not bloomed," *Markova: Her Life and Art*, Anton Dolin.
166. "The fact that had to be faced," Memoir notes from Markova's archives.

Chapter 5: Pioneering British Ballet

167. "The thing that a choreographer really needs is an eye," *Frederick Ashton: A Choreographer and His Ballets* (1971), Zöe Dominic and John Selwyn Gilbert.
167. "Peru, with its 'particular interweaving of lightness,'" *Secret Muses: The Life of Frederick Ashton* (1996), Julie Kavanagh.
168. "[Ashton] felt cheated, and said so out loud," Ibid.
169. "I always felt that Fred was," Ibid.
169. "As a child, Freddie Ashton was considered special," Ibid.
169. "she injected me with her poison," *Frederick Ashton: A Choreographer and His Ballets* (1971), Zöe Dominic and John Selwyn Gilbert.
170. "Massine was very aloof and uncommunicative," *Frederick Ashton: A Choreographer and His Ballets* (1971), Zöe Dominic and John Selwyn Gilbert.
171. "Fred had a loose-jointed, delicate physique," Ballet Contexts: "Ashton the Dancer," Leo Kersley, Ballet.co.uk.
171. "Cecchetti's training stayed with me my entire life," Memoir notes from Markova's archives.
171. "I was brought up with the idea, that well," BBC Radio program "Frankly Speaking," 2002.
171. "found himself thrust overnight into," *Secret Muses: The Life of Frederick Ashton*, Julie Kavanagh.
172. "She only had a part-time studio," *Frederick Ashton: A Choreographer and His Ballets* (1971), Zöe Dominic and John Selwyn Gilbert.
172. "an extraordinary cultured woman," "Two Letters," Jane Pritchard, ballet.co/uk.
173. "I remember seeing her, this trim little," interview for BBC Television documentary "Markova" (1981).
173. "I saw her with Diaghilev," Ibid.
174. "notoriously lazy about going to class," *Frederick Ashton and His Ballets* (1977), David Vaughan.
174. "small, nervous and touchingly eager to please." *Come Dance With Me*, Ninette de Valois.
174. "I never had time off, but I didn't seem to require it," Memoir notes from Markova's archives.
174. "Unlike his exact contemporary, George Balanchine," *Playbill Arts*, July 2004, Julie Kavanagh.
175. "Witty and well mannered, Ashton was the ideal escort," *Secret Muses: The Life of Frederick Ashton*, Julie Kavanagh.
175. "whether imitating Garbo," *Playbill Arts*, July 2004, Julie Kavanagh.
175. "a brilliant evocation of the period," *Secret Muses: The Life of Frederick Ashton*, Julie Kavanagh.
175. "I thought I was made for life," *Frederick Ashton: A Choreographer and His Ballets* (1971), Zöe Dominic and John Selwyn Gilbert.
176. "must never lose her essential mystery," *Markova: Her Life and Art*, Anton Dolin.
177. "without pay or well-defined position," *Balletomania: The Story of an Obsession* (1934), Arnold Haskell.
177. "Arnold saw the possibilities of many new books," *Anton Dolin: Autobiography* (1960), Anton Dolin.
177. "At the time, Arnold Haskell's criticisms," Ibid.

177. "My dear Pat," Ibid.
178. "humble member", "inexperienced, half-trained," *Come Dance With Me*, Ninette de Valois.
178. "Nijinska, in particular helped me tremendously" *Frederick Ashton: A Choreographer and His Ballets* (1971), Zöe Dominic and John Selwyn Gilbert.
178. "She [Nijinska] is a beautiful dancer & a dancer above," "Two Letters," Jane Pritchard, ballet.co/uk.
179. "a half-witted canary," *Lytton Strachey: The Years of Achievement 1910–1932* (1968), Michael Holroyd.
179. "Lydia's pranks put us all on edge." *Virginia Woolf* (1994), James King.
179. "I asked her [Lopokova] whether she," *Quicksilver: An Autobiography*, Marie Rambert.
179. "Coming from a generation that considered itself," *Bloomsbury Ballerina*, Judith Mackrell.
180. "'Poor Fred,' she would report to Maynard," Ibid.
180. "He had seen her perform on many occasions," *Secret Muses: The Life of Frederick Ashton*, Julie Kavanagh.
181. "I'll know you." Ibid.
181. "When Sir Nigel gave me leave to," *Markova Her Life and Art*, Anton Dolin.
181. "I'd only just met Fred," *Markova: The Legend*, Maurice Leonard.
182. "It is not Ashton's habit to demonstrate," *Frederick Ashton and His Ballets* (1977), David Vaughan.
185. "I had thought at the time," *Markova: The Legend*, Maurice Leonard.
185. "As Procris, in this ballet," *Dancing Times*, March 1931.
186. "If anyone could dart about the stage," *Dancing For Diaghilev: The Memoirs of Lydia Sokolova*, edited by Richard Buckle.
186. "a friend and mentor, rather than a muse," *Secret Muses: The Life of Frederick Ashton*, Julie Kavanagh.
187. "[Lopokova] suspected that Markova," *Bloomsbury Ballerina*, Judith Mackrell.
187. "Fred came over and asked me," *Markova: The Legend*, Maurice Leonard.
188. "boxed herself into a moral corner," *Bloomsbury Ballerina*, Judith Mackrell.
189. "it was gall and wormwood," Ibid.
190. "Ashton attempted to create a genuinely," *Frederick Ashton and His Ballets*, David Vaughan.
193. "[Ashton] went to Marie Rambert," *Balletomania: The Story of an Obsession*, Arnold Haskell.
194. "I do not remember in all my career," *Ballet Go Round* (1938), Anton Dolin.
194. "Since the laws in pre-revolutionary," *Dance Today*, Israel, July 2000, Ruth Eshel.
195. "[Lopokova] considered that the majority of her," *Bloomsbury Ballerina*, Judith Mackrell.
196. "Working with Markova was an," *Secret Muses: The Life of Frederick Ashton*, Julie Kavanagh.
197. "When I first worked with her," interview for BBC Television documentary "Markova" (1981).
197. "Markova is a genius of phrasing," *Dance Writings* (1986), Edwin Denby.
197. "When young, his weakness lay," *Come Dance With Me*, Ninette de Valois.
197. "Legat, another great ballet master," "My Life as a Dancer," Markova's recorded talk at the Royal Ballet School, London, 9/27/72.
197. "familiarize himself thoroughly with the music," *Frederick Ashton and His Ballets*, David Vaughan.
198. "As far as I can remember," BBC Radio interview: "Myself When Young," with Claire Rayner (unknown year).
198. "She was extremely musical," Ibid.
198. "After we appeared in the *Marriage a la Mode*," BBC Radio program: "Markova Birthday Tribute," December 1970.

198. "I first saw her dance," BBC Television program: "This is Your Life, Alicia Markova," 1/11/60.
199. "The stage at the Mercury Theatre" interview for BBC Television documentary "Markova" (1981).
199. "as intimate as dancing in a cabaret." Eric Johns, *Theatre World*, 1963.
199. "We would come offstage after we danced," *Markova: The Legend*, Maurice Leonard.
199. "In 1927, Ashley bought the freehold," *Quicksilver: An Autobiography*, Marie Rambert.
200. "But don't you think that is life," Radio interview: "Round Midnight," with Brian Matthew, 1986.
201. "I had to live and I always had a great appetite," Manx Radio program: Concert Classics, 12/31/74.
201. "Nobody realizes what the situation," BBC Radio program: Beryl Grey in Conversations with Dame Ninette de Valois, Dame Alicia Markova, and Darcey Bussell, 1/17/93.
202. "One day, Fred, when I got to rehearsal," interview for BBC Television documentary "Markova" (1981).
203. "I just got an impression of being dazzled," Ibid.
203. "in all-over brown leotard, large bushy tail" and "I had to flee the pack by spinning as fast," *Markova Remembers*, Alicia Markova.
204. "At the end of each show," Radio program: "The Alicia Markova Story," 10/3/60.
204. "Dame Ninette and Lilian Baylis," interview for BBC Television documentary "Markova" (1981).
204. "She was always successful," Ibid.
205. "One morning after class," *Speak to Me, Dance with Me* (1973), Agnes de Mille.
205. "Venus was Alicia Markova," Ibid.
206. "drew a distinction between the pictures," "Talk of the Town: Photo Dept." Judith Thurman, *The New Yorker*, 11/14/11.
206. "I enjoy comedy," *Markova: The Legend*, Maurice Leonard.
206. "I always look back with particular pleasure," *Frederick Ashton: A Choreographer and His Ballets* (1971), Zöe Dominic and John Selwyn Gilbert.
206. "I was really thought of as a classical dancer," Radio interview: "Round Midnight," with Brian Matthew, 7/8/81.
207. "She is such an exquisite dancer," *Music Lover*, 12/19/31.
207. "[Façade] was half based on classical dancing," interview for BBC Television documentary "Markova" (1981).
208. "Her most unusual role for the Club," Radio program: "The Alicia Markova Story," 10/3/60.
208. "cast Alicia as the chief lady of easy virtue," *Dance and Dancers* magazine (1955).
208. "Cedric [*sic*] Ashton is the head waiter." *Sketch*, 5/23/34.
209. "The joke was that Fred should set me," *Markova Remembers*, Alicia Markova.
209. "I think her technical ability fascinated me," BBC Radio interview: "Myself When Young," with Claire Rayner (unknown year).
210. "It must have been something of a surprise," *Markova Remembers*, Alicia Markova.
210. "I again was fortunate to work with," "My Life as a Dancer," Markova's recorded talk at the Royal Ballet School, London, 9/27/72.
211. "[*High Yellow*] was very advanced in its day," interview for BBC Television documentary "Markova" (1981).
211. "terror of boring people," *The New York Times*, 8/20/88.
211. "The dances derived by Frederick Ashton," *The Illustrated London News*, 3/12/32.
211. "Another lesson she," Radio program: "The Alicia Markova Story," 10/3/60.
211. "*La Péri*, Persian, come along," *Frederick Ashton and His Ballets*, David Vaughan.
212. "Fred, Billy Chappell—also a Rambert dancer," *Markova Remembers*, Alicia Markova.

212. "In La Péri the drama is interpreted," *Dancing Times*, June 1931.
212. "Markova as La Péri is brilliant," Press quote printed in The Ballet Club program, 1931.
212. "There was never any money to speak of," *Dancers of Mercury*, "The Ballet Club," (1962), Mary Clarke.
213. "in 'cinematic' black and white, incredibly chic," *Frederick Ashton and His Ballets*, David Vaughan.
213. "forced Ashton into understatement," Ibid.
213. "She [Markova] is on the stage when the thing," interview for BBC Television documentary "Markova" (1981).
214. *"Alicia Markova, the lovely Russian dancer," The Modern*, 8/28/33.
214. "Alicia Markova surpasses her considerable," *Time & Tide*, 3/18/33.
215. "[Markova] is more responsive than any dancer I know," interview for BBC Television documentary "Markova" (1981).
215. "She was always like a most beautiful picture painted." Ibid.
217. "Are we becoming ballet-minded?" and "According to Alicia Markova," *Daily Sketch*, 11/7/32.

Chapter 6: Becoming Giselle
219. "Scotsman John Logie Baird," *John Logie Baird: A Life* (2002), Antony Kamm and Malcolm Baird.
221. "It was the size of a postage stamp!" Radio interview: "Round Midnight" with Brian Matthew, 7/8/81.
222. "It's extraordinary what we went through," Ibid.
226. "It has no serious portent at all," *The Sadler's Wells Ballet: A History and an Appreciation* (1955), Mary Clarke.
226. "[T]he leading role gave Markova her finest," *Vic-Wells, A Ballet Progress* (1942), P.W. Manchester.
226. "It really brought out every gift," *Dance Magazine* feature: "Pioneers of the Royal Ballet," Gordon Anthony.
227. "I think of all the ballets I did for her," BBC Radio program: "Markova Birthday Tribute," December 1970.
227. "The Sadler's Wells company at this point was merely," *Dance to the Piper* (1987), Agnes de Mille.
227. "I have spoken to Ninette," Letter from Lilian Baylis to Alicia Markova, dated 6/14/33, in Markova's archive.
227. "Alice did the main corps de ballet work," Interview for BBC Television documentary "Markova" (1981).
228. "It was wonderful, this extraordinary lightness," Ibid.
228. "When the choreographer commences," BBC Radio program: "Markova Reminiscences" (circa 1990s).
228. "Well, you know with me, I'm afraid," Ibid.
229. "She had a very wide repertoire," BBC Television program: "This is Your Life, Alicia Markova," 1/11/60.
230. "It's like an opera singer or a concert pianist." LBC Radio program: interview with Steve Allen, 1/1/96.
230. "I used to get frightfully irritated," Ibid.
231. "doing finger-turns on Ashton's hand," *Dance to the Piper*, Agnes de Mille.
231. "What a great choreographer Bronia," *Speaking of Diaghilev*, Richard Buckle.
231. "She was an amazing woman," Radio interview: "Round Midnight" with Brian Matthew, 7/8/81.
231. "very, very great. . . . Markova has the SOUL!" *New York Post*, 1/5/48.

232. "Her [de Valois's] success as a choreographer," *Balletomane at Large*, Arnold Haskell.
232. "I think of all the artists," *Come Dance With Me*, Ninette de Valois.
233. "Dedicated and devoted, she wasted no time," *Dance and Dancers* magazine, January 1955.
233. "She was friends with everybody," interview for BBC Television documentary "Markova" (1981).
234. "hers was a changeling personality," Ibid.
234. "[T]he world was a difficult place for Antony," *Shadowplay: The Life of Antony Tudor* (1991), Donna Perlmutter.
234. "watched everything with remembering eyes," *Dance to the Piper*, Agnes de Mille.
236. "Break off a piece and wear it," *Markova: Her Life and Art*, Anton Dolin.
237. "I went to the ballet," *Margot Fonteyn: A Biography*, Meredith Daneman.
238. "Peggy as a plump though beautifully proportioned," Ibid.
238. "Markova has exquisite feet," Ibid.
239. "When I first went to the then Vic-Wells," BBC Radio program: "Markova Birthday Tribute," December 1970.
239. "Margot was always rather like," *Margot Fonteyn: A Biography*, Meredith Daneman.
240. "obstinate" and "strangely lacking in warmth, charm," Ibid.
240. "I remember her first performance," Ibid.
241. "Ashton read the glowing reviews," *Four Saints: Gertrude Stein, Virgil Thomson, and the Mainstreaming of American Modernism* (1995), Steven Watson.
242. "the propaganda of Mr. Arnold Haskell." Unidentified London newspaper clipping, Markova archives.
242. "All those concerned with the Society," *The Camargo Society*, Katherine Sorley Walker, *Dance Chronicle*, 1995.
245. "yards and yards of white tulle," *Giselle and I*, Alicia Markova.
245. "A combination of sad circumstances," Ibid.
245. "Suddenly she remembered I was to dance," Ibid.
247. "What Baylis had to offer in return," *Lilian Baylis: A Biography*, Elizabeth Schafer.
247. "We were lucky that from the beginning," *Dance and Dancers* magazine, January 1955.
249. "threatening to cut me off from Giselle," *Giselle & I*, Alicia Markova.
251. "One night Ashley took a box to see," *Quicksilver: An Autobiography*, Marie Rambert.
252. "The actual classical Italian variation," Radio interview: "Round Midnight" with Brian Matthew, 7/8/81.
252. "To most of us [Markova] was," *Vic-Wells, A Ballet Progress* (1942), P. W. Manchester.
252. "When I was a youth," From the *Sunday Pictorial* (precursor to the *Sunday Mirror*), 4/11/1934.
253. "He advised me against it," *Frederick Ashton and His Ballets*, David Vaughan.
253. "But you know how it is in America," Ibid.
254. "I'm afraid our Ashton has grown," *Secret Muses: The Life of Frederick Ashton*, Julie Kavanagh.
254. "Some people thought Markova miscast," *London Referee*, 6/7/34.
254. "talented, enthusiastic, extremely intelligent," *Helpmann: The Authorized Biography* (1981), Elizabeth Salter.
255. "a grim story in the vein of *The Fall of the House of Usher*." *London Times*, 4/4/34.
255. "It was a series of 32 of this," BBC Radio interview, "Woman's World," Linda Van Alpen, April 1980.
256. "Everyone who sees Markova, that exquisite ethereal," *Dance and Dancers* magazine, January 1955.
256. "I used to have my meal," LBC Radio program: interview with Steve Allen, 1/1/96.
257. "Dame Ninette was very worried about me," Radio interview: "Markova Reminisces" (circa 1990s).

257. "Oh, I know. I have something I will send her" and "I'll always remember at Sadler's Wells," Ibid.
258. "knew the secrets of the *fouettés!*" *Markova Remembers*, Alicia Markova.
258. "'real Markova weather.'" *Bayswater Chronicle*, 12/1/34.
261. "willing to fight hard, and dirty," *Lilian Baylis: A Biography*, Elizabeth Schafer.
262. "Good luck to you." *Tonight and Every Night*, Vivian Van Damm.
262. "I would have been happiest of all if our two Companies," *Giselle & I*, Alicia Markova.
263. "It was obvious that no merger," *The Sadler's Wells Ballet: A History and Appreciation*, Mary Clarke.
263. "not for him." Ibid.
266. "When I first made contact with her," "Dick Cavett in New York," PBS, 1981.
267. "I look forward to the day," *Home and Empire* magazine, July 1935.
267. "Markova is, in my mind," *Dance and Dancers* magazine, January 1955.

Chapter 7: Leaving the Nest

271. "I want you to do lots of well paid work," From a contract letter Lilian Baylis wrote to Alicia Markova, from Markova's archive.
271. "I am so happy that you want to return," Ibid.
271. "We just feel that we would hate to lose you," Ibid.
273. "Helpmann shared the dance world's admiration for Astaire," *The Astaires: Fred & Adele* (2012), Kathleen Riley.
273. "[H]e should have ruined his career," *Balletomania Then & Now* (1977), Arnold Haskell.
273. "I don't want people to say about me," Ibid.
274. "dangerous for Serge," Letter from Lopokova to Keynes, 1/14/24, from *Lydia and Maynard: The Letters of Lydia Lopokova and John Maynard Keynes* (1990), Polly Hill and Richard Hill Keynes.
274. "also made an effort to tutor Dolin," *Diaghilev: A Life* (2009), Sjeng Scheijen.
274. "[A]s a partner Dolin has always," *Balletomania Then & Now*, Arnold Haskell.
275. "I danced many times for Lilian Baylis," *Anton Dolin Autobiography* (1960), Anton Dolin.
276. "Markova, if she is honest," *S. Hurok Presents: A Memoir of the Dance World* (1953), Sol Hurok.
276. "Though Alicia has always said that Anna Pavlova," *Markova Her Life and Art*, Anton Dolin.
276. "all he [Diaghilev] really wanted was a few extras," *Last Words: A Final Autobiography* (1985), Anton Dolin, Kay Hunter.
277. "Dolin was internationally known," *Portrait Gallery* (1990), Agnes de Mille.
278. "Saturday evening I finished dancing," *Anton Dolin Autobiography* (1960), Anton Dolin.
278. "This is the first time that a British ballet," *Birmingham Mail*, 8/22/35.
280. "'Oh, Mr. Dolin,'" *Anton Dolin, Autobiography*, Anton Dolin.
280. "Who is this Markova?" *Markova Her Life and Art* (1953), Anton Dolin.
280. "MARKKOVA—THE SUPEREME ARTIST," *Glasgow Daily Express*, 8/7/35.
280. "DRAMATIC MARKOVA," *Glasgow Bulletin*, 8/9/35.
280. "MADAME MARKOVA, the famous ballerina," *Glasgow Daily Express*, 8/9/35.
284. "When the royal couple," *Portrait Gallery*, Agnes de Mille.
284. "I dreaded being surrounded," *Giselle & I* (1960), Alicia Markova.
285. "I wouldn't say we match at all." Radio interview: Concert Classics (1974).
285. "On the stage we had a similar mental approach," *Markova Her Life and Art*, Anton Dolin.
285. "never felt a need to be secretive," *Shadowplay: The Life of Antony Tudor* (1991), Donna Perlmutter.

285. "I had always understood that Dolin," *Speaking of Diaghilev* (1997), John Drummond.
286. "Neither was seen without the other," *Markova Her Life and Art*, Anton Dolin.
286. "I wonder dear if you will ever know"and (289) "I wonder if you would write the forward to it," Personal letters from Anton Dolin to Alicia Markova, from Markova's archive.
290. "I didn't want to be recognized on the business side," Radio interview: "Round Midnight" with Brian Matthew, 7/8/81.
290. "bulging muscles that make most ballerinas," *Birmingham News*, 10/23/37.
291. "TIGHTS MADE TOO TIGHT," *Yorkshire Observer*, 1/18/38.
292. "It was generally Dolin," *Markova The Legend*, Maurice Leonard.
293. "A friend who took her on a drive," "Secrets of a Dancer," *Leeds Mercury*, 9/4/35.
293. "Dolin would take the company practice," *Markova The Legend*, Maurice Leonard.
294. "I think dear the suggestion should come from you" and (295) "The world is before us now." Personal letters from Anton Dolin to Alicia Markova, from Markova's archive.
296. "simply because her dresses had to be properly hung," *Anton Dolin: Autobiography* (1960), Anton Dolin.
297. "had a far wider range than Spessiva," *Markova Her Life and Art*, Anton Dolin.
297."there is no one living whose performance," *Anton Dolin: Autobiography* (1960), Anton Dolin.
298. "You were quite wonderful (except at Beaulieu)," Personal letter from Anton Dolin to Alicia Markova, from Markova's archives.
298. "Don't run away with the idea," *Markova: The Legend*, Maurice Leonard.
299. "He was a terrible man," Ibid.
299. "The immediate years to come," Preface to *Alicia Markova* (1935), Gordon Anthony.
300. "It was always hard for me to remember," *Choura: The Memoirs of Alexandra Danilova* (1987), Alexandra Danilova.
300. "She would come over and give you," *Frederic Franklin: A Biography of the Ballet Star* (2004), Leslie Norton.
301. '"Aren't they sweet children?" "Fairy Godmother of the Ballet," *The Daily Mail*, 11/12/36.
301. "You see, many things have to be taken," "Women Stars," interviewed by Leila S. Mackinlay, 1936.
301. "Mme. Nijinska really started me thinking about the role," "Alice's Wonderland," *The Sunday Times*, London, 7/7/68.
302. "It is the most complete ballet," Radio program: "The Alicia Markova Story," 10/3/60.
302. "declaring forcefully that I did not seem to know," *Giselle & I*, Alicia Markova.
302. "It's the first time," BBC Radio program: "Markova Birthday Tribute," December 1970.
303. "That particular pantomime is one," BBC Radio interview: "Myself When Young," with Claire Rayner (unknown year).
303. "Ballet used to be a very closed world," Speech to the Women's Canadian Club, 10/22/63.
306. "It is a little disconcerting," "Markova—Our Only Prima Ballerina," interview by Eric Johns, *Theatre World*, January 1935.
307. "FAMOUS BALLERINA AT THE CIRCUS," *West Lancashire Evening Gazette*, 6/3/36.
312. "We must have more fun in ballet," *Yorkshire Evening Gazette*, 11/28/35.
313. "But it was counted as money well spent," *Tonight and Every Night The Windmill Story* (1952), Vivian Van Damm.
313. "the 225-foot vessel was said at that time," "Julius Fleischmann Dies at 68; Stage Producer and Art Patron," *New York Times*, 10/24/68.
314. "Massine always gave himself the best parts," *Choura: The Memoirs of Alexandra Danilova*, Alexandra Danilova.

314. "You've danced for eight years," BBC Radio interview: "Myself When Young," with Claire Rayner (unknown year).
315. "British ambassador for dance," Ibid.
315. "I've been so fortunate," Forces Radio interview with Tommy Vance, 12/12/78.
316. "Danilova is not only a prodigious technician," *Dance Writings* (1986), Edwin Denby.
316. "My nose doesn't dance!" *Frederic Franklin: A Biography of the Ballet Star* (2004), Leslie Norton.
318. "Massine did not want Dolin," Ibid.
320. "Markova's Dresser has never seen a Ballet." *Bristol Evening World*, 11/16/37.
321. "If you don't, you begin to wonder," *Bristol Evening Despatch*, 12/10/37.
321. "close to forty of them were immediately let go by Massine," *Rene Blum & The Ballet Russes* (2011), Judith Chazin-Bennhahum.
321. "There are so many stars," *De Basil's Ballets Russes* (1983), Kathrine Sorley Walker.
321. "an important addition to his company," *Markova Remembers*, Alicia Markova.
322. "Two aspects of Massine's method were especially," *Massine: A Biography* (1995), Vicente Garcia-Márquez.
322. "If he [Massine] had an idea, he would absolutely break," *Choura: The Memoirs of Alexandra Danilova*, Alexandra Danilova.
322. "He would say to me, 'Are you free,'" "Big Dame, Tiny Feet," *The Telegraph*, 6/26/02.
324. "For many years Lifar has been the darling," *PIC Magazine*, 12/13/38.
325. "[O]n his first entrance, Lifar ran around the stage," *Ballet Mystique: Behind the Glamour of the Ballet Russe* (2000), George Zoritch.
325. "If Albrecht had left me," *Choura: The Memoirs of Alexandra Danilova*, Alexandra Danilova.

Chapter 8: Only in America

329. "Jealousies," *Impresario: A Memoir by S. Hurok* (1946), Sol Hurok and Ruth Goode.
330. "He [Diaghilev] taught the company," Excerpt from Markova's speech for "The Diaghilev Exhibition," 1955.
330. "one night a hand came out," *Impresario: A Memoir by S. Hurok*, Sol Hurok and Ruth Goode.
332. "There was an immediate change of pace and mood," *De Basil's Ballets Russes* (1982), Kathrine Sorley Walker.
332. "He was not gracious, neither was he unpleasant," *Dance to the Piper* (1951), Agnes de Mille.
333. "He considered lifting a ballerina or supporting her," *Choura: The Memoirs of Alexandra Danilova*, Alexandra Danilova.
333. "His eyes used to click like cash register signs," *Margot Fonteyn: Autobiography* (1977), Margot Fonteyn.
334. "toity tousand dollars" and "nervous about 'thicket' sales." Ibid.
335. "I thought this—this—I've only seen this," interview for BBC Television documentary "Markova" (1981).
336. "A threat of possible violence," *S. Hurok Presents: A Memoir of the Dance World* (1953), Sol Hurok.
336. "In Act II, Giselle has to pick two flowers," Memoir notes from Markova's archives.
337. "In Act II he [Lifar] insisted upon carrying," Ibid.
337. "Markova triumphed that night in Giselle," *Impresario: A Memoir by S. Hurok*, Sol Hurok with Ruth Goode.
338. "She [Markova] was described by the critics as 'breathtaking,'" *The New Yorker*, Barbara Heggie, 4/15/44.
341. "Lifar, like many people holding important posts," "'ICARE': Remembering Serge Lifar," Dance Research: The Journal of the Society for Dance Research, Vol. 20, No. 2 (Winter 2002), by Clement Crisp.

342. "Some of Markova's enthusiasms," *The New Yorker*, 10/22/38.
344. "Magnificent scenery and costumes," *Boston Post*, 11/9/38.
345. "Tamara was with us." *Frederic Franklin: A Biography of the Ballet Star*, Leslie Norton.
346. "It was in America that Alicia," *Choura: The Memoirs of Alexandra Danilova*, Alexandra Danilova.
346. "From then on, Massine posted a notice," LBC Radio program: interview with Steve Allen, 1/1/96.
347. "There was a marble floor in one auditorium," BBC Radio interview: "Conversation Pieces," 4/7/88.
347. "The company made efforts of several kinds," *The One and Only: The Ballet Russe de Monte Carlo* (1981), Jack Anderson.
348. "Like the frosting on your cake," *Seattle Post-Intelligencer*, Suzanne Martin, 1/20/41.
348. "Sergei Denham courted high society," *The One and Only: The Ballet Russe de Monte Carlo*, Jack Anderson.
349. "SOCIETY GREETS BALLET OPENING," *Boston Post*, 11/9/38.
349. "In a crush of ermine, mink, orchids," *The Seattle Daily Times*, 1939.
350. "The curtain came up and all the girls," LBC Radio program: interview with Steve Allen, 1/1/96.
352. "She [Markova] really conquered the critics," interview for BBC Television documentary "Markova" (1981).
354. "On the call-board the first day," *The Music News*, Mary Mack, March 1940.
354. "I've rehearsed for a new ballet," Radio program "Markova Reminisces" (circa 1990s).
355. "Massine, sitting out in front," "Alicia Markova, Greatest Classical Dancer of Modern Times Creates Sensational New Role," Marya McAuliff, 1940.
355. "There are some remarkable feats," "Diaghilev Protegee [*sic*]—gives ballet world new classic role", *The Music News*, Mary Mack, March 1940.
356. "was as important as that of the composer," *My Life in Ballet* (1968), Léonide Massine.
356. "I pointed out to him," Ibid.
357. "He [Matisse] suggested that Shostakovich's music" and "The Man and Woman, danced," Ibid.
357. "He [Matisse] was the first person to work," *Women's Wear Daily*, 4/12/65.
357. "white was for Russia, black for fascists," *Choura: The Memoirs of Alexandra Danilova*, Alexandra Danilova.
358. "Markova's translation of Massine's conception was a revelation," *Cleveland News*, William Gates, 1939.
358. "A fine musician she," "Diaghilev Protegee [*sic*]—gives ballet world new classic role", *The Music News*, Mary Mack, March 1940.
358. "The audiences today identify me as a romantic," BBC Radio program: "Frankly Speaking," 2/21/59.
359. "Those first days of war were very dismal," "Under War Clouds," A. E. Twysden (early 1940s).
362. "Nobody knew whether we would reach New York," "Britain Had Never Had A Ballerina Before Me," *The Daily Mail*, Louette Harding, 12/1/02.
363. "I would always ask what the shortages were," BBC Radio: "Conversation with Dame Ninette de Valois, Dame Alicia Markova, and Darcey Bussell," 1/17/93, host Dame Beryl Grey.
364."Hastily I auditioned a number of young dancers," *My Life in Ballet* (1968), Léonide Massine.
365. "We used to call it 'Hurok's Special,'" interview for BBC Television documentary "Markova" (1981).
365. "I had bought a large Lincoln," Ibid.
365. "Because ballet was, in the late 1930s," *Markova Remembers*, Alicia Markova.

365. "Just before we were leaving the Metropolitan, the list," interview for BBC Television documentary "Markova" (1981).
366. "It all had to be down to the absolute minute," Ibid.
371. "I have never danced for an audience," *Choura: The Memoirs of Alexandra Danilova*, Alexandra Danilova.
378. "the dapper, delirious Catalonian placed in one window," *Time* magazine, 3/27/39.
378. "On a table, a telephone transformed into a lobster;" *The Secret Life of Salvador Dalí* (1942), Salvador Dalí.
379. "I got along quite well with Léonide Massine," Ibid.
380. "Dalí centered the décor on an enormous swan," *Massine: A Biography*, Vicente Garcia-Márquez.
382. "[T]hese dancers would execute a shuffle," "Behind The Scenes" Walter Terry, *New York Herald Tribune*, 9/22/40.
382. "I want you should be Hurok attraction." *Portrait Gallery: Artists, Impresarios, Intimates*, Agnes de Mille.
383. "It was an adventure," BBC Radio: "Conversation with Dame Ninette de Valois, Dame Alicia Markova, and Darcey Bussell", 1/17/93, host Dame Beryl Grey.
383. "We used to room together," BBC Radio interview: "Conversation Pieces," 4/7/88.
383. "It was in Hollywood," Ibid.
383. "I was exposed to a broad range of ideas and interests," *Choura: The Memoirs of Alexandra Danilova*, Alexandra Danilova.
385. "On her head she wore a balloon," Ibid.
385. "Waterloos," "Alicia Markova: A Sketch for a Portrait," Clement Crisp," Dance Research, 2006.
385. "The rule was: You may die, but you must not be ill," *The Sunday Telegraph Magazine*, interview with Duncan Fallowell, 4/30/2000.
385. "'Alicia Markova' for the two were shopping together," "The ballerina and The Mirror," A. E. Twysden, *The American Dancer*, July 1941.
387. "I had no star billing with the Company," *Anton Dolin: Autobiography* (1960), Anton Dolin.
389. "I was thrilled to see this transformation taking place," *Markova Her Life and Art*, Anton Dolin.
389. "dull and ordinary" and "scarcely opened her mouth." Ibid.
390. "He was Irish, extrovert and temperamental," interview with Jane Kelly for London's *Daily Mail*, 5/21/96.
390. "dancers and slippers," *Markova Her Life and Art*, Anton Dolin.
392. "basking in her fame," Ibid.
392. "He was very grand at these séances," *Portrait Gallery: Artists, Impresarios, Intimates*, Agnes de Mille.

Chapter 9: Spreading Wings

393. "was absolutely void of any idealism," *The Last Impresario: The Life, Times, and Legacy of Sol Hurok* (1994), Harlow Robinson.
394. "Comfortably and advantageously positioned as an," "Sol Hurok: America's dance Impresario," by Harlow Robinson, *Dance Magazine*, 11/1/94.
395. "By 1941," *The Last Impresario: The Life, Times, and Legacy of Sol Hurok* (1994), Harlow Robinson.
397. "'S. Hurok Presents' was like a seal of approval," *American Ballet Theatre* (1978), Charles Payne.
397. "He admired Hurok," Ibid.
398. "Sevastianov saw to it that dancers," *Shadowplay: The Life of Antony Tudor* (1991), Donna Perlmutter.

399. "took full advantage of the fact that dancers, *The Last Impresario: The Life, Times, and Legacy of Sol Hurok*, Harlow Robinson.
400. "*From my side, there is no reason,*" Anton Dolin letter to Alicia Markova, dated February 14, 1938, from Markova's archive.
400. "*I should have been with you & you with me.*" Anton Dolin letter to Alicia Markova, dated November 7, 1938, from Markova's archive.
402. "[T]he souvenir program would be printed," *American Ballet Theatre*, Charles Payne.
403. "The difference between the two companies," "The American Ballet," Edwin Denby, *The Kenyon Review*, Vol. 10, No. 4.
404. "This was not a new experience for St. Denis," *Ted Shawn: Father of American Dance* (1976), Walter Terry.
405. "The first performances were held in the summer of 1933," Ibid.
405. "Creatively and artistically," *How Beautiful Upon the Mountain, a History of Jacob's Pillow* (1944), Ted Shawn.
406. "Again, I listed Jacob's Pillow with the real estate dealers," Ibid.
407. "As it was late in the season," Ibid.
409. "Her artistry was akin in spirit," "From Jacob's Pillow—memories of Alicia Markova," Anthony Fay, *The Berkshire Eagle*, 8/16/81.
410. "transcendent" and "It was all right." *Portrait Gallery*, Agnes de Mille.
411. "plan was that a new, non-profit-making, artistic," *How Beautiful Upon the Mountain, a History of Jacob's Pillow* (1944), Ted Shawn.
412. "There are no preparations for the steps;" *Markova Remembers*, Alicia Markova.
413. "Make-up is another aspect," "Markova's New Career," Eric Johns, *Theatre World*, 1963.
413. "I gave in," BBC World Service Radio, Tribute to Pavlova on "Outlook," 1/31/85.
414. "Having seen Pavlova dance her immortal version," "Murray's Music" column, *Brighton Gazette*, 6/12/54.
415. "The music followed Pavlova," *Giselle & I*, Alicia Markova, introduction by Carl Van Vechten.
415. "Carl Van Vechten took a series of color photographs," "A Royal Ballerina" P. W. Manchester, *Ballet News*, June 1981.
416. "The most important thing of all is the training," BBC Radio program, "Markova Reminisces" (circa 1990s).
417. "One could buy a Stradivarius," "Thirty Years of Alicia Markova," *Dance and Dancers* magazine, January 1955.
417. "Dolin actually seemed to PULL his partner out of the air," "Queen of the Dance," Carl Van Vechten, *Saturday Evening Review*, 4/2/5/53.
417. "The great Markova boom," Ibid.
418. "I always speak of you on Pearl harbor Day." From a personal letter to Alicia Markova in Markova's archive.
418. "In Rio, we'd gone to the cinema," BBC Radio program: "Conversation Pieces," 4/7/88.
418. "When we used to go to the Stage Door Canteen," Radio program: "Round Midnight" with Brian Matthew, 1986.
419. "I shan't forget those days," "The Night Markova Learned to Jitterbug," *T.V. Times*, interviewed by Leslie Bird (unidentified year).
419. "Why is it they always think we need pop stuff?" interview for BBC Television documentary "Markova" (1981).
420. "We thought you should know how very happy," Excerpt from letter from Bette Davis to Alicia Markova on "Hollywood Canteen" letterhead, from Markova's archive.
420. "This letter comes from a G.I. Joe" and "You'll be up there with Gene Tierney!" and (421) "kindness and enthusiastic cooperation," Excerpts of letters from soldiers to Alicia Markova, from Markova's archive.

421. "Wartime, here as abroad," *Dance Writings*, Edwin Denby.
423. "full companies and full orchestras," *Impresario: A Memoir by S. Hurok* in collaboration with Ruth Goode.
423. "The dancers hurried to the railroad station," *American Ballet Theatre*, Charles Payne.
427. "A Russian girl I know who works in a defense plant," "Markova's Dance Rhythm: Tudor's "Romeo and Juliet", *Modern Music*, May–June 1943, Edwin Denby.
428. "felt it essential to visit the local beauty parlor," "Markova—Lady With Twinkling Toes," feature story from unidentified newspaper.
430. "It was a subject close to his heart," *S. Hurok Presents: A Memoir of the Dance World*, by Sol Hurok.
430. "the quintessential Jewish artist of the 20th century," "Art: Fiddler on the Roof of Modernism: Marc Chagall: 1887–1985, Robert Hughes, *Time* magazine, 4/8/88.
430. "No word sounded sweeter to me," *My Life* (1922), Marc Chagall.
430. "invited by the Museum of Modern Art." "Marc Chagall among friends in Philadelphia," Stanley Meisler, *Los Angeles Times*, 4/24/11.
431. "was so intrigued by the theme," *My Life in Ballet*, Léonide Massine.
432. "I used to go to the market with Chagall often," interview for BBC Television documentary "Markova" (1981).
432. "Chagall adored fantasy," *Markova Remembers*, Alicia Markova.
433. "Massine was unmerciful," *Choura: The Memoirs of Alexandra Danilova*, by Alexandra Danilova.
433. "I knew that the pain was part of the artistic," Personal notes from Markova's archive.
433. "murderous lifts," *Massine: A Biography*, Vicente Garcia-Márquez.
434. "Extraordinarily colorful and dramatic," *The Borzoi Book of Ballets* (1946), Grace Robert
434. "the American stage painters' union would not have permitted Chagall," *Marc Chagall* (1978), by Sidney Alexander.
434. "sale of the Chagall backdrops," "Massine's 'Aleko'," by Leland Windreich, *Dance Chronicle*, 1985.
434. "It took me thirty years to learn bad French," "The Elusive Marc Chagall," *Smithsonian Magazine*, December 2003.
434. "Not knowing enough English," Telegram from Marc Chagall to Alicia Markova, from Markova's archive.
435. "priestess of evil," *Giselle & I*, Alicia Markova.
435. "The great surprise of Aleko," *The Borzoi Book of Ballets* (1946), Grace Robert.
435. "When I transferred," Radio program: "Round Midnight" with Brian Matthew, 1986.
436. "I said to Antony, I don't think," Ibid.
437. "In the golden dress with its heavy pleats," "A Royal Ballerina," P. W. Manchester, *Ballet News*, June 1981.
438. "wouldn't hear of such a lie." *Shadowplay: The Life of Antony Tudor*, Donna Perlmutter.
439. "Oh, I adored when he conducted," Radio program: "Round Midnight" with Brian Matthew, 1986.
439. "Her new Juliet," "Ballet Theatre; Graham's 'Punch and Judy,'" *Modern Music*, January–February 1942, Edwin Denby.
439. "For once, there was a Juliet," *The Borzoi Book of Ballets*, Grace Robert.
440. "On February 9, 1942, the company," *American Ballet Theatre* (1978), Charles Payne.
441. "Anyone who has seen Markova's transcendent," *The Borzoi Book of Ballets* (1946), Grace Robert.
441. "Alicia Markova is, by practically unanimous consensus," *Time*, May 17, 1943.
442. "We recognize in her the greatest," "Miracle that is Markova," John Martin, *The New York Times*, 4/11/43.
442. "Dancing in the humid air five nights," *Anton Dolin: Autobiography*, Anton Dolin.

443. "to confirm his contention that," *American Ballet Theatre*, Charles Payne.
447. "That was supposed to be the show of all shows," interview for television documentary "Markova", aired 6/14/81.
448. "All it takes to make a lot of money," *The Nine Lives of Billy Rose: An Intimate Biography* (1968), Polly Rose Gottlieb.
449. "DARLING FEEL NOTHING SHOULD BREAK OUR," Western Union telegram from Anton Dolin to Alicia Markova, 1/19/44, from Markova's archives.
449. "to get back in harness," Letter from Antony Tudor to Alicia Markova, from Markova archive.
450. "Long distance call for Miss Markova," *Markova Remembers*, Alicia Markova.
454. "WILL YOU COME TO MY VICTORY PARTY," Western Union telegram from Elsa Maxwell to Alicia Markova, 8/14/44, from Alicia Markova archives.
455. "Greer Garson always," interview for BBC Television documentary "Markova" (1981).
456. "I played charades with Gene Kelly," "The Night Markova Learned to Jitterbug," *T.V. Times*, London, 1950s.
456. "Very good friends of mine," BBC Radio program: "Round Midnight" with Brian Matthew, 7/8/81.
456. "I have no desire to be an actress," "Markova Here for Ballet," *New York News*, 5/22/44.
458. "Oh, he was wonderful," BBC Radio program: interview with Dame Beryl Grey, 1/17/93.
458. "The lift would come up," Ibid.
458. "a little tedious," interview for BBC Television documentary "Markova" (1981).
459. "To me dancing should be beauty." "Alicia Markova Talks of Dancing," *Picture Plays and Players* magazine, 1945.
460. "Jose Greco, a famous dancer himself," Faces & Places column, unidentified New York newspaper, 1944.
463. "I Can't Ask a Man," *Evening News*, London (unidentified year).

CHAPTER 10: TAKING FLIGHT

466. "slightly exaggerated" and "if it was a narrow skirt," *Choura: The Memoirs of Alexandra Danilova*, Alexandra Danilova.
468. "Hurok still maintained that it was impossible," *American Ballet Theatre*, Charles Payne.
473. "had not retained any control over," Ibid.
474. "For this we met in the studio," *Markova Remembers*, Alicia Markova.
476. "thereafter I never traveled without," Ibid.
476. "conspiring with local managers to undermine Hurok," Ibid.
482. "primal instincts—greed and vanity," *No Intermissions: The Life of Agnes de Mille* (2000), Carol Easton.
486. "the size of an average broom-cupboard." *Markova Remembers*, Alicia Markova.
486. "I had a left wooden leg," interview for BBC Television documentary "Markova" (1981).
487. "[T]he heat, it was agony," Ibid.
488. "On the way back I think we stopped at Trinidad," interview for BBC Television documentary "Markova" (1981).
488. "I fly on stage!" LBC Radio program: interview with Steve Allen, 1/1/96.
488. "Dolin and I were the first dancers to fly everywhere." "Our First Ballerina", by Duncan Fallowell, *The Sunday Telegraph*, 4/30/2000.
489. "big wads of cotton wool to stuff in your ears," "Alicia Markova: A Room of My Own," *London Observer Sunday Magazine*, 3/28/87.

489. "[A]t the pace were now working," *Giselle & I*, Alicia Markova.
489. "there is going to be shooting today." *Markova Remembers*, Alicia Markova.
489. "So we missed luncheon and the possibility," Ibid.
492. "I could not look on it as anything," Ibid.
492. "I take the entire blame for it," *Autobiography: Anton Dolin* (1960), Anton Dolin.
492. "To add importance," Ibid.
494. "With all his vast experience," Ibid.
495. "We are doing our best and trying," *Autobiography: Anton Dolin* (1960), Anton Dolin.
496. "Are you trying to be the richest girl," *Markova: The Legend*, Maurice Leonard.
497. "Whenever people would say to me," BBC Radio program: "Conversation Pieces," 4/7/88.
498. "in an abandoned warehouse and give," *The New York Times*, 10/12/46.
498. "I remember opening a door next to my suite," *Markova Remembers*, Alicia Markova.
500. "New York is a pair of evening shoes," "Why I Love London, Alicia Markova," Roy Nash, *The Star*, London, 12/2/57.
500. "They tell me that it's almost impossible," "Ballerina Danced To Fame by Prescription," Bessie Hackett, unidentified Manila newspaper, 1948.
501. *"I do hope that you will soon come,"* Letter from Frederick Ashton to Alicia Markova, 11/27/46, from Markova's archive.
501. "I disagreed, being of the opinion that," *Autobiography: Anton Dolin*, Anton Dolin.
502. "Well, *he* has gained in vulgarity," Ibid.
502. "Madame Markova is not a great believer," *Model Housekeeping* magazine, October 1959.
504. "Barely has Covent Garden experienced," *Theatre World*, August 1948.
506. *"My Darling Alicia,"* Letter from Arnold Haskell to Alicia Markova, January 1949, from Markova's archives.
507. "Two stalwarts of British ballet," *Weekly Scotsman*, 1/13/49.
507. "It was *cold*," Radio interview: "Round Midnight" with Brian Matthew, 7/8/81.
507. "An experiment in ballet presentation," *Daily Telegraph*, 1/4/49.
509."Madame Markova has reduced the necessity for," "Traveling light with two dozen costumes," *Natal Mercury*, 5/3/49.
510. "Markova-Dolin cocktails." *Giselle & I*, Alicia Markova.
512. "Now I had to carry on with our tour," *Giselle & I*, Alicia Markova.
514. "With bookings coming in from all over the colony," "Ballet Comes to Nairobi," Humphrey Claydon, *Dancing Times* magazine, October 1949.
514. "A ballerina's life, of course," "Alicia Markova Tells Her Own Story, A peep into a ballerina's life," unidentified British magazine, 1951.
515. "The flat belonged to [film actress] Constance Cumming's," "Our First Ballerina", by Duncan Fallowell, *The Sunday Telegraph Magazine*, 4/30/2000.
515. "pioneers of arena ballet." *Markova Remembers*, Alicia Markova.
517. "always created this aura of serenity," *Markova: The Legend*, Maurice Leonard.
518. "I never like to see people in my dressing room," "Intimate Confessions of a Ballet Dancer," Alicia Markova, *The West Indian Review*, 1949.
518. "At seven," "Getting Ready for Ballet Takes Longer than Show," *Toronto Star*, 1939.
519. "My friends often laugh at me," "Alicia Markova Tells Her Own Story," 1950, unidentified magazine.
519. "Never become a ballet impresario," *Braunsweg's Ballet Scandals: The Life of an Impresario and the Story of the Festival Ballet* (1974), Julian Braunsweg as told to James Kelsey.
520. "Dolin was very excited about the offer." Ibid.
522. "more than redeem a certain thinness," *Birmingham Mail*, 10/18/49.
522. "Markova thought the corps," *Braunsweg's Ballet Scandals*, Julian Braunsweg.
523. "I began discussions with Markova and Dolin," Ibid.
524. "No, but with your names I can get money." Ibid.

524. "I wasn't ill and I had the choice," *Autobiography: Anton Dolin*, by Anton Dolin.
524. "Anton Dolin was willing to carry on," "Ballet star ill, 20,000 tickets will go back," *London Evening Standard*, 6/12/50.
526. "indecisive, temperamental, inclined to be lazy," *Braunsweg's Ballet Scandals*, Julian Braunsweg.
527. "Susan—she's three—is just like Alicia," "Alicia Markova's Sister Looks Back," Doris Barry, *Birmingham Gazette*, 10/18/49.

Chapter 11: Taking Charge

530. "If I took a month's holiday," "Markova—Our Only Prima Ballerina," interview by Eric Johns, *Theatre World*, January 1935.
536. "I learned economy on stage from Alicia," *Markova: The Legend*, Maurice Leonard.
536. "I was always aware of the enormous responsibility," BBC Radio program: "Markova Birthday Tribute," December 1970.
536. "There was never any foot stamping from her," *Markova: The Legend*, Maurice Leonard.
537. "pared to the core," *Giselle & I*, Alicia Markova.
538. "Regarding ballet on film, which question followed," London Ballet Circle lecture, 12/19/54.
539. "I buy all my clothes by weight." *Daily Graphic*, 5/29/51.
539. "How does she transport all her hats?" *Daily Record*, 10/18/50.
539. "What does a ballerina do when," *Evening Argus*, 8/29/51.
540. "most perfect feet in the world." *Scottish Daily Express*, 10/2/51.
540. "[Dolin] was an extrovert, happy at parties," *Braunsweg's Ballet Scandals*, Julian Braunsweg.
541. "perhaps the next Anton Dolin," *Autobiography: Anton Dolin*, Anton Dolin.
541. "being a Diaghilev to my John Gilpin," *Last Words: A Final Autobiography* (1985), Anton Dolin, Kay Hunter.
542. "For thirty-three years, since 1950," Ibid.
542. "Sir Anton Dolin died on November 25, 1983," Ibid.
542. "It's you and Alicia the public will buy tickets for," *Autobiography: Anton Dolin*, Anton Dolin.
544. "He's too young and inexperienced," *Braunsweg's Ballet Scandals*, Julian Braunsweg.
544. "Quite a few people have bought seats to see Gilpin," *Autobiography: Anton Dolin*, Anton Dolin.
544. "My God, he is young!" Ibid.
544. "She was a great friend of Markova's," *Braunsweg's Ballet Scandals*, Julian Braunsweg.
545. "I feel that is Fonteyn's ballet," "Dancers in Profile: Alicia Markova," *Dance Magazine*, June 1952.
545. "I do not feel hot enough for that," *Autobiography: Anton Dolin*, Anton Dolin.
547. "the impeccable style and sense of period," "Giselle: 1950: Three interpretations, by J.R. Austin, Tempo, No. 18 (Winter 1950–51), Cambridge University Press.
547. "still in her sable coat," *Autobiography: Anton Dolin*, Anton Dolin.
548. "She had a voracious appetite and was," *Braunsweg's Ballet Scandals*, Julian Braunsweg.
549. "John's affairs of the heart," Ibid.
551. "*because* of you & because of us" and "knowledge and sanction" and "I ask nothing for myself," Excerpts from personal letters from Anton Dolin to Alicia Markova, from Markova's archive.
551. "What about the corps, the soloists," *Braunsweg's Ballet Scandals*, Julian Braunsweg.
552. "the internationally famous English ballerina," "News in Pictures," Movie Magazine *The Daily Film Renter*, 1952.
556. "You are always missed by me," Letter from Anton Dolin to Alicia Markova, May 18,1952, from Markova's archive.

559. "I long for the day when you will return happily to 'guest.'" Excerpt from personal letter Anton Dolin to Alicia Markova, 7/27/52, from Markova's archive.
561. "You've danced Giselle for over 25 years." BBC Radio program: "Parkinson Show," 1/11/75.
564. "We presume Starbuck's substitution of trousers," *Dance Magazine*, March 1953.
564. "His imaginative production of 'The Dying Swan,'" *The Stage*, 3/26/53.
565. "Fan mail poured in by the thousands," *Manchester Daily Dispatch*, 3/5/53.
565. "fan mail was so huge," *London Evening News*, 3/17/53.
566. "Markova received an average of seventy letters," *Dundee Evening Telegraph*, 12/10/56.
566. "I have just a room," *Berlingske Aftenavsi*, Denmark, 9/24/55.
567. "Why did you step from your pinnacle," *Winnipeg Tribune*, 1/11/54.
568. "She [Markova] took time to teach and coach the dancers," Royal Winnipeg Ballet Newsletter, unknown year.

Chapter 12: The People's Ballerina

570. "I worked a fruit-machine for over three hours," *London Sunday Graphic*, 11/14/54.
571. "Do you remember me?" *Markova: The Legend*, Maurice Leonard.
571. "Before the kitten arrived, my young niece," *Dundee Evening Telegraph*, 12/10/56.
572. "Markova received £30,000 for ten performances," *The Evening News*, London, January 1954.
572. "For the first time since the days of Pavlova," *Manchester Evening Chronicle*, 3/13/54.
581. "Dolin did, as Markova says in her account," *American Ballet Theatre*, Charles Payne.
581. "how infuriating Alicia could be," *Autobiography: Anton Dolin*, Anton Dolin.
582. "When Markova danced as a guest of Ballet Theatre," *American Ballet Theatre*, Charles Payne.
582. "Markova was so clear in what," *Balanchine's Complete Stories of the Great Ballets* (1977), George Balanchine and Francis Mason.
583. "It may well be a date to write down," *The New York Times*, 5/2/55.
587. "It isn't every day a ballet dancer can stand in," *San Francisco Chronicle*, 3/4/55.
592. "the most wonderful experience," Personal letter from Alicia Markova to Stanley Burton, 11/18/58, from Markova's archive.
593. "Viv darling," Letter from Doris Barry to sister Vivienne Marks, November 1957, from Markova's archive.
594. "Dear God," Alicia Markova's personal note, from Markova's archive.
595. "ALICIA MARKOVA: She does not dance," *Ballet: A Decade of Endeavor* (1956), A. H. Franks.
598. "Viv darling" and "Alicia thank goodness" and (599) "Things have been very uncomfortable," Letters from Doris Barry to sister Vivienne Marks, from Markova's archive.
602. "Again and again the public gasped with admiration," *Ha'aretz*, June 1958.
603. "I don't think, in the last fifty years," *Braunsweg's Ballet Scandals*, Julian Braunsweg.
604. "Stanley darling," Personal letter from Alicia Markova to Stanley Burton, 9/28/58, from Markova's archive.
605. "I had a half an hour program once a week," Manx Radio program, 1974.
605. "Well, I think she might have made," BBC Television program: "This is Your Life, Alicia Markova," 1/11/60.
606. "A dancer's discipline," *Women's Own* magazine, unidentified year.
607. "Reporters asked me at the airport," BBC Radio interview: "Myself When Young," with Claire Rayner (unknown year).

Postscript

611. "I don't believe you have to raise your voice," "My New Career at 53," unidentified London newspaper, August 1964.

613. "Not long ago I had an audience," *New York Sunday Post*, 4/4/65.
615. "My New Career at 53," unidentified London newspaper, August 1964.
616. "When I first went to London," BBC Radio program: "Markova Birthday Tribute," December 1970.
616. "Opera ballet is a real challenge," *Des Moines Register*, Iowa, 11/5/63.
617. "One wish? I wish my day could start later," *Women's Wear Daily*, 4/11/65.
619. "where David McLain heads one of the most vital," *The Saturday Review*, 8/28/71.
619. "she gave "the illusion of moving," "Markova at the Met," Edwin Denby, *Dance Magazine*, December 1952.
619. "My little dance on the moon wasn't so good." *Markova: The Legend*, Maurice Leonard.
619. "I was there with a full professorship," Manx Radio program: "Concert Classics," 12/31/74.
620. "She remained married to her art," *The Independent*, 12/3/04.
620. "I find it very exciting if one can," BBC World Service, "Tribute to Pavlova," Outlook, 1/31/85.
623. "had mixed emotions. While saddened," *Frederic Franklin: A Biography of the Ballet Star* (2004), Leslie Norton.

Suggested Bibliography for Further Reading

Anderson, Jack. *The One and Only: The Ballet Russe de Monte Carlo.* London: Dance Books Ltd., 1981.

Braunsweg, Julian, as told to James Kelsey. *Braunsweg's Ballet Scandals: The Life of an Impresario and the Story of the Festival Ballet.* London: George Allen & Unwin, 1974.

Buckle, Richard (ed.). *Dancing for Diaghilev: The Memoirs of Lydia Sokolova.* London: Columbus, 1960; San Francisco: Mercury House, 1989.

Chazin-Bennahum, Judith. *Rene Blum & The Ballets Russes: In Search of a Lost Life.* Oxford and New York: Oxford University Press, 2011.

Daneman, Meredith. *Margot Fonteyn: A Life.* New York: Viking, 2004.

Danilova, Alexandra. *Choura: The Memoirs of Alexandra Danilova.* New York: Knopf, 1987.

de Mille, Agnes. *Dance to the Piper.* Boston: Little, Brown, 1951; London: Columbus, 1987.

de Mille, Agnes. *Portrait Gallery.* Boston: Houghton Mifflin, 1990.

de Valois, Ninette. *Come Dance With Me: A Memoir 1898–1956.* London: Readers Union Hamish Hamilton, 1959; Princeton: Princeton Book Co., 1981.

Denby, Edwin. *Dance Writings.* New York: Knopf, 1986.

Dolin, Anton. *Markova: Her Life and Art.* London: W. H. Allen, 1953; London and New York: White Lion, 1973.

Dominic, Zöe, and John Selwyn Gilbert. *Frederick Ashton: A Choreographer and His Ballets.* London: George G. Harrap, 1971; Chicago: Regnery, 1973.

Drummond, John. *Speaking of Diaghilev.* London and Boston: Faber and Faber, 1997.

Fonteyn, Margot. *Margot Fonteyn: Autobiography.* New York: Knopf, 1976.

Fonteyn, Margot. *Pavlova: Portrait of a Dancer.* New York: Viking, 1984.

Garcia-Márquez, Vicente. *Massine: A Biography.* New York: Knopf, 1995.

Homans, Jennifer. *Apollo's Angels: A History of Ballet*. New York: Random House, 2010.

Hurok, S[ol]., and Ruth Goode. *Impresario: A Memoir.* New York: Random House, 1946.

Hurok, Sol. *S. Hurok Presents: A Memoir of the Dance World*. New York: Hermitage House, 1953.

Jackson, Kenneth. *WWII & NYC*. London: New York Historical Society with Scala Publishers Ltd., 2012.

Karsavina, Tamara. *Theatre Street*. New York: E. P. Dutton, 1961 (rev. ed.).

Kavanagh, Julie. *Secret Muses: The Life of Frederick Ashton*. New York: Pantheon, 1996.

Kerensky, Oleg. *Anna Pavlova*. New York: E. P. Dutton, 1973.

Leonard, Maurice. *Markova: the Legend*. London: Hodder and Stoughton, 1995.

Mackrell, Judith. *Bloomsbury Ballerina: Lydia Lopokova, Imperial Dancer and Mrs. John Maynard Keynes*. London: Weidenfeld & Nicholson, 2008.

Markova, Alicia. *Giselle and I*. New York: Vanguard, 1960.

Markova, Dame Alicia. *Markova Remembers*. Boston: Little, Brown, 1986.

Mason, Francis. *I Remember Balanchine*. New York: Doubleday, 1991.

Massine, Léonide. *My Life in Ballet*. London: Macmillan, 1968.

Money, Keith. *Anna Pavlova: Her Life and Art*. New York: Knopf, 1982.

Nijinska, Irina, and Jean Rawlinson (transl. and ed.). *Bronislava Nijinska: Early Memoires*. New York: Holt, Rinehart, and Winston, 1981.

Norton, Leslie, with Frederic Franklin. *Frederic Franklin: A Biography of the Ballet Star*. Jefferson, N.C. and London: McFarland, 2004.

Payne, Charles. *American Ballet Theatre*. New York: Knopf, 1978.

Rambert, Marie. *Quicksilver: An Autobiography*. London: Macmillan, 1972.

Robert, Grace. *The Borzoi Book of Ballets*. New York: Knopf, 1946.

Robinson, Harlow. *The Last Impresario: The Life, Times and Legacy of Sol Hurok*. New York: Viking, 1994.

Scheijen, Sjeng. *Diaghilev: A Life*. New York: Oxford University Press, 2009.

Vaughan, David. *Frederick Ashton and His Ballets*. New York: Knopf, 1977.

Walker, Kathrine Sorley. *De Basil's Ballets Russes*. New York: Atheneum, 1983.

Index

INDEX

INDEX